PENGUIN BC

THE PENGUIN BOOK (

Christopher Silvester is a freelance writer. He was educated at Lancing College in Sussex and at Peterhouse, Cambridge, where he read history. For many years he was a reporter for *Private Eye*, and he has contributed to several newspapers and magazines. He is the editor of *The Penguin Book of Interviews: An Anthology from 1859 to the Present Day* (1993), *The Literary Companion to Parliament* (1996) and *The Penguin Book of Hollywood* (1998).

THE PENGUIN BOOK OF

·

COLUMNISTS

·

EDITED BY
CHRISTOPHER SILVESTER

PENGUIN BOOKS

To my darling mother, whose support was crucial to the prompt completion of this book; to my father, for his unwavering support; and to my sister, for her unrelenting faith in my endeavours.

PENGUIN BOOKS

Published by the Penguin Group
Penguin Books Ltd, 27 Wrights Lane, London W8 5TZ, England
Penguin Books USA Inc., 375 Hudson Street, New York, New York 10014, USA
Penguin Books Australia Ltd, Ringwood, Victoria, Australia
Penguin Books Canada Ltd, 10 Alcorn Avenue, Toronto, Ontario, Canada M4V 3B2
Penguin Books (NZ) Ltd, Private Bag 102902, NSMC, Auckland, New Zealand

Penguin Books Ltd, Registered Offices: Harmondsworth, Middlesex, England

First published by Viking 1997
Published in Penguin Books 1998
1 3 5 7 9 10 8 6 4 2

Introduction copyright © Christopher Silvester, 1997

All rights reserved

The acknowledgements on pages vii – ix constitute an extension of this copyright page

The moral right of the editor has been asserted

Set in 10/12pt Monotype Garamond
Typeset by Rowland Phototypesetting Limited
Bury St Edmunds, Suffolk
Printed in Great Britain by Clays Ltd, St Ives plc

CONTENTS

ACKNOWLEDGEMENTS

I owe a considerable debt to Roy Greenslade, who started out as my collaborator in this project but who was obliged to withdraw as a result of his many other commitments. His extensive knowledge of newspaper lore was especially useful in drawing up the original proposed list of contents, although that list was subsequently expanded to include other columnists of whom neither of us had previously heard, and it has also been pared back in certain respects.

I have to acknowledge that the inspiration for this book came from Karl E. Meyer's *Pundits, Poets and Wits* (1990), an anthology of American columnists which was published in the United States. While Karl stretched further back in time to include the pamphleteers of the American Revolutionary period and restricted his selection to seventy-two columnists, I have confined myself to a narrower historical period while ranging further afield within the English-speaking world and attempting to include as many columnists as possible. In New York, I stayed for some of the time in the apartment belonging to Karl and his wife, Shareen Brysac, and had access to his substantial library of books about newspapers in general and about columnists in particular. Another person who lent me books by humorous columnists was Mike Barfield, who is an expert on the works of the British humorists D. B. Wyndham Lewis and J. B. Morton (who, successively, wrote the 'Beachcomber' columns for the *Daily Express*). I can thoroughly recommend Mike's own anthology of late 'Beachcomber', *Cram Me With Eels!: The Best of Beachcomber's Unpublished Humour*.

Others who assisted me in various ways include Bruce Palling by drawing my attention to the work of Khushwant Singh; Brian Rostron by telling me about Casey Motsisi of *Drum*, and Anthony Sampson, one of Motsisi's editors, by lending me a precious and not easy-to-come-by collection of Motsisi's columns from that magazine; Francis Wheen by telling me about George Orwell's wartime column for *Tribune* and by lending me *Colonnade*, the rare collection in book form of Tom Driberg's columns; Michael Bywater by giving me a copy of his columns from *Punch*, *The Collected Bargepole*; and Alan Watkins by giving me a copy of his collected rugby columns, *Sportswriter's Eye*. Geoffrey Robertson QC and his wife Kathy Lette directed me to the work of two Australian columnists, Charmian Clift and Ross Campbell. Both Richard Ingrams and Alan Watkins rescued me from embarrassment by forcefully advocating the inclusion of certain columnists: Richard championed Peter Fleming ('Strix' from the *Spectator* in the late 1950s) and Sir John Junor from the *Sunday Express*; while Alan sang the praises of Henry Fairlie in his mid-1950s *Spectator* phase, and reinforced the case for Junor. Stephen Glover was a source of encouragement and enthusiasm for this project, and a frequent provider of hospitality.

The institutions where I conducted my research were the London Library; the British Library; the Newspaper Library, Colindale; and the New York Public Library.

There is one other contribution I must acknowledge. During the time I was researching this and other projects in the United States, I was without a home of my own in London. However, I was fortunate to find two very wonderful and tolerant friends in Jeff Montgomery and Valerie Gladwin, who allowed me to stay with them in their Notting Hill flat intermittently for weeks on end over the past year and a half. The comforts which made the completion of this book possible owe much to them.

•

The editor and publishers wish to thank the following for permission to reprint copyright material:

ABC Publications for permission to reprint columns by Phillip Adams from *Classic Columns* (1994), originally appearing in the *Australian*; **Estates of Joseph and Stewart Alsop and Lois Wallace Literary Agency** for permission to reprint columns originally appearing in the *New York Herald Tribune*; **The Earl of Arran** for permission to reprint columns by his father originally appearing in the *Evening News*; **Lynn Ashby** for permission to reprint columns from *As I Was Saying* (1984), originally appearing in the *Houston Post*; *Atlanta Journal-Constitution* for permission to reprint columns by Ralph McGill; **Bailey Archives** for permission to reprint columns by Casey Motsisi originally appearing in *Drum*; **Jeff Bernard** for permission to reprint columns originally appearing in the *Spectator*; *Black River Falls* **[Wisconsin]** *Banner-Journal* for permission to reprint excerpts from columns by Charles Low Cloud; **Estate of Erma Bombeck and the Aaron M. Priest Literary Agency** for permission to reprint columns by Erma Bombeck; *Boston Globe* for permission to reprint columns by George Frazier; *Boston Herald* for permission to reprint columns by George Frazier; **Jimmy Breslin** for permission to reprint columns originally appearing in the *New York Daily News*; **Michael Bywater** for permission to reprint columns originally appearing in *Punch*; *Charleston Post and Courier* for permission to reprint excerpts from columns by Frank Gilbreth, Jr; *Charlotte News and Observer* for permission to reprint columns by Kays Gary; *Chicago Sun-Times* for permission to reprint columns by Carl Sandburg originally appearing in the *Chicago Times*, and columns by Mike Royko originally appearing in the *Chicago Sun-Times*; *Daily Mail* for permission to reprint columns by D. B. Wyndham Lewis and Collie Knox; *Daily Mirror* for permission to reprint columns by William Connor and Keith Waterhouse; **Enoch Pratt Free Library** for permission to reprint one column by H. L. Mencken originally appearing in the *Chicago Tribune*, in accordance with the terms of the will of H. L. Mencken; **Ernie Pyle Fund of the Scripps Howard Foundation** for permission to reprint columns by Ernie Pyle; **Express Newspapers** for permission to reprint one column by Viscount Castlerosse and John Junor originally appearing in the *Sunday Express*; and columns by William Barkley originally appearing in the *Daily Express*; **Gordon Wright Publishing** for permission to reprint columns by George Mackay Brown originally appearing in the *Orcadian*; **Guardian and Observer Ltd** for permission to reprint columns by James Cameron, Michael Frayn, Paul Jennings and Jill Tweedie; **Pete Hamill** for permission to reprint columns originally appearing in the *New York Post*; **Harold Ober & Associates** for permission to reprint 'Income Tax', © 1950 by Langston Hughes, copyright renewed 1978 by George Houston Bass; **HarperCollins** for permission to reprint one column by E. B. White from *One Man's Meat* (1944); **President and Fellows of Harvard College** for permission to reprint columns by Walter Lippmann originally appearing in the *New York Herald Tribune*; **I H T Corporation** for permission to reprint columns by Dorothy Thompson originally appearing in the *New York Herald Tribune*; **Michael Nolan** for permission to reprint columns by Flann O'Brien originally appearing in the *Irish Times*; © **Shaun Johnson** for permission to reprint columns originally appearing in the *Star* and *Saturday Star*; *Kansas City Star* for permission to reprint columns by Bill Vaughan; **King Features** for permission to reprint columns by Damon Runyon and Walter Winchell originally appearing in the *New York Daily Mirror*; **Mrs Edna Lerner** for permission to reprint columns by her husband Max Lerner originally appearing in the *New York Post*; **Little, Brown & Company** for permission to reprint one column by I. F. Stone from *In a Time of Torment, 1961–1967* (1967), originally appearing in *I.F. Stone's Weekly*; **Los Angeles Times Syndicate** for permission to reprint columns by Art Buchwald, Jim Murray and Harry Shearer; **Trustees of Mark Boxer's children** for permission to reprint two caricatures originally appearing in Alan Watkins's *Brief Lives*; **MAT Publications** for permission to reprint columns by Lennie Lower and Alexander Macdonald originally appearing in the *Daily Telegraph* [Sydney]; **Karl E. Meyer** for permission to reprint columns by Ernest L. Meyer from *Making Light of the Times* (1928), originally appearing in the Madison [Wisconsin] *Capital Times*; **Nation** for permission to reprint one column by Christopher Hitchens; **New Republic** for permission to reprint columns by Richard L. Strout; **New Statesman & Society** for columns by Robert Lynd and Arthur Marshall; **New York Times** for permission to reprint columns by Russell Baker (© 1973, 1979), Meyer Berger (© 1954, 1957), Arthur Krock (© 1952, 1962), John Leonard, Red Smith (© 1978), Simeon Strunsky (© 1936, 1943), Anna Quindlen (© 1988, 1991) and William Safire (© 1974, 1979); **Peters, Fraser & Dunlop** for permission to reprint column items from *The Adventures of Mr Thake* (1934) by J. B. Morton originally appearing in the *Daily Express*, and for columns by Auberon Waugh originally appearing in the *New Statesman*; **Private Eye (Pressdram) Ltd** for permission to reprint a caricature by Willy Rushton; **Record [Hackensack, New Jersey]** for permission to reprint columns by William A. Caldwell; **San Francisco Chronicle** for permission to reprint columns by Lucius Beebe, Royce Brier, Herb Caen and Charles McCabe; **Posy Simmonds** for permission to reprint a caricature originally appearing in the *Guardian*; **Spectator** for permission to reprint columns by Harold Nicolson, Peter Fleming, Ferdinand Mount, Auberon Waugh and Peregrine Worsthorne; **Telegraph Group** for permission to reprint excerpts from columns by Michael Wharton originally appearing in the *Daily Telegraph*; **Tribune** for permission to reprint columns by George Orwell; **Tribune Media Services** for permission to reprint columns by Dave Barry, Eugene J. McCarthy and Andy Rooney; **Calvin Trillin** for permission to reprint columns originally appearing in the *Nation*; **Universal Press Syndicate** for permission to reprint columns by James L. Kilpatrick originally appearing in *Newsday*; and columns by Eugene J. McCarthy originally appearing in the *Washington Star*; **Viking Press** for permission to reprint columns by Ben Hecht from *1001 Afternoons in New York* (1941), originally appearing in *PM*; **Vineyard Gazette** for permission to reprint one column by Joseph Chase Allen; **Wall Street Journal** for permission to reprint columns by Vermont Royster; **Washington Post Writers Group** for permission to reprint columns by Ellen Goodman originally appearing in the *Boston Globe*; **Keith Waterhouse** for permission to reprint columns originally appearing in the *Daily Mail*; **Alan Watkins** for permission to reprint columns originally appearing in the *New Statesman*, the *Independent* and the *Independent on Sunday*; **Francis Wheen** for permission to reprint one column originally appearing in the *Observer*; **Sidney Zion** for one column originally appearing in the *Soho Weekly News*.

INTRODUCTION

In the introduction to an earlier book, *The Penguin Book of Interviews* (1993), I was able to draw upon the work of historians of journalism who had already pinpointed the first journalistic interview – Horace Greeley's interview of the Mormon leader Brigham Young in 1859. No such landmark has been agreed upon as the first column, for the very good reason that the column is an outgrowth of the traditional essay and a refinement of that genre. Some columns, it is true, have not been essays so much as causeries,[1] or something akin to leaves from a commonplace book, although the majority of columns in this anthology, notwithstanding certain stylistic differences, might very well have appeared as essays in an earlier age. However, the column, whether in newspapers or magazines, properly belongs to the age of mass newspaper consumption which started around the middle of the nineteenth century and which entailed a change in the methods by which the essay was delivered to readers.

For my own purposes, in making the distinction between the column and the essay I have relied upon the following criteria. Firstly, a column appears in the same publication, on a regular basis, usually in the same position and with the same heading and by-line. The presence of the column is reassuring, therefore, not primarily because of what it has to say, but because of its appearance in a particular spot, on a particular day or days, and at an approximately predictable length.

Secondly, the columnist is conscious of an audience in a way that an essayist is not; indeed, a column is more of a performance than an expression of intellectual argument, and it tends to react to contemporary events and shared experiences. 'The columnist is writing for an audience, and a deadline,' says the Australian columnist Phillip Adams, 'not for eternity.'[2]

Thirdly, the column has sometimes been categorized as 'personal journalism', in which the personality of the writer is a self-referential element in the text along with the subject matter.[3] As Hallam Walker Davis put it in his journalism handbook, *The Column*:

> ... there is one thing that all good columns have, and have in abundance. That thing is the 'individuality' or 'personality' or 'ego' of the columnist. If this indefinable thing is pleasing and positive and challenging, the column's success is assured ... all good columns bear the imprint of the ego of the columnist, an ego that is a live thing, much to be reckoned with.[4]

Opinions are given the imprimatur of a personality with whom the reader becomes familiar and friendly, although this personality may be a fictional character. The essayist or pamphleteer who wrote pseudonymously in the seventeenth or eighteenth centuries generally did so in order to avoid prosecution or to abide by some notion of literary decorum, while a columnist who writes pseudonymously today is often adopting a persona so as to convey his theme more tellingly.

THE HISTORY OF THE COLUMN

One result of the early nineteenth-century Romantic movement in the arts was a greater contemplation of the self. This, combined with the needs of mass-market newspapers to vary the diet of straightforward news, was a spur to personal journalism. The earliest columns, which were humorous in content, seemed to emerge organically from the increased pagination of newspapers and the specialization in their subject matter. Previously, such humorous articles had appeared randomly, wherever there was space available in a particular edition, but now they were granted a fixed abode. The most significant boost to the early development of the column was the formation during the American Civil War of newspaper syndicates – clearing-houses for editorials, articles and serial fiction, which were partly the result of new and more effective copyright laws.

Bill Nye is the first columnist in this book. A humorist of the American frontier, his early columns appeared in various western papers and his later columns in the New York *World* were also syndicated by the American Press Association. One historian has averred that the first regular humorous column was 'Lakeside Musings' by H. T. E. White, which began in the *Chicago Tribune* in 1885.[5] Yet at around the same time in England, J. M. Barrie, who would subsequently become world-famous as the creator of *Peter Pan*, was writing two columns a week for the *Nottingham Journal*, one short essay and one causerie, both under the pen-name 'Hippomenes'. It is agreed, however, that the first columnist who achieved nationwide fame *qua* columnist was the American Eugene Field, whose 'Sharps and Flats', a mixture of light verse and essay humour, adorned the *Chicago Daily News* in the 1890s. Field inspired several others to become practitioners of the craft. George Ade certainly acknowledged Field's influence, as did Don Marquis, who acknowledged Ade's influence as well. Indeed, it was the vibrant Chicago press and not that of New York which was the seedbed of the modern newspaper column. Ade's column, 'Stories of the Streets and Town', appeared in the *Chicago Evening Post* in the mid-1890s, and Finley Peter Dunne's 'Mr Dooley' dialogues, between the eponymous Irish saloon-keeper and his friend 'Hinnessy', appeared in the *Chicago Journal* during the same period.

In 1895 William Randolph Hearst founded his first syndicate, which distributed 'Mr Dooley' and a home-grown columnist from Hearst's *San Francisco Examiner*, Ambrose Bierce. It was succeeded in 1915 by another Hearst syndicate, King Features, which later handled such luminaries as Arthur 'Bugs' Baer, Mark Hellinger and Walter Winchell. Other syndicates founded in the early part of this century include the Bell Syndicate, which distributed Ring Lardner's weekly humour column and the McNaught Syndicate, which distributed Will Rogers's weekly articles.

In the mid nineteenth century, newspaper editors had often been their own proprietors and had been in the habit of writing fulminatory editorials laced with personal vim. With the separation of the roles of editor and proprietor, editorials became more sedate and formal, and so the newspaper column became the domain of vigorous, splenetic opinion, sometimes even going against the editorial grain of the particular title in which it ran. The column 'has been during the recent war [1914–18], and it is today,' wrote Lucy Maynard Salmon in 1923, 'the part of the newspaper where a writer can in seriousness, without the cloak of a jest, and without fear or favor express opinions quite at variance with the conventional opinions held by the public or possibly by the newspaper itself'.[6] The 1920s saw the invention of the 'op-ed' page, or the 'page opposite editorial' – an innovation which was credited to Herbert Bayard Swope, the executive editor of the New York *World* – so that the opinions of a paper's prominent columnists now stood alongside its official voice.

The *World*'s op-ed page was a showcase both for the liberal essayist Heywood Broun and for the 'linemaster' Franklin Pierce Adams, or 'F.P.A.' Several early columns were forums for light verse and humorous items conducted by a 'linemaster'. Most famous of these were Bert Leston Taylor's 'A Line o' Type or Two' in the *Chicago Journal* in 1899; F.P.A.'s 'The Conning Tower', which started in the *New York Tribune* in 1914; and Don Marquis's 'The Sun Dial', which started in the *New York Sun* in 1912.

Between the wars, two new breeds of columnist were spawned: the syndicated Washington correspondent and the Broadway columnist. Walter Lippmann, whose thrice-weekly political analysis was syndicated out of the *New York Herald Tribune*, epitomized the first of these, while Walter Winchell, whose hybrid of commentary and gossip column was delivered in a unique, frenetic slang style and syndicated out of the *New York Daily Mirror*, typified the second.

Two humorous columns were so successful that their creators abandoned them after only a short time to concentrate on writing books instead. Curiously, both of them were satirical columns about American army life. During the First World War Edward Streeter created the hapless infantryman 'Bill', whose 'Dere Mabel' letters to his sweetheart were first published in a military post magazine, the *Camp Wadsworth Gas Attack*, then published as a book after Streeter had sailed for France. The book became a massive bestseller. Similarly, during the Second World War Marion Hargrove was the protagonist of his 'In the Army' column for the *Charlotte News*, and his published collection, *See Here, Private Hargrove* (1942), was one of the leading American bestsellers of the 1940s.

In Britain, where syndication did not exist, several prominent columnists emerged between the wars: Viscount Castlerosse, whose celebrity and opinion column appeared in the *Sunday Express*; Tom Driberg's 'William Hickey' reportage column for the *Daily Express*; J. B. Morton, the *Daily Express*'s 'Beachcomber'; the *Daily Mail*'s humorous columnist, D. B. Wyndham Lewis; 'Candidus' in the *Daily Sketch*; and 'Cassandra' in the *Daily Mirror*. Otherwise, a number of the best British columnists have been found in the pages of the weekly magazines.

The output of columnists in Britain has traditionally been meagre compared to that of their American counterparts. Although Spencer Leigh Hughes wrote a daily column of roughly 1,200 words for around twenty years, William Hickey appeared daily from the mid-1930s until the mid-1940s, and Cassandra wrote a daily column from the mid-1930s to the early 1960s (with a break during the Second World War), yet some Americans wrote five days a week, or even seven days a week, for several decades. Max

Lerner produced a column of about a thousand words, five days a week from 1941 to 1959. Westbrook Pegler, another daily columnist, reckoned his monthly output at 25,000 words. The sports columnist Red Smith recalled 'the years when a daily column meant seven a week. Between those jousts with the mother tongue, there was always a fight or football match or ball game or horse race that had to be covered after the column was done. I loved it.'[7]

Also, American columnists tend to last longer than their British counterparts. Although there are some British columnists today who have been at it for decades (such as Bernard Levin, Auberon Waugh, Katharine Whitehorn, Alan Watkins and Keith Waterhouse), there are few who can match the longevity of, say, a Red Smith or a Walter Lippmann. There are several reasons for this. One is that the culture in America is disposed to think more highly of columnists than the culture in Britain; and despite some of the salaries paid to Fleet Street columnists, nothing can compare to American syndication for enriching a columnist. Added to that is the American lecture circuit, on which my first columnist, Bill Nye, was much in demand as a performer. Another reason for longevity is that if the newspaper where a columnist has originally appeared decides to drop him or is itself closed down, he will none the less be sustained by the syndication system. Barring illness or mental deterioration, 'columning' is a job for life in America, whereas in Britain it is more likely to be one among many roles that a journalist performs during the course of his career.

Another peculiar difference between the two traditions is the tendency of American columnists to be recruited from among the ranks of sportswriters. Ring Lardner, Arthur 'Bugs' Baer, Heywood Broun, Westbrook Pegler and Jimmy Breslin were all sports-writers before they became columnists, yet I can think of no general columnist in Britain who was once a sportswriter. Why this should be the case is not clear, except that sports-writing, like column-writing, is more highly regarded in America than in Britain.

The Role of the Columnist

One historian has suggested that 'the pasquinade seems the forerunner of the "colyum" '.[8] A pasquinade was a publicly posted piece of satirical writing, either short or long, named after Pasquino, a Roman tailor who wrote lampoons of his city's wealthy and powerful citizens. Certainly, there have been many columnists who have continued to thumb their noses at prominent personalities and institutions, but the role of the columnist has been a varied one. As the same historian has put it, the columnist may change 'from teacher or entertainer to the passive onlooker who records the pleasantries of every-day life'.[9]

Fecundity of opinion is one quality that is generally required of the columnist. 'The man never lived who had something to say every day of his life,' wrote Damon Runyon. 'By something to say, I mean of course, something worth listening to or reading. But if editors took to leaving out columnists when they have nothing to say, every columnist would be reduced to about three appearances per week and some less and that would not be good for the columning racket.'[10] Bob Considine found a different solution, albeit a temporary one, when in 1973 he wrote a column which, in its entirety, read as follows: 'I have nothing to say today.'

Yet, while columnists are expected to be opinionated, they are also expected to be less than wholly consistent. They are not, after all, engaged in building a coherent system of thought so much as in ventilating their opinions in response to events and experiences. At his highest, the columnist is not merely an entertainer. Nor is he, however, a mere purveyor of dry, impersonal arguments, as the American columnist Max Lerner recognized:

> The intelligent newspaper reader has come increasingly to ask for a commentary on the running stream of tendency underneath what happens from day to day. He has become impatient of pompous and anonymous editorializing, in which the whole body of editors – speaking through some chosen oracular vessel – collectively seethe with indignation, or point with scorn, or find some course of action dangerous and unsound. He wants to know who thinks what and why on a variety of subjects, and he wants each commentary to flow from a main body of beliefs about human nature and American culture and the world we live in.[11]

By the 1930s the *Philadelphia Public Ledger* columnist Jay House was able to declare that 'The country has come to be so pediculous [i.e. lice-infested] with columnists that the average citizen can scarcely put a foot forward without stepping on one.'[12] Explaining the context in which Will Rogers's columns of cracker-barrel wisdom and cynical humour gained such popularity in the 1920s, one commentator has emphasized the columnist's role as interpreter: 'In an era when radio news coverage was rudimentary and television news unknown, the masses depended almost exclusively on newspapers for information and upon columnists for insight and interpretation.'[13]

The British political columnist Peter Jenkins displayed the same insight when he wrote that the political columnist 'spends a great deal of his time reading the papers on behalf of his readers, trying to make a pattern out of torrents of words'. However, Jenkins identified several important differences between English and American political columnists. 'Fleet Street's idea of a column was, and largely still is,' he wrote in 1977, 'a star turn with the emphasis on turn: the columnist's job was to take an ego trip to entertain his readers, preferably by annoying them, with strong opinions on each and every subject.' Columnists in America, on the other hand, have traditionally been taken more seriously and have enjoyed greater influence than British columnists. There are some columnists, particularly political columnists, who have been influential with men of power. President John F. Kennedy was once heard cursing 'that goddamned Arthur Krock', and President Lyndon Johnson courted the venerable Walter Lippmann. Once, when he had just ordered 50,000 more troops into Vietnam, Johnson apparently muttered, 'There, that should keep Joseph Alsop quiet for a while.' It was not only political columnists who had the capacity to unnerve politicians. Theodore Roosevelt struck up a correspondence with Finley Peter Dunne and was anxious not to be mocked by Dunne's philosophizing saloon-keeper, Mr Dooley. Again, the awesome power of the syndication system provides the explanation, as Jenkins understood. 'A man addressing the readers of, say, 150 newspapers three times a week could see just about anybody he wanted to see in Washington, and have his telephone calls returned. Moreover, the syndicated columnist would often be if not the sole the chief source of political information apart from the news agencies in most of the newspapers in which he appeared.'[14]

Writing in the late 1930s, Heywood Broun explained how he felt compelled to abandon whimsicality and become a serious commentator:

> . . . Unlike Nero, I did most of my fiddling before Rome burned. I was left a tuneless minstrel in a world which proceeded to go into convulsions. Suddenly it was no longer possible to write about bullheads or crickets or the manner in which autumn comes to the maples of Hunting Ridge. It seemed a little silly to write about a fish and put it into a paper which was filled with assassinations, riots and revolutions.
>
> In the old days I sat down ten or twelve days in advance of the deadline and tried to imagine that I was Charles Lamb. Naturally I never made the grade, but presently it was no dice even if you did. Being whimsical or arch while Rome burns is even worse than meeting the fire with violin tunes.
>
> I became a commentator because I was conscripted by the march of events. I do not regret the change in all ways . . .
>
> Now I stay up till all hours to get the morning papers and find out who is dead and where the shooting is. On many occasions it is quite possible to get genuinely aroused about some snide performance by the captains and the kings.
>
> I'm not kicking. All I want to know is would it be too much to ask for the privilege of writing once a month about cabbages and sealing wax or anything else which has nothing to do with the class struggle or the New Deal? Excuse it, please.[15]

The American columnist George Will has said that he most admires those columnists who 'have written about the "inside" of public matters: not what is secret, but what is latent, the kernel of principle and other significance that exists, recognized or not, "inside" events, policies and manners'.[16] For Max Lerner, the columnist is part social historian, part social theorist, and part man of letters.[17] For the Australian Max Harris, writing in the 1960s and early 1970s, the main concern was 'the act of cultural diagnosis' and 'trying to define what is happening in the Australian ethos at any given moment, and in establishing what it means . . . The columnist's job is to see the wood despite the daily trees.'[18]

Other columnists have been more dismissive of the notion that the columnist is a purveyor of instant wisdom. 'Of all the fantastic fog-shapes that have risen off the swamp of confusion since the war [the First World War],' wrote Westbrook Pegler, 'the most futile, and, at the same time, the most pretentious is the deep-thinking, hair-trigger columnist or commentator who knows all the answers offhand and can settle great affairs with absolute finality three days or even six days a week. As nearly as I can figure it, this trade began as a sort of journalistic vaudeville intended to entertain the customers and exert a little circulation pull of a slightly higher tone than that of the comics.'[19] The irony is that Pegler was describing precisely the sort of commentator that he himself would become, especially after the Second World War.

In the early days of the Second World War, having established himself as a screenwriter in Hollywood, Ben Hecht returned to column-writing with a daily column for the New York paper *PM*. In introducing a published collection of these columns, he exuded humility about his role:

> It was my status as a catch-as-catch-can newspaper sage that fascinated me during the editing and compiling of this book. For in thinking of my own status I fell to thinking also of the status of other sages. I thought of all the year's harangues, disputations, crystal-gazings, and cries of doom and despair that will make up the newspaper files of 1940 to 1941. And I wondered how sage-like we would sound tomorrow.
>
> The newspaper files have never been a great fountainhead of philosophy. I have often looked through them and marveled at the curious chemistry that seems to work on the thoughts of journalists. Their most heady fulminations, their banshee prophecies and endless grandiloquence have a way of paling with the days and usually ending up dead on the bier of time.
>
> There is in this an ancient lesson for writers, to wit, that the wind is less permanent than the sea and that all the alarms which disturb us, however powerful and even historic, are of ephemeral interest compared to the littler plots of human relationship.
>
> Concerning the newspaper sages of my own day I am certain that when the future pauses to rummage among the columns we filled it will be amazed, as it always has been, by how little we saw, how confused we were, and how nimbly we met the high winds of our hour by standing on our heads.[20]

Another writer who chose not to keep silent once the Second World War was under way was Carl Sandburg, who jumped at the opportunity to write a weekly column for the *Chicago Times*. He, too, felt humble about his pronouncements: 'It did not then follow that a watchtower arose shedding light over the national scene, bringing order out of confusion. The result rather was a Portrait of a Man in a Fog, at times, or again the piece of writing offered represented the best lucid memorandum occurring to the writer for that particular weekend moment of time.'

Laying bare one's weaknesses and frustrations in an endearing way, along with one's perceptions, is an essential element in the vocation of the general columnist, as Max Lerner realized:

> To be a general columnist is to exclude nothing human from one's perspective, and to treat the personal seriously and the serious personally . . . In season and out a general columnist is fair game on two counts. Since he exposes his prejudices and frailties constantly, he invites their further exposure by others; and since he makes a show of being omniscient, he invites the reactions which will disprove his competence in any area and prove his fallibility in all. One of the most cherished natural rights of Americans is the constitutional right to make a target out of a columnist . . . A general columnist, by his nature, must roam widely and set down his assertions, not just his doubts and torments. Remember that he is not sitting in judgement as an expert who has mastered what there is to know on the subject. He is only a traveler who has made unsuspected discoveries for himself in the realms of gold, and he wants to share them.[21]

Tom Driberg listed the qualities he felt were required in a columnist. First came 'a strong, coherent, philosophic view of life . . . The columnist in modern society, whether he is anti-capitalist or anti-socialist, will therefore tend to be irreverent, sceptical, pungent: like Socrates, a gadfly.' Second, 'he should have his own style'. Third, 'he must be interested in a large variety of special subjects'. Fourth, 'he must not be domesticated'. Fifth, 'he should go abroad at least once a year, for at least a few weeks'. And sixth, 'he should have highly sensitive antennae' to protect him from the blandishments of the professional publicity agent.[22] Max Lerner believed that 'awareness' was the crucial quality in a columnist: 'Like the novelist and the philosopher, he must lay himself open to experience, from every direction and on every dimension. Nothing can replace this awareness.'[23] By way of contrast, O. O. McIntyre was dismissive of the notion that the columnist was uniquely distinguished from other journalists: 'The idea that columning requires special gifts is one of the magnificent myths of the trade. Most of us took it up as people take up soliciting life insurance – after everything else we tried was a flop.'[24]

More recently, the syndicated American columnist George Will has stated that the columnist must have 'three seductive skills: he must be pleasurable, concise and gifted at changing the subject frequently'.[25] He has also described writing columns as 'in part, but only in part, the art of complaining usefully' and referred to 'the columnist's basic stance of thorough disapproval of all conduct but his own'. The columnist can go beyond what other journalists do and he can use his own shortcomings as an aid to promote wider understanding. In the estimation of Hallam Walker Davis:

> They [columns] contribute to the health and sanity of thinking. As a rule they champion common sense and laugh absurdity out of court. The good reporter and the good feature writer do not encourage us to inquire into things. Even the editorial writer does not often ask us to look on both sides. But the columnist is ever flipping things upside down and wrong side out and inviting us to look and laugh – and think, even.[26]

THE ROLE OF THE READER

If columnists can have a powerful effect on readers, then it is partly because they have an appeal that is unique among journalists. 'The reader likes the column because it reveals a daily insight into another man's soul – and he finds this other soul likeable,' explained C. L. Edson in 1920. 'Mencken says (in his column in the *Smart Set* called "Reputation Generale") that "friendship does not make men approve each other. But mutual approval causes men to become friends." '[27]

Friendliness towards readers is not always guaranteed. Instead, the columnist and the reader sometimes serve as foils for one another. The relationship may be a tempestuous one, but it is a relationship none the less, wrote Hallam Walker Davis in 1926:

> The attitude of the columnist toward his reading public is a marked one. He may be chummy with his readers, take them closely into his confidence, and write to them intimately of intimate things. He may use 'you' and 'I', or the editorial 'we', until the reader feels himself engaging in a fireside chat instead of reading a paper. Or the columnist may go to the other extreme and apparently ignore his readers, tossing his

material out with seemingly no concern as to whether anybody ever looks at it. He may choose subjects and employ manners that highbrow, it would seem, at least nine-tenths of the readers of his paper. Or he may assume a nonchalant attitude and appear half in earnest and half not. Or he may indulge in the great American sport of 'kidding'. He may treat you in any way that a human being may treat you.[28]

The long-standing columnist Phillip Adams has given thanks for 'the opportunity to meet with a great many readers each and every week, who, bless their hearts, recognize that you're involved in a process rather than an event. So they forgive you your bad columns, or even runs of bad columns, waiting patiently until you deliver another goodie.'[29] For many years Jill Tweedie's column on the 'Guardian Women' page appeared above the 'Open Space' correspondence column, which carried the letters provoked by her previous column or columns.

Again, Max Lerner shows an acute understanding of the reader's importance as grit in the columnist's oyster:

> The relation of columnist to reader is an intensely close and personal one. 'You come between my wife and me,' a husband has sometimes said. 'We read you often in bed at night, and we argue about what you write.' I like being read that way. Sometimes a column is read and discussed by a whole group of friends. Over the years my mail has been heavy, with generous letters, indignant letters, eccentric letters, argumentative letters, philosophical letters, and letters giving the reader's experience with life and love and asking for advice. The columnist is seen as companion, commentator, guide, friend, even psychiatrist. He gets often a not quite incomprehensible, but always welcome, amount of devotion. His readers use him partly to articulate what they have themselves been thinking, partly as an opinion litmus test: by matching their judgements with his, setting them side by side, they have a way of confirming their own trend of thinking – or condemning his.[30]

Eleanor Roosevelt used her own 'My Day' column to pay tribute to one of the most popular columnists of the 1940s, Ernie Pyle, who had been felled by a Japanese bullet in Ie Shima:

> To thousands and thousands of people all over the world, his column has brought the best understanding of the human side of our fighting men.
>
> Mr Pyle wanted above everything else to see them and to be with them in the Pacific. I am glad he had the opportunity but, like many others, I shall miss his column, with its gracious understanding of human beings. I shall never forget how much I enjoyed meeting him here in the White House last year and how much I admired this frail and modest man who could endure hardships because he loved his job and our men.[31]

Another columnist who died in the Pacific in the Second World War, leaving behind an affectionate readership and radio audience, was the Washington correspondent Raymond Clapper. Unlike Pyle, Clapper was more of a commentator and an analyst, although he slightly resented the fact that he was expected to flourish opinions on everything:

In writing a column one feels he is letting his readers down unless he has a hard-hitting opinion to serve up six days a week on the regular deadline. The writer who appears in print these days without clubbing his readers over the head with an opinion is put down as an odd fellow, with something missing, as if he had walked down the street without a necktie.[32]

Because of his humility about holding opinions, as much as for his sharp analysis and clear prose style, Clapper was dubbed the 'Everyman's Columnist'. This problem of lacking resolute opinions on all subjects tends to haunt columnists. Of course, some columnists – one thinks of Westbrook Pegler or Lucius Beebe or Auberon Waugh – rarely seem to experience any doubt or confusion about what to think, while others, whether deliberately or not, make a virtue out of their bewilderment. Howard Vincent O'Brien, who wrote a daily column for the *Chicago Daily News* from 1935 until his death in 1947, forged a powerful link with his readers, as one of his colleagues reflected, not by displaying expertise and conviction but by laying bare his sense of uncertainty:

Superficially O'Brien's columns presented him as a confused man – one who did not know quite what to make of the contradictions and complexities and absurdities of the modern world . . .

The more he wrote, across the years, about the readiness with which he changed his mind on public issues, the more confidence his readers had in him. He was what they would like to be if they only had a little more courage.

This identification of a reader with a writer made tens of thousands of people accompany O'Brien spiritually as he lost his son in the war, as he lost much of his own eyesight and as, at last, he lost his own life, little by little, to that least understandable of Man's problems, Death.

And he wrote that moving and noble column about the unfathomed disease which was upon him with precisely the same inquiring courage, the identical lack of self-importance with which he had written about everything else.[33]

Another columnist who was appreciated for her combination of warmth, fallibility and wit was Erma Bombeck, who covered what she dubbed 'the utility room beat' and wrote over 4,000 syndicated columns from 1965 until her death in 1996. Her friend and fellow syndicated columnist Art Buchwald, writing after her death, identified the familiar point of view which made her so widely liked and admired:

Her columns invited people in. The only person she ever made fun of was herself. She met readers where they live – their tract houses, their car pools, their kids' band concerts and PTA meetings. Her columns struck a chord. I bet they were clipped from the paper and stuck to more refrigerator doors than those of any other columnist in history.[34]

This judgement was echoed by yet another columnist, Ellen Goodman:

A lot of columnists write words to end up in the Congressional Record or on the President's desk or at the Pulitzer Committee's door. But Erma Bombeck went us all one better. Her words won her the permanent place of honor in American life: the refrigerator door.[35]

The Australian Charmian Clift was another columnist who developed a special bond with her readers, as Nadia Wheatley, who has edited two collections of Clift's columns from the 1960s, has pointed out: 'Charmian Clift was addressing a reader who had a lot in common with Charmian Clift, and indeed she firmly declared that she was writing to please herself. This is, I think, part of the key to Clift's amazing appeal, for if the writer treated the reader as if she were her equal and her intimate, this was of course true – because her reader was to some extent herself.' One of Clift's readers told Wheatley: 'I had the strangest feeling that Charmian Clift was in fact a friend, someone I knew. When reading [her essays] I felt that they were accounts of things we could have talked about (given the chance) over a cup of tea in the kitchen.' As Wheatley has explained, the relationship between Clift and her readers was symbiotic: 'From week to week the Clift reader met familiar characters (Clift's husband, her children, some of her friends, her cat Jeoffrey, and of course the columnist herself) who lived and acted against a background of everyday family life and current political events ... If in a sense the Clift column functioned as a kind of serial story, the audience, through their letters, were also part of the drama.' Wheatley recognized that 'the dialectic of the essay-response-essay added to the serial nature of the column' and that 'the letters could provide solutions'.[36]

Yet some columnists believe that there is no audience superior to oneself and that second-guessing readers, let alone indulging them, is a delusion. Shirley Povich, who wrote a daily sports column for the *Washington Post* from 1933 to 1974, claimed to have given nary a thought for the readers:

> You're not writing for a public, you're doing it for a newspaper, for yourself, for your pride, for your satisfaction. Never think that you're writing for the people out there. Anybody who believes this is riding for a fall. You're writing for that white sheet of paper in the typewriter, for your newspaper, and for yourself. There's nobody out there.[37]

THE SUBJECT MATTER OF THE COLUMNIST

Jay House wrote that 'the columnist continually dramatizes himself'.[38] Among subjects which have proved to be perennials are the difficulties of writing a column (see Charmian Clift on p. 401) and procrastination about sitting in front of the typewriter (see Patrick Campbell on p. 384); the time it takes to write a column, whether as a means to mock working hours legislation (see Raymond Clapper on p. 189) or time-and-motion study (see Bill Vaughan on p. 329), or as itself a means of procrastination (see E. B. White on p. 176).

Another limitless source of inspiration is the columnist's family and pets. Heywood Broun wrote with tenderness and wit about his mother's staunchly conservative views, and even a political columnist like Richard L. Strout once wrote a column about his mother as an index of political and cultural change. Broun also wrote numerous columns about his baby son. 'To be sure there were days when the kid did not come through,' he later explained. 'Some of the brightest things he ever did in print were sheer invention.

Accordingly I have decided that when he comes to man's estate ten percent of the net ought to be a fair return. I mean ninety percent for the agent and entrepreneur.'[39] For Erma Bombeck, family life in a Midwestern suburb was her entire subject matter, but it was sufficiently loamy to produce a thrice-weekly column for over thirty years. When O. O. McIntyre wrote about the death of his dog, he attracted a postbag of some 30,000 letters of commiseration.

The much-married Charles McCabe could be relied on to broach the subject of marriage and ex-wives from time to time, while the Australian columnists Lennie Lower and Leon Gellert both made frequent mention of their spouses – indeed, Gellert always referred to his as 'A Certain Party'. The American columnist Ben Beagle refers to his spouse as 'the greatest station wagon driver of them all'. A few columnists have written about their romance with the bottle and the physiological consequences thereof. Jeff Bernard, in his 'Low Life' column for the *Spectator* was engaged for over twenty years in writing what one person has characterized as 'the longest suicide note in history'. Bernard's intention was to celebrate his wayward life in defiance of those puritanical busybodies who wished to reform him. Even the apology line 'Jeffrey Bernard is unwell', so obviously euphemistic – which appeared when his column, for whatever reason, did not – was a gesture of defiance.

Self-dramatization is one thing, self-exposure, or the exposure of one's family and friends, is another, although it is a fine line that separates the two. Jeff Bernard teetered on the brink between the one and the other. A more recent development in the direction of self-exposure is the columnist, generally female, who eviscerates herself in public, laying bare her emotional insecurities and traumas, and charting the progress (or deterioration) of her relationships with men. 'I myself used to write one of these slice-of-one's-own-life newspaper columns,' Laura Thompson has explained in an article on this phenomenon. 'I know, therefore, how desperate one can become for material and how quickly the ethical dilemma arises: how much of the currency of my personal life can I spend, in order to earn a living.' These columnists fascinate as they infuriate. One hears expressions of envy at the apparent ease of their task and horror at the fierceness with which they go at it. 'We are transfixed, in fact, by the columnists' daring: by their willingness to spill their guts in trying to entertain us.' Thus far, this is more a British than an American phenomenon, and such columnists evidently have difficulty – how could they not? – in sustaining their acts. Zoe Heller, whose column in the *Sunday Times Magazine* epitomized this sub-genre, could not make it beyond a couple of years. 'And, according to her final column . . . ,' Thompson continued, 'Zoe Heller gave up the job not just because she was sick of getting letters from weirdos who felt that they, too, had been to bed with her, but because she had had enough, quite simply, of remaking her life as copy.'[40]

METHODS OF COMPOSITION

Every columnist has his own way of translating his thoughts and personality into written form. 'It seems that I'm column-inching my way towards ten million published words in newspapers and magazines,' Phillip Adams has declared. 'Not a bad effort for a writer who doesn't write. Not a word. Not ever. My writings are technically mumblings, words confided to a little hand-held dictating machine that I carry with me everywhere.'[41]

Keeping up the flow of ideas is not so much the problem as being able to discriminate, according to Max Lerner:

> The hard thing is not to think up a topic, but to pick one out of the many that thrust themselves at you each day, out of the reading of the wire copy and the papers, out of books, travel, dreams, out of conversation and the ordinary contacts of an ordinary day. I keep a notebook and a file into which I jot down ideas for columns as they occur to me. Before I write I look through the papers, and often some headline event will converge with one of these ideas. Most often I have to choose between a half dozen or dozen that have some possibilities. Sometimes I try them out by trying to outline several, and I choose the one that seems to go least lamely.[42]

Red Smith compared writing a daily sports column to sitting down at a typewriter and opening a vein. Others have laboured long and hard to achieve their effects. Westbrook Pegler was rarely able to stop thinking about his column. He took over four hours on each one. 'The columnist was as insistent on neatness as he was neurotic about other people's noise,' wrote a biographer, 'and he felt obliged to retype any page containing the slightest error.'[43] Heywood Broun was envied by his fellow writers for his speed of composition – once memorably dashing off a column while sitting out a few hands of cards. Indeed, Broun disapproved of columnists who took great pains, as is shown in this criticism of his colleague Pegler, because he felt it detracted from their general task of learning about the world:

> Peg told me once that he sometimes spent as much as four or five hours in the creation of a column. This seemed to me a shocking confession for any man who came up from a city room. It is too much time for Peg to put in with himself. It is too much time for anybody to waste upon the works of Westbrook Pegler. The daily commentator who takes too much pains with his writing has insufficient energy left to get out and find something to write about. A column ought to be something more than hem-stitching a pattern around the phrase 'the second Louisiana Purchase'. It may be all very well for Shakespeare and the musical glasses to tinkle sweetly but a newspaperman ought to go clanging down the street along with the hook and ladder. He will seldom be lucky enough to have a four-alarm fire come dropping down his chimney.[44]

Carl Sandburg also believed that excessive care would be an inhibition to forceful commentary. Looking back on his weekly columns in 1943, he explained: 'Much is overwritten. Much would have been better done had there been no deadline to meet. Much would have had meritorious brevity and bright gleam had it been put off into some vague period of an afterwhile when again the same questions would arise: "Why take a chance? What's the use?" '[45]

The working methods of the Australian columnist Charmian Clift required a slow build-up to the actual writing of her weekly essay:

Part of the regular crisis of literary paralysis was the problem of finding exactly the right topic. To get around this, Clift kept files of press-cuttings, recording both major events and odd things that took her interest. She also kept files of the many letters (some of them loopy, or even poisonous) that readers sent her, so she could tap back into her source. And she asked questions: of taxi-drivers, of grocers, of prawn-sorters, of society matrons, of friends and of friends of her children.

And then each week, maybe as late as Wednesday or Thursday, she decided what it was that *this* piece would be about. Once this was established, she would do a quick handwritten checklist. Next there was the mad consulting of encyclopaedias, the search through reference books, the picking of family brains: what *was* that story that Lily used to tell of so and so, and how green was such and such, and where did that line of poem come from, and when was Ur of the Chaldees?

Then she would make up to five pages of densely typed notes, listing bits of information drawn from historical, scientific and anthropological sources, as well as from her extensive and eccentric general knowledge. Yet if Charmian Clift had a talent for ordering and distilling information, her great strength was her lateral turn of mind. So as she jotted down facts and figures she would spin off into memories, anecdotes, quotations or word associations. And in the same way as she addressed her reader directly in her column, she talked to herself in her notes . . .

Finally, after the research and the speculation, would come the writing. Again this would be a laborious process, requiring draft upon draft before all the facts, the opinions, the questions, the examples were stitched together into four foolscap pages of prose that would be ready for the Saturday deadline.[46]

A complete contrast to this all-encompassing approach is that of Jay House, who eschewed preparation, working 'close to the bell' and striving 'for a thirty-minute margin', and instead trusted to a faculty that emerged only while he was performing:

> . . . I never jot anything down. I never even take mental cognizance of it. My subconscious is trained to sop up everything calculated to be of any present or future value to me. Maybe it is, primarily, because I am lazy and hate to take trouble that I regard formal preparation for the day's task casually . . . My chief concern is that I shall not permit tomorrow's work to 'ride' me. That I shall not take it home with me, sleep with it or be conscious of it when I awake in the morning. And so, when I have finished the day's work I do not think of it again until it is time to do another one. I do not spend my leisure thinking up smart cracks to put in the paper. I spend it trying to have a good time . . . My habit is to go to work around two o'clock in the afternoon. Nearly always I am through by four o'clock or four-thirty. I never know what I am going to write. I have never seen the day when there was anything to write. But while I am tucking blank paper into the typewriter and lighting a fresh cigar, I feel out my mood and reach for the topic or topics that seem to stir it or to be in accord with it.
>
> I sometimes devote as much as five minutes to such speculation. After that I start writing. I have never been able to write in leisurely or detached fashion. When I do write I write my head off. There are dead and gone Remingtons that still bewail the

beatings I gave them. And an afternoon's work takes as much toil from me physically as would five rounds in the prize ring. I get over it quicker, that's all.[47]

While some columnists, particularly those who have started out as reporters, crave the camaraderie of the city room and continue to ply their trade from a newspaper office, most have written their best work under widely varying conditions. Max Lerner listed the different examples from his own experience:

> ... at home if I am there, in Boston when I am teaching at Brandeis University, in a score of foreign countries, on planes and trains, at terminals, in hotel rooms, or sitting out on the lawn if I am writing in the summer, at our house at North Sea, Long Island, or on the beach while the children are swimming. I am not one of your conditioned writers who can work only under some routine. I usually write late at night, between midnight and 3 a.m., but I snatch the time whenever it offers, and I work best under the pressure of a deadline.[48]

The pressure of a deadline was essential to the British columnist Robert Lynd, who explained in this passage how the columnist finds himself under a perpetual pall:

> ... even if I had a week in which to write an article, I should find it difficult to begin writing till the last hours of the last day of the week. Expected to deliver my article by the first post on Thursday morning, I still found myself late on Wednesday night doing my utmost to dodge the necessity of work. How often have I succeeded so well that I have had to set the alarum-clock for six and go down and compel myself to tackle the detested task on a wintry Thursday morning! This, the young should be warned, though it looks a lazy life, is not an easy life. The reluctant worker has not an hour of the twenty-four free from the shadow of work. He finds himself under the necessity, at some time or other, of working at every hour of the day − if it happens to be the last hour permitted by the printer − writing in such places as railway trains and on washstands in the bedrooms of provincial hotels. The only compensation for such a miserable state of things is that it raises our opinion of human nature by revealing to us the incomparable patience of editors.[49]

Of course, little of this matters to the reader − as long as the friendly columnist is there in his regular place, to interpret or to entertain, to comfort or to provoke.

The golden land of the columnist has always been the United States, though other countries such as Britain and Australia have produced a respectable crop, while the golden age of the columnist was between the wars, before television created new types of entertainment and its own brand of personality. It may be something of an illusion, but today's columnists *en masse* seem anaemic and lacklustre in comparison to their forerunners from that period. While most regional and local papers in the United States continue to throw up engaging columnists, the British press now is overpopulated with second-rate performers. It is primarily for those who enjoy the column as a genre yet feel dissatisfied with the current generation of columnists, that I have edited this collection.

NOTES

1 A causerie is a piece of writing in a chatty, conversational manner.
2 Phillip Adams, Introduction to *Classic Columns* (1994), p. iii.
3 Of course, there are some brilliant essayists who choose to write only occasionally, or in myriad publications, but who none the less engage in 'personal journalism': such individuals have been of no concern to me in preparing this anthology. Both Stephen Leacock and Robert Benchley had syndicated columns for a brief time in the early 1930s, but they were both essentially peripatetic humorists.
4 Hallam Walker Davis, *The Column* (1926), pp. 4–5.
5 Lucy Maynard Salmon, *The Newspaper and the Historian* (1923), p. 61n.
6 Lucy Maynard Salmon, op. cit., p. 62.
7 Red Smith, 'Writing Less – and Better', *New York Times*, 1982; reprinted in Karl E. Meyer, *Pundits, Poets and Wits: An Omnibus of American Newspaper Columns* (1990), pp. 290–91.
8 Lucy Maynard Salmon, op. cit., p. 10.
9 ibid., p. 62.
10 Damon Runyon, 'Private Thoughts of a Columnist', King Features, *c.* 1945; reprinted in Karl E. Meyer, op. cit., pp. 203–5.
11 Max Lerner, Foreword to *Public Journal: Marginal Notes on Wartime America* (1945), p. vii.
12 Jay E. House, 'Case Notes of a Columnist', *On Second Thought* (1937), p. 41.
13 Introduction to James M. Smallwood and Steven K. Gragert (eds.), *Will Rogers's Daily Telegrams, Vol. 1 – The Coolidge Years 1926–1929* (1978), pp. xiv–xv.
14 Peter Jenkins, 'Inside Story', *Guardian*, 3 June 1977; reprinted in Richard Cockett and Brian Brivati (eds.), *Anatomy of Decline* (1995), pp. 23–5.
15 Heywood Broun, 'How I Got Into This Racket', in Heywood Hale Broun (ed.), *Collected Edition of Heywood Broun* (1941), pp. 322–3.
16 George F. Will, 'Journalism and Friendship', *Newsweek*, January 19, 1981; reprinted in Karl E. Meyer, op. cit., pp. 369–71.
17 Max Lerner, 'The View From a Column', Foreword to *The Unfinished Country: A Book of American Symbols* (1959), p. xvii.
18 Max Harris, *The Angry Eye* (1974), pp. 4–5.
19 Quoted in Oliver Pilat, *Pegler, Angry Man of the Press* (1963), p. 155.
20 Ben Hecht, 'Afternoon of an Author', Introduction to *1001 Afternoons in New York* (1941), p. 10.
21 Max Lerner, op. cit., pp. xv–xvi.
22 Introduction to Tom Driberg, *Colonnade* (1949), pp. 11–12.
23 Max Lerner, op. cit., p. xx.
24 O. O. McIntyre, quoted by Ray Long in Preface to *Another 'Odd' Book: 25 Selected Stories of O. O. McIntyre* (1932), p. xii.
25 George F. Will, 'Ten Years in a Column', *Washington Post*, December 18, 1983; reprinted in Karl E. Meyer, op. cit., pp. 367–9.
26 Hallam Walker Davis, op. cit., pp. 6–7.
27 C. L. Edson, *The Gentle Art of Columning: A Treatise on Comic Journalism* (1920), p. 125.
28 Hallam Walker Davis, op. cit., p. 162.
29 Phillip Adams, op. cit., p. vi.
30 Max Lerner, op. cit. p. xx.

31 Eleanor Roosevelt, 'My Day', April 19, 1945, from *Eleanor Roosevelt's My Day, 1936–1945* (1989), p. 393.

32 Raymond Clapper, November 21, 1940; from Olive Ewing Clapper (ed.), *Watching the World* (1944), p. 57.

33 Lloyd Lewis in 'Howard Vincent O'Brien Considered', *All Things Considered* (1948), pp. xvi–xvii.

34 Quoted in *Forever, Emma: Best Loved Writing from America's Favorite Humorist* (1996), p. 250.

35 ibid., p. 261.

36 Nadia Wheatley, Introduction to Charmian Clift, *Being Alone With Oneself, Essays, 1968–1969* (1991), pp. 6–13 passim.

37 Interviewed in Jerome Holtzman (ed.), *No Cheering in the Press Box: Recollections – Personal & Professional by Eighteen Veteran American Sportswriters* (1974), pp. 127–8.

38 Jay E. House, 'Case Notes of a Columnist', *On Second Thought* (1937), p. 41.

39 Heywood Broun, op. cit., p. 322.

40 Quotations in the preceding paragraph from Laura Thompson, 'The Company of Wolves', *Guardian*, 27 May 1997.

41 Phillip Adams, op. cit., p. iii.

42 Max Lerner, op. cit., p. xviii.

43 Oliver Pilat, op. cit., p. 129.

44 Heywood Broun, 'Square Peg', *Collected Edition of Heywood Broun* (1941), p. 500.

45 Carl Sandburg, *Home Front Memo* (1943), p. 275.

46 Nadia Wheatley, Introduction to Charmian Clift, *Trouble in Lotus Land, Essays, 1964–1967* (1990), pp. 10–11.

47 Jay E. House, op. cit., pp. 41–3.

48 Max Lerner, op. cit., p. xviii.

49 Robert Lynd, 'A Thousand and One "Middles" ', *New Statesman and Nation* [New Statesman Retrospect], 14 April 1934.

BILL NYE

Edgar Wilson Nye (1850–96) was born in Maine and taken to live on a farm in western Wisconsin at the age of two. After school he was briefly a miller's helper, a law clerk, a teacher and a newspaper reporter. In 1876 he went to Laramie, Wyoming Territory, as assistant editor of the *Laramie Daily Sentinel* (at $12 a week) and he immediately began writing humorous columns for the paper. In late 1877 he left the *Sentinel* and attempted to set up in business as an attorney, but he had to continue writing for the *Laramie Times*, the *Cheyenne Sun* and the *Denver Tribune* to support himself. However, in 1881 he returned to a full-time job in journalism as editor of the *Laramie Boomerang*, a Republican paper with a circulation of 300 and both daily and weekly editions. His columns were collected in book form in *Bill Nye and Boomerang* (1881) and *Forty Liars and Other Lies* (1882). Nye spent seven years in Laramie, obtaining a government appointment as postmaster, enjoying the frontier life and honing his skills as a humorist, but after a bout of spinal meningitis he was advised that the altitude of Laramie was deleterious to his health and so he decided to return to Hudson, Wisconsin, the nearest town to the farm where he had spent his childhood. Before leaving, he made sure to assemble a bundle of his clippings, which later formed the substance of *Baled Hay* (1884) and *Remarks by Bill Nye* (1886). In 1885 he began contributing a weekly letter to the *Boston Globe* and in 1887 the New York *World* also took his column. By the early 1890s, Nye was the most famous humorist in the United States; his column was syndicated to roughly sixty papers; and his annual income from column-writing and lecturing reached $30,000. Indeed, the combination was too much for his weak disposition and he was taken ill on stage in Paterson, New Jersey, and hounded to the rail depot by a gang of rowdies who believed him to be drunk. He was exhausted and some months later suffered a stroke, dying soon afterwards, at the age of only forty-five.

Suggestions for a School of Journalism
From *Bill Nye and Boomerang* (1881)

A number of friends have personally asked me to express an opinion upon the matter of an established school of journalism, as spoken of by ex-Mayor Henry C. Robinson, of Hartford, Connecticut, and many more through the West who are strangers to me personally, having written me to give my views upon the subject, I have consented insofar that I will undertake a simple synopsis of what the course should embrace.

I most heartily endorse the movement, if it may be called such at this early stage. Knowing a little of the intricacies of this branch of the profession, I am going to state fully my belief as to its importance, and the necessity for a thorough training upon it. We meet almost everywhere newspaper men who are totally unfitted for the high office of public educators through the all-powerful press. The woods is full of them. We know that not one out of a thousand of those who are today classed as journalists is fit for that position.

I know that to be the case, because people tell me so.

I cannot call to mind today, in all my wide journalistic acquaintance, a solitary man who has not been pronounced an ass by one or more of my fellow-men. This is indeed a terrible state of affairs.

In many instances these harsh criticisms are made by those who do not know, without submitting themselves to tremendous mental strain, the difference between a 'lower case' q and the old Calvinistic doctrine of unanimous damnation, but that makes no difference; the true journalist should strive to please the masses. He should make his whole life a study of human nature and an earnest effort to serve the great reading world collectively and individually.

This requires a man, of course, with similar characteristics and the same general information possessed by the Almighty, but who would be willing to work at a much more moderate salary.

The reader will instantly see how difficult it is to obtain this class of men. Outside of the mental giant who writes these lines and two or three others, perhaps . . .

But never mind. I leave a grateful world to say that, while I map out a plan for the ambitious young journalist who might be entering upon the broad arena of newspaper-dom, and preparing himself at a regularly established school for that purpose.

Let the first two years be devoted to meditation and prayer. This will prepare the young editor for the surprise and consequent profanity which in a few years he may experience when he finds in his boss editorial that God is spelled with a little g, and the peroration of the article has been taken out and carefully locked up between a death notice and the announcement of the birth of a cross-eyed infant.

The ensuing five years should be spent in becoming familiar with the surprising and mirth-provoking orthography of the English language.

Then would follow three years devoted to practice with dumb bells, sand bags and slung shots, in order to become an athlete. I have found in my own journalistic history more cause for regret over my neglect of this branch than any other. I am a pretty good runner, but aside from that I regret to say that as an athlete I am not a dazzling success.

The above course of intermediate training would fit the student to enter upon the regular curriculum.

Then set aside ten years for learning the typographical art perfectly, so that when visitors wish to look at the composing room, and ask the editor to explain the use of the 'hell box,' he will not have to blush and tell a gauzy lie about its being a composing stick. Let the young journalist study the mysteries of type setting, distributing, press work, galleys, italic, shooting sticks, type lice and other mechanical implements of the printer's department.

Five years should be spent in learning to properly read and correct proof, as well as how to mark it on the margin like a Chinese map of the Gunnison country.

At least fifteen years should then be devoted to the study of American politics and the whole civil service. This time could be extended five years with great profit to the careful student who wishes, of course, to know thoroughly the names and records of all public men, together with the relative political strength of each party.

He should then take a medical course and learn how to bind up contusions, apply arnica, court plaster or bandages, plug up bullet holes and prospect through the human system for buck shot. The reason of this course, which should embrace five years of close study, is apparent to the thinking mind.

Ten years should then be devoted to the study of law. No thorough metropolitan editor wants to enter upon his profession without knowing the difference between a writ of *mandamus* and other styles of profanity. He should thoroughly understand the entire system of American jurisprudence, and be as familiar with the more recent decisions of the courts as New York people are with the semi-annual letter of Governor Seymour declining the Presidency.

The student will by this time begin to see what is required of him and will enter with greater zeal upon his adopted profession.

He will now enter upon a theological course of ten years. He can then write a telling editorial on the great question of What We Shall Do To Be Saved without mixing up Calvin and Tom Paine with Judas Iscariot and Ben Butler.

The closing ten years of the regular course might be profitably used in acquiring a practical knowledge of cutting cord wood, baking beans, making shirts, lecturing, turning double handsprings, preaching the gospel, learning how to make a good adhesive paste that will not sour in hot weather, learning the art of scissors grinding, punctuation, capitalization, prosody, plain sewing, music, dancing, sculpting, etiquette, how to win the affections of the opposite sex, the ten commandments, every man his own teacher on the violin, croquet, rules of the prize ring, parlor magic, civil engineering, decorative art, calsomining, bicycling, baseball, hydraulics, botany, poker, calisthenics, high-low jack, international law, faro, rhetoric, fifteen-ball pool, drawing and painting, mule skinning, vocal music, horsemanship, plastering, bull whacking, etc., etc., etc.

At the age of ninety-five the student will have lost that wild, reckless and impulsive style so common among younger and less experienced journalists. He will emerge from the school with a light heart and a knowledge-box loaded up to the muzzle with the most useful information.

The heyday and springtime of life will, of course, be past, but the graduate will have nothing to worry him any more, except the horrible question which is ever rising up before the journalist, as to whether he shall put his money into government four percents or purchase real estate in some growing town.

Requesting a Remittance
From *Bill Nye's Thinks* (1888)

Along toward morning, 1887
Washington, DC

Cashier, World Office, New York

My dear sir: You will doubtless be surprised to hear from me so soon, as I did not promise when I left New York that I would write you. But now I take pen in hand to say that the Senate and House of Representatives are having a good deal of fun with me. You will wonder at first why I send in my expense account before I send in anything for the paper, but I will explain that to you when I get back. At first I thought I would not bother with the expense account till I got to your office, but I can now see that it is going to worry me to get there unless I hear from you favorably by return mail.

I have not written anything for publication yet, but I am getting material together that will make people throughout our broad land open their eyes in astonishment. I shall deal fairly and openly with these great national questions, and frankly hew to the line. Candor is my leading characteristic. If you will pardon me for saying so in the first letter you ever received from me, I believe there is nothing about my whole character which seems to challenge my admiration for myself any more than that.

I have been mingling with society ever since I came here, and that is one reason I have written very little for publication, and did not send what I did write.

Yesterday afternoon my money gave out at 3:20, and since that my mind has been clearer and society has made fewer demands on me. At first I thought I would obtain employment at the Treasury Department as exchange editor in the greenback room. Then I remembered that I would get very faint before I could go through a competitive examination, and, in the meantime, I might lose social caste by *wearing my person on the outside of my clothes*. So I have resolved to write you a chatty letter about Washington, assuring you that I am well, and asking you kindly to consider the enclosed tabulated bill of expenses, as I need the money to buy Christmas presents and get home with.

So far I have not been over to the Capitol, preferring to have Congress kind of percolate into my room, two or three at a time; but unless you can honor the enclosed waybill I shall be forced to go over to the House tomorrow and write something for the paper. Since I have been writing this I have been led to inquire whether it would be advisable for me to remain here through the entire session or not. It will be unusually long, lasting perhaps clear into July, and I find that the stenographers as a general thing get a pretty accurate and spicy account of the proceedings, much more so than I can, and as you will see by enclosed statement it is going to cost more to keep me here than I figured on.

My idea was that board and lodgings would be the main items of expense, but I struck a low-priced place, where, by clubbing together with some plain gentlemen from a distance who have been waiting here three years for political recognition, and who do not feel like surrounding themselves with a hotel, we get a plain room with six beds in it. The room overlooks the District of Columbia, and the first man in has the choice of beds, with the privilege of inviting friends to a limited number. We lunch plainly in the lower part of the building in a standing position without restraint or finger-bowls. So board is not the principal item of expense, though of course I do not wish to put up at a place where I will be a disgrace to the paper.

I saw Mr Cleveland briefly last evening at his home, but he was surrounded by a crowd of fawning sycophants, so I did not get a chance to speak to him as I would like to, and don't know as he would have advanced the amount to me anyway. He is very firm and stubborn, I judged, and would yield very little indeed, especially to

Yours truly,

Bill Nye

PS The following bill looks large in the aggregate, but when you come to examine each item there is really nothing startling about it, and when you remember that I have been here now four days and that this is the first bill I have sent in to the office during that time, I know you will not consider it out of the way, especially as you are interested in seeing me make a good paper of the 'World,' no matter what the expense is.

I fear you will regard the item for embalming as exorbitant, and it is so, but I was compelled to pay that price, as the man had to be shipped a long distance, and I did not want to shock his friends too much when he met them at the depot.

Expense Account

To rent of dress suit for the purpose of seeing life in Washington in the interest of the paper	$4.50
To charges for dispersing turtle soup from lap of same	1.00
To getting fur collar put on overcoat, in interest of paper	9.00
To amount loaned a gentleman who had lived in Washington a long time and could make me a social pet (I will return same to you in case he pays it before I come back)	5.00
To lodgings two nights at 25 cents	.50
Six meals at 15 cents	.90
Pen and ink	.20
Postage on this letter	.08
Bronchial troches, in interest of paper	.20
Car fare	.60
Laundry work done in interest of paper	.30
Carriage hire in getting from humble home of a senator to my own voluptuous lodgings	2.00
To expenses of embalming a man who came to me and wanted me to use my influence in changing policy of the paper	180.00
To fine paid for assault and battery in and upon a gentleman who said he wanted my influence, but really was already under other influence, and who stepped on my stomach twice without offering to apologize	19.00
Paid janitor of jail next morning	1.00
Paid for breaking the window of my cell	.50
Paid damage for writing humorous poetry on wall of cell so that it could not be erased	2.00
Total	$226.78

•

J. M. BARRIE

Sir James Matthew Barrie (1860–1937), the novelist and playwright, was born in Tayside and educated at Edinburgh University. In 1883 he applied for the job of leader writer on the *Nottingham Journal* and when requested to submit some samples of his work he sent the paper one of his university essays. For a salary of £3 a week, he wrote a daily leader, a column signed 'Hippomenes' on Mondays, another column under the heading of 'The Modern Peripatetic' on Thursdays, and various articles and reviews. These were then reprinted in the paper's Saturday supplement. He kept up this output for some eighteen months. He subsequently wrote for the *St James's Gazette* in London and published autobiographical novels, before turning to the stage. His plays included *The Admirable Crichton* (1902), *Peter Pan* (1904) and *Dear Brutus* (1917). He was created a baronet in 1913 and served as Rector of Edinburgh University from 1930 until his death.

Interruptions
Nottingham Journal, 18 February 1884

It is not, perhaps, generally known that the ship yclept 'The Flying Dutchman' is manned by the inhuman monsters who at an earlier period of their existence frequented public meetings for the purpose of calling out 'Hear, hear' at inappropriate intervals. Until such interruptions absolutely cease the vessel must career hopelessly through the seas, and that is, no doubt, the reason why, according to the legend, 'The Flying Dutchman' is to sail for ever. The public-meeting fiend we shall have with us always. He is the thorn in the flesh of all politicians in the House of Commons and out of it, the dark cloud in the orator's clear sky. The impassioned statesman is in the middle of a noble peroration, he pauses to take a breath, and the fiend is upon him. 'Hear, hear,' he shouts, exulting in his infamy; the orator gets confused, forgets precisely where he left off, stutters, blushes, becomes white and nervous, and his chance is spoilt. The fiend has done for him. No seat in the House of Commons for him now, though when he entered the hall everything seemed in his favour. The cup had been at his lips, when the fiend snatched it from him. Sometimes, indeed, the orator is more than a match for the fiend. Sheridan was on one occasion tormented by a hearer, who insisted on shouting out 'Hear, hear' at the end of every sentence. One of us must make a fool of himself, was the conclusion at which the dramatist finally arrived, and he had no sooner reached that point than he made up his mind which one it was to be. 'Where,' he took occasion to exclaim, 'can we find a more foolish knave or a more knavish fool than he?' 'Hear, hear,' screamed the fiend, whereupon Sheridan bowed gratefully to his victim and thanked him for the information. 'If the gentleman in the third seat from the front,' exclaimed a maddened public speaker on another occasion, 'would not call out "Hear, hear" quite so frequently, perhaps we should all "hear" a little better.' This was a villainous pun, but it is one of the few puns on record for which there was justification.

Paris was laughing the other day over an interruption that covered with confusion both perpetrator and victim. The scene was a law court in the gay city, and an eloquent young advocate was pleading the cause of his client in a way that brought tears to the eyes of many of his hearers. It was felt, in short, that a second Cicero had arisen, and so silent was the court that a pin falling would have made a clatter. It was not generally known that the eloquent pleader was reciting his speech from memory, so natural was his affected emotion, so impassioned his appeals, but this was nevertheless the case. He had even taken the precaution of distributing printed copies among the reporters, so that his speech should read properly in the morning's newspapers. 'And now,' he exclaimed, 'I feel myself wholly unworthy to occupy the proud position I hold this day. The onerous nature of the task makes me tremble lest I should not do my unhappy client justice, and I cry "would to God that an abler advocate would take my place".' Here he faltered, put his handkerchief to his eyes, and seemed overcome with emotion. Unfortunately one of the reporters did not understand, and, fearing that the lawyer had forgotten what came next, he hurriedly looked up the place in his copy of the speech to prompt him. 'But the tears I see even now,' he exclaimed in a loud whisper, 'in the eyes of my unhappy client nerve me to the task.' Of course the tables were dissolved in laughter, and the eloquent pleader found that an untimely interruption had been sufficient to rob him of a reputation.

A public-meeting friend of my acquaintance used to attend every meeting in his neighbourhood for the purpose of calling out 'Hear, hear', 'Question', 'Order' and 'No, no', and always turned to the newspapers of next day with anxiety to see if his share in the proceedings had been reported. Where they were attended to, he carefully preserved copies of the newspapers, and there can be little doubt that this is the most singular case of literary vanity known since the introduction of printing. Interruptions, however, are not confined to public meetings, being, indeed, as common and as annoying in the drawing room as in the lecture-hall. The wittiest retort of the eighteenth century was certainly the young officer's cruel answer to Pope's interruption, 'And what, sir, is a note of interrogation?' The reply was, 'A note of interrogation is a little crooked thing that asks questions.' Equally good in its way was the manner in which a Scotch lawyer in London turned the tables on a facetious judge. 'In plain English my lo-ard,' began the lawyer when the judge interrupted him with, 'In plain Scotch, you mean, Mr McNab.' 'Ah weel,' answered the other, 'in plain common sense.' The late Dr Kenealy once showed himself more than a match for his enemies in the House of Commons. Instead of commencing his speech with 'Mr Speaker,' he simply began, 'Gentlemen,' whereupon, of course, there were loud cries of 'Order, order', 'Address the chair.' The offender turned politely to his neighbours, and begged their pardon for calling them gentlemen. On the hustings Lord Beaconsfield, when he was the comparatively obscurer Disraeli, was interrupted by an impertinent elector calling out, 'What do you stand on?' 'On my head, sir,' replied the candidate for a seat in the House, 'which is more than you will ever do.'

You may be telling a capital story, and the fool among your audience laughs before you come to the joke. This is one of the most exasperating of all interruptions, in that it carries a certain humiliation with it. You had announced before you began the anecdote that it was funny, and the fool has laughed out of good nature. Probably when you have

explained that the best of it has to come yet, the fellow laughs again, and this time at
the right place, but his amusement gives you no satisfaction, you are aware that his
hilarity is forced, and the more he giggles the more you grind your teeth. Your story
has been a failure, and all because of an interruption. An aggravating case is when in
the middle of your anecdote, you are interrupted by some friend who wants to know
the christian name of the person it happens to be about, or some such trifle. The man's
christian name has nothing whatever to do with the point of the story, and having
explained this pettishly you hurry along to the finale. But it is no use. The fiend is not
listening to you, he is meditating on that christian name, and his only remark when you
have finished your anecdote is that it is a pity you should have forgotten who it was
about. On the stage it cannot be particularly pleasant for the actor to be interrupted by
the laughter of his audience when he means to be pathetic, and vice versa. Yet Jefferson
used to be greeted with 'prolonged laughter' in 'Rip Van Winkle's' most pathetic scene.
In church I sit opposite an elderly lady who always begins to cry when her pastor raises
his voice. He does not seem to find this an interruption, but I do.

The Modern Peripatetic
Nottingham Journal, 6 March 1884

They talked as they walked,
They read as they run.

The glue that keeps the world together is self-esteem. It is terrible to think of what
might happen did Smith some time take it into his head that it was not worth his while
to try to outdo Robinson, or Brown that life would still be worth living though his
income was fifty pounds per annum short of Jones's. Self-esteem takes the form of a
vehement desire to rise superior to our neighbours, and in all Great Britain there is not
in all probability a single street which does not contain at least one superior family. A
superior family is one that esteems itself so very much, that it cannot avoid looking
down on its surroundings, and it is perfectly happy in the knowledge that its drawing
room is one foot by one and a half larger than any other in the vicinity.

Self-esteem sometimes takes the guise of patriotism. In one of the western isles of
Scotland there is an elderly clergyman who prays every Sunday for himself and his
congregation, and 'the neighbouring island of Great Britain'. This is only self-esteem,
an attempt to make the best of one's lot, to persuade oneself that his brass is gold, and
his ducks swans. No doubt the devout clergyman referred to is some relation to that
other minister of the gospel, who asked God to restore George III to health for three
months after he was dead.

Macaulay's schoolboy is pushing his way into notice again though other persons
could be worse spared. Admit even that there are precocious schoolboys who, like
Professor Robertson Smith, read the Greek Testament at six years of age, they are a
curse to other people if a blessing and a joy for ever to their parents. Infant phenomena
are all very well in Dickens's novels – if you come to think of it you will find one

phenomenon in each – but in real life they are a trifle wearisome. This is true perhaps of phenomena generally. In fiction we all revel in Charles O'Malleys and the like, but if they were persons of flesh and blood we would rejoice to see them in durance vile.

Children are not interesting when they are prodigies, but when they are funny without meaning it. Nevertheless that was perhaps a clever child rather than an unintentionally funny one who on having to solve an arithmetical problem about a dozen loaves asked his teacher if it was a baker's dozen. There was something subtle, too, in the boy who being asked by a contemptuous inspector if he had ever seen nothing, replied promptly, 'Yes, when I shut my eyes.' Only Scotchmen will appreciate the humour of the ragged boy's answer to his Sunday-school teacher's question, 'What do I mean when I say "Man is mortal?" ' The whispered reply was, 'He's awful fou' ma'am!' These scraps may have appeared in print before, though I fancy not.

The best story of the kind is told in Dean Ramsay's 'Reminiscences'. At a house where a dinner party was to be given the child of the establishment announced to his mother that, unless he was permitted to appear at the banquet, he 'would tell yon'. The alarmed mother gave him a seat beside his father, and whenever there seemed a probability of his being refused any dish that struck his fancy he remarked emphatically that if he did not get his fair share he 'would tell yon'. That boy had never enjoyed himself so much in his life, his agonized mother permitting him to gorge upon whatever he liked rather than have him shame his parents in the presence of their guests. When he asked his father to pass the wine, however, she rebelled, and then the ungrateful child announced that he 'would tell yon'. Getting upon his feet he shouted out at the top of his voice, 'My new breeks [trousers] was made out o' the auld curtains!' Sensation and curtain.

A young lady sat in a chair surveying herself in the mirror. When she had been there for a couple of hours or so, she murmured thoughtfully, 'Now I know what papa means when he talks about Mutual Admiration Societies.'

It is rather strange to see the newspapers constantly appearing with the heading 'A Female Impostor'. Are not all women impostors more or less? And is 'a female impostor' not just a long way of saying 'a woman'? The very latest of 'female impostors' is one who is making hay while the sun shines, where it so seldom does shine – in the East End of London. She goes about soliciting donations for free dinners for the metropolitan poor, and though she gets the donations, the poor do not seem to get the dinners. All benevolent persons are warned against her, and she is to be detected by her 'fair hair and tight-fitting Newmarket ulster'. Alas, what a number of impostors have fair hair and tight-fitting Newmarket ulsters!

There are some smart young men in this world; indeed, if the one did not contrive to undo the work of the other there would be no living at all. Among those who love to combine business with intellectual study is a Glasgow student, who, having taken down his moral philosophy professor's notes with exceptional care, has recently had them printed under the title of 'Aids to the Study of Moral Philosophy'. Curiously enough, Professor Caird has a notion that he, rather than one of his students, should derive pecuniary benefit from the publication of his works, and, as a consequence, the

Sheriff of Glasgow is at present insisting that all copies within the control of the publisher must be destroyed at once. Enterprise in undergraduates is sometimes misdirected.

•

EUGENE FIELD

Eugene Field (1850–95) was born in St Louis, Missouri, and although he enrolled successively at Williams College, Knox College and the University of Missouri, he never earned a degree. In 1873 he joined the *St Louis Evening Journal* as a reporter, staying there for a couple of years, then he spent a year as city editor of the *St Joseph Gazette*, and thereafter was an editorial writer for the *St Louis Times-Journal*. It was here that he wrote his first column, 'Funny Fancies', which lasted for four years. Next, he moved to the *Kansas City Times* for a year as managing editor, and then to the *Denver Times*, in the same role. At Denver, he wrote a column for the second time, this one called 'Odds and Ends'. In 1883 he moved to the *Chicago Morning News* to become a full-time columnist. His new column, which was profoundly influential on future columnists, was at first called 'Current Gossip' then changed to 'Sharps and Flats'. It appeared six days a week and usually ran to 2,000 words, embracing serious and humorous commentary in both prose and verse forms. A collection of his columns was published in two volumes as *Sharps and Flats* (1900).

'Sharps and Flats'
How Milton Dictated to a Typewriter
Chicago Morning News, May 18, 1889

It befell anon that Mistress Milton grew grievously aweary for the labour wherewith her father taxed her, for there is none that shall not comprehend that the labour of transcribing doth presently vex the brain and weary the hand, such being especially the case when she that is so burthened is a proper wench of tender age. Therefore, on a day whiles the birds made merry music in the boscage without, and the young folks were at diverting play, Mistress Milton leaned her head upon her hand and heaved a sigh that bespoke uncomfortableness within.

'Marry, dochter mine,' quoth old John Milton, 'I see that you are aweary.' He spoke after the manner of his kind, for, truth to say, he colde see not at all, in that he was blind, but, as all men knowe, they that be blind speake continually of how that they see when they do not see, their sight being, as I you tell, of the understanding, and not, as you might think, of the visual organs.

'In sooth, father, I am sorely spent,' saies the dochter. 'Whiles the others be at their sweete employments, lo, here sit I all days and halfe the night, with no thing to divert me but the music of thy voice and the abominable scratching of this quill. Thy voice, deare father, is ever precious to me, and it is plaisaunce to me to do thy will, but I am weak in the flesche, and I pine to serve thee in a way as profitable and as proper, but more easier withal.'

'Tell me thy meaning, childe,' quoth he.

'I have heern tell of an engine wherewith these writings I do may be done more quickly than I do them now,' she saies. 'As matters be now, my hands and frock are stained with ink continually, and there are full many and grievous corns upon my fingers from usage of this quill; but this engine whereof I speak is so devised that one may use it the compass of a day and transcribe whole folios therewith, yet shall his hands and his raiment be as clean as a newly washed sheep's liver.'

'Where shall soche an engine be boughten?' he asked the wench.

'In the street yonder, near the sighn of the Blue Swan, over against the King's Tavern,' she quoth, 'and the price therefor is one pound six.'

'Odds boddikins! 't is a passing pretty sum,' he cried. 'I like not vain costliness; but, if it pleaseth thee, buy and fetch the engine whereof thou art enamoured.'

Now by this lesson are we shown how precious swift this father was to do what seemed pleasing in the eyes of his dochter, and it was a righteous thing, trewly, for that a father sholde do his dochter's plaisaunce is most sweete and proper, and I do defend the same, for a dochter is ever a joy and a blessing, and which is not a sonne, being continually minded, whiles yet he is a boy, to ramp and to rash and to roore like a hejeous wild beeste and to raise Sheol generally, a most lamentable and dangerous thing withal.

But when that this engine whereof Mistress Milton spake, and for which she bargained in the sum of one pound six – when that this engine ben brought home and ben put in the father's study, grievous was the torment that befell the father, who, having always heard nony sound but the merry scratchings of his dochter's quill whiles that she wrote the lines that he spake, was sorely astound and vexed by the profane clickings of this worldly engine. Yet, for a space, he bore his suffering as well soever as he colde, and his dochter did with exceeding merriment take down his dictacion in this wise as followeth, to witt:

'A gulf profound as that Serbonian bog – '

'Lackaday!' cried Mistress Milton, 'and in what fashion do you spell "Serbonian"?'

'S-e-r-b-o-n-i-a-n,' quoth he, and thereunto he added, 'with an upper-case S.'

'Zooks! I put it in a lower-case,' saies she; 'but, marry come up with a wanion! I can change it anow.'

Then did Master John Milton proceed with the dictacion again: 'Betwixt Damatia with a cap D and Mount Casius old with a cap C, where armies whole have sunk semi-colon the parching air – hist, what sound was that?'

'What sound, father?' asked Mistress Milton.

'Heard you no sound as if of a bell? Methinketh there is someone at the front door.'

'Nay, nay, father,' quoth the dochter. 'The bell whereof you heard the sound is the bell of this engine here, which warneth me that I am come unto the ende of a line, else but for which bell sholde I speedily be writing over the side of the paper upon no thing but the wind.'

Thereat was Master John Milton mightily displeased, nor wolde his temper be comforted until that he had had a goodly glass of mulberry wine. Yet even this wolde not assuage his discomfiture, for with the clicking of the keys of the engine and the jingling of the bell of the same he was vexed continually until, finally, he fell into a distemper that had like to carried him off. Still wolde he not rebel against the machine, for that he loved his dochter so.

But on a day it befell that the machine gave a sodaine snap and wolde not go nony more.

'What is the matter of the machine?' asked Master John Milton.

'In sooth, I wot that one of the taipes been brasted,' saies his dochter.

'Thank God!' cried he. 'Take it away from this once happy home.'

Then did he discourse unto his dochter of how that he had suffered for her sake, and he forbade her the machine, which same he did declare to be an instrument of Satan and a device for lazy peoples.

'But, father,' saies Mistress Milton, 'Gath and Joe Howard and thy other competitors do use the like of this machine, and you must use it, too, or, forsooth, you shall not be able to keep up with the procession.'

'My dochter,' quoth the old man, full solemnly, 'I have been in the epic-poetry swim for going on forty years, and this lesson have I trewly learned: That he that wolde make enduring literature can make it in one way alone; that no ingenuity can devise a way whereby the labour and the pains of this ennobling art shall be lessened one whit. As in groans and in tears and in anguish all mortal men are brought forth into mortality, so with exceeding labour only and slavish diligence withal are immortal words brought forth unto immortality; likewise, also, as the mother loveth best the child that grieveth her most poignantly in travail, so that which issueth with the mightiest labour from the brain is of the brain most sweetly beloved and reverenced. Take thou this thing away, my dochter, and let us twain toil on as we were wont to do, hardly, mayhap, and with exceeding slowness, yet patiently withal, and having in our hearts the sure confidence of immortality.'

•

FINLEY PETER DUNNE

Finley Peter Dunne (1867–1937) was born in Chicago, the son of an Irish immigrant carpenter and a bookish mother. He entered journalism in 1884 as an office boy and reporter for the *Chicago Telegram*, and over the next ten years he worked for five Chicago papers. In 1893 he began writing a column for the *Chicago Evening Post* which consisted of dialogues involving an Irish-American former policeman-turned-saloonkeeper, Mr Martin J. Dooley, who kept a saloon in Bridgeport, on the south-west side of Chicago. In 1892 Dunne had begun using a vernacular dialect for writing editorials about corruption so as to avoid libel suits. 'It had occurred to me,' he later explained, 'that while it might be dangerous to call an alderman a thief in English no one could sue if a comic Irishman denounced the statesman as a thief . . . if I had written the same thing in English I would inevitably been pistoled or slugged.' This was the style that Dunne adopted for his Dooley columns. Dooley is a wonderfully self-important pontificator who regales his Irish working-class clientele, in particular one Mr Hennessy, with his expansive views; but this does not stop Dunne, through Dooley, poking fun at war enthusiasts, sanctimonious reformers and moral hypocrites. Although at first Dooley seems like a brilliant caricature, he gradually emerges as an honest and humane creation.

On the Victorian Era

From *Mr Dooley in Peace and War* (1878)

'Ar-re ye goin' to cillybrate th' queen's jubilee?' asked Mr Dooley.

'What's that?' demanded Mr Hennessy, with a violent start.

'Today,' said Mr Dooley, 'her gracious Majesty Victorya, Queen iv Great Britain an' that part iv Ireland north iv Sligo, has reigned f'r sixty long and tiresome years.'

'I don't care if she has snowed f'r sixty years,' said Mr Hennessy. 'I'll not cillybrate it. She may be a good woman f'r all I know, but dam her pollytics.'

'Ye needn't be profane about it,' said Mr Dooley. 'I on'y ast ye a civil question. F'r mesilf, I have no feelin' on th' subject. I am not with th' queen an' I'm not again her. At th' same time I corjally agree with me frind Captain Finerty, who's put his newspaper in mournin' f'r th' ivint. I won't march in th' parade, an' I won't put anny dinnymite undher thim that does. I don't say th' marchers an' dinnymiters ar-re not both r-right. 'Tis purely a question iv taste, an', as the ixicutive says whin both candydates are mimbers iv th' camp, "Pathrites will use their own discreetion."

'Th' good woman niver done me no har-rm; an', beyond throwin' a rock or two into an orangey's procission an' subscribin' to tin dolllars' worth iv Fenian bonds, I've threated her like a lady. Anny gredge I iver had again her I burrid long ago. We're both well on in years, an' 'tis no use carrying har-rd feelin's to th' grave. About th' time th' lord chamberlain wint over to tell her she was queen, an' she came out in her nitey to hear th' good news, I was anounced into this wurruld iv sin an' sorrow. So ye see we've reigned about th' same lenth iv time, an' I ought to be cillybratin' me di'mon' jubilee. I wud, too, if I had anny di'mons'. Do ye r-run down to Aldherman O'Brien's an' borrow twinty or thirty f'r me.

'Great happenin's have me an' Queen Victorya seen in these sixty years. Durin' our binificent prisince on earth th' nations have grown r-rich an' prosperous. Great Britain has ixtinded her domain until th' sun niver sets on it. No more do th' original owners iv th' sile, they bein' kept movin' be th' polis. While she was lookin' on in England, I was lookin' on in this counthry. I have seen America spread out fr'm th' Atlantic to th' Pacific, with a branch office iv the Standard Ile Comp'ny in ivry hamlet. I've seen th' shackles dropped fr'm th' slave, so's he cud be lynched in Ohio. I've seen this gr-reat city desthroyed be fire fr'm De Koven Sthreet to th' Lake View pumpin' station, and thin rise felix-like fr'm its ashes, all but th' West Side, which was not burned. I've seen Jim Mace beat Mike McCool, an' Tom Allen beat Jim Mace, an' somebody beat Tom Allen, an' Jawn Sullivan beat him, an' Corbett beat Sullivan, an' Fitz beat Corbett; an', if I live to cillybrate me goold-watch-an'-chain jubilee, I may see some wan put it all over Fitz.

'Oh, what things I've seen in me day an' Victorya's! Think iv that gran' procission iv lithry men – Tinnyson an' Longfellow an' Bill Nye an' Ella Wheeler Wilcox an' Tim Scanlan an' – an' I can't name thim all: they're too manny. An' th' brave gin'rals – Von Molkey an' Bismarck an' U. S. Grant an' gallant Phil Shurdan an' Coxey. Think iv thim durin' me reign. An' th' invintions – th' steam-injine an' th' printin'-press an' th' cotton-gin an' the gin sour an' th' bicycle an' th' flyin'-machine an' th' nickel-in-th'-slot machine an' th' Croker machine an' th' sody fountain an' – crownin' wur-ruk iv our civilization – th' cash raygisther. What gr-reat advances has science made in my time an' Victorya's! F'r, whin we entered public life, it took three men to watch th' bar-keep, while today ye can tell within eight dollars an hour what he's took in.

'Glory be, whin I look back fr'm this day iv gin'ral rejoicin' in me rhinestone jubilee, an' see what changes has taken place an' how manny people have died an' how much betther off th' wurruld is, I'm proud iv mesilf. War an' pest-lence an' famine have occurred in me time, but I count thim light compared with th' binifits that have fallen to th' race since I come on th' earth.'

'What ar-re ye talkin' about?' cried Mr Hennessy, in deep disgust. 'All this time ye've been standin' behind this bar ladlin' out disturvbance to th' Sixth Wa-ard, an' ye haven't been as far east as Mitchigan Avnoo in twenty years. What have ye had to do with all these things?'

'Well,' said Mr Dooley, 'I had as much to do with thim as th' queen.'

•

AMBROSE BIERCE

Ambrose Bierce (1867–1913?) was born in San Francisco. At the age of twenty-five he joined the Union Army as a private and was discharged a lieutenant four years later. He became a feature writer and editor for various periodicals and was also an accomplished short story writer. He started out his career as a columnist on the *Wasp* in the 1880s (his opinion columns appeared under the heading 'Prattle', but his *Devil's Dictionary* also began in columnar form) and later he was hired by William Randolph Hearst to write for one of his papers, the *San Francisco Examiner*. His columns for that paper covered politics, military affairs and cultural matters; they appeared regularly from 1887 to 1901 under different headings (first 'War Topics', then 'Prattle' again, then 'The Passing Show') and were caustically critical of the jingoism of the Spanish–American War which Hearst's papers encouraged, although Bierce refrained from attacking Hearst himself. Bierce disappeared in Mexico in 1913.

'Prattle'
San Francisco Examiner, November 13, 1898

After every election both sides fall to explaining the result. It was due to this, it was due to that or the other – there are just as many explanations as there are men who know nothing about it. The significance of all this is obvious: it means that in this country of government by public opinion no way is provided to ascertain public opinion. The party 'platforms' tell us so much that they teach us nothing. So anxious are their scheming authors to 'catch suckers' that they use as many kinds of bait as they can dig in and about the party barnyard, and sometimes add exotic worms from the barnyard of a neighbor – a practice known as 'fusion.' It should be clear to common sense that if a party professes more than one 'principle' there is no knowing which one attracted or repelled the voter. Who knows, for illustration, whether the Republican success of last Tuesday was due to a more general desire to express approval of the Administration's war work than to rebuke it, or to a continuing popular distrust of 'free silver' (if popular distrust of free silver ever existed) or to something else. This explaining 'victories' and 'defeats' (how, in a count of noses, is anybody 'victorious' or anybody 'defeated'?) is clotted nonsense: that could be done by Omniscience only; and Omniscience, I take it, is less concerned to explain why more men voted for Republicans than for Democrats than to find out why anybody voted at all.

In the tiresome tumult of interests and sentiments which we are pleased to call 'politics' there has been in my time but one contest of principles in which it seemed worthwhile for a serious man seriously to engage. The struggle between freedom and slavery affected earnest souls with a compelling fervor. Great-hearted and great-minded men felt the stress, marched to the polls and thence to the camp. There was a chance of action consistent with self-respect for even the pessimist and cynic. In those turbulent days it meant something to be a Republican – and something else to be a Democrat, though there came to be two kinds of Democrats. A 'War Democrat' closely resembled a Republican in all but the hope of Federal office.

There were not many of them in the North; the party was mostly babbling of peace and compromise, and a considerable section was openly disloyal, inviting repression by the iron hand – which every Republican joyously brandished and on fit occasion abundantly applied. The bloody nose was abroad in the land, the cracked crown ever to the fore, addressing itself to public attention. Men sometimes forgot their interests in promotion of their principles, and to the general welfare subordinated their own, and in a sunburst of patriotic devotion Artemus Ward declared his readiness to sacrifice all his wife's relations.

What is a Democrat now? What a Republican? The best we can do in answer is to imitate Swift's definition of the word 'deacon': 'one who performs diaconical functions.' A Democrat is one who votes the Democratic ticket, a Republican one who acts with the Republican party; more enlightening description there is none. Two years ago the man to whom the free coinage of silver at a ratio at which it has never been coined was pie (or crow) was called a Democrat to distinguish him from the Republican, to whom it was crow (or pie). We prated of gold and we prated of silver – shouted of them, shrieked of them and fought for them; but when the ballots were counted we knew as little how the country stood on the silver question as we knew before, and we know no more today. In each party 'platform' the peculiar financial doctrine of the party – or rather the financial doctrine that immediately on formulation became such – was so complicated with others that the whole work resembled a ball of interwoven snakes, whereof none is accessible for individual killing. Moreover, as to 'bowing to the will of the people,' 'accepting the decision of the majority' and so forth, that is about the last thing that the outvoted American voter purposes doing. Convince him that any political doctrine of which his party is proponent was killed at the polls and its memory becomes very precious to him. From that moment he lives but to revive it and put it in training for another trial of strength. It owes its eventual burial only to the imperious necessity of promoting progress by begetting something worse.

A few years ago the country was blazing controversy about 'Protection' and what all agreed to call 'Free Trade.' That is to say, the Republicans proposed to tax importations an average of forty-seven percent of their value, the Democrats forty-three percent. Over this ridiculous 'issue' the sovereign (and intelligent) electors brass-banded, bonfired, shouted their teeth loose, vilified and fought for months! That excess of four percent in the taxation of foreign merchandise was the idol of Republican devotion, the black beast of Democratic detestation. One of the 'State Central Committees' of this commonwealth was kind enough to ask me to write a 'campaign song,' on my own terms. I am glad to say that Heaven put it into my heart to reply without resentment. Eventually one of the parties to this momentous contest achieved a 'glorious victory' – I do not recollect which one. The country was saved and the principles of political righteousness advanced a half-inch.

Signor Luccheni, the gentleman who thought it expedient to insert a three-cornered file in the heart of an Empress,* is good enough to explain his action: he is of the opinion that no one ought to live who will not work. But, Signor, observe: work is a means to an end, and the end is life. Having life without working, the Empress was in the position of a man who has been carried in a wagon to the place to which he wanted to go. Being already there, should he go back to the place whence he came and make the journey again, on foot? It is no wiser to think that one should live by working only than that one should move by walking only. In the government of this world God has so ordered it that not only, as the illustrious Sam Patch said, 'some things can be done, as well as others,' but a few of them can be done in more than one way. One can make an honest living by work, or by being an Empress; as one can murder with a bomb or a file. Trusting that on further consideration of the matter you will not fail, Signor, to discern the error of your view regarding the moral basis of the right to live, I nevertheless congratulate you on the certainty that in your own case life and labor will henceforth go hand in hand to that glorious goal of the anarchists' ambition, a felon's grave. And may loving hands fill it up with other anarchists.

In the horrible scenes of the North Carolinian 'race war' the patriotic 'Expansionist' has a means of mental expansion. If here in our own country we can get on with the Negroes only by killing them, how will it be with the Negroes and Negroids of Cuba and Porto Rico? – more brutal, more ignorant, more unthrifty and less accustomed to our ways than the Blacks of the Southern States. How will it be with the Japanese, the Chinese, the Portuguese and the natives, in Hawaii? How with the seven or eight millions of nondescripts in the Philippines? The Japanese may return to their own country; the Chinese may be deported to theirs, if a country be left to them; the Portuguese problem may be solved by assimilation – or, preferably, assassination. But the other races will have to 'go,' in another sense. Their mandate is exhausted. Before the American the

---

* Luccheni assassinated Empress Elizabeth of Austria in September 1898.

dark-skinned Intertropican will as certainly perish as does the red Indian, as will the black man-and-brother whose doom is foreshadowed in the bloody doings at Wilmington and Greenwood. But, like the red Indian, the Intertropicans (the lambs-to-the-slaughter Hawaiians excepted) will die hard; and, like the red Indian, they will see that a good many of us die with them. There is hardly a township between the Atlantic and the Pacific that has not been the scene of an Indian 'massacre,' the price we have had to pay for possession. We shall be lucky to pay less in the Caribbean and to pay only ten times as much in the East Pacific. Eventually, doubtless, perhaps in a score of generations, these various incompatibles will be effaced, but by that time we may ourselves be 'one with Nineveh and Tyre.'

These dismal forecasts assume that we are to 'settle' in our new possessions – that our people are to go there to live and engage in trade and the industries, paying to Nature our fine for trespass – our tribute of life and character to climate. If content to hold these islands as mere dependencies for the trade which follows the flag, governing them by the strong hand, as Great Britain her crown colonies, the attrition of races may be avoided and Nature's plan of a reservation for degenerates in the horrid zone promoted. In any case the Expansionist of today revisiting earth a century hence in his character of trusty will see that which will make him open his smarting eyes and lift his incinerated hands to signify his sense of the unexpected and untoward.

France did not care for Fashoda* and was thinking about giving it up anyhow.

Tesla, the electrician, says he has a practical invention by which ships can cross the ocean without men. But what we need is an invention by which men can cross the ocean without ships. The necessity of going on a ship frequently leads to detection and detention.

By the way, the several 'wizards' of electrology did not play leading parts in the Yanko-Spanko war, as they promised to do. Tesla did not destroy any Spanish ships by pointing a horseshoe magnet at them, nor did Edison discharge any electrified water from a garden hose among the surprised infantry. It looks as if the military authorities regarded the wizards with such coldness as the Gentiles use, or lesser breeds without the law. Always it has been so: soldiers in the seats of the mighty affect a contumelious disesteem of civilian war-ways. Mr Edison's noble scheme of translating to another and warmer world an entire ship's crew of the opposition by firing from a for'd and an aft gun, by simultaneous electrical discharge, two shots connected by a chain (the unhappy foemen lining up on deck to incur the ensuement) was surely worthy of a trial by a humor-loving Department on a consenting enemy.

Among incidental phenomena of the war nothing has been more gratifying than repression of the freaker freaking on his freak. And of all freakers appealing with lifted hands for an averted attention the electricity freaker has been most clamorous and importunate. And of all electricity freakers, importunate or merely noisy, Mr Edison is easily first. This pet of the newspapers and purveyor-in-ordinary to his serene abominableness the faker is ever on the vocal firing line with proposals for disaster to those whom it has commonly been found most difficult, as Bill Nye might have said,

---

* The French withdrew from this Sudanese town in November 1898, leaving it to the British.

to disast – an armed enemy, to wit. He was too busy discovering the electrical properties of the cat's back in a cold day to go to Santiago, but if Toral's army should have the temerity to march upon Key West, or Cervera's fleet sail to Chickamauga, he'd do, and he'd do, and he'd do! The fellow is a military impostor; he cannot harm a toad. As a scientist he is no better, being destitute of reputation among scientific men. His observation and understanding never transcend the metes of electrology, and they coterminate at the beginning of common sense. One is so fatigued of Edison with his nickle-in-the-slot ingenuity that one hails with delight the disinterested futility of Tesla.

Extract from a story in a popular magazine:

> On receiving his proposal she attentively considered it, he remaining on his knees without further remark; then she looked at him candidly and called him 'William,' which she had never done before. Accepting this as an augury of success he in his turn called her 'Isabella' and a heartfelt silence ensued, broken only by the consciousness Mrs Durane would be coming to look for them. When it had expired Kelson rose from his knees and she from her feet, and without a word of explanation they wended their way to the summer-house, where he kissed her several times and they considered their troth substantially plighted.

•

GEORGE ADE

George Ade (1866–1944) was born in Kentland, Indiana, the son of a bank employee. As a child he devoured the works of Dickens and read Mark Twain in subscription books. He was educated locally and won a scholarship to Purdue University, an agricultural school, where he met John McCutcheon, who was later to illustrate Ade's articles. After seven weeks studying law he went to work for the Kentland *Morning News*, a Republican paper. He then worked for a patent medicine business before becoming a reporter for the *Chicago Morning News* (which later became the *News-Record*, then the *Record*) covering strikes, political conventions and prizefights, and developing a distinctive and lively style. In 1893 he wrote a column of anecdotes and stories about people visiting the World's Fair in Chicago. This was so successful that he was given the opportunity to extend this into a daily column called 'Stories of the Streets and of the Town', which ranked alongside Eugene Field's 'Sharps and Flats' column, also for the *Record*. He and McCutcheon lodged together and plied the streets together, Ade writing his 1,200–1,800-word column in pencil, McCutcheon drawing sketches. His column was notable for its quirkiness and its ear for the vernacular, and collections were soon issued in a series of 25 cent paperbacks. Ade and McCutcheon embarked for Europe and produced twice-weekly articles under the heading 'What a Man Sees Who Goes Away from Home'. In 1895 Ade began to introduce regular characters into his 'Stories'. First there was 'Artie' Blanchard, a young office employee, and when the 'Artie' stories were published in book form they attracted the praise of the literary critic William Dean Howells. 'Artie' was followed by 'Doc' Horne, a bombastic remittance man, and 'Pink Marsh', a Negro bootblack who worked in a barbershop. His columns also included burlesque detective tales, skits on golf, and some short stories which H. L. Mencken later declared were 'two or three of the best short stories ever written in this republic'.

In 1897 he wrote the first of a series of columns called 'Fables in Slang', perhaps his most popular series. These were often written in the first, not the third, person, and Ade said that 'it was a great lark to write in slang – just like gorging on forbidden fruit. The bridle was off and all the rules abolished.' After a while, the 'Fables' appeared in Ade's column once a week, and when they were collected in a book their author achieved national fame – the Kansas editor William Allen White wrote to Ade saying: 'I would rather have written *Fables in Slang* than be President.' In 1900 Ade quit the *Record* and concentrated on writing plays and musical comedies.

'Fables in Slang'
The Fable of What Happened the Night the Men Came to the Women's Club

From *The Best of George Ade* (1985)

In a Progressive Little City claiming about twice the Population that the Census Enumerators could uncover, there was a Literary Club. It was one of these Clubs guaranteed to fix you out with Culture while you wait. Two or three Matrons, who were too Heavy for Light Amusements, but not old enough to remain at Home and Knit, organized the Club. Nearly every Woman in town rushed to get in, for fear somebody would say she hadn't been Asked.

The Club used to Round Up once a week at the Homes of Members. There would be a Paper, followed by a Discussion, after which somebody would Pour.

The Organization seemed to be a Winner. One Thing the Lady Clubbers were Dead Set On. They were going to have Harmony with an Upper Case H. They were out to cut a seven-foot Swath through English Literature from Beowulf to Bangs, inclusive, and no petty Jealousies or Bickerings would stand in the Way.

So while they were at the Club they would pull Kittenish Smiles at each other, and Applaud so as not to split the Gloves. Some times they would Kiss, too, but they always kept their Fingers crossed.

Of course, when they got off in Twos and Threes they would pull the little Meat-Axes out of the Reticules and hack a few Monograms, but that was to have been expected.

Everything considered, the Club was a Tremendous Go. At each Session the Lady President would announce the Subject for the next Meeting. For instance, she would say that Next Week they would take up Wyclif. Then everyone would romp home to look in the Encyclopedia of Authors and find out who in the world Wyclif was. On the following Thursday they would have Wyclif down Pat, and be primed for a Discussion. They would talk about Wyclif as if he had been down to the House for Tea every evening that Week.

After the Club had been running for Six Months it was beginning to be Strong on Quotations and Dates. The Members knew that Mrs Browning was the wife of Mr Browning, that Milton had Trouble with his Eyes, and that Lord Byron wasn't all that he should have been, to say the Least. They began to feel their Intellectual Oats. In the meantime the Jeweler's Wife had designed a Club Badge.

The Club was doing such Notable Work that some of the Members thought they ought to have a Special Meeting and invite the Men. They wanted to put the Cap-Sheaf on a Profitable Season, and at the same time hand the Merited Rebuke to some of the Husbands and Brothers who had been making Funny Cracks.

It was decided to give the Star Programme at the Beadle Home, and after the Papers had been read then all the Men and Five Women who did not hold office could file through the Front Room and shake Hands with the President, the Vice-President, the Recording Secretary, the Corresponding Secretary, the Treasurer, and the members of the various Committees, all of whom were to line up and Receive.

The reason the Club decided to have the Brain Barbecue at the Beadle Home was that the Beadles had such beautiful big Rooms and Double Doors. There was more or less quiet Harpoon Work when the Announcement was made. Several of the Elderly Ones said that Josephine Beadle was not a Representative Member of the Club. She was Fair to look upon, but she was not pulling very hard for the Uplifting of the Sex. It was suspected that she came to the Meetings just to Kill Time and see what the Others were Wearing. She refused to buckle down to Literary Work, for she was a good deal more interested in the Bachelors who filled the Windows of the new Men's Club than she was in the Butler who wrote 'Hudibras.' So why should she have the Honor of entertaining the Club at the Annual Meeting? Unfortunately, the Members who had the most Doing under their Bonnets were not the ones who could come to the Front with large Rooms that could be Thrown together, so the Beadle Home got the Great Event . . . The men managed to get Rear Seats or stand along the Wall so that they could execute the Quiet Sneak if Things got too Literary. The Women were too Flushed and Proud to Notice.

At 8:30 p.m. the Lady President stood out and began to read a few Pink Thoughts on 'Woman's Destiny – Why Not?' Along toward 9:15, about the time the Lady President was beginning to show up Good and Earnest, Josephine Beadle, who was Circulating around on the Outskirts of the Throng to make sure that everybody was Happy, made a Discovery. She noticed that the Men standing along the Wall and in the Doorways were not more than sixty percent En Rapport with the Long Piece about Woman's Destiny. Now Josephine was right there to see that Everybody had a Nice Time, and she did not like to see the Prominent Business Men of the Town dying of Thirst or Leg Cramp or anything like that, so she gave two or three of them the Quiet Wink, and they tiptoed after her out to the Dining Room, where she offered Refreshments, and said they could slip out on the Side Porch and Smoke if they wanted to.

Probably they preferred to go back in the Front Room and hear some more about Woman's Destiny not.

As soon as they could master their Emotions and get control of their Voices, they told Josephine what they thought of her. They said she made the Good Samaritan look like a Cheap Criminal, and if she would only say the Word they would begin to put Ground Glass into the Food at Home. Then Josephine called them 'Boys,' which probably does not make a Hit with one who is the sloping side of forty-eight. More of the Men seemed to awake to the Fact that they were Overlooking something, so they came on the Velvet Foot back to the Dining Room and declared themselves In, and flocked around Josephine and called her 'Josie' and 'Joe.' They didn't care. They were having a Pleasant Visit.

Josephine gave them Allopathic Slugs of the Size that they feed you in the Navy and then lower you into the Dinghy and send you Ashore. Then she let them go out on the Porch to smoke. By the time the Lady President came to the last Page there were only two Men left in the Front Room. One was Asleep and the other was Penned In.

The Women were Huffy. They went out to make the Men come in, and found them Bunched on the Porch listening to a Story that a Traveling Man had just brought to Town that Day.

Now the Plan was that during the Reception the Company would stand about in little Groups, and ask each other what Books they liked, and make it something on the order of a Salon. This Plan miscarried, because all the Men wanted to hear Rag Time played by Josephine, the Life-Saver. Josephine had to yield, and the Men all clustered around her to give their Moral Support. After one or two Selections, they felt sufficiently Keyed to begin to hit up those low-down Songs about Baby and Chickens and Razors. No one paid any Attention to the Lady President, who was off in a Corner holding an Indignation Meeting with the Secretary and the Vice-President.

When the Women began to sort out the Men and order them to start Home and all the Officers of the Club were giving Josephine the frosty Good Night, anyone could see that there was Trouble ahead.

Next day the Club held a Special Session and expelled Josephine for Conduct Unbecoming a Member, and Josephine sent Word to them as follows: 'Rats.'

Then the Men quietly got together and bought Josephine about a Thousand Dollars' Worth of American Beauty Roses to show that they were With her, and then Homes began to break up, and somebody started the Report that anyway it was the Lady President's Fault for having such a long and pokey Essay that wasn't hers at all, but had been Copied out of a Club Paper published in Detroit.

Before the next Meeting there were two Factions. The Lady President had gone to a Rest Cure, and the Meeting resolved itself into a Good Cry and a general Smash-Up.

MORAL: *The only Literary Men are those who have to Work at it.*

•

SPENCER LEIGH HUGHES

Spencer Leigh Hughes (1858–1920) was born in Trowbridge, Wiltshire, the son of a Wesleyan minister who moved to a new part of the country every few years. For this reason Hughes was educated in Yorkshire, leaving school at the age of fourteen and working for ten years in a firm of Ipswich engineers. In 1885 he set up the *Ipswich Advance*, a halfpenny fortnightly paper, doing the editorial work out of the Reform Club, and he wrote his first article under the heading 'Sub Rosa' for the *Suffolk Chronicle*. Before long his work was spotted by Frederick Wilson, proprietor of the *East Anglian Daily Times*, who recruited him to the staff of the London *Star* and soon afterwards to the staff of its sister title, the *Morning Leader*.

Hughes spent eighteen years in the press gallery of the House of Commons, including several years as a member of the Lobby, before himself being elected to Parliament as a Liberal. From 1892 to 1915 he contributed his daily 'Sub Rosa' column to the *Morning Leader*, writing thousands of columns and in his own estimation 'about ten million words'. His column was much admired by one British Prime Minister, Sir Henry Campbell-Bannerman, who once quoted approvingly from it in a Cabinet meeting. Shortly after the column ceased, following the merger of the *Morning Leader* with another title, Hughes received a letter from a young man who wrote: 'While the second battle of Ypres was being fought I lay under the gable of a barn and read "Sub Rosa" with the German eighteen-pounders whizzing over our heads, endeavouring at the time to compose what I am pleased to call my mind.'

'Sub Rosa'
Morning Leader, 9 March 1910

The Tory orator of these later days finds great comfort in saying that the respectable Liberalism of twenty years ago is now extinct, and that the Liberal leaders of the past would shrink with horror from the proposals of their successors. Praising Mr Gladstone is now one of the favourite tricks on the Tory platform. Not long ago Sir Gilbert Parker went one step further, and proclaimed the great superiority of Sir William Harcourt over the Ministers of today. And someone else, whose name I have forgotten, brought the game up to date by saying that while everyone could trust Sir Henry Campbell-Bannerman no one could rely on the word of Mr Asquith.

This is a very old trick, which has been played for generations, and will no doubt continue to be played for generations. They revile a man so long as he lives, and then when he is dead they beslaver his memory with mock eulogy in order to revile someone else. I have shown on more than one occasion what a striking contrast there is between what Tories said about Mr Gladstone, Sir William Harcourt and Sir Henry Campbell-Bannerman when those statesmen were alive, and what is now said about them when the game is to slander their successors. And now I wish to call the attention of the reader to a curious document, more than seventy years old, which shows that all which is now said about the modern Radical used to be said about the old-fashioned Whig.

I suppose there is not a single hack stump orator of the Tory Party today who would not say that while the Whigs were possibly mistaken in regard to their views on some matters they were at least honourable and high-minded gentlemen. One can imagine a peripatetic tub-thumper, hired to defend the House of Lords, saying that the Whigs, with all their faults, were sound on the Constitution, they respected our institutions, they would have been appalled had they heard the atrocious sentiments of 'your Lloyd George' or 'your Winston Churchill'. (The cheap orator always says 'your' this or that when he wishes to express the utmost disdain.) Those old-fashioned Whigs would never have threatened the aristocracy, but in these terrible and Socialistic days – and so on and so forth, until the eloquent gentleman thinks he has said enough for his money.

Well, the document I have mentioned is dated 1837, and contains an address to the electors of Nottingham, signed 'A Thinking Man'. The gentleman not only thought, but he also put his breathing thoughts into burning words, and he leads off in this way:

To the Electors of Nottingham
CONSERVATIVES
Will you vote for Hobhouse and secure a triumph to the perjured and pernicious Whigs?

> Believe me, the wild and visionary notions of Mr Eagle on the Church Question, whether they be sincere or assumed, can do no real harm, their antidote lies in their certain ruin, both to the Aristocracy and the People.

In this opening passage we find that the Whigs of 1837 – men like Melbourne, Lord John Russell, Palmerston, Macaulay – were denounced as perjured and pernicious, while certain proposals in regard to the Church were wild and visionary, involving the ruin of the aristocracy and the people. How familiar it all seems!

The passage which I have quoted is, however, mild when compared with what the thinking man of Nottingham proceeded to say. Here is a pleasant allusion to those old Whigs who are now held up as examples to be imitated by the reckless Radical politicians of today:

> Already they have contrived to throw the odium of their own cupidity upon the Upper Senate. Already they have more than hinted at the Abolition of the Hereditary Peerage.

I was not surprised to find that the Church was in danger in those days, for it always has been in danger – as I think Carlyle has pointed out. But I was not prepared for this sad revelation about the Whigs of seventy years ago, that they were hinting at tampering with the hereditary principle. Recent noble orators had led me to suppose that this blasphemous suggestion had quite a modern origin, and was put forth by 'your' Lloyd George or by 'that' Winston Churchill. And now I find that the Whigs at the time of the accession of Queen Victoria were at least contemplating with approval a policy so unhallowed.

Let us return, however, to the thinker of Nottingham, whose thoughts breathe more than ever and whose words burn more fiercely as he goes on. Thus I find him saying about these same old Whigs who are recommended as an example of moderation to modern Radicals:

> Their policy teems with destruction to every principle of Constitutional Freedom, and Social Harmony. They legislate for a class whose selfish instinct will very shortly throw the firebrand alike into the Palace and the Cottage.

That may be said to have 'done it'. Really, I do not see how the present Ministers, even if they were as wicked and as vile as the sanctified Lord Hugh suggests that they are, could be greater monsters than were the Whigs of 1837. They cannot, however hard they may try, do much more than destroy every principle of Constitutional Freedom and Social Harmony and at the same time polish off Palace and Cottage alike.

And now we come to the closing passage, the peroration of the thinking man of Nottingham:

> Save your country and assert the independence of the Borough by spurning back upon the Whigs the man whom they would force upon you. Unless you unite with the People this Borough will be as close as the worst of those included in Schedule A.

The modern reader may think that the excited gentleman leaves off on rather a tame note, but the allusion to Schedule A may have meant more to him than it does to us.

And he was certainly on sound old lines when he urged that the rejection of the Whig meant the salvation of the country.

As I have already said, this appeal to the men of Nottingham is dated 1837, and we have seen that they were invited, nay, urged impetuously, to spurn back a certain Mr Hobhouse, who was described as the representative of the perjured and pernicious Whigs. The appeal was made in vain. Either the men of Nottingham did not regard Mr Hobhouse as perjured and pernicious, or if they did so regard him it would appear that they liked that sort of thing. In any case the Member for Nottingham from 1834 to 1847 was Mr J. C. Hobhouse. Possibly, when the result was known, the thinking man declared that Nottingham had become even as the very worst of all the boroughs that were ever included in Schedule A. As to that history is silent.

My reason for mentioning the matter is this – the document shows that the very men who are now brought out as models for the edification of modern Radicals were reviled by the Tories of their day in precisely the same manner as the modern Radicals are reviled by the Tories of today. And it is at least conceivable that the industrious Tories in 1980 will be bawling away to their unhappy contemporaries that in 1910 the leaders of the Liberal Party were statesmen, a little mistaken perchance in regard to this or that matter of detail, but sound at the core – patriots who would shrink from the doctrines of those nonentities who had followed them. This will be in accordance with well-established precedent, it will illustrate continuity of policy, and will carry on a great tradition.

It is comforting also to remember that though the triumph of the perjured and pernicious Whig was secured in Nottingham on the occasion in question, it was not followed by the disasters foretold by the gloomy and thinking man. Was it not John Bright who said that the worst of great thinkers is that they so often think wrong? We are not entirely without constitutional freedom, and there is still some social harmony left. The palace is intact, and I believe there are more (and better) cottages today than there were in 1837 – in spite of Free Trade.

'Sub Rosa'
To Introduce Nearly 500 Celebrities
Morning Leader, 4 May 1915

I wonder who first wrote an autobiography. Whoever it was he (or it may be she) has had a great succession, and today a man is regarded if not as a freak yet as more or less a crank, if by the time he is middle-aged he has not told the public all about his schooldays and his youth. Autobiographies are therefore now turned out in instalments, for the impatient author cannot keep back the intellectual treat he has in store for the public – and yet he cannot tell the whole truth until his course is nearly run. And this accounts for the appearance of such a work as 'Twenty Years of My Life', by Mr Douglas Sladen (Constable and Co.) – a title that might be used by a gentleman just released from a long sentence at Portland.

Everyone will hope that the author will enjoy other scores of years before anything like a complete autobiography can be produced. Carlyle either said, or said that someone else had said, that 'the life of man, the life even of the meanest man, it were good to remember, is a poem'.

And I believe Tammas also observed that the life of any man if written faithfully, by himself or another, would be interesting. Possibly these remarks have encouraged this passion, or rage, for men to tell us all about themselves – how they will never forget their feelings when they first went to school, the trembling hopes with which they posted the first proffered contribution to the Press, the rapture caused by the first appearance in print, and so on.

Mr Douglas Sladen's book is remarkable both within and without. On the outside the reader is confronted by a noble crest and coat of arms, I will not say worthy of the Kaiser, because I know that would annoy the author, but quite a big thing in the heraldic line. And it is set off by two Latin mottoes. This superb display may be something of his very own, or something that belongs to his family, tribe, clan, university or political club, I cannot say – perhaps it has something to do with the fact that Mr Sladen is the author of *Who's Who*, and that he may be said to have started or created a new era by producing that work. Indeed, I believe that a higher standard of conduct has been attained by men trying to make themselves worthy of admission in its pages.

In any case, I can tell him I was so much impressed by the outside of this new book that I hesitated for some time before opening it. It was not that I supposed the inside would be inferior, but I could not tear myself away from the fascinating, almost hypnotizing, effect of that gorgeous coat of arms. My knowledge of heraldic terms is not great enough to enable me to explain all there is in this work of art. The reader may, however, take it from me that there are all kinds of things there – indeed, everything that no gentleman's coat of arms should be without – and perhaps a little more.

And inside the book we are introduced to quite a crowd of people – all, or nearly all, of the very best. They are people of the sort that can get into *Who's Who* without much trouble. At the end of the book the author has very thoughtfully arranged a list of these notables – men and women – and there are 435 of them. As the book contains 360 pages, the reader will see that there has been no stint, nothing niggardly, in the way of introducing celebrities. They come not single spies, but in the other way. And they vary in many ways – the list containing Prince Alamayu, Mr Balfour, King Edward VII, Bill Nye and Lord Willoughby de Broke.

The full list should be 436, and not 435, for though Mr Douglas Sladen's name does not appear in the table at the end he does mention himself now and then. That is quite right, and, indeed, unavoidable, in a book of an autobiographical nature. Let me take one or two notable points that are here communicated to the public. Mr Sladen's maternal grandfather was Sheriff of London when Queen Victoria was married. That is just the sort of thing that a man has a right to record about an ancestor. Some men have had ancestors who, though never Sheriffs themselves, have been brought into touch with those officials. Possibly if Mr Sladen were to search back far enough he could discover some of that sort (in spite of that coat of arms), but the author of *Who's Who* cannot be expected to make any such exposures.

Here is another remark taken from these pages which shows the candour that adds a charm to autobiography: 'I have never been to Manchester.' He is but a trifle short of three score years of age – he owns up like a man to the fact that he was born in 1856 – and yet in all his wanderings he has never seen that famous city! I cannot make out whether he makes this announcement in a spirit of contrition, or boastfulness, or of mere indifference. All I will say about it is that the loss has been mutual, and that I hope the day may soon come when the long-deferred visit will be made – with civic reception, band and coat of arms reproduced in the local papers.

Of course, when a book of 360 pages introduces 435 notables (not including the author), it naturally contains a great many tales. This book is full of tales, of all sorts, some very good, and others, of course, not quite so good. Here is one which I venture to class among those that are not quite so good:

> I once heard a Bishop, who in those days was a smug and an Oxford Don, remark to a circle of delighted undergraduates, 'My brother Edward thinks I'm an awful fool.' As his brother Edward was captain of the Eton Eleven and amateur champion of something or other, there is no doubt that his brother Edward did think him an awful fool.

That is all. When I first read the tale I thought that perhaps I had missed a line, so I went through it again carefully – but once more I failed to 'get the hang' of it.

No doubt the fault is mine, but even now the tale seems incomplete – or if complete it is not quite the sort of tale that one would think it worthwhile to print. Granted that the Oxford don was an awful fool, and that his brother Edward thought so, and said so, we may ask, 'Well, what abaht it?' Again it does not follow that because the name of a celebrity appears in the list at the end there is much about him in the book. For instance, I noticed this reference: 'Churchill, Rt Hon. Winston, 175,' so I turned to page 175. Mr Churchill's name is not there, but there is an allusion to the fact that Lord Willoughby de Broke is, or was, of the opinion that the First Lord of the Admiralty is a 'rat' – and that is all! It is just the sort of thing he would say.

•

A. G. GARDINER

Alfred George Gardiner (1865–1946) was born in Chelmsford, became a reporter in Bournemouth, and later moved to Lancashire, where he joined the *Northern Daily Telegraph*, a liberal paper in Blackburn, serving as a leader writer and as editor of its weekly edition. In early 1902 he was invited by his former proprietor to become editor of the *Daily News*, another Liberal paper, which was owned by George Cadbury. He quickly raised its circulation from 30,000 to 80,000, and by 1915 had taken it to 800,000. He also wrote a column for the paper on Saturdays. However, in 1919 he was rebuked by one of the paper's new owners, Henry Cadbury, for his attacks on the Prime Minister, Lloyd George, on the grounds that an editor should not himself criticize. Gardiner resigned the editorship, but kept his salary and stayed on as a columnist. Starting in 1914, he wrote columns as 'Alpha of the Plough' on Tuesdays for the *Star*, which were published in collected form as *Leaves in the Wind* (1919), *Many Furrows* (1924), *Pebbles on the Shore* (1916) and *Windfalls* (1920). His Alpha columns were characterized, as he put it, by 'intimate triviality' and gave him the 'opportunity to go on holiday with my pen and escape for an hour or two once a week from the maelstrom of the war'. He also wrote Saturday columns for the *Daily News*, which were collected as *The War Lords* (1915). He would write his columns either in his study at home or in the Committee Room on the Reform Club mezzanine, where he would compete with Hilaire Belloc for a favourite table.

'Alpha of the Plough'
On Umbrella Morals

From *Pebbles on the Shore* (1916)

A sharp shower came on as I walked along the Strand, but I did not put up my umbrella. The truth is I couldn't put up my umbrella. The frame would not work for one thing, and if it had worked, I would not have put the thing up, for I would no more be seen under such a travesty of an umbrella than Falstaff would be seen marching through Coventry with his regiment of ragamuffins. The fact is, the umbrella is not my umbrella at all. It is the umbrella of some person who I hope will read these lines. He has got my silk umbrella. I have got the cotton one he left in exchange. I imagine him flaunting along the Strand under my umbrella, and throwing a scornful glance at the fellow who was carrying his abomination and getting wet into the bargain. I daresay the rascal chuckled as he eyed the said abomination. 'Ah,' he said gaily to himself, 'I did you in that time, old boy. I know that thing. It won't open for nuts. And it folds up like a sack. Now, this umbrella . . .'

But I leave him to his unrighteous communings. He is one of those people who have what I may call an umbrella conscience. You know the sort of person I mean. He would never put his hand in another's pocket, or forge a cheque or rob a till – not even if he had the chance. But he will swop umbrellas, or forget to return a book, or take a rise out of the railway company. In fact he is a thoroughly honest man who allows his honesty the benefit of the doubt. Perhaps he takes your umbrella at random from the barber's stand. He knows he can't get a worse one than his own. He may get a better. He doesn't look at it very closely until he is well on his way. Then, 'Dear me! I've taken the wrong umbrella,' he says, with an air of surprise, for he likes really to feel that he has made a mistake. 'Ah, well, it's no use going back now. He'd be gone. *And I've left him mine!'*

It is thus that we play hide-and-seek with our own conscience. It is not enough not to be found out by others; we refuse to be found out by ourselves. Quite impeccable people, people who ordinarily seem unspotted from the world, are afflicted with umbrella morals. It was a well-known preacher who was found dead in a first-class railway carriage with a third-class ticket in his pocket.

And as for books, who has any morals where they are concerned? I remember some years ago the library of a famous divine and literary critic, who had died, being sold. It was a splendid library of rare books, chiefly concerned with seventeenth-century writers, about whom he was a distinguished authority. Multitudes of the books had the marks of libraries all over the country. He had borrowed them and never found a convenient opportunity of returning them. They clung to him like precedents to law. Yet he was a holy man and preached admirable sermons, as I can bear witness. And, if you press me on the point, I shall have to own that it *is* hard to part with a book you have come to love.

Indeed, the only sound rule about books is that adopted by the man who was asked by a friend to lend him a certain volume. 'I'm sorry,' he said, 'but I can't.' 'Haven't you got it?' asked the other. 'Yes, I've got it,' he said, 'but I make it a rule never to lend books. You see, nobody ever returns them. I know it is so from my own experience. Here, come with me.' And he led the way to his library. 'There,' said he, 'four thousand volumes. Every – one – of – 'em – borrowed.' No, never lend books. You can't trust your dearest friend there. I know. Where is that *Gil Blas* gone? Eh? And that *Silvio Pellico*? And . . . But why continue the list? . . . He knows. HE KNOWS.

And hats. There are people who will exchange hats. Now that is unpardonable. That goes outside that dim borderland of conscience where honesty and dishonesty dissemble. No one can put a strange hat on without being aware of the fact. Yet it is done. I once hung a silk hat up in the smoking-room of the House of Commons. When I wanted it, it was gone. And there was no silk hat left in its place. I had to go out bareheaded through Palace Yard and Whitehall to buy another. I have often wondered who was the gentleman who put my hat on and carried his own in his hand. Was he a Tory? Was he a Radical? It can't have been a Labour man, for no Labour man could put a silk hat on in a moment of abstraction. The thing would scorch his brow. Fancy Will Crooks in a silk hat! One would as soon dare to play with the fancy of the Archbishop of Canterbury in a bowler – a thought which seems almost impious.

It is possible, of course, that the gentleman who took my silk umbrella did really make a mistake. Perhaps if he knew the owner he would return it with his compliments. The thing has been done. Let me give an illustration. I have myself exchanged umbrellas – often. I hope I have done it honestly, but one can never be quite sure. Indeed, now I come to think of it, that silk umbrella itself was not mine. It was one of a long series of exchanges in which I had sometimes gained and sometimes lost. My most memorable exchange was at a rich man's house where I had been invited to dine with some politicians. It was summertime, and the weather being dry I had no occasion for some days afterwards to carry an umbrella. Then one day a sensation reigned in our household. There had been discovered in the umbrella-stand an umbrella with a gold band and a gold tassel, and the name of a certain statesman engraved upon it. There had never been such a super-umbrella in our house before. Before its golden splendours we were at once humbled and terrified – humbled by its magnificence, terrified by its presence. I felt as though I had been caught in the act of stealing the British Empire. I wrote a hasty letter to the owner, told him I admired his politics, but had never hoped to steal his umbrella; then hailed a cab, and took the umbrella and the note to the nearest dispatch office.

He was very nice about it, and in returning my own umbrella took all the blame on himself. 'What,' he said, 'between the noble-looking gentleman who thrust a hat on my head, and the second noble-looking gentleman who handed me a coat, and the third noble-looking gentleman who put an umbrella in my hand, and the fourth noble-looking gentleman who flung me into a carriage, I hadn't the least idea what I was taking. I was too bewildered by all the noble flunkeys to refuse anything that was offered me.'

Be it observed, it was the name on the umbrella that saved the situation in this case. That is the way to circumvent the man with an umbrella conscience. I see him eyeing his exchange with a secret joy; then he observes the name and address and his solemn conviction that he is an honest man does the rest. After my experience today, I think I will engrave my name on my umbrella. But not on that baggy thing standing in the corner. I do not care who relieves me of that. It is anybody's for the taking.

●

H. L. MENCKEN

H. L. Mencken (1880–1956) was born in Baltimore, where he spent his entire life. The son of a cigar manufacturer, he was educated at a private school and graduated at the age of fifteen from Baltimore Polytechnic Institute, where he had, somewhat eccentrically, studied both journalism and chemistry. He spent three years working in the family factory, but in 1899 he joined the editorial staff of the *Baltimore Morning Herald*. He performed a variety of roles – police and fire reporter, city hall reporter, and drama critic – and wrote a splendid memoir of this period in his career, *Newspaper Days, 1899–1906* (1941). He progressed upwards through the executive ranks and by 1906 was editor of the *Herald* (by then the *Evening Herald*). Six months later, however, the paper closed and Mencken was made Sunday editor of the *Baltimore Sun*.

He had started writing columns on the *Herald*, under various titles ('Terse and Terrible Texts', 'Knocks and Jollies', 'Untold Tales' and 'Baltimore and the Rest of the World'). At the *Sun*, he wrote editorials for the first few years, graduating to a column signed 'H.L.M.' in 1910 and a controversial column, called 'The Free Lance', the following year. While serving as co-editor of *Smart Set* – one of the most influential sources of American literary criticism, including his own contributions – from 1914 to 1923, he continued writing his *Sun* column until it was dropped in October 1915 after he defended the sinking of the *Lusitania*. The *Sun* sent him to France as a war correspondent in January 1917, but a couple of months later he resigned to join the *New York Evening Mail* as a thrice-weekly columnist. In 1918 he returned to the *Sun* as an editorial adviser and from then until 1938 he wrote a weekly column, called 'Monday Article'. From 1924 to 1928 he also contributed a column to the *Chicago Tribune*. His principal targets were mass democracy, puritanism and political humbug. He wrote numerous books and was a prolific free-lance.

The Telephone Nuisance
Chicago Tribune, April 10, 1927

The other day I was summoned to the telephone to answer a long-distance call from Cleveland. I could recall no business with anyone in that great city, but the local operator (rather unusually) spelled and pronounced my name correctly, and so I put the receiver to my ear and waited. Four or five minutes passed. There was, it appeared, some sort of trouble on the line. I could hear the local long-distance operator howling at the Cleveland operator, and the Cleveland operator whispering back. At the end of nine minutes the Cleveland operator addressed me directly. She was sorry, she said, but the call could not be completed. The unknown in Cleveland, growing tired of waiting on his end, had gone out to lunch.

What is to be made of such manners? Here was a man who summoned me uninvited from my work, let me wait with a telephone to my ear for ten minutes, and then calmly walked off. Who he was I don't know, and shall probably never know, for I served notice on the telephone company on the spot that no long-distance call from Cleveland would be answered at my house for six months. But, though one town is thus shut off, all the rest remain open, and at regular intervals I'll hear from them. On days when I am hard at work against time, and making heavy weather of it, I'll be hauled to the telephone to wait upon the peppery dialogues of long-distance operators, and the pleasure of bounders I don't know and don't want to know. Idiots who, if they wrote me letters, would get no answers, and who, if they came to my house, would be kicked out by my chaplain, will be free to call me up day or night, and if the experience of the past counts for anything scores of them will do it.

The thing, indeed, becomes an unmitigated curse. The telephone has become as great a boon to bores as the movies are to morons. It enables them to practice their depressing art and mystery upon anyone who has a telephone in his house, whether they know him or not, and they take advantage of the privilege up to the extreme limit of human endurance. It has been rarely, during the last few years, that I have sat down to a meal at home without suffering their intrusion; it has literally never happened that I have escaped them during two consecutive hours of work.

My home is in Baltimore and my office is in New York. In the latter city the excessive number of calls, especially during the morning hours, makes the service very bad, but that fact doesn't seem to discourage the town nuisances in the slightest. The moment I get to my office in the morning the shrilling of the bell begins, and it keeps up without pause until late in the afternoon. Often it is so bad that I find it almost impossible to get through my mail. As for any work requiring a greater alertness and concentration, it is wholly out of the question. Day after day I am forced to flee to my hotel for enough quiet to get through the banal operations whereby I make a living.

There are, of course, devices for escaping this barrage. Many men have secretaries to take their telephone calls. When a call comes in the secretary finds out who is calling and then asks for instructions; it is not until after that that the boss himself is reached. I practice the scheme myself, but it has many disadvantages. For one thing, the secretary's report on a call is almost as distracting an interruption as the call would have been itself. For another thing, the secretary of a man who does any actual work in his office is very busy herself, and the calls greatly interrupt and impede her work. And for a third thing, it seems to me to be grossly impolite to force a man making a legitimate call to wait while its legitimacy is being discussed.

But in New York, I fear, politeness is a lost art. It is the almost universal custom in the town to relay calls through secretaries. One hears that one is wanted by Mr Blank, and then one discovers that one is talking to his secretary. While she goes to fetch him, one waits. At least two times out of seven, in my experience, the connection is broken while he is being sought, and so the whole business is in vain. Five minutes later the secretary calls again, and it is repeated. I have had as many as four such calls in a row.

Time consumed: twelve minutes. Penalty for the attendant swearing: 10,000 years in hell.

Of late a new complication is invented. The bore instructs his secretary to call up his chosen victim, and the secretary asks the switchboard operator to get his number. When the victim gets to the telephone he finds that he is talking to the operator, and so he has a double wait: while the operator gets the secretary, and while the secretary gets the bore. It frequently happens that the bore forgets the call in the meanwhile, and cannot be found. Or he has gone into conference. Or he is operating upon some other victim, and his line is thus busy.

Naturally enough, such elaborate hocus-pocus is mainly practiced by third-rate men – that is, by the sort whose calls are seldom of any importance. The secretary fever now rages in the United States, and every white-collar slave has one. They transact, indeed, nine tenths of the business of the country. One of the chief occupations of these secretaries is calling up people who don't want to be called. Their idiot employers obviously get a magnificent satisfaction out of this privilege. It makes them seem busy and important. It puts them on a footing of equality with their betters. So the bells jangle all day long, and men with actual work to do are driven half frantic.

The schemes that have been proposed for getting rid of the nuisance are all full of defects. There is, for example, the plan of putting in a so-called silent telephone – that is, one whose number is not listed in the book. But it has the disadvantage of cutting off many calls that are really necessary and would be welcome; moreover, it does not impede the bores, for all the true professionals know every silent number for miles around. There is, again, the plan of having no telephone at all. But that is cutting off one's nose to spite one's face. The telephone, in the modern world, is far more than a mere convenience; it is an absolute necessity. Without it one wastes more time than it ever wastes itself, even when it rings all day. And one misses many charming contacts, and many sweet titbits of gossip.

The true remedy, I think, lies in other directions. What is needed is a national secret organization, with members bound by a bloody oath to avoid telephone calls whenever possible and to boycott all persons who makes them unnecessarily. Even without this secret organization much could be accomplished. On July 1 next, at noon precisely, I shall put into effect a plan of my own. From that instant I shall answer no calls made by switchboard operators or secretaries. The instant I hear the dulcet feminine inquiry, 'Who is this?' I shall hang up, and for ten minutes thereafter I shall answer no calls at all.

This scheme, to be sure, will annoy many of my friends, but I am sure that they will bear with me: they must suffer that I may survive at all. I am as busy as they are, and yet I never make telephone calls by way of a secretary. Whenever I wish to call anyone I make the call myself, and am at the telephone, ready for discourse, the instant the party called responds. This seems to me to be only common politeness. Nevertheless, it appears to be somewhat rare in the world, and especially in New York. Very often, so calling a man, I find him surprised into temporary speechlessness by the fact that I am talking to him myself. He expects a preliminary parley with a secretary. He is prepared to give his full name and address, and to answer various other questions. When I bust in upon him at once he is somehow shocked.

But life in this grand and incomparable republic would be far more comfortable if such shocks were so common that they ceased to shock at all. The telephone is undoubtedly the most valuable of American inventions. It is worth a dozen airplanes, radios and talking machines; it ranks perhaps with synthetic gin, the movie and the bichloride tablet. But here again, once more and doubly damned, we become slaves to a machine. What I propose is simply a way of liberation.

•

BAIRD LEONARD

Mrs Harry St Clair Zogbaum (1889–1941) – 'a witty woman', as A. J. Liebling described her – wrote a column called 'Stuff and Nonsense' under the pseudonym Baird Leonard for the New York *Morning Telegraph* during the early 1920s. She wrote a book called *Simple Confessions* (1930) and edited *Cora Scovil's Lady's Book* (1940).

'Stuff and Nonsense'
[New York] *Morning Telegraph*, March 4, 1922

Lines to Some Snappy Publishers

Boni and Liveright, thee I sing
    In airy cadence guaranteed;
You never publish anything
    That people do not want to read.

When literary food I lack
    And to the bookshop gaily go,
Your firm name on a volume's back
    Is all I need on earth to know.

Now am I totally inclined
    To like you for your taste alone:
Your gilt initials, intertwined,
    Form – as a monogram – my own.

Imaginary Letters

126 East 64th St,
New York City,
March 3, 1922

My dear Niece:
    Your letter telling me of the collapse of your father's fortune has just arrived. I am sorry to hear it, but not surprised. Poor dead Robert has been prone from boyhood to

believe implicitly in the myth about the end of the rainbow. I dare say he will go on believing in it, even though deprived of all means of financing his journey. But that has nothing to do with you, and I hasten to give you the advice for which you ask concerning the course of your immediate procedure.

You must know well that your Uncle John and I stand ready to give you a home and to maintain you indefinitely in the style to which you have been accustomed. But I gather from your letter and from my knowledge of your independence of spirit that you would never accept it. I have accordingly taken an inventory of your talents, in an attempt to hit upon one thing to which you may apply them most advantageously. And I think I have found it.

If you had asked me the same question ten or fifteen years ago, the answer would have been simple. A dozen avenues, if not royal roads, to economic independence would have been open to you. You might have started a kindergarten in Bayville for the children of your friends; you might have taken in a few music pupils, or sought employment in a publishing house, or learned stenography. Strict application along any of those lines would have, in time, assured you of a comfortable maintenance and a position of dignity in the community. But I cannot, in honesty, advise you to attempt any of them now. After weighing the matter carefully, I have decided that you will attain your fullest felicity as an individual and your maximum power as a breadwinner if you become a domestic servant.

It is a business axiom that commercial success comes from dealing in a commodity which everybody must have. If the demand is greater than the supply, all the more fortune attends the venture. I need only direct your attention to the advertising columns in the Sunday papers.

You had, if I remember rightly, a course in domestic science when you were in boarding school. Even if you hadn't, a lack of such training would by no means stand in your way. If you could have seen the roast with which your Uncle John and I struggled last night . . . But I digress.

As a schoolmistress or stenographer or social secretary – in fact, in any one of the vocations hitherto supposed to be suited to indigent gentlewomen, you would be poorly paid and subject to the whims of your employers. As a domestic servant, you will regulate your own salary and bend your employers to your own inclinations. If you happen to be an exceptionally good servant, your price will be greater than rubies. Friendships will be broken on your account, and bribery and corruption will enter your life.

Please do not get the idea that your social position and authority will suffer in the slightest degree. They will be enhanced, if anything. The women for whom you work will defer to you in every way. Many of my friends are surrendering their own suites to their servants, retiring themselves to the miniature bedroom and bath originally accorded domestics by short-sighted Manhattan architects. It will be your privilege to order artichokes for yourself when the family is having boiled spinach. When in need of a stimulant, your access to the carafes will be easy – no master these days dares own keys to sideboards and cellarettes. Silk stockings and French lingerie, which you could not afford if you were following a profession, will be yours for the taking. What is more, your mistresses will expect you to take them. You will be given tickets to the opera, the theatre and the motion pictures at regular intervals, driven to and from church in a motor, and presented frequently with objects of definite material value. It will also be possible for you to choose the persons with whom you come in contact. Your aversion to any particular guest will be instantly marked by your employers. Your regulation of the numbers who come to the house is a simple matter. In fact, the power of the domestic has advanced to the point where it is having an effect on the birthrate.

It goes without saying that you will not suffer from personal comparison. You will be expected to make a better appearance in street clothes than your mistress. And you will have a great deal of time to yourself concerning which you will never be questioned.

In short, my dear niece, I know of no other calling which you can follow in which you will so fully enjoy the liberty and advantages which have always been yours. Your literary ability may enable you to turn your experience as a servant to excellent account as a side issue. It has become the fashion for anybody who does anything whatsoever to make literary capital of his adventures and experiences.

Think over what I have said, and let me know when you have reached a decision. I know of at least twenty homes into which you can step without ten minutes' notice.

Devotedly yours,
Caroline B. Wexford

•

RING LARDNER

Ring Lardner (1885–1933) had a well-off Michigan farmer as his father and a preacher's daughter as his mother. He was educated at Niles High School and briefly at the Armour Institute of Technology in Chicago, where he obtained distinction in rhetoric. He joined a company of minstrels based in Niles, writing music and lyrics for their shows, and after a brief spell with the local gas company, he fell into journalism by accident. His brother Rex had been working on local papers and the editor of a rival paper came looking to hire him. Rex was on vacation and so Ring volunteered his services, falsely claiming to have helped his brother with newspaper work. He was hired as 'society reporter, courthouse man, drama critic and sporting editor' for the South Bend, Indiana, *Times*, on a salary of $12 a week.

He stayed there for two years, writing without by-line, during which time he started reporting baseball games. He joined the *Chicago Examiner*, and between the autumn of 1907 and the summer of 1911 he went on the road with baseball and football teams, switching to the *Chicago Tribune* in 1908. He inherited Hugh E. Keough's daily humour column, 'In the Wake of the News', in 1913 and wrote it for several years until short-story writing became his staple living. His first 'Weekly Letter' column for the Bell Syndicate, about 1,000 words written in the voice of one of his 'wise boob' characters, was published in 150 papers and read by eight million people. He tended to avoid baseball, preferring to write whimsy and political satire. Two later attempts to revive his column-writing career were failures: his four-times-a-week column called 'Ring's Side' for the New York *Morning Telegraph* (for which he was hired on an annual salary of $50,000 in 1928) ran to only thirty-eight pieces, while his six-times-a-week 'Night Letter from Ring Lardner' for the Bell Syndicate and the Chicago Tribune–New York Daily News Syndicate ran out of energy and content after only three months in 1931. Thereafter, he concentrated entirely on fiction. Admired and befriended by F. Scott Fitzgerald and Ernest Hemingway, he died at the age of forty-eight from heart disease, after four miserable years of illness.

On Prohibition

From *First to Last* (1934)

When it was suggested that I write something about prohibition, I snapped at the idea as a starving dog goes after a deck of cards. Here was a subject that had escaped the attention of other members of the writing graft, and you don't have to be so skillful in the handling of a given theme if the theme itself is sufficiently novel.

I thought I could tear off two or three thousand words almost as fast as I could type. I forgot that even a mental contact with the Demon or anything pertaining to same always filled me with an almost overwhelming desire to abstain from work for a period of thirty-four days. So the composition of this article has been a tough job and not a siesta, and I ask my friends to bear that in mind while they are thinking what a tough job it is to read it.

I do not believe I am betraying a confidence when I say that there are, in this country, several organizations whose aim is to effect the modification or repeal of the Eighteenth Amendment.

Nearly every citizen who isn't living under an assumed name has received invitations to join one or more of these tongs. If I have been asked once, I have been asked twice. But I have consistently declined to go into them because I figure it is silly to interfere in any way with the efforts of the Drys to knock their own pet legislation for a nose dive. If they fail, it will be time for outsiders to step in.

But they won't fail. They are experienced Gummers and we should be grateful that they are not enlisted on the side of some more salutary statute such as the one which restricts husband-killers to four kinds of dessert during the week of penal servitude.

The Drys of our land are to a large extent identical with the people who have fought the good fight for purity and decency in books and plays. If their war on rum is conducted only half as shrewdly as the struggle against literary and dramatic dirt, we boy scouts need have no fear. You can hardly name one legitimate show of the past season that could possibly give offense to any 125-year-old paralytic who was unable to attend it, and parents are safe in leaving a volume of Milne or Guest on the living-room table, while the children are away at kindergarten.

With a modicum of the same energy and skill applied to the anti-alcohol campaign, the Pros will soon have it fixed so a person can't buy a drink from a horse. It were folly for an amateur to offer advice to these needle-witted strategists, but it does seem to me that if the idea is to stop tippling by homicide, bigger results could be obtained, and at less expense, through the withdrawal of artillery and snipers from the border and the free and untrammeled admittance of all the stuff the consumer wants.

The price of what is screamingly called liquor would shortly drop to a point where even actors could afford it and the consequent fatalities would outnumber those resulting from the present system by at least a hundred to one.

Moreover, this sort of war of attrition would be carried on at little or no cost to the government; the customers would have to pay for their own demise unless they died before they settled, in which case the laugh would be on the bootlegger, where it belongs.

But even if the current scheme is adhered to, I believe it should be carried out with more thoroughness and zeal.

In the first place it should be under the auspices of the War Department instead of the Secretary of the Treasury. Revolvers, shotguns, small-bore rifles and pea-shooters ought to be supplanted by long-range cannon, and bullets that can kill only one man or child at a time, replaced by high explosives, shrapnel and all the latest delicacies in the way of gas.

Electrically charged wire should guard the Canadian border from ocean to ocean and the Mexican border from the Pacific to the Gulf. Scout planes and observation balloons should locate Canada's distilleries and direct our shell fire, and the fields of hay from which the liquor is made could be destroyed by poisoned confetti.

The entire eastern half of the Dominion to the north of us might be inundated by a company of volunteers under Capt. Gertrude Ederle, who would stand at the bottom of Niagara Falls and splash the water back as fast as it came over. Our aces could drop souvenir postcards from George Creel assuring the Canadians that we have no quarrel with them as a nation, that all we want is peace without whisky, and that this is merely a war to make the United States safe for the soda fountains. An armistice would be granted, we'd tell them, as soon as they pledged themselves to eliminate entirely the alcoholic content of the stuff they have been selling to our importers. This would mean a reduction of nearly two percent.

Some of the wartime regulations should be in effect once more. No meat on Mondays; no heat on Tuesdays; no sweet on Wednesdays; no wheat on Thursdays; no treat on Fridays; and no eat on Saturdays. Censorship of all mail passing between us and Canada and Mexico; four-minute speeches; adoption of Belgian orphans; purling; saving fingernail parings to fill in the shell holes on the Texas and the Minnesota thoroughfares.

I do think, though, that this war should be made much more bearable and entertaining to the stay-at-homes by the adoption of a liberal policy in regard to press dispatches. I never did understand what good was accomplished by the exclusion of the names of people and places from the dull, daily stories from France in 1917 and 1918.

The theory seemed to be that if the Grand Rapids 'Herald' printed the news that Hendrick Van Hooten of Holland, Michigan, was in hospital at Châlons-sur-Marne with anthrax, a German spy employed by the Grand Rapids Furniture Company would call up the Kaiser who would thus suspect that a division containing Michigan regiments was, or had been, somewhere near Châlons. Wilhelm would then confer with Ludendorff on what style of defense to use against Michigan's passing game with Van Hooten on the sidelines.

Let's cut down on caution this time; the danger of disclosing military secrets would be more than offset by the certainty of improving the country's morale with a few human-interest stories such as:

El Paso, Tex. Aug. 2 – Corporal Charley Judson of Company B, Fourth Regiment of the Eighth (Hawkeye) Division, American Prohibitionary Force, was being congratulated by his buddies tonight for shooting the left ear off a two-year-old child who was crossing the bridge from Juarez with a peculiar waddling gait. Corporal Judson said he had witnesses to prove that the fellow had been seen drinking out of a bottle; he fired at his ear instead of his heart because he just wanted to frighten him. The bottle was found to contain a little over an ounce of a liquid identified as milk. 'Yeh?' said the Corporal, who has a certain dry humor. 'Well, milk don't make people walk funny.'

Sault St Marie, Mich., Aug. 2 – Miss Muriel Chapin of this place was scattered all over the Northern Peninsula today by a machine-gun squad in charge of Capt. Felix Lord of Houghton. The captain picked up one of the girl's lips and showed it to his colonel, H. R. King of Calumet. The lip was a pale red. 'That's what fooled me,' said Captain Lord. 'It's just some kind of rouge, but I thought it was grenadine.'

Niagara Falls, N. Y., Aug. 2 – A depth bomb dropped by Lieut Ed. Frawley of Herkimer demolished a barrel that was seen shooting the Falls late today. Frawley suspected that the barrel was full of liquor, but it developed that the contents had been John E. Gardner and wife and two children, a Buffalo family out for an outing. 'This was self-defense if there ever was one!' declared Lieut Frawley. 'I acted only after assuring myself that the barrel was shooting the Falls.'

Plattsburg, N. Y., Aug. 2 – A bearded man on a bicycle was stopped here today by Clarence Dutton, an M.P. of the A.P.F. Dutton demanded the man's name and the man said he was Eli Kolp, a farmer residing three miles south of Plattsburg.

'Then why are you wearing a beard?' asked Dutton.

'I look funny without one,' replied the bicyclist.

'You look funny with one,' retorted Dutton. 'You look suspicious to me. How do I know what you've got in those tires?'

'I've got nothing but some air. I'll open them and let it out.'

'I'll let some into you,' said Dutton, shooting him full of holes.

The bicyclist was later identified as Eli Kolp, a farmer residing three miles south of Plattsburg.

•

D. B. WYNDHAM LEWIS

Dominic Bevan Wyndham Lewis (1894–1969) was born in Wales, the son of a clergyman, and was studying at Oxford with every intention of going into the Law when the First World War broke out. He enlisted as a private in the infantry and was shell-shocked twice in France. In 1919 he joined the *Daily Express* to write the 'By the Way' column, signing himself as 'Beach Comber'. In 1923 he defected to the *Daily Mail*, where he wrote a similar satire in the form of a weekly column called 'At the Sign of the Blue Moon', which he continued throughout the

1920s and 1930s. He later wrote a humorous column for the *News Chronicle* as 'Timothy Shy', as well as a miscellany column for the society paper *Tatler* (and *Tatler-Bystander*). He also wrote biographies of Louis XI of France, François Villon, Ronsard and James Boswell.

'At the Sign of the Blue Moon' By Numbers

From *At the Sign of the Blue Moon* (1924)

On such a day as this, my little ones – a burning blue August day, with the golden cornfields hardly whispering in the stillness of noon and a drowsy sound of bees in the air – on such a day it is pleasant to lie on some thymy sun-kissed hill in Sussex and meditate on the undoubted fact that only a few leagues away, over the Hampshire border, Mr Sidney Webb, President of the Board of Trade and author of *Industrial Democracy*, *Problems of Modern Industry*, *English Poor-Law Policy*, *History of Liquor Licensing* and other works of passion and ecstasy, is also solacing himself from the cares of State with a country holiday. Bring, Nymphs, fresh Blue-books! And you, sunburnt rustic deities, prepare new statistics! But let us have no drunkenness and no revelry, but only that which is done neatly and in strict order, while on the grass the well-clothed Fauns trip to a Fabian song.

Musing a long time (not without tears) on this and endeavouring to evoke within my quaking mind the spectacle of Mr Sidney Webb crowned with rose leaves at some country festival, I naturally began next to think of that rural feast which Grandgousier gave on the day when the great Gargantua was born. To this feast (as you know) all the burghers of Sainnais were invited, as well as those of Suillé, of Roche-Clermaud, of Vaugaudray, of Coudray, of Montpensier and of Gué-de-Vede; and after feasting they went pell-mell to the Grove of Willows, where on the green grass they danced to the sound of merry flageolets and sweet bagpipes, so joyously (says the misguided Rabelais) that it was a heavenly pleasure to see them frolic so – '*C'estoit passetemps celeste les voir ainsi soy rigoller.*'

Alas! How unproductive! How economically wasteful! How far removed from the glorious ideals of the Industrial State! We (Mr Webb and myself) would not have deprived these citizens of reasonable recreation; but how much better, my friends, to have had them, each labelled and clothed in a neat combination suit of official grey, capering in unison at the direction of a State Controller of Joy! It makes us sick to think of those careless, wasteful ages before Manchester became what she is today: a glory to mankind.

I mentioned this yesterday to Professor Dogbody, one of the most earnest Fabians I know – the famous Dogbody who was thrown out of the Folies-Bergère for shouting in a loud voice 'Is this Co-Operation?' He told me that in Spain, in Italy, in France, and even in some parts of England this passion on the part of the producing and consuming classes alike for uncontrolled revelry (especially in agricultural districts) still exists.

'Tck, tck,' I said sympathetically.

'Happily,' said the Professor, producing a sheaf of blue papers, 'I have had some opportunity of putting into practice in the village of Hogsnorton, where I have been living for that purpose, the principles so admirably set forth in Euphemia Polk's *Need Joy Be Unconfined? A Plea for Rational Amusement in the Co-Operative Commonwealth*. The inhabitants at first, indeed, stubbornly refused to evince Joy on the days I set apart for that purpose, but I was determined that these days should be observed. With the aid of a capable Committee, including Mrs Struggles, Professor Bodger, Miss Volumnia Bibb, Mrs Martha Dillson Dudbody, of Athens, Pa., and Canon Boom, we examined and assessed every inhabitant of the village individually, afterwards classifying them as follows:

'Class A (Joy-value 40 per cent) – Fit for general joy-making, including such specified occupation as laughing, dancing, and any other approved by the Committee's Controller.

'Class B (Joy-value 30 per cent) – Fit for moderate joy-making, including the specified occupations in Class A.

'Class C (Joy-value 20 per cent) – Fit for light or sedentary joy, such as songs in the Co-Operative Commonwealth Official Song Book, to be sung at the Controller's discretion.

'Class D (Joy-value 0.5 per cent) – Totally incapacitated for any kind of organized joy whatsoever.

'Among this last class,' continued Professor Dogbody, trumpeting through his nose, 'were, I regret to say, several aged and hairy men of agricultural occupation who not only refused point-blank to be gay when requested peremptorily to do so by my Committee, but added mutinously that they would be gormed if they did. Canon Boom at once replied by having them drawn up in a line and ordering them to sing in chorus the 'Laughing Song' (No. 98 A) from the Official Song Book, which goes:

> We are so merry and gay, tra la,
> We laugh and dance and sing:
> Controlled in every way, tra la,
> And drilled in everything.
> All non-productive gladness we
> Unanimously spurn;
> Our breasts with mass hilarity
> Co-operatively burn!

> (*Chorus, to be sung while dancing – see chart*
> pp. 87–9, Sec. 23 (A) (I.).)
> Tra la tra la tra la tra la!
> Hooray hooray hooray!
> Huzza huzza huzza huzza!
> Three cheers for Sidney Webb!

'And on their again refusing (this time with rural oaths) to evince gaiety and move their limbs in the dance in the manner prescribed, we had them at once expelled from the village. It is now a pleasure to a serious and well-nourished mind,' said the Professor with strong emotion, 'to observe our weekly festival. One-two. One-two. Should any inhabitant neglect to smile on these occasions he (or she) is at once placed in solitary confinement with all the recent Blue-books pertaining to Local Government and the Factory Acts, and on a second offence soundly beaten. Here, indeed, is the Ideal State!'

'Indeed, indeed yes,' I said fervently.

There was a pause.

'You spoke just now of Rabelais,' said Professor Dogbody, coughing slightly. 'You may be interested to know – possibly the public might be interested to know – that I have been asked by Mr Eustace Smiles –'

We both raised our hats reverently.

'– to bring out a new Vegetarian Edition of Rabelais. It is our belief that the substitution of nut dishes and various proteid-containing foods (such as tapioca, Meggo and Gloxo) for the various rich meat and flesh foods which form the extensive banquets over which this writer gloats to such a great extent in his works would not only improve their tone but make them a definite power for Good. At the same time we feel that his extravagant praise of wine (such as the wine called Chinon Grillé), if directed so as to praise instead the virtues of Milko, or some such beverage rich in vitamins, would materially assist our Movement; for a nut diet does not heat the blood or minister to the baser passions.'

So saying, Professor Dogbody, after performing a few deep-breathing exercises, grasped his umbrella firmly and went away.

But I remained for some time revolving many things, observing the disorderly arrangement of the trees, the untidy luxury of the hedgerows, the uneven skyline of the great Downs above me, the ragged flight of the rooks going home with such hoarse and uncoordinated cries, the imperfect alignment, far away through a gap in the hills, of the long waves which rolled and broke on the shingle. Such things are distressing to a trained and tidy mind. I contemplated Nature for a little time very coldly and unfavourably through an eye-glass, with pursed mouth, just like a Fabian who might be, by some mischance, caught suddenly up to Paradise; and then I went home to tea.

'One Thing and Another'

From *Take It to Bed* (1944)

Snook

When Oriane, Duchesse de Guermantes, gave her evening parties in the 1900s, for which the bluest blood of the Faubourg St Germain scrambled to get a card, the principal refreshment served was orangeade. Patrician *morgue* and absolute power enabled that sweetheart to treat the most exclusive society in Europe thus, in the days when Russian Grand Dukes on the razzle would chuck vintage champagne and liqueur brandy by the bucketful over fluffy ladies in Maxim's, for fun. A superb snook by the Duchess, we've often thought.

Why no modern leader of Society, combining economy with chic, has yet begun boldly to imitate Oriane de Guermantes we can't understand (and how like you to point out that somebody has, long ago, but naturally we wouldn't know). Cocktails are getting fouler and fouler and even Labour leaders are complaining. Sherry suburban grocers would blush for is being inflicted on palates which a year ago rejected with cries anything but a fine solera or the driest of manzanillas, and orangeade even out of a bottle would be no worse than some of the vermouth we've come across lately. You may say that orangeade, though launched by a duchess, would be the death of the average modern party, which may be true, and mightn't be a bad idea, either. Friends wouldn't dislike each other so much if they didn't meet so often at cocktail parties. Ring up Myra and say Dusty is screaming that he won't go to the Faughaughtons' again unless somebody puts everybody's head in a haybag.

Racket

A rich reek of whisky and tartuffery having surrounded General Gordon's name since Lytton Strachey took him in hand, it was agreeable to read a *Times* letter praising this great soldier on the fifty-seventh anniversary of his heroic death at Khartoum.

Whether Gordon ever hit the bottle as Strachey affirms we can't say, never having examined sources. Probably not – but how picturesque! Old Testament in one hand, decanter in the other – how amusing, how rhythmic, how chic! And how it inspired the booksy rabble immediately to cash in on debunking every other great figure in history, digging feverishly in the refuse heaps of Grub Street and being very, very careful not to check their evidence! However, they've faded out now.

Poor little Lucrezia Borgia, most slandered of blondes, had to wait nearly 400 years before a scientific historian like Funck-Bretano probed the case and found her biographers had been handing on the tales of hired anti-Borgia pamphleteers. Mary Queen of Scots, for whom, as Dr Johnson said, any decent man would be glad to die, was cleared only about forty years ago. The booksy racket badly needs the attentions of the LCC Sanitary and Public Health Department, we've often thought. Ring WATerloo 5000 and ask for Dusty.

Smoke

Pipe-smokers are not as yet rallying with any marked enthusiasm round Sir Stephen Tallents, BBC, and his war-economy watercress-and-lavender experimental ersatz blends, which he admits are not 'very palatable'.

You may have noted that the best-selling booksy boys who have capitalized the large-sized briar so extensively – it shows the public they're bluff, manly, forthright and honourable, a photographer explained to us – are hanging back rather ostentatiously. Maybe some of them, having sponsored various tobaccos for advertising purposes, are scared of the Tobacco Ring's bodyguards if they're caught backing the Tallents experiments. Or maybe, now booksy publicity has fallen off, they've dropped manipulating those pipes and taken to chewing, like Ibsen. Did you know Ibsen habitually chewed American plug? A French critic some time ago dug up the odious fact, which for us explains all Ibsen's drama, just as the fat, rich Havanas Trollope habitually chain-smoked while working explain the works of Trollope. Old Daddy Ibsen, chewing and spitting through his whiskers and thinking up yet duller and snuffier dramatic situations – no wonder his lily-handed admirers never mention it, the shy wild ducks.

Nobody has yet (apropos the Tallents scheme) suggested dried tea-leaves, on which most pipe-smokers begin at an intempestive age. Or horrible, lousy, fiery, leathery, yellow homegrown tobacco, such as chaps who grow it sometimes foist proudly on you. Or the nearly similar seats of old cane chairs, which Barrie's friend smoked, or said he did. Or Magaliesberg, the dark, dry, crumbly, linen-bagged Boer tobacco you dislike at first but by degrees grow to esteem, and which South Africa ought to export a bit more. Whatever the Tallents herb laboratory ultimately digs up, the result could hardly perturb anybody who in the last war smoked army ration tobacco, which tasted like the unwashed beards of very old damp enemies of God blended by epicene witches from Bloomsbury under a bloodshot moon (*la sangrienta luna*) on a wet February night outside a Liberal club in Manchester.

Echo

Subaltern after hard-up subaltern faces a court-martial on cheque charges, and more and more sergeants (as Mr William Hickey of the *Express* remarked) stay in the ranks, where they're better off.

While the War Office is still 'considering' paying junior army officers a decent living wage, that item of 17s. 6d. for 'hire of furniture' in a typical monthly mess-bill quoted by Mr Hickey seems to us to strike a charming old-world note. It smacks, in our unfortunate view, of Buller's long baggage-trains in the Boer War, blocking communications with truckloads of rugs and carpets and plush hangings and mahogany tables and leather armchairs and Fortnum crates and grand pianofortes and cases of regimental plate and all the other essential campaign mess-furniture the army lugged along to South Africa, unless survivors lie. The average officers' mess of 1942 would hardly have been deemed suitable for stabling by some of those Olympians, by all accounts. It was the last Monocle War, after all; we mean ornamentally and symbolically, as malicious Continental caricaturists of the period saw it, and how.

We've no grudge against the monocle as a necessary and practical engine of war, and we know a chap who runs an infantry brigade like clockwork with its help at this moment. But it seems in its romantic, symbolic, or Boer War aspect to go naturally with that 17s. 6d. – which would almost buy the entire furniture of some Spartan messes – and the suspicion strikes us horribly that this may be the war, after all, for which the Warbox is still stealthily preparing. Up with those pom-poms, there! Where's that heliograph? Damme, they've put up wire, the unsportin' hounds! Play us a bit of Chopin, Colonel.

Tax

Exactly ninety-nine years ago next month the country was staggering under a fiendish blow. At every well-appointed British breakfast table high-browed, severe, egg-faced, whiskery figures, pale with indignation and despair, clutched *The Times* with quivering fingers and moaned aloud, while Mamma behind the silver urn hushed the children and, outside in the hall, John and Thomas stood petrified, like statues, rolling glassy eyes in wild surmise. Peel had introduced a tax on income for three years at the rate of 2d. to 8d. in the £, the City was dumbfounded, and England was ruined.

There were no vivacious boys in Fleet Street in those days to paint jolly pictures of the Briton dancing along to the Inland Revenue, carolling like a bird and laughing his head off. It's only in the last quarter of a century, apparently, that we've grown to love our income tax. The Victorians were sick with hatred and fear, the Stock Exchange reeled, and even the St Pancras Guardians, those benefactors, paused in their brisk selling of pauper infants to the mines and wondered if the Millennium had really arrived as advertised; or so we conjecture from a few yellowed newspaper files we looked up the other day.

The moral is so obvious that it would take a far less brilliant pen than ours, as the youthful Mr Beerbohm once remarked, to point it. Meanwhile all we ask on the citizenry's behalf is that the gossip-boys (who exaggerate) lay off that old merrie-merrie. Even when you pay income tax simultaneously in three countries, as we once did, the sensation amounts to nothing more than what the Schoolmen would call 'morose delectation'. (End message.)

Maestro

That gay little exchange in the House the other day between Sir Kingsley Wood and Sir William Davison on the subject of the public hangman's fees (laughter) made us wonder what has happened of late to M. Deibler, executioner of the Republic, who was putting in for a rise in a rather injured way about ten years ago, though whether the skinflint Republic gave it him we don't remember.

Deibler's official top hat and dignified, sure technique gave French executions a *ton* which reminded all present that his office was of high antiquity, as his historic title, 'Monsieur de Paris', implied. The only Monsieur de Paris who ever let the profession down, so far as we know, was his fifteenth-century predecessor who dented the great two-handed Sword of Justice on the neck of the Constable de St-Pol. Whether the mob hooted M. de Paris as the mob hoots a star matador who makes a clumsy or unforgivable kill is not recorded. M. Deibler's job was less difficult by far, and our own State expert in the High Works has few problems to solve, they say, barring one in elementary physics involving strains and stresses.

The Commons boys seemed to enjoy this little Grand Guignol interlude so much, a chap in close touch tells us, that when all those politicians, financiers, usurers and others responsible for our recent distresses come up for public execution, as after the last war, some MPs are likely to press for incidental music and a cold buffet.

•

ARTHUR 'BUGS' BAER

Arthur 'Bugs' Baer (1886–1969) was born in Philadelphia, the seventh of fourteen children. He had to leave school at the age of fourteen to work, first taking a brief course at the School of Industrial Art, then earning $12 a week drawing flowers for lace designs. For six years he created lace patterns, becoming a snappy dresser, a beer drinker and a pool shark in the process; but at the age of twenty he left to be an office boy on the *Philadelphia Public Ledger* for a mere $2 a week. Although he soon moved up to be a staff artist, he was sacked after a curious incident. He had been asked to take a colleague who was feeling queasy out for some fresh air. As they walked along the waterfront, the colleague darted up a gangplank, followed by Baer, and the duo found themselves transported to Wilmington, Delaware. Next, he moved to the *Washington Times* as a sports columnist, where he earned his nickname by drawing cartoons involving an insect shaped like a baseball. He was hired to write a sports column called 'Rabid Rudolph' for the New York *World*, a task that he managed to achieve in five minutes – principally because he was rewriting the columns he had written in Washington. One famous sentence describing how a baseball player, Ping Bodie, was thrown out trying to reach second base – 'His head was full of larceny but his feet were too honest' – appeared in a *World* column, but 'the laugh was, that the year before I had written the same thing about Germany Schaeffer, second baseman of the Washington Senators'. Still, it was a memorable phrase, not just one Baer remembered, and it was because of his aptitude for such quips that he graduated to writing a syndicated, daily humour column for the *World* called 'One Word Led to Another'. After the First World War, during which he served in the artillery at Camp Zachary Taylor, he signed to do a Sunday column called 'The Family Album' for Hearst's *New York American* newspaper. Later, his daily column, still called 'One Word Led to Another', was distributed through Hearst's King Features Syndicate. 'His whole work is a cable-language of his own,' wrote the critic Gilbert Seldes. 'He is neither a satirist nor an ironist. What he has is an exceptionally oblique outlook upon the world and an elliptical expression which gives the same effect as small and agreeable galvanic shocks.'

'The Family Album'
The Tragic Conclusion of Cousin Alex's Go-hither Attitude on the Discomforts of Home
From *The Family Album* (1925)

Yes, that's Cousin Alex in his sample clothes. Alex was a very neat dresser and he was always looking in the fashion magazines to see what our well-dressed men were going to drink this summer.

He was a traveling man for a big Danbury firm and only came home to sober up. He lived in hotels and Pullman trains so much that he often longed to get married and settle down.

But when anybody started to talk about the comforts of home, he would immediately pull his bachelor ideas up around his ears and get mad.

He'd say that all the comforts of home propaganda was pro-alimony literature gotten up by lawyers and their confederates.

He said he never got a good cup of coffee at home in his life and everything was so burned they ought to use a fire alarm for a dinner gong.

It used to be mutton on Monday, veal on Tuesday and all those et cetera things, and you had about as much choice as coal on the chute. Talk about forcible feedings, home cooking was force without any feed.

But in a hotel a man can look at the bill-of-menu and he could order what he wanted and the waiter didn't want to be kissed and the manager of the hotel wouldn't burst into tears if he threw a plate at the cashier and missed. He said it was easier to dine with gentlemen than like one.

Hotel owners never asked guests to get up early in the morning and make the furnace fire, and so far as mending clothes was concerned, he said he never knew what real comfort was until he had lost all the buttons off his red flannel underwear.

They'd put enough starch in the cuffs to support a broken leg and if the neckband was any tougher they could chip diamonds with it. And anybody who wore a home-laundered collar did so with suicidal intent.

If you wanted your trousers mended your wife would slash a piece out of your coat to match it. Then she would have to chop up your vest to fix the coat and by the time they got through matching patches you looked like you were made up to play a busted sofa in the church cantata.

Hotel tailors overcharge you, all right, but they do things quick and they get their mistakes back on time.

And it's more fun fighting with strangers than with relatives, because once in a while the cops think you are right. And if you want to sleep late there ain't nobody to hammer on the door and ask if you're awake, and no kids playing leapfrog on the chandeliers. When a man is feeling sick in a hotel he don't have to ask any questions and that angel's ministering hand on the fevered brow might be all right in poems, but cracked ice was a darned fine imitation, and don't pull any of that Thomas Edison questionnaire business.

Alex wasn't exactly against family institutions, but when a man is away from home so long he forgets the language. He used to say that home comforts and privacy were legends handed down from the time when folks lived in jungles, and that life in hotels and upper berths proved the Darwinian theory enough to please him.

He lived in upper berths so much that any time he came home he used to go up on the roof and dress on the chimney. Once he went down to Coney Island and got on the merry-go-round and left his shoes with the ticket taker. When he called on any of our neighbors he would leave his shoes in their vestibule, and he got mad if they weren't shined when he said good-bye to come home.

His habits were so single that it surprised everybody when he got married to a widow with four children. That's her on this page with those seven little boys and girls. All hers. You know you've got to marry a widow to find out just how many children she really has got, because all widows seem to think that children should be subtracted and not seen.

When Alex discovered that he had married one of those University Extension families, he got mad and claimed the widow had mobbed him instead of married him. All the kids went on their honeymoon with Alex and his new bride, who was new to him.

This was the first time that Alex had ever taken out a road show that was so big you needed an advance agent. When he got to towns he seemed surprised that there wasn't any billing up on the fences.

When you talk to him about home comforts, he don't say anything, but his eyes look like his ears are glad that he is still a traveling salesman.

'The Family Album'
Uncle Joe's Gambling Instincts Succumb to the Bow Wow
From *The Family Album* (1925)

That's Uncle Joe. He was awfully stingy and so lazy that his best suit was his working clothes.

He wasn't a bad-looking man, and didn't inherit the big family mouth. He used to say that grapefruit was invented for people with big mouths who really liked oranges.

You could tell any of our family wherever you went, because their mouths looked like china closets with the doors open, and once in a while there was a gold tooth that looked like a collar button on the keyboard of a piano.

Uncle Joe had some bad habits. He would gamble on anything, dice, cards or horses. He was always going to make a big winning some day on the Honduras Lottery. He had his house papered with elapsed lottery tickets and had some left over to make rugs with.

He said that if he ever knocked off the big prize, he would save his money and have every bank in the country laying eggs for him.

But he never got within an adding machine of the prize number. Once he had 67,987 and 27,189 won and he took his ticket and tore it up slowly as if he realized that it meant just as much in pieces as it did whole.

The truth is that it did, because those Honduras people never gave any money away. Some days you would hear that George Smith, at No. 1619 Twelfth Street, won $50,000. But when you inquired at that address there wasn't no George Smith living there, and if he did he was six months behind in the rent.

Uncle Joe used to play those lotteries every month like people took baths. You couldn't convince him that it wasn't as crooked as the chimney on a shanty in a hurricane.

He would swear off the lotteries and cuss everybody in Honduras – man, woman and strangers. Then he would go right out and buy another ticket and promise to pay for it as soon as he won the prize.

Every month he would get a big sheet of paper from Honduras with a mess of numbers on it. He would read it, and then look at the number on his ticket. His head would keep bobbing back and forth from the paper to his ticket until he looked like a crow in a cornfield watching out for farmers.

But it was something like a Quaker arsenal, with nothing but blank cartridges in it.

Uncle Joe never won anything on the lottery, but he didn't stop until our Government made it illegal for any foreign country to swindle US citizens when there were so many home industries waiting for their chance.

After lotteries turned sour in the US Mails, Uncle started in to bet on the races. He made what bookmakers call laundry wagers.

Laundry wagers are something about betting on the cuff and the bookmakers used to laugh at Uncle when he would motion for them to give him fifteen to one, which would make thirty to two for two cuffs.

After that, he got discouraged and took to childish gambling like pinochle and casino. All us folks used to try to get him to stop figuring out percentages with a borrowed lead pencil, but he went right on trying to pencil his way into some money.

He got so that he and three other men would hang out in the back yard playing poker without any cards. They went through all the motions, dealing and raking in chips, and mom thought that maybe Uncle was going what they call cuckoo.

She sent me around for the doctor to look him over and after seeing the shape of Uncle's head, the Doctor asked how long it had been shaped that way. Mom told the Doctor that Uncle's head was that way all his life. So the Doctor told her that it would never get any worse because it was that bad at the start and after a mouse was drowned it couldn't get any wetter.

What finally cured Uncle of the gambling habits was being bitten by a bulldog.

The dog bit him on the left leg.

Uncle had two legs but one of them was wooden. The right leg was the timber one and the left leg was meat.

When the dog bit him on the meat leg, Uncle got out his pencil and figured close. He doped that for once in his life he started with an even chance. With a fifty percent chance of being bitten on the wooden leg the dog had picked out the other.

So he quit gambling. If he couldn't win with a fifty percent chance, he figured that he might as well quit gambling altogether.

And he did.

'One Word Led to Another'
Beautiful New World is the Nuts
New York Journal-American, January 12, 1944

I've had two weeks of the first year of the beautiful world-to-be. And I find no more change than in the shape of a cruller.

Taxes are still in the upper brackets. And starch is just as fattening.

In the old days the butcher weighted his thumb with the pork chops. Now he can hide one with his thumb.

A man must make twice as much as he is worth in order to live half as well as he is accustomed to. And water pipes burst between zero and thirty-two above.

The only way you can get the back of your shoes shined is to stand on your head in the boot-black chair. And you are solvent if you can borrow enough on your 1945 salary to pay your 1943 income tax.

Chivalry is practically extinct. Old ladies still try to beat me to a seat in the street-cars. And no genius has yet perfected a self-cleaning bird cage.

In this beautiful new world-to-be I find that commuters arrive at shows late and leave early. Thus giving your bunions a giving-over east and west. There has been no change in the taste of a two-minute egg except it takes longer.

In the old days your wife ran up a millinery bill but got a new hat with it. Now they saw her old hat in half and charge her double for both chunks. I admit the butter was bad in the old time lunchwagons but there was plenty of it. Now they trot out a little piece of butter they call a pat. It sure is pending.

What's become of southern cooking and western hospitality? Where is the piece of liver the butcher once threw in for the cat? Where is the butcher? By the way, where is the cat? Does it taste like liver?

No, I'm afraid there has been a relapse all along the beautiful new line and we are being taxed for it. It may be still too early to judge but not to accuse. My furnace is colder than the handle on a hammer-head shark because there is no coal in my bin. And there is no coal in my bin because the miners started their beautiful new world a year too quick.

I'm an optimist all right. And I know that everything will come out all right in the end. But I'll be on the other end.

•

J. B. MORTON

John Cameron Andrieu Bingham Michael Morton (1893–1979) was born in Tooting, south London. The son of a journalist, he was educated at Harrow and attended Oxford, but had to leave during his first year in order to support his ailing father. At the outbreak of the First World War he was writing stage revues. He enlisted as a private in the army and was sent to the front in 1915. He was at the Somme in 1916, was sent home with shell-shock and spent the remainder of the war working for the MI7b intelligence branch and the Ministry of Labour. In 1919 he joined the editorial staff of the *Sunday Express* as a book reviewer, and in 1922 switched to the *Daily Express* as a reporter, a role which he did not enjoy. He shared an office with D. B. Wyndham Lewis, the paper's literary editor and the 'Beach Comber' who wrote the 'By the Way' humour column, and when Wyndham Lewis left he recommended Morton to fill his shoes. Morton wrote a daily column of around 600 words, six days a week, from 1938 until 1975 when he was fired by the then editor, Alistair Burnett. A single column would contain several paragraphs: some were part of separate, long-running sagas, and others were stand-alone items. Over the years, 'Beachcomber' (as it was now rendered) created numerous comic characters including Mr Justice Cocklecarrot, Captain Foulenough, Lady Cabstanleigh and Dr Smart-Alick; and his columns have been republished in numerous collections. I have chosen here one of the earliest comic creations from 'Beachcomber', the pompous clubland figure Oswald Thake.

The Newhaven Saga
From *The Adventures of Mr Thake* (1934)

A paragraph in a local newspaper informed me yesterday that the private yacht *Adventuress*, owned by Mr Arthur Chelmsford, had been overhauled and redecorated and was lying in Newhaven Harbour; also that there was to be a yacht-warming party shortly, given by the wealthy owner. Among those expected to attend was Mr Thake. A cruise would follow.

I at once wrote to my friend Mr Thake, telling him that an account of the cruise would be most interesting if he could spare the time to send me a line or two occasionally. This he promised to do.

Newhaven harbour

Dear Beachcomber,

We are what is called, I believe, lying-to, here in Newhaven Harbour, on my old friend Arthur Chelmsford's yacht *Adventuress*. Don't ask me to describe the boat, as I am a mere tyro in nautical matters. We are a happy party. There's Tom Watson, Mrs Chelmsford, Anita (the daughter), Vill, the novelist, an American woman called Mrs Bailey, and, of course, the professional crew. I understand that if the tide is favourable we may start tomorrow. Arthur asked us where we'd like to go. I plumped for Dieppe. The others were divided between Etretat and Cornwall. Of course, I suppose it all depends on the wind. We looked at the charts, but they were Greek to me.

After dinner we went on deck and examined the town through our binoculars. Nothing much to see. Later we got the wash from a tug-boat, and Mrs Bailey went to lie down till it was calm again. What on earth will she do when we are really at sea?

Bridge afterwards, which Vill spoilt by telling stories all the time. Arthur went up to inspect the light on the mast before we turned in, and held his handkerchief out to test the wind. There wasn't any.

Yours ever,
O. Thake

PS – Tell Saunders to address my letters PO, Newhaven, not P and O – the fool!

Newhaven harbour

We did not set sail this morning after all, as Mr Bailey, the American woman's husband, arrived late last night, and wasn't awake early enough for the start. He is an Englishman, and behaves queerly. He began shouting 'Land, ho!' during breakfast. Considering we were only about two feet from the quay, the joke fell rather flat. He next said there was a groundswell, and Chelmsford said flatly that you couldn't have a swell in harbour. To which Bailey retorted, 'What about Thake?' Vulgar, and not very funny.

I must say one feels rather a fool in yachting clothes in harbour. A small boy kept on tormenting me this morning by shouting, 'What about it, Commodore?' And when I asked him coldly what about what, he asked me whether I'd caught many sharks in the Bay of Biscay. Then an old longshoreman kept on saluting me and spitting, and once he said to the boy, 'Jim, clean the Admiral's boots for him.' Then they both laughed. So I went below, and found them all playing bridge.

In the evening we had the same old discussion about where we should go to the next day, but Vill said there was rain about, and Mrs Chelmsford and Anita talked of slipping off to London to buy clothes. It's rather haphazard. And when the captain was summoned we found he was ashore. He returned late at night, and woke us all up by singing 'Annie Laurie' at the top of his voice.

A life on the ocean wave, eh? Ah, well.

Newhaven harbour

It seems to me we might as well be on land for all the sailing we do. After breakfast yesterday Arthur Chelmsford said, 'I think we'll get the anchor taken up and push off.' He rang for the captain, but apparently the crew were ashore, and nothing could be done. So we got into the dinghy, and Bailey and Arthur rowed us about the harbour. We got into the way of a smack, and there were hard words, and Bailey broke an oar against the wall of the quay.

After lunch we sat on deck, but as the tide went down we had nothing to stare at but a slimy wall and green steps in one direction, and the side of a Channel boat in the other.

When the Channel boat started we all cheered, and Tom Watson shouted, 'Bring us back a parrot!' Arthur tried to run up a flag, as a compliment to the Channel boat, but when he pulled the rope, up went an old sailor's jersey that had been hung out to dry.

Mrs Bailey is down with hay fever, of all things. Mrs Chelmsford and Anita motored to London to do some shopping and are returning tonight. The longshoreman and the horrid little boy came back this afternoon, and kept on calling me Commodore and Admiral. The boy yelled out, 'Haul on her, me bucko boys,' so I turned away. I wish we could get out to sea. It seems so stupid, all this.

Newhaven harbour

We nearly got off today.

The sails were actually put up, and we were all gathered on deck, when the captain said the motor had broken down. I was so angry that I said, 'Hang it all, can't we sail? What are all these sails for?' To which he replied that both wind and tide were against us. Really! I give it up. We spent the afternoon playing bridge again, and when I went on deck for a breath of air, that awful boy shouted, 'Take 'er into the wind, Captain. Dirty weather ahead!' I turned my back and pretended to be studying a crane. The motor is being repaired, so we may get off tomorrow.

Newhaven harbour

We are in a perfectly absurd situation on board here.

It has turned out that the captain, recommended to Arthur Chelmsford by some agency or other, is no more a sailor than the man in the moon.

Yesterday, when he was ordering the crew about, we noticed that his language sounded queer. For instance, he told one man to 'Try and hang up that big sail at the end there,' and another, to be sure and let him know when the anchor was loose. Of course the crew laughed. Then he put the helm over the wrong way, and we got foul of a tug. After that we had to give up the attempt to start, and returned to harbour with our tail – or should I say, rudder? – between our legs. Chelmsford sacked the captain, who confessed that he was a lorry driver out of a job.

He is no loss, as he frequently got intoxicated, and once sang a ribald song outside Mrs Bailey's cabin door.

To crown a disappointing day, no sooner were we moored to the quay again than the boy and the longshoreman arrived. The boy asked if we had brought back any copra, and the longshoreman spat and said, 'You'll have to declare it all, Bo'sun.' What can one reply to such nonsense? Really!

Bridge as usual in the evening. Tom Watson, to relieve the boredom, as he said, produced twenty-three aces from his sleeve. The joke did not go down very well, as the Chelmsfords play at Marshall's Club.

Shall we ever taste the brine, as it were?

Newhaven harbour

While we were playing bridge yesterday morning – Mrs Chelmsford and Anita having gone ashore to church – one of the sailors came in and said wind and tide were ideal for a start.

We all rushed on deck and began to get things ready. Finally, our preparations were complete, but we could not start without the ladies. Just as we were despairing, we saw them coming along the quay, but the fool of a sailor who had taken the dinghy to bring them back in did not see them, and rowed to the wrong place.

We shouted and waved, and Tom Watson set the fog-horn going. At last the sailor spotted them, but instead of waiting for him, Mrs C and Anita walked farther along to watch the Channel boat going out. We had the anchor half up in our excitement. But all the muddle so infuriated Arthur that he shouted to the sailors, 'Drop the dammed thing back again We'll never get off!'

And then what should come along as the last drop of bitterness in our cups but that diabolical little boy, shouting, 'Make four bells, Nelson, my lad!' And the infernal longshoreman spat and grinned. What a fiasco!

PS – Tell Saunders to send some bridge-markers.

At last! I feel the foam in my face, and the wind buzzes in the rigging. What adventures await us? We set sail this morning, gliding majestically out of harbour. This letter will probably be posted from France, for which we are headed. The ladies are lying down as we are rocking somewhat. We are just clear of the harbour. Ah, open sea!

Later. Can you believe it? This letter will be posted in Newhaven after all. Hardly were we outside the harbour when Arthur discovered that the dinghy had been left behind. So back we came to get it. And now it's raining, and there's nothing for it but bridge once more. Arthur intends to try again tomorrow. That wretched boy saw us return, and shouted out, 'What cheer, Ulysses!' Then he yelled, 'A sail! a sail!' and the longshoreman spat and grinned. Really!

PS – Tell Saunders I said bridge-markers, not book-markers. The dolt!

We should have put to sea this morning, only the ladies were rather knocked out by the recent heat, and decided to stay in bed. I got a bit sick of bridge, because Tom Watson won't play seriously. Yesterday, for instance, he just tore up his hand and pretended to cry, because he said he had no lovely picture-cards. Well, I had a look at the log, and I must say it doesn't read much like a seaman's record of peril and adventure.

Arthur keeps it himself, and so far this trip is nothing but a list of his bridge losses, and a memento about Anita's birthday.

After lunch I got a sailor to row me ashore, but there was nothing to do in Newhaven. I bought some books and papers and came back. And just as I was getting on board the yacht again that imp of a boy called out to the longshoreman, 'Fire off them guns, mate! Here's the Admiral coming aboard.'

I feel quite ashamed of being still here, after more than a week, but nobody can say we haven't tried to get to sea. Something always interferes at the last moment. I hear we are to be off really and truly at dawn tomorrow, so I must turn in early. My nephew Blakeney writes saying he pictures me bounding over the deep. Little does he know!

Newhaven harbour

I am getting this posted before we start, for we are really off this morning. Sleep is impossible, as the din on deck is terrific. When you get this we shall be at sea, and really, I shall be glad. That interminable bridge!

Breakfast is all disorganized, as all the sailors are on deck working at the sails, and I can hear that fool, Tom Watson, shouting silly naval terms. Plucky Mrs Chelmsford went up to help, but got a bang on the ankle with a coil of rope, and Arthur ordered her below – only as a joke, of course. I've been up, but feel the deck is no place for amateurs this morning. You can hardly move for ropes and masts and sails. Besides, that satanic boy was on the quay, and as soon as he spied me he yelled out, 'What cheer, Jellicoe, me lad!' and pretended to do a hornpipe. I'd tan his young hide if I caught him!

Apparently they got the sails up out of place. I mean they put them on the wrong masts, I suppose, because it all had to be done again. I popped up just now and asked Arthur where we were going, but he snapped at me, and said as long as we got clear of this cursed harbour he didn't much care where we went. Then he got wild because Anita had been scribbling her crossword puzzles all over the charts.

I must stop now, as the motor is chugging, and they're getting ready to pull the anchor out. The longshoreman will post this. Now I'm going up on deck to watch the start.

Newhaven harbour

I am not in the best of tempers. Little did I think that today would find us back again in that horrible harbour at Newhaven.

I really did think we had managed to get free, and when we cleared the harbour mouth and saw the open sea ahead of us we raised a cheer. There was a light breeze blowing – I don't know any directions at sea, but I fancy it was south-easterly – anyhow, the sailors said we could stop the motor and rely on the sails. This we did, but progress was so slow that we all voted for the motor again. Well, would you believe it? It wouldn't start. It had broken down again. With infinite trouble we got back to harbour to have it repaired – and who do you think greeted us on the quay? Why, that limb of the devil, that inhuman boy, singing 'Hearts of Oak', and asking what we had brought him from the Bahamas.

So here we are again, playing bridge, confound it, while the motor is being mended by a sandy-haired mechanic who whistles shrilly the same old tune until you nearly go mad. 'Pon my soul, I almost prefer a holiday on terra firma, eh? Really.

PS – Tell Saunders not to address letters 'c/o the *Adventuress*'. I know that's the yacht's name, but I get chaffed by the party, who pretend to misunderstand.

Hôtel Incroyable, Dieppe

I write, as you see, from Dieppe, but I have a confession to make. It happened like this:

Yesterday morning, while we were playing bridge on deck, and the mechanic was mending the motor, we all became aware of the longshoreman and the little boy. They were on the quay and were talking audibly. The longshoreman said, 'Sonny, that's a bucko ship, if ever I saw one,' and the boy said, 'You bet, Tom. They could tell some tales of derring-do.' Then the man said, 'Their sweethearts must get tired of waiting while the ship's away on one of those long cruises. Think of the peril, sonny.' And the boy replied, 'Sharks, Tom, and whales, monsoons, typhoons, and things.' 'Tropical heat. Nights of sleet and snow, with the spars all frozen,' said the man. 'Chilblains,' said the boy. 'Yes, and sunstroke,' said the man.

Well at that moment Arthur threw down his hand and shouted, 'I can't stand any more of this! We're all getting on each other's nerves.' It reminded me of a scene in one of those Gold Coast plays.

The outcome was that we packed up, left the yacht, and caught the Channel boat. Not very heroic, I admit, but better than sitting in harbour, and being insulted by that dreadful boy and his accomplice. So here we are, staying at a big hotel on the seafront, and looking forward to a bit of fun at the casino.

Hôtel Incroyable, Dieppe

I had a wretched dream last night. I was back in that awful harbour at Newhaven, on the *Adventuress*, and the boy and the longshoreman were grinning and saluting sardonically. It shows how the experience of those days got on my mind, doesn't it?

Arthur says if the weather holds he intends to go back to England and to try our cruise all over again. But when I think of the hours spent at bridge, and all the fuss and boredom, I can't face it.

Yesterday, for no reason I could see, Tom Watson led me up to a French actress who is staying here and introduced me. I had nothing to say, of course, and as she was a very pretty girl I felt a frightful fool. Then she said, 'Your friend tells me you are a great sailor.' I was tongue-tied and could only nod. She mistook this for shyness and modesty, and said she loved sailors because they were so exciting. My tongue still stuck, and I felt awful. And then a man whom she introduced as her brother asked me about sighting guns at sea. I said with a laugh that I'd never sighted anything at sea. What a situation to be in!

I suspected Tom Watson of one of his practical jokes, and determined to turn the tables. I beckoned to him, and told them he was a great writer. They were delighted, and asked what he had written. Just as I walked away I heard him say that he wrote under the name of John Galsworthy, and was the author of *Peter Pan*. Well, I leave him to get out of it as best he can. It's his kettle of fish, and he must lie on it.

Later. Here we are once more in this abominable harbour. No sooner were we off the Channel boat and in the *Adventuress* once more than the boy and the longshoreman started again. 'They look weatherbeaten,' said the boy. 'Tropical suns,' said the longshoreman. 'Think they've brought back any ivory?' asked the boy. 'Shouldn't be surprised,' said the longshoreman. 'Wonder what those cannibals are like out there,' said the boy. 'Fearful,' said the longshoreman. 'Blood-curdling yells in the dark.' 'And serpents hissing,' said the boy. 'They're not half brave to risk it all,' added the young rascal. 'England's proud of 'em,' said the longshoreman.

Isn't it enough to make a man feel a fool?

•

FRED C. KELLY

Fred Charters Kelly (1882–1959) was born in Xenia, Ohio, and educated at the University of Michigan. He wrote a humorous column for the *Cleveland Plain Dealer* and subsequently a daily syndicated Washington column, the first of its kind, called 'Statesmen, Real and Near', for about thirty leading newspapers from 1910 to 1918. He also wrote daily syndicated editorials called 'Kelly-grams'. During the First World War he was an FBI agent for eighteen months and he later ran a farm in Peninsula, Ohio. Apart from collections of his humour, his books included a biography of the Wright brothers, authorized by Orville Wright, and a biography of George Ade, the Chicago columnist and playwright.

When a Man is Honored
From *But, on the Other Hand – !* (1928)

In Washington, not long ago, I met an old acquaintance who had just been appointed to an important public office. His desk was banked with flowers and he was busy opening great stacks of congratulatory letters.

To all appearances he had arrived somewhere and was entitled to strut a little.

When we were all alone, I asked him: 'How does it feel suddenly to become a person of importance?'

'You may be surprised to know,' he replied, solemnly, 'that this is about the most tragic day of my life.'

I looked at him closely and saw that he meant exactly what he said.

Of course I asked him to explain.

'What does all this mean?' he asked, disgustedly, with an inclusive wave of his hand at the spacious office, mahogany furniture and expensive fixtures. 'It means simply that I have been thrown off like a chunk of clay from the wheel of fortune and happened to alight at this spot. Here is an office that I had nothing to do with creating. I was appointed, not so much as a tribute to my ability in the line that will be required here, as because I chanced to be a friend of a politician who thought he was doing me a favor. If it were a little factory that I had built up from nothing and this were the main office I might feel proud. If this were the day on which I had succeeded in having published a book of poems, or in painting a good picture – anything at all, so long as it were creative – I might be elated. But all this fuss being made over me because I have taken a public office in which I feel scant interest – bah!'

And he was almost in tears.

Then it dawned on me that here was one more dramatic explanation of why so few officeholders ever amount to much.

If they were creative geniuses, they wouldn't be there.

Too often a public office is a landing place for a misfit.

Such ability as he had lay in the line of getting himself elected rather than in accomplishing much afterward.

I remember a man in my native county who inherited a prosperous big farm. Because of his commanding lack of business sense, he ran through with his money in a few years and his farm passed into other hands.

But he was an agreeable fellow and a great hand-shaker. Everybody felt sorry for him and wanted to see him have a chance to earn a decent living. So the voters made him a county commissioner, where he could handle public business in the same slipshod, inefficient way that had made him a failure in running his own farm.

Mad Dogs and Open Minds

From But, on the Other Hand – ! (1928)

For many years I have been hoping to learn the exact truth about so-called mad dogs. Is there really such a thing, or is a mad dog, like a haunted house, invariably a creation of somebody's excited imagination?

My point here isn't to tell the facts, but rather to emphasize the difficulty of arriving at facts. After years of trying to determine if the mad dog business is a myth, I'm still unable to make up my mind one way or another. I'm inclined to believe that all mad dog stories are untrue, and yet all the while in the back of my head is a sneaking suspicion that maybe I'm somehow wrong.

Once I was sent out to investigate a report about a mad dog biting a boy and throwing him into convulsions. I learned that the dog had acted strangely because of a bone wedged in between two back teeth. It had snapped at a boy, but no harm resulted until the boy's mother grew excited and gave the boy to understand that he would probably die. Then the poor boy nearly died of fear.

After that I got into the habit of writing letters to people who figured in mad dog stories. Almost invariably, when sifted down, the first reports proved to be groundless.

I talked to many pound-keepers and agents of the Society for the Prevention of Cruelty to Animals. All assured me that though often bitten by dogs reported as mad, they had suffered no ill effects. I wrote to Bellevue Hospital, in New York, and learned that in nearly thirty years they had had only one or two cases diagnosed as hydrophobia, due to dog bites. It seemed conceivable that those few cases might have been wrongly diagnosed. I learned from Johns Hopkins Hospital, in Baltimore, one of the most famous in the country, that they had never had a case of hydrophobia.

Competent dog doctors assure me that there is no truth in stories that a mad dog will refuse water or froth at the mouth. If he doesn't drink water, it is only because his throat is too swollen. Many diseases might cause a dog to froth at the mouth, they say, but hydrophobia isn't one of them.

Such evidence makes one suspicious of all mad dog reports. Yet once in a long while, some intelligent person tells me a story that seems too well supported to discredit. I decide that maybe there's something in these mad dogs tales after all. After years of seeking facts, I'm still in doubt.

I mentioned all this to a friend who is a philosopher. After I had lamented my inability to arrive at the truth about mad dogs, he said: 'You are probably in a healthier mental state about mad dogs than about almost anything else. You seek truth as a goal, but know that you don't know. You're still open-minded. The trouble with most of us about all subjects isn't that we can't make up our minds, but that we have made them up and then closed them to further evidence. We are nearly always too sure of our facts. Never worry about not being too cocksure.'

How Loudly Does Your Town Applaud?
From *But, on the Other Hand –!* (1928)

One of the most successful platform talkers in the United States told me recently that he can sense the civic pride of a city by the amount of applause he receives.

In a general way, audiences in smaller cities do not give him as much applause as do those in larger places and he believes the reason is that smaller cities are more likely to have an unsuspected inferiority sense. Nobody in the audience would admit even to himself that his town isn't just as good as any. Yet, my informant declares, the audience in a small city is inclined to imagine wrongly that the lecturer doesn't amount to much or else he wouldn't have come there. Members of the audience actually doubt if their town is good enough for a first-class lecture. Half suspecting that the lecture isn't really good, naturally the audience isn't enthusiastic in its applause.

On the other hand, audiences are larger in the smaller cities and most of a lecturer's revenue comes from them rather than from metropolitan centers. A New York or Chicago lecture is almost never profitable. Of course, a lecturer likes to speak in these larger places to have that fact to refer to in advertising himself elsewhere. But he can get a bigger crowd in a city where a lecture is more of an event – where there are fewer counter-attractions.

This same man went on to explain that a city which has recently had a rapid growth and advanced within a few years from a small town to become a place of greater consequence is especially likely to be sparing in applause. Such a town feels its oats and desires to show that it cannot be hoodwinked by anything short of the best. It prefers to show by restrained enthusiasm that it can be dignifiedly discriminating.

All of which reminds me of a girl I used to take to theaters. She never applauded anything unless she had previously read a favorable review of it in a large city paper. Her lack of enthusiasm nearly made a morose man of me and I was glad when she married a brown-derbied traveling man and moved far away.

Why Do Juries Ever Agree?

From *But, on the Other Hand — !* (1928)

I often hear lawyers and others express surprise that a jury in a legal controversy has been unable to agree upon a unanimous verdict.

But isn't it a wonder that any jury ever does agree?

Twelve men are called in from their regular tasks to listen to a controversy in which there are two definite sides.

Two contestants who have been unable to agree have hired two lawyers who disagree for a fee.

They summon witnesses, one group for each side, and the testimony of these witnesses probably does not hang together. In fact, half the witnesses have been called for the purpose of offsetting the testimony of those on the other side.

Thus we have clients, lawyers and witnesses who do not agree.

Clients and lawyers presumably have seen the futility of trying to agree or they wouldn't have gone to all the trouble and expense of taking the case into court.

Possibly they have tried to effect a settlement by compromise but were so far apart that the only thing left to do was to try the case before a jury.

These jurors are mere average folk, of only average intelligence.

They sit and listen to evidence from witnesses who do not agree, and arguments by lawyers who do not agree, on behalf of clients as far apart as the poles.

From this mass of conflicting evidence, the jurors are expected to favor only one side.

They are asked to do what contestants and lawyers who have known all about the case for a long time have found impossible.

I marvel that any group of twelve men ever succeed in being of one mind on a verdict.

It's a wonder that most cases aren't thrown out of court because there is no chance of getting a jury that can agree.

Why Pests Forge Ahead

From *But, on the Other Hand — !* (1928)

In Chicago recently I talked with an old friend at lunch about mutual acquaintances at a state university. He asked me if I remembered a certain man.

Immediately we both laughed.

'I know you're thinking the same thing I am,' he said. 'Of course he was the biggest pest in college. Everybody agreed that he was a hopeless ass. Remember how he annoyed everybody at dinner by trying to do all the talking? He strutted when he walked, patronized most of us and irritated even the girls by his superior airs. Yet — what do you suppose became of him?'

'Is he a dressmaker's husband?' I asked.

'No, he's a leading lawyer here in Chicago. Highly successful, mixed up in all sorts of profitable enterprises and his name is almost a household word.'

That aroused my curiosity and since then I have been making a canvass of friends regarding men who in college days were conspicuous asses. I asked one man after another if he could remember who was the outstanding joke of the class. Then I asked what happened to these men.

Almost invariably the egregious asses have turned out well. Many of them, it seems, are now prominent citizens, well known clubmen and pillars of their communities.

In other words, young men who have plenty of gall and, in consequence, may appear to possess only nuisance value, are fairly certain to get along comfortably. They may irritate their fellow travelers on this planet, but they are so sure of themselves that they do not hesitate to step in where a more agreeable person might wait until invited. Being aggressive and full of self-confidence, they forge ahead.

Here is perhaps a field for statistical study. I wish every college class would list the two or three more noticeable pests and then report in, say, twenty years, how such men are making out.

•

ERNEST L. MEYER

Ernest L. Meyer (1892–1952) was born in Denver, Colorado, and brought up in Milwaukee. After spells as a journalist-compositor on a Washington State paper, as a police reporter in Chicago, and as editor of the literary magazine at the University of Wisconsin, he joined the Madison, Wisconsin *Capital Times* in 1920, where he served as managing editor, then as telegraph editor. He also wrote a column called 'Making Light of the Times', which was a whimsical miscellany of anecdotes and commentary, until 1935. From then until 1941 he wrote the same column under the title 'As the Crow Flies' for the *New York Post*. He was telegraph editor at the *Daily News* and wrote a weekly column for the *Progressive* (Madison, Wisconsin).

'Making Light of the Times'
Statistics are Lovely Things
From *Making Light of the Times* (1928)

['*Eight years of Prohibition in the United States have abolished raw poverty and drunkenness. Prohibition has increased the number of college graduates 150 percent. Prohibition is responsible for the fact that there are twenty-five automobiles in the country today where there was only one before Prohibition.*' – *From an address by Warren G. Jones, president of the Wisconsin Anti-Saloon League at the Madison dry rally.*]

Having been commissioned by the Anti-Hipflask League of America to prove statistically the success of Prohibition, it is with considerable satisfaction that I herewith report the results of my findings:

1. There are at present in the United States 685 radio broadcasting stations, and some 20,000,000 receiving sets. Less than twenty years ago, in the wet era, there were no radio broadcasting stations and no receiving sets. Prohibition did it.

2. In the days of the wide-open saloon there was in the whole country not a single case of transmitting photos over wires by the television system. In fact, it is indisputable that liquor made just plain, ordinary vision difficult. According to the researches of Prof. Erasmus Ackenbacken of Prague, an ordinary wire, soaked in alcohol for forty-seven days, is incapable of normal sight, succumbing to what is known in the medical profession as 'angularitis conjunctivitis,' or cock-eyedness. With the adoption of the eighteenth amendment scientists were at last able to find wire that wasn't soaked in rum toddies or slo gin fizz. As a result we have television photography. Another triumph for Prohibition!

3. One of the most noteworthy achievements of Prohibition is the effect on aviation. Ten years ago, in the vile days of Schlitz beer, there was not a single case of a successful cross-continental air flight. All the pilots would stop off at Milwaukee.

4. Added to this victory for Prohibition is another achievement: the economy wave in fashion. The booze generation with its cloudy vision submitted tamely to the era of long skirts and balloon sleeves. But with Prohibition, as men came to see more clearly, there arose a demand for short skirts. As a result of the economy in cloth the vicious tweed ring of New York has been routed, and enough wool is saved annually to pull over the eyes of 8,887,000 registered voters and win the election for the Republicans.

5. Another advance which must be laid at the door of Prohibition is the recent tremendous achievement of flagpole sitters. There is no case on record anywhere which indicates that in the saloon age a man could sit more than eighteen hours on top of a flagpole without shinning down for a load of schnapps, kümmel, absinthe frappé and cloves. Police documents show that the few hardy souls who could shin up again would teeter groggily on the flagpole and sing maudlin and indecent songs, until they fell off and broke their records in two places. But since the dry law went into effect we have grown a noble and virile generation of flagpole sitters, who can sit there for three days and three nights without a wink or a wobble or a jigger of Jamaica rum. Prohibition wins again!

•

WILL ROGERS

William Penn Adair Rogers (1879–1935) was born on a ranch near Claremore, Oklahoma to wealthy parents, both of whom were part Cherokee. He attended Scarritt College in Neosho, Missouri, for a year, and then, a year later, the Kemper Military Academy in Booneville, Missouri, but soon ran away. He first gained attention as a cowboy who performed in Wild West shows and vaudeville (he was a rope-trick artist and comedian with the Ziegfeld Follies) before turning to newspapers and magazines as a writer, as well as to radio and the movies. From 1922 until his death in 1935 Rogers wrote weekly articles for the McNaught Syndicate, which were ultimately published in about 600 daily and weekly newspapers. In October 1926 he also started writing a daily 'telegram' column, a feature which had begun in the *New York Times* a few months earlier and which was also syndicated through McNaught. From 1926 to 1930 he was guaranteed a weekly fee of $1,700 for his combined daily and weekly columns; thereafter, he received $2,500 per week.

His weekly articles often began with the self-deprecating phrase 'I only know what I read from the papers . . .' – although he had forthright opinions on extraordinarily varied subjects, including politics, economics, diplomacy, crime, public figures, social affairs, Hollywood and whimsy. If he received no inspiration from the events of the day, he would raid the Aladdin's Cave of his anecdotal memory and his own helter-skelter daily routine of travels and encounters with other celebrities. Sometimes editors would blue-pencil phrases or passages that they found politically unacceptable, but they were not allowed to change his distinctive style and eccentric spelling and punctuation. 'That's the way I write it,' he explained, 'and that's the way I want it to lay.' Indeed, the deliberate gaucherie of his style was utterly in keeping with his crackerbarrel nostrums and robust common sense. 'When I first started out to write and mispelled a few words, people said I was plain ignorant,' Rogers wrote. 'But when I got all the words wrong, they declared I was a humorist.'

His columns were usually written up against deadline and there was virtually no circumstance that prevented him from filing them. As he waited for a gallstone operation in his hospital bed, he dictated three 'telegrams'; and when he came round from the operation he jotted down another. He had always been a keen flyer; indeed, he was the first civilian to fly across the United States from coast to coast. He was the sole passenger on an airplane piloted by aviator Wiley Post when it crashed in Alaska, killing them both – in a brilliant stroke, he was in the midst of composing one of his weekly articles at the time.

Christmas is Over, Hooray!
Tulsa Daily World, January 6, 1929

Well, all I know is just what I read in the papers. The holidays got by without much publicity. Xmas was awful quiet after the excitement of the late election. It looked like there was a lot more interest in Smith and Hoover than there was in Santa Claus. I guess Xmas is getting kinder old and we will have to scare up something new to take its place. The trouble with this generation is they are getting too wise. That is they are getting too wise about things which they ought not to get wise about, and learning none of the things that might be any good to 'em afterwards. We kid the idea of Santa Claus now, where as a matter of fact it was one of the greatest illusions and ideas we ever had. We lost it and nothing has taken its place. Even to presents, why in the old days just any little rememberance was the very thing we wanted and needed, but now with all this Republican prosperity, nobody can't give you anything you need, for you already got it.

Nowadays if a person, either woman or man, has a Flask why there just ain't much left for you to get for them. Children used to be tickled to death with a $1 drum. Now they want a Saxaphone accompanied by eight lessons. A doll that would shut its eyes when you laid it down was just about the last word in presents for a little girl. But now it's a Party dress with a vanity case to match.

A little iron train with some coal cars would keep a bunch of children out of some other kind of devilment till away along up in April. But now it's got to be one with tunnels and bridges and electric towers and will blow the fuses out in your whole house the first time you hook it up. And then the disgusted Father will be asked why he didn't get an Aeroplane that would fly instead of a plain old train.

Xmas cards was invented by somebody that wanted to sell more stamps and wanted to break the backs of Mail carriers. You pay a lot of money to get what is supposed to be an exclusive design, and the first mail brings you twelve just like the ones you are mailing out. That makes you sore at Xmas from then on no matter how great things break from then on. It just don't look like there is much left of the old time Xmas, but Sox and Neckties and handkerchiefs. That's about the only things that have really stood the gaff of modern advancement. Mothers, childrens and friends' presents have undergone a great change, but the old Father still can rest assured that he can dig in the ribbon-wrapped package and drag out three (near linen) handkerchiefs, a missfit pair of sox or a red Tie.

New York got away pretty good this time in the way of deaths from bad alcohol.

Hoover spent his Xmas out on the broad Ocean on a Battleship. But that even don't do you much good nowadays to try and get away from everything. That Radio gets you even out there.

Mr Coolidge he picked out an island down in Georgia to get away from 'Happy New Year Mr President' in Washington.

He went down there hunting, where they had some game big enough to hit. You know on Thanksgiving he went to Virginia, but the quails didn't fly where he figured they would. So he wanted something a little bigger. A Republican President in Georgia is kinder a novelty, even if he don't hit anything but a Democrat.

But all these trips shows you to what lengths these Public men will go to get away from other Public men. He has sit in that White House and seen so many Senators coming up that long front walk, that I bet he would like to go and visit Trotsky in Siberia for a year. You know there is nothing in the World as alike as two Senators. No matter how different their politics, how different the parts of the Country they come from, they all look alike, think alike, and *want* alike. They are all looking for an appointment for some guy who helped them get theirs. One blind one brought his dog the other day and Coolidge said, 'Even the dog looked like he had a friend back in the home kennels that he would like to see brought on and made a White House pet.'

So you just can't blame Calvin for proposing that we get our Presidents a place where they can go and forget the following monologue: 'Now Mr President there is a man in my State that really worked very hard for your election and we really owe him this appointment. The Government is really losing by not having him work for them.'

'Who is he working for now?'

'Oh he isn't working for anybody now.'

'Well then the country is losing his valuable services as much as the Government. So we better just let him lay off. I don't like to take such a good man away from the people.'

Say, was any of you in that Prohibition contest that that fellow Mills won? His wife likes to beat him, and none of the things she had in hers was anything like the thing he had in his. Then a Boy out in Hoover's home town won the prize for Amateurs. That is people who had never tried to enforce it. He said the way to do it was by education. Teach 'em that it was wrong.

But the Professional that won the Twenty five thousand, he said, 'Make it so expensive that the Bootlegger couldn't make any money on it.' Why, the higher price anything is the bigger profit the middle man makes on it. A Man that sells potatoes don't make near as much as the man that sells Automobiles. The Bootlegger makes ten times more profit on it than the Saloon-keeper used to when it sold cheap. So it don't look to me like either one of these Scenarios were anywhere near right.

Education never helped morals. The most savage people we have are the most moral. The smarter the guy the bigger the rascal. And the minute a thing is high priced, you immediately create a desire for it. You give liquor away tomorrow like water and the novelty of being drunk would be over in a week, and nobody would touch the stuff. It's like Golf, you let the poor all get to playing it and you watch the rich give it up. So make the Government make it, and give it away, and we will all be disgusted with it. Americans don't like common things.

Beating Wall Street
Tulsa Daily World, November 10, 1929

Well all I know is just what I read in the Papers. Awful lot of news percolating here and there. This Stock Market thing has spoiled more appetites lately than bad cooking. Some fellow named Roger Babson a month or two ago predicted that lightning was going to strike the margins, and because it dident do it the day his warning come out, why they all give Roger the laugh and said 'This Country is too big and prosperous to have any let up in prices.' Well it looked like Roger had pulled a bone and he had to stand for a lot of kidding. But as the old saying, 'He who laughs along toward the finish, generally carries more real merriment in his tones.' So as things have turned out why it looks like the whole market has just tried to help Roger Babson make a sucker out of his detractors.

Now that Stock Market is all a puzzle to me. I never did mess with it. One time in New York last year when everybody was just raking in money with a shovel, so they all told me, well Eddie Cantor the Actor of Jewish contraction, I had known and been a friend of Eddie's for many years and I was hearing that Eddie was piling up a fortune that Rockefeller couldent vault over. So I hold out some dough on Mrs Rogers out of the weekly stipend and I go over to the New Amsterdam Theater one night and call on Eddie.

When I was admitted I felt like a Racketeer that had finally gained admission to J. P. Morgan's sanctum. Eddie thought I had come to persuade him to play a benefit for some improvedent christians (as I had often done with him in the past). But when I quietly whispered to him that I wanted him to make a few dollars without telling jokes for them (or what went for jokes) I told him about the amount that I had been able by judicious scheming to nick from Mrs Rogers. Knowing her he wouldent believe that I had been so shrewd, and immediately he said, 'You don't need me, just keep this thing up and grab it off from her. What does it matter whether you make it from Wall Street or her?'

But I told him I wanted to get in on this skinning of Wall Street. Everybody was doing it and I wanted to be in at the killing. I dident have anything particular against Wall Street, but knowing the geographical and physical attributes of the Street, I knew that it was crooked. (You can stand at the head of it, and you can only see to the bend. It just won't let you see all of it at once as short as it is.) I just said to myself I would like to be with the bunch that has the credit of straightening this Alley out.

Well Eddie had just that day made fifty thousand according to closing odds on the last commodity. I says show me the fifty. He then explained to me that he hadent the money, that that's what he could have made if he had sold. But he hadent sold, as tomorrow he should make at least another fifty, or even if he only made forty-nine why it would help pay for burnt cork. Then he explained the stock market to me in a mighty sensible way, he told me who had told him this, but anyhow it had repeated well, so I will repeat it to you.

The Stock market is just like a sieve (one of those pans with holes in it). Everything and everybody is put into it, and it is shaken, and through the holes go all the small stuff. Then they load it up again and maby hold it still for awhile and then they start shaking again and through the little investors go. They pick themselves up, turn boot-legger or do something to get some more money, and then they crawl back in the hopper and away they go again.

Well that made a mighty pretty Scenario. But I said, that's only the Boobs that go through the hole. I am going to grab a root and hang on with the big boys. He dident much want to take my money, knowing how hard I had worked for it, both from the Theater Manager and Mrs Rogers.

But I went on telling him I was forty-nine years and had never in my life made a single dollar without having to chew some gum to get it. So he says, 'Well I will buy you some of my bank stock. It's selling mighty high and with this little dab you got here you won't get much of it, but it's bound to go up, for banks make it whether the market goes up or down. Even if it stand still they are getting their interest while it's making up its mind what to do.'

So he said I will get you some of this. You don't need to pay me for it, just let it go. Put it away and forget about it. Then some day when you want you can send me a check for it.

Well I shook hands and told him that I had always known and said that he was the greatest Comedian on the stage but now I knew that he was the best financier we had in our profession. Well I went back to my own dressing room at my Theater and I never was as funny in my life as I was that night. I had Wall Street by the tail and a down hill run.

I stayed up the next night till the papers come out to see what *our* Bank had closed at, and after reading it stayed up the rest of the night wondering if Eddie could possibly be wrong. Well one little drop brought on another, till one day I received a letter from Eddie's Broker saying my check would come in mighty handy and for me please remit undernamed amount.

Well in the meantime I had used most of the money celebrating the fact that I had bought the stock. In fact I had really spent most of it in advertising Eddie and his humanitarian qualities. Each night I begin to get unfunnier and unfunnier. This strain of being 'In the Market' was telling on me. Eddie could laugh at a loss and still remain Komical. But when there was minus sign before my lone stock, I just was not unctious.

I dident want to tell Eddie. But finally I sent for his personal Aide De Camp and told him that on the morrow when the market opened, among those desiring to dispose, I would be among those present. I got out with a very moderate loss. Next day it went up big. But the whole thing is no place for a weak-hearted Comedian, and from now on when Eddie wants to help me, he can just give me some of his old jokes.

•

GENE HOWE

Gene Alexander Howe (1886–1952) was born in Atchison, Kansas, the son of Ed Howe, owner of the *Atchison Globe*. Educated at public schools, he was expelled from high school and joined his father's paper as a reporter and typesetter. He was fired for drinking and went into exile for four years, working on the Portland *Oregonian*. His father invited him back to Atchison and in 1911 sold the *Globe* to him. In 1924 Howe founded another paper in the Texas Panhandle, the *Amarillo Globe*, and two years later he acquired the *Amarillo News* and merged the two titles. He edited the *Amarillo Globe-News* from 1924 to 1935 and wrote a column for it under the heading 'Old Tack', in the persona of Kernel E. Rasmus Rookus Tack. He wrote about his wife O. W., his wastrel son Aloyious, and his contrary daughter Lollapalooza. He told stories about Amarillo and, occasionally, about such outlandish places as New York. There were plenty of jokes about Borger, a nearby oil boom town where shootings were a frequent occurrence. So fond was Howe of his column that he resigned from the job of editing the paper in order to concentrate on Tack's musings.

'Old Tack', *Amarillo Globe*
From *Them Texans*, by Kernel E. Rasmus Tack, The Tactless Texan (1927)

I have been asked whether religion has ever penetrated into the plains of Texas. All I can say is that the other week in the vaudeville at The Fair theater a Miss Thompson was featured. She played the violin as she danced and was billed as the 'Dancing Melodist'. In the Sunday paper it came out as the 'Dancing Methodist'.

There are so many Methodists in Amarillo that the *Globe* considered it good policy to get out an extra to correct it.

Borger is the oil city that grew from prairie to a city of 25,000 people in less than six months. Nothing but oil could do it. Of course Borger was tough.

The city was built around the oil derricks and whenever there was an explosion the people in town didn't know whether it was a man or an oil well being shot.

The Santa Fe shipped an immense lot of tonnage into Borger as more than 1,200 oil wells, costing better than $50,000 each, were put down in one year in the Borger and surrounding pools.

For the year 1926 Borger and Chicago were the two largest shipping points on the Santa Fe. Borger and Chicago also were the two largest shooting points.

When Borger was going its best a tenderfoot from the east happened in. Several of the citizens undertook to initiate him but they made a mistake. After the smoke of the battle had blown away, several of the local bad men were candidates for the hospital. This particular tenderfoot happened to be from Chicago.

When a man moves from Borger to Amarillo it takes him at least three weeks to learn to walk on the sidewalk when walking from his place of work to home or vice versa.

A Texan is a man who goes to New York to see the sights and becomes one of them.

Any town can have a boom if its citizens will pay each other too much for lots.

The most weazened-up man I know goes about preaching that it is most dangerous from a health standpoint to engage in kissing.

I agree with him that there isn't anything quite as dangerous as kissing but I'm not thinking of the germs. The most exuberantly healthy people I have ever known are the greatest kissers I have ever known. They are in much more danger of being shot than of catching some contagion.

Lollapalooza is so up-to-date that she is having her hairlip bobbed.

The Panhandle of Texas, which isn't but has the reputation of being the blowingest place on the continent, has never had a cyclone. The explanation given by Texans is that occasionally a tornado does try to slip in from either Oklahoma or Kansas but that the regular Panhandle breeze chases it away.

Again O. W. has had her way and I have promised her solemnly that on the first of the year I will swear off eating with my knife. I have tried it several times and suffered so terribly that I had to give it up. But I do appreciate that times are changing in Amarillo and the Panhandle and that new things are here to stay. It has become so in Dallas that one can eat with a fork even in the most public restaurants without any risk of being insulted. In Fort Worth it is still dangerous and in Amarillo until lately it was regarded as well nigh fatal.

Amarillo Globe, July 5:

Old Tack was phoned this morning by a most worthy woman who lives on South Polk Street. She has a most beautiful home, most elegantly furnished but she is in the direst distress and is most unhappy because of an unwelcome visitor. A skunk has taken up its abode in her home and has declined all invitations to leave.

The skunk appears in the house several times each day. It frolics about on the Turkish rugs and is friendly and as tame as a young kitten. The lady telephoned this morning and asked for my help. She said she was afraid to shoot or cage the skunk for fear of arousing its displeasure. She is planning a house party for early next week and she says she must be diplomatic and not violent.

I once read a treatise by Ernest Seton Thompson on skunks. As I remember, he said that skunks are not ill-tempered and are most kindly until riled. He wrote, as I remember, that he had a family of skunks in his backyard and he very often transferred them from one pen to another by lifting them by the tail. A skunk held aloft by the tail is indeed harmless, he stated. He never had an accident, he wrote.

If the skunk continues to visit, I will be delighted to volunteer my services. I have faith in Mr Thompson's writings and will be very glad to carry away the skunk. Just send for me lady.

From the *Amarillo Globe*, July 6:

(Note by the Editor: Mr Tack did not have time to complete his column this morning as he received a message to hurry out to a certain house on Polk Street. He was informed that the skunk was playing about in the parlor. Later Mr Tack appeared in front of the *Globe* office and sure enough he had Mr Skunk. He was carrying it by its tail and while it was not embarrassing Mr Tack it could be plainly seen that the animal was infuriated. Mr Tack said that Mr Thompson's plan worked to perfection. He stated that, humming a lullaby, he approached it quietly. The skunk actually purred in reply and rubbed up against his ankle. Mr Tack then grabbed the tail firmly and hoisted.

But Mr Tack says he has failed to remember what Mr Thompson said about turning the animal loose. It was suggested to him by Mr McDaniel that he drop it off the roof of the fourteen-story Herring Hotel. It was said that the skunk would be so stunned by the fall that it most likely would be rendered hors d'oeuvres. Mr Tack was plumb elated over the suggestion and when last seen was taking wide strides down Fillmore in the direction of the Herring.)

From the *Amarillo Globe*, July 7:

(Note by the Editor: It is to be regretted that Mr Tack's column is again missing. Mr Tack cannot be located at home and an inquiry at the Herring has developed no specific information. It has been learned that the top two floors of the Herring have been closed. No statement could be had from the management as to the reason.)

From the *Amarillo Globe*, July 8:

(Note by the Editor: Readers of the *Globe* will be pleased to learn that Mr Tack is at his home and that in a statement issued to the press this afternoon he said he would be at his office by next Monday or Tuesday. Mr Tack, it seems, slipped when he was hiking up the stairs between the thirteenth and fourteenth floors day before yesterday. In his eagerness to save himself from a nasty fall he released his hold on the tail of the skunk to grasp a railing. Those who saw the skunk say it was an unusually large and vigorous specimen.)

I believe in fitting my children for life's struggles. Aloyious put in three years at journalism college and now he is preparing to open up a news stand.

An old story being told of an Amarillo man who has just recovered from a very dangerous siege of illness. For a time the doctors would have given him up if his credit hadn't been extra good.

And when he was at his worse a minister visited him.

'Bill,' said the minister, 'you had better renounce the devil.'

'Not now, preacher,' whispered Bill, 'I'm not in any condition to make any new enemies.'

Well, folks, I had a major operation yesterday evening at home. Our family doctor, a veterinary surgeon, snagged out my tonsils. It was performed at home and I took a major anaesthetic. I had a total eclipse.

My bedroom faces north, and from it one could see the flames of that big fire we had out our way last night. But when I came out from under the dope O. W. had all the blinds pulled down. I inquired as to the why of it.

'There's a big fire outside,' she explained, 'and I thought perhaps that just when you came to if you saw them flames that you might have thought you had died.'

Them Texans, Vol. II, by Kernel E. Rasmus Tack, The Tactless Texan (1928)

'Who is O. W.?' I was asked the other day. I thought, of course, that everyone knew that O. W. is the woman who proudly wears the doubtful honor of being the wife and helpmate of Kernel Tack.

Me and O. W. were born on adjourning farms on the west bank of the Missouri river in Kansas. Across the river is Missouri and we knew many of the 'bottomites' who lived about the lakes. Many of the Missouri husbands, young and old, refer to their wives as their 'old woman'. Both of us were brought up to it.

I had an ambition to be literary when I was very young and instead of taking up manual labor as did other young men of my acquaintance I entered a newspaper office. The best people in our neighborhood rarely agreed on anything of importance but they had no difficulty coming to the unanimous opinion that I would never amount to much. Most everybody thought O. W. was making a mistake when we were married. And I will say that for the first few years we had a most grievous time of it. I surely did provide a sorry living.

I took myself very seriously. I thought I could write and I drifted from one newspaper to another. I did not make the slightest progress until I happened to drop into Amarillo away down here in Texas. And then one day I got to laughing at myself as others must have laughed at me. I started writing up myself and O. W. and our children and somehow or other the idea must have taken hold.

Anyhow, folks, we're eating higher up on the hog here in Texas than we ever did in any other place we ever lived. And O. W. and Lollapalooza and my aristocratic, formidable-appearing mother-in-law and the other Tacks are so grateful for the change for the better in their diet that they don't mind it a bit. In fact they glory in it. The status of our table improved with the start of Old Tack's telling the truth about what goes on in this household.

We haven't made much real progress otherwise since we have been here but we at least don't have to skimp in the matter of vitamins. And furthermore, I'll venture that O. W. makes as many trips to the beauty parlors as any lady in Amarillo. And when the new Turkish bath opened the other day in the basement of the new Fisk building, she was the first customer. And Lollapalooza is taking pianist lessons three times a week from Emil Meyers.

The trouble with the Panhandle of Texas is that we never have a rainy spell when it doesn't rain too much and that it never gets dry without staying dry too long.

The women in this country will never vote wet.

There never was a time when women had so much to spend and the men spend so little.

Now that the saloon has passed, there ain't much a man can spend. He buys a suit or two a year, shirts and shoes and his cigars and cigarettes don't cost but little. If he still likes his licker, more than likely he is making it at home, and this doesn't cost him much. For example what I formerly spent over the bar O. W. now spends at the beauty parlors and dry-goods stores. The women and children certainly have come into their own.

When we had saloons they weren't hardly nobody but the very rich who wore silk stockings. Nowadays if a girl would appear on Poke Street in cotton stockings there'd be a riot. I don't know of no women folks so poor that they don't have some silk about them.

Old Tack has a keen sense of humor. O. W. has a keen sense of rumor.

There is a man out at the county hospital suffering from shell shock. He is from Borger.

Them Texans, Vol. III, by Kernel E. Rasmus Tack, The Tactless Texan (1929)

Lollapalooza has reached an age where she is becoming interested in boys. Her idea of romance is a boy who has slicked-back hair and one who can dance and looks somewhat like those make-believe heroes you see in the movies.

But I'd like to wager that twenty years from now her idea of romance will be a husband whose check is good at the bank. The sheiks worth while are the ones who are out hustling to make a living for the wives and children at home. To me they are much more heroic than the insipid, spoiled screen idols who serve no good purpose in life except to make wives dissatisfied with their husbands. I dislike to have O. W. go to a movie as it means that for two days she will go about the house heaving deep sighs and being cross and cranky with Old Tack. I can't help it that I don't look like Buddy Rogers. And just between us, folks, O. W. isn't any Greta Garbo herself.

*

O. W. and Lollapalooza early in November begin to have a wild look in their eyes. They are restless to start the Christmas trot.

Them Texans, Vol. IV, by Kernel E. Rasmus Tack, The Tactless Texan (1930)

Latest remark by Congressman DePriest: 'I've a good mind to make a tour of the South to tell some of the Crackers what I think of them.'

I'm not smart and I don't know nothing much except as to the weather but one thing I know sure as certain is that Congressman DePriest isn't going to make a tour of the South to tell the people of the South what he thinks of them.

A hick town is any place smaller than the town in which you live.

Yes, I was in a speakeasy. What is a speakeasy? I don't know as to where it derived its name, but it's nothing more than a saloon. It is said there are 38,000 of them in New York City. Before Prohibition there were 10,000 saloons.

A friend of mine who lives in New York took me to a speakeasy close to one of the main streets in New York when I was there on a visit several months ago. It was nothing more or less than a long old-time bar with a brass foot rail and plate glass in back and all the trimmings. Beer was on draught and any kind of liquor could be had.

As the friend and myself crowded in close to the bar a red-faced bartender leaned over and whispered to me: 'Please remove your hat,' he said.

And of course I did, but I surely did say to myself that this was the first time in my life I was ever requested to remove my hat in a saloon. The reason was that there were quite a few women in the place and they were drinking, just the same as the men.

This is the truth if I ever told it.

Speakeasies are so numerous along certain streets in New York that those not operating saloons are putting up signs.

'This is not a Speakeasy; this is a Tailor Shop,' is a sign I saw over the entrance to one building.

•

HERBERT SIDEBOTHAM

Herbert Sidebotham (1872–1940) was born in Manchester and educated at Manchester Grammar School and Balliol College, Oxford. He trained as a barrister but never practised, preferring to join the *Manchester Guardian* as a leader writer in 1895. After writing on military affairs for the *Manchester Guardian* during the Boer War and the First World War, he joined *The Times* as a political commentator in 1918. He wrote columns for the *Sunday Times* (as 'Scrutator'), for the *Daily Sketch* (as 'Candidus') and for the *Daily Telegraph* (as 'Student of Politics'). His 'Candidus' columns were collected as *The Sense of Things* (1938).

Like Madam's Hat

From *The Sense of Things* (1938)

Lord Baldwin does not believe in 'progress' – at any rate, not in the sort of progress that the nineteenth century used to swear by and which we now put in inverted commas. At a Worcestershire dinner he told the story of how, when he was taking his wife out to the theatre, his car was caught in a block, and it took him half an hour to get from Downing Street to Shaftesbury Avenue. He unburdened himself later to a policeman who had been looking after his car. 'What a marvellous age we live in,' said Lord Baldwin. 'When I was young I could have got there in seven minutes in a hansom; now we take half an hour. In years to come, we shall never get to the theatre at all.' It is just what you or I might have said. But only a policeman could have made so apt a reply as, 'Very good, sir.' Only three words, but full of a profound if not very explicit philosophy. He may have meant that blocks did not begin with motor cars, but were just as bad, or worse, with the old horse traffic, and that, as Lord Baldwin had got his facts wrong, it was no use discussing his inferences. Or he may have meant that, as it was not for him to bandy an argument with his betters, it was polite to leave it at that.

Progress produces results very like those that follow the purchase of madam's new hat. It is a beautiful hat, considered absolutely. Its shape and colour are alike charming – so charming that they show up the relative shabbiness of the costume and a new dress has to be bought to match the hat. So with progress, except that you cannot remake the world to match the new discovery. To match the motor car, one would need another Fire of London which would burn down all the buildings and force us to lay out the streets on a new and better plan. Cars are cheap and the rebuilding of London is prohibitively dear, with the result that the increase of speed actually lengthens the time that it takes to get from one place in the town to another. Nor is the invention of the internal combustion engine a solitary example of this law. I would not say a word against the telephone, but has anyone honestly cast up the time that is consumed by the telephone and compared it with the time that is saved? Because a message gets through more quickly, it by no means follows that time is being saved.

On the other hand, it is true that some scientific inventions do create an opportunity of increased leisure. If mechanical inventions were given free rein, it might be quite possible to get the same output that we now get from an eight-hour day in six or even four hours, and think what a gift those extra hours would be if the leisure were used wisely. It will be objected that shorter hours would mean more unemployment. But would it? It would create more employment for the men who would have to make the machines, and for those who would have to serve us in our extra hours of leisure.

Have the two sides of this account ever been scientifically balanced one against the other? It might be well worth doing. My impression is that the tendency of mechanical and scientific invention is not so much to diminish employment as to change its character. As the numbers of men required for a given amount of production are diminished, the numbers required for the processes of transport, sale and marketing, and for new and subsidiary trades that the reduction of hours creates are proportionately increased.

Blonde – That Was

From *The Sense of Things* (1938)

I understand that the platinum blonde is passing and that red hair is to be the new mode. Will it be good news to those who already have Titian-red hair of their own, or will their pleasure be dashed by the thought that after their long languishing in fidelity to Nature the art of the hairdresser will soon take away their advantage of Nature and force them to share it with everyone else?

Fashion, which is made by the desire to be different from other people, ends by making us alike. Perhaps it is as well. If there were a fashion exclusive to Nature and unattainable by art, the women of the world would be divided between those doomed for ever to be out of fashion and those who could not help being in it and could not make a new one, and the second state would be as bad as the first. Art and artifice are wise in the inconstancy which gives every colour of hair and complexion a turn of popularity and then turns every advantage of Nature into a disadvantage as soon as it has been enjoyed long enough. For it is common observation that Nature is never so hopelessly out of date as when it has just ceased to be fashionable. Women's fashions are more rapid in their revolution, but they repeat the laws of changing taste in other departments of life.

I wonder how far these changes of taste are commercial or purely capricious or the logical reflexes of fossilized history that is part of our make-up. It is an old saying that there is no arguing about tastes. If you ask anyone whether he likes red hair or flaxen or black best, he will tell you without a moment's hesitation.

Some of these dislikes may be instinctive and have been acquired through long-forgotten experiences in his ancestry. The hatred of red hair which was general and unreasoning in my youth perhaps goes back to memories of some fierce Danish or Viking invader with his warlike fury and his berserker rage. It may be that those whose ancestors experienced it have something in the blood that now expresses itself in a dislike of hair that happens to be red like his. Similarly, the recent cult of the platinum blonde may be an unconscious echo of the state of mind that prevailed when the fair Saxons were dominant, when fairy stories were made, and the only type of beauty that was prized was the fair type.

But perhaps it is idle to attempt to rationalize these instinctive preferences, or to make the changes of fashion correspond with the forgotten cycles of historical change. Their motive may be purely commercial, for the oftener they occur the oftener it is necessary to visit the hairdresser or to buy a new hat. Or the reason for the variations may be in the nature of woman herself, intensely conservative where men and the general structure of society are concerned, but a restless innovator in her own appearance, a lover of change for the sake of change and without reference to any aesthetic standard. Personally, I shall welcome the change of colour fashion in hair from straw and bleached to red – provided it is a rich, glowing red and not a sandy shade. But even if red hair were as ugly in my eyes as, in fact, it can be beautiful, given the skin to match, I should still welcome the change just because it is one, and because it is the privilege of women to refute Nature by art and prove themselves equal to conquering every prejudice.

Waiting for Disaster

From *The Sense of Things* (1938)

Mr Winston Churchill says that the day will come when the ground will decisively master the air and (I quote his own tropical language) the raiding aeroplane will be almost certainly clawed down from the skies in flaming ruins. Let us hope so. But what astounds me is the fatalism of these politicians. Mr Churchill puts ten years ahead the day on which human mammals will be safe from human birds. But apparently until the mechanics of ground defence are topsides of air attack we can do nothing but turn ourselves into birds, equip ourselves with hideous gas masks and tax ourselves to the bone to pay for it. The bombardments of Madrid demonstrate that no amount of raids is sufficient to break down the morale of a civil population.

If that be so, why wait ten years before applying the obvious moral, namely, to abolish methods of war that are evidently going to be indecisive anyhow? The strongest Power in the air for the next ten years cannot make itself immune from attack in the air, for the aeroplane is essentially a means of attack, not of defence. The degree of risk depends on considerations with which the mere size and numbers of aircraft have comparatively little to do – on the nearness of your vital spots to the enemy, on whether you are in the main an agricultural or an industrial country, and whether your population is scattered or centred in large towns. By these tests Russia is probably the least vulnerable, but this country, France and Germany are all equally exposed to attack.

If Berlin is more distant from the starting-point of attack than London, and our own people are thickest on the ground, Germany is at an equal disadvantage as compared with Russia, and she is, moreover, liable to attack from two sides, whereas all our danger comes from one side only. Is it not, therefore, to the advantage of all four Powers in Western Europe (including Italy) that they should disarm themselves of methods of war which will probably be indecisive anyhow, and increase the horrors of war out of all proportion to the dividend of military gain? Is there one of them that would not agree that immunity from attack by air is enormously preferable to the dubious, remote and fractional advantage in attack?

If we were not fatalists we should act on that belief. There is no chance of anyone attaining that measure of security in the air that our sea power gave us at sea. Why not, therefore, agree that, as the balance of mischief is so excessive, we will jointly insure ourselves against this particular form of mischief and do it earlier and relatively cheaply rather than later and at ruinous cost? I am not arguing against our own rearmament. I regard rearmament in the air as essential to the safety of our communications overseas. To me air power is another form of sea power. I am thinking, not of the legitimate functions of air power in association with the operations of armies and fleets, about which argument may be possible, but of the specific danger of air raids on the civilian population, about which there is no argument possible. That could be abolished at a stroke to the advantage of all. Why do we wait?

●

O. O. McINTYRE

Oscar Odd (pronounced 'Udd') McIntyre (1884–1938) was born in Plattsburg, Missouri, and grew up in Gallipolis, Ohio. He was not a success at school, although he did publish the school paper. Straight from school he joined the *Gallipolis Journal* as a typesetter and reporter, then attended a business school in Cincinnati for a couple of years, before becoming a reporter for an Ohio paper, the *East Liverpool Morning Tribune*. From there he moved to the *Dayton Herald*, where he started as a police reporter. He was always dashing past the publisher's desk in the paper's front office, hoping to avoid attention. 'Who's that fast-stepping boy who dashes in and out all the time as if he's heading for a three-alarm fire?' the publisher inquired. 'That's Oscar Odd McIntyre,' someone explained. 'Make him city editor,' said the publisher. By 1907 he was combining the roles of managing editor, city editor and telegraph editor. Next, he moved to the *Cincinnati Post* as telegraph editor, under Ray Long as managing editor. When Long took over *Hampton's* magazine in 1909 McIntyre followed him as his assistant, but the magazine folded and McIntyre became copy-editor of the *New York Evening Mail*. He was the paper's city editor at the time of the sinking of the *Titanic*, and was responsible for organizing coverage of the disaster. Amazingly, after so many years' newspaper experience, he was fired for poor spelling. However, this turned out to be a blessing in disguise, since he began writing sketches of New York life from the point of view of a young man from a small town, while earning his bread-and-butter as a publicist for the Majestic Hotel. In 1922 he began syndicating his 'New York Day by Day' column and he also started writing a monthly column for *Cosmopolitan*, which was then under the direction of his old chum Ray Long. By the 1930s his syndicated column was appearing in 500 papers across America and he received up to 3,000 letters a week from readers – one column, about his dog Junior, who had been run down by a motorist on Fifth Avenue, elicited some 20,000 letters. He never supplemented his income with lectures or radio work, yet he was, after Arthur Brisbane, the highest-paid columnist in the country. As a result, McIntyre and his wife were able to live splendidly, with a Park Avenue apartment, a chauffeur to drive them around, and annual trips to California, Texas and abroad.

I Wouldn't Trade Jobs with Hoover

From *Another 'Odd' Book: 25 Selected Stories of O. O. McIntyre* (1932)

After fifteen years of conducting a syndicated newspaper column, I would not trade jobs with anybody. That goes for the Prince of Wales, the Christmas-tree salesman and Rudy Vallée. Such enthusiasm is not difficult to explain. I had my try at many things and my yesterdays proved a nightmare of imperiled vision and defeat. All my occupational efforts fizzled until a freakish destiny catapulted me into the columning business.

And then I discovered the fulfillment of every lazy man's dream – to live without work. My todays are actual play, a happy succession of new interests, new thrills.

I have no clock to punch. I get up when I please, go where I please and retire in the same fashion. My office is where I take the lid off my typewriter – on a railroad train, in a steamer cabin, a hotel room or even an airplane.

In fifteen years I have visited the office of the gentlemen who syndicate my wares but once and that – ha, ha – was to sign a contract with an increase in salary.

The only order I ever received from them was a telegram on the eve of a departure for Europe with the command: 'Have a good time!' There's a tough set of instructions, boys.

It has all been so soft that there are times when I skip around pinching myself, expecting to wake up back where I probably belong – at a newspaper copy desk, wearing a green eye shade and wondering if a harassed boarding-house lady will listen to reason.

As one of the many he-Cinderellas of modern journalism I am conscious that it may not last. Any day I expect to feel like the fellow with the high bicycle when the safety arrived.

Something new, something different is bound to come and attract the readers of newspaper columns just as naturally as the automobile followed the buggy. That is the inescapable law of progress.

But I have had my fun and if the eclipse arrives tomorrow or the day after I'll always believe I have been numbered among the lucky guys in a turbulent world.

My quixotic adventure in newspaper columning was launched from a hall room, four flights up and all the way back. I had reached that drab depth of poverty wherein I indulged in self-haircuts and peeked covetously at the morning bottle of milk at the neighbor's door across the hall.

But my world was young and with that sublime optimism of youth I sang my song of the city on a one-lunged typewriter. After eight months of utterly futile metropolitan minne-singing without attracting the attention of a single newspaper editor I was ready, aye, determined, to quit and trek back to the little Ohio town whence I came – a failure. But fate as usual hung on the thread of coincidence!

It was a letter from the editor of a Bridgeport, Connecticut, paper, bless him, agreeing to accept my offer of three months' trial service free that turned my frail journalistic craft out of rough seas into pleasant waters. I carried on. And am I glad?

Had I surrendered when all human logic told me to quit, I probably would be sitting at some obscure desk in a corner of a busy editorial room. So it is that what looked to be the most forlorn of syndicated newspaper hopes reaches an audience of more than twenty millions.

When I think of that vast audience I face an agonizing and complete mental sterility. The ideas will not come. My deliverance from this dilemma came about through an interview with a celebrated actor, who told me he saved himself from the tortures of stage fright by playing solely to a single person in his audience.

In this fashion, for many years, I have in my thought been addressing the people of my native village. Everything that I write is a daily letter home.

And in trying to interest the people I know so well I discovered that I was interesting, to a certain degree, people I had never met – not only in small towns but in every large city in America, including New York.

It is trite to say that people are the same the world over, but in columning you find that is amazingly true. For instance, I have discovered one column topic with a universal appeal. That is food.

A new dish or a new method of cooking an old dish is sure fire. Such gastronomic garrulities have brought me letters from a President of the United States, a housewife on the Kansas prairie, a rajah in India, a cowboy in Texas and the late Chauncey Depew.

It is, however, an article about a dog that brings the most letters. No person is so willing and eager to write his protests or congratulations as the dog lover.

Strangely enough, readers outside New York are more responsive to stories about the Bowery, Greenwich Village and aristocratic Park Avenue than about the street that whips the universe – Broadway. Coincidentally, the topic that seems to interest the native New Yorker more than any other concerns household innovations.

My mail averages a hundred letters a day. Most of it is of an interrogative or complimentary nature but there is always a sprinkling of mean-tempered and anonymous epistles.

For more than a year, for example, my column has been clipped from a San Francisco paper daily and mailed to me with critical notations in red pencil: 'You are rotten!' 'What trash!' et cetera.

Daily, too, for many months comes a tender missive from a lady who, touched by some mental twist, believes me to be her long-lost twin brother. A prisoner in San Quentin seems convinced I helped him to blow a safe, and a storekeeper in Des Moines wants $40 I borrowed 'when we were in the navy.'

Whenever I mention a longing for such old-fashioned yum-yums as gingersnaps, apple butter or sorghum molasses the response is immediate. Samples arrive from everywhere. Without any design whatever, I mentioned several years ago that my idea of a perfect gift for men was a dressing-robe. I received fourteen. Incidentally, my automobile is not what it used to be.

Solely because I am a columnist, I am invited to first nights of stage and movie offerings, openings of night clubs, hotels and such. And – pardon the hysteria – I have been invited to cross the continent in a private airplane, to fly to Mexico and Cuba in the same fashion, and I have refused three trips around the world.

Come look over my shoulder at excerpts from the morning mail!

From Seattle, Washington: 'If you ever come to Seattle, a fried-chicken dinner with all the trimmings – including preserved plums – awaits you.'

From Prescott, Arizona: 'I am on the last lap of a three-year chase of the cure. Your column has been a daily comfort.'

From Ogden, Utah: 'I am eighteen and am considered a beautiful type of blonde. I have $400 to spend on a ten-day visit to New York. If you will show me the town I will pay all the expenses.'

From Atlanta, Georgia: 'I can imitate ten different kinds of wild animals and more than a dozen birds. Everybody says I should go on the stage. If you will arrange it I will give you my first two weeks' salary.'

From Portland, Maine: 'I have told certain people here I am an intimate friend of Irvin Cobb. If you can get him to write me a letter, signing it, "Your Pal – Irvin," I will send you a certified check for $100.'

From Cincinnati, Ohio: 'I have been out of work and am ill. I need $500 to put over a patent. Unless you raise this amount for me I intend to kill myself.'

Thus does a columnist's daily mail offer its sweep of emotion. It is a constant reminder that the bulk of humanity is kindly and tolerant. I have thousands of unseen friends, many whose lives are epics of courage in affliction, who take time to cheer me on the way.

There are as many thousands more who look to my daily efforts to add a touch of sunshine to the drab realism of life. Indeed, I know of no job offering so many sacred obligations.

It is no concession to a mock modesty to say that I wish I were far worthier of such a trust but I can honestly say I am very, very humble.

'New York Day by Day'
From *The Big Town: New York Day-by-Day* (1935)

A fierce rain thudding down. Nothing more soothing than watching rain from a cozy window chair. Every home should have a sheltered balcony for shower gazing. A queasy day, but now midnight and big drops pelt and zig-zag the pane. Serenity. Rain, rain, rain!

About the only thing left that is simple is rain. Or perhaps dawn. I laid down a book to watch the rain. One George Buckley told me to read: *Little Man, What Now?* A drama of two defeated hopefuls in love written with a sparkle of Aesopian brevity. All my life I've tried to write briefly. And failed.

The most poignant line in literature encompassed two words: 'Jesus wept.' And how marrowy terse the Sermon on the Mount and Lincoln's Gettysburg address. G. K. Chesterton sits down to every new novel declaring, 'I will be brief.' Yet rarely is. It's an art few master. But about rain –

Willie Collier once appeared in a frolicsome tarantara *Caught in the Rain*. The plot is vague but the title is a honey. Catchy. The success of Jeanne Eagles's play, *Rain*, was half in its title and the constant downpour. An editor tells me poems ticking of rain always click with readers.

Of all phenomena rain has the most superbly ordered rhythm. No matter what one writes about it, however, the contrast is jerky. For instance! This ramble.

San Antonio, Texas, and San Diego, Cal., have the most salubrious climate the world over. I enjoy both and have frequently hymned their praise. Yet more fascinating than either is Havre, France, where it drizzles or pours 300 days of the year. The late Grant Clarke taught me to walk in the rain. It should be done slowly with pocketed hands and head bared. Often when a storm broke he would quit some night club and round the reservoir in this fashion and come back dripping with water – and sometimes lyrics. 'Dirty Hands, Dirty Face' came to him on such a jaunt. His famous song.

Have you noticed at sea how sailors love rain? Even with protection near, they will stand sopping in a deluge. Afterward their scoured faces have a new light, fresh vigor. Victor Herbert loved the rain. Several times exposing himself to the torrents laid him low with pneumonia. Earl Carroll is a disciple of Old J. Pluvius. Henry L. Doherty, in the first penthouse in town, had a roller-coaster bed that slid out to the touch of a push button to a tin-roofed portico, where he could hear the patter on the roof.

I know a rain worshipper who gives credit to one of those sudden showers, that so thoroughly disorganizes New York, for twelve years of married bliss. A bachelor, he was eddied under Dutton's book-store awning on Fifth Avenue. He talked to a chance lady, walked her a few blocks when the sun came out. So they were married, have five beautiful children and a most contentful home. He lives next door.

Hugo Halling and I once spent part of a night in a Bowery flop-house during a slashing rain. The suspicious aloofness of bums in a huddle seemed to melt with the rainfall. The low, fetid room was soon chirping like an insect obbligato on a summer night. One expanding gentleman with an arbored mustache proved himself authentically the father of a person of means. He was of life's miscellany, with no trade and a drifter, but not a boozer. I wrote his son of the encounter. He never spoke to me again. But when I see him I stare. And he reddens!

One remembers old friends in the rain. At breakfast Jerome Beatty mentioned Fred Schneller as an important politician in Cincinnati. A man by that name was extremely kind to me when I gawked out of the hedge to that Ohio city, a gar-mouthed country boy with cockle burrs in my hair. I never saw him again, but I learn he is the same Fred Schneller. So, inspired by the rain, I am going to write him of appreciation I was then too shy to express. Most of us should be more gracious to the stranger in town. In those formative, bewildering days, a cheery word means much.

The rain has stopped. Across the way a slinking cat comes to the curb and puts a shine on its morning face. There's a juniper tang in the dawn air. One of those refreshing days when incompetents dream of starting the Great American Novel.

'New York Day by Day'

From *The Big Town: New York Day-by-Day* (1935)

It's magnificent relaxation for a writer to let thought go womp and dash off anything that rustles through his mind. From a painting by Picasso to a seasoned housefly. That's the mood for today. Abandonment of the sequence of direct narrative. A preface to nothing!

No foreboding pangs about the final paragraph. Nothing to do but drift. I can write that Gene Fowler often walks through town wearing carpet slippers and let it go at that. And there's that sudden freak of consciousness that makes me wonder if the plural of mongoose is mongeese.

No. A dictionary is handy and it's mongooses. It is fun to clear the mind and set down the first idea that pops. Here it comes: I hope there's chocolate ice cream for dinner! Lloyd Enochs sends in a book on thimble magic – a list of 500 evanishments. Stimulating. Magic.

As stimulating as an uproarious laugh I heard in the public library the other day. He was at a table reading and of a sudden doubled with guffaws. I tip-toed to see what touched off such hilarity. He was reading that old timer, *David Harum*.

I recall one earthy gem from that volume. Something like this: 'A reasonable amount of fleas is good for a dog, keeps him from broodin' over bein' a dog.' With Kin Hubbard in Heaven, there is too little homespun humor any more. Such as Kin's twinge of esprit: 'Nuthin' excitin' has happened in this town since Apple Week.'

But flippancy, as expressed by the Broadway breed of Cantor–Jessel wise-crackers, is slowly going the way of high-powered banking. Even youngsters are acquiring a sober outlook. The 24-year-old son of a friend joined me in an evening walk. He wants a farm in Minnesota and a selected library. Maybe he's in love.

Twenty-four! I was married at that age. And spent two days' salary for the rubber-tired hansom – was I smearing it on! – from Cincinnati to the church in Newport, Ky. We both became conscious of a faint scent in the vehicle, a lavender odor. That was the venerable hackman's contribution to romance. He was one of those garrulous 'seein' as how' talkers. I wonder what life did to him!

I hear Stuart Price is over at the Waldorf. We were born in the same Missouri town and his brother Jay is a close friend. Yet I hesitate to phone. A strange man – Stuart Price. Most of his life has been spent in the Orient and he's somewhat the mystic. Kindly, cultured, an intimate of governing figures in the dramatic chessboard of the Far East, he shrinks from contacts, floating around in an air of abstraction. He's the sort who loses a handful of cuff buttons a year. Sometimes he looks through you in passing. Or suddenly walks out of a room and next you hear he's in Sumatra.

Flits of thought: Al Smith grows stout . . . It strikes me John Golden and Brock Pemberton are staunchest of the dwindling list of legitimate producers . . . I fell heir to Pemberton's drama editing job when he left the old *Evening Mail*. I wondered why he quit. He was getting $45 a week. I, $35. Next I heard he was producing *Enter Madame*, which made a fortune. I was still decorating the outer rim of the copy desk. He sent first-night seats E.1–2. I went in a rented tuxedo.

A name swims into ken – Grace Tyson. Wasn't she a vaudeville actress with a redhead partner named McWatters? Flashy fashion-plate act. A statuesque blonde who resembled the belle of our town, Buzette Newsome. She could suddenly twist her face and look like a monkey. Maybe it wasn't Grace but it was Tyson. She had the breezy personality of a Lee Tracy. McWatters and Tyson – where are they?

My barber Anthony grossed $602.40 at what he calls his 'tonsorial studio' near Herald Square last week. He quit a job at depression depths because he had faith in America. I sat directly behind Jack Dempsey at the Schmeling–Baer fight. Three seats on my left Jack Sharkey, loud-mouthed, uncouth, defiant. Dempsey, silent, chewed a frayed cigar nervously, his black scowl in dullest glower. He's still the most picturesque figure the ring produced. And shows a more alert flair for promotion instinct than Rickard. Or any snatchers at the Rickard crown. Dempsey seems one ex-champ who won't end up with a benefit. This kind of a column means so much. That is when you quit!

•

DON MARQUIS

Donald Robert Percy Marquis (1878–1937) was born in Walnut, Illinois, and only attended college for a year. An admirer of midwestern columnists Eugene Field and George Ade, his ambition was always to be a columnist and early on he wrote an unpaid column for an Illinois weekly where he also worked as a printer. After a year working for the Census Bureau in Washington, DC, he spent the next decade on papers in Washington, Atlanta and New York City, although not as a columnist but as a reporter, editor and rewrite man. However, within a year of joining the New York *Evening Sun* as editor of its magazine page, he started his humorous column 'The Sun Dial', which ran in that paper until 1922. His fellow columnist Christopher Morley later paid tribute to Marquis in the introduction to *The Best of Don Marquis* (1946): 'In the recurrent hodiernity of the Sun Dial, from 1913 to 1922 in the New York *Evening Sun*, six days a week, bedeviled by a million interruptions and beclamored by all agreeable rattles, the social riveters who gang round a man trying to work, Marquis created something utterly his own.' In 1922 Marquis moved to the *New York Tribune* (later the *Herald Tribune*) where his column again ran six days a week, this time under the heading 'The Lantern'. Over the years he created several characters with which he was able to poke fun at contemporary values – Hermione, the breathless, do-gooding pseudo-intellectual; Clem Hawley, the 'Old Soak', who reminisced about life before Prohibition; and archy the cockroach, whose wisdom was often superior to that of man. Marquis abandoned daily journalism in 1925, but his 'Sun Dial' characters continued to flourish in book form.

Mamma is so Mid-Victorian

From *Hermione and Her Little Group of Serious Thinkers* (1916)

We've been taking up Hedonism lately – our Little Group of Modern Thinkers, you know – and it's wonderful, just simply *wonderful*!

Though Mamma – poor dear Mamma is so hopelessly old-fashioned – has entirely the wrong idea about it.

'Hermione,' she said to me the other evening, after the little talk, '*what* did the lecturer call himself?'

'He's a Hedonist,' I said.

'Indeed!' she said, 'and what sort of modern impropriety is Hedonism? Is it something about Sex, or is it something about Psychics?'

I simply couldn't speak.

I just gave her a look and walked out of the room. It is absolutely useless to attempt to explain anything to Mamma.

She is so Mid-Victorian!

And Mid-Victorianism has quite gone out, you know. Really. The loveliest man gave us a talk on the Mid-Victorian recently, and when he was done there wasn't a one of us that didn't go and hide our Tennysons and Ruskins.

Although I always *will* like 'Come into the Garden, Maud.'

But he did it with such *humor*, you know. Isn't a sense of humor a perfectly *wonderful* thing?

A sense of humor is a sense of proportion, you know – he brought that out so cleverly, the anti-Mid-Victorian man did.

Though so many people who have a sense of humor are so – so, well, so *queer* about it, if you get what I mean. That is, if you know they have one, of course you're naturally watching for them to say humorous things; and they're forever saying the sort of things that puzzle you, because you have never heard those things before in just that way, and if you *do* laugh they're so apt to act as if you were laughing in the *wrong* place!

And one doesn't dare *not* to laugh, does one? It's really quite unfair and unkind sometimes! Don't you think so?

We took up a volume on the Analysis of Humor one winter – our Little Group of Serious Thinkers, you know – and read it completely through, and before the winter was over it got so there wasn't a one of us that dared *not* to laugh at anything any other one said and – well, it got rather ghastly before spring. Because even if someone wanted to know if a person needed an umbrella someone else would laugh.

Well, I must be going now. I have a committee meeting at three this afternoon. We're going in for this one-day Women's Strike, you know – our little group is.

'The Sun Dial'
archy interviews a pharaoh
From *Archy and Mehitabel* (1927)

boss i went
and interviewed the mummy
of the egyptian pharaoh
in the metropolitan museum
as you bade me to do

what ho
my regal leatherface
says i

greetings
little scatter footed
scarab
says he

kingly has been
says i
what was your ambition
when you had any

insignificant
and journalistic insect
says the royal crackling
in my tender prime
i was too dignified
to have anything as vulgar
as ambition
the ra ra boys
in the seti set
were too haughty
to be ambitious
we used to spend our time
feeding the ibises
and ordering
pyramids sent home to try on
but if i had my life
to live over again
i would give dignity
the regal razz
and hire myself out
to work in a brewery

old tan and tarry
says i
i detect in your speech
the overtones
of melancholy

yes i am sad
says the majestic mackerel
i am as sad
as the song
of a soudanese jackal
who is wailing for the blood red
moon he cannot reach and rip

on what are you brooding
with such a wistful
wishfulness
there in the silences confide in me
my imperial pretzel
says i

i brood on beer

my scampering whiffle snoot
on beer says he

my sympathies
are with your royal
dryness says i

my little pest
says he
you must be respectful
in the presence
of a mighty desolation
little archy
forty centuries of thirst

look down upon you
oh by isis
and by osiris
says the princely raisin
and by pish and phthush and phthah
by the sacred books perembru
and all the gods
that rule from the upper
cataract of the nile
to the delta of the duodenum
i am dry
i am as dry
as the next morning mouth
of a dissipated desert
as dry as the hoofs
of the camels of timbuctoo
little fussy face
i am as dry as the heart
of a sand storm
at high noon in hell
i have been lying here
and there
for four thousand years
with silicon in my esophagus
and gravel in my gizzard
thinking
thinking
thinking
of beer

divine drouth
says i
imperial fritter
continue to think
there is no law against
that in this country
old salt codfish
if you keep quiet about it
not yet

what country is this
asks the poor prune

my reverent juicelessness
this is a beerless country
says i

well well said the royal
desiccation
my political opponents back home
always maintained
that i would wind up in hell
and it seems they had the right dope
and with these hopeless words
the unfortunate residuum
gave a great cough of despair
and turned to dust and debris
right in my face
it being the only time
i ever actually saw anybody
put the cough
into sarcophagus

dear boss as i scurry about
i hear of a great many
tragedies in our midsts
personally i yearn
for some dear friend to pass over
and leave to me
a boot legacy
yours for the second coming
of gambrinus
                                archy

SIMEON STRUNSKY

Simeon Strunsky (1879–1948) was born in Vitebsk, Russia, and at the age of seven was brought by his parents to live on the lower East Side of Manhattan. He was educated at Columbia College, where he received an AB in 1900. His first job after graduation was as a department editor for the *New International Encyclopaedia*, but he also contributed articles as a free-lance to various newspapers and magazines. In 1906 he joined the editorial staff of the *New York Evening Post* as an editorial writer and columnist. In 1920 he was made editor of the *Post* and his editorials were instrumental in persuading his proprietor to switch allegiance from the straight Republican ticket to the Cox–Roosevelt ticket in the 1920 presidential election campaign. Strunsky left the *Post* in 1924 after it had been sold and joined the *New York Times*. He continued to write editorials as well as a column for the Book Review called 'About Books – More or Less'. In 1932 he took over an existing column called 'Topics of the Times', which he wrote until he was overcome by illness in 1947. A witty and genial writer, he was brilliant at deploying statistics in a way that did not cause his readers to glaze over, and his knowledge of history enabled him to counteract the mythology of the New Deal which dominated the period in which he wrote his *New York Times* column. Although he had started out as a Socialist, he gradually became what he called a Tory, debunking those who sought to debunk the Republican record and defending traditional American institutions. I have chosen one of his 'On the Other Hand' columns from the humour magazine *Puck*, as well as a couple of his 'Topics of the Times' columns.

'On the Other Hand'
Puck, April 17, 1915

At this point in the war debate several tempers gave signs of cracking and it became necessary to change the subject.

'Supposing,' said the man whose dinner we had been eating, and who had played neutral all evening by passing around the cigars and saying nothing, 'supposing one were to write a history of the United States during the last ten years and wanted a tag that would describe the period, the Age of Something or Other, you know. What would he call it?'

Everyone around the table was glad to shake off the war madness and the suggestions piled in; so did the objections. Someone said it should be the Age of Roosevelt, but our host insisted that the name would only hold from 1906 to about 1913. The Roosevelt man moved to amend by substituting the Age of Uplift, and again our host declared that while the term was long enough it wasn't wide enough, not quite universal, beside being rather colorless and tinged with highbrow. Someone who pretends to do something down in Wall Street proposed the Age of Rotten Business and offered to tell us his average annual income since the winter of 1907, but that was not going back far enough. I proposed the Age of Bernard Shaw which began safely back in 1903 or 1904 and was still going; and I proceeded to point out how the Shaw outlook upon life would fairly describe the outlook of most intelligent people and of some who were not.

'Not of enough people,' said the man who had supplied the dinner and the topic and so was in a position to domineer. 'Shaw does not get down to the masses. I want a name that does. Let me put it another way. Take a modern young woman of nineteen, not an exceptional woman, just a daughter of the people. In 1906 she was ten. Between these two dates lies the formative period of her life. Now what one name is there which during these years of growth and ripening impressions has again and again laid its stamp on her spirit – the name that she has probably heard most often and that certainly has aroused the readiest emotional response? A name that mustn't be looked up in the reference books for detail, as the best of us would have to do for a complete list of Shaw's plays or Mr Roosevelt's enemies, but the mere mention of which brings up a vivid picture, a complete fund of information?'

'Since it is plain,' said the Wall Street man, 'that this is not a debate but a conundrum, and that our friend has the answer up his sleeve, I move that discussion be closed. What *would* you call it?'

'The Age of Thaw,' said our host. 'Harry K. Thaw.'*

It was a triumph; thoroughly prepared, no doubt, carefully led up to, like one of von Hindenburg's victories, but quite as definite and complete. Our silence showed that, and the man of the house was noticeably gratified.

'No other name,' he said, 'comes so intimately home to the generation in whose hands the fate of the country will lie during the next ten years, the generation that is buying Arrow collars and tickets for "Daddy Longlegs," that is to say, the young flesh and brawn of this nation. I clipped a short paragraph from the morning paper the other day. It was about a little girl of ten who was knocked down by a motor truck and killed. She had run up from the street to tell her mother that Harry Thaw was acquitted on the charge of conspiracy and her mother sent her back for an "extra." She was killed on the way. My first impression was that no fate could be more pitiful than to be killed while buying a Thaw "extra." But the story was too somber and I dismissed it from my mind. I fell to thinking, rather, of the little girl who was ten years old back in 1906 and whom her mother sent out for one of the earliest Thaw "extras," and she was not killed. I find myself tracing her spiritual growth through the years. In 1907 she was not too young, perhaps, to be interested in Harry Thaw's picture and to glean the first fragmentary meaning out of the testimony which the Brooklyn *Eagle* printed in full – the beginning, by the way, of the new realism in the press which has thrived so well and made it so easy to discuss eugenics.'

That, of course, was prejudice. He went on: 'In 1908 this little girl of mine was nearly twelve and in a position to follow intelligently the details of the second trial. She was in her third year at high school when Judge Somebody issued Harry's third writ of habeas corpus, and she had entered the senior class when Judge Somebody Else dismissed the writ. She was growing into full womanhood. That winter she was permitted to be taken to the theater by her first admirer, and is it altogether unlikely that they went to see Mrs Evelyn Nesbit Thaw dance at Hammerstein's? Today she is probably married –

---

* Thaw shot and killed the New York architect Stanford White, who had 'ruined' Thaw's wife prior to their marriage. His wealthy family hired the best lawyers and he evaded the death penalty by pleading temporary insanity. He escaped from a mental institution but was later found sane by a jury and released.

the children of the masses still marry young – and she makes an excellent wife, and in the late afternoon, when her work is done till dinner, I imagine her going downstairs to buy a Thaw "extra." Or am I wrong?'

'Young women today read a great many other things,' said the Wall Street man.

'Of course they do,' he said. 'The war, woman suffrage, Mary Pickford, dress, Bernard Shaw; and they discuss these things with intelligence and interest. But it is conversation. The thrill of actuality, the personal sympathy that comes from having grown up with a thing – that is a different matter. As a Formative Influence, is there anything else that can compare with Harry and Matteawan?'

Having made his point he grew amiable: 'And for the social historian, the scholar, these last ten years are quite as properly the Thaw Age. Take most of the things we have been interested in – Wealth and its relation to the Social Structure; our Courts, our Juries, our Lawyers, our Doctors, our close affiliation of Progress with Lunacy, the Stage – how far away can you get from the Thaw touch?'

He passed the cigars and we all agreed.

'Topics of the Times'
New York Times, June 14, 1936

Controversy rages about the new autobiography of John Middleton Murry. Out of the dust of battle a pair of old maxims emerge, recognizable if somewhat mussed up. It makes a difference whose ox is debunked. What is sauce for the bourgeois is sauce for the artist.

Mr Murry was the husband of the late Katherine Mansfield and the intimate friend of D. H. Lawrence. His book is about these two, with many others, and himself. Undeniably it belongs in the literature of exhibitionism, but it has merits which are not denied by those critics who call it a disgusting book and a revolting book. Ralph Thompson in the *New York Times* was gentler, both with the book and its author. Mr Thompson could not help noticing that even before Mr Murry's memoirs were published over here 'the local reception committee was in none too friendly a mood.'

Why are most of the reviewers harsh with Mr Murry? One of them says there has seldom been such a shocking example of the kiss-and-tell school. Another reviewer goes to the heart of the matter. He says too much has been written about the private vagaries of high-strung artists like D. H. Lawrence and Katherine Mansfield. 'Concentration on their art rather than on their idiosyncrasies ought to be the program from now on.'

From this admirable dictum by Harry Hansen in the *World-Telegram* there can be no dissent. The only important thing about a writer is his books. They will not only contain the best of the man but the only thing that is accessible to the general public. For every person who knew D. H. Lawrence or Katherine Mansfield in the life, a hundred or a thousand know their books. By his work alone the artist must live, if he does live. But that is also true of statesmen, soldiers and railroad builders.

This is where the debunked ox and the sauce for the gander come in. If it is right and proper that the biography of an artist should be concerned with his art, it must be equally desirable that the career of a queen and empress should be appraised by the manner in which she ruled an empire. The biography of a general should be concerned with the manner in which he won battles and their historic consequences. The biography of a great revolutionist should play up the successful revolution he led and the nation he helped to build. It should not lay too much stress on his false teeth and his fondness for the ladies. The biography of a railroad builder should be chiefly interested in his railroads.

But who does not recall the debunkage school of biography which a little while ago was cavorting all over the place and all over history? It got its inspiration from Lytton Strachey's *Queen Victoria*. Before it ran itself out of breath there was not a plaster saint left intact in the annals of the nations . . .

To the short way of the debunkers with George Washington, Abraham Lincoln and Ulysses S. Grant objections were raised here and there. It was contended that the new biographers, by making pitifully little men out of Washington, Lincoln and Grant, only made these men incomprehensible. If George Washington was really a man of very limited powers, why don't we have performances like Valley Forge and Yorktown all the time?

If we are to remember Abraham Lincoln chiefly as a man of coarse speech addicted to long spells of physical and mental lassitude, why don't people turn out a dozen things as good as the Gettysburg Address every day in the year? If the character of U. S. Grant will not stand close examination, it makes one wonder what kind of character must a man have to win a war and write two big volumes of memoirs while dying of cancer.

It is well for Mr Murry to remember that the important thing about the D. H. Lawrences and the Katherine Mansfields is their work and not their private neuroses. But that is also true about the Washingtons, Lincolns, Grants. If ever the debunkage school lifts its head again the book reviewers will please remember that nobody's ox should be gored and what is sauce for the bourgeois is sauce for the artist.

'Topics of the Times'
New York Times, July 25, 1943

Secretary Ickes, angry at the charges of bureaucracy against the Administration, asked a rhetorical question the other day. He asked if the critics of the bureaucrats are seeking to bring back the days of E. L. Doheny or Albert B. Fall. Suppose now that a person took his courage in his hands and violated the rule of rhetorical questions and gave the unexpected answer. Suppose he said, in reply to Secretary Ickes' inquiry about bringing back the days of Teapot Dome, 'Yes.'*

The immediate effect would no doubt be general astonishment and horror. But the further consequence could not help being a salutary discussion of bureaucrats versus dishonest public officials in a democracy. Suppose we compared the world as it looked in 1925 and the world as it looks today. It might contribute to clearer thinking about today's fundamentals.

---

* Teapot Dome was a corruption scandal in the late 1920s involving the sale of federal oil reserves by Secretary of the Interior Albert B. Fall.

Which would you rather have in Washington? Ten honest bureaucrats or eight averagely honest, dull officials plus two corrupt officials like Albert B. Fall who sold out to the oil interests? Up to twenty years ago there could be only one answer. Democracy's deadly enemy was corruption in office. Honest government was the whole duty of the citizen. No alternative purpose was conceivable. Either we had good government, which meant honesty and efficiency, or we had bad government, which was inefficient and venal. But that was before the world had learned the meaning of totalitarianism.

Today we know only too well what totalitarianism means. People know that it is no longer a choice between 'honest' government and corrupt government. It may be a choice between honest government without freedom and free government punctuated by Teapot Dome and Tammany Hall. There the correct answer is by no means clear. Or rather the answer to most of us is clear. As between the orderliness of fascism and the confusion and waste of democracy plus Tammany Hall plus Teapot Dome, people are now saying that they will take Tammany and Teapot Dome. We do more than say it. It is the very foundation of our action. That is the thing for which America is now fighting.

It is not true that the only kind of America worth defending is the 'better' America which we expect to build after the victory has been won. This war is justified if fought only for the defense of America as it is in 1943. It would be a justifiable war for the America of 1939 and of 1925, which is approximately the date of Teapot Dome. It is a justifiable war because it is being fought in defense of the whole American record through the years, white and black.

What is that record and what is that nation? Our discontented college youth of a few years ago, educated by two decades of savage devaluation of America, complained because we had no flaming American ideal to compete with the dynamic ideal which Hitler and Mussolini and the Japanese official murder fraternities provided for their own youth. But if our young people had looked at the American record in the whole and in its essentials, they would have found an American purpose to enlist their loyalty and stir their pulses. The country which we are defending today was there five years ago, and twenty years ago.

What is this America that we are now fighting to defend? For more than a year after the collapse of France, England alone held the gate against Hitler. Without the English stand America would have had no time to become the arsenal of democracy. But without the good hope of American aid England might have been unequal to the mighty task. We are the hope of the world today in the sense that we have the final say. We have the casting vote for victory, and we have cast it for humanity and civilization.

That is the kind of America people are asked to defend – the old hope, the old record. When our young people a few years ago envied the flaming faith in the hearts of Hitler's and Mussolini's young men, did they happen to note the identity of the country to which the victims of Hitler's and Mussolini's crusading faith were fleeing for refuge? The refugees came to America, as the refugees have been coming to America for more than 300 years. The victims of the Hitler terror did not stipulate for a better America before they consented to seek refuge here. Our old American Status Quo was plenty good enough for them. Our old American Status Quo gave them life, liberty and livelihood.

What, then, do we seriously mean that America of the 12,000,000 unemployed ten years ago is the hope of the world? Yes.

America of the Economic Royalists and utility pirates the hope of the world? Yes.

America of the Ku Klux fanatics, of the Negro lynchings, of the Dillingers and the corrupt politicians – this America the hope of the world? Yes.

One need not take America's word for it. Ask the people of Britain, Russia, China and the conquered and martyred nations of Europe what they think of the American record.

•

JAMES M. CAIN

James Mallahan Cain (1892–1977) was born in Annapolis, Maryland, and was educated at Washington College, where he received his AB in 1910 and his AM in 1917. He joined the *Baltimore Sun* as a reporter, but soon afterwards enlisted in the army and sailed for France, where he became editor of the *Lorraine Cross*, a weekly army paper for the American Expeditionary Forces. In 1919 he returned to the *Baltimore Sun* and reported on the labour dispute in the West Virginia coalfields, even becoming a miner and a union member so as to assist his understanding of the issues. Next, he joined the New York *World*, where he remained for the following seven years until it closed. Subsequently, he contributed articles to Mencken's *American Mercury*, the *Ladies' Home Journal* and *Liberal* magazine. He is best known for his crime novels and the films that were made from them – *The Postman Always Rings Twice* (1934), *Mildred Pierce* (1943) and *Double Indemnity* (1943) – but he was also a columnist for the New York *World* and, later, for the Hearst syndicate.

Panhandling
New York World, December 14, 1930

Some weeks ago, in the belief that if panhandling is unavoidable it had as well be done in a competent way, and inspired by a particularly fine exhibition of the art given at my own expense, I lay down in this place a set of rules by which I thought the citizen could be relieved of his money with a minimum of pain to the beneficiary and, more importantly, to the citizen. They were as follows: That the person in need of funds learn to frequent show windows, excavations and other places where knots of people would be likely to collect; that he become adroit at little humorous remarks that would bring a smile to the face of someone of these spectators and that, with the ice thus broken, he proceed to make his touch, confident that whatever else a man might go back on he would not go back on a smile.

I am by no means prepared to admit that this is a poor scheme – on the contrary. I think it is a very good scheme, for, as I have said, it works when it is tried on me. Nevertheless it is now my duty to reveal that I have discovered a much better scheme.

I say 'discovered.' This, of course, is a careless phrase: actually it discovered me, to the tune of 25 cents and not even a 'thank you' at the end. But that is part of its surpassing beauty, so I think it would simplify things all around if I were to allow it came to my notice, and then proceed to the conclusions that are to be drawn from it.

It all happened very quickly, as I was leaving the house the other morning on my way to work. I was a little late as usual, and not really in the humor for the delays incidental to philanthropy. But, as I turned west on Nineteenth Street I knew I was going to engage in philanthropy whether I was in the humor for it or not. For in front of me was a battered little man, a most preposterous little man, who seemed to be on his way to some destination of the greatest importance to him and at the same time to be going nowhere in particular. He was the kind of little man, if I make myself clear, who is able to go nowhere with all the bustling dignity that the rest of us exhibit going somewhere. When he saw me he stopped. A look of annoyance appeared on his face – he became aware of his surroundings with the bored start that a process server might give when at last he sighted his quarry.

I stopped too: it seemed the least I could do under the circumstances. Then without saying a word he stretched out his hand, at the same time turning his face away with the expression of disgust that one shows in the presence of some disagreeable rite, like the removal of a dead cat from the gutter. Then he stood there. When I had fished the 25 cents out of my pocket it was I who walked over to him, not he who walked over to me. The 25 cents received, he moved on without saying a word.

And I – what did I do? I moved on with a light, gladsome feeling in my heart, not because I had given a needy brother 25 cents but because the needy brother had vetoed all talk, before, during and after, on his part, and all mumbling don't mention it's on my part; it boiled down to handing over the money, really the easiest part of the whole transaction. I am convinced that many another citizen would prefer to be approached in exactly the same way. In the first place, the very curt manner of it acknowledged the hard realities of the situation. I have spoken before about the Judas Iscariot feeling that comes over one when a man asks for money on the street, that horrible feeling of guilt that reduces you to gulps and stutters and makes you claw feverishly for your coins with the single thought that you may hand one out and get away. It is the same feeling that you had when you were a little boy and papa caught you in a lie and asked you all sorts of stern questions, which you were utterly unable to answer for the reason that you were helpless to say anything at all.

Well, why should you feel guilty under these circumstances? In my opinion, you feel guilty because you are guilty. It is all very well, when Dec. 31 rolls around and you cast up what you have done in the year, to pat yourself on the back about the long hours you have worked and the admirable way in which you have performed your tasks. But God, up in heaven, knows this is all hooey. That you happen to have 25 cents in your pocket at this moment is nine-tenths luck. The man before you probably worked hard too and performed his tasks quite as admirably as you. Yet there he is and here you are. There is no reason in the canon of eternal justice why he should not be here and you there; nor is there any assurance, for that matter, that in 1940, when we have the next cycle of Republican prosperity, those are not the identical places where the two of you will stand. So you feel guilty with good reason, and why a man who is for a moment behind the game should be so very polite about borrowing a few chips from the man who is ahead is a little hard to see. Indeed, it is something of a relief when he treats you like a felon, for at least the air is somehow cleared and you breathe freely.

In the second place, there are some situations so stark that they are utterly sublingual. When you win a new love, or leave an old one, when your belly is full, another man's empty – what is there to say? My battered little friend said nothing and for that I am profoundly grateful.

Good Resolutions
New York World, December 28, 1930

Placing feet on desk and lighting cigar, our citizen decides the time has come to have a showdown with himself on a certain matter. Thinks to self, this stuff about New Year's resolutions may be all hooey, but one thing is certain, and that is he's not saving enough money. God knows he's making plenty. Not as much as last year, but still plenty. Fact of the matter, if anybody had told him ten years ago that he'd be making as much as he's making now, he'd have thought they were kidding him. And where is it? It isn't anywhere. It isn't anywhere. Well, cut out the fancy talk and say what you mean: It ain't nowhere. That's where it is, it ain't nowhere.

Here you've let a whole year slip by, and all you've put in the saving account is $117, and you can't count that because you've let the checking account drop so low you've had to pay the service charge three months running for not having a minimum balance of $500. A swell businessman you are. Whoever said you were a businessman anyhow? Say boy, you got to cut this out. You got to remember you got a family. Suppose you should die? Would you like Ethel and the kids to go out and sell apples? No? Yeah? Well, that's what they'll be doing if you don't get a shake on. Apples, nice red apples only a nickel apiece. A nickel, a nickel, a half a dime, the twentieth part of a dollar.

Frowns, thinks to self he could maybe cut down on his cigars and find a cheaper place for lunch. Thinks to self, will you for God's sake get your mind on this and act like you were awake? Suppose you cut out all the cigars? Suppose you didn't eat any lunch? How much would that save? About $7 a week. Here you're up against a tough proposition and you're wasting time with foolish schemes for saving $7 a week. Come on, snap out of it. You've got to get at this thing comprehensively. Likes sound of this, mutters it over several times to self: Comprehensively, comprehensively, comprehensively. That's the stuff. Comprehensively . . .

Feels he is getting somewhere now, knits brow, puffs at cigar. Tries to think how you go about a thing comprehensively. Wonders how the big shots go about it.

Puts feet back on desk, thinks, well then, how about Ford? Anyway, he won't turn into Hoover on you, soon as you look at his picture. Has hardly thought of Hoover before word pops out at him: Facts. Thinks to self, a fine guy you are, not to think of that sooner. Of course that's what you need, facts. Facts. Opens desk drawer, gets out old bank statements, begins to riffle through checks. Takes pen and piece of paper, begins to write down items beginning from first of year:

Snowdrifts Laundry	$13.62
J. Rossi (ice)	5.25
NY Telephone Company	5.60
Consolidated Gas Company	2.48
NY Edison Company	1.85
Elco Realty Corporation (rent)	160.00
Cash	1.02

Wonders what that cash item was for. All right, never mind, we're getting somewhere now. Turns over next check, finds it is to Robert P. Hill for $10. Thinks to self, what the hell. Robert P. Hill, hey? Robert P. Hill. Don't know any Robert P. Hill. Looks at signature, wonders if it is forgery. Looks OK but when them crooks start to forge your name they do it so good you couldn't even tell it yourself. Thinks to self, no wonder you couldn't save any money. Facts, hey. I'll say we're getting facts. Facts and then some. Wonders whether he ought to send wire to bank. Guesses as check is nearly a year old the bank couldn't do anything now. Better call the Detective Bureau, though. Picks up telephone, starts to call Spring 3100, feels pretty important that he can remember the number quickly like that. Puts phone down quickly, thinks to self, now wait a minute. We'll just make sure about this thing. Gets out old checkbook, begins to riffle through stubs. Finds Snowdrift, Rossi, Telephone, Consolidated, Edison, Elco, Cash, begins to get pretty excited. Is sure next stub will not be marked Robert P. Hill. Turns leaf, finds next stub marked Robert P. Hill.

Well, what the hell?

Something wrong somewhere.

Picks up phone, calls wife, finds out Robert P. Hill is Dr Hill, the dentist. Says all right, just wanted to know. Is unable to get mind on checks any more. Says, listen bimbo, to hell with facts. There's only one way to save money, and that's to save it. Hoover, hunh. Sure he's got plenty of facts, and look at him.

Dictators

New York American, October 24, 1934

It is surprising, and in a way gratifying, this loud razz that has greeted Mr Hoover's book, *The Challenge to Liberty*. It is surprising, because this country has a habit of being too polite to its public figures, and it is gratifying because the razzers have laid their fingers squarely on the main point, which is that Mr Hoover never showed any passion for liberty in the days when he could do something about it, and thus, in his present dither over it, seems a bit late, to say the least of it.

But a book, after all, is not merely a thesis. It is also the presentation of a thesis, a job of literary carpentry in its own right, and I wish somebody would go into this question of how badly Mr Hoover writes. A half hour of his style, I confess, completely exhausts me. He has a genius for what Walter Lippmann used to call flat-wheel sentences, dreadful strings of words that torture your eye, rasp your ear, and leave your mind groping for their meaning, if any.

In addition, he is the kind of writer who never quite says it. He selects the word 'work,' decides that doesn't quite do it, and puts 'and struggle for' on top of it. 'Those principles of' comes glibly enough, but it has a plural in it, so that 'Americanism' doesn't quite seem to match up right, and gets 'an individual accomplishment' to keep it company.

But by this time the thing is in a dreadful snarl, and it takes three lines about the forefathers, involving a whole flock of do's, with 'ands' in between, to unwind it and nail it down so he can go on to another one of exactly the same kind.

Of course such men never write, in any accurate meaning of the word. They dictate. And the mouth is such a spendthrift, so accustomed to send its words flying down the wind with no thought that they will never come home to roost, that it is incapable of the economy, the careful calculation of effect, that real writing demands and must have.

If stenography were abolished, and big shots compelled to hitch up to their typewriters as lesser hacks do, the quality of their prose might be distinctly improved or, more likely, they would decide not to write the book at all, which is probably what the situation really calls for.

•

HEYWOOD BROUN

Heywood Campbell Broun (1888–1939) was born in Brooklyn, New York, the son of a well-off printing contractor, and was educated privately at the Horace Mann School and Harvard. He had written about sport on vacation from college in 1908 and instead of completing his degree he became a baseball and Broadway reporter for the *New York Morning Telegram*. He was sacked for requesting a raise in salary. Thereafter, he was a copyreader, then a baseball writer, then a theatre critic, then a war correspondent, all for the *New York Tribune*. In 1921 he joined the New York *World* as an op-ed page columnist ('It Seems to Me') and stayed until his resignation over a dispute with his proprietor in 1928. From 1928 until shortly before his death, his column appeared in the *New York Telegram* and was syndicated by Scripps–Howard Newspapers. He was the archetypal liberal columnist and took up unpopular causes, such as that of the alleged anarchists Sacco and Vanzetti, who were executed – this led to his sacking from the *World*. As the founding president of the American Newspaper Guild, he was frequently to be found on picket lines and in 1930 he stood for Congress as a Socialist, all of which infuriated his conservative mother. Broun wrote that his mother 'would make an excellent agitator herself, but she doesn't want to see anyone else agitate ... When the revolution comes it's going to be a tough problem what to do with her. We will either have to shoot her or make her a commissar. In the meantime we still dine together.' One of his columns was so admired by President Roosevelt that FDR read it out for his annual Christmas broadcast to the nation the day after it appeared, much to Broun's delight. In 1938 he started his own weekly tabloid, the *Connecticut Nutmeg* (later called simply *Broun's Nutmeg*). He took his column to the *New York Post* in 1939 but completed only one for that paper before he died of pneumonia.

'It Seems to Me'
Joe Grim

From *Sitting on the World* (1924)

Joe Grim, a small catfish or bullhead, was hooked in the lake north of Stamford at 3:30 Saturday afternoon. He would have been thrown back at once because of his meagerness, but H. 3d [his young son, Heywood Hale Broun], who had assisted in the capture a little, protested. This was his first fish and he wanted to take it home.

The hook remained in the mouth of Joe Grim, and for a time he swung suspended by a loop of line over a nail in the wall of a local cabin. He was then wrapped in tissue paper and placed in a heavy burlap bag on the back seat of a small sedan. The journey to town consumed two hours and a half, and the springs of the car are not so good.

H. 3d also insists that I sat on Joe Grim during the greater part of the journey, but I don't think so. I am pretty sure it was the chocolate cake.

At half-past six Joe was taken out of the burlap bag in the kitchen of the town house, and to the surprise and consternation of all beholders it was observed that he still breathed. Immediately the hook was removed from his mouth, and he was placed in a laundry tub. Once in water, Joe Grim not only revived but swam about furiously, and within half an hour ate a hearty meal of shredded wheat, which was supplied to him at my suggestion, as there were no worms available in the house at the moment.

Joe Grim is still alive and, as far as I can tell, happy. His career has been an inspiration to me. When water was denied to him during the long ordeal in the automobile, he breathed and lived on willpower. His gills clamped tight as iron doors each time that the spirit within him pounded to be let out of torrid torture into the empty glare of nothingness. Perhaps he had been told of cool, green, muddy pools which are eternal. But Joe gasped and choked to hang on to the now which he knew. And after watching this little catfish I feel that anybody is a damn fool to die.

I plan to put Grim into a pail of water and take him back to the lake north of Stamford. Of course, he doesn't actually have to have water. He could sit up on the driver's seat or even wriggle along behind this car, which has a good deal of carbon in the engine. Still, I think a pail of water would be a courtesy.

When Joe Grim gets back to his lake, what tales he will have to tell! After the first month or so I rather fear that he may grow a little tiresome. Because he suffered so much he will inevitably have to garnish his adventure with significance. There will be a moral, a purpose, a philosophy. Perhaps Joe will tell the other bullheads that he fought in a war to end war.

And naturally he will organize. By and by belatedly, he will run for something and be opposed by bullheads who have never ridden in sedans or lived in laundry tubs. This will bring in the religious issues, and Joe will be badly defeated.

However, in his community there need be no protracted period of waiting for the coming of a younger generation, and every new fish born into the lake alive will be compelled to hear at least once the tale of the covered wagon and the trek across the continent. And these little catfish will be allowed to swim close and gaze at the scar across the mouth of old Joe Grim, who fought and bled back in the days when bullheads were bullheads.

Joe has rather dampened my enthusiasm for fishing. Certainly I shall never venture to eat any catfish caught in the lake north of Stamford. If the filet so much as bobbled under the knife I would draw back from the table with the horrible conviction that here again was Joe Grim and that he had somehow survived the frying pan and the bread crumbs.

But even beyond that I am disturbed by the evidence that fish so much want to live on. There is no such passion in my angling. It is not fair that I should thwart and crush great eagerness for existence for the sake of the extremely mild diversion which I get from fishing. They told me that the fish cared very little and that they were cold-blooded and felt no pain. But they were not fish who told me.

Fishing is something less than the duel pictured by the complete angler. The match-making decidedly is open to criticism.

'But sometimes the fish gets away,' explains the angler.

That is not enough. A good draw or, at the very best, a moral victory is the most a fish can expect. The rules should be altered. If there is to be adequate chivalry in the pastime no man should be allowed a rod and line until he has first signed an agreement that every time he fails to pull a hooked fish out of the water he himself will accept and signalize defeat by jumping into the lake. The man gets the fish or the fish gets the man. I can see no other fair way.

And even after my amendment has been adopted there must be a congress to consider justice to the worm. He is exploited by both fish and fishermen. For him there is not so much as the cold comfort of a moral victory. He stakes his life upon a roulette wheel which carries just two numbers. One is zero and the other is double zero. The worm may be taken with the hook or without the hook. You can't expect a worm to get excited about a sport with such limited potentialities as far as he is concerned.

And my experience is that he doesn't get excited. I have seen many a worm carry his complete boredom right into the jaws of an onrushing fish. He will neither fight nor fly. He tries to dignify his death by being sullen about it.

'But,' I can imagine a fish saying in rebuttal, 'your remarks are most unfair. Worming is a truly sporting proposition. Sometimes you don't get the whole worm.'

'It Seems to Me'
There is No Hiding Place
World-Telegram, September 23, 1939

'Senator Borah,' says an editorial in the Hearst papers, 'reveals his own strict neutrality, both as an eminent member of the Senate and as the ranking member of the Senate Foreign Relations Committee, by not mentioning by name the combatants in the European war.'

This, I agree, is the ultimate in isolation. Indeed, it goes all the way back to an ancient tribal taboo under which even the names of individuals were secret lest they fall into the clutches of evil spirits. But no harm could come to Tom or Dick or Harry if the demons had no identifying tag around which they might weave a spell. If there were safety in such a retreat from reality, it would, without question, constitute a magnificent way of life. Death itself could not prevail if its existence might be obliterated by never mentioning it even in whispers. And here would be the sure way to abolish poverty, disease, fear and every other misery known to man. In passing a graveyard the practitioner of this magic would either refer to the place as a conservatory or keep silent. And possibly even the pauper would feel no belly pains if he could only stuff his ears against the sound of words such as 'breakfast,' 'dinner' or 'a crust of bread.'

We might even pretend that Hitler and the guns and bombers over Europe are all part of some nightmare not worth discussion among the wakeful. Keep a stiff upper lip and pinch yourself, and Fascism will fly out the window.

To be sure, this theory was given quite a workout for a number of years in the matter of venereal disease. Nice people never mentioned the maladies. Newspapers co-operated in cutting out all shocking words and gave no space to any stories of the situation in hospitals and homes. Unfortunately, syphilis and gonorrhea did not disappear when sent to Coventry.

And I very much fear that the canker of conflict cannot be cured by the device of pretending that here in America its echoes are quite inaudible.

Only the other day I was rereading *Lost Horizon,* and one episode in Mr Hilton's book had a prophetic quality. I can't remember whether it was included in the motion picture version. You may remember that the head of the monastery was an ancient who had managed to add centuries to his life by an ability to withdraw not only from the world but actually from consciousness during trancelike periods in which there came to his muted senses not even so much as the ticking of a clock. And he urged the hero to follow in his steps. His argument was based upon the fact that the world outside was about to destroy itself and that there should be a small corner of the earth where civilization might be preserved as if in a vacuum. Ideals might be kept alive within that small valley protected by its giant mountains and in a kingdom whose existence was unknown.

It was a romantic conceit. It is a story; there really is no such land and no such valley. The author quite frankly put his tale forward as a fantasy. It would be nice, and all of us, I imagine, might like it very well to dwell with Senator Borah in a big apartment at No. 277 Linden Avenue, Shangri-la, somewhere in Tibet. But there is a man called Hitler. There is a Nazi nation. There is a Russian bear that has stepped beyond his borders – for what purpose time will tell.

It is not a dream that bombs fall from the sky and kill and blister. Buildings burn. Women mourn. It is expedient that we pray and work for peace here at home. It will be well, if it lies within our power, to call the nations out of conflict.

But we will be useless even to our own interests if we close our eyes and pretend our world ends at the misty line where some wooded American hill keeps its rendezvous with the sky. That is not the end of the world or the end of the road. There are sounds louder than the ticking of the clock. Time and space cannot be discarded, nor can we throw off the circumstances that we are citizens of the world. The blood of one is the blood of all. Our Lord dies once again.

The Fifty-first Birthday
Broun's Nutmeg, December 9, 1939

When I woke up the morning of December ninth at seven minutes past nine I found I was fifty-one years old. It would be pleasant but untrue to say that I could detect no change in myself. Calling for a mirror, a dish of ham and eggs and a sloe gin rickey I crawled out of bed more gingerly than usual.

I took the mirror first and was pleased to observe that when held close to my lips a slight mist could be detected upon its bright surface. But upon surveying my entire countenance the glass grew tarnished. I looked like hell and accordingly I quickly changed the order and substituted a second rickey for the slice of ham. At fifty-one it is well to keep a weather eye upon the diet.

Canceling all business appointments, I decided to go back to bed and check up on my spiritual accounts. This, I fear, is a symptom of being past fifty. The tendency to self-examination begins to gnaw in and express itself in the question so long and happily unheeded, 'Did I do right or wrong?' But this self-criticism is sedative rather than tonic because all too often the half-centenarian under cross-examination tends to answer, 'Well, what else would you expect me to do under the circumstances?'

Perhaps this is one of the greatest weaknesses of the aged. We wander about with arched back hoping for a friendly pat from someone who will say, 'Don't let them kid you. I've known worse jerks than you are.'

I've only tried it one way but in my opinion it is better to have your fifty-first birthday drop on your head like a ton of bricks than to have senescence do a sneak-up on you. That, I am told, is the trouble with clean living. Persons afflicted with this complaint enter the icy water a toe at a time. Surely there is less shock in plunging in head first with a high nonny and a hoopla.

Still, if I were a go-getting evangelist I would keep a little list of men who had just passed fifty. They are suckers for any Billy Sunday. When a man is halfway home he begins to fret and ask himself, 'Whatever did I do with my religion?' And often you will find him searching through the clothes closet and turning the pockets of his last year's winter overcoat inside out.

But at fifty-one I have more faith than I ever had before. People are better than I thought they were going to be – myself included. In mere physical exertion there may be some let-up. Instead of the daily constitutional of a hundred yards it will be twenty-five from now on. But at fifty-one I'm a better fighter than at twenty-one. Things which once were just a sort of sentimental solace are now realities. Brotherhood is not just a Bible word. Out of comradeship can come and will come the happy life for all. The underdog can and will lick his weight in the wildcats of the world.

The Last Column
New York Post, December 15, 1939

The horsemen and the footmen are gathering at the capital from many quarters of the country to see the major political event of 1940. I think that they have the correct candidate in mind and the likely party, but why pick on the city of Washington?

The more we announce our repugnance to dictatorial processes, eagerness to avoid these governmental devices may lead us into the very blasphemies which we purport to shun. For instance, it is held that the decision as to whether Mr Roosevelt shall run for a third term can only come after a very definite word from him. I do not agree, although I grant that to a mild extent it is up his alley. The public seemingly was dissuaded from following after the feet of Calvin Coolidge. It was said that Mr Coolidge did not choose to run. You couldn't tell it by his feet. I'm not sure he actually meant it. I think that a small determined band of one man or less might have sneaked up to Calvin's room the night before he refused the nomination and by threatening him that refusal would have meant being ridden into the White House on rails, the young man might have given way to the cowboys. But there were no cowboys.

Now, of course, we know Franklin D. Roosevelt a good deal better than Calvin Coolidge. Indeed, his newspaper mind is singularly open to the convenience of correspondents. Some of them don't think he is going to run, because they don't think he wants to run. A few believe it is more or less a matter of social hygiene. Naturally, anybody who knows anything about it thinks that if he is nominated he will be re-elected, and that's the way to bet.

We do Mr Roosevelt a great disservice by constantly speaking as if the decision to run or not to run were his to make. If you please, that simply isn't in his province. He is a great man, but he is the servant of the people and they will have to tell him what he should do.

Franklin Delano Roosevelt moves about the world as a man with great charm because he has the gift of being able to listen to someone as if he were really paying attention. This piece of good manners is occasionally unfortunate. It flatters men into speeches which are far too long and often convinces a Washington visitor that he has scored a signal point, although in all truth his message was not much appreciated.

But if public men in Washington got together to wager on the basis of their international acumen, I have no doubt that Cordell Hull would play, that Borah could be nagged into it, that Johnson would not abstain, and that Roosevelt would be willing.

Now, if you think of yourself as among the group best situated to lead your country in a particular crisis, it is decidedly an unpatriotic duty to throw that leadership away until you know in which direction it is going.

There seem to be very many evidences now that Roosevelt is less keen for a third term than he was previously. If the chance to act as an international mediator does not come before the conventions of 1940 are held, it is not likely to come at all. And the third term of any American President may be a constant grim-lipped enterprise of keeping our own barbed wire up when it is smashed by passing shell raids. Who wants such a third term in his right senses? Nobody. But to hold the office marks the man in history. Your son, and your son's son can look it up in the almanac, and there it will read, under some farmer's joke, 'I told you,' the boy said, 'that my great-grandfather Fred used to be President of the United States. That's how he got his start. Now he is working in the shops in Wichita.'

Depend upon it, there won't be very much of a show when Roosevelt makes up his mind yes or no on the third term issue. He'll go into a room and there will be three persons there: the President, his better nature and his devotion to his country. That should be a committee quite satisfactory to anyone.

•

JAY E. HOUSE

Jay Elmer House (1870–1936) was born in Plymouth, Illinois, and was self-educated. He started out as a country printer, then became a country editor, and in 1901 he wrote his first newspaper column. He was Republican Mayor of Topeka, Kansas, from 1915 to 1919, and from 1919 until his death he was a syndicated newspaper columnist for the *Philadelphia Public Ledger* and the *New York Evening Post*. Apart from general commentary and 'old ego stuff', he liked to reminisce about his childhood in the rural wilderness and one of his favourite occasional columns took the form of a dialogue between Lash and Bill, a couple of rubes.

Chronology of a Column
From *On Second Thought* (1936)

Column established August, 1901.

First letter saying column is 'slipping' received September, 1901. Similar letters received at intervals of two weeks or less, 1901 to 1932, inclusive.

First letter saying the column is 'funny' received September, 1901.

First letter saying the column is inane and stupid received September, 1901.

Many thousands of letters of both kinds received 1901 to 1932, inclusive.

Pretty Prairie WCTU [Women's Christian Temperance Union] passes resolution condemning the column for its attitude toward public morals and memorializes the Zenith *Morning Star* to discontinue it.

Reporters on the *Morning Star*, in informal convocation, decide the column won't last till Christmas. City editor reported to have said: 'I hope it doesn't; he's a good reporter.'

First letter assailing the columnist for being a tool of the capitalistic interests received September, 1901. They've been coming in ever since at the rate of forty or fifty a year.

First letter accusing the columnist of catering to his employer in order to hold his job received October, 1901. The matter has been a favorite topic with letter-writers ever since.

First abusive anonymous letter received October, 1901. Hundreds of such letters received, 1901 to 1932, inclusive.

State Suffrage Society, in convention assembled, condemns columnist for his facetious attitude toward woman suffrage and expresses the opinion that he is doing his newspaper great harm.

Belief that he is doing his newspaper great harm expressed by many others, 1901 to 1932, inclusive.

Musical Art Society passes resolutions, 1905, condemning the columnist and appoints a committee to visit the publisher to ask him to direct the former's activities into some other channel. The Musical Art Society was more tolerant than most; it didn't ask that the columnist be fired.

Many persons demand that columnist be removed from his job for speaking lightly of the initiative and referendum, the recall, and the recall of judicial decisions, 1908 to 1912, inclusive.

Governor of State demands columnist be fired for stating he had seen liquor sold over a bar in presumedly dry territory, 1911.

Governor summons columnist to give testimony, 1912, and has him committed to jail for refusal to answer.

Columnist released from jail on writ of habeas corpus, 1912.

The Rev. Robert Gordon preaches sermons branding columnist as a menace to society, 1913, 1914, 1915.

Lillian Mitchener Good Government Club assails columnist for his evil practices and associations, 1915.

Courtesies of the Elks Club parlors, where the club held its meetings, withdrawn from it on the ground that it had assailed a brother Elk.

Frank B. Brown condemns columnist for being inimical in his attitude toward union labor, 1915, 1916, 1917, 1918.

Through the efforts of Mr Brown and others, a monster mass-meeting was assembled at the city auditorium with the purpose of forcing the columnist to change his attitude, 1916.

The column is sneered at by the New York intelligentsia, 1920 to 1932, inclusive.

Many persons write the columnist, 1920 to 1932, rebuking him for his attitude toward prohibition and casting reflections on the quality of his citizenship.

The column is sneered at by Communists, 1925 to 1932, inclusive.

The column is sneered at by Socialists, 1905 to 1932, inclusive.

Columnist is branded as unethical and Brookhartian by the Kewanee (Ill.) *Star*, the Webster City (Ia.) *Freeman-Journal*, the *Editor and Publisher* and 197 other journals for writing a private letter in which he stated he had been served liquor in thirteen out of fourteen homes in Zenith, 1929.

Webster City (Ia.) *Freeman-Journal* brands columnist as a spokesman for the Eastern interests, 1928, 1929, 1930.

Thousands of persons write, 1901 to 1932, inclusive, saying they intend to stop taking the paper because of the columnist's connection with it. A total of two persons stop taking it on that account.

Governor of Kansas refutes scandalous stories about drinking in his State and brands columnist as a liar, 1929.

One hundred thousand persons, estimated, tell columnist the column is the only thing they take the paper for, 1901 to 1932, inclusive.

At the rate of one thousand a year, 1901 to 1932, inclusive, clients write to the columnist commending the column for its sanity, its common sense and good humor.

'On Second Thought'
From *On Second Thought* (1936)

A client has written me in part as follows: 'As a person, if you are the smarty show-off which you portray, I shouldn't care for you.' I don't think I'm a smarty or a show-off. I'm a sort of dual personality. Part of the time I'm old John Brown. The remainder of the time I'm Pocahontas. In my writing I am cocky, irreverent and contumacious. That is a calculated attitude derived from judgement and experience. It has the effect of making a lot of people hate me. A columnist may not live on love alone. If he leaves any impression whatsoever upon the world for which he writes, he must occasionally stir some part of his reading clientele to anger and denunciation. Cheers hearten a man. But jeers are just as essential. They help maintain his sense of balance and proportion and keep him whittled down to his actual size.

In my character as old John Brown I stir people up. But when I'm Pocahontas, by which I mean when I am in contact with and in social relation to other people, I'm just a friendly dog, panting from heat and hoping somebody will pat me on the head. I am, it is true, something of an exhibitionist. But my exhibitionism is restrained and in good taste. At least, I think it is.

A man gets an education through assimilation. He acquires a vocabulary in the same way. School and college confer neither upon him. Formal education merely fertilizes the young mind and prepares the seed bed for the growth of knowledge. Because of this preparation the college man, everything else being equal, learns quicker than the one who hasn't gone. The non-college man has a three- or four-year handicap to overcome. He is, in the beginning, about that far back of the college man. By the time he is thirty, perhaps before, he has pulled up even.

My aversion to listening to public speeches probably is in large measure due to the fact that I have heard so many of my own. In one period of two years I gave 415 public talks ranging in length from five to twenty minutes, and they were all bad. Ed Howe once observed that nobody has ever said anything bright or witty into an ear trumpet. I go farther. I say nobody has ever said anything bright or witty over a telephone.

The greatest white team of black-face actors was McIntyre and Heath. Five minutes of McIntyre and Heath was better than ten years of that which now passes for comedy by radio performers. Of course, that is just an opinion, but if anybody tells me the new comedy is better than the old, I shan't bother to argue'with him. We'll shoot it out.

I have always been against government in business for the reason that a government bureau can make the simple feat of reporting one's age and birthplace as complicated as the act of keeping five balls, an Indian Club, a lighted lamp and a horseshoe in the air at one time. An income-tax statement is an example of what I mean. I have tried, always, to make out an honest one. If I am to go to the penitentiary for some trifling error, or some irregular computation, I ask to be sent to Leavenworth. The nights are often cool in Leavenworth and I know a lot of nice people there. They'd send me little gifts of apples and maybe some Indian beadwork. I like apples.

I am tired of motion-picture actresses who claim to be good friends with the husbands they are divorcing. A woman doesn't divorce a friend. She divorces a man she doesn't like.

There has been a good deal of scandalous talk about the younger generation, but it's a wise child that knows more than its parents knew at the same age.

The small-town woman, like the Northwest Mounted, always gets her man. In a city, a man may elude a woman by hiding from her. In a small town there is no place in which a man may hide himself.

Again I caution you that it's not a great life if you don't weaken. It's only a great life if you do weaken. If you question the truth of the foregoing pronunciamento, take a look around at the fellows who never have.

There has recently been a good deal of talk about the insidious effect of contract bridge on conversation. 'People don't talk any more,' they say. 'They just play contract.' The effect on the human mind is supposed to be deleterious. I do not share the general alarm. I was around when contract was whist and the polite card game was euchre. My recollection is that conversation never did amount to much.

It may or may not be worth remembering that had not Ananias shown unusual facility and skill as a liar, he would have been forgotten long ago.

Marriage is a ceremonial which, in many cases, merely reveals to the contracting parties the fact that they could have got along very well without each other.

Old Ego Stuff

From *On Second Thought* (1936)

I have smoked the same brand of cigars for nearly thirty years. They are made in a little factory out West and retail at two for a quarter. I have never found a medium-price cigar anywhere that approached them in excellence. I can sleep soundly for ten or twelve hours and often do so. I do not recall having arisen when I could not have turned over and gone to sleep again. I was the first resident of the Yankee Ridge vicinity to wear a derby and my appearance in one when I was fifteen years old created a good deal of coarse and invidious comment. For some obscure reason the derby, although it is worn by many, has always rested under a cloud. I can cook hardboiled eggs, but that is my only culinary achievement. When I was a boy, somebody was always trying to eat a quail a day for thirty days. It was considered a great sporting event which resulted in many wagers being laid and to which much newspaper publicity was given. I do not know why eating a quail a day for thirty days was considered an achievement and I do not recall that anybody succeeded in performing the feat.

The quail eaters finally were obscured by the celebrated Dr Tanner, who was, I believe, the first man to fast forty days. After Dr Tanner succeeded in his widely advertised feat, many others attempted it. Some of them were successful and thus kept themselves in the headlines for considerable periods of time. I recall that the first thing Dr Tanner asked for at the conclusion of his fast was watermelon. Charles J. Guiteau, who assassinated President Garfield, asked for raspberries on the morning he was hanged and got them.

The *Police Gazette*, which has folded its wings, was almost exclusively a barbershop publication. I never knew anyone, outside a barbershop, who bought it or subscribed to it. Those who wished to read the *Police Gazette* dropped into a barbershop and read it while awaiting their turns. Knickers are to me the most uncomfortable garment. A stiff-bosomed shirt, on the other hand, causes me no discomfort or annoyance whatsoever. When I lived in the very small town of Foster, Mo., a good many years ago, every resident of the town who was anybody owned a silk hat, which he wore on Sundays and holidays. A few of the leading citizens wore silk hats every day. I never succeeded in getting to the bottom of the mystery. It may be that I failed through lack of diligence. There must have been a reason.

I never knew a farmer who said, 'By heck!' On the other hand, I have known any number of farmers whose favorite expletive was 'By gonnies!' Years ago, I owned a bulldog named Kelly. Kelly followed me to the theater, where he would, somehow, elude the doorman and come down the aisle to the seat which I regularly occupied and sit beside me during the performance. He was very well behaved, ordinarily, but would sometimes go into a barking fit when things grew exciting on the stage. He preferred the legitimate drama and would seldom remain through the entire performance of a musical show. An Airedale named David, which I subsequently owned, always escorted me to my streetcar when I went downtown in the morning and always awaited me at the car stop when I returned in the evening. For five or six years after I gave him to a friend and left town he waited for me at the car stop every evening. Everybody else writes about his dogs. Why shouldn't I write about mine? The first time I really got 'into the money' was when a proprietary medicine concern in Indiana paid me $60 a week for gathering testimonials and writing advertising copy.

I do not attempt to account for the decrease in the amount of wild game. All I know is that I am not responsible for it. I have never paid to see a wrestling match, and my alibi for the few occasions on which I have accepted complimentary tickets is that my presence was obligatory and that I was there in a professional capacity. I shall do nothing to secure the passage of a law imposing a penalty on those who attend wrestling matches, but I think there should be such a law. The conversation of half the people I know is as futile as that of 'Lash and Bill.' And that goes for much of my own conversation. In my boyhood the favorite Kansas lubricant was alcohol diluted with water and sweetened with as much rock candy as a given portion would dissolve. The favorite drinking places were in the shade of hedgerow or the back stalls of livery stables. Blackberry brandy ran diluted alcohol a fairly close second.

I don't happen to enjoy horseback riding and I wish people would stop telling me what fine exercise it is. They're just wasting breath and my time. The pitching bronchos which I 'forked' in an earlier day spoiled horseback riding for me for all time. I didn't have a very high opinion of baseball umpires, either, until after I tried to umpire a couple of small-time professional baseball teams. I have been wholly unable to understand why it is called the busy bee. A bee works six weeks in a year and loafs comfortably in its hive the balance of the time.

The saxophone has been around longer than most people imagine. The first one I saw was in the instrumentation of the Pittsfield (Ill.) Silver Cornet Band in 1891. It took the saxophone quite a while to get into society, but it finally made it. In my very brief experience in a brass band I played the second tenor horn. You can't get any lower than that – in a band. In that day it was equivalent to playing right field on a baseball team. Right field has become a position of considerable importance. They used to let anybody play it.

I'm glad the tailcoat is coming back, being one of those who can wear tails without exciting invidious comment. Another thing I long for is the opera hat. I used to get untold enjoyment out of 'plopping' an opera hat. But I never was any good at marbles nor better than a very mediocre croquet player. What I have always liked to do best, and what I am better at than anything else, is nothing at all. Domestic geese shed their quill feathers every year. Probably wild geese do so, although I am unable to speak authoritatively on the matter. When I was a boy on a farm there was a story that goose quills could be sold for five cents a dozen. I followed the geese around one spring and picked up sixty quills, but I was unable to find a market for them. I don't believe there was any such market.

George Washington's fortune has been growing every year since I began reading abut it. When I first heard of the Washington fortune, now some forty years ago, it was estimated at $100,000. The most recent estimate of it that I have read is $4,000,000. Would it not be a good idea to settle upon some satisfactory figure and stick to it? Palpably, for two or three generations back the young have been habitually misled concerning Washington's money. A caller just paid me the compliment of saying, 'I don't see how you do it every day.' I have to do it every day. They'd have me back covering 'police' if I didn't. I don't want one created especially for my benefit – it shall never be said of me that I encouraged crime – but I'd like to report a good murder trial again. The first newspaper writing I ever did was reporting the trial of Willie Sells for the murder of his family. I was a boy in the back shop of the Grigsby City *Clarion*. The editor told me I might as well lay off and attend the trial. 'You'll do it anyway,' he said. So I got the job of reporting it for a Kansas City paper. The check in payment for my labor was $35. When I got the check I didn't suppose I'd ever have to work again. I thought I had all the money in the world.

There's no use pretending; I don't like artichokes. I'm not even sure I like broccoli. I was recently offered two pianos as a gift, but the condition attached made it impossible to accept. If I took one I had to take both. I might find room for one piano, but I can't possibly find room for two. I was sorry to disoblige the lady, but the dimensions of my apartment are fixed and immutable. On a train recently I saw four men playing seven-up. But even seven-up has felt the influence of the jazz age and is the worse for it. They now play it with the joker in the deck. And that reminds me that I, too, have succumbed to the influences of the jazz age. I've forgotten how to play euchre.

And crokinole, which is never heard of nowadays! Well do I remember the winter Cottonwood Falls went wild over the game. I will do anything within reason, but I positively will not embark on any enterprise, pleasurable or otherwise, through which I am compelled to put up a tent in which to sleep at night. Cooking picnics do not attract me, either.

To the Ladies

From *On Second Thought* (1936)

'Why are you so sarcastic about women?' writes one of them. Well, we aren't. We're just truthful as we see the truth. We say it to their faces instead of behind their backs. It is a sort of habit now, but we suspect that in the beginning we were prompted by an ulterior motive. Somehow we discovered that the best way to attract and hold the attention of women was to tell them the truth about themselves. A columnist must live. Or at the least, he wants to live. To do so he must attract attention from somebody.

We may say, by way of putting out a backfire, that we greatly admire women. They are the salt and savor of existence. They are life's fragrance and much of its beauty. But we do not worship them; we just like and appreciate them. And we think that any gent who does worship them is a good deal of a sucker.

Women who think much about it, or think about it at all, have an exaggerated idea of themselves. For this the hypocrisy of the men and their lack of courage are largely responsible. It is the conventional thing to respect and venerate women and place them on a pedestal. It is a sort of pseudo-gallantry which the average man affects because he thinks it is the thing to do. Privately he may detest a woman, but publicly he bows low and kisses her feet. He is afraid somebody will talk about him if he doesn't.

The truth about women probably is that they are no better than men. They are no more honest, no more patriotic, no more concerned about public or private welfare. A government by women would be no better than a government by men. The chances are it wouldn't be as good. Government, after all, is the science of organization and getting along with it. Women lack something of the faculty of men for organization. Men get along with each other. Women don't. Therefore men will always direct affairs, and because they are better constituted to direct affairs they should do so.

There comes a time in the life of a majority of women when their hands, in a manner of speaking, lie idly in their laps. For them the hard drive of domestic life is over. To a considerable extent they have paid their obligation to it. Their children are reared and probably married and out of the way. The interests which have held them are measurably discharged. But such a woman cannot sit idly by. She must do something. And so she goes in either for culture or for doing good. The probability is that she will go in for doing good. Her idea of doing good is to reform the men. She joins an organization – or a dozen organizations – with that end in view. Thereafter she is busy and, if it were not for her continual contemplation of the horrible atrocities committed by men, she might be happy. But, men being what she thinks they are, she rarely is happy.

We don't know, nobody knows, how many such organizations there are. All that is known is that they run into legions. We don't object to them. Of a fact, our attitude is encouraging. We want everybody to be happy. If women are not exactly happy in their reform and uplift work, they at least have the consciousness of having tried to do their duty by humanity as they see it. And that, we are sure, is one grand feeling, although we have never experienced it. If we, now and then, laugh softly at their efforts – if we giggle a little at their attempts to enlarge triviality to the stature of vital and significant issues – that is good for them. That is to say, it would be good for them if they paid any attention to it. It might prevent them from taking themselves too seriously, and nothing is so fatal to effective results as a too-serious approach.

At any rate, all we have ever contended in respect to women's activities in the larger affairs of life is that they should first reform the women. After that, if they have any time left, they may go ahead and tackle the men.

One of the conventions to which most men subscribe is that no gentleman may speak ill of a woman. We'll accept that convention if we may enlarge it to read: 'No gentleman may speak ill of a man or a woman.' And after a little meditation, we have decided to ask that another amendment be added to the foregoing admonition. It is that no woman shall speak ill of another woman. Men bound to each other by the ties of close personal friendship do not publicly criticize each other. Nearly every woman's friend criticizes her to others. We suggest that a society or association be formed to discourage and, if possible, to abolish the practise of publicly clawing at each other indulged in by women between whom friendships exist.

Again may we observe, we aren't sarcastic about women. To us women are grand. But we find we get along better with them by just being ourself. And that is a good code of conduct for any company, male or female. We don't feel any of the mock heroics which so many men affect in their contacts with the attractive sex and we don't pretend to feel them. We do try to be polite and friendly and companionable. And it is our theory that what women like in men is frankness and honesty, not flattery.

•

WALTER MURDOCH

Sir Walter Murdoch (1874–1970) was born in Aberdeenshire, Scotland, and went to Melbourne, Australia, in 1884, where he completed his education at that city's university. After graduating he worked as a private tutor and schoolmaster. In 1904 he became a lecturer in English at his alma mater and in 1912 he was appointed to the chair of English at the newly established University of Western Australia, at Perth. In 1905 he started contributing a weekly column, 'Books and Man' (signed Elzevir), to the *Argus*. He continued this until 1913 and resumed it in 1919, carrying on until 1938. He was also a prolific free-lance reviewer under a variety of pseudonyms, a contributor to the *Western Australian* as well as the *Argus*, and a broadcaster. Over the years his newspaper columns were collected in several books and five of them were combined in his *Collected Essays* (1938). A further collection, *My 100 Answers* (1960), contained a series of essays in miniature from his *Melbourne Herald* syndicated column. From a Presbyterian background, Murdoch was a liberal humanist who attacked pretension and the 'suburban spirit', and subscribed to 'the sacred duty of growling'. His great-nephew is the media magnate Rupert Murdoch.

Our Prominent Citizens
From *Moreover* (1932)

Sometimes, in a mood betwixt merriment and malice, I like to toy with the thought of certain high and puissant personages – prominent citizens, of immense importance in their own little day and in their own little world – coming back to the earth where they strutted so pompously, to learn for themselves how they are honoured by posterity. What tremendous surprises there would be! What gnashing of teeth!

It is pleasing, for instance, to see incredulity, stupefaction, dismay, and chagrin chase one another across the solemn countenance of Sir Thomas Lucy as it is borne in upon his dull mind that his name would have been wholly blotted out from men's remembrance had it not been for an obscure young scapegrace from Stratford, who is supposed (on the flimsiest of evidence) to have poached on his preserves.

Or, again, one's delighted fancy plays with the picture of the placid, smiling, self-satisfied face of Sir William Temple, statesman, diplomat, scholar, squire, political thinker, writer of polished prose, finest of fine gentlemen, all rolled into one. 'I was a world's wonder,' his face seems to say; 'whoever is forgotten, I, at least, must be remembered by the planet of which I was so conspicuous an ornament.' Certainly, your honour; of course you are remembered; but not for your statesmanship or your scholarship or your rounded periods (which nobody now reads), or your urbane manners; for these things none of us cares a doit. You are remembered for the sake of a delightful girl who wrote you some charming letters before she was eccentric enough to marry you; and you are remembered still better for the sake of a quiet, inconspicuous young man who acted for some years as your amanuensis – a somewhat pallid youth, a dyspeptic, with disagreeable manners; his name – which may very well have slipped your memory, you have so many grand friends to recall – was Jonathan Swift.

Or, once more, do but look at yonder magnate; grave, soberly clad, ceremonious; plainly a man of consequence and authority. He seems surprised and a little pained that you do not at once take off your hat to him. 'Has the world lost all its manners, all its respect for the eminent?' he asks. 'Surely you know me? The world's memory must be indeed short if I am forgotten. I flatter myself I was, in my time, not the least of England's merchant princes. As Chairman of the East India Company for the first twenty years of the nineteenth century, I swayed the destinies of Empire, and –' 'But

I say, I say – hold on a minute; this is really interesting. The first twenty – why, good heavens! You must have been there in Lamb's time!' 'Lamb – what sort of a lamb? What in the world are you talking about?' 'Why – yes, of course – Lamb was a clerk in the India House – accountancy branch – during those very years. Perhaps you can tell me some new story about him, or even remember some jokes he made. This is really thrilling!' 'God bless my soul, sir, do you imagine that I – I who directed the counsels of the Company – knew the name of every pettifogging quill-driver in the Company's employ, and listened to their miserable jokes?' 'Oh, well, I'll look up Lamb's *Life and Letters* and see if your name is mentioned . . .' At this the magnate flies back, indignant, to the shades.

Once more – does it not strike you as queer, to say the least of it, that a poor devil of a Paris university student, who seldom had enough to eat, who had less than no morals, whose companions were thieves and murderers and their appropriate womenfolk – a grimy fifteenth-century *apache* who happened to have the knack of making verses – should be the one man of his time and country to achieve immortality, and that for his sake, and for his sake only, so many grave and pompous and tremendous seigneurs of the day should be given a kind of minor immortality? And not only such big-wigs, but a number of disreputable little-wigs as well, have climbed into remembrance on this youth's lean shoulders. What, but for him, should we know or care about that gallows crew – about Master Guy Tabarie, or about Colin des Cayeul (described in the documents as *fortis operator crochetorum*, a powerful operator of picklocks), or about Regnier de Montigny, the best-born and blackest-hearted scoundrel of the gang? They swung on gibbets, all that precious company; and, by all accounts, deserved no better fate. They were not even distinguished criminals; they were squalid, commonplace ruffians, and there is no earthly reason why their names should be known to anybody today except that their companion in iniquity was one of the great poets of the world. For his sake, too, we remember his poor old mother, whom he seems to have loved even while he was breaking her heart with his ill-doings, and for whom he made the great Ballade; and the good priest who adopted him, gave him his name, educated him, and forgave him seventy and seven times. And for his sake – coming back to my point – we remember the various bishops and magistrates and other exalted personages who presided at his trials and condemned him to the greater and the lesser torture, and, having condemned, incontinently dismissed him from their lordly minds. What would they think, I repeat, if they came back to earth and found their names remembered, not at all for their own sweet sakes, but because for a moment they crossed the path of a lean and desperate cutpurse who made scandalous rhymes, by name François Villon?

'Take physic, pomp,' says the disillusioned Lear; and this is the physic for you, O people of importance; the right purge for your high-blown pride. This is that honest mirror for magistrates, that candid looking-glass wherein whoso gazes will see clearly his own complete insignificance. This is the primer from which you great ones of the earth may learn humility; and it has lessons for us obscure nonentities as well; for we are apt to let ourselves be foolishly irritated by the ineffable airs you give yourselves – till we remember that Time and Death set all to rights, and that in a century or less you will be as entirely forgotten as we ourselves, unless our names, yours or ours, happen by some quaint accident to be embalmed in a footnote to the biography of one of the real immortals.

•

BOB DAVIS

Robert Hobart Davis (1869–1942) was born in Brownsville, Nebraska, the son of a missionary clergyman who had come from New England to minister to the Indians. He was brought up on the prairies and at the age of fifteen he travelled to Carson City, Nevada, where he worked for his older brother (older by twenty-five years), who was the publisher of the *Carson City Daily Appeal*. His $5-a-week job was to deliver the paper to its 300 subscribers, who were spread along an eight-mile road. To ease this burden he reached an agreement with a local livery stable to do his round on their unbroken mustangs. By nineteen he had acquired the skills of a compositor and he moved to San Francisco, where he worked successively as a reporter on the *Chronicle*, the *Call*, the *Examiner* and the *Bulletin*. In 1896 he went to New York where he obtained a job on the *New York Journal* under Arthur Brisbane, but it had always been his ambition to work for Pulitzer's New York *World* and in 1898 he won a one-story contract with the Sunday *World* to write an exposé of the Beef Trust and its provisions of rotten meat to American soldiers in the Spanish–American War. In 1903, by which time he had become managing editor of the *New York Sunday News*, he was lured to join Pulitzer's *Morning World*. Before long, however, he was recruited by the magazine magnate Frank Munsey as fiction editor for all his titles and in this capacity over the next decade and a half he saw the launch of *All Story Magazine*, *Scrap Book*, *Railroad Man's Magazine*, *Woman*, *The Ocean*, *The Live Wire* and *The Cavalier*.

In 1925 Munsey decided to make Davis into a roving reporter for the *New York Sun*. When Munsey died later that year, his successor, William Dewart, confirmed Davis as the *Sun*'s peripatetic columnist: 'The whole world is your assignment. My only instructions are that you see everything and write about it in your own vein. To you in the future this whole earth is to be a local story.' Davis's column, which was called 'Bob Davis Recalls' and, later, 'Bob Davis Reveals', ran three times a week on the editorial page from 1925.

'Bob Davis Recalls'
Diamond Jim Brady's Costly Gesture to a Bride
New York Sun, June 16, 1927

In a recent issue of the *New Yorker* appeared an article from the pen of Morris Markey, in which the life of James Buchanan Brady, otherwise 'Diamond Jim,' was presented with skill and grace. Viewed as a biography, it was quite enough and revealed the monumental jewel exhibit to the present generation impartially. Aside from the fact that Mr Brady was born in dire poverty and died fabulously rich in precious stones, it was evident that it required a lapidary instead of a valet to get him in and out of his wearing apparel.

Mr Markey also stated that Diamond Jim was an abstemious man. And so he was – but at what price!

What follows is probably the only unpublished chapter in the life of that famous tee-totaler. Pardon this digression, but it is necessary to go back to the year 1906, at which period a socially prominent New Yorker made a pilgrimage with Homer Davenport to the Arabian desert in search of fine horses. After six months' absence the travelers returned with four stallions. Davenport retired to his stock farm at Morris Plains, New Jersey, while his companion announced his engagement to a beautiful New York débutante.

Shortly thereafter the wedding day was set and the usual preparations were made for one of those quaint ceremonies known as a bachelor's farewell dinner. It was to be along heroic lines of parsimony.

To me fell the delightful responsibility of arranging the banquet, which was to provide for sixteen covers.

'Go as far as you like,' said the groom-to-be with a grand wave of the hand, 'and make it memorable. Think up something novel. Everything in season or out of season is yours to command. There is just one point to keep in mind. Diamond Jim Brady is one of the guests, and never took a drink of intoxicating liquor in his life.'

'What shall we have for him, a quart of bluing?' I asked. 'No. A gallon of orange juice, his favorite beverage. Otherwise it's up to you.'

After twenty-four hours of deep thought I formulated the gigantic idea of seating the guests in a circle, the center of which would be occupied by a miniature reproduction of the Arabian desert, a waste of sand across which camel trains would be seen heading for an oasis. Among the dunes Arab tents were to be set, tribesmen riding fiery steeds, spears tipped with banners placed on the yellow ridges, jackals prowling, groups of nomads camped here and there. The scene was set upon an enormous pane of French glass, over which, in clean yellow sand, the conformation of the desert was laid. From a property man in one of the theaters I secured a whole tribe of lead Arabs, toy tents, tropical trees, prancing horses and lumbering camels. Wherever a tent was pitched we brushed the sand away so that the glass showed through. Underneath small electric light bulbs were stationed so that after turning out the room clusters there remained only a faint suggestion of bivouacs in the ghostly desert night. It was just such an elaborate and perfect creation as Max Reinhardt or Belasco or Urban would have worked out had they been invited. It seemed a pity that only sixteen people in the whole city of New York were to sit around that achievement. The center of the table being open allowed us room to adjust the electrical paraphernalia, all of which were concealed by the undulating yellow sand.

The place selected for the banquet was the old Delmonico restaurant at Twenty-sixth Street and Fifth Avenue, taken over at that time by J. B. Martin; second floor, in the small dining room overlooking Madison Square. It required only two days to set a desert scene that looked at least a million years old. An hour before the guests arrived we gave J. B. a rehearsal and convinced him that we held the Arabian country in the hollow of our hands. If the great Englishman Lawrence could have gazed upon that scene he would undoubtedly have written a better book. However . . .

At the spot certified for the use of Diamond Jim Brady I caused to be set a one-gallon cut-glass pitcher, full to the curved lip, of golden orange juice. There were other juices for other guests, and so on ad infinitum.

At eight o'clock the guests were admitted to the banquet room. Four hours elapsed between the first and the last toasts. It was a rare farewell to bachelorhood, a night of friendly declarations. The guests saluted the groom. A young man lifted his glass and held it high.

'Your health and the happiness of the bride. To your fortune and to her beauty I drink this toast.' He drained the chalice. 'And none other lip shall touch this shimmering rim; none other hand shall hold this stem aloft. I have spoken.' He broke the glass in twain and threw it into the sand. That was the signal for similar manifestations of finality. Glass after glass was broken and added to the discard. It sounded like a barrage of exploding electric light bulbs. Mr James Brady caught the contagion and picked up his supply of orange juice.

'Let's make it a loving cup,' he rumbled, and straightaway tossed a fifteen-pound cut-glass pitcher and two quarts of its soft drink into the heart of the palm-lined oasis. There was a crash of vast dimensions. The Arabian desert cracked into two sections and a sand storm broke into space. The whole tribe, including horses, camels, tents and banners, pitched headlong into the gaping chasm on an avalanche of falling sand. The electric light equipment short-circuited and spat three static protests, leaving the room in darkness. Somebody started for the door and collided with a stand of imported wine glasses, decanters and objects of the drinking art. Chairs began to crack, electroliers fell prone and serving tables splintered. Remarks were made, but to nobody in particular; just made, that's all. Somebody struck a match and fifteen other gentlemen followed that light into the hall, where a dozen waiters stood transfixed. Cab, sir? Cab, sir?

I remained to explain and asked for the account. Tomorrow the estimate would be ready. The bill for the sixteen covers was a-plenty, whereas the item of $485 for 'incidentals' seemed to be trivial for what occurred during that one minute of darkness.

For a teetotaler Diamond James Brady put on quite a show.

'Bob Davis Reveals'
Over-eating on the High Seas

From People, People Everywhere! Footprints of a Wanderer (1936)

On the Rolling Deep

Once upon a time John L. Sullivan [world champion bare-knuckle fighter 1882–93], suffering from a fit of temporary indigestion, summoned the head waiter and spake as follows: 'I've got to lay off on the grub. The paunch can't stand being packed like a full house. Get me the breakfast card and I'll show you where to make the first cut.'

The flunky complied with that alacrity which the Boston Boy required of all his servitors.

'Now put your fingers on the spot where it says "Corned beef hash." '

'Here it is, sir,' replied the man with the menu, 'seventeenth line from the prunes.'

'All right,' said the then retired champion, 'what follows on the four next lines? Hurry up.'

'Broiled tripe, veal cutlet, chipped beef in cream and Salisbury steak so called.'

'What's Salisbury steak?'

'Hamburger.'

'The hell it is?' queried the gladiator, for the moment startled. 'If that's the case, why don't you call it that? Now listen, young feller, just cut out them four lines from the hash to the hamburger and bring me everything above 'em and below 'em. Yours Truly, John L. Sullivan, is going on a diet.'

Despite the threat to push his chair back from the table, when this noblest Roman of them all passed out of the picture, he tipped the slab at 270 pounds and girthed fifty inches. So much for Sullivan.

Now let us look into the valiant gastronomic performances of those who go down to the sea in ships, not the captain, the crew and the midshipmite, but the passengers who enter the dining salon or eat in their berths, and crash the snacks at eleven a.m. and four p.m., to say nothing of the sandwich bunkers piled in the bar-room when the witching hour draws near.

During all of my 300,000-odd miles sailing the bosom of the deep, in all zones and on every ocean (regardless of my esteem for good cooking, wherever it may be found), I am filled with wonderment as to why at least seventy-five percent of these floating gluttons escape foundering or how they foil actual starvation when at home. No man or woman residing ashore could possibly by the widest stretch of imagination consume – or even pay for – the quantity of food parked in the abdominal cavity by the average mortal on shipboard. After carefully surveying the activities of these hapless wretches, who will live to regret – if they are not overtaken by apoplexy – I attribute their baneful indulgence to the economic fact that the original cost of a steamship ticket includes all the provender a traveler can pack into his digestive tract.

There are flashes of ironic humor in the excuses behind which these cormorants take refuge for their indiscretions: 'The sea air gives me an appetite.'

'At last I can now take time to have breakfast in bed.'

'A cup of bouillon and a biscuit at eleven in the morning whets one's appetite for lunch.'

'I never used to care for afternoon tea. Now I'm rather looking forward to it.'

'They tell me that an empty stomach is an invitation to seasickness.'

'Thank heaven for refrigeration and cold storage. One need have no fear of ptomaine.'

Buoyed up by the conviction that no speed regulations impede, the tourist with both feet on the accelerator rolls down the broad highway, adding weight, blood pressure and minor symptoms that flesh is heir to; onward to the inexorable hour when in the words of Spenser: '. . . His belly was upblown with luxury, and eke with fatness; swollen were his eyne.'

A majority of these sufferers, left to their own devices or restrained by the high cost of living, would on their native heath be quite content with a diet of coffee and rolls, ham and eggs, one roast, vegetables in season and bread pudding or a piece of pie for sweets.

If handed a bill, at à la carte prices, for what they consume on an ocean liner, three-fourths of the passengers would jump overboard and swim ashore with the speed of porpoises. These are they who, given opportunity, willingly tax their constitutions but resist to the bitter end a tax upon their purse.

A man whose whole life has been lived in an environment of frugality and self-denial will step up to a cold buffet in the grand dining room and in the manner of a piano virtuoso, with both hands spread in full octaves, point out four cold cuts, two salads, one deviled egg, one stuffed sweet citron and two kinds of cheese with a single jab.

I have seen whole families double-shoot the menu from soup to nuts, with hunks of pie carrying a load of ice cream towering like the Taj Mahal and then, as though fearing a famine, carry away to their state-rooms an assortment of fresh fruit and whatever bon-bons and raisin clusters had escaped the main event.

It is not unusual to see a thin woman, accustomed to a meager bill of fare at home, let go all holds of herself at sea and shoot the works at table. Woe betide the waiter who draws a first-trip-at-sea female who finds herself immune to mal de mer. In catch-as-catch-can wrestling with a menu she can qualify as a devouring angel ready and willing to compete for the world's diamond belt at catch-weight eating.

After a novitiate of from four to six days, depending upon weather, previous experience and downright resistance, it finally dawns upon those who are not absolute morons, that with but one mouth and a single digestive apparatus, human greed sooner or later must face the limit beyond which none may proceed without paying the high penalty exacted for rapacity.

It is far better to eke out with John L. Sullivan's repudiated corned beef hash and let it go at that, than to wander down the primrose paths above, below and into the mysterious purlieus of the culinary frontier which mortal man wots not of save at his peril, the banishment of pleasant dreams and the acquisition of composure that is denied the overfed.

'Bob Davis Recalls'
Details of How I Twice Saved a Goddess of Liberty
From *Over My Left Shoulder* (1926)

In presenting this hitherto unpublished fragment of history it is necessary for me to go back to Park Row, which I infested during the declining hours of the nineteenth century. At that time the wage scale for reportorial work was $7.50 a column. Exclusive matter unearthed by a quill-driver working under his own steam brought as high as $15, with extra kudos for pictures. Small wonder that we pried into the day's doings in the hope of uncovering buried gold.

One afternoon while basking in the studio of the late John LaFarge on Tenth Street I learned that the model who posed for Bartholdi's statue of Liberty Enlightening the World had arrived in America and was residing in a modest apartment house uptown. That was enough. I had visions of not less than four columns of text and illustrations to the tune of $60. What a story!

'THE GODDESS OF LIBERTY ALIVE AND IN THE US.'

It was a frightfully hot August day, but I lost no time hastening to the address.

Unfortunately the apartment was on the fourth floor and the premises lacked an elevator. Nevertheless, I puffed up to the eyrie, to which I was admitted by a statuesque, large-boned lady, who was unquestionably at one time a beautiful woman. There still remained certain professional graces discernible even to my unpracticed and inartistic eye. At once I made clear the purposes of my call and became comfortable in a wicker chair by an open window.

'It is with the regret that I am not able to be of service,' said she in broad French accents, 'for it is not true that I posed for your beautiful statue in this New York harbor. It is that I come here to see your fair land only. Many American artists to me known in Paris speak well of America, so it is here I am at last. A model in the atelier of M. Julian? *Oui.* In the studio of Bartholdi? No. Still I am resemble the Goddess of Liberty.'

She shrugged her manly shoulders and folded her blacksmith's arms with a serene air. Had the bronze statue looking out to sea fallen from its granite pedestal I could not have been more disappointed. But 'twas all in the day's work, so I made preparation to depart. 'No, no,' I must partake of refreshments. From a tin ice-box my hostess produced a block of ice cream, some lady fingers and a bowl of nectarines, which fruit, by the way, affects me as nesting partridges work on a pointer.

While we sat there reviewing the world's art or touching modestly on the low cost of modeling in the local studios, the faint odor of smoke assailed my nostrils. There seemed no immediate cause for alarm, so I consumed two more nectarines and another slice of ice cream. The smell of burning wood grew stronger. Catacornered from where I sat I could see the kitchen, in the far end of which was a dumbwaiter with the door half open. From the shaft I discerned a thin feather of smoke emerge lazily and curl into the room. Leaning back in my chair to get a better view, I saw a heavy, black puff billow up, mushroom and follow in its wake. Here was genuine cause for alarm.

'*Madame,*' I said, summoning all my reserve, 'if you have any valuables or papers that you wish to save, secure them at once and come with me.'

'Come with you, *monsieur?*' she said frigidly. 'Why?'

'Because this building is on fire,' I replied.

A puff of smoke crossed the threshold.

'*Mon Dieu!*' shrieked the visiting model, throwing up her heroic arms and falling full length on the floor. She collapsed with all the resiliency of half a refrigerated beef. There was no time for restoratives, no occasion for delay, no just cause for desertion. I hauled her upward, got my shoulder under the still shapely waist and staggered to the door, seizing my straw hat in transit. Out into the narrow hallway and down the first flight I bore her, visualizing the red demon roaring up the dumbwaiter shaft. The idea of rescuing a lady who resembled the Goddess of Liberty steeled me to go on. At the second landing my straw hat fell off and got under my feet. I kicked it away, but it came back and entangled me. All the way down that cheap lid impeded my movements. I stepped into it and out of it a dozen times, rending and ripping its beauty with each stride. I began to perspire like a sprinkling cart. At the next landing the hat with almost human intelligence actually made the turn with me, and the more to cement our association the rim slid up my leg. I went slowly downward with the model, from step to step, the fragments of the villainous hat still pursuing. As I approached the ground floor I saw through a reek of sweat that almost blinded me a figure at the foot of the stairs staring up in wonderment. Little did he know that Hercules the Second was almost all in.

'Vot you doing mit dot voman?'

'Saving her life,' I snorted. 'The place is on fire.'

'Ach! Dot is der smoke from der basement furnace. Every vonce in a vhile it does dot. Take her back.'

The comely cargo stirred and sighed her entire length. What a situation. There was I in a most imbecile role masquerading as a hero. I had saved her life to all intents; now I had to save her reputation. Oh, very well! Turning, I started back to the fourth story with the lady recovering consciousness. At the second landing she began to swoon again. She appeared by that time to be fainting in installments.

All the way back I stumbled on the fragments of my straw hat, scattered up and down the stairway. It was like climbing into a hayloft. I arrived at last at her apartment. I dropped her ungallantly on a sofa, opened all the windows to let out the harmless smoke, ate the cool remaining nectarines and left the place for ever.

When I got to the street a total stranger gave me the once over and asked me why I wasn't wearing a hat. 'The first thing you know,' he volunteered, 'sunstroke will do its dirty work and then: Nutty. Go get yourself a lid.'

'It may be news to you, Mister, but I am already nutty,' said I coldly, 'and so far as hats are concerned I just kicked a perfectly good one down four flights of stairs – and up again.'

●

ROBERT LYND

Robert Wilson Lynd (1879–1949) was born in Belfast, the second of seven children. His father was a Presbyterian priest and his mother was the daughter of a minister. He was educated at the Royal Academical Institute and Queen's College, Belfast, but whereas his family background was Unionist, he became a Nationalist and a Socialist. In 1908 he became the assistant literary editor of the *Daily News* and in 1913 its literary editor, contributing a light essay to the paper on Saturdays. At the same time he started writing a weekly essay for the *New Statesman*. In a 'New Statesman Retrospect' in April 1934 he was able to look back on twenty-one years of writing weekly articles of approximately 1,500 words each for the *New Statesman*. He began in 1912 as a book reviewer and a couple of months later started writing regular 'middles' (i.e. middle articles, which appeared between the leading articles and the reviews). At first, these 'middles' were a cross between an essay-column and an editorial, unsigned and using the editorial 'we'. During the First World War, however, Lynd abandoned the editorial 'we' and began to sign his articles 'X.', later changing this to 'X.X.', and later still (because 'X.X.' was the name of a brand of stout) to 'Y.Y.' Kingsley Martin, his editor for many years, described his column as 'neither wholly literary nor political but almost as good as Lamb', while Leonard Woolf said that Lynd was 'one of those impeccable journalists who every week for thirty or forty years turn out an impeccable essay ... like an impeccable sausage about anything or everything or nothing'. He carried on writing his weekly column until 1945 when he joined the staff of the *News Chronicle* as a book reviewer and essayist. He also wrote literary essays under the pseudonym 'John O'London' for *John O'London's Weekly*. His columns were published in thirty book collections between 1908 and 1945.

Changing One's Mind
From *In Defence of Pink* (1937)

Lord Balfour towards the end of his life told his niece, Mrs Dugdale (who has written his biography), that, looking back, he could remember having changed his opinion about scarcely anything. When I read this, I could not help wondering whether he was to be envied or not. Nothing surely could make a man more serenely happy than to feel that in the crises of his own or his country's life he was nearly always right. You may think that this would lead to complacency, but complacency, though widely condemned by the moralists, is at least a very agreeable sensation. The man who has never seen cause for changing his opinions lives in the sunshine of his own rightness, and this is reflected in his disposition. Even in the hour of defeat, it is something to know that one is right. In the hour of victory, it is intoxicating – at times almost fatally so.

Yet who that has changed one of his opinions after another looks back longingly to the opinions he has abandoned? Most of us are inclined to congratulate ourselves rather on having escaped from folly into wisdom. We look back to our early tastes in literature, for example, and feel no regret in having got rid of a good number of them. There are, I suppose, people who are born with perfect taste – who never worshipped an idol with feet of clay – but they are rare even among the fastidious. For, especially when one is young, there are all sorts of reasons for enjoying books that have nothing to do with good taste. If one is a pious child, one can enjoy a poorly enough written story about the dying ten-year-old son of a burglar, at the end of which the hard heart of the parent melts into a Christian softness. I have been moved by many such stories, and thought them better literature at the age of ten than I think them now. I have also changed my opinion about the excellence of penny dreadfuls, and I do not rate Marie Corelli and Hall Caine quite so high as I rated them in the early nineties. Kipling became a god to me for half a dozen years; then, chiefly for political reasons, he became a vulgar rhetorician; finally, passions having cooled, I could enjoy his humour and his imaginative energy and cease to care what his opinions on politics were. This, I think, is a normal process in our taste for books. We come to lose interest in what we once loved passionately, and we come to love passionately what once bored us.

I remember how many attempts I made to read *David Copperfield* before I could get on with it. Even though I had liked others of Dickens's novels, I found *David Copperfield* heavy going. I persevered, however, and suddenly one day broke through into an enchanted world. When once you are converted to *David Copperfield*, I doubt whether you can ever change your opinion about it again. To the end of life it remains one of the six greatest novels. I found no similar need to change my opinion about Scott and Thackeray; I liked them from the beginning, and though I no longer like them so extravagantly, I still hate to hear them belittled. Jane Austen, on the other hand – what girlish stuff she seemed to be to a schoolboy just learning to smoke in the prime, so to speak, of manhood! It took me a long time to enjoy the niceties of Jane Austen.

Looking back, indeed, I see my life as one long series of changes of opinion. I remember when I thought the verse of Mr W. B. Yeats all but nonsense, and how it was succeeded by a time when I worshipped him. I remember the ecstasy and, after that, the boredom, of reading Swinburne. I remember when Emerson changed from a prophet into one of the great unread. One cannot help feeling a little sad at times at the thought of all the great writers one has deserted. One feels that one owes a certain loyalty to writers who once lit up the world for one, and that there is an element of treachery in neglecting them. How pleasant it is to open one of their books now and then, and to be able to feel, while rereading it: 'Yes, he's good – not so good as I once thought him, but still good.' But even then, the old rapture can seldom be rekindled. Whitman, Emerson and Carlyle – they remain men of genius, but not on the old gigantic scale. That, perhaps, is the penalty of having mingled didacticism with literature. We become sated with the teaching till we have no more appetite for it. Even Swinburne was in his way a teacher – a teacher of Victorian heresies. His teaching intensified the rapture of his disciples and the weariness of those who came after them. Much the same thing occurred in regard to the paintings of G. F. Watts. Men who found inspiration in him in the nineties now look for it in vain. Time has changed their opinions for them. The great teacher has vanished, and a great enough painter does not remain to make up for the loss.

It is obvious, of course, that our present opinions about once-loved writers and painters to whom we have turned Laodicean may be as wrong as we think our former opinions were. They may be due not to the improvement of our taste but to our fickleness. At the same time, we cannot help believing that our present opinions are right. We are as complacent as the most consistent Conservative. Exalted by our latest opinion, we feel like a man who, having missed the way again and again, has found the right way at last. You will notice this in some cases of religious conversion. I once knew a man who passed from Methodism to Atheism, and from Atheism to Unitarianism, and from Unitarianism to Catholicism, and who was equally confident at each stage that by changing his opinions he had found truth at last. He regarded me as hopelessly stupid when he vainly tried to thrust Ingersoll down my throat, and he afterwards regarded me as equally stupid when he fruitlessly assaulted me with quotations from Newman's *Grammar of Assent*. It would have been useless to say to him: 'You admit that you were wrong before. You may be wrong again.' Few people believe in the possibility of their being wrong again.

In this respect, I am as complacent as anyone. At least, in matters of politics. I have changed my political opinions a number of times and never once had I the slightest doubt that my new creed was as patently true as an axiom in Euclid. Who that has ever experienced the raptures of Liberal Unionism can fail to remember what an inspired gospel it seemed? Bliss was it in that dawn to be alive. From that I passed on and became what I called an Imperialist Russellite Socialist. I was confident that if everybody else became an Imperialist Russellite Socialist – and I saw no reason except their blindness to argument why other people should not do so – the world would be transformed and we should all settle down to the enjoyment of liberty, equality and fraternity, while the organ in the Ulster Hall played *Rule Britannia*. Veering somewhat in my opinions, I then became an International Nationalist, and I can assure you that once more I was vehemently convinced that I was right. I did not care twopence what I had believed in the past. I had now found the key to the world's salvation.

Unfortunately, I have not Mr Gladstone's lifelong capacity for conversion, and I cannot experience the ecstasy of being converted to any of those new creeds that have burst into existence during my middle age. I see all about me, however, younger men and women undergoing the marvellous experience of conversion, and I cannot but wonder whether, from a purely hedonistic view, they are not even more to be envied than the changeless Lord Balfour. To go through life without ever being converted to anything seems a mark of insensitiveness. The ideal world would be a world in which everybody was capable of conversion and in which at the same time the converts would admit the possibility that they might be mistaken. That, unfortunately, is impossible. It is of the essence of conversion, or change of opinion, that the convert should know that he is absolutely and indubitably right. I myself sometimes wish that the people who are not sure that they are right would form a league to control the people who know that they are right and turn this splendid knowledge to the world's advantage. But then I have reached a point at which I am not sure that my latest opinion is right. I do not even feel sure that my opinion that my latest opinion may not be right is right.

A Sermon on Shaving

From 'Y. Y.': An Anthology of Essays by Robert Lynd (1933)

No man can shave every morning for twenty or thirty years without learning something. Even if he is too lazy or too incompetent to shave himself, and submits himself to barbers, he can hardly escape learning something about human nature by the time he is middle-aged. For barbers contain in their ranks every variety of human nature. I have known barbers who were angels; I have known barbers who were devils. Some of them have a touch as light as a falling feather; others wield a razor like a weapon of the stone age, and are not content unless they are allowed to flay as well as to shave you. The latter, I confess, are rare in the more expensive hairdressers' shops; but, if you are economical or poor, and go into one of those little shops in which before the war a shave used to cost three-halfpence, you will in the course of time discover a kind of shaving which makes you feel as if a mob were rushing over your face in hobnailed boots. I do not say that the poor man's barber is always, or even usually, so brutal as this, but undoubtedly the barber whose customers often allow their beards to grow for two or three days at a time gets used to a more determined sweep of the razor in order to clear away so stiff a field of stubble. He cannot suddenly alter his methods for a thin skin that looks as if it scarcely needed to be shaved at all. To such a skin his very shaving-brush feels as if it were made of darning-needles, stabbing the flesh at every touch. His charge is so small that he has no time for the delicacies, and at the end of the shave you find yourself with soap in your nostrils, blood on your jaws, and tears in your eyes. Then you rub into your wounds, so as to make them smart, a piece of alum that has been rubbed into ever so many other wounds, and you wipe your face with a dirty towel that has wiped ever so many other faces. And you come out into the air, glad to be alive and resolving never in future to go to any but the most expensive barbers.

I do not speak as one who is accustomed to being shaved by a barber. I no longer have the courage. In my twenties, however, when I was more indolent, I used constantly to find myself in barbers' shops even though, as the razor touched my face, I was not always free from such apprehensive thoughts as: 'Suppose the barber should suddenly go mad?' Luckily, the barber never did, but I have known other and comparable perils. There was that little French barber, for instance, who shaved me during a thunderstorm and who sprang into the air at every flash of lightning. There was also the drunken barber who felt for my cheek with the razor as a drunken man reaches out for something and misses it. Having at last brought the razor down on my face, he leaned on it to steady himself, and, by leaning hard, even succeeded in shaving a certain patch on my right jaw. I did not dare so much as to utter a protest while the razor was on my skin. Even a whisper, I felt, might unnerve and overbalance the man, and my jugular would be severed before he knew he had done it. No sooner, however, was the razor temporarily withdrawn from my face – *reculer pour mieux sauter* is, I think, the way the French describe it – than in a nightmare voice I gasped out: 'No more. No more. That will do, thank you.' He looked down at me with stupid, heavy eyes, and swayed gently with the open razor in his hand. 'You won't say anything to the boss,' he said. 'Nasty touch of influenza. Been trying to cure it. Get into trouble if you say anything.' I looked at the razor and spoke, like Harold, King of the English, under duress. 'Right,' I said. That happened a good many years ago, and I am still in doubt whether I acted as an honourable citizen either in making or in keeping such a promise. I was so exceedingly frightened, however, while the man was trying to shave me, that I am afraid it never entered my head to consider my duty as a citizen. Self-preservation, they say, is the first law of nature, and at the moment I cared about nothing except escaping at the earliest possible moment from that terrible chair. As I passed out into the street I did not even mind the fact that a piece of my face was clean-shaved while the rest of it was not. I consoled myself for not reporting the barber with the thought that perhaps he would not have to shave anybody else that day, that perhaps the next customer would only want to have his hair cut, and that not very much damage could be done during a haircut. Still, these very casuistries show that my conscience was pricking me. It continues to prick me till the present day. Life is full of difficulties if you do not happen to possess the heroic virtues. Never is it more so, believe me, than when you are being shaved by a drunken barber.

It was not, however, perils of this kind – perils, surely, worthy of being added to that catalogue with which Othello used to thrill the ear of Desdemona – that finally decided me never, if I could avoid it, to allow a barber to shave me again. If I now shave myself, it is owing to that middle-aged nervousness which disguises itself in such words as 'hygienic'. I dislike being touched with shaving-brushes and razors that have been used on other people's faces. I knew a man who had to grow a beard as the result of a small poisonous cut that he got at a barber's, and I do not wish to have to grow a beard. If one did not mind having a beard life would obviously be simpler. But most of us, even in these days, would rather do almost anything than grow beards. Much as the average man hates shaving, he hates the notion of growing a beard still more. In this he is entirely unreasonable. He does not know why he dislikes beards any more than he knows why he dislikes medium-boiled eggs. It is clear that a beard is a labour-saving device, but even in an age of labour-saving devices the very laziest of us will have none of it. Again, it is obviously natural to grow a beard, and for a man to shave is to defy nature no less than for a woman to use lipstick. A beard is also of service in hiding the imperfections of the human face, and a face with an evil mouth and a weak chin may look positively noble in the shelter of a beard. There is, indeed, everything to be said for wearing a beard that could appeal to so slothful and uncomely an animal as man. Yet we go on shaving, and know not why, and if one of our friends appears with two days' growth of beard on his chin, we regard it as evidence of a deficiency in his character. There is an iron law of shaving. You must either not shave at all or you must shave every day. Here there is no room for the moderate man, the lover of compromise, the good-natured being who likes to make the best of both worlds. If you do not shave at all you will be respected. If you shave regularly every morning you will be respected. But if you attempt to strike a nice balance and shave one day and grow a beard another, both camps will combine to denounce you as though you were something unclean. I have never been able to understand why it should be considered unclean to let the beard grow for three days and clean to let it grow for thirty years. There must be some powerful reason why moderation is praised in every other sphere of conduct but is anathematized in this. It is a matter on which I – possessing, as I have said, none of the heroic virtues – bow to public opinion, and I find myself shaving at the mirror every morning as though I were a slave obeying orders. It is a waste of time. I dislike doing it. But if I did not, I should feel an outcast. Shaving is my daily act of hypocrisy. It enables me to feel a better man without being one.

The sermon I wish to preach on shaving, however, is not a sermon against hypocrisy. It is a sermon against putting your trust in any one thing, as though it alone were necessary to perfection, and it came into my head in this way. I bought a safety-razor some years ago, because everybody else seemed to have a safety-razor. For a time it gave me not only the pleasure of a new toy but, I honestly believe, the pleasure of a perfect shave. Months passed, however, and I became dissatisfied. I began to realize that I used to be able to shave better with an ordinary razor. Then I heard somebody saying that, in order to get a good shave, the important thing was not only to have a perfect razor but to have a perfect lather and that So-and-so's soap was the best; and so I went out and bought So-and-so's soap and, for a week or two afterwards, noticed a marked improvement in my morning shave. Once more, in the course of time, I became dissatisfied, and, on this occasion, when I began to attack So-and-so's razor and So-and-so's soap, I was told by my friends: 'The great thing is to have a perfect shaving-brush.' I immediately bought a good shaving-brush, and applied So-and-so's soap according to the directions on the paper that was wrapped round it, moistening the face with cold water before using the soap, and, with the help of So-and-so's razor, had the first series of satisfactory shaves that I had had since the war. Were it not for the soap, even a sharp razor would not give me a perfect shave. Were it not for the brush, even the soap would be ineffective. Were it not for the razor, of what use would the best brush in the world be? Hence I tell myself: 'Do not expect too much from any one thing.' We are always putting our trust in one thing or another as though it were the key to perfection, but the truth is we cannot attain to the inner sanctuary of perfection without a whole bunch of keys. You would imagine that a perfect shave was fairly easy of achievement for a serious-minded man, but it has taken me half a lifetime to discover the secret of it. The perfect life, or the perfect State, is probably even more difficult of attainment, and we make the same mistakes about them, over-emphasizing the importance of one thing and overlooking the importance of others. We attempt to save civilization by means of birth-control or private enterprise or nationalism or internationalism, as though any of these things was good in itself except in company with other equally important things. The fanatic believes that if he mentions the word 'birth-control', or 'republicanism', or 'Communism', he has given you the clue to paradise. But it is possible to imagine human beings miserable with birth-control, miserable in a republic, and miserable under the dictatorship of the proletariat. You cannot build a house with only one wall, and you cannot build a perfect State with only one principle. At least, so I thought as I soaped my face with perfect soap and a perfect brush, and shaved it with a perfect razor. If there had been such a thing as a golden rule, there would have been no need of ten commandments. I am not sure that even ten are not too few. And he who neglects one neglects all. This I said to myself emphatically, dogmatically, this morning, while shaving.

•

MARK HELLINGER

Mark Hellinger (1903–47) was born in New York and educated at public schools. He was expelled from Townsend Harris High School for organizing a student strike, and worked in various capacities, as a waiter, then as a writer of songs and advertising copy for direct-mail, before starting to contribute to *Zit's*, a theatrical weekly. In 1923 he became a nightlife reporter for the newly launched *New York Daily News*. Within six months he had established a column for the *News* called 'About Broadway', vigorously feuding with crooner Rudy Vallee and sportswriter Paul Gallico to excite the interest of readers. Then in 1930 he switched to the *New York Daily Mirror*, where he started a general Sunday column, 'All in a Day', which mixed short stories, anecdotal reflections, and showbusiness items. His column was syndicated by King Features. He went to Hollywood in 1937 as a writer-producer for Warner Brothers and produced several films there. In 1944 he became a war correspondent for the Hearst papers, and after the war he set up his own production company in Hollywood. However, he never abandoned his Sunday column. His columns were collected in *Moon Over Broadway* (1931) and *The Ten Million* (1934).

The Dame on the Seventh Floor

From *Moon Over Broadway* (1931)

He was a man of no particular rarity. His life, like that of countless others in this city, was strangely the same – hour after hour and day after day. Born of poor parents, he had entered the cotton business as soon as he graduated from high school. When he was twenty-one, he married. At the age of thirty-eight, he had three children and a wife who grew stouter and more nagging with each passing year.

His income, while not tremendous, was more than sufficient for his needs. He carried $30,000 life insurance. His home life was so evenly regulated that it fairly cried aloud for a bit of hellishness.

During the winter he attended the movies once a week and a Broadway theater once a month. When summer rolled around and he felt hot and uncomfortable, his wife took the children and went to the mountains.

Respectable, that's what he was. Very respectable. The same days. The same nights. He sensed a certain restlessness. He didn't know what it was.

If you had told him it was unhappiness, he would have laughed at you . . .

While lunching one noon he met Margie. It wasn't a flirtation, really. It was just that she was so pretty and was sitting right across the table from him. He had his paper open and it accidentally knocked over her glass of water. He apologized. She said it was nothing at all.

Then she smiled again. And he smiled. Then they talked about the weather. Soon they were talking about Margie. She was a cloak model, she said. Been in New York just a short time and didn't have many friends. He felt sorry for the poor kid.

The following noon he met Margie again. And again the next day. And again on the next. He was happier now. The day seemed to move faster. Margie's face was continually before him.

Soon there was a night on Broadway. Margie took him to a cabaret where she said she had been once before. There were girls who danced before him in scanty clothes. And there was the gin that Margie kept pouring into his glass. He thought that Margie drank too much. And he told her so, too.

'Maybe, honey,' she had responded, looking deep into his eyes, 'it's because I'm in love for the first time in my life. I'm so much in love that I'm unhappy. Don't ask me with whom. Maybe I don't want to say.'

His heart beat wildly. He knew it was he of whom she was speaking. He pressed her hand tightly – and took another drink. He, too, was in love . . .

Some two months later, he was a constant visitor at Margie's apartment. He knew now that he was mad about this girl. When she was in his arms, he was content. This was love. Real love.

When he thought of his home and his wife, he hated them both. Not a drop of gin around the place. Too damned respectable. His wife was fat and dumpy. And stupid, too. Nagging all the time. What fun could he have with her in a cabaret or a theater? None. Absolutely none. But Margie – ah, she was different!

In the back of his mind was the thought that he would get a divorce and marry Margie. This was the only happiness for him.

Still, he was cautious. Nobody knew of his affair. Even the elevator boy in Margie's house knew nothing about it. Margie lived on the seventh floor – and he always rode to the ninth and walked down to her apartment. He was doing it more for her sake, he told himself, than for his own. It wouldn't do to have people talk about this sweet kid.

Coming down from the ninth floor one night the elevator boy looked at him. The boy stopped the car and asked him if he'd like to have a little fun. The man in love asked what was meant by fun.

'O,' responded the boy, 'there's a dame on the seventh floor who's always glad to entertain a gentleman. You know what I mean' – and here he gave a knowing wink – 'plenty of gin and all that. I've steered plenty o' guys up there an' they all said everything was jake. Want me to interdooce you?'

Smilingly, the man in love asked for the number of the apartment. Suddenly he fell back. His eyes widened with horror. A strange choking sound came from his throat.

The boy had given the number of Margie's apartment.

Two hours later the police entered Margie's apartment. Both Margie and the man in love were dead. There had been a struggle. The man had shot her and then killed himself. The case was clear.

Two of the reporters talked it over outside the door.

'I just came from the dead guy's house,' said the first. 'It's a shame. Got a nice wife, three kids and a pretty home. Too bad. I guess Broadway got him.'

'Yeah,' agreed the second. 'Guess Broadway got him.'

New Year's Eve on Broadway

From *Moon Over Broadway* (1931)

New Year's Eve on Broadway. 1931. The poet's dream. The bootlegger's heaven. The hat check girl's julep of joy. Lights. Love. Laughter. Tickets. Taxis. Tears. Bad booze putting hics into hicks and bills into tills. Sadness. Gladness. Madness. New Year's Eve on Broadway.

I stood in front of the Astor Hotel and watched the crowds go this way and that, that way and this. The way of the whirled, you know. Everybody so happy. Or seeming so happy, which is the next best thing. Pushing. Milling. Grinning.

Set that frail flivver shoot past that powerful Packard. Two people in the Packard. Nine in the Ford. Men selling trick mustaches. And ticklers. And balloons that blow up into chickens. It's nearing midnight. Those horns. And claxons. And sirens. Such a din!

Take a deep breath of that cold, fresh air. Boy, it's great to be alive. On New Year's Eve.

'Spare a quarter, mister?'

Funny question to pop out of the air at that moment. Seemed almost out of place. Here was someone who was begging for money when all the others were spending money to beg for happiness.

I turned toward the voice. The man didn't look like the ordinary beggar. Small cap. Blue suit that was by no means a total wreck. A small overcoat wrapped tightly about him. He might have been fifty years of age. Or fifty-five. Or sixty, for that matter.

'I'm not a real beggar, mister,' he was saying. 'Just trying to get enough to tide me over for a day or two. These days are not the same for an old-timer like me. Broadway's different from what it used to be.'

He was telling me, was he? Oh, well. I handed him a dollar on the chance that he'd talk. The dollar was well invested. He talked. And he said something.

'You know,' he mused, 'New Year's Eve always sets me thinking. Same as it does most folks, I guess. Makes me feel sorta sad inside. Not 'cause I'm broke for the time being. Not at all. I feel funny 'cause life ain't what it used to be.

'My mind runs back over the years. It seems like yesterday they were celebrating the start of a new century. New Year's Eve in 1900! Say, young feller, those were days on Broadway that were real days!

'Right across the street was Rector's! Ah, that was a place. No stupid dancing in those days. Just music and wine and the girl. But you remember Rector's, don't you? Sure. Everybody remembers Rector's.

'Look over there at that Times Building. Yes, it's beautiful in a way. But not as beautiful as the old Pabst restaurant that stood there in 1900. Say, they're all coming back to me – every one of those old landmarks.

'The old St Cloud Hotel where the Knickerbocker Building stands now. The celebrated Metropole Hotel is now an idiotic jewelry store. The Rossmore Hotel is a haberdashery. And so on down the line. All gone. And what for?

'Martin's chop house – open morning, noon and night. Charley Schloss's café. The Aulic Hotel. Engel's chop house. And down further, at Thirty-third Street, was Trainor's Hotel. Steaks – sirloin, I mean – for fifty cents, and a huge lettuce and tomato salad for fifteen cents. Say, those were happy times!

'Hammerstein's Victoria Theater stood right there on the corner of Forty-second Street. Famous people played there. Real artists and celebrities of the day. And now what have you got? Movies! Brain food for fools. Bah!

'And the women. Ah, they were real then. And the styles were beautiful. High necks and long trains. Pompadours. None of your painted flappers with dangling cigarettes. Just women as God intended 'em to be.

'The men have changed too. And for worse. If a man took two small drinks of whiskey in 1900, he was drinking a lot and kept it quiet. Any man who carried a flask was a cheapskate. Today the man who doesn't carry a flask is the cheapskate – and the more he drinks, the more he brags about it. It's all wrong.

'Look at those damned taxis rushing around like a pack of demons. In the good old days, you had your hansom cab or your victoria. Those were vehicles for ladies and gentlemen. You went across Forty-second Street in a horse car, nobody ever dreamed of that nuisance they called the subway and – '

The old-timer interrupted his narrative abruptly. He looked at me for a moment and then broke into a broad grin.

'Say, I'm telling you about 1900 – and here we are standing in front of the Astor Hotel this very minute. I remember the New Year's Eve of that year 'cause I was married two weeks later. And if that ain't enough to make a man remember things, I don't know what is.

'Yes, sir. It seems to me I was standing right close to this spot that night talking to some people who lived in the Cumberland flats, which occupied this block before they built the Astor. I'd had a bit too much wine, I guess, 'cause I can remember an old man coming down the steps and shaking his cane at me for something I did.

'I have to laugh when I think what I told him. "Say," I yelled, "why don't you go to bed? This is New Year's Eve – a night for the young fellows."

'Well, sir –'

Came the sudden shriek of a motor horn and the grinding of brakes. The old-timer, carried away by his enthusiasm, had stepped off the curb. A battered machine, carrying some ten young people, had barely missed hitting him. Only a sharp turn of the wheel had saved the old-timer from losing his memories for ever.

A young girl sat in the rear of that machine. Pretty as a picture, she was sprawled over two of the boys while her legs dangled contentedly over the right rear fender. And as the old-timer slipped and almost fell, the girl howled with laughter.

'Hey, pop,' she screamed, 'you wanna watch your step. You got one foot in the grave and you ain't wise to yourself.

'Get hep, baby. This ain't no night for grandpas to be chasin' around.'

The crowd laughed. Crowds always do. Such a funny girl. Great kid really. Called the turn all right. 'No night for grandpas.' Ha, ha. Ho, ho.

A whistle. A blinking light. Traffic. More noise. And when I looked around the old-timer had vanished. His story was finished. Out for another dollar, no doubt.

Oh, well. Just another episode. Lights. Love. Laughter. See them go! Take another breath of that cold, fresh air. 1931. It's great to be alive. On New Year's Eve . . .

•

VISCOUNT CASTLEROSSE

Viscount Castlerosse (1891–1943) was the son of the 5th Earl of Kenmare and was born in County Kerry, Ireland. He was educated at St Anthony's School, Eastbourne; briefly, at the Royal Naval College, Osborne; at Downside; and at Cambridge, where he acquired a passionate interest in gambling and good living. He served in the Irish Guards during the First World War and was badly wounded on the Belgian border – one of his arms was thereafter disabled. In 1915 he befriended Lord Beaverbrook who frequently helped him out of financial problems over the years, but who also found him a career when he induced him to write for one of his papers, the *Sunday Express*. In 1926 Castlerosse began writing a 3,000-word column called 'The Londoner's Log' on page two of the *Sunday Express*. For the next fifteen years, with hardly a break, Castlerosse maintained this output. 'It was described popularly and erroneously as a gossip column, but it was something more than that,' Castlerosse's biographer, George Malcolm Thomson, has written. 'It might contain gossip about others, but it was essentially a self-portrait.' Indeed, its protagonist was an eligible bachelor who roved the West End of London, the South of France or America's Palm Beach, expressing his fascination with the rich, his sympathy for unfortunate gamblers, his wariness of marriage and his delight in human foibles.

'The Londoner's Log'
Sunday Express, 1 May 1936

It might be worse!

You might be Raymond Vaudé, a French thief who escaped last year from Devil's Island. He is in Paris now – to give himself up to the police 'if only he can get justice'.

He will not get that. Nobody does.

But it is the picture in my morning paper I am thinking of. Vaudé is sitting in a café – typical Paris café.

It looks as if it were in the Place de l'Opéra. It might easily be the Café de la Paix, where you can sit all day and watch people pass and hear them talk.

Bless us, it is more than a year since I was in Paris, which is a long time. I wonder if the German refugees still congregate in the cafés round the Opéra. Like a lot of jackdaws they used to sit chattering away, and some of them laughing – at themselves as often enough.

It might be worse!

You might be one of those German Jewish refugees!

Bad enough for them now, but if war ever breaks out it will be intolerable, for they who only wish to make friends will become the world's enemy.

Outside Germany they will be Germans, and in Germany – just Jews?

Every man who has warmth in his heart has sympathy for these unfortunates, but they are not a particularly attractive lot.

A friend of mine was on the Committee of Assistance in Paris for German Jewish refugees some time ago, when this sort of thing was comparatively new. One of these fellows burst into his office and said: 'Do you know what they have done now? Jews in Germany are not allowed to bathe in public baths before three o'clock.'

'It might be worse,' said my friend. 'It might be that Jews must bathe before three o'clock.'

It is a curious habit we have over here of massing Jews together under one head.

In fact, they vary racially as much as Gentiles.

Who was it who told me that he was sitting in the Café de la Paix one hot summer's day, so hot that the taxicab drivers were drowsy and the newspaper boys droned?

Oh! Yes! It was Don Pedro de Zulueta who was my informant. Suddenly a pistol cracked, a taxi stopped, a woman lay bleeding, dying in the cab. By it was a man with a smoking revolver in his hand.

Cries of angry rage from the crowd. The assassin obviously on the point of being lynched. Then, wrenching himself free, he jumps on the top of the cab.

'It is my wife – she has been unfaithful to me,' he cries.

Immediately silence reigns. The crowd disperses, muttering: 'It was his wife, she was unfaithful to him.'

Interest dies – the husband lives.

A typically French scene? Don't you believe it – it is only typical of the stories that Don Pedro likes telling.

I have not seen the Don for some time. Is he still living in Bournemouth? But who wants to live anywhere but in or near London?

No man should be bored in London, for at the worst there are so many people and things to avoid in London.

For years I have meant to study London. There are so many places that Londoners never see. The Tower, for instance, or Hampton Court. I have never seen Hampton Court, which omission I realize must be rectified.

What is the best 'life' of Cardinal Wolsey? It has suddenly occurred to me that I have never read one.

I may state that my taste in historical reading veers towards the vivid – I could never see any literary charm in Bradshaw, whereas I have revelled in Lytton.

I note that my friend Charles Graves had an action against *Lilliput* for infringement of copyright and won it. Some weeks ago I myself infringed the copyright of *Lilliput*.

Do you remember I wrote an article on the costs of becoming a barrister? Instead of ringing up a barrister and asking him, I lifted the facts from *Lilliput*. Yes, just another sad case of how:

> Perched on the eagle's towering wing,
> The lowly linnet loves to sing.

In order that there should not be any confusion, I am the lowly linnet. Is that an apology? It is meant to be.

You cannot quite tell how people will take apologies. Only last week I was travelling on the Underground when I accidentally trod on a sturdy old lady's foot. She gave vent to such a howl that the whole carriage was startled.

'I am sorry, madam,' I said. 'I hope I did not hurt you.'

No answer! And what was worse the aged woman continued to glare with all the fury of an enraged lioness. Then up spoke a dispirited-looking man who was sitting next to the injured and angry lady.

'It ain't no good, guv'nor, she's deaf, you'll 'ave to kiss 'er,' he said.

I did nothing of the sort, for even lowly linnets do not peck Vesuvius when erupting.

Lowly linnets notice things which are hidden from the general public. Sweet peas, for instance!

I did not know till quite recently that the popularity of sweet peas only dates back just over thirty years or so.

In 1902 Mr Salis Cole noticed in Lord Spencer's garden a pale pink upright sweet pea. All modern sweet peas are bred from that original.

It may surprise you to know that sweet peas are not just flowers to look at and sniff, but in some ways are as saucy as glamour girls. Certain sweet peas make good mothers, others do not. Likewise all sweet peas do not have the reputation of being good fathers.

Sad though it is, many a sweat pea could echo those words: 'Mother was a Quaker, father was a rip.'

The facts of life are exactly similar in essentials in the sweet pea as in the matings of kings and queens.

The reason for all this knowledge is that the lowly linnet had a long and most interesting conversation with Mr H. T. Wilkins, who knows all about sweet peas.

As we were talking, up came A. C. W. Fells, who must be the world's patience champion. I say this because it took him thirty-two years to invent a mangold. It is now as perfect as can be.

Perfection is a queer thing – it is apparently only to be discovered in aged married couples who have never caught each other out.

'Scottie', i.e. Legge, told me the other day of a fellow countryman of his whose wife died and how he buried her and how the lawyer came with the will in which she left everything to him, with the statement, 'No woman ever had better or truer husband.'

As the old Scot read this he murmured, 'And to think that all these years I was never sure whether she loved me or not.'

Note: Is it the springtime? Or is it a fact? Anyway, wherever the lowly linnet goes he sees pretty girls. Last Thursday there were battalions of them going to weddings.

There were also quite a number of lovely women at *Idiot's Delight* last week. The lowly linnet had heard a great deal about the play and had even had the honour of meeting Tamara Geva at dinner.

However, going to the theatre is quite an undertaking, for the linnets are not birds who favour high teas. We song birds are ritualists, and dinner is part of that ritual.

Another theatre terror is the length of the play. There have been occasions when it seems to the unfortunate audience that they were doomed to a life sentence.

That is where the cinema scores. A linnet can twitter over his dinner, get a glass or two of encouraging wine down his throat, stick a cigar into his beak, present himself at the cinema at 9.35 and enjoy himself till eleven o'clock.

The perches are fine, too, at the cinema, much better than in our old-fashioned theatres.

However, despite the fact that we had the worst seats in the Apollo Theatre, despite the fact that after the first act the temperature of the atmosphere rose to a million degrees over boiling point, despite the fact that my companion had no place to park his long legs, despite the fact that the lady next door laughed at every line in the play, whether it was funny or not – *Idiot's Delight* was fine.

You know the story? It takes place in an hotel at the point where Switzerland, Italy and Austria meet. Do not, fair reader, look that up in an atlas – imagine it.

We are on the Austrian side of the border and war breaks out.

Of course, we have the director of the armament firm in Achille Weber, played by Hugh Miller.

Have you ever thought what would happen if, by some miracle, the world were disarmed and all the battleships were sunk and the cannons and the tanks were dumped into the sea?

It would be fine provided we kept at peace, but if we went to war the mortality would be terrible.

A thousand years ago the percentage killed in battle was twenty times higher than it is now.

Some say Genghis Khan was responsible for the death of 20,000,000 people during his lifetime.

I sojourned for one night and day during the last war at Modane, which was the frontier station, high up in the mountains, between France and Italy.

I spent the morning fishing in a little stream there. They were the most peaceful hours of my life, and I shall always remember them. Modane could tell many curious tales. I wonder one of those frontier officers does not take pencil in hand.

Note: Frere Reeves came to luncheon last week. He is a partner in Heinemann's, the publishers. A good life, dealing with interesting people. Sometimes when publishing a book by J. B. Priestley, they do not have a contract at all – just word of mouth.

After all, the dealings in the Stock Exchange are done verbally. Poor lambs, stock-brokers, have indeed been feeling the draught. It is estimated that during the last year the dealings in that institution were down no less than 4,000 million pounds.

Frere told me how Oscar Wilde once went to see a publisher. After the visit he said to A. E. W. Mason: 'When I arrived the publisher was wearing two gold watch chains; when I left he was wearing three.'

I was just trying to think as I was writing the above of a mellow man, and casually, [Hollywood producer] Walter Wanger's name occurred to me.

As I thought of him I opened *Time*, which had just arrived, and there read that Walter Wanger had been divorced by his wife, Justine Johnstone Wanger, on the grounds that he 'was abrupt, surly, and discourteous'.

I have often wondered what head waiters are like in their home life. Does the natural rudeness of man break out or does politeness become second nature?

Also, how they manage to have any home life at all. It seems to me that they are on the job from midday to midnight, and after. And if you have been up after midnight those morning hours hardly count at all.

Well, now, children, the time has come to stop, particularly as tonight there will be celebrations. Even lowly linnets occasionally give their wings a bit of a swing, and why not? – for as MacDonald says in his *Book of Dreams*:

> A bird knows nothing of gladness,
> It is only a song machine.

Finally, at 8.45 p.m. on Sunday night, that is tonight to you, join with me in a toast, namely: 'Damnation to all cats.'

Perhaps a little explanation may be necessary. Remember even Mr Wanger was misunderstood.

•

WESTBROOK PEGLER

James Westbrook Pegler (1894–1969) came from a humble background in Minneapolis, Minnesota. The son of a newspaperman, he left Loyola Academy in Chicago at the age of nineteen to join a press association in that city. Before the First World War he moved to the International News Service and covered the 1912 Republican convention at which Theodore Roosevelt announced his departure from the party. He was a United Press correspondent during the war, but also served for two years in the navy. Back in civilian life he turned to a new beat, writing about sports. He lasted in this role until 1933 when he graduated into column-writing for the Scripps–Howard Newspapers syndicate and later for Hearst. His column, entitled 'Fair Enough', chose as its targets big government, fascism, labour unions, gangsterism, Eleanor Roosevelt and his rival columnist (and erstwhile friend) Heywood Broun (who was nicknamed 'Old Bleeding Heart'). The tone of the column varied, too. Sometimes it was satirical, sometimes indignant, sometimes crusading, and sometimes it was rabid. One racketeer, who was on his way to prison after being exposed in Pegler's column, complained that he had been 'peglerized'. His column later degenerated into anti-Communist ravings.

'Fair Enough'
The Harpoon
From *'T Aint Right* (1936)

Garmisch-Partenkirchen, Germany, February 19, 1936
It is going to be pretty hard to do this, but right is right, as President Harding said, and I feel that I have done the Nazis a serious injustice, so this is my apology.

Two days ago these dispatches reported that the quaint little Bavarian town of Garmisch-Partenkirchen has the appearance of an army headquarters a few miles behind the Western Front during an important troop movement. That was wrong, and I can only plead that I was honestly mistaken and the victim of my own ignorance.

Those weren't troops at all but merely peace-loving German workmen in their native dress, and those weren't army lorries which went growling through the streets squirting the slush on to the sidewalks but delivery wagons carrying beer and wieners and kraut to the humble homes of the mountaineers in the folds of the hills. It is a relief to know this and a pleasure to be able to report that, after all, the Germans did not conduct their winter Olympics in an atmosphere of war, which would have been very injurious to the Olympic ideal of peace through sporting competition.

My information comes from a kindly Bavarian cobbler in a long black overcoat who was standing in a cordon of cobblers along the main street on Sunday afternoon during Adolf Hitler's visit to the town to pronounce over the closing ceremonies the benison of a great protector of the world's peace.

'Are you a soldier?' I often inquired, for I had been told that in Germany strangers often mistake for soldiers people who have nothing to do with the military establishment.

'Why me?' he asked. 'No, I'm a cobbler. All of us in the black costume are cobblers.'

'Then why do you dress in military uniform?' I persisted.

'That's where you are wrong,' said my cobbler friend. 'This isn't a military uniform.

It's a shoemaker's uniform, and this big clothes stabber in the scabbard at my side, which may look like a bayonet to you, is merely a little knife which we use when we cobble.'

'But,' I asked, 'why do you march in military formation through the streets of international friendship?'

The cobbler controlled his impatience and explained that for hundreds of years the cobblers of Bavaria had worn the same distinctive costume, which looks military to the uninitiated. And why, then, do they march like troops and form imposing cordons around the streets to hold back the crowds during the Olympic Games?

The answer is that they don't really march at all. They just walk in step in columns of fours, because they like to walk that way. And it is an old custom of theirs to form cordons of military appearance along the curbs and just stand there by the hour for pleasure.

'But what about those other troops in the brown uniforms?'

'Troops?' said my friend. 'Those are not troops. Those are gardeners who have always worn brown suits, which seem to be military but aren't. Just peace-loving gardeners is what they are, and those blades which you see hanging from their belts are not bayonets, either, but pruning knives. It is an old Bavarian tradition.

'They, too, like to go for long walks in columns of fours, and drill with spades, as soldiers sometimes drill with rifles, but they are not soldiers, I assure you, my friend. They are just kind-hearted gardeners who wouldn't hurt a potato bug. It is interesting to see them strike spades when they come to the end of a stroll in columns of fours. To some people unacquainted with our local customs they may seem to be performing a military drill with their spades, but nothing could be further from the truth.

'I hope it never comes to the attention of our Herr "Putz" Hanfstaengel, of the Foreign Propaganda Department, that you mistook our cobblers and gardeners for soldiers on the scene of the Olympic Games, because if there is anything that annoys him it is to see Germany accused of militarism in foreign papers.'

Thus far two of my military corps had been explained away as harmless and altogether peaceful workmen, but I thought I had him when I mentioned the men in the gray uniforms, also with scabbards at their sides, who seemed to be regular infantry. He laughed uproariously at this.

'Oh, those!' he said. 'Those aren't infantry. How could you make that mistake? Those are plasterers, and those tin hats which you undoubtedly mistook for shrapnel helmets are an ancient tradition of Bavarian plasterers. Sometimes the plaster falls down, and it would knock them for a lot of loops if they didn't wear something for protection. Wait till I tell the foreman of the plasterers – I suppose you have been calling him the general – that you mistook his boys for soldiers. He will laugh himself dizzy.'

Still, there were other men all dressed alike in blue gray, with wings embroidered on their clothing. Undoubtedly those would be soldiers of the aviation branch, wouldn't they? But my friend the peace-loving cobbler in the black suit, which looked very military but wasn't, enjoyed another pleasant hysteric over that one, too. Those, he said, were poultry farmers, and the wings on their collars merely represented the harmless fowl in their barnyards.

It is not easy to be proven wrong in a serious matter. I had seen as many as 5,000, perhaps even 10,000, men in apparel which seemed to be that of soldiers, and had recklessly accused the peace-loving Nazi regime of converting the winter Olympics into a military demonstration, which would have been a grave breach of manners. My troops had been explained into gentle civilians, and the marching to which I had referred had turned out to be nothing but an habitual method of going for nice long walks.

The motor trucks still seemed questionable, however, for they were painted in camouflage like the lorries used in the war.

'Yes, I know,' my friend the cobbler explained, 'but we have painted our motor trucks in eccentric designs and colors for hundreds of years. It makes them look nicer.'

A foreman of the cobblers came by at the moment, and my friend put his hand to his cap in a gesture which resembled a military salute. I asked him about this, but he said he was only shading his eyes.

The Nazi Press Bureau released the other day a quotation from a dispatch to the *New York Times* insisting that anyone reporting the presence of troops at the Olympic Games was a liar. I guess that's me, but the mistake was natural, as you can see, and I hope pardonable. When thousands of men seem to march but don't, in clothing and tin hats which seem to be military uniforms but aren't, and carry harmless utensils which appear to be bayonets, any stranger is likely to make the same mistake.

'Fair Enough'
Golden Spoon

From *The Dissenting Opinions of Mister Westbrook Pegler* (1941)

Nobody has ever put a finger on the exact spot where Mr Roosevelt is a pain in the neck to a large proportion of those Americans whom he describes as economic royalists and well-fed clubmen.

The element of rich men whom I have in mind are members of the Horatio Alger school who started from scratch as typical, one-gallus, Whitcomb Riley barefoot boys. They got their rudimentary knowing in a one-room or two-room schoolhouse, learned swimming in Goose Crick, split kindling, pumped and carried water by hand and in their high school years sold papers, worked in quarries, laid paving blocks, mowed lawns, shovelled snow and coal and dragged out ashes.

In every possible way they hustled to make an honest quarter or a dollar, always with the ambition to become successful or, in a coarser word, rich. College in those days was for the rich or the uncommonly studious and dogged poor, and the college boy of Mr Roosevelt's own class, backed by rich parents, was known somewhat contemptuously as a rah-rah or a Cholly and was depicted in the comic papers with a big, fuzzy chrysanthemum in his lapel and sucking the handle of his walking stick.

Horatio Alger was the most popular boys' author of the time, and, like some of our most opulent fiction writers of today, he wrote the same story over and over. It was called *Bound to Rise*, *Dick Mordaunt's Career* or *Upward and Onward*, but it was always the story of the boy with the widowed mother or no parents at all who worked hard, suffered much, conquered temptation, and in the last chapter wore a gold watch and chain. The hero was an insufferable little prig, and nobody ever tried to copy his morals, but his success was dream stuff and he was the inspiration of many men who are now either rich or quite well to do and who got that way playing the game according to the rules which were unanimously recognized and against heavy odds.

Many of them had to quit school early to take the responsibility of supporting their mothers and younger brothers and sisters, and when at last they met the one and only and decided to get married they moved into a boarding-house or furnished room or rented a little house or flat furnished up with installment plan furniture bought at extortionate rates of interest.

Mr Roosevelt himself never spent a day in a public school in all his life. The public schools never were and are not now good enough for the Roosevelts, and when Mr Roosevelt had done with nurses and tutors he went to a dude school called Groton, which prepared him for Harvard, and after he had married and had taken his bride for a honeymoon tour of England, France, Italy and Germany, they returned home in time for him to go to Columbia Law School.

'My mother-in-law,' writes Mrs Roosevelt in her book, 'had taken a house for us. She had furnished it and engaged our servants.'

Later, Mrs Roosevelt writes, 'For a while we had, as waitress, my father and mother's waitress,' and, again, 'During the next few years we observed in summer much the same routine. We visited my mother-in-law at Hyde Park for a time and then went up to stay with her at Campobello. Ordinarily my husband sailed up and down the coast in the little schooner *Half Moon* and took perhaps one or two short cruises.'

In 1908 the President's mother thought their little house too small and therefore bought a plot in New York and built another for them. Later she also bought and gave to Franklin Roosevelt and his young wife an estate on Campobello Island, including a house completely furnished, even to china, glass and linens.

For Mr Roosevelt to sail his own schooner around Fundy when he had never yet assumed the task of supporting his own wife unassisted was all right, but let some other man cock a funny cap over his eye and toss off such words as 'Ahoy!' 'Port!' and 'Starboard!' on a yacht bought with his own money in enjoyment of his own success and he is not merely ridiculous but an enemy of the great common people of whom the President is paradoxically one.

There are those who call Mr Roosevelt a traitor to his class, but that cry comes from the hereditary rich who grew up endowed and, as he did, looked to their mothers and fathers for support and luxuries long after they had ceased to be children. The class that I have in mind take pride in having made their own way. They are proud to have taken care of their own parents, and every crack from him about well-fed clubmen and economic royalists evokes from them the soul-satisfying and contemptuous taunt, 'mamma's boy.'

'Fair Enough'
Spelvin's Income Tax

From *The Dissenting Opinions of Mister Westbrook Pegler* (1941)

The income tax reviewer called on George Spelvin, American, today, to go over his return for 1936, examine his private papers and ask some questions about his dreams and his personal life, and met a strange rebuff.

'Nothing doing,' Mr Spelvin said. 'Absolutely nothing doing.'

'Now, don't be like that,' the reviewer said. 'It's the law, and you will only make trouble for yourself.'

'Absolutely nothing doing,' Mr Spelvin insisted. 'I am sore.'

'What are you sore about?' the reviewer asked.

'I'm sore about this "Where did you get that $5?" and "What did you do with that four-bits?" when Jimmy Roosevelt and the boss himself and Henry Morgenthau get special treatment.'

'But they have to pay income tax,' the reviewer said.

'Yes, and so do I,' said Mr Spelvin, 'and I have paid it, but now you want to take up my time asking a lot of questions that are none of your business, and how do I know you aren't going to go out and get tight some night and spill a lot of gossip about me? And, moreover, I don't like the way they acted down in Washington when they were combing a lot of other people but refused to go into Jimmy's return or the President's or Henry's. That Republican Congressman said he had trustworthy reports that Jimmy made a big income selling insurance to people who wanted to stay in right with the administration, but when he wanted to put an expert to work on Jimmy's returns, the way you want to pry into mine, the committee said, "Nothing doing." Well, all right, nothing doing on his or the President's or Henry's, nothing doing on mine. I'm like Popeye. I'll do anything they do.'

'But, for gossakes,' the reviewer said, 'Henry Morgenthau is my boss. Can you picture me going in and acting like that with the Secretary of the Treasury?'

'Henry ain't my boss,' said Mr Spelvin. 'I only know the committee refused to let an expert like you go over Henry's returns, the same as the experts went over other people's, after Ham Fish challenged him. It's one thing to throw down a lot of papers like an inventory of the Pennsylvania Railroad and say, "There it is. Help yourself, chum," but it's something else to turn loose an expert to see what the figures mean. Henry said people had established losses by exchanging stocks, and he said this was unethical. And the record says Ham Fish charged before the committee that Henry did it himself before the law was changed. Well, did he or didn't he? Why not let an expert decide? What is the reason for all this bashfulness? Brother, I'm bashful myself.'

'But surely you don't think there's anything funny about the President's returns,' the reviewer said.

'Well, what makes you guys always think mine are so funny, then?' Mr Spelvin demanded. 'You seem to get a lot of laughs out of me. Well, I've got the same kind of a sense of humor, and I want a couple of laughs. You can't ever tell where you are going to turn up a laugh.'

'What have you got against Jimmy, anyway?' the agent asked.

'Nothing,' said Mr Spelvin. 'I don't even know the guy. But I'll ask you one: What have you mugs got against me and a lot of other suckers? Always nosing around like a house dick, asking trick questions, pulling trick clauses on guys. Listen, brother. I haven't got any family connections or political connections, and any time I sell a bill of goods it's Spelvin working. I don't even belong to the Elks. I don't like that way of doing. You tell them for me it's unethical.'

'Well, I am going to have to turn you in,' said the agent.

'Go ahead,' Mr Spelvin said. 'I am just practicing Mr Roosevelt's preaching, and they can't hang you for that. I am hell on unethical conduct and special privilege.'

'Fair Enough'
Red-baiting

From *The Dissenting Opinions of Mister Westbrook Pegler* (1941)

At a lunch in Kansas City lately the speaker, a Mr Collins, told of a man standing at a bar who tore out of the place and ran for home when a voice at the door cried, 'McGuire, your house is on fire.'

'He had run six blocks,' Mr Collins said, 'before he suddenly dug his heels into the ground, skidded to a stop and said, "Hell, my name isn't McGuire!" '

Mr Collins was making the point that we are all slaves of habit in thought, and I use his story to open the question of red-baiting and ask why reds or Communists of various shades should enjoy an immunity which is not given the members of any other political faith and which the reds themselves allow to nobody who disagrees with them.

Why not bait reds? Out of sheer carelessness a superstition has been allowed to grow to the size of a robust principle that of all the political elements in this country the reds alone must be treated with special courtesy and that it is un-American and a mark of gross ignorance to criticize those whose sole purpose and constant effort is to install here the bloody terror of Moscow.

The favorite attack of the reds themselves, which they have made popular even with persons who are not reds but only want to be fair, is to assert that the red-baiter is a political bigot who recklessly flogs liberals and Socialists in his sweeping denunciations of the bolos.

I will grant that this has been known to happen, with the stipulation, however, that many liberals and Socialists keep very bad company and that many reds, wise in the uses of protective coloration, pretend to be liberals and Socialists. But, considering that the reds despise the liberal and Socialist, their concern for these elements obviously is false. Since when have they been so solicitous for liberals and Socialists? They bait liberals and Socialists themselves.

On the other hand, the reds are notoriously careless in their generalizations, for to them everyone who is not a red, or pink enough to be useful as a decoy, is a Fascist. They violently abuse as Fascists many ordinary Democrats and Republicans whose detestation of Fascism is known to be as fierce as their hatred of the Moscow horror.

Yet, thanks to the American habit of accepting ideas without examination, they have enjoyed the benefit of a tradition that red-baiting is beneath the political chivalry of true Americans. Our papers, even the most conservative, often have uttered self-conscious denials of any such intention when, in decent loyalty to their principles, they should have ripped and slashed the reds with the same loose-jointed abandon that the bolos use against all and sundry.

This inhibition dates back to the time of A. Mitchell Palmer, but should be overcome because it imposes an unnecessary handicap in a scuffle with an opponent who fights tomcat style and observes none of the ethics which he demands of others.

Chicago and Los Angeles, in the *Tribune* and the *Times*, respectively, possess two of the most intemperate and highly colored reactionary papers in the country, but these are models of calm and patient fairness by comparison with the least vicious of the red publications. The bolo editor has no financial responsibility to deter him from libel, and a sentence for criminal vilification would be martyrdom and thus a victory according to his peculiar system of scoring.

And direct controversy is avoided in respect for ex-Senator Jim Watson's quaint but indisputable dictum that nobody ever won a personal contest with a skunk. That is one reason why red-baiting should be avoided, but it is a purely personal and not very noble one, and it certainly is not binding on anyone who wants to take the risk.

Herbert Hoover, Al Smith, Mr Roosevelt, Jim Farley, William Green, Hearst, the duPonts, Tom Girdler and hundreds of other prominent men, the Elks, Odd Fellows, Kiwanians and Kluxers, the Democrats, Republicans, Kansans and graduates of Princeton all may be criticized, denounced and derided and often are. Such being so, it is not only fair to bait reds but dishonest to treat them with special restraint.

•

TOM DRIBERG

Thomas Edward Neil Driberg (1905–76) (later Baron Bradwell) was born in Crowborough, Sussex, and educated at Lancing College and Christ Church, Oxford. Already a Communist, he worked at party headquarters during the 1926 General Strike and spent a vacation from university as a reporter on the *Sunday Worker*, a party publication. After coming down from Oxford, he obtained a position on the *Daily Express* as assistant to the paper's gossip columnist Dragoman, who wrote the 'Talk of the Town' column. In May 1933 Beaverbrook put an end to 'Talk of the Town' and created a new column, 'These Names Make News', by William Hickey (after the bibulous and womanizing eighteenth-century diarist of the same name). The essence of this new column was personalized reportage, and over the next ten years Driberg covered almost every subject and travelled in Europe and the United States. In 1942 he was elected as an Independent MP for Maldon and the following year he was sacked from the *Express*. He quickly found a berth elsewhere, writing 'Tom Driberg's Column' for *Reynold's News*. He later wrote a column for the *People*.

'William Hickey'
My Double Quits
Daily Express, 4 November 1947

'I want to introduce you to Mr William Hickey, of the *Daily Express*.'

Yes; but the words were spoken *to* me.

I was led up to a bar against which a young man was leaning. He was 'Hickey'.

It was an interesting situation. Last weekend a reader rang up, asked had I been at a certain music-hall on Saturday night, behaving in a 'rather lively' way?

I hadn't; thought it amusing – but when two other readers rang up and said someone claiming to be Hickey of the *Express* was going to see same show nightly, standing drinks lavishly in the bar, boasting of this column (!), bunching one of the girls in the show, I thought I'd better look into it; set off for the South London Palace, near the Elephant and Castle. Private detective and two friends went with me. Detective lurked in the background, venerable, bald. Friends joined in the fun.

We led the young man up the garden for about an hour. It gave me keen pleasure to say to him all the silly things that are always said to me: 'What an interesting life you must have . . . What a lot of interesting people you must meet.'

He was admirably ready with the correctly *blasé* answers; said what a bore it was, for instance, to have to go to lunch today with Sir C– C–, eminent arms magnate, instead of playing shove-ha'penny in the pubs at Putney (where he lives).

Friend, recalling my visits this year to USA and Spain, asked about them. On USA, 'Hickey' side-tracked the talk to Walter Winchell. On Spain he said, 'Oh, I never went anywhere near the front . . .'

'Oh, but,' said friend, 'I thought you wrote . . . ?'

'You mustn't believe all you see in my column,' said 'Hickey'. 'Why, I might write that I'd had four light ales in this bar when I'd really had ten!'

Friend kicked me surreptitiously, smirked disgustingly. 'Hickey' hastily got on to the safely speculative subject of Spanish women.

'How do you *get* such a job?' we asked earnestly. 'What are the qualifications?'

'Oh, you just have to have a flair, old boy,' said 'Hickey'.

'The screw's jolly good,' he added. 'But it's a hell of a life. Most of the money goes to the brewers in the end anyway . . .'

I winced, glimpsing an awful Hyde-caricature of my own relatively (but only relatively) Jekyll way of life.

The time for the Grand Dramatic Exposure drew near. I didn't feel a bit heroic; nor think him a bit villainous. His puny evasions made me sorry for him. I looked at his shabby coat, floppy felt hat, weak chin, rather pleasant face, nicotine-stained fingers. He was obviously just a fool. He had plenty of money; there was no question of any offence, of obtaining cash or credit by false pretences. But why pick on me?

Interval was ending. Bar was emptying. Round us were gathered several people whom 'Hickey' had imposed on, including the pretty, blonde, eighteen-year-old show-girl whom he was courting.

I said: 'I think this has gone on long enough. Will you tell me why you are passing yourself off as Hickey?'

He did not look at me or the girl, looked straight ahead, said in a low voice, 'I don't know what you mean.' He didn't want her to hear, took me aside; made no attempt to bluff it out.

Within a few minutes we knew a good deal about him. I won't print all the details. He says he makes his money backing dogs.

'But why did you do it?' I insisted.

It was because of the girl. 'I wanted to *be* somebody,' he said.

'Be yourself,' I said.

'Well, I thought she wouldn't look at *me*,' he said – so I trotted out all the old platitudes about anyone worth having loving one for oneself, etc.

He wouldn't go back to see her, said, 'I can never face her again. I just worship her. I've let her down.' (He was a little too dramatic.)

I told him I might send him an injunction. But I don't think he'll do it again.

Impostor, friends, I then went off for a drink up West. The awful thing was that we didn't remember till after midnight about the poor old private detective. He's probably still hanging about the Elephant.

'William Hickey'
I Take My Boo
Daily Express, 17 March 1939

We know how things are in central Europe; it may surprise some to hear that in London, already, a journalist cannot safely go to a public political meeting.

Go *as a journalist*, I mean: to represent and report for his paper, sitting quietly at the press table.

On Wednesday night Sir Oswald Mosley, Fascist leader, spoke at a meeting at St Pancras Town Hall. I had never heard him speak. I had heard that he was a good speaker. So I went along. (It was arranged by telephone with his organization, now called British Union, that we should send a representative.)

One of Mosley's stock grievances is that he doesn't get enough publicity. After this experience I am not surprised if the press stay away from his meetings.

This is what happened . . .

The meeting was nearly over. Many questions had been asked, some pointed, some foolish; they had been dealt with efficiently by A. Raven Thomson, the Fascists' Political Director, whom Mosley had put in charge of the meeting when he left after his own speech.

The tone of questions and answers had become predominantly anti-Semitic; whenever Jews were mentioned, there were howls and roars of exultant hatred.

I was sitting at one of the two press tables just below the platform; my companions were two reporters from local papers.

Suddenly, from about half-a-dozen rows behind us, a man got up and asked, raucously, 'What is Mr Hickey of the *Daily Express* doing at the press table there?' – and either he or, in the confusion of voices which now broke out, another man added, 'Will he give a fair report of this meeting?'

There was a babel of surprised and angry cries. Fingers were pointed at me, eyes glared. I felt like the subject of a Bateman drawing. At the same time, I felt indignant as well as embarrassed: it is a universal tradition of British public meetings that the press table should be regarded as neutral ground.

Raven Thomson held up his hand. 'Now, now,' he said, 'we don't want any personalities about people at the press table . . .'

There were interjections. I have been present at many scenes of violence, but I don't think I have ever heard such bestially savage cries and yells. It was difficult to distinguish the words, but I heard 'Jew!' and 'He's a Jew' and, from a witty woman, 'Hickeystein'.

To try to answer would have been useless. I am not a snake-charmer. I sat quietly, while a colleague kindly took down in shorthand whatever could be heard.

Raven Thomson went on to say that he had been 'keeping an eye' on me during Mosley's speech, that he envied reporters their job, that while 'our Leader' had been making his fine speech we had sat there twiddling our pencils, not taking it down; 'I wish I could get a job like that.'

This was hard, not only on me (I had filled seven and a half pages of a notebook with small writing) but on my colleagues, who had both taken copious shorthand notes of the speech and were already busy writing their stories.

I held up my notebook, open, to him.

'Yes, I know, you made some notes,' he said; 'but it struck me that you were just writing down those points which might be twisted against Mosley' – a curious admission of vulnerability, had it been true.

He went on to a little harangue about freedom. The press had a right to be there; they were invited; 'but we do wish they'd do a little more for us sometimes in exchange for the unfailing courtesy they receive at our meetings.'

Courtesy!

It would be interesting, he added, to see what report of the meeting the *Daily Express* printed.

While he was speaking a steward – a quiet, good-mannered chap – came and whispered to me: would I please leave with him by the side-door near where we sat; he and his colleagues would see me out to the back.

I asked why; what was wrong with the main door?

'Well, we don't want any trouble,' he said. 'Some of the boys might get rough.'

Meanwhile, Raven Thomson had announced to the audience that the police wanted them to leave by another side-door. We gathered that there was a hostile crowd outside the main door. 'It will be more convenient by this door,' said Raven Thomson, 'and if you go out this way you won't need your gas-masks.' (Laughter.)

The meeting ended with 'God Save the King'. The press stood up. The press did not join in the shooting-up of hands which accompanied the last line; nor in the shouts of 'Hail [or was it Heil?] Mosley!' which followed like an Amen.

I was taken round by devious passages, coming face to face behind the platform with Raven Thomson. I said to him, 'Thank you for your courtesy from the platform, anyway.' He looked taken aback. Maybe he thought I was being sarcastic. Actually I was at least grateful for his half-hearted attempt to quell his mob.

As we left, I said to one of the stewards, 'I should have thought your chaps would be better disciplined.'

'They will be,' he said, reassuringly. 'But you know what they are . . .'

I do now.

Now, I'm afraid I haven't much room left for the full report of Mosley's speech that they wanted.

We do not write often about the Blackshirts. They take an exaggerated view of their own news-value. There are all sorts of little political and religious sects and cliques and clubs whose meetings we cannot possibly report.

But Mosley is in his way a picturesque figure. I had planned a fairly detailed analysis of his oratory. I am sorry that his own followers have robbed him of it; I can hardly be blamed for having dwelt on that unseemly scene, both as a matter of public interest and having myself been, apparently, in danger of a beating-up.

He is certainly a sure and effective orator. He spoke for seventy minutes, without notes, without hesitation, without losing his hearers' attention. (If their applause did show signs of flagging, he could always whip it up by a sneer at the Jews.)

He began in an admirably quiet, mellow, colloquial style (no 'Ladies and gentlemen'): 'Well, Sir Samuel Hoare's "golden age in Europe" has certainly begun with a bang.'

He stood with hands open on hips, or in his coat pocket. It was only towards the end that his gestures became really melodramatic. He spoke of Jewish financiers; he crouched and snarled, with clutching hands. He spoke of his party ('born of blood and soil'), of men who had 'found their souls in the comradeship of the Blackshirt movement'; he drew himself up, hand to heart, face gazing up into the light, voice ringing out sonorously.

Certainly I didn't take down all his speech. Sometimes I only noted his favourite words – 'shackles', 'holocaust', 'tentacles', 'revolution', 'aliens'. All the rest of the nation, it seems, is – consciously or not – in a great 'conspiracy' against the Blackshirts.

He got in some excellent cracks at the government. His sarcasm is broad and schoolboyish. Sir John Simon is always 'Soapy Simon'. He repeats the same joke several times – probably a wise thing to do, with that type of audience.

He said that the British Government had 'said to the Red Government in Spain: "Fight to the last – Britain's behind you, France is behind you, democracy's behind you, Ellen Wilkinson's behind you." ' (Loud laughter.)

I am sure the British Government would be as surprised as I was to learn that they had ever said anything like that.

He doesn't hesitate to take credit when it's only questionably due: that no one in Parliament that day had 'dared to ask for war' about Czechoslovakia showed how 'effective' the Blackshirts' work had been!

The way he said it all was in the best tradition of demagogy. What he said was an odd mixture of sense and nonsense. He has obviously studied the Opinion column of the *Daily Express* attentively: his views on empire development might have been quoted straight from it.

His defence of Nazi aggression would find less general agreement. Not only should the German colonies be given back; he would not be alarmed if Germany built naval and air bases in Africa – Britain being strong enough to live in 'manly friendship' (a phrase used four times) with a strong Germany. It was 'sheer cowardice' to think otherwise. 'I here and now give notice,' he said, 'that on the day British Union assumes power all treaties that tie the British people down will be shattered the same afternoon.' He has, as they say, hopes.

So we came to question time, when the scene already described occurred. One question got the answer that Masons, Oddfellows and so on would be allowed by Blackshirts, 'so long as we have no proof that seditious matters are discussed at their meetings'.

I ought perhaps to add that I am not a Jew, but that, judging by what I have seen of British Fascists, I would rather be a Jew than a Fascist.

For what it is worth, I welcome their hostility.

'William Hickey'
Eagle in Dove's Clothing
Daily Express, 10 July 1939

There are many influences which help the Nazis just now – some unintentionally, some with the intention disguised.

There was that Indian paper I mentioned the other day, which prints only Axis radio programmes. The BBC write to tell me that they have taken this matter up, that the editor has agreed to publish their programmes too in future. They are right: it is rarely better to let hostile propaganda go unanswered.

There are other papers nearer home which, under guises as harmless as that Indian radio journal's, are helping the Nazis directly or indirectly.

There is the weekly *Peace News*, organ of the Peace Pledge Union, whose membership is 127,644.

PPU was founded by a great idealist, the late Dick Sheppard. The bulk of its supporters are idealists too, pacifists of the purest sort; many clergymen and well-meaning intellectuals are among them.

They are exceedingly active just now. They hold many meetings. They have set up a network of 'advisory bureaux' all over the country. They distributed leaflets to militiamen enrolled last month.

All that may do little harm . . .

But, for a newspaper one of whose primary objects may be supposed to be the defence of freedom of conscience, *Peace News* devotes a remarkably large amount of space to material friendly to Nazi Germany.

It publishes weekly an anonymous column by 'The Plain Man'. This week 'The Plain Man' deals with Danzig. He doesn't think there will be a war about Danzig. He seems to think Hitler will get it. His view is that small nations must continue to be 'thrown to the wolves' until there is 'a world movement towards a better scheme of' – apparently – colonial distribution.

Last week 'The Plain Man' pleaded for 'understanding' of Goebbels and his demand for 'deeds not promises' from London. He suggested – a little naively, even for a plain man – that if only Britain would lead resharing of world's wealth, would give up territorial or other advantages gained in the last war, would disarm, Nazi leaders wouldn't work up anti-British feeling in Germany.

I bet they wouldn't.

Other items in *Peace News* are:

Series on Hitler by Wilfred Wellock, who argues that Hitler doesn't want conquest or world domination but merely 'economic independence' for Germany; and says of the Nazi leaders, 'We must assume that they possess, or would develop when the necessity arose, an ideal of social greatness for their country.'

Statistics to show that crisis is the fault of democratic Powers for owning too much raw material.

Plans for 'friendly visits to Germany' this summer.

Reprint of article written by Bertrand Russell during last war, on technique of 'non-violent resistance': military invasion of Britain by Germans should not be opposed, would thus be made to look 'ridiculous'; co-operation in German administration of Britain should be refused – so Germans, thought Russell, would find the job too difficult and go home in despair!

•

DOROTHY THOMPSON

Dorothy Thompson (1893–1961) was born in Lancaster, New York. The daughter of a Methodist minister, she was dispatched in her teens to live with an aunt in Chicago, where she attended the Lewis Institute. In 1914 she graduated from Syracuse University and went to work for the New York State Suffrage Association in Buffalo, New York. She saved money and in 1920 was able to buy her passage to Europe, where she became a free-lance reporter for the International News Service, the *New York Evening Post*, the *Christian Science Monitor* and the *Manchester Guardian*. In 1925 she became the *New York Evening Post*'s bureau chief in Berlin, and while there she met her future husband, the American novelist Sinclair Lewis. She returned with Lewis to the United States in 1928 to combine domesticity with occasional free-lancing, but the urge to be once again in the European fray was too much and she and her husband went back there in 1930. Thompson interviewed Hitler for *Cosmopolitan*, which was not one of her better assignments, since she dismissed him as a force not to be reckoned with. However, in 1936 she began a three-times-a-week column for the *New York Herald Tribune*, 'On the Record', in which she criticized Nazism and warned against appeasement. Syndicated to about 170 papers, her column was an influential voice against the isolationist mood in the United States. By way of contrast, she also started writing a monthly column about domestic matters for the *Ladies' Home Journal* in 1937. In 1940 she left the *Herald Tribune* for the *New York Post* and the Bell Syndicate. After the war she took up the Palestinian cause and was unfairly branded as an anti-Semite. The *Post* dropped her column in 1947, but the Bell Syndicate continued to carry it until 1958. She also wrote numerous books.

'On the Record'
Cassandra Speaking
New York Herald Tribune, March 17, 1939

I SEE BY THE PAPERS

New York Times   October 7, 1938

Prime Minister Chamberlain in a speech to the House of Commons on October 6, 1938 (after Munich):

'. . . To accuse us of having by that advice betrayed Czechoslovakia is simply preposterous. All we did was to save her from annihilation, to give her a chance of a new life as a new state which, even although it involves the loss of territory and fortifications, perhaps she may be able to enjoy in the future and develop a national existence in a neutrality and security comparable to that which we see in Switzerland today.'

We are, at least, no longer susceptible to shocks over what is happening in central Europe. We feel pain and sorrow. But we do not share the perennial and amazing surprise of Mr Chamberlain.

On February 18, 1938 – that is more than a year ago now, and before the entrance of Hitler into Austria – I wrote:

'Write it down. On Saturday, February 12, 1938, Germany won the world war, and dictated in Berchtesgaden a peace treaty to make the Treaty of Versailles look like one of the great humane documents of the ages.

'Write it down. On Saturday, February 12, 1938, militarism, paganism and despotism started on the march across all of Europe east of the Rhine.

'Write it down that the world revolution began in earnest – and perhaps the world war.

'Why does Germany want Austria? For raw materials? It has none of consequence. To add to German prosperity? It inherits a poor country with serious problems. But strategically, it is the key to the whole of central Europe. Czechoslovakia is now surrounded. The wheat fields of Hungary and the oil fields of Rumania are now open. *Not one of them will be able to stand the pressure of German domination . . .*

'It is horror walking. Not that "Germany" joins with Austria. We are not talking of "Germany." We see a new Crusade, under a pagan totem, worshiping "blood" and "soil," preaching the holiness of the sword, glorifying conquest, despising the Slavs, whom it conceives to be its historic "mission" to rule; subjecting all of life to a collectivist, militarized state. Persecuting men and women of Jewish blood, however diluted it may be. Moving, now, into the historic stronghold of Catholic Christianity, into an area of mixed races and mixed nationalities, which a thousand years of Austro-Hungarian Empire could only rule tolerably with tolerance.'

On September 21, I wrote an 'Obituary for Europe' and on October 1, following the Pact of Munich, I wrote 'Peace – And the Crisis Begins!' which was severely criticized in some quarters for its failure to rejoice over the peace. I said:

'What happened on Friday is called "Peace." Actually it is an international Fascist *coup d'état*.

'The "Four-Power Accord" is not even a diplomatic document. It is certainly not a normal treaty. It is such a fantastic piece of paper that it is difficult to describe except as a hurriedly concocted armistice made in advance of a war to permit the occupation by German troops of a territory which by sheer threat and demonstration of force they have conquered by "agreement."

'*There is not the most elementary consideration of justice . . .*

'The pressure of the Nazis in contiguous territories occupied by German troops, their immense and cunningly organized propaganda, their house-by-house and name-by-name political organization; the ever-present threat that if the territories go German the political minorities will be exterminated, will assure the outcome of these plebiscites. *One might just as well cede them to Germany in the first place . . .*

'Even on the basis of what by internal evidence would seem to be a rigged report [the Runciman Report], Germany is guilty of provoking what was nearly an all-European war. And the punishment for this guilt is that she received everything that she was going to fight the war over.

'*This "everything" is more than the Sudeten territories. It is more than a free hand in the east. It is the domination of Europe* . . .

'In this whole affair, described as an attempt to keep peace, the democratic process has been completely suspended. In both Britain and France the facts have been suppressed by the exercise of government pressure on the controlled radio and on the newspapers. The people of England and France are confronted with a *fait accompli* without even being able to gain in advance possession of the facts on which it is based! . . .

'*Not only is Czechoslovakia dismembered – what is left is destroyed as a democratic republic. It will be utterly impossible for the new state to exist under the conditions created.*'

On October 17, in 'The Case of Cardinal Innitzer,' the prophecy of Heine was recalled:

'It is the greatest merit of Christianity to have assuaged the joy of the German in brutal bellicosity, but . . . when, one day, the Cross of Christ is broken, the savagery of the old warriors, the wild berserker wrath, will break forth anew in all the barbaric fury of which our Nordic poets tell in song and saga. Even today the talisman of Christianity has begun to rot, and the day will come when its power will piteously collapse. Then will the old stone gods arise from the accumulated rubbish of the past . . . When that day comes . . . take good care, Frenchmen, and do not interfere with those affairs which we are settling among ourselves. Take care neither to fan the fire nor to quench it . . . Do not laugh at my advice . . . the advice of a dreamer . . . German thunder is admittedly German: it is not very agile . . . but it will come one day, and . . . you will hear an explosion such as has never yet occurred in the history of the world.

'The hour will come, when, like spectators in an amphitheater, the nations will crowd around Germany to watch the great tourney.'

Chamberlain umbrellas are being advertised to wear in one's coat lapel this spring. I am not wearing this symbol. I recall what happens to umbrellas when carried in cyclones. They blow inside out and have been known to bear their carriers into the whirlwind.

'On the Record'
Chamberlain and Alice
New York Herald Tribune, April 5, 1939

I SEE BY THE PAPERS

New York Times   April 1, 1939

Prime Minister Neville Chamberlain, speaking to the House of Commons on March 31, 1939: '. . . I now have to inform the House that . . . in the event of any action which clearly threatens Polish independence . . . His Majesty's Government would feel themselves bound at once to lend the Polish Government all the support in their power.'

There is a reason why *Alice in Wonderland* is pre-eminently *the* English classic. It is a tender and humorous glorification of the age of innocence.

Alice is the very well-brought-up, polite and extremely reasonable English child who finds herself in a world full of unreasonable foreigners – a world where the bottles labeled 'Drink Me' are not marked 'poison,' the way all bottles in the nursery medicine closet ought to be, and which, nevertheless, when you drink their contents, 'shut you up like a telescope.'

If the bottle had only been decently marked, as a proper English bottle would have been, Alice would not have drunk it, 'for she had read several nice little stories about children who had got burnt and eaten up by wild beasts and other unpleasant things, all because they *would* not remember the simple rules their friends had taught them; such as that a red-hot poker would burn you if you hold it too long, and that if you cut your finger *very* deeply with a knife it generally bleeds, and she had never forgotten that if you drink much from a bottle marked "poison" it is almost certain to disagree with you sooner or later.'

However, as you remember, this bottle was not marked 'poison,' so Alice ventured to taste it, and 'finding it very nice (it had, in fact, a sort of mixed flavour of cherry tart, custard, pineapple, roast turkey, toffee and hot buttered toast), she very soon finished it all.'

Now, what happened to Alice after that was that she became only a fraction of her former size, and since this sudden diminution made it impossible for her to do some of the things she very much wanted to do, she sat down and cried. But being a well-brought-up little English child, she took herself severely to task, saying, 'There is no use crying like that!'

And we learn that Alice was in the habit of scolding herself and even sometimes of boxing her own ears 'for having cheated herself in a game of croquet she was playing against herself, for this curious child was very fond of pretending to be two people. "But it's no use now," thought poor Alice, "to pretend to be two people! Why, there's hardly enough of me left to make one respectable person!" '

And you remember that, pulling herself together and seeing a box marked 'Eat Me,' Alice figured that she might as well eat it, 'for if it makes me grow larger I can reach the key, and if it makes me grow smaller I can creep under the door. So either way I can get into the garden.'

For those who find it difficult to understand Mr Chamberlain I recommend a rereading of the English classic.

Mr Chamberlain followed the 'Drink Me' policy at Munich, and the 'Eat Me' policy in the House of Commons last week and this.

It is called the muddling-through policy when translated into political terms, and is totally ununderstandable to anything except an English mind. It is a combination of responsibility without reasoning.

It has its uses in English statesmen. I use the word 'English' advisedly. It is certainly not Scottish. And it is, above all, not Welsh or Irish. One can perfectly imagine Mr Chamberlain at six as the masculine twin of Alice. One cannot imagine Mr Lloyd George as anything but a very distant relative. Its usefulness is that the qualities of Alice – her niceness, her reasonability and her incredible foolishness – attract the English people.

If Alice makes a mistake it is because of her innocence, because she is really much too nice to live in a world full of falsely labeled bottles and boxes, perverted nursery rhymes, vicious old Father Williamses and ugly Duchesses. She is confused and misled, but in the end it all turns out to be a nightmare.

And she wakes up in her secure nursery, comforted by her tea, recalling the shriek of the gryphon, the choking of the suppressed guinea pigs and the distant sob of the miserable mock turtle as a fantastic experience.

Yes, Alice is beloved by England because of her unconquerable simplicity.

And so, strange as it may seem to any type of mind except the English, it is extremely probable that Mr Chamberlain is stronger in his leadership because he turned out to be wrong than he would have been had he been always right.

At any rate, as the result of making incredible blunders, one has Monday's spectacle in the House of Commons, where an entire nation, from the Labor Opposition to the most Bourbon Tories, is united behind the counterpart of Alice.

Perhaps this uncoerced unity, which has been convinced not by using its reason but purely empirically, will turn out to be of more importance to history than all the lost strategical bases. Perhaps, to paraphrase another English poet, there is some method in this madness. For mad it certainly appears to be.

The nation which was not prepared to defend Czechoslovakia, a country which had meticulously kept all of its international engagements, is now prepared to defend Poland, a country which has pursued a most dubious diplomatic course and which is at least as difficult to defend.

Some will look for every explanation except the simple one. But I am inclined to believe that the simple explanation is the true one.

It is very difficult to believe that when Chamberlain went to Munich he did not know that he was giving Hitler a free hand in the east and that he did not know exactly what giving that free hand would mean. But since Mr Chamberlain is English it is possible that he really thought that Hitler would behave like an Englishman and take what he wanted in such a way as not to shock and horrify the world, and stop at the right moment.

I doubt whether Mr Chamberlain has ever in his life met anybody who was not either just a gentleman or a 'gentleman in trade.' But Hitler is neither a gentleman nor a trader.

I am inclined to believe that when Mr Chamberlain said, on the eve of Munich, 'If I were convinced that any nation had made up its mind to dominate the world by fear of its force, I should feel that it must be resisted,' he meant it – but didn't believe. Since then he has come to believe.

What has made him believe has been the *method* of Hitler. What has made him believe is the speed of Hitler.

If Chamberlain had ever read *Mein Kampf* – which I am reasonably sure he has not done – he might have been aware a long time ago. But, being English, even that is doubtful. For the English mind believes only what it sees. It believes in the event, not in the plan.

And the German mind has its equal weakness. It believes in the plan and fails to observe the event.

That is perhaps one reason why Germany won all the first battles but lost the last war. It is not written in history that this will always be so, but it is curious that Hitler, who prides himself on having invented something absolutely new in diplomacy and who attacked Wilhelm's Germany for its idiocy in making an enemy of England and Russia at the same time, has managed to repeat Wilhelm's mistakes.

•

COLLIE KNOX

Collie Knox (1897–1977) was born Columb Thomas Knox, the son of a King's Counsel, Vesey Knox, and a step-nephew of Sir Max Beerbohm. He was attending Rugby when the First World War broke out, and went immediately to Sandhurst. He served in the Queen's Royal Regiment and chose to be attached to the Royal Flying Corps. After an accident in which his stringbag aircraft crashed a thousand feet to the ground, he suffered from a slight speech impediment. He continued a career as a regular soldier, working as an ADC to Sir George (later Lord) Lloyd, Governor of Bombay (on £900 a year 'and all found, including whiskey'), and later Sir Geoffrey Archer, Governor of Uganda. In the mid-1930s he plunged into journalism, writing his first article for the *Morning Post*, then joined the *Daily Express* as a £5-a-week sub.

He sold his idea for a radio column to A. L. Cranfield, editor of the *Daily Mail*, and by 1937 was 'already one of the most famous features in daily journalism'. His radio column, in which he regularly lambasted the BBC, was 2,000 words and ran five days a week, and drew a massive postbag (said to be 35,000 letters in one year). In 1937 he started a more general Friday column called 'Week-End Broadcast', characterized by a chatty, intimate style and dealing with sundry topics: 'I believe in writing my Friday articles in the way one talks to a friend. I do not labour under the delusion that I have a Message, that I am a Crusader, or that God is my younger brother, and I am happy that I have not lost my sense of humour.'

In 1939 he went to the Ministry of Information and in 1941 was made director of ENSA [Entertainments National Service Association] public relations. Also in 1941, he joined the *Star* to write a weekly Saturday column. In 1945 he returned to the *Daily Mail* as a special columnist, mainly dealing with showbusiness, and stayed there until 1955 when he resigned his £4,000 job because he objected to his column appearing below an article by someone else. None the less, he still had a writing contract with the Newnes–Pearson magazine group, a column in *Home Notes* and a 2,000-word Saturday column in the New York *Morning Telegraph* (which earned a letter of appreciation from FBI chief J. Edgar Hoover, no less).

'Week-End Broadcast'

Daily Mail, September 1939
From *Collie Knox Recalls* (1940)

We are tried friends who have so much to say to each other that they feel almost tongue-tied. One false word . . . one failing hold on ourselves and we shall be over the abyss into the wrong kind of emotion . . .

In a day . . . an hour . . . we put aside the pettinesses to which even the best of us are at moments subject and we dedicated our lives anew . . . to the biggest job we have ever tackled. To see the thing through to the end. To keep faith with our King and our leaders . . . for was it not written of Kings and of tyrants . . .

> 'Twixt kings and tyrants there's this difference known:
> Kings seek their subjects' good, tyrants their own.

And it is well that we bear on our mental banner . . . which we shall keep held well before our eyes . . . that every tyrant since the world began has believed in Freedom – for himself.

I say in all sincerity that this is the first time in history that this nation has ever waged a war against Germany on behalf of the German people. It is so indeed. The unhappy dupes and slaves of the Swastika Skull and Crossbones – crushed and oppressed, spied upon, and inhumanly served – look with anguished eyes to the day when Freedom and Right shall prevail.

Their spirits are weak and their minds are dulled . . . but our spirits are strong and our minds are of one purpose. We strive towards a happy issue out of all our and their afflictions, wrought by thugs and madmen. For our turn would assuredly have come . . . had we not cried 'Halt', or, in the words of the taxi-driver who drove me home the other day, 'Arf a mo', 'Itler.'

The peoples of the world will surely echo with Shakespeare . . .

> For what is he they follow? truly, gentlemen,
> A bloody tyrant and a homicide;
> One rais'd in blood, and one in blood established . . .
> A base foul stone . . .
> One that hath ever been God's enemy.

My taxi friend – who fought in the last war and was bitterly communing with himself because his wife threw his tin-hat in the dustbin two years ago – said to me, 'This is a business and no mistake. You know, I'm sorry for that chap Hitler's people: they only want to live in peace like we do. It's a rotten shame. Poor blighters.'

I feel that all of us who think straight at all – and most of us have cleared our minds of cobwebs by now – agree with the taxi chap. Has not our Prime Minister – his eve of war broadcast will never be forgotten – himself broadcast to Germany: 'We are not fighting in this war against you, the German people, for whom we have no bitter feeling'?

Our land is full with refugees who have during the last years given up their homes and careers because they refused to bend the knee to the monster's rule. They came here and have tried to tell us what is going on, hoping that more of their own folk would revolt against intolerable conditions. They are grateful to this country – as they well may be – and for all this talent and brains we shall, I know, find a use. And we must be kind and 'understand'.

It is a wonderful thing to me that a country begins a war in such a spirit. And it makes one feel mighty proud . . . and if I go on saying too much what I feel about US I shall go plunging over that abyss I mentioned a moment ago, and that would not do at all.

This is no Khaki War. No drums are sounding. No flags are being waved. No hysterical crowds are screaming heroics and uttering death-defying threats. Whether we wear a neat blue suit, a navy or army uniform, or any uniform at all, we are all 'in it'. We are doing what we can . . . It is no use talking about a 'civilian population' any more. There are no civilians.

I have known one war, and, like others who knew it too, never thought we would see another. Our feelings now are too deep for words. Things were different then . . . and when we were boys in a uniformed struggle we were all very excited and thought it all too thrilling for words. Poets wrote sarcastic things about 'scarlet majors at the base' (often with truth), and about comfortable people in England who 'toddled home to die in bed'.

And I recall a very cleverly drawn cartoon depicting an enormously fat man, with seventeen chins and a red nose, sprawling in a large club armchair, drinking a treble brandy and soda, and shouting, 'We will fight to the death.'

Other times, other habits, of very truth. No one is comfortable now. Indeed quite apart from personal danger . . . things are extremely uncomfortable. We have all of us got to rearrange our lives. We must get up earlier . . . we must go to bed earlier. There will be hours of acute boredom, and hours of acute fright . . . there is no use boggling at the truth.

So we must learn – and such is our extraordinary adaptability, we very soon will learn – to make our own entertainments and to read those books we never had time to read before, and to build up inward strength. Those, I mean, who are not in the Services . . . though all are, or will be shortly, in Service.

I do so concur with the opinion put forward a day or two ago by a writer who can speak with authority of the last war, that it is to be hoped there will be no 'White Feather' nonsense this time.

A band of hysterical and giggling girls banded themselves together to go up to any man of 'military age' (we are all of military age now) in the street, or wherever it happened to be, and to hand him a white feather if he were not in uniform. They did not last long, for public opinion drove them to more useful 'war work', and on one occasion two of them narrowly escaped being thrashed in public.

Once I was with a fellow . . . he was not in uniform, though I was . . . and one of these girls gave him a white feather. He accepted it with a bow and then told the idiot girl that some hours earlier he had had the honour of being decorated by the King with the Victoria Cross at Buckingham Palace. Which was true. I leave you to imagine the girl's face.

Much later on I myself had the unhappy distinction of being awarded the charming emblem of cowardice. At the Carlton Grill, it was, if I remember. As I had just come out of eight months in hospital after impinging upon the earth in an aeroplane from a very unpleasantly great height, I was not too pleased.

No, there must be none of this. There must be no probing into other people's business. Energies must be directed aright . . . energy is needed . . . mental and physical. And when it is not active it must be conserved.

It makes me smile a bit when I remember how, during past years, some people have said, and kept on saying, 'Ah, this generation is not like the last one.'

This generation is, of course, exactly the same. As usual, the most unlikely young men and women are in the front of the queue. As usual, the men and women who have kept their counsel are proved to have been 'making ready' for a long time.

A pal of mine has annoyed me faintly for some time past by constantly telling me that if war should ever come again he would never volunteer for any service. 'No damned fear,' he would exclaim, 'not for me. I've had enough. Let the younger fellows do it if they want to.'

A few days ago I was walking down Pall Mall . . . the shady side . . . when I cannoned into a hasty person who appeared to be late for several trains all at once. He looked very hot and cross and was about to consign me to perdition when he recognized me.

'Oh, hallo,' he panted. 'Can't stop. Going to the War Office . . . to see if there is anything I can do. What are you going to do? Oh, good. Well, good-bye.' And off he rushed . . . I need not tell you who it was.

I met him again – at a club . . . for we must all eat – and he was in a fury because the War Office had told him he was at present over age . . . and that a game leg and one eye were handicaps. I thought he would burst.

The nights are not much fun. We all know that. We have just got to lump them . . . and remember that our defences are in tip-top order . . . and that those gay, shining balloons hanging in the sky are ready to trip up an enemy.

Funny thing, I do not know if it will interest you, but I was present at the inauguration of the balloon barrage system . . . in 1917 it was. Since then, of course, it has been altered and perfected, but it was the idea from which these shiny helpmeets have emerged. It was on Barnes Common. Beautiful day it was . . . just like yesterday.

I was connected with the Air Defence then, and Lord French and the General Commanding and myself drove down in the Field-Marshal's car to see the first testing of these balloons. All was set . . . and we stood in the middle of the common . . . when something went wrong. And two balloons very like the ones you see today broke loose. Two aircraftmen unhappily held too long on to the guy ropes, and they were carried up with the balloons.

One man fell a hundred feet only a few yards from us. The other, poor chap, hung on till he was a speck in the sky, and let go over Croydon. The wires holding the balloons swished and whistled across the grass, trailing like spiders' legs from the sky, and if we had not rushed for a tree we would have been caught up, too. Lord French never spoke, but went back to his car. He looked very white . . . but I recall I said to my general afterwards that those two aircraftmen who had been killed would one day be hailed as pioneers. That their lives would not have been in vain.

My mood was not particularly prophetic just then.

Our heads are useful to us. They may or may not be particularly beautiful, but they serve their purpose. We would fare ill without them. So it behoves us all to 'keep them'.

When the first air raid warning sounded . . . the first thing I heard was a woman in a flat in the block where I dwell shouting at the top of her voice. She yelled for her chauffeur to get the car ready. 'We must get back to the country at once' . . . and she let high heaven know that truly and thoroughly she had lost her head.

Her screamings affected even the stoutest of us, as is natural . . . so that my neighbours, who were calm and ready to go down into the shelter, began to get jittery. That kind of panic is catching.

If any of you at such an emergency come across men or women who behave in that fashion I advise you to have no truck with them. It will be no time to stand on ceremony or to observe that exquisite politeness towards our fellow creatures which so distinguishes us. The pouring of a bucket of water over a panic-spreader can be well recommended . . . for its cold, icy shock restores the mind to its level balance. Perhaps two buckets of water are even more efficacious.

Near where I dwell is a police station house wherein live members of that Metropolitan Force who are justly called 'wonderful' by all visiting film stars who know their onions. The other morning . . . about three a.m., wasn't it? . . . they welcomed us all inside to their heavily sandbagged fortress with smiles and that humorous resignation which is the mark of every true Briton when any circumstance gets beyond his personal control.

We must have looked a funny lot as we struggled in and sat down on wooden benches. Some of us displayed a pretty taste in pyjamas and dressing-gowns, and one girl was tastefully arrayed in grey flannel trousers and a crimson sweater. The police officers, some in uniform and some not in uniform, gave one an impression of confidence which would have surprised them considerably.

One 'shelterer', a woman, talked a great deal too much . . . but that was nerves, of course. She was very bright indeed and bored one member of my household so profoundly that he went off to sleep sitting up.

But she was doing her best . . . was the bright lady.

Do you notice at all that you feel more thirsty than usual? Must be the reaction after an hour or two of pulse-quickening at the thought of 'what might be'. Personally, when I got home after the All Clear I could have filled the Albert Hall and drunk it.

Yes, the nights are not pleasant just now. The sun is more than ever our friend and we look at him and say, 'Well, as long as you are shining away we are more or less safe.' And then he sinks to rest, and, whether we admit it or not, we would gladly bid him stay a little longer.

We must not be afraid of feeling afraid. It is natural indeed at an emergency moment to get that pit-of-the-tummy sensation as if a horse had just kicked us with stunning accuracy. But it passes. Everything passes. And we come out into the light.

Well, we have our Big Job to do and we must get on with it. And not pause nor draw back till it is done. Till justice and humanity rule again and men and women may go about their days, and their nights, in safety and peace.

For the strangers in our midst we shall have consideration and sympathy. For one another we shall have comradeship and cheer.

Already are emerging the Great Qualities . . . and they shine like a blinding light amid the present darkness.

•

DAMON RUNYON

Damon Runyon (1884–1946) was born Alfred Damon Runyan in Manhattan, Kansas. He acquired his new surname when a printer misspelled it and he was advised to dispense with his first name because it made his byline too unwieldy. In 1887 his family moved to Pueblo, Colorado, where he was later a reporter for the *Pueblo Evening Press*. He enlisted in the US Army in 1898 and was posted to the Philippines, writing for a military paper, *Manila Freedom*, and a magazine called *Soldier's Letter*. He rejoined his newspaper in Pueblo the following year and was a journeyman reporter for various local papers until 1905 when the *Denver Post* hired him as a sportswriter. He was sacked, and then given a job by the *Rocky Mountain News*. Within a few years his short stories were being published by magazines like *Collier's* and *McClure's*, and in 1910 he moved to New York as a sportswriter for Hearst's *New York American*. He could not help injecting humour into his reports and consequently, in 1914, was given a humour column called 'Th' Mornin' Mornin' '. In 1928 his column changed its name, first to 'I Think So', then to 'Between You and Me', with a greater emphasis on his favourite sports, boxing and horse-racing. The famous Broadway stories for which he is best known today were published in the *Saturday Evening Post*, *Collier's* and *Cosmopolitan* from 1929 to 1940. In the 1930s he started writing a sports column called 'Both Barrels', then abandoned that for a general syndicated column called first 'As I See It' and later 'The Brighter Side'. In addition, he wrote another column for the *New York Daily Mirror*. His column-writing made Runyon a rich man who could afford a home in Florida and several racehorses. He died of cancer and his friend Walter Winchell founded a cancer fund in his name. His ashes were scattered over Manhattan from a plane, and after his death his Broadway stories were made into the musical *Guys and Dolls*.

The Insidious I

From Short Takes: Readers' Choice of the Best Columns of America's Favorite
Newspaperman (1946)

My autobiography, or life story, is one thing you can bet I will never write.

If I told the truth, a lot of persons, including myself, might go to jail. If I held out the truth or just told it half way, a lot of my pals who now have confidence in me would be saying: 'That Runyon is a scaredy-cat and a phony bum. As long as he was going to write his life at all, why didn't he write it on the emmus.'*

---

* Meaning 'on the level'. Hollywood talk.

Of course an even more potent reason why I am never going to write my own tale is that there is no sure money in that tripe. It is purely speculative. It might sell but the odds are against it.

It is pretty difficult to find a bookie in New York nowadays to get a market on this proposition but I imagine the price of publication against any book selling to a profit is easily 50 to 1 and up, depending on the author.

I think you could write your own ticket on an autobiography.

I am frankly a hired Hessian on the typewriter and have never pretended to be anything else and when I write something I want to know in advance how much I am going to be paid for it and when.

I am aware that there are many other writing fellows, especially in the newspaper columning dodge, who write out of sheer altruism and who pick up their weekly wage envelopes merely as a matter of form. But not Professor Runyon. The professor wants his. I think I am less spurious than those muggs who let on that their journalistic pursuits are guided by motives far above mere gold.

However, a note from a publishing house which says it is interested in my autobiography helps solve a mystery for me. For years I have been wondering who tells people to write autobiographies. Many a time as I have skimmed through the pages of such a tome, I have said to myself, How can anybody as inconsequential in the world and with as little to say as this guy have the gall to spoil all this white paper?

Well, obviously the publishers tell them, which partly absolves a number of persons against whom I have been nursing the most sinister designs. I do not know who tells the publishers. That is something I am going to investigate at the earliest opportunity.

Maybe many a fellow is going along through life minding his own business and keeping his affairs to himself as he should when some publisher or his representative sneaks up behind the poor bloke and whispers in his ear:

'Look – why not write your autobiography?'

That does it. The fellow immediately becomes a frightful bore.

I say there ought to be a national committee to which book publishers should be required to submit the names of persons they contemplate asking for autobiographies, the committee to survey each candidate on his experiences before a single line is permitted to be set down on paper. The approval of the committee should be something not easily secured.

I do not think my material would ever pass on the basis of importance. My life has been made up of trivialities. I have accomplished no great deeds. I have met no considerable number of the high muck-a-mucks of the world, and when I did I was always too self-conscious to hear what they said.

Of course, I could tell about the time Butch Tower was playing vaudeville in Grand Rapids, Michigan, when a furniture dealers' convention was being held there and he shot craps on a blanket on the floor with them with such success that, after examining both sides of the blanket and all sides of the dice, they suggested that Butch ought to give them a handicap by hanging the blanket on a line across the room like a sheet up to dry.

So the blanket was rigged like the walls of Jericho in the movie *It Happened One Night* when, as you probably remember, Clark Gable, the lucky dog, was in bed on one side of the blanket and Claudette Colbert was in bed on the other side. And the furniture dealers made Butch stand on one side of the blanket which was hung head high and hurl the dice plumb over it.

And what do you think happened? What do you think happened?

Why, Butch cleaned those furniture dealers from top to bottom. If they had been betting their own merchandise, he would have been able to furnish a ten-room house.

Not on Speaking Terms

From *Short Takes: Readers' Choice of the Best Columns of America's Favorite Newspaperman* (1946)

I was in the Stork Club with Mike Todd and Lenny Lyons, the Broadway columnist, when Billy Rose, the theatrical producer, stopped at our table and gave me a real big double-breasted hello, the kind you usually reserve for a creditor, unexpectedly encountered.

He also gave Lenny Lyons a hello, not as big as mine yet adequate because he sees Lenny oftener than he does me, and hellos are naturally graduated according to frequency of expenditure on one object. But Billy Rose did not give Mike Todd even a little bitsy hello.

In fact, he did not as much as glance at Mike Todd and Mike Todd did not glance at Billy Rose, and I think it is a pretty good trick for two persons not to glance at each other in a space so limited that a glance and a half make a crowd. Then I remembered that Mike Todd and Billy Rose have not spoken to each other in several years because of some business difference.

I would say that this state of affairs has its compensations for other theatrical producers because if Todd and Rose got together in a field in which they are regarded as the smartest guys of a new era, they might make it very tough on all rivals. However, I suppose some of their mutual friends find the non-speaking business a trifle awkward.

Personally, I think the best thing to do in a situation such as I have described above is to preserve an attitude of moderate cordiality, neither over-warm nor yet unduly cool. Then when one guy goes along you can make some remark about him that will convince the fellow you are with that you are on his side, though afterwards when you run into the other gee you can let him know that it was not your fault that he found you with that fellow.

I mean, one has to be diplomatic in such matters. I do not think a person is required to take sides openly when two friends are not speaking to each other, though in the days when I was a great hand for not speaking to people I felt had done me dirt, I was inclined to dispute this theory as pursued by a certain member of my family, to wit Mrs R, whose name I am not supposed to mention in my writings but who is away at the moment and will not see it.

She is of very friendly disposition and I have known her to stop in the street and chat gaily with some mugg I was not speaking to while I stood glumly on the sidelines hoping the bum would drop dead. (No! No! Not you, Mrs R! The mugg.) Her answer to my reproaches was that if she stopped speaking to everyone I was not speaking to, there would be long periods when she would be doomed to non-communication with human beings.

I suppose she had the right slant, though one time when I stopped to talk to a dame, she was not speaking to, her reactions were most peculiar. She said that was different. Some day I am going to ask her how it was different. But in any event, I am now speaking to everyone. I have found it less of a strain than not speaking to someone.

There is an art in not speaking to people without seeming obvious and self-conscious about it, and a greater art to carrying off meetings in company with those you are not speaking to without making everyone else feel awkward. I think George Smith, a well-known box-office man of sports events in New York, had a simple solution to that problem.

George used to issue a calendar every year as a holiday greeting and also to inform his friends because it said: 'I am not speaking to the following persons,' then listing the usually not inconsiderable number of those who got no hellos from George. I think he has discontinued the practice of late years, possibly because of the paper shortage.

Harry Leon Wilson, the author of *Ruggles of Red Gap*, and numerous other works, had another system. Harry would set you down in his own mind. He might leave you one evening with words of affection and the following morning when you were looking for a five-gallon hello, would pass you without a nod.

That meant you were suspended from his hellos and you might never know the reason. Then one day he would hello you just as if nothing had happened and you knew you were reinstated. Once Harry had practically everyone he knew suspended for a month and he went around rather lonesome.

John J. McGraw, in his heyday as manager of the New York Giants, did not speak to his third baseman, Charley Herzog, and any communication between them was through a third person. One day McGraw forgot their relations and yelled 'bunt' to Herzog who was at bat but, instead, Charley hit a home run, saying McGraw had no right to address him directly and he wanted to show his displeasure.

I was of a mind to try to act as mediator between Todd and Rose and get them to make up. Then I reflected that if I were successful they would compare notes and find out what I said about one to the other, and both would stop speaking to me.

Around with Winchell

From Short Takes: Readers' Choice of the Best Columns of America's Favorite
Newspaperman (1946)

Winchell kept me out until broad daylight two nights hand-running mostly just walking around. I do not mind awaiting daylight in some pleasant deadfall but walking around is no good for me and Walter cannot show me that it is of any benefit to him, either. Because while he walks around a heap, he always has a beef about not feeling any too well, and he gets balder by the minute.

Of course, I was on to Winchell while he was walking me around. I knew he wanted company and that he wanted to talk. I made the ideal companion inasmuch as I am unable to articulate and he did not have to listen to my replies.

Once I wrote out an answer to one of his statements and he paused under a street light to read it; then he said you are dead right, Runyon. But I saw Walter was looking at it upside down and nobody can read my handwriting upside down, and very few right-side up, and anyway he should have denied what I said, so I did not attempt any more answers. I just walked and listened, and listened and walked, and I am sure he has had no finer audience in years.

I reckon Winchell likes to talk more than any other man alive with the possible exception of Herbert Bayard Swope, the dashing gentleman who was editor of the New York *World* for years and more recently a big figure in horse-racing, and always the bon vivant and raconteur and what-have-you.

It used to be held that a collision of the conversational immovable object and the verbal irresistible force would be a meeting between Swope and 'Hurry-Up' Yost, the Michigan football coach, and finally Grantland Rice arranged it at his home one evening years ago.

The result was supposed to have been a victory for Yost as Swope finally took his hat and left but I thought the decision unjust because Yost was strictly a one-subject man and would talk about nothing else, the subject being football, which I contend is one of the dullest in the world, while Swope is an all-around gabber and generally pretty interesting.

I think Winchell could have spotted Yost six all-American elevens and Swope an encyclopedia and still out-talk them both, but that is just a personal opinion and no formal contest can ever be arranged though I got an informal line on Winchell as opposed to Swope the other night.

Winchell was sitting at a table in the Stork Club with me and right next to us was a party that included Irving Berlin, Alfy Vanderbilt, Oscar Levant and Swope with their women folks. Swope was posted with his back to us. But presently Swope was turning around to talk to Winchell and Winchell was leaning over to talk to Swope until he was practically in the other party and Swope was in ours, and it was quite a give-and-take until I noticed the women folks acting a little restless over this invasion of privacy, and so was I.

It was after the women folks got up and sort o' swept Swope out of the place with them (with the chats unfinished) that Winchell decided we ought to take a stroll. At first he wanted me to go cruising about with him in his auto in which he can pick up police calls and hurry to the scene of the crime but I was too smart for that. Winchell at forty-eight still loves the game of cops and robbers as much as a little boy.

So we walked from the Stork over to Hanson's drugstore at Fifty-first and Seventh Avenue, a small establishment through which filters the early morning life of Broadway, and as we walked Winchell talked, mostly in reminiscence. I know of no man who is more entertaining than Walter when he is in the mood, nor one who has greater store of experience on which to draw.

En route we passed that towering citadel of a warehouse at Fifty-third and Seventh Avenue which I imagine must contain more tales than any other building in the whole world and we found the embrasure-like windows open. Peering in we saw a porter at work 'mid massive furniture and drapes, probably truck in storage.

'I've passed here a thousand times in twenty years and I never saw those windows open before,' said Winchell, and I nodded my own testimony on this point. He was silent for the first full minute since we started out, apparently lost in thought and then he said: 'The history of the Winchells from the time I started newspaper work on Broadway is stored in there. Little things that we didn't want to throw away but couldn't carry around with us – furniture, books, pictures, toys – trifles and mementoes. I haven't seen that stuff in years but we keep paying charges on it. But what was I saying before I interrupted myself?'

'It was something about you and Hellinger in the old El Fay Club,' I said.

'Do I bore you?' Winchell asked, suspiciously. 'Or are you becoming a milksop and a weakling and want to go to bed? It's only six-thirty. How about a spin through the park? No? All right. Now about Hellinger and I that time –'

•

HAROLD NICOLSON

Sir Harold Nicolson (1886–1968) was born in Tehran, the son of a British diplomat, and was educated at Wellington College and Balliol College, Oxford. He served as a diplomat from 1909 to 1929, when he moved into journalism as editor of Londoner's Diary on the *Evening Standard*. He left after little more than a year and devoted himself to writing biographies. He also became a National Labour MP in 1935, surviving in the House until 1945. From 1939 to 1952 he wrote the 'Marginal Comment' column for the *Spectator*, which was highly acclaimed. Otherwise, he is most famous for his remarkable *Diaries and Letters 1930–1962* (1966–8).

'Marginal Comment'
Spectator, 24 February 1939

I was reading the other day the memoirs of a former American diplomatist. It was not an interesting book since its author possessed little memory for, or insight into, serious things. But he did care about food. He wrote lovingly, in the manner of Colonel Newnham-Davis, of vanished restaurants in four continents. Fascinated as I am by all forms of human snobbishness, I find restaurant snobbishness one of the most subtle and entrancing. We all know the type of man who will talk with maddening dignity of Foyot or Voisin, of Larue or La Pérouse, 'as they used to be before they were discovered by the tourists'. We know that other type who will dismiss those once-famous establishments and will claim that the only place where one can get a decent meal in Paris is with Madame Aubert in her flat on the Boulevard Raspail – 'only of course you must let her know in advance'. We know the cosmopolitan who assures us that the *bouillabaisse* at Bregaillon is better than that at the Reserve; that nowhere in Paris can one obtain such food as at Dijon railway station; that for sucking pig one must go, not to the Casa de Botion in Madrid, but to the Eritana in Seville; and that the only place where any sensible or educated man can expect to enjoy his *mousaka* is at Tokatlian's (not at Istanbul, of course, but in the branch establishment at Therapia). To such a man the most unprovocative turbot at a London club will evoke memories of *glachi de carpe* at Capsa's; and the most honest partridge will tempt him to tell really tiresome and exhausting stories about how, in Iran, they make *fessinjan* out of the little *tihu* of the desert flavoured with the juices of the walnut and the pomegranate.

I am not myself much of a restaurant snob, yet it is a sorrow to me that I am never recognized by head-waiters. I have moments of envy for those of my friends whose appearance in any restaurant from San Francisco to Omsk lashes the staff into an orgy of welcoming adulation. Yet there is (or was) one head-waiter in the world who used to call me by my name. I refer to Olivier of the Paris Ritz. Some years ago I was walking in Paris when I met Captain Edward Molyneux. I asked him to luncheon. He said, 'Where shall we go?' I said, 'We shall go to the Ritz, because Olivier is such a friend of mine.' We went to the Ritz. We entered the restaurant. It was as I expected. Olivier hurried towards us with his ducal smile. It was Edward Molyneux whom he greeted first, but I did not mind that; in fact I relished the delicious anagnorisis which would follow. He then turned to me. A fleeting cloud of perplexity crossed his sunny features, to be followed immediately by a burst of delighted recognition. '*Mais voyons donc,*' he said, '*c'est Monsieur Bonstetten!*'

I return to my American diplomatist and the subject of food. This adaptable citizen of the United States found that he could enjoy his food everywhere, even in Japan; but not in England. He contended that the muffin was the only edible product of the English kitchen. I remember that even Monsieur André Maurois (that undaunted anglophile) had said more or less the same. With infinite delicacy he had advised his fellow-countrymen, if they desired to feel happy in England, to dispense with luncheon and dinner; they would find that our breakfast and tea foods were delicious. In fact, Monsieur Maurois with that courtesy which befits a Knight of the British Empire, could not say enough about the excellence of our teas. Yet a certain stigma remains behind. Man cannot live by teas alone, and it is regrettable that we as a nation, in that we possess the finest foodstuffs in the world, should make such a hash of our raw material. Many friendly foreigners have tried to explain away our indifference to the art of cooking. It was M. André Simon (if I recollect aright) who suggested that our lack of culinary tradition was due to the fact that forks were only introduced towards the end of the reign of James I. Yet cooking does not really depend on forks; to this day the Moors eat with their fingers and yet their dishes are among the best on earth. Others have contended that the ordinary Englishman has an insensitive palate. This is untrue. The British working man can detect immediately the slightest variation in his beer or tobacco. Others again suggest that it is the puritan tradition which is responsible, and that to enjoy one's food appears to us tantamount to lusting after the pleasures of the flesh. If this were the reason, then the Americans would be equally impervious to cooking. Whereas in fact they fuss inordinately about their terrapin, their squabs and their sweet-scented salads.

The explanation is, I think, that we, owing to our climate and our curious habit of taking physical exercise, have strong appetites. Few things are so inimical to good cooking as animal hunger. I am confirmed in this theory by the history of cooking. Our savage ancestors, when they killed a reindeer, tore it limb from limb. The Homeric heroes were only slightly more advanced. What they liked was 'a sheep's back and fat goat's, and a great hog's chine rich in fat'. These crude viands were grilled on spits upon a gridiron, even as *kebabs* are grilled in the village of Hissarlik today. It was only when appetites became jaded that the art of cooking began. Even Alcibiades can scarcely have indulged in anything more subtle than olives, garlic, cuttlefish, radishes and little white beans. When the Romans found their empire and lost their digestions, cooking became a most important element in their civilization. Apicius committed suicide when he discovered that he would have to moderate his diet, and the many devices adopted by the Romans for the stimulation of appetite and the relief of indigestion prove that hunger was a delight that the richer Roman never knew. From Rome, after many centuries, the art of cooking passed, with Catherine de Medici, to France. Great names arose. There was Bechamel, butler to Louis XV; there was Vatel, chef to Condé; there was Carême, chef to Alexander I, to Talleyrand and to Baron Rothschild; there was Alexis Soyer, chef to the Reform Club, who, during the hungry forties, invented a dish of *truffes de Périgord* boiled in champagne and garnished with *foie gras* which cost five guineas a guest.

This French invasion of London did immense harm to our national cooking. Tomato soup started calling itself 'Pompadour' or 'Portugaise' and pea soup 'Demidoff'. In place of the fish pies and oyster patties of coaching days we entered upon our dining-car period. Even the wet but harmless brill was covered with a pink sauce tinted with cochineal, which in itself is the product of dried beetles from Mexico. We gave up cooking and started to cover up what we had cooked. All flavour having been boiled and roasted out of our foodstuffs, we began replacing it by pungent artificial sauces. Thereafter came the tin age. Indolence allied itself with hearty appetite in order to consummate the defeat of whatever tradition of good cooking may have existed in these islands. It was then that Sir John Orr launched the nutrition movement. I should like to feel that Sir John will one day oust the tin-opener. I am not optimistic. The hand that wields the tin-opener also votes.

•

ERNIE PYLE

Ernest Taylor Pyle (1900–1945) was born on a farm near Dana, Indiana. He was educated at Indiana University, and edited both his school paper and his campus humour magazine before training as a reporter on the *Laporte Herald* (Indiana). After three months there, he joined the *Washington Daily News*. Having married, he bought a car and travelled around America with his wife for ten weeks in 1926, writing a regular feature about their experiences. Subsequently he worked on the copy desks of the *New York Evening World*, then the *New York Evening Post*, but in 1927 he returned to the *Washington Daily News* as telegraph editor. He wrote a column about aviation and in 1929 became aviation editor. He was the paper's managing editor for a while. Again he did an American tour with his wife and wrote a series of columns about it, and in 1935 the paper decided to make him a permanent roving columnist, publishing his pieces six days a week. In 1939 the column was syndicated by Scripps–Howard. He went to England to report the home front in 1940 and returned to America the following year to resume his travel column, but when the United States entered the war after the bombing of Pearl Harbor he became a war correspondent, though with this difference: he wrote his dispatches in the form of a column about the human aspects of the war. Eleanor Roosevelt was a great admirer and considered that he 'could make the men in the army more human than any other writer'. He reported from North Africa, Sicily, Italy and France. By 1941 Pyle's wife had suffered a nervous breakdown and for the next few years she had been in and out of institutions; as a result, according to his biographer Lee Miller, Pyle was reluctant to return home. After being awarded the Pulitzer Prize in 1944 and making a brief visit home, Pyle reported from the Pacific, where he was killed by a Japanese sniper on Ie Shima. (Pyle had been dressed in civilian clothes and was mistaken for a political or official figure.) At the time of his death his column was being syndicated to over 400 daily papers and about 300 weeklies. One of his fellow correspondents in North Africa, A. J. Liebling, reckoned that Pyle had been encouraged by Scripps – Howard to take greater risks and spend more time near the front line, and as a result his nerves were a-jangle. 'His trips to the front,' reflected Liebling, 'were perhaps a kind of Russian roulette that he played with himself. (I must say that he never seemed to me a reckless man; he protracted the game.)'

Ringed and Stabbed with Fire

London, December, 1940

Some day when peace has returned to this odd world I want to come to London again and stand on a certain balcony on a moonlit night and look down upon the peaceful silver curve of the Thames with its dark bridges. And standing there, I want to tell somebody who has never seen it how London looked on a certain night in the holiday season of the year 1940.

For on that night this old, old city was – even though I must bite my tongue in shame for saying it – the most beautiful sight I have ever seen.

It was a night when London was ringed and stabbed with fire.

They came just after dark, and somehow you could sense from the quick, bitter firing of the guns that there was to be no monkey business this night.

Shortly after the sirens wailed you could hear the Germans grinding overhead. In my room, with its black curtains drawn across the windows, you could feel the shake from the guns. You could hear the boom, crump, crump, crump, of heavy bombs at their work of tearing buildings apart. They were not too far away.

Half an hour after the firing started I gathered a couple of friends and went to a high, darkened balcony that gave us a view of a third of the entire circle of London. As we stepped out on to the balcony a vast inner excitement came over all of us – an excitement that had neither fear nor horror in it, because it was too full of awe.

You have all seen big fires, but I doubt if you have ever seen the whole horizon of a city lined with great fires – scores of them, perhaps hundreds.

There was something inspiring just in the awful savagery of it.

The closest fires were near enough for us to hear the crackling flames and the yells of firemen. Little fires grew into big ones even as we watched. Big ones died down under the firemen's valor, only to break out again later.

About every two minutes a new wave of planes would be over. The motors seemed to grind rather than roar, and to have an angry pulsation, like a bee buzzing in blind fury.

The guns did not make a constant overwhelming din as in those terrible days of September. They were intermittent – sometimes a few seconds apart, sometimes a minute or more. Their sound was sharp, near by; and soft and muffled, far away. They were everywhere over London.

Into the dark shadowed spaces below us, while we watched, whole batches of incendiary bombs fell. We saw two dozen go off in two seconds. They flashed terrifically, then quickly simmered down to pin points of dazzling white, burning ferociously. These white pin points would go out one by one, as the unseen heroes of the moment smothered them with sand. But also, while we watched, other pin points would burn on, and soon a yellow flame would leap up from the white center. They had done their work – another building was on fire.

The greatest of all the fires was directly in front of us. Flames seemed to whip hundreds of feet into the air. Pinkish-white smoke ballooned upward in a great cloud, and out of this cloud there gradually took shape – so faintly at first that we weren't sure we saw correctly – the gigantic dome of St Paul's Cathedral.

St Paul's was surrounded by fire, but it came through. It stood there in its enormous proportions – growing slowly clearer and clearer, the way objects take shape at dawn. It was like a picture of some miraculous figure that appears before peace-hungry soldiers on a battlefield.

The streets below us were semi-illuminated from the glow. Immediately above the fires the sky was red and angry, and overhead, making a ceiling in the vast heavens, there was a cloud of smoke all in pink. Up in that pink shrouding there were tiny, brilliant specks of flashing light – antiaircraft shells bursting. After the flash you could hear the sound.

Up there, too, the barrage balloons were standing out as clearly as if it were daytime, but now they were pink instead of silver. And now and then through a hole in that pink shroud there twinkled incongruously a permanent, genuine star – the old-fashioned kind that has always been there.

Below us the Thames grew lighter, and all around below were the shadows – the dark shadows of buildings and bridges that formed the base of this dreadful masterpiece.

Later on I borrowed a tin hat and went out among the fires. That was exciting too; but the thing I shall always remember above all the other things in my life is the monstrous loveliness of that one single view of London on a holiday night – London stabbed with great fires, shaken by explosions, its dark regions along the Thames sparkling with the pin points of white-hot bombs, all of it roofed over with a ceiling of pink that held bursting shells, balloons, flares and the grind of vicious engines. And in yourself the excitement and anticipation and wonder in your soul that this could be happening at all.

These things all went together to make the most hateful, most beautiful single scene I have ever known.

A Long Thin Line of Personal Anguish

Normandy beachhead, June 17, 1944

In the preceding column* we told about the D-Day wreckage among our machines of war that were expended in taking one of the Normandy beaches.

But there is another and more human litter. It extends in a thin little line, just like a high-water mark, for miles along the beach. This is the strewn personal gear, gear that will never be needed again, of those who fought and died to give us our entrance into Europe.

Here in a jumbled row for mile on mile are soldiers' packs. Here are socks and shoe polish, sewing kits, diaries, Bibles and hand grenades. Here are the latest letters from home, with the address on each one neatly razored out – one of the security precautions enforced before the boys embarked.

Here are toothbrushes and razors, and snapshots of families back home staring up at you from the sand. Here are pocketbooks, metal mirrors, extra trousers and bloody, abandoned shoes. Here are broken-handled shovels, and portable radios smashed almost beyond recognition, and mine detectors twisted and ruined.

Here are torn pistol belts and canvas water buckets, first-aid kits and jumbled heaps of lifebelts. I picked up a pocket Bible with a soldier's name in it, and put it in my jacket. I carried it half a mile or so and then put it back down on the beach. I don't know why I picked it up, or why I put it back down.

Soldiers carry strange things ashore with them. In every invasion you'll find at least one soldier hitting the beach at H-hour with a banjo slung over his shoulder. The most ironic piece of equipment marking our beach – this beach of first despair, then victory – is a tennis racket that some soldier had brought along. It lies lonesomely on the sand, clamped in its rack, not a string broken.

Two of the most dominant items in the beach refuse are cigarettes and writing paper. Each soldier was issued a carton of cigarettes just before he started. Today these cartons by the thousand, water-soaked and spilled out, mark the line of our first savage blow.

Writing paper and airmail envelopes come second. The boys had intended to do a lot of writing in France. Letters that would have filled those blank, abandoned pages.

Always there are dogs in every invasion. There is a dog still on the beach today, still pitifully looking for his masters.

He stays at the water's edge, near a boat that lies twisted and half sunk at the water line. He barks appealingly to every soldier who approaches, trots eagerly along with him for a few feet, and then, sensing himself unwanted in all this haste, runs back to wait in vain for his own people at his own empty boat.

Over and around this long thin line of personal anguish, fresh men today are rushing vast supplies to keep our armies pushing on into France. Other squads of men pick amid the wreckage to salvage ammunition and equipment that are still usable.

---

* Pyle's previous column about D-Day – not the preceding column in this anthology.

Men worked and slept on the beach for days before the last D-Day victim was taken away for burial.

I stepped over the form of one youngster whom I thought dead. But when I looked down I saw he was only sleeping. He was very young, and very tired. He lay on one elbow, his hand suspended in the air about six inches from the ground. And in the palm of his hand he held a large, smooth rock.

I stood and looked at him a long time. He seemed in his sleep to hold that rock lovingly, as though it were his last link with a vanishing world. I have no idea at all why he went to sleep with the rock in his hand, or what kept him from dropping it once he was asleep. It was just one of those little things without explanation that a person remembers for a long time.

The strong, swirling tides of the Normandy coastline shift the contours of the sandy beach as they move in and out. They carry soldiers' bodies out to sea, and later they return them. They cover the corpses of heroes with sand, and then in their whims they uncover them.

As I plowed out over the wet sand of the beach on that first day ashore, I walked around what seemed to be a couple of pieces of driftwood sticking out of the sand. But they weren't driftwood.

There were a soldier's two feet. He was completely covered by the shifting sands except for his feet. The toes of his GI shoes pointed toward the land he had come so far to see, and which he saw so briefly.

Japs Do the Silliest Things

In the Marianas Islands, February 23, 1945

There are still Japs on the three islands of the Marianas chain that we have occupied for more than six months now.

The estimate runs into several hundred. They hide in the hills and in caves, and come out at night to forage for food. Actually many of their caves were so well-stocked that they could go for months without getting too hungry.

Our men don't do anything about the Japs any more. Oh, troops in training for combat will go out on a Jap-hunt now and then just for practice, and bring in a few. But they are no menace to us, and by and large we just ignore them. A half dozen or so give up every day.

The Japs don't try to practice any sabotage on our stuff. It would take another Jap to figure out why. The Japanese are thoroughly inconsistent in what they do, and very often illogical. They do the silliest things.

Here are a few examples. One night some of our Seabees left a bulldozer and an earth-mover sitting alongside the road up in the hills.

During the night, the Japs came down. They couldn't hurt anybody, but they could have put that machinery out of commission for a while. Even with only a rock they could have smashed the spark plugs and ruined the carburetor.

They didn't do any of these things. They merely spent the night cutting palm fronds off nearby trees and laying them over the big machinery. Next morning when the Seabees arrived they found their precious equipment completely 'hidden.' Isn't that cute?

On another island, there were many acts of sabotage the Japs could have committed. But all they ever did was to come down at night and move the wooden stakes the engineers had lined up for the next day's construction of buildings!

There is another story of a Jap who didn't take to the hills like the rest, but who stayed for weeks right in the most thickly American-populated section of the island, right down by the seashore.

He hid in the bushes just a few feet from a path where hundreds of Americans walked daily. They found out later that he even used the officers' outdoor shower bath after they got through, and raided their kitchens at night.

There was a Jap prison enclosure nearby, and for weeks, peering out of the bushes, he studied the treatment his fellow soldiers were getting, watched how they were, watched to see if they were dwindling away from malnutrition.

And then one day he came out and gave himself up. He said he had convinced himself they were being treated all right, so he was ready to surrender.

And here's another one. An American officer was idly sitting on an outdoor box-toilet one evening after work, philosophically studying the ground, as men will do.

Suddenly he was startled. Startled is a mild word for it. For here he was, caught with his pants down, so to speak, and in front of him stood a Jap with a rifle.

But before anything could happen the Jap laid the rifle on the ground in front of him, and began salaaming up and down like a worshiper before an idol.

The Jap later said that he had been hunting for weeks for somebody without a rifle to give himself up to, and had finally figured out that the surest way to find an unarmed prospective captor was to catch one on the toilet!

But don't let these little aftermath stories mislead you into thinking the Japs are easy after all. For they are a very nasty people while the shooting's going on.

On Victory in Europe*

And so it is over. The catastrophe on one side of the world has run its course. The day that it had so long seemed would never come has come at last.

I suppose emotions here in the Pacific are the same as they were among the Allies all over the world. First a shouting of the good news with such joyous surprise that you would think the shouter himself had brought it about.

And then an unspoken sense of gigantic relief – and then a hope that the collapse in Europe would hasten the end in the Pacific.

It has been seven months since I heard my last shot in the European war. Now I am as far away from it as it is possible to get on this globe.

This is written on a little ship lying off the coast of the Island of Okinawa, just south of Japan, on the other side of the world from Ardennes.

---

* This rough draft of a column, prepared in advance of VE-Day, was found on Pyle's body when he was killed.

But my heart is still in Europe, and that's why I am writing this column.

It is to the boys who were my friends for so long. My one regret of the war is that I was not with them when it ended.

For the companionship of two and a half years of death and misery is a spouse that tolerates no divorce. Such companionship finally becomes a part of one's soul, and it cannot be obliterated.

True, I am with American boys in the other war not yet ended, but I am old-fashioned and my sentiment runs to old things.

To me the European war is old, and the Pacific war is new.

Last summer I wrote that I hoped the end of the war could be a gigantic relief, but not an elation. In the joyousness of high spirits it is easy for us to forget the dead. Those who are gone would not wish themselves to be a millstone of gloom around our necks.

But there are many of the living who have had burned into their brains for ever the unnatural sight of cold dead men scattered over the hillsides and in the ditches along the high rows of hedge throughout the world.

Dead men by mass production – in one country after another – month after month and year after year. Dead men in winter and dead men in summer.

Dead men in such familiar promiscuity that they become monotonous.

Dead men in such monstrous infinity that you come almost to hate them.

These are the things that you at home need not even try to understand. To you at home they are columns of figures, or he is a near one who went away and just didn't come back. You didn't see him lying so grotesque and pasty beside the gravel road in France.

We saw him, saw him by the multiple thousands. That's the difference . . .

•

CHARLES LOW CLOUD

Charles Round Low Cloud (1872–1949), a Winnebago Indian, was born in West Wisconsin and attended Carlisle Indian School in Pennsylvania from 1893 to 1898. From then until the early 1930s he made his living from casual farmwork and interpreting. In 1920 he became a weekly columnist for the *Black River Falls Banner-Journal*, writing 'The Indian News' and signing himself as 'Indian Report', a role in which he continued for thirty years. His columns were written with the syntax of the Winnebago and offered a mixture of local gossip, Winnebago folklore, observations about the seasons and local flora and fauna, and spirited critiques of politicians and their misdeeds. Occasionally, Charley Low Cloud would get drunk and find himself in jail, but he was always able to keep readers abreast of his personal situation. 'Not much news this week,' he once explained, 'Indian report in jail.' And on another occasion: 'There are no Indian news since fourth of July . . . I have not done anything wrong, but have fourth of July drinking.' Despite his problems with punctuation, excerpts from his column were often reprinted in publications further afield, such as *Collier's* magazine and the *New York Times*. 'The only punctuation he knew, I guess, was periods,' his editor, Mrs Harriet Noble, said after his death. 'We always printed his column just as he brought it in, handwritten on a scrap of paper.' During the Second World War, his column was sent to all servicemen of

Jackson County including Indians serving as far away as Italy and Guam. When Charley Low Cloud died from stomach cancer, his publisher paid for a granite gravestone to commemorate him in Decorah Indian Cemetery, next to the Indian Mission there.

'The Indian News'

From *Charles Round Low Cloud: Voice of the Winnebago* (1973)

January 18, 1933

Too bad news. A baby boy was born last Thursday afternoon by Mr and Mrs Edwin Greengrass. Passed away last Saturday afternoon . . . We can not help when our time come they have to go.

March 8, 1933

Quite number Indians very sorry for John Levis passed away a few days ago, and Mr Levis sure is a good man for every Indians know him. He never cheat any Indians or make fun of their, always had a good square deal with them because he is Democrat side, honest for everybody.

February 21, 1934

The Indian History has been told by our old Indians. They said always they had one 'Trader' that is mean white man had deal with them or think that help the Indians, but always cheat them, make money out of them and of course white men are smart, pretty well educated, finish school, High school, college, and university, know how to highway robbery, know how to bank robbery, know how to defraud poor people, know how to lie to other people. Make people think he is honest.

August 5, 1936

Lots of talk about coming election one side give good talk and other the same. Which one best, I don't know. The only way is to lie down and wait. The Indian can know from the past, and when high collar people get their office they all forget what they promised to the people. All they want that office is salary money, and I think, white people their god is money . . .

March 27, 1940

We don't know who is right Democratic or Republicans. Our first President, George Washington, the people want him third term to hold the chair of United States president but he told the people that was enough two term not the third term. Therefore I think George Washington gave us that law. If anybody vote for third term, he or she will be think only himself to know anythings nobody else.

December 4, 1940

President Roosevelt, did you notice? Last two years when they set the day of Thanksgiving day always he change a week head or less a week and may be they change Christmas day too.

January 8, 1941

There were two boys were arrested at Wood county last fall, use Rotten law, because white people think, the Indian don't know any things at all. There is one deer has been killed during deer season, lay there more than a month, so these two boys saw this deer several times. Finally they went there to look for that deer hide, see if they can make use of that. Perhaps game warden come out from brush, they had a gun with their hand and they ready to shoot if any one say anything. These two boys arrested for killing a deer, fine $100 and cost or 90 days in wood county jail. They were stay there 90 days, Archie Elk and Willie Wilson. They said pretty bad for Winnebago Indians at this Wood county, always against hard, and one white man was drunk, drive into another car one Saturday evening, was arrested over Sunday and Monday they let it go, cost only twenty five dollars.

February 12, 1941

Bad news. Martin White Bear of Red Wing, Minnesota, he was here in the town and went from there to Dells Dam at the Green family's place. They have been use intoxicated and when the whiskey is all gone they drained some out of the radiator in alcohol. They said they fixed it up and drink it. Mrs Maggie Day and Frank Green died at same night . . . Martin White Bear, they could not find where he went and he left his car at Neillsville . . .

April 23, 1941

We have some true story. There are many things we could not tell how it happened, when these things going along our own life at present, for instances, our working classes people, when they get a job, any kind project to work at it, and some medium classes people, they hold the office in the town. They sit in the chair and hired some type writer, about half dozen ladies or more. They received a good wages for the month and working classes people they get only half that much, these medium classes, sit in the chair. Low classes in working hard every day. They can not make any thing extra, just only work for a living, in order not to starve to death, that is all . . . We Wisconsin Winnebago tribe, we would like to have any thing help from Agency office, we never get anything we want, when we do go over there to see them, when they tell us the way, we want any thing, always tell us just opposite, we fail.

Our administration and legislature, they want to help the foreign country. They ought to look for first our own country and some places rich people, just rediculous low classes people.

October 22, 1941

Luke Green of Dells Dam passed away . . . He is a nice old man and he has been sick
since 1936 . . . He is 83 years . . . He is real Indian, never go to school any kind white
man way. He used to say 'I would not try to do white man way, too crooked.' The
sympathy goes to his two son . . .

July 22, 1942

This is show the white people would like to cheat these Indians pretty bad at all the
time and even store keeper too. One day last week Mrs Jennie Decorah bought some
sugar, eight pounds for canning stuff. When she come home she weigh again, only six
pounds, this was not storeman himself but his hires, in the store.

November 4, 1942

The rationing of coffee, tea, sugar and meat. The Indians don't mind the rationing
because the woods are full of tea and meat. The Indians learn all sweet stuff from the
white man. When meat rationing comes around the red man will be happy because his
meat is in the woods. The white man think they own all the wild game, but God created
Indian here in this country, also wild game. When Christ. Columbus landed on our
shores he was not put off but landed and asked the first man he met and that was an
Indian. He asked him for some meat and the Indian told him to go and kill a deer.
There was no game warden because the wild meat belong to the Indians. White man
cheated the Indians. Today if an Indian kill a wood chuck and game warden see him
the Indian is put in jail for about 90 days. When white man kill a chicken or pig or cow
nobody say anything. Indian has no money to fight any law, white man makes his own
law.

January 13, 1943

One our soldier boy was wounded in action, William White Bear at New Guinea, and
another boy was missing, George Green has been kill or capture. These two boys
volunteer early part this second world war.

   They are helping United States army, and at the same way when they fought confederate
and union. Help the Union, and the same when 1861–3 fought out west Indians and
same way 1917–18 at first world war and several wounded and some killed and some
poison gas after they come home, and Winnebago tribe always help the United States
army.

March 29, 1944

The politic has been talking about some time ago, but I think it will be pretty good idea
Democrat side. Suppose they know how to do the things on this world. Democrat are
always they had one certain man nominade and Republican had four or five different
men nominade. Then I think most all Republican in this country but they divided too
many men and other party they had one man to vote for.

October 4, 1944

Some old Indians feel sorry for these things happened. When Wilson administration and of those men Indian bureau, they had mistaken try to make Indian farmer. The Winnebago had a million dollars in US Treasure and these Indians got 5 per cent interest on it, that interest made annual payment of about 20 dollars for capita every fall. This was best for Indians welfare but those fellows thought it wise to pay out the Winnebago all this money, so they can farm. That was not right because this money was spent unwisely and mostly wasted, it come out at time when things were high. These fellows made mistake try to make a farmer out of these Indians and two or three Indian farmers, Mr George Lowe of Jackson county, Mr John Smoke of Monroe county, Mr John Stacy of Clark county. These three men has been working their own farm. We don't know what could make out of these Indians. Try to make any things out of these, carpenters, mason worker, or brick layers, doctor or horse doctor.

January 3, 1945

Bad News. Milwaukee paper say a report asked F. D. R. where find Atlantic Charter. He say no Atlantic Charter, just think so, and I think somebody been stole or may be get lost and this more jobs for to find out these things. If lost in ocean may be eat it up fish already, then fish get sick too.

January 10, 1945

David Little Soldier pass away Jan. stroke Jan. 24, 1944 evening on left 31, 1944, in the evening, and he had side body. It would not take very long to come end of his life. His family and some other relatives all of the shocks to know this only a few days he had been sick and pass away. He is sixty-eight years old on time of his death . . . He is nice old man, he don't use intoxicated, everyone feel sorry for him everyone who heard this unexpected this bad news.

June 20, 1945

I saw a letter from one soldier from oversea. Says 'I enclose $3 for subscription to the *Banner-Journal* with the hope that it will continue to be embellished by the journalistic genius of your Indian reporter'. This was Captain J. S. Tracey, United States America.

April 24, 1946

As I understand, that some places has been discussed about politics, about our government. The other day I saw in the news paper, says the boys organization, and we ought to have all young people in congress and senate be better started our government. I will now tell my opinion this case. I think just opposite what they are thinking, and I think it would be better government if they continue these old experience to know what to do the best for our government. You know that too, and yourself, if any man do some things they can not do best they should do until he or she had experience, to know how to do best way. Therefore we should try to be best way, Republicans party instead Democrats and we ought to have free country again, not to use any kind stamps.

May 8, 1946

There are good many stories we remembers but white people never tell true anythings since Columbus think discovers this country 1492 and they think they own this country without paying any things. It is just like some children playing some where, some older people come in, spoil all their places, without their consent.

September 25, 1946

Some time when man get old he give every things away. Uncle Sam same thing, this kind. He give four billion away. He ever say what to do with this money. If make these all ten dollar money and tie together, may be it reach Millston, some say reach Milwaukee, another say it go around the world. Children going school take pencil and find who right. May be Democrat not want to know.

This Democrat want high wages sit on rocking chairs. He makes the price every things what working people raised them and stockholder. This what makes many farmers give up farms works.

December 4, 1946

Big question nowadays, what become of all Democrat. Every body shame to admit he was one. Moses Paquette say he see somethings in brush by his place, maybe last Democrat hiding. Moses says he is going to pay bounty on it if he can't trap it before long. This is we heard at Olson Cafe.

March 26, 1947

We have many things change right round corner. Blame for Congress or Uncle Sam, or presidents of the US. Some time ago closed Indian school and now we had some relief from the government for to get some medicine for the Indians, that been closed too, and I have been ask our Sub agency Mr Morrin. He said there is no more money, money all gone. I told him President Truman signed a loan money Turkey, and Greece, for some 240 millions dollars to loan some other country. As I understand once US Constitutions is on basic on the History. May be they all forget them.

September 24, 1947

The white people think the Indians do not know anythings about law, made by the white people they can change at any time they want to and white people go the money, that what makes think big head. Last Monday Eli Young Thunder has been lost his horses several days, finally somebody told him they got them at William Klein's place, so he went there right away and he saw the horses but not Bill until last Monday, he charges him $25 to feed horses and damages, but Ray Gilbertson told him he will pay only $12 and now then when the farmers round here this area. The Indians trying to keep a garden, but the farmer cattles come up, eat all up and Indians go to tell lawyer but told them if they want anythings, not to go in, the stuff should be a fence round, not open place.

December 1, 1948

'Thanksgiving' – We know one thing, there are our old Indian used to tell them our Winnebago Indian descent from at the beginning when first white people came in this country, stop a few rods from the sea shore. They called some Indians out there, so they talked to them, they wanted landed on the ground, and they told them alright, so they landed and lived there. This was on Monday and they wash themselves all day, so they used to call on Monday is 'wash day' and those white people when they lived there always ask them whenever they want cut wood, make logging camp or fire wood. When the Spring came, try to raise some thing, they asked again, they wanted plowed eight inches deep into the ground, if they found any things they said they can take it back to the Indians, and when all done these things and in the Fall or Harvest time, these white people every one donated food stuff and called to the Indians have a dinner. These for 'Thanks' for the Indians, because rented the ground to raised the stuff, and after that they always have given 'Thanks,' every fall, but now these Winnebago tribe still they remember yet.

•

WILLIAM RANDOLPH HEARST

William Randolph Hearst (1863–1951) was born in San Francisco, California. The son of a wealthy miner, he was educated at Harvard University, where he was business manager of the *Harvard Lampoon* before being expelled for playing practical jokes on professors. After working for Joseph Pulitzer's New York *World* for a couple of years, he persuaded his father to let him buy the *San Francisco Examiner*, which he transformed into one of the highest-circulation daily newspapers, and in 1895 he acquired the *New York Morning Journal*. From there he went on to accumulate a vast media empire, but in 1940, following the death of his trusted lieutenant Arthur Brisbane, who had written a daily, front-page, homiletic column for Hearst's papers, he decided to write a replacement column, 'In the News', which ran from 1940 to 1942. People evidently thought it strange that such a powerful man should deign to write a column, and when asked about it all Hearst would volunteer by way of explanation was: 'I suppose I have the bear by the tail.'

'In the News'
The Lemmings*
June 24, 1940

In Norway there is a little animal, a lemming – something like a squirrel or a beaver or a rat.

---

* Written after the fall of France in World War II, when Nazi invasion of the British Isles seemed imminent, this article attracted world-wide attention. It was republished in beleaguered England as a stimulus to the national morale.

It goes back, far back, into prehistoric times – back before the glacial eras, back to the geological period when there was no English Channel, when England was connected by land with the continent of Europe, and the river Thames flowed across the west of Europe and emptied into the Rhine.

Then, before the great ice caps wore the land away, Norway extended much farther into the ocean towards the British Isles than now; and the British Isles extended farther towards Norway, and there was no great body of water between Norway and Scotland – only a narrow strait that a little rat could swim.

So the little lemmings lived in Norway, in those early geologic days, and they multiplied there and became numerous.

As the years went by, some of them adventured away from the main herd.

They marched over hill and dale, marched through forests and scrambled across steep gorges, and clambered up high cliffs and down again.

Unremittingly they marched towards the sea.

Some mysterious instinct guided them, some inherited habit led them always towards the west, always towards the sea.

Finally they reached the ocean strand.

There, across the narrow ocean strait, lay the British Isles.

A little lemming from a high sand dune could see the isles.

A little lemming could swim that narrow strait.

So into the ocean they plunged, driven by that inexplicable instinct.

And most of them reached the other side.

Some perished. The weaker succumbed.

It is the sad way of the world.

It means, of course, the 'survival of the fittest.' It is best for the survivors.

It is Nature's way of improving the race of mice and men. Nature is cruel – sometimes incomprehensible.

Then years upon years passed. The ice ages came, and the little lemmings walked across from Norway to the great isle of Britain.

Then the ice melted and the little lemmings had to swim again – had to swim a wider and constantly widening sea.

The ever breaking waves, the ever surging sea, washed and washed away the land.

The coasts of Norway and Britain in the course of the ages have receded farther and farther away from each other.

However, now as formerly, every ten or twenty years, the little lemmings march across hill and dale, across mountain and vale, until they reach the sea.

They can no longer perceive the coast of Scotland from the high dunes of Norway – no, not from the highest mountain over which they cross – but they know that it is there.

The mysterious instinct, the inherited habit of millions of years, tell them it is there, but also, do not tell them how far away, how hard to reach.

So the army of lemmings draws up its serried ranks upon the beaches of the Norseland, and prepares for its fate.

It is doubtless harangued by its leaders, who tell the lemmings how brave they are, how heroic – how they are the chosen rodents of the world, the only pure-blooded race of Aryan lemmings alive.

Exhorted to do their duty to their country and their fellow lemmings, the little animals plunge into the wide waters and swim and swim, and die in the depths of the insatiate sea.

The lemmings should beware of the sea.

They are brave; they are devoted; but they cannot contend with the sea.

They bide their time. They march successfully across the land.

They reach their land objectives encouragingly.

Then, stimulated by success so far, they plunge into the sea and disappear.

Herr Hitler – Chancellor Hitler – General Hitler – Imperator Hitler – beware of the sea.

You have marched successfully across the land – over hills and dales – overcoming all difficulties.

You have stridden with heavy heels through Poland.

You have stamped your way through Norway, where the lemmings live.

Take warning from the lemmings.

You have waded across the canals of Holland.

You have marched over the plains of Belgium.

You have smashed through the Maginot line and crashed your way through the once-smiling valleys of France.

You are a victor as far as you have gone.

You are one of the great conquerors of the world; but beware of the sea.

The sea is a greater conqueror.

It can engulf armies, as it engulfed the hosts of Pharaoh.

It can swallow up the invaders of its isles, as it swallows up the foolhardy little lemmings.

The might of Spain wrecked itself upon the sea.

The power of Portugal sank itself into the sea.

The forces of Holland and of France beat themselves to froth and fragments on the wave-worn chalk cliffs of England.

The sea protects its own – beats back the invader – wraps the enemy in its curling arms, and drags him to the depths.

Beware of the sea.

It has been for centuries the defense of the maritime nations.

It has been not only the main defense of the British Empire, but of America as well.

The rocks are its redoubts; the waves its trenches.

The lands are little compared to the expanses of the seas.

Those nations which have tamed the sea have made it part of their dominion.

They have trafficked on its calm waters. They have ridden safely on its storms.

The Tritons are their brothers; the Nereids are their sisters.

Poseidon is their ally.

Beware of the marshaled forces of the sea.

Again, do not depend too much upon an ever-favoring fortune on the land.

Fortune is fickle. Reverses will occur. Allies will prove faithless.

Hannibal was a mighty conqueror, too.

He lost at Zama, and died a fugitive.

Napoleon, a still greater conqueror, lost at Waterloo, and died a prisoner at St Helena.

The fates do not spin any thread without a break. Sometimes the spindle fails.

Make peace.

Make peace, a long and stable peace, reared on the firm foundations of the right – built on the even cornerstones of generosity and justice.

If the Versailles Treaty made war certain, do not make another war more certain by terms that are more harsh.

No victory of force will 'last a thousand years.'

No peace of injustice will endure even a generation.

March no more across the land with brutal tread.

Crush no more with iron heel the helpless nations of the earth.

Stand firmly on the ground of peace and equity.

Turn back from further venturing.

You have reached the sea.

'In the News'
The Gay Nineties
November 25, 1941

Your columnist often wonders why people are prone to ridicule the Gay Nineties.

The eighteen-nineties were a period of great and genuine gayety, and of unusual and universal prosperity, and of mighty and manifold achievement throughout the nation.

It was in the nineties that the modern automobile was invented, and to a large degree perfected.

The automobile is quite a respectable contribution to the welfare of the world.

We laugh, stupidly enough, at these early automobiles, but without those first successful achievements in motor-propelled vehicles we would not have the highly developed automobile of today.

It was in the Gay Nineties that Edison invented the moving picture.

In 1891 he applied for a patent for taking motion pictures on a band of film.

That was certainly a splendid contribution to the benefit and to the business of the world.

In the Gay Nineties occurred the brief and brilliant Spanish–American War, as a result of which the United States rescued the American isle of Cuba from European domination and oppression by Spain, and in which war the American Navy 'mopped up' the Spanish fleets and swept them from the seas.

Only a few American men were killed in that short and conclusive campaign.

But the army and navy of the United States firmly established as a proven fact the dictum of Cleveland that the fiat of the United States was law on this continent and in this western hemisphere.

An era of great glory as well as great gayety were the Gay Nineties.

An era of great wealth created by American individualism and distributed liberally in good wages.

It was the period of the full dinner pail.

McKinley was the 'advance agent of prosperity,' and the McKinley tariff bill kept American money in this country to build up American industry and raise the workers' standard of living to a standard of luxury.

Our funds were not then distributed as handouts to foreign nations to build up foreign industries in competition with our own, nor were our tariff walls laid low to let in the products of cheap foreign labor.

An era of constructive American government, of glorious American achievement and of great prosperity and gayety were the nineties.

If that is something to be laughed at, we would all like to laugh a little at our own era – and not have so many trials and tribulations to weep and wail about.

Not all the achievements of the Gay Nineties were material achievements.

American art was at its highest and soundest point.

Abbey and Sargent were painting their marvelous murals in the Boston Library.

F. D. Millet and Howard Pyle were at their best.

Maxfield Parrish was coming into his own.

Sargent's splendid portraits, painted in London, and Abbey's great painting of the coronation of Edward VII carried the high reputation of American art throughout the world.

What have we in American art today to compare with these great creations of the Gay Nineties?

Nothing but some meaningless hen tracks defacing clean canvas and made by fakers for fools.

If we can laugh at the Gay Nineties, just imagine the convulsions of raucous laughter that will rock the frames of future generations when they look at the pitiful productions of the so-called modernistic art of today.

Music, too, was at its highest and sanest point in America in the nineties.

The productions of the great operas in the Metropolitan Opera House of New York were superior to those of London or of any great musical center anywhere.

And Emma Eames, the American soprano, was probably the ranking operatic star of the world.

What is our music of today?

Little but a jitterbug jangle of inharmonies – a distortion of melody made to gear and dovetail with the physical contortion of the modern dance.

This discordant noise known as jazz originated as a joke and has developed into a tragedy.

American literature in the Gay Nineties was elegant, eclectic – and wholesome.

The American stage occupied a lofty position from which it has regularly and rapidly deteriorated.

Nor can the deterioration of the stage be attributed to the prevalence of the moving picture.

Indeed, on the contrary, the superior popularity of the moving picture can partly at least be attributed to the vulgarity and general degeneracy of the stage.

Small chance for the nineteen-forties to laugh at the eighteen-nineties, except in the matter of costume.

But always the fashions of today are the freaks of tomorrow.

So things were not so backward in the Gay Nineties as the critical nineteen-forties would have us believe.

Human beings were very much the same then as now.

Some conditions perhaps were worse – some better.

America at least was American.

•

E. B. WHITE

Elwyn Brooks White (1899–1985) was educated at Cornell University, where he edited the *Sun*. He started writing for the *New Yorker* in 1925 and began contributing to its unsigned editorial column, 'Notes and Comments', the following year. His themes were those of Thoreau: 'man's relation to Nature and man's dilemma in society and man's capacity for elevating his spirit'. He 'beat all these matters together' in order to create 'an original omelette from which people can draw nourishment in a hungry day'. He was still contributing to 'Notes and Comments' in 1976. From 1938 to 1943 he also wrote a monthly column called 'One Man's Meat' for *Harper's Magazine*.

'One Man's Meat'
Memorandum
Harper's Magazine, October 1941

Today I should carry the pumpkins and squash from the back porch to the attic. The nights are too frosty to leave them outdoors any longer. And as long as I am making some trips to the attic I should also take up the boat cushions and the charts and the stuff from the galley and also a fishing rod that belongs up in the attic. Today I should finish filling in the trench we dug for the water pipe and should haul two loads of beach gravel from the Naskeag bar to spread on top of the clay fill. And I should stop in and pay the Reverend Mr Smith for the gravel I got a month or two ago and ask him if he has seen a bear.

I ought to finish husking the corn and wheel the old stalks out and dump them on the compost pile, and while I am out there I should take a fork and pitch over the weeds that were thrown at the edge of the field last August and rake the little windfalls from under the apple tree and pitch them on to the heap too. I ought to go down to the shore at dead low water and hook on to the mooring with a chain and make the chain fast to the float, so that the tide will pick up the mooring rock and I can tow the whole thing ashore six hours later. I ought to knock the wedges out from the frames of the pier, put a line on the frames, and tow them in on the high water. First, though,

I would have to find a line long enough to tie every frame. If I'm to do any work at the shore I ought first to put a cement patch on the leak in my right boot. After the frames are on the beach another fellow and myself ought to carry them up and stack them. And there is probably enough rockweed on the beach now, so that I ought to bring up a load or two for the sheep shed. I ought to find out who it is that is shooting coot down in the cove today, just to satisfy my own curiosity. He was out before daybreak with his decoys, but I do not think he has got any birds.

I ought to take up the wire fence round the chicken range today, roll it up in bundles, tie them with six-thread, and store them at the edge of the woods. Then I ought to move the range houses off the field and into the corner of the woods and set them up on blocks for the winter, but I ought to sweep them out first and clean the roosts with a wire brush. It would be a good idea to have a putty knife in my pocket, for scraping. I ought to add a bag of phosphate to the piles of hen dressing that have accumulated under the range houses and spread the mixture on the field, to get it ready for ploughing. And I ought to decide whether to plough just the range itself or to turn over a little more on the eastern end. On my way in from the range I ought to stop at the henhouse long enough to climb up and saw off an overhanging branch from the apple tree – it might tear the paper roof in the first big wind storm. I shall have to get a ladder of course and a saw.

Today I certainly ought to go over to the mill and get four twelve-inch boards, twelve feet long and half an inch thick, to use in building three new hoppers for dry mash feeding to my pullets, which are now laying seventy-eight percent and giving me about eighty dozen eggs a week. I should also need one board which would be an inch thick, for the end pieces and for making the ends of the reels. I shouldn't need anything for the stands because I have enough stuff round the place to build the stands – which I had better make twenty-three inches high from floor to perch. If I were to make them less than that, the birds on the floor would pick at the vents of the birds feeding.

I ought to get some shingle nails and some spikes while I am at it, as we are out of those things. And I ought to sharpen the blade of my plane if I am going to build some hoppers. I ought to take the cutting-off saw and have it filed, as long as I am going over to the mill anyway. On the way back I ought to stop in at Frank Hamilton's house and put in my application for government lime and super, because I shall be passing his house and might just as well take advantage of it. Frank will ask me to sit down and talk a while, I imagine.

It is high time I raked up the bayberry brush which has been lying in the pasture since the August mowing. This would be a good chance to burn it today because we have had rain and it is safe to burn. But before burning it I ought to find out whether it is really better for the pasture to burn stuff like that or to let it rot for dressing. I suppose there is so much wood in it it wouldn't rot up quickly and should be burned. Besides, I was once told in high-school chemistry that no energy is ever lost to the world, and presumably the ashes from the fires will strengthen my pasture in their own way.

I ought to take the buck lamb out of the flock of lambs today, before he gets to work on the ewe lambs, because I don't want them to get bred. I don't know just where to put him, but I ought to decide that today, and put him there. I should send away today for some phenothiazine so that I can drench my sheep next week. It would probably be a good idea to try phenothiazine this time, instead of copper sulphate, which just gets the stomach worms and doesn't touch the nodular worms or the large-mouth bowel worms. And I ought to close the big doors on the north side of the barn cellar and board them up and bank them, so that the place won't be draughty down there at night when the sheep come in, as they are beginning to do. I have been thinking I ought to enlarge the south door so that I won't lose any lambs next spring from the ewes jamming through the narrow single opening, and this would be the time to do that.

Today I ought to start rebuilding the racks in the sheep shed, to fix them so the sheep can't pull hay out and waste it. There is a way to do this, and I know the way. So I am all set. Also I ought to fix up the pigpen down there in the barn cellar and sweeten it up with a coat of whitening, so that I can get the pig indoors, because the nights are pretty cold now. The trough will probably not have to be rebuilt this year because last year I put a zinc binding all round the edges of it. (But if I *shouldn't* get round to fixing up the pen I should at least carry a forkful of straw down to the house where the pig now is – I should at least do that.)

This would be a good day to put in a new light in the window in the woodshed, and also there is one broken in the shop and one in the henhouse, so the sensible thing would be to do them all at once, as long as I have the putty all worked up and the glass cutter out. I ought to hook up the stove in the shop today, and get it ready for winter use. And I ought to run up the road and see Bert and find out why he hasn't delivered the cord of slabwood he said he was going to bring me. At any rate, I ought to make a place in the cellar for it today, which will mean cleaning house down there a little and neating up, and finding a better place to keep my flats and fillers for my egg cases. Incidentally, I ought to collect eggs right now, so there won't be any breakage in the nests.

It just occurred to me that if I'm going to the mill today I ought to measure the truck and figure out what I shall need in the way of hardwood boards to build a set of sideboards and a headboard and a tailboard for my stakes. I ought to bring these boards back with me along with the pine for the hoppers. I shall need two bolts for the ends of each sideboard, and one bolt for the cleat in the middle, and two bolts for the ends of each of the head- and tailboards, and there will be three each of them, so that makes fifty-four bolts I shall need, and the stakes are about a inch and a half through and the boards will be three-quarters, so that makes two inches and a quarter, and allow another half-inch for washer and nut. About a three-inch bolt would do it. I better get them today.

Another thing I ought to do is take that grass seed that the mice have been getting into the barn and store it in a wash boiler or some pails or something. I ought to set some mousetraps tonight, I mustn't forget. I ought to set one upstairs, I guess, in the little north-east chamber where the pipe comes through from the set tubs in the back kitchen, because this is the Mouse Fifth Avenue, and it would be a good chance for a kill. I ought to gather together some old clothes and stuff for the rummage sale to raise money to buy books for the town library, and I ought to rake the barnyard and wheel the dressing down into the barn cellar where it will be out of the weather, because there is a lot of good dressing there right now. I ought to note down on the calendar in my room that I saw the ewe named Galbreath go to buck day before yesterday, so I can have her lambing date. Hers will be the first lamb next spring, and it will be twins because she is a twinner. Which reminds me I ought to write Mike Galbreath a letter. I have been owing him one since before Roosevelt was elected for the third term. I certainly should do that, it has been such a long time. I should do it today while it is in my mind.

One thing I ought to do today is to take a small Stillson wrench and go down the cellar and tighten the packing nut on the water pump so it won't drip. I could do that when I am down there making a place for the slabwood – it would save steps to combine the two things. I also ought to stir the litter in the henpen in the barn where the Barred Rocks are, and in the henhouse where the crossbred birds are; and then fill some bushel baskets with shavings and add them to the litter in the places where it needs deepening. The dropping boards under the broody crops need cleaning and I should do that at the same time, since I should be out there anyway. As far as litter is concerned, a man could take and rake the lawn under the maples where there is such an accumulation of leaves and add these dry leaves to the litter in the houses for the birds to scratch around in. Anything to keep their minds occupied in healthy channels.

Today I intend to pull the young alders in the field on the north side, as they are beginning to get ahead of me. I must do that today, probably later on this afternoon. A bush hook would be a good tool for that. I should also clean up the remaining garden trash and add it to the compost, saving out whatever the sheep might eat, and should remove the pipe from the well under the apple tree and store it down below in the barn.

I also think I had better call up a buyer and get rid of my ten old hens, since we have canned all we are going to need. After the hens are gone I shall no longer need the borrowed range house that they are living in and I can get two long poles, lash them on behind the truck, and load the house on and drag it up to Kenneth's house. But it will be necessary to take an axe and flatten the ends of the poles so they won't dig into the highway, although the tar is so cold now they probably wouldn't dig in much anyway. Still, the thing to do is do it right.

Another thing I should try to manage to do today is to earmark the two pure-bred lambs. That will be easy enough – it just means finding the ear tags that I put away in a drawer or some place last spring and finding the special pliers that you have to use in squeezing a tag into a sheep's ear. I think I know where those pliers are, I think they are right in my cabinet next to that jar of rubber cement. I shall have to get the lambs up, but they will come without much trouble now because they are hungry. I *could* take the buck away at the same time if I could think of a place to put him.

Today I want to get word to Walter about the ploughing of the garden pieces, and I had also better arrange down cellar about a bin for the roots, because on account of the extra amount of potatoes we have it will mean a little rearranging down there in order to get everything in. But I can do that when I am down tightening the nut on the pump. I ought to take the car into the village today to get an inspection sticker put on it; however, on second thoughts if I am going to the mill I guess it would be better to go in the truck and have a sticker put on *that* while I am seeing about the lumber, and then I can bring the boards back with me. But I mustn't be away at low water otherwise I won't be able to hook on to the mooring.

Tomorrow is Tuesday and the egg truck will be coming through in the morning to pick up my cases, so I must finish grading and packing the eggs today – I have about fifty dozen packed and only ten to go to make up the two cases. Then I must nail up the cases and make out the tags and tack them on, and lug the cases over to the cellar door, ready to be taken out in the morning, as the expressman is apt to get here early. I've also got to write a letter today to a publisher who wrote me asking what happened to the book manuscript I was supposed to turn in a year ago last spring, and I also should take the green chair in the living room to Eliot Sweet so that he can put in some little buttons that keep coming out all the time. I can throw the chair into the truck and drop it by his shop on my way to town. If I am going to take the squashes and pumpkins up to the attic I had better take the old blankets which we have been covering them with nights, and hang them on the line to dry. I also ought to nail a pole up somewhere in the barn to hang grain sacks on so the rats won't be able to get at them and gnaw holes in them; empty sacks are worth ten cents for the heavy ones and five cents for the cotton ones, and they mount up quite fast and run into money. I mustn't forget to do that today – it won't take but a minute.

I've got to see about getting a birthday present for my wife today, but I can't think of anything. Her birthday is past anyway. There were things going on here at the time and I didn't get around to getting her a present but I haven't forgotten about it. Possibly when I am in the village I can find something.

If I'm going to rebuild the racks for the sheep it would be a good idea to have the mill rip out a lot of two-inch slats for me while I am there, as I shall need some stuff like that. I ought to make a list, I guess. And I mustn't forget shingle nails and the spikes. There is a place on the bottom step of the stairs going down into the woodshed where the crocus sack which I nailed on to the step as a foot-wiper is torn off, and somebody might catch his foot in that and take a fall. I certainly should fix that today before someone has a nasty fall. The best thing would be to rip the old sack off and tack a new one on. A man should have some roofing nails if he is going to make a neat job of tacking a sack on to a step. I think I may have some but I'd better look. I can look when I go out to get the Stillson wrench that I shall need when I go down to tighten the packing nut on the pump, and if I haven't any I can get some when I go to town.

I've been spending a lot of time here typing, and I see it is four o'clock already and almost dark, so I had better get going. Specially since I ought to get a haircut while I am at it.

●

BEN HECHT

Ben Hecht (1894–1964) was born in New York City, the son of Russian Jewish immigrants, but graduated from high school in Racine, Wisconsin, after his family had moved there. In 1910 he dropped out of the University of Chicago after only three days to work for the *Chicago Journal*, hunting down pictures of criminals and their victims. His adventures during the next eleven years are described in his memoir, *Gaily, Gaily* (1963). He did some reporting for the *Journal* and in 1914 joined the *Chicago Daily News* as a reporter. In 1921 he began writing a daily column of human interest features and short stories for the *Daily News*, called 'One Thousand and One Afternoons'. These were collected in a book of the same title in 1922 and in another book, *Broken Necks* (1926). His famous play, *The Front Page*, co-written with Charles MacArthur, opened on Broadway in August 1928, and during the 1930s Hecht spent much of his time in Hollywood as a screenwriter, associated with such films as *Scarface, Underworld, Notorious, Spellbound* and *Wuthering Heights* – he won two Oscars for screenwriting. In 1941 Hecht returned to column-writing, this time for the New York afternoon tabloid *PM*. Hecht and his wife, Rose Caylor, were Jewish (she was descended from eleven rabbis), and his new column was frequently concerned with Nazism and the plight of his fellow Jews. While most Jews worshipped Roosevelt for his humanitarianism, Hecht described him as 'the humanitarian who snubbed a massacre'. After the war he supported the Irgun, the Zionist resistance group which attacked the British in Palestine, and as a result the British boycotted his films. A selection of his *PM* columns was published as a book called *1001 Afternoons in New York* (1941).

The Fatal Truth

From *One Thousand and One Afternoons* (1922)

Those journalistic surveyors of the Broadway glitter have always a tender, columnar tear for the has-beens. The croaking old-timer trailing his faded press notices down Carnival Street is always good for a fiddle solo or a hatful of adjectives.

I will promise, however, not to break your heart with the saga of Highwater Sam, who has been tucked away for six months in the cooler. The charge was pickpocket. The judge was His Honor Mr Saul Streit of General Sessions. And there was none to weep – not even Highwater Sam, who is a rangy and cadaverous rogue as devoid of the finer sentiments as a dead turtle.

The press paid obeisance to the event with the brief announcement that what was unquestionably the oldest pickpocket in the city had been sent to jail. But one item mentioned something that startled me. It said that this tottering old purse pincher had been long known as Highwater Sam.

Long known, indeed! Twenty years ago I recall the Yellow Kid, prince of the get-rich-quick lads, proclaiming that if he were ever to take his hat off to anyone it would be Highwater Sam – the most dazzling roper, inside man and inventive genius in the order of the golden fleece.

The name Highwater Sam had been bestowed in his heyday because of a minor sartorial quirk. Although arrayed always like unto a Solomon of the boulevards, Sam did his strutting in highwater pants. Whenever he passed a mirror, which was often, it was his pleasure to hike his pants up well above his ankle bones. The sobriquet was inevitable in that sharp-eyed world where Sam gloried and drank deep.

Here were faded press notices, indeed! Six months in the cooler for poke snatching! A fine, heart-gripping finale for a dazzler who had clipped them for fifty grand apiece in the wire-tapping game, who had run through a dozen fortunes wheedled out of suckers, with nimble tongue and derring-do.

I called on Sam and found him a little sour. But after an hour the venerable light fingers thawed and obliged with the story of his downfall. I have seldom heard a prettier one.

'Yes sir,' said Highwater, 'I was in the money, like you say. Wine for the house every evening. Diamond collars for dames. The works. Broadway was a street in those days. And then overnight I blow up. No, it wasn't the coppers. There never was a copper smart enough to nail me when I had the touch. And it wasn't dames. I had all their numbers. It was me – Highwater Sam – person-ally. Something busted inside, here,' and he tapped his spavined bosom, 'and my nerve and everything else went with it. Why, I even holed up in a sanitarium for six months, that's how hard I was hit. And since I come out – well, you can see what a lug I am.

'I'll tell you what happened. You see, I figured out a new kind of store, the smartest I ever heard of. It was a high-class fortune-telling joint in Miami. I stuck a broad of mine in and called her Madam Zubediah – sees all, knows all. And I gave her a split.

'She worked up a classy trade. It was the Florida boom days, and suckers were breaking their necks to toss it away faster than you could catch it. The madam had an easy part. All she had to do was read the future for the gimmick. Tell him after a squint into the crystal globe that great good fortune was coming to him out of his meeting with a guy wearing a black derby hat and smoking a big cigar.

'Well, a few hours later when this favorite of the gods is stretched on the beach stands baking his fanny a guy asks him for a match. The guy is smoking a big cigar. The guy is also wearing a black derby, which is a novelty on any beach. And the guy is me. It wasn't a heavy racket but good and steady and strictly up and up. No cops, no fixers, no squawks.

'Well, after I get my light we get to talking and I put on the cry. I'm stuck with a lot of bogus land in Texas, I tell him, and here I am in Miami with millions to be made and me out of it. It all ends up that the sucker, inflamed by madam's spiel about the good luck coming out of a black derby, follows me to the hotel. We have a few drinks and I unload a lot of bona fide paper giving him the undisputed possession of forty no good acres in Texas and he hands over a check for ten grand like a gentleman. It's foolproof. The paper is genuine. The acres are there and what's more I own them. The name of this hungry sucker is Charles O. Kirby.

'Well, I'm eating my poached eggs at the pool a week later when I see it in the newspapers. A new oil gusher has popped in Texas and is owned by Charles O. Kirby and an oil company is already offering him 200 grand for it. But he ain't selling. He's got forty acres of land and he drills them for five years. And it ain't one, it's seven oil gushers, until I couldn't stand it any more and went to the sanitarium.

'When I come out, I'm through. I'm scared to lie about anything. I get dizzy when I

start sellin' something. I tried roping but something always cracks up when I start a
phony spiel. I'm frightened. And I still am. I ain't told a lie in fifteen years and this is
the result – six months for lifting a $5 wallet.'

Highwater Sam, still tearless, said good-bye to me. And as I was leaving I took a look
at his pants. The cuffs were frayed and dragging on the floor.

Birth of a Nazi

From *1001 Afternoons in New York* (1941)

I heard my old friend Willy von Russwurm-Schleichen on the air last night. He was
speaking from Berlin. Reception was none too good, but I gathered that Willy was a
colonel now and that he felt happy. He spoke of the fulfillment of the glorious German
dream.

I've kept listening to the short-wave broadcasts for some time hoping to hear someone
I once knew. Willy is the first and only one I've bagged. He apologized for his absence
from the front by informing us all he had been wounded in Greece – wounded in body,
he said, but in spirit only uplifted – and told us all that he hoped before the war was
won to be able to rejoin his regiment and help rewrite the destiny of the world with
German valor and Nazi idealism. That's a long sentence, but that's the way Willy talked.
German sentences, like German daydreams, aim to embrace as much as they can. In
Willy's anaconda-like strophes the phrase '*der Nazi Idealismus*' rang out eleven times clear
as a bell. It was my first time to hear this phrase. It's possible that Willy, who was once
a great admirer of the poet Stefan George, coined it.

Maybe all Nazis aren't like Willy von Russwurm-Schleichen, and maybe they are.
Maybe what I know about this once elegant youth has no bearing on the secrets of Nazi
'idealism' and its triumphs to date. But, having bagged Willy, glowing on the air like a
bridegroom, I'll tell what I remember about him and try to remember in the telling that
all men are created in the image of God.

I met Willy when he was not nearly so idealistic as he is now. He was twenty years
old and drinking heavily at the Adlon Hotel bar in Berlin, and this was one a.m. in
March 1919. He was in a lieutenant's uniform, and he was standing alone in the empty
barroom when I came in with Dick Little (Richard Henry Little), in whom the souls of
Mark Twain and d'Artagnan got mixed up for a generation.

'It's funny,' said Dick, 'to see a German drinking hard liquor and by his lonesome. I
wonder what's ailing this handsome Hun.'

And, having called my attention to the most troublesome story I ever put on the cables,
the great humorist and war correspondent said he was weary and bade me good night.
Mr Little not only went to bed, but he stayed there for several days, having been hit on
the head earlier in the evening with the butt of a pistol. This had happened after Dick
had been riding around for several hours looking for a revolution. He had found it.

Willy von Russwurm-Schleichen's hand kept shaking as he lifted his tenth glass of
bourbon. I was at his side, pleased as always to meet a German, drunk or sober, who
spoke good English.

'I am drinking,' said Willy suddenly, 'because I wish to be dead. I wish never to see the sun again. From tonight on I am under a curse.'

I asked Lieutenant Willy why he felt that way. After several more drinks he answered: 'I have been on a machine-gun. Moabit Prison. Killing. Twelve hundred men, and women, and boys. They are in handcuffs. They march across the prison yard. There are two machine-guns. One is mine. We shoot. They fall down – one, two, three. Like dominoes. They lie on the ground but keep moving. A hand. A foot. A head moves. They lie handcuffed on the ground, still moving. We shoot again. The moving stops. Two, three more rounds, and so – they are finished moving.'

Willy said all this in one breath.

'Who are the prisoners?' I asked.

'German,' said Willy. 'German men. German women. *Spartakisten*. They were in the *Putsch* in Alexanderplatz. Last week. Captured. Put in prison. No trial. General Noske gave the order for their execution today. At nine o'clock tonight they walk out into the prison yard. Handcuffed. Some are singing – the young ones. Some of the women scream. Nobody can run. They walk ten yards away from the machine-guns. They stand in a line, and we shoot. One by one they tumble forward. Then the soldiers clear the yard. Another hundred are brought out, handcuffed. We kill another hundred. At midnight I was released from duty. There were still 200 to kill.'

I verified Willy's story, and put it on the cables. I called it the White Terror because the 1,200 who were executed were what passed for Reds in those days. They were Berlin working men and women, and their sons.

The story was denied by President Ebert of the then republic, and I was ordered out of Germany for cabling false news. I went to Weimar instead, where the National Assembly was in session. Here Hugo Haase, head of the Independent Socialist Party, made good my story in a speech – hurling the actual names of the 1,200 butchered Germans at the government. (Herr Haase was assassinated later while on his way up the Reichstag steps to take his place in that honorable forum.)

When I saw Willy von Russwurm-Schleichen again, he was sober but shaky. He was still under a curse. We used to go around to the nightclubs together, and Willy would sit brooding. He would recite a stanza from his favorite poet, Stefan George, and stare moodily at the perforated peach in his champagne glass.

'From what I have done I will never recover,' he used to say to me. 'It is hell to remember the moonlight in the Moabit Prison yard.'

Then the music would play, and Willy would place his girl's hand against his cheek, and his eyes would fill with tears.

There was no trace of the young lieutenant of one a.m., 1919, in Willy, as his voice came over the short waves last night. And as I listened, I knew where one Nazi's idealism had been born – in the moonlit yard of Moabit Prison, while killing 1,200 of his brothers and sisters.

Testament of a Reporter

From *1001 Afternoons in New York* (1941)

I saw Jack Dempsey knocked out of the ring in Atlantic City and come back to win.

I saw Ben Jeby, knocked down three times, climb back on his feet and land a haymaker.

I saw Pepe Ortiz tossed on the horns of a bull, land on his feet, and, running blood, wave his *toreros* aside to make the kill himself.

I saw the coal miners of Herrin, Illinois, walk unarmed into the barking guns of the militia, fall in heaps of dead, and win their strike.

I saw Blackie Weed stand on the gallows and spit in the sheriff's face, laugh when they tightened the rope around his neck, and go through the trap still guffawing.

I saw Joe Gans riding in an ambulance to his death-bed with his fists still clenched and twitching and his chin still tucked down against Bat Nelson.

I saw Chris Haggerty of the AP climb an icy telegraph pole in the Dayton flood, tap out his last message: 'Dayton, Ohio – AP everywhere,' and slide unconscious to the earth.

I heard Hugo Haase stand up in the first National German Assembly at Weimar and proclaim: 'I am a German who believes the might of guns will only win for us an ignoble place in the human family. If this is treason, kill me.' They killed him on the Reichstag steps in Berlin.

I saw Lou Gehrig bat out his last homer with his spine tied in a knot.

I saw Jesús María Lopez, before the firing squad in Chihuahua in 1928, smoke his last cigarette, grin at the leveled rifles, and say: 'Your bullets, my friends, will have no effect on the thoughts in my humble head. They will continue in other humble heads.'

I saw Teddy Roosevelt, shot in the morning by an assassin, stand up that night in a Milwaukee auditorium and, with a bullet still in his midriff, deliver the finest oration of his career. If anything happened to him as a result of the morning's accident, he cried to the throng, he hoped their mourning would be tempered by the memory of what a hell of a good time he had had out of life.

I saw Ben Welch, blind as a bat, come prancing out on the Palate Theater stage and crack jokes that convulsed his audience.

I saw Eugene Debs, the Socialist leader, come out of the Atlanta jail and say: 'America is the greatest country in the world with the brightest future. I only hope nothing happens to dim that future.'

I saw George Gershwin writing his last tunes for the *Goldwyn Follies* with a brain tumor driving an ice pick through his skull.

I saw Billy Petrolle, twice beaten, come back in his old Indian blanket in Madison Square Garden and whale the daylights out of Jimmy McLarnin.

I saw the garment workers in Chicago march singing into a double wall of mounted police, get trampled to death, and win their strike.

I saw a survivor of the *Titanic*, a servant girl from Galway, who told me how her friends in the steerage had died. Unable to find places in the lifeboats, they had crowded into the forbidden but now deserted precincts of the first-cabin saloon, taken possession of the elegant piano, and played and sung Irish tunes as the ship went down, themselves with it.

I saw Bill Haywood on the night he skipped bail and fled from his native USA to die in Russia. He was under sentence as a radical. I met him in the gallery of a burlesque theater. He had been touring the town having a last look at the country he loved. 'They put on a great show here,' he said, chewing on a bag of peanuts. 'I always like to come to places like this just to watch those bums in the audience laugh.'

I saw an AEF [American Expeditionary Force] soldier on a hospital cot, with both legs off and a fake jaw riveted to where his face had been, move his mouth stiffly and squeak like a mama doll: 'We won.'

I've seen these and many things like them.

Along with the endless saga of misfortune that hits the eye of the reporter, he gets to see the queer stamina of little people in big troubles. He is given a privileged look at the undaunted moments that are the soul of human history. He sees a lot of disaster and wreckage, but if he keeps his eyes open he usually gets a look at the flag of man still flapping away above some corner of the shambles.

I've seen this flag a hundred times where it never belonged. I've seen it come out of the many big and little hells in the hearts of people and straighten up in victory. And I'll see it again. I'll see England win.

•

SERGEANT YORK

Alvin Cullum York (1887–1964) was born in Pall Mall, Tennessee, one of eleven children. His father was a blacksmith. An ace rifle- and pistol-shot, York was raised as a fundamentalist Christian and when he joined the army in the First World War he refused to be a sniper on religious grounds. However, on a single day in October 1918, when his company was pinned down by German machine-gun fire, he became the greatest American hero of the war. He killed seventeen Germans with rifle shots and another eight with pistol shots and would have breezily continued to pick them off had not a German soldier who had already been captured persuaded the rest to surrender. Thus, Sergeant York and seven other US infantrymen went back to base with 132 prisoners. Upon his return to America he was fêted, and was given a 396-acre farm by the State of Tennessee. He later helped to found the American Legion and wrote his memoirs, the proceeds from which went to finance the establishment of a college and Bible school under the auspices of the Alvin C. York Industrial Institute. His story was made into a film, *Sergeant York* (1941), starring Gary Cooper. During the Second World War he wrote a short daily column for the Chicago Times Syndicate.

'Sergeant York Says'
Chicago Times Syndicate, January 9, 1942

Pall Mall, Tenn., Jan. 8

The Jap attack on us was like somebody grinding a file across our teeth and we've been twisted up with fury and pain. Maybe it has made a lot of us lose sight of the main line.

We're going to give Japan a royal pounding, naturally, but we've likewise got a bigger, deadlier enemy to curl up. We know that whatever Japan does comes from higher up the fork. Trace the dirty water back to the head and you'll find Hitler's Germany bubbling.

It's like when a man finds a gap deliberately cut in his fence-wire and somebody's pigs rooting in his garden patch. The man gets busy and drives those pigs out, but he doesn't stop there. He looks for the fellow who cut the wire and turned the pigs in. You can herd pigs out, but if you leave the fence cutter loose, they'll keep coming back.

So my notion is, the big job we and our Allies have is to put up Hitler's meat above all. It'll be hog-killing weather for the others mighty soon after that.

•

RAYMOND CLAPPER

Raymond Clapper (1892–1944) was born in Kansas. His father was a farmer and a factory labourer. From an early age Raymond hero-worshipped William Allen White, the famous Kansas newspaper editor and sage, and he worked as a printer's devil while at grade school. At seventeen he became a printer himself before enrolling at Kansas University. While there he was a correspondent for the *Kansas City Star* as well as managing editor of the *Kansan*, the daily paper of the university. In 1916 he was hired by United Press to go to Chicago, and subsequently covered newsbeats in Milwaukee and St Paul before going to Washington where he worked on the White House and Congress beats. In 1929 he became Washington manager of United Press and in 1933 he published a book, *Racketeering in Washington*. Also in 1933, he left United Press to join the staff of the *Washington Post* as its Washington bureau chief, and a year later he started a daily column for the paper, telling his wife that he would 'make it like a news story right on the nose of the news but put into it what I'd like someone to tell me if I was living out in Kansas about day-to-day background in Washington'. His daily 'Between You and Me' column was syndicated through Scripps–Howard Newspapers and the United Feature Syndicate from 1936 to 1944. What lifted Clapper 'out of the ruck of columns', wrote *Time* in 1940, was 'his knack of translating some event into sound sense on the very day that people want to hear about it. Somehow he manages to move a half step further than the mass mind.' By 1943 he was being syndicated to 176 papers with a readership of ten million, and he was being described in magazine profiles as 'Everyman's Columnist' and 'The Average Man's Columnist'. In later years he was able to supplement his syndication income with White Owl sponsorship for a radio version of his column. Attached to the US Navy, he was killed in a plane crash during the invasion of the Marshall Islands in the Pacific.

'Between You and Me'
Washington Post, November 12, 1937

During twenty years of political reporting in America I have observed all sorts of national politicians in action, but I have never encountered anything as puzzling as the worship of the German people for Hitler.

Soon after I arrived here in Berlin I saw Hitler in action before an audience of 20,000. Nazi political theatricals are unmatched in America. We have nothing like the impressive entrance of the color guard advancing through a lane of black shirts, followed by lines of brown shirts marching in to fill the side aisles. Finally the stage is set. There is a period of breathless silence. The rear doors are flung open and with the whole audience standing with arms extended in the Nazi salute, Hitler, a man of slightly less than medium height, wearing a raincoat, strides down the center aisle.

Hundreds, with arms still outstretched in salute, scramble toward the aisle to see him more closely. He returns the salute by flipping his arm upward very quickly, looking straight ahead, poker-faced, as if in a trance.

He mounts the platform and faces the audience. It strikes the foreigner as an anticlimax because as Hitler stands there after this impressive military build-up, with no flicker of a smile on his face, there is some hint of comic appearance – undoubtedly arising in American minds because his mustache suggests Charlie Chaplin.

Hitler begins to speak. His voice has no arresting quality, none of the smooth resonance of Roosevelt's nor the sharply penetrating huskiness of Al Smith – the two most effective political speakers I have ever heard. But soon his tempo increases until his words are pouring out in torrents, his neck cords bulging. Interrupted by applause, he twists his neck and rolls his eyes upward while waiting to resume.

I have observed countless audiences and never have I seen more intense or more sustained attention. Not a head turns away. Laughs and applause burst forth from all parts of the hall with the bursting impact which comes only from spontaneity, not from claque leaders. I have never seen an audience more a unit. There were only two persons in the hall – Hitler and the audience – completely meshed in their mutual responsiveness. As he left, the crowd again surged to the center aisle to be near him.

I hear of underground grumbling, but I believe Hitler has the fanatical devotion of a large majority of the German people. The others are forced into acquiescence but they are the minority. I am told that in rural Germany children pray to Hitler at night. He is the German god, a brooding, fanatical figure, who becomes more incredible as you read his *Mein Kampf*.

His secret must include his obvious sincerity, his fanatical devotion to Germany. Also he has by military and diplomatic aggressiveness restored the pride of the German people. Then he has put everyone back to work, literally. It may be unsound work, armaments, work camps, or what, but everyone is working. Factory chimneys pour out smoke even on Sundays, as I saw around Essen. This may be at suicidal cost, but the machinery is turning. Theatricals, propaganda and compulsion are not enough to account for the enthusiasm for Hitler. He is the miracle man to the German people.

Although no one questions that he could carry a truly free election overwhelmingly, he is open in his contempt for democracy. He says bluntly that he must have unquestioning obedience. He gets it. Most of it is offered gladly, the rest forced by the iron hand. This phenomenon seems natural to an ignorant people but not to the intelligent, advanced German nation. Yet there it is.

As an American, believing in democracy, I see these things with one reaction. No human being is wise enough to deserve to hold millions of his fellow men in his absolute power, without their right to question or change.

In Germany as in Russia, whole peoples have been thrown back into the age of despotism. They have lost all semblance of control over their own destinies. The only thing to be said in favor of these systems is that physically an attempt is being made by these dictators to improve the conditions of life. Modern dictators have that in their favor as against the old despots.

In return they rob their subjects of the right to think, deprive them of the opportunity to think. Newspapers, books, magazines, education are all shaped to permit these people to know only what the dictator wants them to know, to hold only the opinions he wants them to hold. No man deserves to have such power. But they have it.

And the strangest thing of all is that if you put it to a vote, in either Russia or Germany, the people would not change it.

Well, they can have it. All of it.

'Between You and Me'
Washington Post, December 5, 1938

Hey, Elmer! Mister Andrews, what are you trying to do to us with your wage-and-hour law?

On my desk is a formal office notice concerning your wage-and-hour law, to wit:

'All persons on the pay roll are asked to place themselves on working schedules of forty hours a week, and are hereby notified that no one must work in excess of forty-four hours per week without express permission. Whenever permission is granted and an employee does work in excess of forty-four hours, he must report to Mrs Jeffries the extent of such work, not later than Monday following the week in which he worked overtime.'

So instead of writing a column, I must write up last week's report for Mrs Jeffries, our efficient office manager.

Sunday. Came in late. On way to office got idea for a column about the divided Republicans. Easy subject. Made a mental note to use some of material obtained from Kenneth Simpson in New York several weeks ago, also something editor Harold Johnson of Watertown, NY, said in a letter, and a slant from a conversation with Tom Dewey before election. Snatches of something I heard recently in Kansas and Minnesota came back to mind and fitted in, along with several odds and ends from conversations with various politicians here and in other cities during last few weeks. By the time I reached the office I had the column fairly well worked out in my head, and it took me a little more than an hour to write it. Then I was through.

Monday. Decided last night to write another column about politics but today a congressman came in and talked for an hour about the defense problem and the public attitude toward it. So I scrapped the political idea to write about defense. I remembered something Representative Louis Ludlow had said about his war referendum, and some questions which had occurred to me while reading *The Ramparts We Watch* on an airplane from Chicago to Washington two weeks ago. Dictated mail, went to lunch, returned, and knocked out column in about an hour. But after looking it over thought it was clumsy and rewrote part of it. Total writing time about two hours.

Tuesday. Planned some time ago to write on Republican National Committee meeting today. Arrived at office 9:30 a.m. Dictated mail, then to Carlton Hotel for Republican meeting. Stayed for luncheon (free on Republican National Committee), listened to speeches, hung around all afternoon talking with politicians. Took fifteen minutes out to interview some of them on radio. Had material and outline all in mind on returning to office at 4:30 p.m. Through writing at 5:45. Went to cocktail party and listened to two Supreme Court justices, John L. Lewis and conservative publisher Eugene Meyer in free-for-all argument about where capitalist system is headed. Discovered they didn't know any more about it than the rest of us, which is going to help me in my work, I hope. Then to buffet supper for new Philippine delegate, who is the John D. Rockefeller of the islands, and he talked informatively on Philippine and Pacific questions. Background and ideas there for several future columns. Home shortly before midnight. Writing time one hour fifteen minutes.

That's half of my week. Wednesday a friend of Justice Brandeis came to office indignant about pressure to get him off bench so Frankfurter could go on. After checking by long distance and several local calls, had material for a column about that. Thursday attended monopoly hearings but wrote about free congressional sugar junket to Florida on basis of several telephone conversations. Friday wrote about patent question which O'Mahoney committee is about to investigate, drawing material from following: (1) File which I have been accumulating for several years; (2) conversation with a businessman friend on beach at Rehoboth, Del., during last summer's vacation; (3) discussion with a businessman whose firm is being investigated by the monopoly committee; (4) data from O'Mahoney committee investigation. Writing time two hours.

For the week, that adds up to ten or twelve hours' writing time. As for the rest, I can't figure how much is work and how much is play. They are much the same in this business. We get some of our best material over highballs, and when I'm in the office, I'm practically loafing.

So, Mrs Jeffries, if it's all right with you, it's all right with me just to put me down for forty hours flat. We won't count thinking time, so-called, and ideas that come out of the shower bath. And if one of Elmer's investigators comes around to paste a $10,000 fine on you with six months in jail for the second offense, I'll lie like hell to get you out of it. After all, much as I like the wage-and-hour law, I have a family to support and I can't afford to give up newspaper work to become a timekeeper.

'Between You and Me'
Washington Post, January 27, 1942

As I read the Roberts report on Pearl Harbor, I kept thinking that would be a hell of a way to run a newspaper.

I don't know anything about military affairs. But I have been around newspaper offices all my life. A newspaper office is organized to be ready for the unexpected. We hire an army and navy to protect us from the unexpected. But I never saw a newsroom that was as slack and sloppy as the Roberts report shows the army and navy at Hawaii to have been.

Go through any well-run newspaper office and you will find galleys of type, with headlines and art, all ready to be thrown into the paper at an instant's notice. Let a flash come through about the sudden death of any prominent figure and the paper will be ready to roll within a few minutes.

A newspaper office always goes on the assumption that the worst is about to happen the next minute. An incredible amount of planning, labor and watchfulness goes into this side of a newspaper – much of it in vain. But it is necessary if you are not to be caught asleep when a big story breaks.

I remember when Carl Groat, now editor of the *Cincinnati Post*, was manager of the United Press bureau at Washington. After the Shenandoah dirigible disaster he sent a reporter to camp on a death-watch at the Navy Department whenever a dirigible made a flight. The man-hours which reporters spend on death-watches and on chasing down tips which do not materialize, the newsless days they put in hovering around prominent figures just so they will be on hand in case something happens, are all part of the routine of being prepared for the unexpected.

Around Scripps–Howard newspaper offices is the old story of the Oklahoma City hanging years ago. The sheriff was all ready. Most of the reporters in town were on hand. But one city editor sent a reporter out to watch the governor, who was opposed to capital punishment. Ten minutes before the hanging was to take place, the governor commuted the sentence. The newspaper which was on the job had its newsboys selling papers to the crowd waiting in the jail yard to see the hanging that had been called off.

Newspapers are prepared always for the unexpected. Hawaii seems to have operated on the conviction that the unexpected couldn't happen.

More than that, the Roberts report shows appalling lack of coordination between the army and navy. The army thought the navy was patrolling. The navy thought the army had its detection service operating. Neither bothered to check with the other – or maybe they were not on speaking terms.

In any newspaper office the first business of the managing editor is to see that his city editor and his telegraph editor clear with each other on space. If the city editor went on his own and the telegraph editor sent wire copy to the composing room to his heart's desire, you would have enough type set to fill three newspapers. If a big local story breaks, the telegraph editor's space is reduced. If a big telegraph story breaks, the city editor takes a cut in space. The two subordinate executives must work together.

I have always thought civilians should be extremely sparing in their advice about military affairs, which seem so simple and yet are so intricate. But the Roberts report shows two glaring situations which come down, in civilian language, to sloppy operation. First, the army and navy acted on the assumption that the unexpected would not happen, when they should have assumed the opposite. Second, the two services were totally uncoordinated, and neither knew what the other was doing – or, in this case, not doing. And the air force, so supremely important in the new warfare, apparently was regarded by both as a minor auxiliary.

•

ROYCE BRIER

Royce Brier (1894–1976) was born in River Falls, Wisconsin, and spent a year at the University of Washington (1914–15). In the early 1920s he became a short-story writer, then he studied for a year in the Orient, the Middle East and Europe. From 1926 to 1937 he was a reporter for the *San Francisco Chronicle*, and from 1937 to 1975 he was the paper's interpretive news columnist; he also directed the editorials from 1942 to 1953. Apart from that he was the author of several books. His columns appeared either as 'Royce Brier Writes' or 'This World Today' on the front page and continued inside; or as 'Looking Around . . .' in the Sunday *Chronicle*'s *This World* magazine supplement.

'Looking Around'
This World [San Francisco Chronicle], March 1, 1942

If one hasn't anything else to do during the periods of waiting for something, there is no more fascinating subject possible than the American psychology under the impact of this war for survival.

Furthermore, it is cheap, and we will be in need of some cheap diversions when the rubber wears out. It requires a few newspapers and magazines, a little chatting with friends and neighbors, and perhaps with strangers in the cocktail bars. Then a little occasional rumination. And a little American history.

It's too big and too majestic in its course for any of us to chart confidently, and as participants in it we are moreover biased and very fallible. But study of it is much more effective than being surprised at every manifestation of the national idiosyncrasy.

Roughly, the Civil War psychology was similar, granting the special variations. There was the slow buildup of resolve, interspersed with moments of dismay and even despair. There was the slow drift of conviction, step by step, from one position to a more uncompromising one. In retrospect the former positions always looked timid and ineffective, and no solution for the problem in hand.

And most of this progressive education came mostly by the teaching of events, seldom by debate among men, or even the persuasion of so clear and logical a man as Abraham Lincoln.

This persistent alteration of war psychology was as true of the Revolution. There were opponents of a break with England, men who tried to save the colonies from the horrors of war, which they said were worse than the oppression of an absolute imperialism. Nor were they all Tories. Some wanted a little war, not a war for independence but a war to teach George III and his ministers a lesson about freemen.

Indeed, they were in the majority as the war opened, and Washington himself was not conspicuous in the independence faction. Many good patriots who fought through the seven long years with great tenacity, in 1775 considered Samuel Adams and other advocates of a complete break as crackpots.

But Samuel Adams was right and the majority were wrong, and while the writings of such as Tom Paine were powerful, events were what forced the inevitable Declaration.

This alteration of convictions under the impact of events is one of the fundamental traits of human nature, in fact it makes children into men and women. And we will do well if we leave a good margin for it in this conflict, and thereby escape a good deal of astonishment at ourselves.

We don't know how we will change our convictions in this war from month to month and from year to year if need be, because we don't know what the controlling events will be. We only know that the events will occur, and that every one of them will deal us a blow, knocking the props from beneath stubborn beliefs derived from earlier events.

Every day in the news, in how we interpret events to ourselves and to our friends, in efforts at interpretation of which this column is but one in thousands, we see this change manifesting itself, and watching it is quite as interesting as watching the little roulette ball spin.

'This World Today'
About Some of Those Civilian 'How to Win the War' Plans
San Francisco Chronicle, March 12, 1942

Well, folks, you may have noted in your idle moments that everybody and his brother now has a way to win this war. Not you and I, but those other fellows.

As for yours truly, it is a most embarrassing juncture. For yours truly, when coming on the payroll some time back, was instructed to plant himself quietly in a corner and interpret the news, and let human society take care of itself.

Consequently he hasn't given much serious thought to the matter or unfolded yet any really comprehensive scheme for cleaning this situation up. In some contemplative moments this has seemed to him a blessing, as the situation is a trifle intricate, if not unmalleable.

But as this hasn't awed those other fellows, there's no reason why anyone at all should be awed, so maybe it isn't as intractable a riddle as it at first appears.

So, there are some who say the way to win the war is to get aid to General MacArthur, and some who in various ways would cure morale, saying it's green around the gills. Some would grant independence to India, and some would wait until Hitler and Stalin had slugged each other cold as turkeys, and then move in and polish them off.

Most everybody would attack, but not quite everybody. Most everybody is sick of taking a mauling, and the thought of dishing out a mauling to somebody else is nice. There are a few, however, who don't feel quite this way, though they are plenty devious about saying so. They are like the wife who is a weekly police court visitor, complaining her old man is beating her. She knows a beating when she takes one, all right, but that isn't the point. She loves him.

First, let's take the miracle. This has been one of those Alamo things, lifting us right out of our shoes. It's levitation, no less.

Hence it may not be astonishing if spots begin to weave before the eyes, and a fixation wells up, and a gospel that that's the war. So what've we given MacArthur and his boys? Not an old casing or a two-pound sack of sugar. So, fellow-Americans, how long goes it? Just so long as you don't drop a postcard to your congressman.

You drop a postcard to your congressman, reminding him you know MacArthur's on Bataan, if some dopes don't, and boy, you'll see action!

Action? Why, we'll put so many ships into Bataan's capacious harbors the fish'll strangle and gargantuan cranes will be unloading crated fighter planes till the brownies'll think we're building three more pyramids. And take a look at those greedy British, hanging on to the *Queen Mary* and *Queen Elizabeth* like they were the Bank of England!

Know how many men one of those babies will handle – 20,000 is how many. Say, if those miserly, extortionate British would leave go of those babies for a month, we'd make five trips easy loaded to the scuppers, and roll 'em right up in the surf, and what do you think 200,000 rootin', tootin' Yanks would do to them brownies?

All right, listen. They go to Indo-China and take. They'd go to Australia and take – that is, take it back, though it's just another island and ain't worth much. They might even take Hawaii back, or with reinforcement whoop across Asia and invade the Balkans, eh? It wouldn't be important, but it'd give them practice. Are we mice or men?

And say, since when has Europe been important to us? Not since 1776, maybe not since 1492. Let 'em fight. They've always been fighting. They're no good. Read your history. Besides, they're half Russians or Germans, and the rest are English or French, who're about the same. That only leaves Monacans.

Therefore, phooey on Europe and phooey on Africa, too. It's across an ocean and everybody carries spears, and nobody ever threw a spear across an ocean. Dakar's got fleas and Libya's got sand. *Raus mit ihm!*

That leaves China and India. But China's been jumping Japan for years, isn't it? – anyway, before we ever heard of a war, so that's their fight. Did we start it? Furthermore, Chinese are being born faster than they die, so what's the complaining about?

But India's another story, as Imperialist Kipling said. There's a land struggling for independence, and we know something about that, we who were at Valley Forge. If George Washington were alive, he'd be in Calcutta this minute. Sensible men won't need proof of that (and won't get it, either). More, there's strategy involved, and nobody sees it. If we really want to lick the brownies (who've had a dirty deal, though really one must hold them off a bit at the moment) – if we really want to lick them, turn India on 'em.

India is populous. There are just lots of people down there, and lots of people win wars, witness Germany and Luxemburg. But the only way to turn India loose on the brownies is free it. Right today. All English out by sundown. Well, look – if the British don't free the Indians, the Japanese will. They've already said they would, dropped pamphlets from planes saying so flatly. Can't you read plain Hindustani?

Last of all, the great question. American morale, of course, that's all we care about. Many more people are interested in winning the war by morale, than in winning it by specific strategy, like Bataan, Dnieper exhaustion or India. You have to be an expert on those, but practically anybody's an expert on his morale and that of his fellow-Americans.

So this ought to be easy, and lo! it is. Last summer, you remember, there was a morale flurry. We had some, but not the soldiers. Give them more ice cream and more Grable and Lamour, and they'd turn into wildcats.

And this is a funny one, because you see these lugs riding around in jeeps right now with their tin hats, and they look like they've got more morale than a jungle full of gorillas. Put them in a Bataan foxhole and in one hour flat they'd have the knack and be knocking the brownies kicking, like Joe, the Filipino.

But now we, who wander disconsolately around in mufti, haven't got any morale. Well, life is strange, as somebody must have remarked once.

And then the alarming thought occurs, what if morale isn't talking about your own morale or worrying about one another's morale? What if it's something else? Like, just seeing a job to be done, and deciding you can and will do it, then moving in and doing it, without much conversation, excepting an occasional low warning to those standing in the way, or crying, that they'll get hurt if they don't get to hell back under the covers.

Not that it's a way to win the war. Oh, no. This wasn't to be another way to win the war, anyway. That requires a good deal of reading up, so maybe some other time.

'Looking Around'
This World [San Francisco Chronicle], September 5, 1943

Well, the newspaper boys in Berne have certainly chanced on a toothsome side-dish in the news, and far be it from a guy whom fate did not select to undergo the rigors of Berne to fail to spread the light. Berne is all right, and the Alpine glow is genuine and doesn't cost three Swiss francs a drink, but there must be a good deal of drudgery and claustrophobia in carrying on the news trade there right now, and the lads can be indulged a little gay copy in the midst of all the sober rush of history.

So it seems a few days ago two gals, a sister act, to wit: Claretta and Miriam Pitacci, were grabbed by the Swiss border patrol about to bow their way out of sunny Italy, and this pair was, one or the other, in the favor of Benito Mussolini during his better days. It was old stuff in Italy, of course, that they were successively Il Duce's mistresses, wherefore the Pitacci family had done very well for itself in the villa-and-jewel department in recent years.

But what was new – though maybe not so new as to be dumbfounding – was that the girls were lighting out for a more healthful climate, in the immemorial manner of the tribe. It will also be a little new to some on this side of the water, but to none in Italy, that the late premier didn't hate the sight of women. The writer boarded the Brussels Express in Paris North station one morning, and while pulling out noticed much running and shouting. In Brussels that evening he gnashed his teeth in frustration to read that some dame had put a slug into some count on the station platform. She said she did it because the count, when ambassador to Rome, came between her and Il Duce. Maybe it was just imagination.

So far as known, none of Ciano's friends have yet shown up at the frontiers, but then, travel conditions are bad. When they do it will be reminiscent of the various French countesses, advisors of various French statesmen, who ducked for Spain in

June, 1940. The trouble with those countesses was they were working for Hitler. We have not yet heard the Pitacci girls were working for us.

The Berne boys dug up Mme Maintenon, consort of Louis XIV, for an analogy, but that was hurry stuff with a cable deadline, and maybe there is a better one, closer to the scene.

The most appropriate romance in history was that of Caesar and Cleopatra, for they were the two most remarkable people of their time. Caesar first met her when he was chasing Pompey to his doom. She was seventeen at the time, a queen and an exile. Certainly she had political motives in enticing the great Caesar, but maybe she loved him, too. He was not a man to be taken lightly by anyone. At any rate, he put her back on her throne in Alexandria, and the next year she went to Rome as his mistress, with their son, Caesarion.

She was at her villa outside Rome when Caesar was assassinated, but she didn't flee immediately. She waited to see how this was going to affect her main concern, the Egyptian throne. The accounts agree that she became 'unpopular,' so she went home. Legend has made a heart-throb of her subsequent romance with Antony, but maybe that's exaggerated. She took very good care of Cleopatra. There's that much analogy, but perhaps no more. Cleopatra had great designs in history (which were ultimately frustrated), and she was a first-rate poisoner and double-crosser for her dynasty's sake. She was no cream-puff out of nowhere.

•

CARL SANDBURG

Carl August Sandburg (1878–1967) is best known for his poetry and his mammoth biography of Abraham Lincoln, but he was also a columnist during two periods of his life. The son of Swedish immigrants, he was born in Galesburg, Illinois, and finished school at the age of thirteen. He hopped trains and was a menial labourer until 1898 when he enlisted to serve in the Spanish–American War. After a period in Puerto Rico he attended Lombard College until 1902, and although he failed to complete his degree he did edit the *Lombard Record*. Between 1904 and 1910 his first four books were published, under the name Charles A. Sandburg, by Professor Philip Green Wright's Asgard Press. From 1907 to 1912 he worked in Wisconsin as an organizer for the Social Democratic Party before joining a Socialist paper, the *Chicago Evening World*, as a reporter in 1911. When it closed he joined a Scripps paper, and when that, too, closed in 1917, he started writing for the National Labor Defence League and was an editorial writer for the *Chicago Evening American*. That same year he became labour reporter and an editorial writer for the *Chicago Daily News*, his home for the next decade or so. He was a film reviewer for several years and wrote a column, first under the heading 'Chips from Carl Sandburg', and later called 'From the notebook of Carl Sandburg'. He started publishing poetry in 1914 and the first two volumes of his Lincoln biography came out in 1926. Having completed the project in 1939, he received the Pulitzer Prize for history in 1940. From 1941 to 1945 he wrote a weekly political column for the Chicago Times Syndicate, and a collection of columns from this period, along with several broadcasts, was published as *Home Front Memo* (1943). In 1951 he was awarded the Pulitzer Prize for poetry for his *Complete Poems* (1950).

For a While We Must Drift
Chicago Times Syndicate, April 13, 1941

One reason why I understand some of my isolationist friends is because I know their language and why they talk like they talk.

Only a little more than a year ago I was using their same line of talk.

Even while Hitler was taking Denmark and Norway, Holland and Belgium, I believed there was a probability, a fighting chance, that once more France and Britain would be deadlocked in a long war like the last one – and the pattern of the war might take the same shape as the last one.

Chamberlain was still Prime Minister of Britain, Daladier at the helm in France, and the sickness and shame of the Munich four-power pact still evident.

The lassitude, stupidity and shame involved in France and Britain handing over Czechoslovakia to Hitler – the infamy of France and Britain letting loyalist Spain go down under the tanks and bombing planes of Hitler and Mussolini – I could not forget these – I remember them now and I hope to go on remembering.

Then France went down.

Then France came under the clammy paws of the Nazis.

Then Britain threw out her reactionaries and stood up and fought and took punishment and did a thing that amazed the world.

For the first time the Hitler timetable was wrecked.

The English Channel, the RAF, and the fleet stopped and held the swiftest and best coordinated war machine that had ever taken the field.

Then slowly across weeks and months the British defense kept on. And I found myself from day to day drifting, my blood and brain saying things they had not said before.

Day by day came the questions: 'If Hitler takes Britain, what kind of a world will it be for us of the United States to live in? Does any man know? If Britain goes down, Hitler takes over unoccupied France, Spain, Switzerland, Sweden, Finland, Yugoslavia, Greece, Turkey, with Italy and Spain as yes-saying partners – and why not? Who is to stop him? Then what? Who will give me a picture of what then follows for this country of ours?

'Who knows how long Soviet Russia then would keep certain oil lands and areas near Germany which Hitler has termed a "rich bread basket"? Are not the Nazis a school, a cult and a philosophy vastly different from that of the Kaiser and the Hohenzollerns? Have they not, as Cardinal Mundelein said, taken the children away from the teaching of the Church? And have they not active spokesmen and defenders in North and South America? And would not these voices be louder and more active than ever if Britain should fall and Hitler take over Europe?

'And what program of human betterments would have much of a chance while we operated as an isolated nation, so armed and so dedicated to national existence that it would not be long before we would have to fight alone a full-sized war or be one more country saying yes-yes to those who wish to regulate our national housekeeping for our own good?'

So I drifted along with those who favored all possible aid to Britain, short of war. From this point on I did more drifting. I believed that when we sent those fifty overage destroyers to Britain we were taking a chance. It spoke our wish that Britain should win enough of her war to still be standing as a nation. It was so near to a declaration of war on Nazi Germany that the point was merely technical as to whether we were in a war or not.

Now what? Now whither am I drifting? Now I find myself approving the war of nerves that President Roosevelt is using on the Nazis. He has given millions of white men, regimented into slavery on the continent of Europe, the hope that arms, planes and supplies from this country may in the end break Hitler's power. Does this mean we send another AEF to Europe? I doubt it, for several reasons. For a year to come – and so much can happen in a year – we will do well to equip all the men now over there anxious to have the use of all we can send. Furthermore, if there should be a call from over there for men, I believe the American volunteer is not extinct. From among our enlisted men, and outside, there could be had in sixty days, I would guess, a half-million young fighting wildcats. And in modern mechanized warfare this half-million would be equivalent to more than the AEF, each man in front combat service requiring forty mechanics, transport, and service and supply men to keep him going.

And there is nothing unusual, unique, or out of the ordinary about my driftings. At times I felt something almost uncanny about the way my driftings were registered in the periodic shifts and gains and losses of the two leading polls of public opinion.

Also I am well aware that the foregoing is an inadequate statement; that what I have tried to say here briefly would require a book with many shadings and modulations. But this is a time when writers ought to try to put on paper for their readers those things moving as shadows in their hearts – and which they are speaking frankly in talk with friends and neighbors.

I agree with my isolationist friends, the handsome Doc Hutchins, the sweet and unimpeachable Lillian Gish, the horselaughing Oscar Ameringer, that if and when we save Britain there will be terrific headaches over what kind of peace is possible to negotiate. They think they know Roosevelt is leading us into war and national suicide. I think they know very little – and maybe next to nothing – about what the picture will be a year from now, even a month from now.

I wish I knew more than I know. I go on drifting. The nation drifts. It is written for a while we must drift. By drifting I mean guessing as to where the national ship of state is going and what will happen to it in the end. Just now I am willing to throw in everything to save Britain. Beyond that I agree with anyone who has a headache.

Hitler and Huey

Chicago Times Syndicate, November 16, 1941

Mein Kampf is a book out of the year 1924. Rudolf Hess took it down as Hitler was serving a jail sentence in a comfortable cell in the fortress at Landsberg on the Lech in Bavaria. That was seventeen years ago. Since then Adolf Hitler has come to be known as the wildest single human tornado that ever tore the map of Europe to pieces, spitting in the wind four ways at once and showing the world how to get on a horse and ride in all directions at once. Where he will end, whether the outside world is to get him or whether one of his own crowd will finish him, is anybody's riddle. In the book *Mein Kampf*, however, we get a self-portrait of him. He tells us how he wants us to think he looks inside and out.

Those who would like good company while reading *Mein Kampf* can enjoy Francis Hackett's *What Mein Kampf Means to America*. Hitler is a statesman, a politician, an evangel, a great executive, organizer and conspirator. Also he is a fraud, a spieler, a charlatan and a lunatic. Hackett calls the turn. Hackett knows when. He spots the paradoxes, the gyrations, the monkeyshines, the doodlebug tricks. In case you don't have the time to wade through the thousand pages of Hitler seeing himself as God's pick of God's best race and breed, Hackett's 280-page book will give you the gist of it. Also his book is a pamphlet and an exhortation. An Irish-born American, he says his say for the hour.

I like his Irish eloquence and his American wrath and wit and scorn. He writes: 'Of the thousands of sweet-minded Americans who have swarmed to read Mrs Lindbergh's book, how many have recognized the ideas in it that are derived from *Mein Kampf*? How many see it as the star-eyed child of that ideological father? . . . Wishing to exclude the Hitler process, she imports the Hitler idea. Her whole intention is honorable, well meant, utterly solicitous for America's welfare, but on every page she evidences the extraordinary degree to which she is under Hitler's influence; and only the person who takes the trouble to read *Mein Kampf* can possibly know this. Which then is better: to consume sugared *Mein Kampf* out of the Lindbergh feeding-dropper or to probe for yourself what the Hitler argument is? You are bound, in any event, to be subjected to Hitler's ideas.'

Quite likely in reading *Mein Kampf* there are things we miss, that we can never understand unless we should go back and be reborn in Germany and live through the years that saw Hitler rise and go to town. However, in reading *Louisiana Hayride* by Harnett T. Kane, we get the accent and we know the game play by play. Here is the living Huey Long, mocking, irresistible, as he laughs, 'Just say I'm sui generis, and let it go at that.' He, too, had the stuff of a dictator. 'Can you handcuff an eel?' Hackett asked as to Hitler, and it would go for Huey Long. An eel, a liar, a monstrosity of shabby and shameless ambitions, there are many parallels in the ways of Hitler and Huey Long. Hitler went into long explanations of how 'the strong man is mightiest alone,' reading the dreams of the people for them and then making them into realities.

To Forrest Davis, Huey Long explained he would be president for four terms. When the people saw how well he was doing, nobody would be able to budge him out in less than that. Long's theory of democracy: 'A leader gets up a program and then he goes out and explains it, patiently and more patiently, until they get it. He asks for a mandate, and if they give it to him, he goes ahead with the program in spite of hell and high water. He don't tolerate no opposition from the old-gang politicians, the legislatures, the courts, the corporations or anybody.'

And then what? Then I'll take Huey Long as against Hitler. The Vienna paperhanger never has laughed. He is subhuman and clammy. Huey Long, the eel and the liar, the patent-medicine seller, laughed, and his laugh yet lingers. If by wile and circumstance he had become a dictator it would have been on a Mussolini pattern rather than a Hitler one.

Huey Long's assassin, Harnett Kane tells us, was 'a quiet, gentle scholar . . . who felt deeply on the subject of dictators and dictatorships. He had done postgraduate work in Vienna when the Social Democratic movement was crumbling, when Dollfuss ordered the destruction of the workers' co-operative apartments. He remembered those days, and he thought bitterly of the days that were now upon Louisiana.'

The dying eel and liar, en route to the hospital, moaned, 'I wonder why he shot me.' That was the poorest wondering Huey Long ever did in his life. Certainly not half the men of Louisiana that he had called 'thieves, bugs, and lice' were what he called them. And it is possible he might have lived on and on had he not let his rash, evil mouth speak follies about the ancestry of the father of his assassin's wife.

•

COLONEL JOHN R. STINGO

James Stuart Aloysius Macdonald was born in New Orleans in 1874. He started out in journalism on the New Orleans *Catholic Register*, a weekly Irish Catholic newspaper, writing about distinguished deceased parishioners and collecting sales returns from news-stands. He next joined the New Orleans daily *Item* and by the age of twenty was its horse-racing handicapper. The managing editor of the New York *Evening Sun* was in New Orleans with his wife, who won $3,400 after following Macdonald's tips. He hired him as turf editor of the *Evening Sun* on $50 a week, but he was soon poached by Arthur Brisbane, Hearst's chief lieutenant, to do the same job for the New York *Evening Journal* on $100 a week. When the governor of New York banned horse-racing in 1906, he travelled west to join Hearst's Los Angeles *Examiner*. He did not return to New York until the end of the 1920s.

From the early 1930s until the mid-1950s he contributed a column called 'Yea, Verily' to the New York *Enquirer* – an afternoon tabloid which later became the *National Enquirer* – in the character of Colonel John R. Stingo, named after a sage from Bret Harte's *Luck of the Roaring Camp*, who would settle disputes among the miners, always concluding with the words 'Yea, Verily'. Instead of a salary, Stingo was paid commissions on the various advertisements that he attracted to his page, and for many years he lived at the Hotel Dixie on Forty-third Street, between Seventh and Eighth Avenues. Although his predominant subject matter was horse-racing, he would occasionally allow himself historical digressions on such events as the burning of the steamboat *General Slocum* in 1904, the charge of the Irish Brigade at Fontenoy in 1745, the defeat of Terry McGovern by 'Gentleman Jim' Corbett at Hartford, Connecticut, in 1901, and the great Rubel Coal and Ice Company hold-up of 1934. Furthermore, he would write a commemorative column each year about the Battle of Gettysburg. As a storyteller, Stingo was an unashamed embroiderer. In 1952 the *New Yorker* columnist A. J. Liebling wrote a series of worshipful articles about Stingo which were later published as a book called *The Honest Rainmaker: The Life and Times of Colonel John R. Stingo* (1989). Liebling adored Stingo's 'damascened style': 'His sentences soar like laminated boomerangs, luring the reader's eye until they swoop and dart across the mind like bright-eyed hummingbirds, for a clean strike every time.'

'Yea, Verily'
New York Enquirer, 1943

Loined in nonchalant Palm Beach kalsomine white duck and tabbing his program with stubby lead pencil, he is watching handy field of sprinters trot postward in Fleetwing Handicap, 3 YO & U 6 furlongs, here this afternoon. He is fifty-three percent owner of newest and best-paying Gold Mine in this America of our'n. And, his name is Eugene Tomaso Mori. Throw-off kid from Mori family that run quaint old Café Mori, Bleecker & West Broadway, New York, for years.

This fabulous Gold Mine of aforesaid Mr Mori is the Garden State Racing Association plant, Camden, NJ. May not be yielding quite the gross bullion of Porcupine's far-famed Hollinger, nor, the Empire shaft, Grass Valley, California, but Garden State has the rich veins and soft yellow stringers indicative of tremendous Bonanza output in years to come. Yes, Mr Mori struck it rich when he made his strike on New Jersey's unbelievably treasure trove Mother Lode ledges only three years ago ... And this, despite most exasperating heartbreaks and setbacks in Construction Operation & Transportation in all Race Track history ...

First, that powerful and bitterly narrow Reform Element which had defamed Jersey State since Dr Lyman Samuel Beecher's bigoted day, brought Heaven and Earth to bear to squelch Mori's enterprises. Tax schedules were enacted and thrown like a Rick in middle of road. Then the wartime necessity killed off Motor Transportation ... Yet, today, this Camden racetrack is pretty snug and nice-away as any you wish to see. And all this time Mori just keeps on smiling while weeding out heavy Tease [Stingo's term for money] and plentee.

I'm out here to Camden's miracle Raceway last week. And what spectacle? Round about eighty-five percent attendance comes from Philadelphia. After youse leave Philadelphia's subway terminal to Camden, then youse heel and toe two and a quarter miles to trackside. Or, perhaps, for a Buck hard, you can claw on to one of the weird Horse drawn vehicles that transport the hungriest Army of Straggling Fortune Hunters over on the March since 'Lucky' Baldwin's Party went over Chilkoot Pass into Klondike in 1898. Like the cavalcade in 'Jim' Cruise's pic, *Covered Wagon*, leaving Platte River in 1849, the Quaker City saffari of dyed in wool Horseplayers sinuously winds down road far as eye could see. All ee samee Oklahoma's 'land rush' on Cimmaron in Indian Territory days.

Moiling and Sweating in Jersey's terrible midsummer's parching sun, here they come, day after day. Women in run over heels, men in bare feet, carrying their boots, sometimes. I've seen seventy-five-year-old wooden wheeled Bonecrackers in locomotion. Also, regular oldtime Hay Wagons, daily Victorias, creaking Democrats, swaying Buckboards, and a collection of busses which must have seen service for Wells Fargo Express in 'Kit' Carson's heyday. But on they come in deathless resolve of a score today. Perfectly oblivious to biblical admonitory suggestion, 'All Horse-players must die broke.' Truly, this present day Pari Mutuel deleria begets a human dementia comparable only to the grand old Bank player who just had to go against Gaff for it was only game in town. And now, as I join out this coolly fastidious Old Boy Mori, in liaison with Col 'Mat' Winn, 'Herb' Swope, 'Packey' Lennon, and George Vanderbilt, to belly Clubhouse Bar for further libation of that heather creamy John Begg liquorial ecstacy, I'm told off a chunk of delectable news.

Come devoutedly wished Peace, this Pennsylvania Railroad, its line between Philly and Atlantic City now running only 500 yards off Garden State's front gates, will haul to Trackside that Philadelphia multitude. Then, attendance will average close to 35,000 and the Handle will break up to, perhaps, $1,500,000 every day. Today, Philadelphia is one of America's red hottest gambo towns in country. May be lot of proverbial Living Dead in old Quarter City but it's surprising how quick come to life when that Paddock Bugle gol darn doth blow.

'Yea, Verily'*
New York Enquirer, 1944

Lakewood, NJ, Mar. 3rd (Special)

We've engaged in, or observed, the Tango Marathon, the Bunion Derby, the Stork Derby, the Flagpole Sitter Contest, Commodore Dutch's Annual Ball, the Pie Eater Handicap, the Frog Jumping Championship, the Irish Royal Hospital Sweep and the Roller Skating Gold Cup, but the White Robin Authenticity setup takes the confectionery.

About middle of last month, 'Bonehead' Barry, the Original, surprised the weary-eyed company at the All Night Drug Store, over in New York, after the shutters had clattered down at Armando's, Duffy Tavern, Golden Pheasant, Stork Club, Paddy the Pig's, El Morocco and Hogan's Irish House, with the astounding assertion that the White Robin had come back to Lakewood. He had been seen by that distinguished Ornithologist, affable 'Abe' Potal, Commander 'Sam' Moorehouse and 'Mike' Todd. Sure sign of early spring and a favorable Training Season for the New York Giants, explained 'Bonehead' Barry. Fitting in nicely with the pattern of things planned by the devious 'Bonehead,' grave doubt and challenging apprehension of Mr Barry's assertion immediately arose. What, a White Robin? Never heard of such a thing. There's no mention of it in Frank C. Menke's *Encyclopedia of Sports*. Impossible, 'Bonehead,' you're sure daffy.

Then old 'Sad Sam' Jackson, the Booking Agent and All Night Sitter Up of substantial

---

* This column tells how the professional gamblers occupied themselves after US racetrack owners were shut down in the last week of 1944 until the end of the war.

repute, offered to lay 3–1 that no one could prove there is such a thing as a White Robin. Quick as lightning for the Overlays, 'Jack' Bart, the Pharmacist, demanded 16–5, and, on acceptance, loaded 'Sad Sam' with a hundred. That started it. The nice fat Schnuckles cut in hefty, too. Night after night, the Mob had been betting off its collective head on the White Robin proposition. Over the All Night Drug Store's steaming Java many a wager, one way or another, had passed on the gentleman's word.

Appears, this 'Buddy' Prior, across at the Golden Pheasant steam beer Peelau, side-kicker of Wingie of Philly, consistently laid against the White Robin proposition, still posting 12–5 right up to five o'clock, yesterday (Friday) morning. Other good Players booked against the White Robin too. Strange how iron-faced Sophisticates will take Gamble Action on anything these days – and nights – with the Horses on motatorium? With plenty a money around the Mob will go for anything. And, so, the White Robin was made to order.

And now 'Bonehead' Barry was going to prove his case – that there is a White Robin, and, that he is back in Lakewood again this Spring as pouty and chesty as ever. This past Wednesday Night the 'Bonehead' declared he had a friend, Lawyer Frank A. Murchison, whose country home on Forest Drive, beyant the Rockefeller Estate, is surrounded by the Red Berried bushes of the Paunsa Tree.

This sends 'em. Schnuckles go for White Robin hook, line & sinker. Soft touch.

The hardy Long Island Thrush, the early Spring visitor, the long-tailed Bluebird, and the Robins thrive lustily on these Red Berries as well as the wild Pidgeons, fast becoming extinct, the Jersey Ravens, and the shiny owl-like Toebills. 'For the past ten days,' says 'Bonehead,' 'the Birds have been appearing in the bushes, opposite the large bay window of the Murchison home, which commands a full view of the red-berried feeding grounds.

'Several red-breasted Robins have been noted, and, for the first time in many Springs the very rare specia, the White Robin. He, or she, is the same in size and contour of brother Red Breast. Has the same song, hop and trot of Mr Redbreast, and, is quite as chesty too. Feeding time is around 7:15 o'clock every morning, soon as the light of Dawn is tolerably clear.' Continuing, 'Bonehead' said, 'It is my Idea to have you Betting Men appoint two Representatives and let Pricemaker Prior nominate the third one. You'll all ride out to the Murchison country manor house in my car leaving Paddy the Pig's ice free Barge Landing at 3:30 a.m.' Agreed. 'I'm taking along Photographer "Ben" Cohen, post-graduate pupil of I. Kaplan, and we'll see what we can do as to proving that there is such a thing as a White Robin.' Readily agreed.

Quickly the Anti-White Robin Mob selected as representatives Oldboy 'Bitzy' Ascher, ancient Bookkeeper for roly poly 'Sam' Boston and 'Jack' Durnell, the Parker & May, Bar Harbor, Me., credit man. The trip was made, the Birds fed as per schedule, and Picturetaker Cohen caught a corking flash of rare White Robin through the Murchison large bay window. The illustration, poised herewith, tells eloquently that there is a White Robin, and, the Payoff of quite some money was made last night on the Committee's Report and this visual confirmation of the fact.

And now the denouement, the finale, the Grand Sendoff, if you don't mind. This ostensibly Silly Johnnie, the red-headed 'Bonehead' Barry, may be knave or fool? I'm just after learning from Tillie the Toiler, in effect, Mr Barry is a Brother of 'Ringer' Barry who did a little Remembrandting on the good racehorse Ahmaudon, $5,000 Claimer, at Havre de Gras, Maryland, ten years ago.

Made this Ahmaudon look like a certain $1,500 Claimer entered in a race that same afternoon. The conspirators got the Price and they reaped the harvest. Without customary Easel or Pastel, somebody could have done a neat job on White Robin. I'm only Saying, that's all. Ever, and always, the Honest Rainmaker, as related in Job, the 2d Verse, is among those with the Prattle of a Babe and the soul of Jimmy Hope, the Bank Robber. Some of the Lads haven't cooled out as yet. Anyway, I lay 'em down, and you guess 'em. Yea, Verily.

•

GEORGE ORWELL

George Orwell was the pseudonym of Eric Arthur Blair (1903–50), who was born into an Anglo-Indian family, and educated at Eton. He served as a policeman in Burma and then back in England he worked as a dishwasher, as a teacher in private schools, and as the keeper of a general store in the countryside. He fought on the Republican side during the Spanish Civil War and was wounded. During the 1930s he acquired a reputation as a novelist and essayist. He was a war correspondent for the BBC during the Second World War, and from December 1943 to February 1945 he wrote a weekly column called 'As I Please' for *Tribune*, the left-wing paper. He also contributed a regular 'London Letter' to the *Partisan Review*. His most famous novels were *Animal Farm* (1945) and *1984* (1949).

'As I Please'
Tribune, 31 December 1943

Reading the discussions of 'war guilt' which reverberate in the correspondence columns of the newspapers, I note the surprise with which many people seem to discover that war is not crime. Hitler, it appears, has not done anything actionable. He has not raped anybody, nor carried off any pieces of loot with his own hands, nor personally flogged any prisoners, buried any wounded men alive, thrown any babies into the air and spitted them on his bayonet, dipped any nuns in petrol and touched them off with church tapers – in fact he has not done any of the things which enemy nationals are usually credited with doing in war-time. He has merely precipitated a world war which will perhaps have cost 20 million lives before it ends. And there is nothing illegal in that. How could there be, when legality implies authority and there *is* no authority with the power to transcend national frontiers?

At the recent trials in Kharkov some attempt was made to fix on Hitler, Himmler and the rest the responsibility for their subordinates' crimes, but the mere fact that this had to be done shows that Hitler's guilt is not self-evident. His crime, it is implied, was not to build up an army for the purpose of aggressive war, but to instruct that army to torture its prisoners. So far as it goes, the distinction between an atrocity and an act of war is valid. An atrocity means an act of terrorism which has no genuine military purpose. One must accept such distinctions if one accepts war at all, which in practice everyone does. Nevertheless, a world in which it is wrong to murder an individual civilian and right to drop a thousand tons of high explosive on a residential area does sometimes make me wonder whether this earth of ours is not a loony-bin made use of by some other planet.

As the 53 bus carries me to and fro I never, at any rate when it is light enough to see, pass the little church of St John, just across the road from Lord's, without a pang. It is a Regency church, one of the very few of the period, and when you pass that way it is well worth going inside to have a look at its friendly interior and read the resounding epitaphs of the East India Nabobs who lie buried there. But its façade, one of the most charming in London, has been utterly ruined by a hideous war memorial which stands in front of it. That seems to be a fixed rule in London: whenever you do by some chance have a decent vista, block it up with the ugliest statue you can find. And, unfortunately, we have never been sufficiently short of bronze for these things to be melted down.

If you climb to the top of the hill in Greenwich Park, you can have the mild thrill of standing exactly on longitude 0°, and you can also examine the ugliest building in the world, Greenwich Observatory. Then look down the hill towards the Thames. Spread out below you are Wren's masterpiece, Greenwich Hospital (now the Naval College) and another exquisite classical building known as the Queen's House. The architects responsible for that shapeless sprawling muddle at the top of the hill had those other two buildings under their eyes while every brick was laid.

As Mr Osbert Sitwell remarked at the time of the 'Baedeker raids'* – how simple-minded of the Germans to imagine that we British could be cowed by the destruction of our ancient monuments! As though any havoc of the German bombs could possibly equal the things we have done ourselves!

I see that Mr Bernard Shaw, among others, wants to rewrite the second verse of the national anthem. Mr Shaw's version retains references to God and the King, but is vaguely internationalist in sentiment. This seems to me ridiculous. Not to have a national anthem would be logical. But if you do have one, its function must necessarily be to point out that we are good and our enemies are bad. Besides, Mr Shaw wants to cut out the only worthwhile lines the anthem contains. All the brass instruments and big drums in the world cannot turn 'God Save the King' into a good tune, but on the very rare occasions when it is sung in full it does spring to life in the two lines:

> Confound their politics,
> Frustrate their knavish tricks!

---

* The German air raids on English towns where places of no possible military value but of historic or artistic interest were hit, e.g. the raid on Canterbury.

And, in fact, I had always imagined that the second verse is habitually
left out because of a vague suspicion on the part of the Tories that these lines refer to
themselves.

Another ninepenny acquisition: *Chronological Tablets, exhibiting every Remarkable Occurrence
from the Creation of the World down to the Present Time.* Printed by J. D. Dewick, Aldersgate
Street, in the year 1801.

With some interest I looked up the date of the creation of the world, and found it
was in 4004 BC, and 'is supposed to have taken place in the autumn'. Later in the book
it is given more exactly as September 4004.

At the end there are a number of blank sheets in which the reader can carry on the
chronicles for himself. Whoever possessed this book did not carry it very far, but one
of the last entries is: 'Tuesday 4 May. Peace proclaimed here. General Illumination.'
That was the Peace of Amiens. This might warn us not to be too previous with our
own illuminations when the armistice comes.

'As I Please'
Tribune, 7 January 1944

Looking through the photographs in the New Year's Honours List, I am struck (as
usual) by the quite exceptional ugliness and vulgarity of the faces displayed there. It
seems to be almost the rule that the kind of person who earns the right to call himself
Lord Percy de Falcontowers should look at best like an overfed publican and at worst
like a tax-collector with a duodenal ulcer. But our country is not alone in this. Anyone
who is a good hand with scissors and paste could compile an excellent book entitled
Our Rulers, and consisting simply of published photographs of the great ones of the
earth. The idea first occurred to me when I saw in *Picture Post* some 'stills' of Beaverbrook
delivering a speech and looking more like a monkey on a stick than you would think
possible for anyone who was not doing it on purpose.

When you had got together your collection of führers, actual and would-be, you
would notice that several qualities recur throughout the list. To begin with, they are all
old. In spite of the lip-service that is paid everywhere to youth, there is no such thing
as a person in a truly commanding position who is less than fifty years old. Secondly,
they are nearly all undersized. A dictator taller than five feet six inches is a very great
rarity. And, thirdly, there is this almost general and sometimes quite fantastic ugliness.
The collection would contain photographs of Streicher bursting a blood vessel, Japanese
war-lords impersonating baboons, Mussolini with his scrubby dewlap, the chinless de
Gaulle, the stumpy short-armed Churchill, Gandhi with his long sly nose and huge bat's
ears, Tojo displaying thirty-two teeth with gold in every one of them. And opposite
each, to make a contrast, there would be a photograph of an ordinary human being
from the country concerned. Opposite Hitler a young sailor from a German submarine,
opposite Tojo a Japanese peasant of the old type – and so on.

But to come back to the Honours List. When you remember that nearly the whole of the rest of the world has dropped it, it does seem strange to see this flummery still continuing in England, a country in which the very notion of aristocracy perished hundreds of years ago. The race-difference on which aristocratic rule is usually founded had disappeared from England by the end of the Middle Ages, and the concept of 'blue blood' as something valuable in itself, and independent of money, was vanishing in the age of Elizabeth. Since then we have been a plutocracy plain and simple. Yet we still make spasmodic efforts to dress ourselves in the colours of medieval feudalism.

Think of the Heralds' Office solemnly faking pedigrees and inventing coats of arms with mermaids and unicorns couchant, regardant and what not, for company directors in bowler hat and striped trousers! What I like best is the careful grading by which honours are always dished out in direct proportion to the amount of mischief done – baronies for Big Business, baronetcies for fashionable surgeons, knighthoods for tame professors. But do these people imagine that by calling themselves lords, knights and so forth they somehow come to have something in common with the medieval aristocracy? Does Sir Walter Citrine, say, feel himself to be rather the same kind of person as Childe Roland (Childe Citrine to the dark tower came!), or is Lord Nuffield under the impression that we shall mistake him for a crusader in chain-armour?

However, this Honours List business has one severely practical aspect, and that is that a title is a first-class alias. Mr X can practically cancel his past by turning himself into Lord Y. Some of the ministerial appointments that have been made during this war would hardly have been possible without some such disguise. As Tom Paine put it: 'These people change their names so often that it is as hard to know them as it is to know thieves.'

I write this to the tune of an electric drill. They are drilling holes in the walls of a surface shelter, removing bricks at regular intervals. Why? Because the shelter is in danger of falling down and it is necessary to give it a cement facing.

It seems doubtful whether these surface shelters were ever of much use. They would give protection against splinters and blast, but not more than the walls of an ordinary house, and the only time I saw a bomb drop anywhere near one it sliced it off the ground as neatly as if it had been done with a knife. The real point is, however, that at the time when these shelters were built it was known that they would fall down in a year or two. Innumerable people pointed this out. But nothing happened; the slovenly building continued, and somebody scooped the contract. Sure enough, a year or two later, the prophets were justified. The mortar began to fall out of the walls, and it became necessary to case the shelters in cement. Once again somebody – perhaps it was the same somebody – scooped the contract.

I do not know whether, in any part of the country, these shelters are actually used in air raids. In my part of London there has never been any question of using them; in fact, they are kept permanently locked lest they should be used for 'improper purposes'. There is one thing, however, that they might conceivably be useful for, and that is as block-houses in street fighting. And on the whole they have been built in the poorer streets. It would amuse me if when the time came the higher-ups were unable to crush the populace because they had thoughtlessly provided them with thousands of machine-gun nests beforehand.

'As I Please'
Tribune, 17 March 1944

With no power to put my decrees into operation, but with as much authority as most of the exile 'governments' now sheltering in various parts of the world, I pronounce sentence of death on the following words and expressions: Achilles' heel, jackboot, hydra-headed, ride roughshod over, stab in the back, petty-bourgeois, stinking corpse, liquidate, iron heel, blood-stained oppressor, cynical betrayal, lackey, flunkey, mad dog, jackal, hyena, blood-bath.

No doubt this list will have to be added to from time to time, but it will do to go on with. It contains a fair selection of the dead metaphors and ill-translated foreign phrases which have been current in Marxist literature for years past.

There are, of course, many other perversions of the English language besides this one. There is official English, or Stripetrouser, the language of White Papers, Parliament-ary debates (in their more decorous moments) and BBC news bulletins. There are the scientists and the economists, with their instinctive preference for words like 'contraindicate' and 'deregionalization'. There is American slang, which for all its attractiveness probably tends to impoverish the language in the long run. And there is the general slovenliness of modern English speech with its decadent vowel sounds (throughout the London area you have to use sign language to distinguish between 'threepence' and 'three-halfpence') and its tendency to make verbs and nouns interchange-able. But here I am concerned only with one kind of bad English, Marxist English, or Pamphletese, which can be studied in the *Daily Worker*, the *Labour Monthly*, *Plebs*, the *New Leader*, and similar papers.

Many of the expressions used in political literature are simply euphemisms or rhetorical tricks. 'Liquidate' (or 'eliminate'), for instance, is a polite word for 'to kill', while 'realism' normally means 'dishonesty'. But Marxist phraseology is peculiar in that it consists largely of translations. Its characteristic vocabulary comes ultimately from German or Russian phrases which have been adopted in one country after another with no attempt to find suitable equivalents. Here, for instance, is a piece of Marxist writing – it happens to be an address delivered to the Allied armies by the citizens of Pantelleria. The citizens of Pantelleria

> pay grateful homage to the Anglo–American forces for the promptness with which they have liberated them from the evil yoke of a megalomaniac and satanic regime which, not content with having sucked like a monstrous octopus the best energies of true Italians for twenty years, is now reducing Italy to a mass of ruins and misery for one motive only – the insane personal profit of its chiefs, who, under an ill-concealed mask of hollow, so-called patriotism, hide the basest passions, and, plotting together

with the German pirates, hatch the lowest egoism and blackest treatment while all the time, with revolting cynicism, they tread on the blood of thousands of Italians.

This filthy stew of words is presumably a translation from the Italian, but the point is that one would not recognize it as such. It might be a translation from any other European language, or it might come straight out of the *Daily Worker*, so truly international is this style of writing. Its characteristic is the endless use of ready-made metaphors. In the same spirit, when Italian submarines were sinking the ships that took arms to Republican Spain, the *Daily Worker* urged the British Admiralty to 'sweep the mad dogs from the seas'. Clearly, people capable of using such phrases have ceased to remember that words have meanings.

A Russian friend tells me that the Russian language is richer than English in terms of abuse, so that Russian invective cannot always be accurately translated. Thus when Molotov referred to the Germans as 'cannibals', he was perhaps using some word which sounded natural in Russian, but to which 'cannibal' was only a rough approximation. But our local Communists have taken over, from the defunct *Imprecor* and similar sources, a whole series of these crudely translated phrases, and from force of habit have come to think of them as actual English expressions. The Communist vocabulary of abuse (applied to Fascists or Socialists according to the 'line' of the moment) includes such terms as hyena, corpse, lackey, pirate, hangman, bloodsucker, mad dog, criminal, assassin. Whether at first, second or third hand, these are all translations, and by no means the kind of word that an English person naturally uses to express disapproval. And language of this kind is used with an astonishing indifference as to its meaning. Ask a journalist what a jackboot is, and you will find that he does not know. Yet he goes on talking about jackboots. Or what is meant by 'to ride roughshod'? Very few people know that either. For that matter, in my experience, very few Socialists know the meaning of the word 'proletariat'.

You can see a good example of Marxist language at its worst in the words 'lackey' and 'flunkey'. Pre-revolutionary Russia was still a feudal country in which hordes of idle men-servants were part of the social set-up; in that context 'lackey', as a word of abuse, had a meaning. In England, the social landscape is quite different. Except at public functions, the last time I saw a footman in livery was in 1921. And, in fact, in ordinary speech, the word 'flunkey' has been obsolete since the nineties, and the word 'lackey' for about a century. Yet they and other equally inappropriate words are dug up for pamphleteering purposes. The result is a style of writing that bears the same relation to writing real English as doing a jigsaw puzzle bears to painting a picture. It is just a question of fitting together a number of ready-made pieces. Just talk about hydra-headed jackboots riding roughshod over blood-stained hyenas, and you are all right. For confirmation of which, see almost any pamphlet issued by the Communist Party – or by any other political party, for that matter.

•

ELEANOR ROOSEVELT

Anna Eleanor Roosevelt (1884–1962), the niece of President Theodore Roosevelt, was born in New York City. She was educated at home and at Allenwood, an English girls' school. In 1905 she married her fifth cousin Franklin Roosevelt, a law student, and she was America's First Lady during Roosevelt's twelve years in the White House. She was also a beacon of liberalism. Starting in December 1935, she wrote a 500-word column for the *New York World-Telegram*, six days a week, called 'My Day', which was syndicated by the United Feature Syndicate. The general manager of United Feature Syndicate coached her through three weeks of practice columns, thereafter she gave over an hour each writing day (usually between two and four p.m.) to dictating her column, sometimes while knitting, sometimes even while eating, often while travelling. She broke her routine for four days after FDR's death in 1945 and missed a copy deadline in 1949. Otherwise, she continued writing the column until her death, switching from the *New York World-Telegram* to the *New York Post* in 1957.

'My Day'
New York World-Telegram, January 7, 1936

Washington

Someone sent me a most amusing present. When I came into my room this afternoon, I thought I was being visited by a zoo, for it was surrounded by four polar bears. On closer inspection, however, I found that the polar bears were guarding a goldfish bowl, with three lovely lilies growing out of the center and a red rose floating to the surface and the goldfish swimming around.

The donor had a sense of humor, for to me a goldfish bowl is certainly suggestive. I doubt if anyone living in the White House needs such a constant reminder, for whether they write themselves, or just trust those who write about them, no goldfish could have less privacy from the point of view of the daily happenings of their existence.

There is, however, one consolation to anyone who lives in the public eye, namely, that while it may be most difficult to keep the world from knowing where you dine and what you eat and what you wear, so much interest is focused on these somewhat unimportant things that you are really left completely free to live your own inner life as you wish.

Thank God, few people are so poor that they do not have an inner life which feeds the real springs of thought and action. So, if I may offer a thought in consolation to others who for a time have to live in a 'goldfish bowl,' it is: 'Don't worry because people know all that you do, for the really important things about anyone are what they are and what they think and feel, and the more you live in a "goldfish bowl" the less people really know about you!'

'My Day'
New York World-Telegram, April 1, 1939

Seattle

What a different point of view one can have on life in twenty-four hours. The night before last, John and Anna and I were still waiting for a baby's arrival, and no one can tell me that is ever an entirely carefree time. No matter how many times we have seen babies come safely into the world, we always think before the event of all the dreadful possibilities that surround all human ventures. When, yesterday afternoon, Anna was safely back in her own room at the hospital and the baby was brought in for John and Anna to inspect together, the sun shone outside. But it would have made no difference, for the sun was certainly shining in our world as far as all the people who love Anna were concerned.

I feel sure that the baby is going to grow up able to take care of himself in life, for he began at once to make himself heard and to move his arms and legs like a little prizefighter. His shoulders are broad too, like his father's, so he ought to carry burdens.

Sometimes I think one's subconscious mind shows the trend of one's thoughts: Anna kept murmuring yesterday, 'So many social problems and I can't solve them,' as though she were searching for the answers and could not get her mind quite focused on them. The baby was saddled at once with responsibility, for the first thing Anna said about him was 'He is so tiny now, but some day he may do something really big.'

Sistie and Buzz came down to see the baby in the afternoon and were a little awed by anything which looked so small, even though we told them what a big baby he is. However, at supper the baby's future status was settled. In discussing the difficulty of adding to the Johns already in the family, Buzz suddenly remembered that Robin Hood had a Little John as his constant companion, so he announced that he would be Robin Hood and the baby would be Little John.

This is one occasion when an event actually occurred in the family and was telephoned to the President before the press was aware of the news. This so rarely happens that I could hardly believe it was possible. Judging from my husband's tone of voice, it gave him great joy to hear it in Warm Springs, Georgia, half an hour after the baby's arrival. And then to be able to announce it to the press.

When you love people very much, isn't it grand to be able to join in their happiness? Like everything else in the world, however, there is a price to pay for love, for the more happiness we derive from the existence and companionship of other human beings, the more vulnerable we are when there is any cause for apprehension. It takes courage to love, but pain through love is the purifying fire which those who love generously know. We all know people who are so much afraid of pain that they shut themselves up like clams in a shell and, giving out nothing, receive nothing and therefore shrink until life is a mere living death.

'My Day'

New York World-Telegram, April 13, 1939

Washington

I had a letter yesterday from a woman who takes me solemnly and somewhat bitterly to task because she finds that I am 'just as silly as other women.' She remarks sadly that those who really suffer in the world today, day in and day out, rarely get any sympathy, but I will write a column on the subject of a passing anxiety when my daughter had a baby. That certainly is sufficiently transient to go by unnoticed, says she, and I have proved myself a foolish sentimentalist.

Perhaps she is right, and I accept her reproof. The pain which results in joy is not to be thought of in the same breath as the kind of pain which simply means a weakening of the power to live with joy. Poor woman! I imagine she is suffering constantly, and it may not be just physical suffering but mental suffering, which can mean even greater torment. A letter such as this makes me wonder how many people have so much to bear themselves that sympathy for anyone else is out of the question.

'My Day'

New York World-Telegram, September 19, 1942

Washington

Wonder of wonders, I have just come across a woman who is not inquisitive. This woman wrote me a little while ago and accused the Student Assembly, held in Washington under the auspices of the United States committee of the International Student Service, of being a strange mixture – in her own words: 'This mob of Hitlerites and ex-Communists.' Quite a mixture!

I answered and tried to tell her something of the truth, but she returned my letter unopened. I wonder if she is just not curious, or so convinced that she knows everything there is to know that she doesn't want to know anything more!

Of course, whatever she believes does no one any harm. I have a theory that when you feel bitterness and rage against other people, even against groups, it is a help to find that it is not necessary. The only harm that comes from self-indulgence in bitterness and anger is what happens to the person so indulging him- or herself. The doctors tell us that there is a chemical change which takes place inside of people who go through such emotions, so it is injurious to the attacker but not injurious to those attacked.

I have had a request from the publicity director of the American Industries Salvage Committee to bring out certain facts about the need for scrap metal. She tells me that four million tons of materials, now hidden away in our homes, are needed on the battlefield.

An old wash pail, for instance, would provide three bayonets. A set of skid chains will provide twenty thirty-seven-millimeter antiaircraft shells. A bicycle tire and tube will make one gas mask. Therefore, the committee begs that you will go rummaging through your house, from garret to cellar, and find everything you no longer use and see that it goes to your local salvage committee. Now that I have told you what the central committee wants you to do, I am going to ask them to do something in return.

I find a great many people who have no idea where their local salvage committee is. They have collected scrap metal and rubber and find no one to notify. I realize all the difficulties of synchronizing all the needs with the collections. I know that eventually all this material we find in our households will be used by industry, but many people are discouraged when nothing is done with the scrap their particular community has collected.

'My Day'
New York World-Telegram, September 25, 1944

Hyde Park

In Oswego, NY, the other day, a local newspaper publisher told us with some pride about the rumor clinic which his paper had established there.

As he described it, the clinic works out very well. For example, when cigarettes are hard to buy in town and someone begins to ask whether the shortage is due to the fact that they are all being bought by the refugees at Fort Ontario, this item is published in the paper and the real answer is given. The real answer, of course, is that the cigarette shortage exists almost everywhere, and is not due to any local condition!

The Oswego advisory committee feels that the newspaper clinic has stopped many rumors which might have caused friction between the people of the city and the people living in the refugee shelter.

I can't help thinking that something of this kind in every community might be wonderfully useful. For instance, a friend of mine tells me that people come up to him constantly and say: 'We know that you are a Democrat. You must be so concerned about the President's health. We hear that he is desperately ill.'

When the President went to Hawaii and the Aleutians, I accompanied him as far as San Diego. I had just returned when I received a letter telling me that the writer heard the President had been very ill in San Diego and had been taken on board a ship to be operated on!

For security reasons, at the time I could say only that I knew this tale was untrue. Now that he has been to Quebec and back, I hope everyone realizes that the people who spread these rumors are not really concerned about the President's health. They are working to create an impression which they think will serve their interests.

Of course, I realize that it is easier to spread rumors now, when a certain amount of secrecy has to be maintained because of wartime conditions. But I think rumor clinics in every town would help to break us of the habit of repeating things which we are not really sure are true.

It is said that gossip is the vice of women. Yet I have lived nearly sixty years, during which I have spent a good part of my time with men, and I have not found that they are any less quick to repeat things about which they know little and which they have not verified. When it comes to gossip about people, I have often wondered if the curiosity of the male members of the family was not one of the real reasons why the ladies gather their little items of scandal to retail at home!

'My Day'

New York World-Telegram, April 17, 1945*

Washington

When you have lived for a long time in close contact with the loss and grief which today pervades the world, any personal sorrow seems to be lost in the general sadness of humanity. For a long time, all hearts have been heavy for every serviceman sacrificed in the war. There is only one way in which those of us who live can repay the dead who have given their utmost for the cause of liberty and justice. They died in the hope that, through their sacrifice, an enduring peace would be built and a more just world would emerge for humanity.

While my husband was in Albany and for some years after coming to Washington, his chief interest was in seeing that the average human being was given a fairer chance for 'life, liberty and the pursuit of happiness.' That was what made him always interested in the problems of minority groups and of any group which was at a disadvantage.

As the war clouds gathered and the inevitable involvement of this country became more evident, his objective was always to deal with the problems of the war, political and military, so that eventually an organization might be built to prevent future wars.

Any man in public life is bound, in the course of years, to create certain enmities. But when he is gone, his main objectives stand out clearly and one may hope that a spirit of unity may arouse the people and their leaders to a complete understanding of his objectives and a determination to achieve those objectives themselves.

Abraham Lincoln was taken from us before he had achieved unity within the nation, and his people failed him. This divided us as a nation for many years.

Woodrow Wilson was also stricken and, in that instance, the peoples of the world failed to carry out his vision.

Perhaps, in His wisdom, the Almighty is trying to show us that a leader may chart the way, may point out the road to lasting peace, but that many leaders and many peoples must do the building. It cannot be the work of one man, nor can the responsibility be laid upon his shoulders, and so, when the time comes for peoples to assume the burden more fully, he is given rest.

God grant that we may have the wisdom and courage to build a peaceful world with justice and opportunity for all peoples the world over.

And now I want to say one personal word of gratitude to the many people who have sent messages of affection and condolence during these last days. My children and I are deeply grateful. I want to say too that the people who waited in the stations and along the railroad to pay their last respects have my deep appreciation.

'And now there abideth these three – faith, hope, charity, but the greatest of these is charity.'

●

* This column appeared following the death of her husband.

THOMAS HORNSBY FERRIL

Thomas Hornsby Ferril (1896–1988) was born in Denver, Colorado, and served in the First World War in the US Army Signals Division, becoming a second lieutenant. He worked first as a reporter for the *Denver Times* and *Rocky Mountain News* from 1919 to 1921, then for the next five years in motion picture advertising, before joining the Great Western Sugar Company as editor of its PR publications, a job he kept until 1968. Meanwhile he forged a reputation as a poet, publishing several collections, winning numerous poetry prizes, and being dubbed 'Colorado's poet laureate'. He also edited the *Rocky Mountain Herald*, a weekly paper which had previously been edited by his father. This consisted of seven pages of legal notices and announcements and the front page, which contained 'the pearls', including from 1939 to 1972, Ferril's column, 'Ideas and Comment'. From 1945 to 1947 he also wrote a column for *Harper's*, called 'Western Half-Acre'. A collection of his columns was published as *I Hate Thursday* (1944).

What Chamberlain Really Muffed

Rocky Mountain Herald, September 16, 1939

I wonder if it occurred to Chamberlain to try to get half an hour alone with Hitler and bop him off. I doubt if they would have frisked Chamberlain for firearms. The practical considerations don't seem insurmountable, but I fear the idea would be rejected on ethical grounds. If you're going to get Hitler, you must do it by approved warfare with thousands of legions of young men murdering each other.

The world is a bit old-fashioned in diplomacy, or perhaps not old-fashioned enough. The grand tradition of bopping off rival dictators, so well approved by the Egyptians, Persians, Greeks, Hebrews and Romans, has its modern counterpart only in such vulgar realists as Dutch Schultz and Al Capone who conducted their diplomacy by the classic code, unsullied by the amenities of nineteenth-century statesmanship.

The Tolerance Mongers

Rocky Mountain Herald, March 10, 1945

I'm prowling through two weeks' accumulation of mail on my desk. The stack includes three appeals to my tolerance – my religious and racial tolerance. You're probably getting the same stuff. It comes from government agencies and humanitarian foundations. It makes me mad and has, I believe, the same effect on others. It is fanning the fires of racial and religious prejudice. Even if it's printed or mimeographed you can't receive such mail without feeling that the person who sent it to you thought it would do you good. He thought you needed it. He thought your cruelty was getting the best of you and he ought to step in.

If we're headed for racial and religious difficulties in America this tolerance campaign is certainly making it worse. It is based on a fundamental delusion evident in many other fields – education, art, agriculture, science, politics, economics – namely the delusion that a desirable objective can be attained directly. Your farm, for example, may be bothered by an ornery little beast called a nematode. Your objective is to get rid of him. But you can't gun for him directly. You have to reorganize your cropping systems, your fertility practices and finally, when you achieve a healthy well-managed farm, he disappears. Or take the artist, the artist in any field. Form and beauty finally determine his success. But if he aims directly at form or beauty he never attains them. His drive must be in the direction of the implications of life, he must supply something that is lacking in the spiritual environment. So doing, form and beauty appear concomitantly, almost as by-products.

This is invariably true of desirable human traits. Kindness is a desirable trait but it cannot be achieved as an end in itself. A hundred other traits must be working in harmonious synchrony to bring about that type of behavior which, in a given situation, automatically results in an act of kindness. Try to make kindness an end in itself and the result is like the 'party manners' of a gross person.

If by tolerance we mean some live-and-let-live habit of mind, it can come about only through a wide and generous understanding of men, it must be a by-product of knowledge and wisdom, it must be grounded in experience.

I see no sensing of this ample context in the minds of the tolerance mongers. They campaign against intolerance the way Carry Nation campaigned against the saloon. They are narrow and single-purposed. They want to make us self-conscious about tolerance, they fail utterly to realize that if you ever become self-conscious about it, you're working against it. A tolerant person never knows he has the trait. It comes as easy as lacing a shoe. It's a spiritual reflex. Think too much about it and you degenerate to the self-righteous snobbishness of Thomas Jefferson when he wrote to Mrs John Adams:

> I tolerate with utmost latitude the right of others to differ from me in opinion without imputing to them criminality. I know too well the weakness and uncertainty of human reason to wonder at its different results.

Big-hearted Tom! You could disagree with him without really being a criminal.

I was talking to a tolerance monger halfway up the OWI [Office of War Information] totem pole the other day. His job was to think up little campaigns, slogans and publicity stunts. These things had enormous 'coverage.' Once an idea was 'approved,' it swept the country, newsreels, radio, newspapers, etc. Decisions had to be right. My informant said, 'You have no idea what a feeling of responsibility and *power* it gives you.' And *power*! The italics are mine. What an insight into that person's mind! Achieving personal power through reordering the lives of others for their own good! Are we living in America or Germany? It's rather frightening, isn't it?

Of Tightropes, Knives and War Crimes
Rocky Mountain Herald, October 20, 1945

I have a disturbing letter from one of my seaboard spiritual advisors. He is, I fear, unaccustomed to being told the truth. In recent correspondence I have referred rather casually to such normal pleasures as tightrope walking, knife throwing and shaving in the bathtub, and he took it for whimsy of the lowest order. Surely I didn't mean it.

Just to keep the record straight, may I advise him that I still carry as a tow-rope in my car the same tightrope I've used since childhood and still use occasionally when nobody is looking. It all dates back to the time when all the kids on our block came under the influence of magnificent Ivy Baldwin who walked the high-wire at Eldorado Springs, 500 feet above South Boulder Canyon. (I think Ivy Baldwin is still living and the Historical Society should certainly write him up. His high dives, balloon ascensions and wire walking were heroic.) We usually strung our ropes between two trees, three or four feet above the ground. Rope walking is much easier than fence or pipe walking, and much more relaxing than golf or bridge. Sneakers are better than any other kind of footgear. Annie Downs once gave me some Japanese tightrope shoes, each made like a mitten with the big toe separated, but I don't like them as well as sneakers.

As for knife throwing, the door to our broom closet has been sacred to this art for years. We allow no putty, plastic wood, or paint to violate its scarred surface. Knife throwing reached its peak in Denver the night Allen True opened his studio beyond Cherry Hills. We even got to throwing axes along toward sunrise and it was all very pleasant. As you grow older, knife throwing is likely to degenerate to ice picks or even darts. It was clear to me that the New Deal was on the skids when Lowell Millett, one of the secret assistants to the President, invited me to do some precision heaving in his basement over in Virginia one evening. I assumed it was to be scout knives, of which I always carry two for social purposes, but imagine, it turned out to be darts – those horrid little things they throw in British pubs for small beer. I meekly asked Lowell if I couldn't at least throw ice picks to assuage my ebbing honor, but he insisted on the damned darts. When a man starts that, his life goes down, down, down. The last I heard, Lowell had sunk to writing editorials.

As for shaving in the bathtub it never occurred to me that any civilized person did it any other way. You do, of course, have to get the right kind of extension mirror from Sears Roebuck. Those who make two separate chores of tubbing and shaving are still slaves of Victorian convention when shaving (unless you were a bearded beauty) was a daily obligation while bathing was a weekly or bi-weekly affectation. Nobody ever thought of linking up the two operations even when they became daily routine. Until Norman Bel Geddes explains that the sentences should run concurrently, our time-saving well-groomed *Esquire* type of man will continue to go through the laborious tubbing sequence and get all dry with towels only to spend another fifteen minutes getting all messed up again shaving over the washbasin.

It's strange to be talking about tightropes – (the savages of Maryland still call them 'type-ropes') – or knife throwing or shaving in the bathtub while the papers are full of this macabre Laval episode in France. Modern civilization is adding something to war which old Cato would approve. In our new concept of what a war criminal is we are restoring the oldest concepts of the Romans and Carthaginians. Perhaps we'll soon be leading the vanquished in chains behind our chariots in public processions.

War itself is the greatest atrocity of all and for a good many centuries we were heading toward the idea that once war was over, it was over, and good riddance. Today it isn't over until the last criminal is punished. This appeals to our sense of justice. But when the paper said the other day that as many as two million war criminals in defeated Germany alone ought to be punished – well, what about our idea that you can't indict a countryside? Is democracy voting against itself? Laval appeals to me as a wicked eloquent eel who deserved what he got and gave those who tried him what they deserved, too. Your feeling that justice was administered turns out to be sadistic, going and coming. There were legendary seeds in his behavior. With favorable germination, martyrdom might be indicated. The good-for-nothing George of Cappadocia who was lynched for cheating the Romans on a pork contract may have been much like Laval. Today he is St George, the patron saint of England.

Traitors are traitors and it's pretty clear how they behave. Where our new definition gets hazy is in the case of an expedient politician who guesses wrong on a political trend in which multitudes guess one way and multitudes guess another. We had such situations on the Kansas–Missouri border in the 1850s and 1860s. Perhaps we should have tried and hanged the leaders who guessed wrong, but we didn't. Only in barbershop quartets did we hang Jeff Davis on a sour apple tree and, as the years went by we admitted that he had a case. Under our modern concept of a war criminal, General Nathan Bedford Forrest should most certainly have been hanged, but today we are very sentimental about this cruel Confederate slave broker who may or may not have coined the expression about getting there 'firstest with the mostest.'

We've come back pretty definitely to the idea that justice depends on the might of the winning side. It's always a tricky matter. Those old Indian chiefs we admire so much, like Chief Ouray, were actually quislings who happened to guess right. We tricked and murdered Sitting Bull because he refused to be a quisling. Our schoolbooks pictured him as a ruthless criminal, so also with Geronimo and the harmless Digger priest Wovoka who, in his simple desert dreaming, had a good many of the ideals of Jesus Christ.

In view of the frightful atrocities the war defendants have committed, it is difficult to stand back and be philosophical about our procedure, but vindictive hysteria might easily carry it to a point where the useful convention of the truce would actually be revised into a pretext for continuing warfare. International justice, as we have come to think of it, might undermine itself by its own crusading. Even that has its points, in view of how international justice has worked in modern times. Carthaginian peace at least put Carthage out of business. The world was made safe for the humanitarian Romans.

●

WALTER WINCHELL

Walter Winchell (1897–1972) was born in Harlem, New York City, the son of Russian Jewish immigrants (he changed his name from Winchel), and educated at public schools, ending in the sixth grade. At the age of thirteen he became part of a trio of singing ushers at a nickelodeon, with Eddie Cantor and George Jessel; the trio was joined by three others and became the 'Newsboy Sextette'. During the First World War he served in the US Navy, carrying secret messages for Rear Admiral Marbury Johnson, and after the war he was in vaudeville with a girl partner. However, he preferred a $25-a-week job as a gossip columnist on the *Vaudeville News* to performing, although his role as a columnist was to become his best vaudeville turn in itself. He wrote two columns for that paper, 'Merciless Truth' and 'Broadway Hearsay'. In 1925 he took his column, now called 'On Broadway', to the *New York Graphic*, the seediest of New York papers, where he also served as advertising manager, drama critic and editor, and amusement editor. In 1929 he moved again, this time to Hearst's *New York Daily Mirror*. Syndicated through Hearst's King Features as 'In New York', the Winchell column sometimes carried other headings, such as 'Portrait of a Man Talking to Himself'. Winchell's brand of gossip was unique in its breathless, intense quality, with a demotic vocabulary of its own – fellow columnist Ben Hecht said that Winchell wrote 'like a man honking in a traffic jam' and H. L. Mencken declared that he was one of the ten most productive coiners of slang words and phrases. He attacked Hitler for his anti-Semitism and mocked him in the belief that he was a 'pansy'. For many years he had a fifteen-minute Sunday night radio show on CBS, in which he read out material from his columns, with an inimitable staccato delivery. In the late 1950s he hosted his own television show, and from 1959 to 1963 he provided the voiceovers for the popular television drama series *The Untouchables*. His subjects were showbusiness, crime, politics, love affairs, the evils of appeasement and, later, the evils of Communism. He compared the Communist menace to the Nazi menace and supported McCarthy's crusade: when McCarthy was discredited in 1954, Winchell was caught in the shadow and his popularity waned. At the height of his success, almost 1,000 papers subscribed to his column. In 1963 the *Mirror* closed and Winchell took his column to another Hearst title, the *New York Journal-American*. Five years later King Features dropped his column and it was syndicated for a while by the McNaught Syndicate, although it now reached only 150 papers. During the Second World War he was made a lieutenant commander.

Broadway Alien

New York Daily Mirror, December 1940

She believes everything she reads in the movie mags. She once went to a nightclub on New Year's Eve and didn't enjoy it. The only time she stays up all night is when she has a toothache. Marriage, in her opinion, is something sacred, not just a breathing spell between gigolos. She thinks 'Lucious' Beebe [New York society columnist (see pp. 393–401)] is the name of a perfume. If she wasn't true to the guy she cared about most, she'd never be able to sleep. It would worry her too much.

When she sees a girl snubbing others or being insulting, she doesn't consider it being sophisticated, but downright rude. She doesn't do charity work just to get her picture in the paper. She's never been to a horse show or dog show at Madison Square Garden – and when she sees scenes from them in the newsreels, they make her yawn. She is familiar with all the latest styles, but cannot afford to wear them.

You never see her sitting in the corner of some Broadway joynt drinking and smoking and trying to appear interested in the conversation of a man who looks as though he might be her father. If you see her at 5:30 in the morning, she isn't on her way to some after-hours spot in Harlem. She's en route to the six a.m. Mass. Tommy Manville never asked her to be his Girl Friday or any day of the week. She thinks a sweater is something you wear at home – to high school or at a football game. Not at the Stork Club.

When a fellow asks her if she'd like a silver-fox stole, she replies: 'What for?' When she goes to the theater, it is to see and hear – not to be seen and heard. The only daddy she knows is the one who married her mother.

She remembers everything she did on New Year's Eve since she was ten years young – and there's nothing she did that she's trying to forget. She thinks a powder room in a restaurant is a place to powder your nose, not to stab a gal-pal in the back. Macoco never took her to El Morocco or on a trip to Acapulco. She heard the risgay lyrics of Dwight Fiske and Belle Barth and blushed. Her name has never been bandied about in a Broadway column or in some comic's routine at The Copa. *Life* and *Look* photoggers have never tried to get pix of her with her dress up to her hips. They know what a waste of time that'd be. The only time she ever got her picture in the paper was when she helped Coney Island reach the 'Million on the Beach' mark. She thinks 'Tony's' is a shoe-shine place. She detests double-talkers, double-crossers, double-entendres and double-Scotches. To her 'going on the wagon' means a hayride with a boyfriend and the gang.

You won't find her father rated in Dun and Bradstreet. In fact, he may not even be listed in the phone directory. Her fingernails never grow to claw-length because they'd get mixed up in the typewriter keyboard. When you talk about 'heels,' she thinks you mean part of your shoes. The fur coat she wears was purchased by herself on the installment plan. It's almost paid for, too. She doesn't go slumming on Second Avenue. She lives there. An 'Escort Service' would fail if it was up to girls like her.

She wore the colors of the flag as an ornament on her dress or coat long before it was fashionable to do so. She thinks phony eyelashes look exactly like phony eyelashes. She never bothers people in the public eye for an autograph. When Joan Crawford gets a bum notice, it makes her ache. Nobody from the fashion pages ever writes up what she wore at the opening night because she goes to the theater after she's read the reviews. And, anyway, they'd never see her because she sits in the balcony and stays there during inter-mission. She smells sweet, not because of any cologne, but because she washes her neck, too. When she says she loves you it comes from the heart – not from a Cuba Libre.

You seldom hear her pulling any of Dorothy Parker's best quips, but if she does she prefaces them with credit to Miss Parker. Nobody ever goes to the bother of telling her shady gags because they'd lay an egg. Her vocabulary of cusswords is limited. When she gets real angry she says 'Holy Smoke!' She reads the best books and understands them, not just an occasional detective story. At the movies she considers it perfectly normal and proper for the boyfriend to hold her hand – not her knee. If you told her you were a press agent she'd respond: 'What's that?' If a fellow ever pinched her any place but the cheek, she'd never say 'Fresh!' – she'd haul off and bang him one. She's definitely not in the social register. She couldn't be – she's the kind of gal who always says 'Thanks' to waiters and busboys.

She's a strange little creature, this kernel of alien corn. She doesn't like being called a dame or a broad. She buys Ernest Hemingway's books to read them, not to have Mr Hemingway autograph them. On her way to the 'Little-Girls-Room' she never pauses to shout 'Daaahhhleeeeeng' to Brenda Frazier or Tallulah. For the very simple reason that they do not know her. She thinks *The Great Dictator* and *Fantasia* are swell, and that the critics are whacky. Two highballs are enough for her and she won't let you pay nightclub prices for a doll or toy. I don't know how she lasts in this town. She stops eating bread, butter and potatoes when she's getting chunky. No avoirpoison for her. She always goes home with the fellow who brought her and she's never called anyone 'Stinky.'

Saroyan, Stein and Dali are not up her alley. She adores Toscanini or Kostelanetz recordings and detests 'Gloomy Sunday.' Her grandfather wasn't with Clive in India and none of her kin came over on the *Mayflower*, but they all made darn fine buck privates when they were needed. Jane Kean would find her dull material for mimicry or satire, but she would have made a swelegant heroine for Harold Bell Wright. She eats onions with hamburgers. She doesn't know Peter Arno or Lois Long and vice versa. She's her own Emily Post and insists you use your knife on that impossible hunk of lettuce. When she goes into a phone booth, it is to call her mother to report she'll be later than she thawt – not to phone some other guy to meet her after she drops the date she's with. She applauds when the American flag is flashed on the screen. She closes her eyes when she dances with you – and stays on key when she hums in your ear. You can bet your life she isn't flirting with the sax tootler over your shoulder. She's the gal your mother was and your sister is.

New York Daily Mirror, November 1946

Jimmy Walker* is dead . . . The papers are filled with accounts of what a great guy he was in spite of his faults. Because he was a friend of mine – and because I like to think I hate hypocrisy as much as he did – I want to offer a correction. He was not a great guy in spite of his faults; he was a great guy because of them.

As a politician, Jimmy had three faults. One, he was too brave. Two, he was sincere enough to live up to his vices publicly. And the most important and final fault of all, he ran into hard luck. It's part of our tradition to make an unlucky politician our scapegoat. But it is too much for the stomach of this reporter to see people try to turn it into evidence of their own virtue.

It might have proven too much for even Jimmy's sense of humor to watch the syrupy better-than-thous pay glowing tribute to their own pseudo-virtue by assuming a forgiving

---

* Jimmy Walker, Democratic Mayor of New York from 1925 until 1932, when he resigned under a cloud, his administration mired in corruption scandals. Nevertheless, he was an immensely popular personality.

and understanding attitude – for a man who had the courage to lead the colorful life they all secretly envied.

As a matter of fact, Jimmy could see so much of every side of a question that he was in frequent demand as an arbitrator. He wasn't anything but simply American. He wasn't pro- or anti-Franco, anti- or pro-Turks, Swedes, Russians or Hindus. He took things as he found them.

He liked everybody and nearly everybody liked him . . . his most bitter critic, Fiorello H. La Guardia, recommended him years after as the impartial arbitration chairman for the garment industry.

The two men were warm friends until the end. They used to sit around and talk about old campaigns like two opposing generals explaining their battle plans to each other. Some men live to confound their enemies – but Walker loved to confirm them as friends.

One reason is that during the trying years, he maintained his sense of humor as well as his dignity. At his investigation, James Finnegan, Brooklyn Independent, accidentally struck Walker on the shoulder with a heavy chair. 'Excuse me, Mr Mayor,' said Finnegan. 'That's OK, Jim,' said Walker. 'I was expecting your shoe – in a different place!'

While a great deal has been said of his affection for Betty Compton, little has been written of his undying devotion to her . . . Nelson for Lady Hamilton, Abelard for Heloise, Gabriel for Evangeline were not more constant. He loved her above mere possessiveness. He shared her memory with the man she later married. They became firm friends, occupied the same apartment and took care of the children she adopted. Both of them were broad enough to accept each other as friends because of their singular love for this remarkable and beautiful woman.

Few men in history are as widely liked as they are widely known – and he was once. His faults were the warm ones: There was nothing cold or calculating in his whole makeup. Love of his fellow man was his chief characteristic.

With this infallible credential there must be someplace, somewhere for someone who could even wear a halo jauntily.

So long, Jimmy. For once, you're too early.

'In New York'
New York Daily Mirror, October 7, 1947

Attention Mr and Mrs United States!
On Friday at the UN Deputy Foreign Minister Vishinsky of Russia held a press conference witnessed by over 400 reporters . . . He accused America of warmongering and he named this newscaster (along with several other Americans) as one of the warmongers 'who should be enchained' and put behind bars . . . The Russian Deputy Foreign Minister also denounced the Marshall Plan as an American attack on the nations of Europe . . . Very notably Mr Vishinsky offered no plan to prevent the war which he says he fears and hates . . . Well, here are some concrete suggestions.

Since when is a loaf of bread for a starving man or a bottle of milk for a sick baby an act of war? . . . We Americans don't think so.

Mr Vishinsky also accused the United States of threatening the world with the atom bomb ... But, in open assembly, we agreed to turn it over to the United Nations, provided there was an International Police Force – and inspection of it ... But Russia vetoed it ... Mr Vishinsky, why no inspection? ... Is somebody carrying concealed weapons? ... And why no great International Police Force – without veto? ... Who's afraid of police – but criminals?

Mr Vishinsky, our country is ready for honest international inspection – any time your country is ... But not before ... We told you that we would submit to international inspection, if you would. Though that would prevent war, your country declined ... A very strange action for a gov't which says it loves peace, Mr Vishinsky.

Your statement that I (and some other Americans) should be enchained is impractical ... Chaining people, as a principle, doesn't work ... Mr Hitler tried that and look what happened to him and the world ... So, as a counter-suggestion, why don't you consider not more chains on Americans but less chains on Russians? ... Before you give us a piece of your mind, Mr Vishinsky, why doesn't your government give the Russian people a chance to speak theirs? ... Since your commissars won't let your people talk, how do you know that they do not think you are the warmongers? ... You say that Winchell would be able to write more cleverly if he came to Russia. Now how could anybody typewrite without hands, Mr Vishinsky?

You also stated that newspaper people could enjoy 'reasonable access' to the Soviet – 'even the unreasonable radio liar Walter Winchell.' Well, I wonder ... Helen Kirkpatrick (the foreign correspondent) in her report significantly pointed out there were many in your press audience who had 'vainly applied for admission to Russia.'

I told International News Service (and the *NY Times*) Saturday I would be glad to go to Russia if anything I could say or write would help stop our two countries from going to war ... But I wouldn't want to go on any of those specially guided vodka tours – as I am not a vodka man, anyway ... I would, however, like to visit your country – along with other American reporters and radio commentators ... And receive the same courtesies your Tass News Agency people receive over here ... Go where they please and so on.

I published a list of newspaper people I'd like to have on this expedition ... They include some of my best friends and severest enemies – and some of Russia's too ... From the extreme Right to extreme Left and even some who are center – of center ... I put all of them on the list to show you people that I couldn't lie, even if I wanted to, with so many of my rivals there to show me up. If you really meant your offer of a trip to Russia I'm ready – let's go ... And, Mr Vishinsky, if you can prove that I am a liar – you will not have to do anything else ... My competitors will do the rest.

There is, however, still another and a final issue, Mr Vishinsky ... *your* statement is either true or false ... Either Secretary of State George Marshall, Senator Austin, Senator McMahon and myself are warmongers – or *you* are a liar.

I do not flatter myself that you intended to pan me personally ... You struck back in a rage at a member of the American press because there is nothing in the world that you and Mr Stalin fear more than a man with a free typewriter and microphone.

But it is not I who should be locked up. It is you, Mr Vishinsky, who are in chains right now . . . I can speak my mind and you cannot . . . Along with 140 million other Americans, I am free to criticize our gov't . . . But if you, third ranking man in the Communist dictatorship, criticized yours, you would be shot, and you know it.

Now let's set the record straight . . . Your chief worry is not keeping Americans from knowing what is going on inside Russia . . . You are afraid to let the Russian people know what is going on in the world . . . You and your Communist-atheist government know that one independent and honest American reporter inside Russia with a microphone is more dangerous to the Communist Party than any atomic bomb . . . And, for once, Mr Vishinsky, you are right.

Man About Town: Who's the London newspaperman (*Daily Mail*?) Perón arrested in Argentina last week for a piece he wrote about Evita? . . . *Brigadoon*'s star, Marion Bell, became Mrs Alan Jay Lerner at Fort Lee Friday . . . Phyllis Holden, who bought playwright Robert Pysel's play, *Quadrille*, will be welded to him at City Hall (with Hizzoner doing the merging) on Wednesday. The groom's pop is a Shell Oil exec . . . W A Capt. Kathleen Nash Durant (released on bail in that huge gem theft abroad) is dwelling here so she can be near her Colonel-groom now jailed on Governor's Island . . . The Colonel Batistas (he was once Cuban Prez) are imaging at Drs Hosp . . . Nick the Greek has finally fallen for a fashion columnist . . . '21' has barred a society columnist for conduct, one presumes, unbecoming a society man.

Pola Negri and Sergi DeKarlo are inseparable . . . Model Jean Sinclair (chums expected she'd become the new Mrs Alexis Thompson) may now altar things with millionaire R. Duff . . . Conductor M. Abravanel (Utah Symphony) married Lucy Carasso (formerly of Paris) on the 20th. He recently baton'd 'Street Scene' . . . Isn't Tallulah's new interest a Chicago airlines exec? . . . Hedy's ex-groom, John Loder, was showing Mrs Anthony Eden (or her double?) the midtown boites Friday after curtain time . . . It must be ironic for Russians to see Vishinsky losing his head. He was responsible for so many Russians losing theirs to the executioner . . . From Hitler's Berlin paper *Beobachter* (in 1934), via the front page: 'Walter Winchell, above, is the New Germany's new American enemy. He tells conscienceless lies about the Führer in hundreds of American newspapers.'

•

BENJAMIN DE CASSERES

Benjamin de Casseres (1873?–1945) was born in Philadelphia where he became a newspaperman at the age of sixteen. He later joined the *New York Sun* as a proofreader, then served as a reporter for the *New York Herald* from 1903 to 1919. Apart from his newspaper work, he also wrote poetry, fiction, essays and criticism. In 1934 he moved to the *New York American*, for which he wrote two columns, 'On the Nail' and 'The March of Events'. He also wrote numerous editorials for the *American* and for other Hearst papers. De Casseres described himself as 'an anti-New Deal Democrat': he was a vigorous libertarian and a sceptic about post-war planning.

He continued his daily column and his editorial writing for the *New York Mirror* through a final year of illness.

'The March of Events'
New York American, May 19, 1944

Speaking of the curious softness that this Administration displays to Red Russia, Mr James M. McPadden asks in a letter to 'March of Events': 'Does the defense of liberty against two madmen demand marriage to a third?'

The two madmen are evidently Hitler and Tojo. The third is Stalin, who is, by the way, not 'mad' at all. He's plenty sane, brother! But Mr McPadden has put the question cogently. I have heard the excuse given that the Administration is merely playing a diplomatic, a military game – a game of international 'expediency' – with Soviet Russia.

However, it is well to remember that this coddling began some years ago when President Roosevelt 'recognized' Communist Russia, and thereby stamped Stalin's colossal prison camp as a legitimate form of government. That was long before Hitler, Mussolini and Tojo had begun their war on the democracies.

As a matter of fact, this Administration has had from the very first a sentimental leaning toward this 'noble experiment' – an 'experiment' on which the Russian people never voted; an 'experiment' that was put over on them by force – in the same way that Hitler put over Nazism on Czechoslovakia, Austria, Norway and France.

If we are now looking for a post-war ally and we are going to deliberately choose totalitarian, anti-American, anti-democratic Russia, then to Mr McPadden's 'madmen' we may have to add a fourth – Uncle Sam.

One of my most hilarious amusements nowadays is putting the verbal and written koombosh of Vice-President Wallace into my mental crucible and discovering what the ingredients of this fantastic fellow are. Throwing into the crucible his 'Seven Freedoms' (trumping his chief by three aces), I find in Henry A. Wallace's character fragments of Moody and Sankey, Karl Marx, Don Quixote, Huey Long, Billy Sunday, Peter the Hermit, Tolstoy, Bill Bryan, Aimee Semple MacPherson, 'Greenback' Butler, Dewitt Talmadge, Lenin, Susan B. Anthony and Houdini.

He is a man properly equipped to lead millions of impressionable and gullible Americans on another messianic 'bender' à la Bryan. Like Bryan, and all social messiahs in fact, Mr Wallace is a supreme type of the sincere demagogue. This with his profound ignorance of human nature and the laws, both human and cosmic, of the world he lives in makes him a power. You folks have no idea of the number of people on earth at any given time who believe implicitly in these social kingdom comers. Their appeal is wholly emotional because these 'saviors' are wholly emotional themselves. They are wishbone thinkers. They are all really drunk on ego-booze, although, as in the case of Mr Wallace, they may never have taken a drop of real booze.

Maybe that's what's the matter with them. They need the humor that is in wine and beer.

The essence of Mr Wallace's 'seven points,' for instance, is freedom from worry and fear. Now, both fear and worry are innate in the very mental and bodily structure of man and beast. Both are the dynamos of change, of 'progress,' of betterment.

'The March of Events'
New York American, May 20, 1944

If I ever want a ready prescription for turning this free American democracy of ours into a socialistic state I shall get the prescription from 'Doctor' Robert Wagner, the German-born US Senator from New York.

I mention the fact that Senator Wagner is German-born not to be 'catty' but because the Germans almost to a man in all ages believe in regimentation, mental goosestepping and the 'divine' origin and mission of the State. All parties in Germany are collectivist and the individualist of the Jefferson–Emerson–Paine type is regarded as a heretic in the land of Hitlers, Kaisers and Bismarcks.

So no matter to what part of the world the German emigrates he carries with him in his blood, bone, brain and gizzard his prenatal state-enslaving reflexes which he calls 'social legislation,' 'welfare legislation' or some such series of weasel words to cover up his propaganda for his age-old superstition that 'be it enacted' is the way of social and political salvation.

Senator Wagner's whole political life is devoted to transferring to our country all the 'socialized' regimenting laws that have been the mental habits of all Germans for a hundred years. He is the author of the National Industrial Recovery Act, Labor Relations Act, the Railway Pension Law, the US Housing Act, and now he has another projected act to wallop as much as twelve percent out of wage envelopes with an additional seven percent for a 'Federal fund' for the purpose of insuring everyone from the cradle to the grave from anything that could happen.

Of course, after Senator Wagner's act has got through taking everything out of the pockets of employers and employees, there will be nothing left for us to do but to get the government to keep us – if the government can find the money after taxing us all to death.

Then will come the Hitler, the Stalin, the Huey Long or the Mussolini to take us all over, bag, baggage and Wagner.

So you can see how Hitler may lose this war and yet win it through enslaving, Teuton-conceived legislation.

Of course, beneficent Senator Wagner has no intention of turning his adopted country into a Stalinized or Hitlerized slave pen. But Hitler and Stalin would also throw up their hands in horror if you ever suggested to them that their 'social legislation' had finally created a nation of robots.

But I'm not an optimist on the home front nowadays. We are being Germanized and Russianized. There is one way to save our skins, Yankee Doodle Americans, and that is to vote back to private life next November all the Wallaces, Wagners, Jekeses and Tugwells, including their too-complacent chief.

'The March of Events'
Auld Lang Syne

New York American, [undated]

The Old 'Red-Ink' Places (Part III): Memories of Little Hungary draw me over to Second Avenue, once the most picturesque and European-like street in New York. Hungarian red wines, steaming hot or ice-cooled, were consumed on the sidewalk cafés far into the summer nights and in winter they were got indoors, while a violinist strolled around, stopped at the tables and played some of the weirdest and most beautiful airs I have ever heard.

Second Avenue preserved its air and entity almost to 1920. Few uitlanders ever visited it. There were Balogh's Café Monopole (happy, laughing Balogh, who one night went behind a cask of red ink and blew his brains out!); the Orpheum (steaming red Hungarian wine and a whole play in Hungarian, Yiddish or something, for ten cents); the Café Royale, with its extensive sidewalk café, and the Café Boulevard, with its wine cellars lighted by candles and its grotesque cymbalum player (Huneker made him the central character in one of his fantastic short stories).

The Boulevard was not, strictly speaking, a red-ink joint. It catered to the Vere de Veres of the East Side.

It was at a dinner of the Sunset Club at the Boulevard that Sadakichi Hartman delivered his epoch-making lecture on temperance and monogamy.

Maria's! A tocsin, a trumpet of resurrection in the ears of all Bohemian, wine-bibbing, roystering New Yorkers. Maria's was in Twelfth Street, and for many years it was a club of the arts and letters. It has become a legend. For thirty years it was a whole Boul' Mich in itself. Who has not dined, wined, sung and high-jinksed it at Maria's is not in the Golden Book of New York Bohemia.

It was the central red-ink joint of every writer, painter, sculptor, architect, composer and newspaper man, including Ibsenists, Marxists, Stirnerites, Shavians and Swin-burnians, that heeled it around New York.

On Saturday night after ten o'clock you couldn't lower a boat in that heaving Red Sea. At four o'clock in the morning you could attach a fire-hose to any mouth in the place and put out a fire a block away.

It was in Maria's that a writing lady whose name shall be inviolate here laid her face on my collar, crinkled to a string, and wept and wept. I inquired. She pointed to a big fellow (a well-known painter) who stood at the piano, his arm around the waist of a young woman bawling out a song.

'That's my husband,' she sobbed. 'Look at him! For two years after we were married he didn't drink a drop and we used to read Nietzsche and Schopenhauer to one another every night. Now he sings in bed, and our dear Nietzsche and Schopenhauer nights are no more!'

Maria's had a recognized toastmaster. For years he was Mickey Finn. Anybody called on had to do something – a song, a story, a dance or a recitation. *Gunga Din* was done to death there. I once recited *The Ride of Paul Revere* in order to soothe the Americans who frequented the place.

'The March of Events'
New York American, [undated]

You think things are happening to you? Well, after you hear the true story of Solomon Mack, from his own pen, you'll think you're living in a chateau on Easy Street.

Solomon Mack was born on September 26, 1735, in Lime, Conn. He wrote the story of his life, the manuscript of which is in the rare documents division of the New York Public Library. But nothing is beyond the marauding brain of Dent Smith, the editor of that astonishing, entertaining and highly literate monthly pocket-size magazine, *Encore*. Mr Smith prints Mack's confession in full. I condense:

PART I

Mack's father dropped dead. Mother died after a lingering illness . . . five children left to the mercy of the world and the Indians . . . Sol, 'bound out,' worked like a slave for his 'master' . . . no education . . . At twenty-one a feversore on his leg. Nearly died of it . . . Enlisted in French and Indian War . . . Got very sick . . . Saw five men hung at once . . . Went farming. Had his oxen stolen . . . English officer was going to run him through with a sword but changed his mind . . . Indians came out of the woods to tomahawk him. He chased them with a staff and howls . . . Got smallpox at Albany while teaming . . . Robbed of two teams . . . Enlisted again. Five hundred killed in action, but Sol escaped when a well aimed musket ball passed under his chin . . . A friend of his had nine bullets shot through his clothes and was scalped, but lived.

PART II

In 1754 Sol lost all his money again . . . Re-enlisted . . . Came out alive . . . Nearly cut his leg off in the woods. Laid up for a whole season . . . Freighted on a boat down the Hudson. Gale wrecked it . . . Broke his wrist . . . Enlisted in the Revolutionary War . . . A tree fell on him. Crushed to a 'pulp,' almost . . . Limb from a tree fell on his head. Nearly dead for days . . . Taken with fits while traveling. Laid on the ice unconscious for four hours . . . Amnesia . . . In the spring seven trees fell on him. Unhurt . . . Went privateering. Chased by five British privateers. Battle. The Red Coats shot away the rigging of Sol's boat and shattered the boat . . . Another battle. Sol's boys killed forty of the enemy. Took refuge in a house where a woman was 'frying cakes.' An eighteen-pounder came through the house from British guns . . . After the war went to Liverpool in a freighter. Terrible hurricane. Caught twenty-five large fish . . . Bought a vessel in Halifax. Great gale. Wrecked on Mount Desert . . .

Now, this Solomon Mack, whose middle name should have been Job, was the progenitor of hundreds of thousands of good Americans, sound in wind and limb. He was the grandfather of Joseph Smith, the prophet and founder of Mormonism, and also of the celebrated Mack family of Illinois, Michigan and Missouri, sturdy pioneers who have made American history.

So if you are discouraged, have puny spells or are losing your 'grip,' ponder on the life of Solomon Mack, rugged individualist – in fact, the dodblasted ruggedest individualist I've ever read about.

•

GEORGE SOKOLSKY

George Ephraim Sokolsky (1895–1962) was born in Utica, New York. His father was a rabbi, who owing to his strong temper never remained in a post for very long. The family soon moved to Manhattan's Lower East Side where Sokolsky was brought up. A precocious talent, the man who would later emerge as an arch-conservative columnist, at the age of ten stumped for the Republican Party in a Tammany Hall stronghold. He graduated from Columbia University in 1917 and in a flush of enthusiasm for the Bolshevik Revolution travelled to Petrograd as a correspondent for the New Republic News Service, but the absence of a mail service rendered the job impossible. To make ends meet, he joined the *Russian Daily News*, an English language paper, as its editor, until the authorities ordered him out of the country. He took a train to Peking and worked as assistant editor of the *North China Star*, in the hope of earning his passage home to the United States, but remained for thirteen years. In 1919 he became a reporter for the *Shanghai Gazette* and during the 1920s he was president of the *Journal of Commerce* in Shanghai. He also contributed articles to the London *Daily Express*, the *New York Evening Post* and the *Philadelphia Public Ledger*. He even married an English-educated Chinese woman (who died in 1933 after bearing him a son). In 1932 he returned to the United States and combined broadcasting for the National Association of Manufacturers with writing a column for the *New York Herald Tribune*. From 1944 until his death his daily column 'These Days' was syndicated by Hearst's King Features. In addition to this he wrote a number of books and was much in demand on the lecture circuit.

'These Days'
Teddy Roosevelt's Sons
New York Sun, July 20, 1944

Quentin, Kermit, Theodore Roosevelt gave their lives for their country. Of Theodore Roosevelt's four sons only one remains alive, Archibald, recovering from shrapnel wounds in this war. 'By their fruits you shall know them ... Even so, every good tree bringeth forth good fruit and the evil tree bringeth forth evil fruit.'

Theodore and Kermit were my friends, both of whom I first met in China where they came year after year, to trek through dangerous country, exploring, hunting, seeking to understand unusual peoples. The Roosevelts were curious about everything upon this earth, inheriting from their father an insatiable anxiety to miss nothing that is or happens.

Both were courageous and sympathetic, but Theodore was the broader in knowledge and wisdom, and had he not been his father's son he might have gone further politically.

He was unquestionably held back by his sire's reputation, for what was in Theodore's nature was regarded by the public as an imitation of his father. He did not, of course, equal his father in breadth and capacity – but who could be the equal of the older Theodore Roosevelt? He was the progenitor of our age, the individual who changed the course of American history and accomplished the rechanneling of our lives without destroying that restraining dam, the Constitution, or the margins of tradition that keep us within the bounds of our particular civilization. No son could quite live up to such a father. That Theodore understood and accepted. 'A good tree cannot bring forth evil fruit, neither can an evil tree bring forth good fruit.'

The Roosevelts, particularly the Oyster Bay Roosevelts, are an amazing tribe of swift-thinking, strong-willed, ardent men and women, who fight for what they think is right and take the consequences. Theodore was heroic in this war. His achievements at Oran and elsewhere in Africa and Italy entitled him to the highest honors, but honors would have meant nothing to him, nor publicity, nor plaudits. The joy of doing was sufficient for this man of action – the joy of doing precisely what he wanted to do and what he believed he ought to do. Just as Theodore senior offered himself and his sons to Wilson, so all the men of whatever age of this Roosevelt clan offered themselves to their distant cousin, Franklin. It is not militarism that sent these Oyster Bay Roosevelts to three wars; it has been an unquenchable love of country – a patriotism that is completely absorbing.

And Ted is dead and Kermit is dead and Archie is wounded and the war goes on and their sons will take their places and fight for the land that old Theodore made safe by building its outposts in Panama, in Cuba, in the Philippines. Theodore senior was called an imperialist and was often regarded as a militarist, but he saw the destiny of his country as the first nation in all this world. He grasped this vision when most men were still unseeing, and it was for that greatness of our land, that primacy of our flag, that his sons have given their lives. Such would be an honorable record in any family.

The Oyster Bay Roosevelts have always been Republicans and the Dutchess county Roosevelts have become Democrats and the families have drifted apart. It is curious that politics should be so strong an impulse in any family; yet the fact is that all Roosevelts are everlastingly in politics. Kermit used to say that he was not in politics, but I am sure that beneath the skin the political virus worked in him as in Ted or in Alice or, for that matter, in Eleanor, who is more an Oyster Bay Roosevelt than she is akin to the President. But the Oyster Bay crowd always were in politics for their country, not for themselves. They never made anything out of it, and except for the Theodore who became President, never got to any places where something could be made. And so each one died for his country, and now that they are dead, we shall assess them for their true worth rather than for the ephemera of partisanship. A great father gave to his country noble sons.

'These Days'
The Right to Think
New York Sun, December 18, 1944

Mischa Auer achieved fame, I fear, by an amazingly pungent pronunciation of the phrase, 'It stinks!' in the play, *You Can't Take It With You*. Since then he has always been cast in the role of a comedian, a hoodlum of fun. But Mischa Auer knows suffering: he is a child of the Russian Revolution. And so, Mischa Auer has been expelled from a Russian–American society in Hollywood because he voted for Dewey and because, as they put it, he uttered reactionary sentiments. And he told them 'It stinks!' as only he can.

Cecil B. de Mille is a great artist whose program on the radio is one of the best and most refreshing. Because he is on the radio, he has to belong to a union. Maybe he has to belong to several unions to earn a living. His union assessed him one dollar for a fund to oppose a public measure that he favored. That dollar represented his conscience. To contribute that dollar meant to impeach his intellectual integrity. As an American citizen, it is his privilege to favor or oppose or ignore any bill before the legislature of his State. His union denied his right to think: it denied his freedom of conscience. It demanded his dollar to oppose what his conscience dictated was right.

And because he would not compromise on a moral question, this union ordered him off the radio. He had paid his dues to the union. He had performed his contract with his sponsors. He had fulfilled his obligations to the network. He had done everything required of him – except to pay an assessment of one dollar on a matter that involved not his relationship to his union but his duties and obligations as a citizen of the United States. And de Mille took the position that he would render unto Caesar the things which are Caesar's and unto God the things which are God's. I do not know whether he will be permitted to earn his living on the radio, but he will have the satisfaction, come what may, that came to those early Americans who dumped chests of tea into Boston Harbor.

These instances of oppression are being multiplied all over the country. A mother telephoned to me to tell of her daughter in a New York city high school who was upbraided, insulted and disciplined by a teacher for bringing an editorial of the New York *Daily News* to class, on the ground that this newspaper was part of the Hearst–McCormick axis. I offered to take the matter up with the Board of Education but the parties ran out on me, frightened.

Another parent writes me that in a Jewish district in Brooklyn children were told by their teachers that if Dewey were elected, the schools would be open on the Sabbath and examinations would be held on the most holy fast day. A publisher sends me proof of a book with a section critical of the New Deal marked out because the printer refuses to set up that bit of type. I asked him for permission to publish the details, names, quotations, etc., and he tells me frankly that he fears he would get into further trouble. I suppose he is afraid of losing his paper allotment. I hear of a private Gestapo in New York going to a publisher to demand that he withdraw a book on Germany which fails to demand the total extermination of the German people on the ground that this anti-anti-everything organization is opposed to anyone who is not for a 'hard peace,' no matter how great the scholarship of the author. I get a circular asking for funds to deposit at Columbia University for general use of a file of books, documents, etc., gathered to fight Pan-Germanism in this country, not now, but for ever more, although this is one of those wars fought to end human hatred.

Oppression, bigotry, persecution are abroad in the land. Haters of freedom of thought have organized for mastery of our minds and spirits. They call themselves liberals; they are the equivalents of Black Hundred reactionaries, poisoners of the wells of human liberty.

•

HOWARD O'BRIEN

Howard Vincent O'Brien (1888–1947) was born in Chicago and graduated from Yale in 1910. His first job was on a publication called *Printer's Ink* in 1911, and for a couple of years he was founder and editor of *Art* magazine. After a stint as an advertising copywriter, he enlisted in the US Army and served in the Field Artillery of the American Expeditionary Force in France from December 1917 to February 1919, attaining the rank of first lieutenant. He joined the staff of the *Chicago Daily News* shortly after the war and worked as a reporter during Chicago's roaring twenties. He was chosen by Al Capone to be his official biographer, but he found this task impossibly frustrating, since whenever he asked a searching question during one of the several interviews he was granted with the gangster, he met with the response, 'I couldn't say that. It wouldn't be fair to my people.' From 1928 to 1932 he was the *Daily News*'s literary editor and its commentator on publishing matters before becoming a general columnist. His first column appeared on 17 October 1932 and continued on a daily basis until 22 July 1947, a record unbroken other than by illness or holidays. 'All Things Considered' included news commentary, essays about likes or dislikes, about odd characters, about his travels in the company of his wife, and about his family. His columns about his son Donel, who was killed in action during the Second World War, were published in 1944 as *So Long, Son*. O'Brien was struck by a disease which attacked his optic nerves and eventually had to write his column in longhand, using a heavy black pencil and writing only a few words to a page so that he could read them back to himself. In 1936, when the publisher of the *Daily News*, Frank Knox, was running for the vice-presidency on the Republican ticket, he was asked by the managing editor to approve O'Brien's column for the next day: O'Brien had come out against Knox and predicted that if he and the Republican presidential candidate, Alf Landon, were elected they would be forced to adopt the same policies for which they were lambasting the Roosevelt Administration. Knox allowed the column to run with the result that O'Brien was admired for his daring and Knox received a good press for his tolerance. In 1947 he was admitted to hospital suffering from cancer and from there he dictated his last columns, which included a moving essay about facing death.

'All Things Considered'
Bootle

Chicago Daily News, March 6, 1935

The pacifists claim that if people knew one another better the cause of war would disappear. I question this when I think of Bootle.

Bootle and I were born in neighboring houses. We went to the same school and were classmates in college. Now we live in the same village. I know Bootle very well, and the mere sight of him makes me ill. From the expression on his face when he sees me I gather that my emotions are reciprocated.

A curiously malignant fate is forever bringing us together. This morning, for example, when Bootle saw me coming down the street, he plunged up to his ankles in slush in order to reach the other side and thus avoid me.

It was no use. Even when we reached the station, and Bootle hastily buried his face in a newspaper, a third party insisted on introducing us. Having done his innocent but dirty work, the third party drifted off, leaving Bootle and me alone.

We were waiting for the eleven o'clock train, and instantly Bootle plunged into a long and unsolicited explanation of why he was taking so late a train. I tried to tell him that I didn't care if he never took a train at all. When he persisted with his explanations, I even went so far as to suggest that his mere existence was irrelevant and immaterial to me.

It was useless. Bootle had a consciousness of sin, and even in my worthless eyes he could not bear to seem a person who took eleven o'clock trains. I have every reason to know that he has no regard whatever for my opinions about anything, yet he cringed like a whipped spaniel before what he assumed must be my accusing glance.

With a pitiful effort to regain his accustomed self-respect, he interrupted his breast-beating long enough to inquire what train *I* usually took. Before I could answer, that supercilious smile I have always found so offensive came over his lips, and he said, 'Of course, with a job like yours, it doesn't make any difference what train you take.'

What he meant by this, of course, was that he had a very important job, while I didn't. I once managed to shake Bootle's faith in that axiom by explaining how it was that I made as much money as he did. This wasn't true, but by some plausible lying I managed to make him think it was, and for a few days he was almost respectful. Then he realized the absurdity of my statements and resumed his normal disdain.

I do not know how hard Bootle works. I suspect that it is not so hard as he thinks it is, and that suspicion has been intensified by his response to my suggestion that his life did not differ noticeably from that of a caged white mouse.

But even if Bootle toils as painfully as his groans would indicate, I cannot, for some reason, become impressed with the fact. Bootle makes early arrival at his office a religious rite. He worships work for its own sake. He looks on loafers as heretics. Whether he knows that people who take eleven o'clock trains are loafers or not, he conscientiously despises them.

Repulsive to people like Bootle is the idea that work is a means to an end. One of the things they fear most is the possibility that the 'masses' may have more leisure. They insist that the 'masses' will be demoralized if their noses aren't kept at the grindstone at least eight hours a day. They are convinced that if the 'masses' aren't obliged to work they will spend their time in mischief.

Of course the Bootles of the world are short of logic. They are contemptuous of a man who will put in an afternoon whittling, but respectful of a man who spends the same amount of time playing golf, bridge, squash rackets, or chasing a nonexistent fox over the countryside.

At the same time they object to having the 'masses' attempt such diversions. The creatures might play golf in derby hats or wear the wrong sort of pants while chasing nonexistent foxes!

A droll lot, the Bootles.

'All Things Considered'
I Look Like Something Out of Dickens
Chicago Daily News, January 24, 1940

Quite early in my life I acquired an aversion for the writings of Charles Dickens. This was due to several things. One was the insistence of my elders that I ought to like Dickens even if I didn't. Another was the fact that a certain amount of Dickens was required reading in school. (This puts Dickens in a class with Shakespeare and Thackeray and Edmund Burke.) But most of all, I suspect, was the creepy feeling I got from the Cruikshank illustrations.

How could I possibly like such people as Micawber and Bill Sikes when they were depicted in so grotesque, not to say repulsive, a manner? Well, I couldn't. Those spindly legs, those hideous beaks, those leering eyes . . . I came to the conclusion, not since altered, that a 'Dickens character' represented just about everything that I did not wish to be.

Imagine, therefore, how I felt at the letter I got this morning. The writer thereof said that he had attended a banquet at which I was one of the guests at the speakers' table.

This man had pointed me out to a friend with whom he was sitting, and had asked if he knew who I was. The friend had scrutinized me carefully and replied, 'Who is he? He looks like a character out of *David Copperfield*.'

After reading this letter and meditating on its significance, I sneaked down to the washroom and had a look in the mirror. What I saw didn't please me. What stared back at me was a face that looked like a Cruikshank drawing – or, even worse, a caricature by Lloyd Lewis, that part-time cartoonist whose pictorial realism outdoes even Hogarth.

It is no fun looking like a drawing by Cruikshank or Hogarth or Lewis; but after all, what can one do about it? I listen to the radio announcer warning me that gray hair is dangerous – 'In these days,' he says, 'people often lose their jobs because of gray hair. C'mon, folks – buy a bottle of this stuff, and if you don't look so beautiful your friends can't recognize you, you can have your money back.'

I listen to this, and I read the advertisements about falling hair. But, having read them, I can only murmur those poetic lines about the moving finger which, having writ, moves on; and I realize that neither piety nor wit nor anything out of a bottle can lure back the snow that rested for a moment upon the desert's dusty face.

I may wear a hat and avoid intercourse with mirrors; but like the lights of Europe, in the prophetic words of Lord Grey, I know that one by one my hairs are winking out.

I cannot truthfully say that I enjoy looking like a character out of *David Copperfield*; but it is obvious that there is nothing to be done about it. And I get a melancholy sort of satisfaction watching the boys with their pocket combs and the girls with their compacts. They don't know it, but they fight a losing battle. Time is at work on them hammer and tongs. Someday they too will look like something out of a book.

They don't want any advice from me; but if they asked for it I would tell them – the boys, anyway – that the best preparation they could make for what is coming is to raise beards. Nothing stymies time like a beard. It hides the worst of wrinkles – the nose-to-lip ones – and keeps secret the consequences of adaptation to synthetic teeth. And hair on the chin somehow compensates for its absence farther up.

This is what I would tell the boys. I wouldn't tell the girls anything. I would leave the girls alone for two reasons: first, because I would have nothing to say; and second, because even if I did they wouldn't listen.

'All Things Considered'
No Peace with My Panama
Chicago Daily News, March 13, 1940

You will recall that south of the border, down Mexico way, I once acquired what the salesman assured me was a hundred-dollar hat. In cash, the price I paid was nominal, but the bargain proved a costly one in the long run.

Wearing a hundred-dollar hat is worse than having a matched string of pearls around your neck. Such a hat isn't precious enough to warrant having a copy made and keeping the original in a safe. On the other hand, it is too valuable to leave much peace in the head on which it reposes.

Distinctly, such a hat is more of a liability than an asset. One forgets what it cost and remembers only what it is 'worth' – which is absurd in itself, since at forced sale you could never realize even a part of what you paid for it.

In the North, Panama hats are not customarily worn during the winter, so there are months mine is laid away and I can forget it. Comes a trip to Florida, however, and my treasure is exhumed.

Its sojourn among the moth balls had left it rumpled and yellow. Obviously it needed attention before it could be applied to its task of causing me assorted anxiety. The question was: where should it be sent for that attention?

The matter was discussed in family council, and I made the point that the proper place for the renovation of a hundred-dollar Panama hat was a place where hats of that quality were customarily worn. Where in all this broad land, I inquired, would one find the largest number of hundred-dollar hats per square yard of territory? What was the nation's center of wealth, beauty and fashion? Why, Palm Beach, of course! So, as Palm Beach was on my itinerary, my hat went in with the spare tire for its fifteen-hundred-mile journey to the cleaner.

Arrived at last in the hub of swank, I hied me with my hat to Worth Avenue – perfect home for a street of de luxe shops. There I entered what appeared to be the most luxurious of the hatteries. To the sales person who approached me – plainly a member of the older Russian aristocracy – I spoke with the hauteur proper to one who would make an impression in a Palm Beach hattery of the higher grade.

'I have here a hat,' I said, 'a hat of Kohinoor quality, if you know what I mean. It is to ordinary hats what a fish pole is to a two-ounce job from Hardy's. For its rehabilitation I would no more take it to an ordinary establishment than I would ask a blacksmith to fix a watch. That is why I have come to you.'

The ex-Grand Duke looked at my hat and passed his delicately manicured fingers across its many rings. Something like awe came into his eyes, and his voice shook as he handed the hat back to me. 'Sir,' he said reverently, 'as far as that hat is concerned, we are blacksmiths. We wouldn't dare touch it.'

Torn between elation at having awed the help in a Palm Beach shop and disappointment at the failure of my mission, I tried another establishment. The results were the same.

I trudged from shop to shop, always being treated with the respect due to the possessor of so valuable a hat, but getting no nearer its cleaning. Apparently what the ex-Grand Duke had said was true – the only place where my hat would get proper attention was New York.

So, believe it or not, my hat, wrapped in tissue paper and securely crated, was started off on the long journey northward. That was some time ago; and it will undoubtedly be some time before I see it again. When it at last returns to me there will be a bill that, I estimate, should be approximately what I paid for the hat in the first place. When I have paid this bill I shall then put the reconditioned hat in with the spare tire and myself start the long journey northward; and I shall not wear the hat until next summer.

A complicated story, this; and I feel rather foolish as I think over its details. But life is like that, and one ought to know that when he acquires hundred-dollar hats he's just letting himself in for a lot of trouble.

'All Things Considered'
Hat Peace at Last
Chicago Daily News, April 16, 1940

These are among the most decisive days in human history, but the human mind is so constituted that it can endure only brief and fleeting intercourse with profundity. Most of its attention is on trivialities.

Thus, though I listen dutifully to Winston Churchill, my thoughts are on my Panama hat. If you have read previous reports on this subject, you know that my hat was transported from Chicago to Palm Beach for cleaning and pressing, and that Palm

Beach, not feeling up to the job, had recommended further travel – specifically, New York.

To New York, therefore, the thing was sent, leaving me practically defenseless against the Florida sun. This was a ridiculous situation, and it did not escape the notice of Mr Robert Carr, eminent Chicago chemist and, as far as is known, the only Democrat in Palm Beach.

He himself was wearing a nobby number of porous straw that he had come by after seeing it on the head of a friend who had paid two dollars for it. Being a man wise in the ways of commerce, he had approached the hat dealer with an offer of a dollar and a half, which, the season getting on, was finally accepted.

This hat was not, of course, so good as my Panama, which was worth, according to the Armenian who sold it to me in Colon, at least a hundred dollars. But when you get down to it, even a cheap hat is preferable to no hat at all. So, embarking on a golf match with Mr Carr, I was well pleased to have the stake established as one hat, the equivalent of his own.

It was a hotly contested match, but I won it by a narrow margin. It took quite a time to play, due to losing balls where, according to the caddies, rattlers abounded; and the Florida season was more advanced at the end than when we started. So when Mr Carr offered a dollar for the hat, the merchant yielded.

Even though the Ohio River and the chill North now lie before me, I am still wearing the Robert Carr Memorial Hat. And in the back of the car, still in its box and occupying more space than a stove, is my hundred-dollar Panama.

I say 'my,' but I'm not sure. It may be somebody else's Panama. It may not be a Panama hat. It may not even be a hat at all. It may be an Easter rabbit or a collection of pressed ferns. Someday I may open the box and find out. For the moment I am adequately sheltered by the Robert Carr Memorial and resolved never again to become the victim of a hat that requires the servicing of experts.

Yesterday a letter caught up with me. It was written by a man who had read of my tribulations with my Panama. He gave me the name of a firm in Milwaukee that could be recommended as a refurbisher of Panama hats.

I wrote this man an appreciative note. It was kind of him to volunteer this information. But I'm through with the business of having my hat do my traveling for me. After this my hat and I travel together. I'm not going to have my hat go one way, while I go another. And I'm through with having inferiority complexes because of a hat too aristocratic for the places I go. I'm a plain man, as ill at ease with a hundred-dollar Panama as I would be with a valet or a rope of pearls. There's something Jeffersonian about the Robert Carr Memorial, something equalitarian and restful. It was certainly made by an automatic machine and is therefore more in harmony with the times than a hat spun by the fingers of a Guatemalan peon. It can be sat on or blow away without darkening the soul like a defaulted bond. There's peace in it – and that's more than I can say of its predecessor.

'All Things Considered'
So Long Son

Chicago Daily News, January 12, 1945

The box came by express the day after Christmas. The children thought it was a belated gift from Santa Claus and jumped up and down, clapping their hands. They thought it was a doll.

The carton was the right size for a doll, but I knew it wasn't a doll. Dolls don't come from the Army Effects Bureau, Kansas City Quartermaster Depot. Besides, I had a letter.

Nobody but the children wanted to open the carton; so it was taken to the attic and for days stayed out of sight if not out of mind. Then, Sunday afternoon, when I was alone in the house, I got a pair of metal shears and snipped the steel tape with which the carton was bound.

It was packed just as he might have done it himself – the coats and trousers neatly folded, the socks and handkerchiefs and underwear all helter-skelter.

On top was the made-to-order dress uniform, as fresh as the day it had come from the tailor. He had been so proud of this extravagance, admiring himself in the close-fitting tunic; and he had looked so smart when he stood with long fingers around his wasp waist, buttons gleaming like fire against the dark green. He had so little time to be proud.

In the corner was a pair of officer's shoes, almost like new. Even less worn were his summer things. He saw no summers in Britain. His work was done before he could hear the skylark or see the meadows 'knee-deep in June.'

At the bottom of the carton was a tattered envelope, stuffed with orders and a diploma of graduation from a Louisiana training school.

Beside it was a leather-bound diary, given him by his mother, with her name on the flyleaf. Eagerly I leafed through its pages. They were blank!

The only other record of his life was a couple of flashlight pictures of himself and comrades – all laughing – snapped in New York 'spots.'

Under them was a small paper bag, torn in the corner. In it were the following:

A jeweler's ring box – with no ring.

The silver wings of a navigator.

A wristwatch, minus crystal, which had stopped at twenty-three minutes to nine.

A pair of sunglasses.

A Yellow Cab identification tag, No. 3233.

Three coins – a nickel, a dime and a threepenny piece.

The winter twilight was settling as I finished the inventory, and my nostrils ached with the sick-sweetish odor of disinfectant. Methodically I unpinned the gold lieutenant's bars and the navigator's wings and snipped off the buttons.

Then I sat staring at the box in which these things had come. It was such a small box to hold all the laughter and tears, all the hope and apprehension, which had been packed into it. So much gaiety and tenderness, so much generosity and fun, such talent and eager inquiry, such virile beauty ... It was hard to believe it had all vanished like the song of a bird at dusk, leaving only a little heap of clothes and a torn paper bag.

It was incredible that of high adventure in a far land nothing was left but a threepence and a watch which had stopped ticking.

'All Things Considered'
God
Chicago Daily News, April 10, 1947

When you lie for hours staring at a blank ceiling; when you no longer know the day of the month – or even the month itself; when fire and flood and rumors of war are things dim and unreal, you find yourself thinking quite a good deal about God.

The God I believe in is different from the God of my youth – a God much harder to comprehend, yet offering a security of faith far greater than the God replaced.

The God of my youth was singularly capricious, and given to oversights of management. He could permit floods in Pennsylvania while burning up the wheat fields of Nebraska. He seemed alternately benevolent and malicious, yet readily diverted by supplication. If properly approached, He would halt the rains in one place, while permitting showers where needed.

Looking back on it, He was a God who didn't know His own mind, and nothing, apparently, was too trivial to move Him. I remember the implicit faith with which I sought His aid in the recovery of a lost pocketknife. This seemed to me as reasonable and seemly as it must have seemed to the clergyman who, last fall, prayed publicly for the success of the local ball team.

That God, who could be wheedled and cajoled into concerning Himself with my small affairs, seemed, at times, unreasonably cruel. He launched His bolts of sorrow and suffering at what seemed to be the wrong targets. And sometimes He seemed moved by what could only be called revenge.

Well, looking back, that wasn't God at all – it was something created in my own image, subject to all my human limitations and weakness.

The God I believe in now is not an individual, swayed by anger and compassion, a vaporous counterpart of our emotions. God is *law*, expressing Himself in an ordered universe; and my racked flesh is part of Him.

When I was young I was troubled by the apparent conflict between science and religion. I was torn between two convictions. But that conflict has disappeared. The fallacy of materialism has been revealed, and scientists, today, are the most essentially religious men I know.

In my youth the problem was to make God conform to my pattern of Him. Now the problem is for me to conform to the pattern of the universe – the pattern of order, the design of immutable law which is 'God.'

To primitive man God revealed Himself in a clap of thunder, riding on a cloud. He reveals Himself now in test tube and microscope; in the physics laboratory and through the lenses of the astronomers.

We know little of Him yet; but however deep we probe, we find Him the same – always. He reveals Himself as order – solid and dependable.

'All Things Considered'
I Balance My Life

Chicago Daily News, July 21, 1947

Having considerable leisure on my hands I have devoted it to stacking of ballots between the good and the bad which fate has ladled out to me in these years. The last eight years or so preceding it were not too agreeable, faced as I was with the prospect of failing vision.

But as I turn the pages back through the beginning of my account book, I find a strangely different story. I had an uncommonly happy boyhood remarkably free from ailment. I was good at games and happy with my playmates. My college career, if not brilliant, was free of disappointment. I was never hungry and never had to look for a job.

These blessings I took as a matter of course, as I did many things until this balancing of the books. I took it as a matter of course, for example, that I enjoyed the devotion of three remarkable women. Only now as I total the debits and credits do I begin fully to realize the quality of love I was accorded by my mother, my wife and my daughter.

Now as I look at the red ink with which the pages of the last few years are liberally adorned, I have a tendency to dissolve in tears of self-pity. Then I look at the many black pages which went before and I feel that I should rise and say, 'Lord, I am still deeply in Thy debt.'

•

LENNIE LOWER

Leonard Waldemar Lower (1903–47) was born in Dubbo, New South Wales. He was seven when his father died and he was later taken to Sydney by his stepfather, where he attended the Barcom Avenue State School, Darlinghurst. After leaving school he joined the Royal Australian Navy and it was during this time that he began to write humour and poetry. His first article was published in a scandal-sheet called *Beckett's Budget*, when he was twenty-three. When he left the navy he did some road-mending work but for the most part he found himself unemployed (he learned to hop trains, an activity known as 'jumping the rattler' in Aussie slang). He joined the *Labour Daily* and began to write a daily column of comment, humour and poetry under the pseudonym 'T. I. Red'. Before long his column was appearing under his own name, and later he switched to the *Daily Guardian* and its parent, *Smith's Weekly*. In 1930 he published a novel, *Here's Luck*, about drunken low-life and disillusionment, which is now regarded as a classic of Australian humour. Otherwise, he devoted himself to writing columns. He left *Smith's Weekly* and undertook an output that was prodigious, at one point contributing eight humorous columns a week, two of which were substantial in length, to the *Australian Women's Weekly*, the *Daily Telegraph* and the *Sunday Telegraph*. When the *Telegraph* sacked him in 1940, he returned to *Smith's Weekly*, where he continued to write columns until his death. The Sydney press were sparing in their plaudits when he died, with only *Smith's Weekly* prepared to declare him 'the greatest of Australian humorists', but his brilliance has since been widely recognized and celebrated in *The Best of Lennie Lower* (1963), *Here's Lower* (1983) and *The Legends of Lennie Lower* (1988).

Chivalry, Thou Art Not Dead

From *Here's Lower* (1983)

Though depression may still be here, chivalry is not dead. Probably because politeness costs nothing.

Abraham Wicks, taxi-driver of this town, drove a well-dressed gentleman from the Quay to the Hotel Australia, the fare being 1/4.

'I'm afraid, I have not sufficient money,' said the fare. 'Will you accept stamps?'

And the taxi-man got five pennies and one shilling's worth of stamps. He took it with that innate politeness so popular with taxi-drivers.

Take our own experiences. We said to the driver, 'We are afraid we are stone, motherless, hearts-of-oak. Will you accept empty bottles, a penknife, and two dirty handkerchiefs?'

'*Oui!*' said the driver (an educated man). 'But I shall have to give you the change in spark-plugs.'

'It is well,' we said.

We turned to go, but the training of a thousand years drew us back.

'You have served us faithfully for the past ten minutes,' we said. 'If ever you need a reference, come out to La Perouse.'

We took off our left boot. 'Some little recognition of your service,' we said.

'Thank you, sir. Thank you!'

We stood on the steps of the Australia and watched him push his taxi back towards the rank. We are glad that it was mostly downhill.

Don's Boyhood Friends

From *Here's Lower* (1983)

It's marvellous the number of people who knew Don Bradman when he was a small boy in short trousers. We met approximately 158 of them yesterday.

They told us: 'I used to say to young Don, "Don, you keep on the way you're going and some day you'll play for Australia." I could *see* that the boy was a born batsman . . .' etc.

Plain bunk, that's all it is. Now, when we knew young Don, *we* used to say to him, 'Don, my boy, you keep on the way you're going . . .'

As a matter of fact, we told the tramguard about it, sitting in the front seat on the way to Watson's Bay.

The driver nearly ran over four pedestrians, and the conductor forgot to collect our fare, thus allowing us a profit of 5d.

We were in the court the other day when the murderer was asked if he had anything to say before being sentenced to death.

'Yes, Judge,' he replied. 'I think that Woodfull and Bradman are two of the greatest cricketers in history.'

Whereupon the whole court cheered madly, and he was let off with a fine, the solicitors waiving costs.

We even heard a rumour that members of the Union Club were kicking each other's hats around the billiard room.

There was a man sacked yesterday from a large Sussex Street warehouse, and pausing at the door, he said: 'Anyhow, I think we'll win this Test.'

So the boss said: 'Bring that man back. He's got brains. We can't afford to lose men like that.'

But it doesn't always work.

We got home pretty late last night, and thinking to get in first, said: 'What do you think! Bradman's 215 umpty not out!'

'Who is this Bradman?' she said, and while we were recovering, 'Anyhow, I don't wish to hear about your drunken friends. Two hundred and umpty not out! Why, *you*! You're only thirty, and you're always out!'

What's a man to do with a woman like that?

Women have no sense of values.

Me and the OAAMCNOC

From The Best of Lennie Lower (1963)

I have long felt the need of a really impregnable excuse for having a night out with the boys. All my excuses are worn so thin that my wife, when I get halfway through, finishes them for me. Which is humiliating to a fellow who earns his living solely by his imagination.

I thought of joining a lodge. I did not know whether to join the Hibernian Society or become a Mason. And, being in doubt about some others, I decided to form my own society.

My name not being Murphy or O'Brien, I was a non-starter for the Hibernian Society, but I was rather attracted to Masonry because of all the little hammers and trowels, and spades and gold-plated things. Still, the goat-riding part of the initiation ceremony perturbed me.

I was informed by a very exalted Mason (I think he was the Chief Rock-chopper and Honourable Foundation Stone Chiseller) that the lodge goat was a nice animal which had been donated by Mr Skuthorpe from his buckjump circus as he was unable to control it. This rather put me off becoming a Mason.

The Antediluvian Order of Buffaloes did not attract me much. I know a few buffaloes, personally.

Then there was the Ancient Order of Foresters. Well, you can't go home late at night and tell your wife you've been out planting trees, or chopping wood, or whatever the Ancient Foresters do.

The Ku-Klux-Klan seems to be a back number these days, and anyhow, there is no scope for an energetic member in this benighted country. What's the use lugging a rope around when there's nobody to lynch?

So I was driven to forming a society of my own. It is the Old and Ancient, Antediluvian, Moth-eaten, Cobweb-covered, Neolithic Order of Complainers.

It is a secret society which has an annual meeting once a week, its object being to stay out as late as possible and assist charity by buying State Lottery tickets. All members of the Order are pledged to save up their old razor blades which will later be melted down into a battleship, thus helping towards the defence of the country.

The signs and countersigns are rather complicated. If you see a man with his vest on back to front, and wearing his wristlet watch around his neck, you will not be far wrong in guessing him to be a member of the OAAMCNOC.

The fist must be clenched when shaking hands, after which the member must turn around three times and then yell in a loud voice, '*Whacko!*' They then exchange bootlaces.

After that they make a moue. I am not quite sure what a moue is, but Phillips Oppenheim is always making people do it. I read only last night that 'The bewitching young Countess made a little moue, and tapped Sir Edward lightly on the arm with her fan.' It must be some kind of knitted thing, because I can hardly imagine the Countess wandering about the ballroom with a hammer and nails. However, I digress. I'm afraid that my passion for literary research work overcomes me at times.

One good thing about my lodge is that you can get buried free. Any time you like. We have a lodge doctor who will give you a medical certificate for a small fee so that you can stay away from work for a week. The fee goes into the Sick and Accident Fund so that any brother of the Order who wishes to have an accident merely notifies the Secretary to the Grand Canyon, who gives his official permission.

The Supreme Hooded Terror (me) has the last word in all disputes. Such a change from home life; I'm sure I'm going to enjoy it.

I am inviting tenders for the headquarters building. The bar will be on the top floor. On the next floor will be the meeting room, then the second (or novices) bar. After that comes the horizontal bar, where you can lie down to drink. Then the swimming pool and an ambulance station in the basement. Thus one progresses by easy stages towards home and mother.

One of the most important positions in the lodge will be that of Grand Chief Sympathizer. Last week I injured my wrist. I wrapped it up in most impressive bandages and put it in a sling and went around the town with an agonized expression. Did anybody rush up to me and say, 'My poor chap! How dreadful to see you so frightfully maimed, and what a blow to literature that it should be your right hand! I'm sure you're being tortured with pain, but I see you are bearing it with a gallant smile'?

Not on your life! They just said: 'Hullo! Been playing up again?' or 'You ought to take more water with it,' and 'How's the other bloke look?'

All this will be altered when the OAAMCNOC gets going. Brothers with sore wrists will go to see the Grand Chief Sympathizer and be sympathized at and with so thoroughly that they will go home and take to their beds for weeks, complete with medical certificate and free burial chart.

Don't miss these benefits. Rip out a coupon!

Model Husband – for a Day!

From *The Best of Lennie Lower* (1963)

That's the worst of these New Year resolutions – they get you into so much trouble. I think it is much safer to give some harmless order to yourself, such as resolving not to drink out of horse-troughs on Sunday. But I wasn't satisfied with something simple like that. I made a grand, sweeping gesture and resolved to be a model husband. And the result: The resolution split up the sides the first day.

For the first few hours I was so good that the wife thought I was sickening for something. Then she came to the conclusion that I wasn't cranky enough to be sick, so she decided that there was another woman in the case, and I was trying to allay suspicion. Following this she searched the house to see what I'd smashed or burnt.

It had her completely puzzled, and when I actually offered to help with the washing-up, she had to sit down for a while to recover.

Having managed to smash the cake-dish which was a wedding present from her mother, and apparently the only one of its kind in the world, I volunteered to do the shopping and go to the butcher's, and I even went as far as to say that I didn't mind carrying flowers.

She gave me the money to do the shopping in a kind of daze, and when I came back with the correct change she swooned away and I had to rally round with the smelling salts. When she came to, she inquired feebly whether I'd called in at the hotel on the way, and I said, 'No.'

'Do you mean to tell me you didn't meet that old school-mate of yours this time! You know, the one you haven't seen for years – the one who insisted on having a drink with you and you couldn't very well refuse?'

'No, dear,' I replied, 'I didn't meet him and, even if I had, I would have told him that you were waiting for me at home and I couldn't leave my little wifie all at home by herself. Now, darling, I'm sure you want me to go visiting your Aunt Jessie. You know, the one with those two blasted brats . . . I mean those two dear little children. I'd love to romp on them. I mean romp with them.'

'Listen, you half-baked hypocrite,' she said, pushing me into a chair, 'what have you done that you're trying to smother up? Tell me, because I'll find out, anyhow.'

I then explained to her about my resolution to be a model husband. She didn't congratulate me – just said it was about time. That's gratitude for you.

After having mowed the lawn and taken the dog for a walk, I rather overstepped the mark when I said I was going to paint the house. I had to withdraw this alarming statement and explain about the high cost of paint and ladders and brushes and things.

All the time I was looking forward, pretty gloomily, to the prospect of afternoon tea at Aunt Jessie's with the confounded kids crawling all over me, eating cake and nursing their filthy lap-dog. And not being allowed to smoke. And listening to Aunt Jessie's complaints about her back.

I was walking about the house, glooming over things and conquering my evil inclinations by not going up the road to see a man about a dog, and wherever I went the wife moved me on with a vacuum-cleaner or a broom or a mop or a duster.

At last she said, 'For the love of Mike, can't you keep out of the way, you clumsy, useless oaf! Why don't you go for a walk or something? Hanging around the house with a look on your face that's enough to make a woman burst into tears!'

'I wouldn't think of going out while you may need me for something, darling,' I said. 'And I don't think it's very nice of you to call me names when I'm only trying to help you!'

'Help me! Yes! Tramping dirt all over the floor just after I've polished it. Hurling cake-dishes about. I believe you did it deliberately. And another thing! Take that long-suffering, martyred look off your face. If you're going to keep this up I'll finish up in the asylum. Now get out, and don't come back till lunch time!'

Very reluctantly and slowly I left the house. I mean to say, I was pretty slow and reluctant until I got around the corner out of sight, and then I ran like mad to the SP bookmaker, and had two shillings each way on a horse, and then had four pints of beer, and came home and burnt a large hole in the carpet, and knocked the ashtray all over the floor; kicked the wife's dog, criticized the lunch, and asked how a man could be expected to keep alive on stuff like that; complained about a button being off my trousers, and wanted to know why the devil there never seemed to be any matches in the house.

'Well! Well!' exclaimed my wife, gazing at me almost affectionately, 'Back to your old form, eh? Well, I must say I much prefer it. And for heaven's sake don't do any more reforming. I couldn't stand it!'

Can you beat it! Anyhow, I'm happy again.

•

JAMES A. JONES

James Alfred Jones (1902–69), known as Jimmy Jones, was born in Lowestoft, Suffolk, and joined the *Cambridge Evening News* at the age of fifteen. He subsequently worked for the *Burnley News* and the *Manchester Evening News* before joining the *Evening News* in London as a general reporter in 1925. He described seeing the 1927 solar eclipse from a peak in Yorkshire, covered a Test series between England and Australia, and over the years was called upon to write sketches of royal weddings, funerals and coronations. He also wrote, over a two-year period, a series of essays, 'Wonderful London', which depicted the many moods and aspects of the capital, and a similar series on 'London's River'. However, his main output was the five-days-a-week column he wrote from 1933 until his retirement in 1965, called 'Courts Day by Day' and signed 'J.A.J.': each weekday he reported from one or other of the London courts, where, according to his editor Guy Schofield, he 'noted the comings and goings of the unfortunate, the silly, the abandoned, and sometimes the vicious'. He had 'a subtle, penetrative mind, a Dickensian gift for the unobvious descriptive phrase, and a compassionate approach . . .' He was sent to cover the opening days of the War Crimes Trial at Nuremberg, and also reported court proceedings in South Africa and the United States. In 1947 *Time* magazine dubbed him the 'Rogues' Boswell'. 'He sees his column – or whatever it is he is about to tackle – in full before ever he begins,' wrote Schofield in the preface to a collection of Jones's columns, 'and once his fingers move over the typewriter the words flow steadily, with little pause and hardly ever a correction or "second thought". And – most astonishing in a professional journalist – his typing is always without blemish!'

'Courts Day by Day'
She Liked Dancing

From *Courts Day by Day* (1946)

Daphne, you could see, was born under a dancing star. There was rhythm in the grace
of her walk, there was vitality in the gleam of her black hair and in the slenderness of
her lissom young form. Her eyes shone. Her shoes twinkled. In the solemnity of the
Clerkenwell court she made almost everybody else look old and dusty and tired.

But not Mr Hopkin. Mr Hopkin, on the bench, has a warm and round benevolence
that glows as brightly as the briefer fires of youth. He turned to Daphne's husband, a
soldier with a troubled air, and he said, 'Well, well, well. So your wife stole all this money
and spent it on clothes. She's fond of dancing and dress, I gather?'

'Yes, sir,' said the soldier.

'What lady isn't?'

The soldier's frown did not lessen. 'She's extravagant on clothes, sir,' he said rather
heavily. 'I've warned her about buying things unnecessarily, but the trouble is I'm in
the army, and I'm helpless. I can't stick up a list of rules as to what she's to do and
what not, can I?'

The notion that a husband could stick up rules for his wife's behaviour obviously
did not find a supporter in Mr Hopkin. 'Of course not,' he agreed. 'Of course you can't.
Certainly not. But perhaps I can help you.' He turned to the detective who had arrested
Daphne, and asked a good many questions. Daphne's only income, it seemed, was the one
pound fifteen she got from the army, and she was trying to keep a flat going on that.

'It's not a great deal in these days, is it?' mused Mr Hopkin, with a shake of his kindly
head, and he looked down at the daintiness of Daphne's black frock. 'But you shouldn't
have taken all that money, should you?' he said. 'After all, it was a friend of yours you
robbed. Why steal all that money?'

'I was tempted, sir,' said Daphne.

'You want nice clothes?'

'Yes, sir.'

'And you like dancing?'

'Yes, sir,' smiled Daphne.

'And your income's small?'

'Yes, sir,' she said.

'Why not work?'

Daphne opened her lips to answer, but before she could speak the woman missionary
of the court spoke for her.

'Perhaps I can help you, sir,' she said to Mr Hopkin in a businesslike voice. 'She used
to work for the ARP, but she was hit on the head during a blitz. She can't do any hard
work now. I can help her to get part-time work, and she tells me she's willing to give
up the flat and go back to live with her mother.'

Mr Hopkin nodded an approving nod, and he addressed Daphne encouragingly.
'Would you be prepared to do part-time work?' he suggested.

'Oh, yes, sir.'

'Sure?'

'Please, sir.'

His accent took on a note of fatherly warning. 'I don't know whether you know it,' he said, 'but you've put yourself in peril of being sent to prison for a long time. If you want these fine things, if you find your present income isn't enough, it's wiser to supplement your income by working rather than by stealing. I shall bind you over for two years, and you must pay back the ten pounds as fast as you can. You understand all that? Yes. I'm sure you do. You're an intelligent lady, and I'm sure you won't steal again.'

Daphne's dancing feet descended from the dock, and with her husband and her mother she went out into the very stolid streets of Clerkenwell.

'Courts Day by Day'
The Sea Lawyer
From *Courts Day by Day* (1946)

Other men, summoned into the solemnity of a court, may be timorous, or confused or stricken dumb with awe. Other men may gape uncomprehendingly when invited to cross-examine a witness, or fall into a stammering incoherence when asked to defend themselves. Other men may be blustering, rambling, whining, offended, pitiful or merely abject.

Frank was none of those things. He walked with tranquil assurance into Thames Police Court, and calmly took his stand in front of the dock. He glanced with restrained approval at the lean tolerant face of the magistrate on the bench, and his expression seemed to say that here was a man after his own heart – a man who could see things steadily and see them whole. Then, serenely, he awaited the words of the clerk.

'Did you drive your wagon and trailer past the red light?'

'No, sir,' said Frank.

'Take the oath, officer.'

The officer took the oath, and told his story in the detached and unwavering manner of all police evidence. Frank listened.

'Officer,' he said.

'Yes?'

'Would you agree with me,' he said, 'that my vehicle is so long, with its total length of fifty-four feet, that when my radiator crossed over the line the light was green, that when my cabin passed over the line the light was buff and that if the light changed to red at all it was as the tail of my trailer crossed the line?'

'I would not,' replied the constable.

'You're sure of that?'

'I am.'

Frank nodded imperturbably, and turned from the constable as though indicating that he had no further use for his services.

But a little of that impeccable calm dropped from Frank as he found Mr Harris gazing at him speculatively. A cockney gleam came into his eyes, and a cockney tang to his voice.

'I think, sir, that the policeman was over-zealous,' he said, with the air of a man giving his candid opinion, without disguises or reserves. 'Your learned worship's self will see that the policeman had been on duty all the morning, without a single catch. He wouldn't like to go back to the station and tell them he couldn't catch anybody at all. Your worship's learned self will understand that, I'm sure.'

Mr Harris laughed openly. 'Well, have you got any witnesses?' he inquired.

'Yes, sir.'

'Let's hear them, then.'

Frank swung round easily to the warrant officer who towered beside him and his manner changed swiftly back to his old, placid assurance. 'Call Carl,' he commanded.

Carl was ushered in from the hall, was steered to the witness-box, and was duly and hoarsely sworn. Then he looked awkwardly at the clerk and visibly nerved himself for the ordeal.

But Frank was once more the learned counsel. Before the clerk could ask the first formal questions Frank had summoned Carl's attention and opened his examination. 'You are Carl, you live at Smith Street, and you are employed by the same firm as the defendant – that's me?' he inquired professionally.

'Yes,' said Carl.

'At two o'clock on the fifth of August this year you were driving a lorry along the East India Dock road? You passed me on the crossing, and you –'

But there Mr Harris raised a smiling objection. 'You mustn't put leading questions to your witness,' he remarked.

'Very well, sir,' agreed Frank.

Clearly, smoothly, he drew the evidence from Carl. On only one point did he find Carl obstinate. Carl would not swear definitely and finally that the policeman was standing a hundred and fifty yards from the lights; and into Frank's voice crept the authentic be-careful-how-you-answer, remember-you're-on-oath, legal note.

'Is it not a fact –'

Once again, amusedly, Mr Harris intervened. 'Now, now, you mustn't cross-examine your own witness,' he observed. Frank grinned again, suddenly and disarmingly, and called for his next witness.

John stood sturdily in the witness-box, and Frank scrutinized him keenly. 'You are my statuary attendant?' he demanded.

'Yes,' agreed John.

Mr Harris interposed again, with an ironical shake of the head. 'You mean he's your mate?' he asked.

'Yes, sir,' said Frank.

'Why call him a statuary attendant, then?'

Frank's tone was deprecatory, the tone of learned counsel bowing to a judge's ruling. 'Well, I didn't want to put it so common before your learned magistrate's worshipful self,' he apologized.

'Oh, there's nothing common about "mate". It's a very good word.'

'Very well, sir.'

He turned back to John, and resumed his examination-in-chief.

Mr Harris pronounced judgment. 'I think there's a doubt in this case,' he said, 'and I shall therefore dismiss it.'

'Thank you, sir,' said Frank.

He walked serenely away towards the door; but though his step was restrained and mannerly his eyes were shining with a cockney delight.

'Courts Day by Day'
A Touch of Ruritania
From *Courts Day by Day* (1946)

James was beyond doubt a figure from one of those romantic and dashing tales of Ruritania. A fur coat hung from the broadness of his shoulders almost to the tips of his shining shoes; his face had the gallantry of youth in its firm chin and its clear blue eyes and its high, clean-cut forehead; and his hair was swept backward in black and virile curls. There was vitality in every inch of him. His very glance was noble. One expected that he would descend from the dock at any moment, mount to the bench and proclaim himself the rightful magistrate of Bow Street.

Mr Fry, however, seemed impervious to romance. He rubbed his chin dubiously, passed a handkerchief across his lips and spoke finally in the accent of a man who had long ago given up believing in Ruritania.

'Well?' said Mr Fry.

'You wish me to speak?'

'If you have anything to say.'

James thereupon looked round him with chivalrous blue eyes, as though assuring himself that Black Erik was not concealed behind the arras; and he unbuttoned his rich fur coat with deliberate fingers. Once more he scrutinized the recesses of the court. All was well. Erik the Black was not there. He then smoothed his curls with a chivalrous hand, and addressed Mr Fry in resonant but faintly broken English.

'In the – the last few years,' he said, 'I have taken a great interest in Russian art and literature, and everything that has – has to do with the Russia of the days before the war. I have taken a great interest in the work of the man who made the jewellery for the Imperial Court, and I have visited the shops in the West End of London which exhibit the Russian Imperial jewellery. It was to see the work of that exquisite artist that I went to a shop the other day.'

Mr Fry appeared greyly perplexed. 'Apparently,' he remarked, 'you gave a false name at the shop, and stole a gold snuff-box from it.'

'Quite true, sir.'

'Well?'

James levelled a burning gaze on Mr Fry. 'I had to give a false name, and the name of a great hotel, before they would show me the things I wanted to see. If I had told them that I was only a chef, and that I had no work and no money, they would have shown me from the door. And then I would never have seen the jewellery of the Imperial Court.'

Still Mr Fry was enshrouded in doubt. 'But you stole a gold snuff-box from the shop,' he murmured. 'You didn't have to steal a gold snuff-box to see the jewellery, did you?'

James shrugged a handsome shrug, and his accent became a little more Ruritanian. 'They wanted me to buy,' he said. 'They brought out the pieces they show only to collectors. They spread many things in trays before me. I saw the jewellery all round me, and I remembered that I had no money and the temptation was too great.'

Mr Fry, having frowned for some time at that dashing young figure in the thick fur coat, turned to the detective in the witness-box. 'Where does he come from?' he asked.

'Devonshire, sir,' said the detective.

'Where did he get that accent?'

The detective made a noncommittal gesture; but James answered himself from behind the bars of the dock. 'I always speak in French and German and Russian to my friends, sir,' he said. 'Perhaps that has something to do with it. My interests are not in the things of this country.'

Mr Fry spoke to the detective again. 'He seems to be rather a clever thief, doesn't he?' he remarked.

'All I can say, sir,' said the detective, 'is that when I arrested him he told me that he wasn't grumbling because he had had a good run.'

With a sigh Mr Fry reached for his pen. 'I think this was a very bare-faced theft,' he said. 'You've been bound over once, and I must discourage people like you who are prepared to be clever thieves. You must go to prison with hard labour for six months.'

James drew himself up with a dignity that should have brought all the people of Ruritania to his rescue. But the only man who spoke to him was the jailer; and, submitting himself nobly to the jailer's command, he went with a shine of fur towards the place where there is no romance.

•

WALTER LIPPMANN

Walter Lippmann (1889–1974) was born in New York City and educated at Harvard University, where he graduated cum laude in 1909. He was briefly a cub reporter on the *Boston Common*, before working as an assistant to Lincoln Steffens, the muckraking journalist, on *Everybody's Magazine*. In 1912 he spent four months as a secretary to the Socialist mayor of Schenectady, New York. Next, he joined the *New Republic* as an associate editor, staying there until 1922, though with leaves of absence to work first for the Secretary of War and for President Wilson, and later (as a military intelligence officer) for General Pershing. He wrote a column for *Vanity Fair* from 1920 to 1934, and from 1922 to 1931 he was part of the New York *World*'s editorial staff, becoming its executive editor in 1929. When the *World* was sold in 1931, Lippmann joined the *New York Herald Tribune* to write a political column, which he called 'Today and Tomorrow'. From 1962 the column was syndicated by the Washington Post and Los Angeles Times syndicates, reaching some 275 papers. He also wrote a fortnightly column for *Newsweek* from 1962 to 1971. He was revered for his intellectual acumen by members of Washington's political élite, and was essentially a New Deal liberal. Towards the end of his career he became a vigorous critic of President Johnson for further embroiling the United States in the Vietnam conflict. He won two Pulitzer Prizes, in 1958 and 1962, both of them for commentary on US–Soviet relations.

'Today and Tomorrow'
A Spell is Broken
New York Herald Tribune, December 4, 1934

It is said that one of the czars of Russia, walking in his park, came upon a sentry standing before a small patch of weeds. The czar asked him what he was doing there. The sentry did not know; all he could say was that he had been ordered to his post by the captain of the guard. The czar then sent his aide to ask the captain. But the captain could only say that the regulations had always called for a sentry at that particular spot. His curiosity having been aroused, the czar ordered an investigation. But no living man at the court could remember a time when there had not been a sentry at that post and none could say what he was guarding.

Finally, the archives were opened, and after a long search the mystery was solved. The records showed that the Great Catherine had once planted a rosebush in that plot of ground and a sentry had been put there to see that no one trampled it. The rosebush died. But no one had thought to cancel the order for the sentry. And so for a hundred years the spot where the rosebush had once been was watched by men who did not know what they were watching.

It is always difficult to know that the rosebush is dead and that you are standing guard at an empty space. This is particularly true of the hopes and fears which sweep across the modern world, and for a time possess men's minds and govern their conduct.

'Today and Tomorrow'
Zigzag Between Right and Left
New York Herald Tribune, February 14, 1935

The latest bulletin from the front is that Mr Roosevelt has taken 'a turn to the right.' Before long there will be another bulletin saying he has turned to the left. For I have a strong suspicion that Mr Roosevelt will continue to use all his political gifts to continue on this zigzag course. Though it is disconcerting to those who want to nail fast the rudder and drive ahead, Mr Roosevelt is no mean navigator and he knows that in the teeth of the wind and amid hidden rocks the good sailor moves most safely if he can tack and turn and maneuver.

As a matter of historical experience, it is clear that a responsible and effective statesman can rarely be classified as all conservative or all radical. George Washington led an armed revolution against the established order and then helped to make a constitution which has conserved the results of that revolution. The Tory Party in Great Britain introduced political democracy into the British constitution. Bismarck established social insurance in Germany. Theodore Roosevelt brought the railroads under regulation; and Woodrow

Wilson, aided and abetted by William Jennings Bryan, presided over the making of the Federal Reserve System, which is now regarded by many conservatives as sacrosanct.

It is all very confusing to those who would like their politics neat and simple, black or white, right or left. But human affairs are more complicated than human formulas and, therefore, especially bewildering to those who are so conservative that, as someone has said, they will not look at the new moon out of respect for the old, and to those who are so radical that, as George Santayana once said, they redouble their effort when they have forgotten their aim . . .

Another point to bear in mind amid all the rumors about the rise and fall of radical or conservative members of the Administration is that it requires one state of mind to grow indignant and to agitate about a social evil, another state of mind to invent a legislative remedy, and still another state of mind to administer the remedy so that the reform sticks and works. A few men, but very few, can agitate, legislate and administer; most men are good at one stage in a reform and not at another. And, therefore, a president who is interested in reforms that endure because they work is bound to use different men at different times. To the men themselves, except those who have some philosophy, this raising of officials to prominence and then reducing them to relative obscurity usually looks like ingratitude, the betrayal of the cause, surrender to the enemy, and what not.

A very good illustration is to be found in the Securities Exchange Commission under the rule of Mr Joseph P. Kennedy. When the abuses of the security markets were being exposed, Mr Kennedy took no part in the exposure, and presumably little would have been done about them if it had depended upon him. Nor is it likely that he would have taken a leading part in the drafting of the legislation. But once the laws had been enacted, the men who had had the courage and the ardor to write them were far from fitted to administer them. They had fought a victorious war, and, like so many warriors, they could not make peace. Then came Mr Kennedy, as suspect by the warriors as a pacifist by triumphant generals, and in a short time, by sheer political and administrative wisdom, he made the new financial system a practicable reality and then insured its survival.

He illustrates very well the remark of F. S. Oliver that revolutions can be successful only if at just the right moment politicians take charge. For it is the politician, using the word in its favorable sense, who knows human nature as it is in normal times and is not so fanatical about principles that he cannot bend them to human nature.

'Today and Tomorrow'
Intermission
New York Herald Tribune, May 28, 1938

Large portions of mankind are under the spell of men who seem to go to bed with their boots on, and are magnificent and grandiloquent even in their sleep. This fact is the great fact of our time, and raises all kinds of immediate and urgent practical issues that have to be met.

But if I read history correctly, the ultimate remedy in such periods as this, when mankind becomes exalted beyond its capacity, is not any one of the logical solutions that reasonable men propose, but a gradual exhaustion of the operatic emotions, a growing indifference to the issues, and, with the coming of a new generation, a loss of interest in the subject matter of the quarrel. That is the way the religious wars of the sixteenth century really ended, in a benign lack of interest in the dispute, in a civilized unconcern with the grandiose claims of the partisans, and in the discovery that there are other and better things to attend to.

It does not seem to me likely that the great issues which now embroil mankind will be resolved either by war or by statesmanship. They are in the deepest sense insoluble in that they arise out of passionate differences about human values. In conflicts of this sort, there is never a decisive victory for the partisans of one view; the ultimate victory is to those who are interested in other human things, in things that finally displace and obscure the burning but insoluble issues. In the sixteenth century it was the view of Erasmus that finally prevailed and brought peace, not that of the irreconcilables on either side of the barricades. And perhaps in our time, if catastrophe can be postponed, it can be averted by the generation that did not start these quarrels and can have no true interest in perpetuating them.

•

IAN MACKAY

Ian Mackay (1898–1952) was born John Mackay at Wick, in Scotland, the son of an engine driver, and educated at Wick High School until he left at the age of fourteen. While at school he rose early to hump coal for neighbours and did a paper round in the evening. His mother spent any extra money she had on books and accumulated a library of 3,000 volumes, in which the young Mackay immersed himself. Mackay worked for a pharmacist for three years before volunteering for the army at seventeen. He served four years in the Royal Army Medical Corps during the First World War, and did his first journalistic work contributing sketches from the trenches to the *John O'Groats Journal* and the *Northern Ensign*.

During the 1920s he took an ex-serviceman's course at London University while sending regular dispatches to the *John O'Groats Journal* under the heading 'Mac's Letters from a London Attic'. Next, he joined the London staff of the *Western Morning News*, serving for a time in the reporters' gallery of the House of Commons. When he joined the *News Chronicle* as its industrial correspondent in 1934 he changed his Christian name to Ian. After eleven years in which he earned the trust and admiration of the trade union movement for his fair and accurate reporting, he wrote a daily commentary on the events of the 1945 general election campaign, which persuaded the editor of the *News Chronicle*, Sir Gerald Barry, to give him a general diary column. Over the following seven years this developed into an essay column and Mackay wrote a million words as a columnist. He died suddenly at the end of a Labour Party Conference, soon after he had given the reply to the traditional vote of thanks to the press. His subjects were serendipitous and quirky and infused with his learning and his love of Greek mythology, Socrates, Shakespeare, Dr Johnson, Dickens, Sherlock Holmes, George Bernard Shaw and music-hall songs.

It Happened One Night
News Chronicle, 15 November 1946

Until I got home last night to find the lights all fused and the old ancestral halls plunged in dire and stubborn darkness, I imagined it was the ceaseless nagging and nattering of that hideous hag Xanthippe that made Socrates such a profound philosopher and dear old man. But after my desperate duel with the powers of darkness under my mansard roof in Marylebone, I am now convinced that the old boy turned to metaphysics and high thinking after he had flattened that famous nose of his against one of the Parthenon pillars on his way home from a party one dark and sticky night.

After my frenzied gropings and stumblings midst a hellish legion of savage stools, sofas, buckets and boxes which slithered and snapped at my heels like clockwork crocodiles, as I floundered helplessly about looking for matches and candles, which were not there anyway, I am prepared to believe everything that Bacon, Edgar Allan Poe and Ambrose Bierce had to say about the dark. In the end I found my bed – after skinning my shins on the iron frame – and slunk in between the sheets feeling about as civilized as a Neanderthal man wallowing down in his cave in the Dolomites ten million years ago.

But it did make me think about the slender hold we monarchs of all we survey really have on old Mother Nature. And one of the ponderous thoughts that kept coming up was that ninety-nine per cent of the miseries of mankind consist of the breakdown of artificial gadgets we have made ourselves in the last hundred years or so – lights fusing, cars breaking down, steamships sinking, trains crashing, phones going wrong, radio sets going dead, lifts not working, cigarettes running short, and so on. It makes you wonder whether all the scientific effort was really worth it, and emphasizes the wisdom of old Thoreau, who maintained that happiness increases in direct proportion to the number of things you can do without. As for myself I have often wondered about the wisdom of a civilization which discovered a method of getting from London to Widnes in four hours without first finding out if the place was worth going to at all.

My Greatest Moments
News Chronicle, 29 July 1947

Yesterday afternoon as I lay among the loosestrife and ragwort in the sparrow-haunted shadows of the Temple Library ruins, trying to concentrate on the Dungeon Scene in *Faust*, I suddenly found my mind wandering in the queerest way to Rita Hayworth and the Lyric, Hammersmith. The air was busy with butterflies, the lawns were glowing with gaily coloured girls, and even the hatchet-faced Chancery lawyers smiled like cold chisels as they watched the seed balloons of the willow herb sailing in silver over the shattered roof of Middle Temple Hall, where Elizabeth smiled on Shakespeare on the first night of *Twelfth Night*.

I had just reached that tempestuous passage, in Bayard Taylor's translation, where Margaret flings her fetters down and cries to Faust – just before the Devil takes him – 'Be quick. Be quick. Save thy perishing child,' when my ears got the better of my eyes and I found myself listening to a lass telling of her adventures in Hammersmith the other night. 'We went to the Lyric,' she said, 'and they gave me the very seat Rita sat in the night before. I was thrilled.' The dear thing fairly glowed with the wonder of it all.

It's queer how contact with the famous affects us all. In my job you would think I would have worked all that nonsense out of my system years ago. Prime ministers, industrial caliphs and trade union rajahs leave me cold, but I still cannot resist a famous clown, artist, film star, murderer, centre-forward or fast bowler. Why, only a year or two before the war I nearly paid double for a bedroom at the Black Boy, Nottingham, when they told me that Don Bradman was the last man in. Then, shall I ever forget that morning in 1940 when I signed in at the Hotel Raphael in Paris, a day or two before Rundstedt took the place over, and the chambermaid told me, as she patted the pillows, that only two hours earlier they had been pressed by the lovely head of little Lily Pons, the world-famous warbler? And there was that great day in Whitehall Place when I hailed a cab and when it stopped, Bernard Shaw stepped out and I stepped in.

Then there was that magic night at Paganis in Great Portland Street, when I got the table just vacated by Puccini and Busoni, who left musical scribblings on the tablecloth among the wine stains and the breadcrumbs. Chesterton I frequently followed, of all places on earth, in a dairy tea shop in the Charing Cross Road, and once I found myself sitting next to Belloc on the top of a Chelsea bus. I can never make up my mind whether my biggest break was when Jack Dempsey mistook me for Carl Brisson in the Savoy Grill, when Horatio Bottomley knocked me down in Long Acre and offered me a five-pound note or the night when I found Charlie Chaplin sitting in my seat in the Press Gallery listening to Baldwin telling us our frontier was on the Rhine.

Best of all such stories, however, was told me during the war by old man Collinson, the Fleet Street taxi-man, who drove his cab through the blitz until he was nearly ninety. One night in 1881 he picked up Lefroy, the Brighton train murderer, at Charing Cross just after he had done the deed, and drove him to Ludgate Circus. When he got out an old man like an eagle got in and cried: 'House of Commons.' It was Gladstone.

Considered Trifles – on a No. 15 Bus
News Chronicle, 21 October 1949

When G. K. Chesterton called one of his best books *Tremendous Trifles* he was not just showing the world that he was the prince of paradox-mongers and high priest of organized chaos who loved to stand on his head to make the rest of the world look wrong side up. He really did believe, not only that trifles were tremendous but that tremendous things, like his own gigantic carcass, were mostly trifles.

G.K.C., however, was no mere snapper-up of unconsidered trifles like Autolycus, though, like that immortal and melodious spiv, he did believe and prove in a prodigious cataract of sparkling verse and blithe, pugnacious prose that a merry heart goes all the way. All Chesterton's trifles were considered ones, no matter whether they were tiny or tremendous, and that is why I think he would have been happy if he could have left Don Quixote and Dickens in the shades for an hour or so yesterday afternoon and travelled with me from Marble Arch to Fleet Street in a number 15 bus.

The morning, which began with brilliant splendour in a frosty flush of sparkling champagne sunshine which danced and glittered on the plate-glass windows, proved to be as false as it was fair and most of us waiting for the bus outside Selfridge's were late, wet, cold and peevish. As I never wear a hat and, like the mysterious man in Sonnet 34, had travelled forth without my cloak, I was soon as soaked as a water spaniel, and my smart American shoes – which I bought in Washington last year when a radiator burned a hole in my good stout English ones – suddenly began to leak. And to top it all the red dye in the cover of *Martin Chuzzlewit*, which I am reading at the moment, began to run until I must have looked like Macbeth or Buck Ruxton with my 'hangman's hands'.

To make things worse I had to write this column before six o'clock and I hadn't one idea in my head. Which only goes to show what happens, even to a garrulous old gossip like me, when he goes on a pub crawl like the one we have just finished.

It was then that the first trifle came to cheer me up. When the conductress asked for my fare at Oxford Circus I just said, 'Fleet Street, please,' and she punched a 2½d. ticket and went away humming 'Confidentially'. I hadn't the heart to call her back and tell her I got on half a mile back, so I decided to cheat the London Transport out of 1½d. and turned to Betsy Prig. Then at the Café Royal I looked up and saw a ravishing young strawberry blonde sheltering in the doorway with a beige bulldog that looked for all the world like A. V. Alexander trying to look like Churchill. She caught my admiring eye through the streaming window of the bus and just as we began to slide away towards Piccadilly Circus and out of her life – I suppose for ever – I'll swear she smiled at me.

By this time life was beginning to look a little rosier and before Mighty Joe Young, the monstrous gorilla with the electric eyes above the Monico, could make me shiver again, there was my sweetheart Myrna Loy smiling at me beneath the hoofs of a red pony from the façade of the Plaza, and Orson Welles glowering at me from a Viennese sewer on the front of the Carlton.

Then as we swung round into Trafalgar Square, there the fountains were flashing back at the rain and the workmen were getting Nelson ready for his annual jamboree, I am sure I saw Mrs Braddock [Bessie Braddock, Labour MP for the Scotland Division of Liverpool] sailing up the Strand like Congreve's Millamant with all her pennants flying. Not that I would suggest for a moment that the redoubtable Mrs Braddock is in any way a trifle; and if that determined lady I saw sweeping past the Corner House like an avenging angel was not Mrs Braddock I hereby apologize to them both for looking so remarkably like each other, and, may I add, so brisk and bonny in the rain.

Mrs Braddock or whoever it was cheered me up no end and when I saw a man coming out of a shop opposite the Tivoli wearing a pith helmet I wanted to get out and do a rumba with him. I expect he was one of Dick Plummer's groundnuts men trying out his new kit. At Aldwych, which I never pass without recalling the night the bomb fell in front of the Gaiety with me cowering in the doorway of Inveresk House – where Winston brought out the *British Gazette* during the General Strike – I thought there was a fire. But it was only the crowd around the Aldwych Theatre looking at the pictures of Bonar Colleano beating up Vivien Leigh and Renee Asherson in *A Streetcar Named Desire*.

When I thought of the old carefree days of the Aldwych farces when Ralph Lynn, Robertson Hare and Tom Walls were always losing their trousers, I wondered what the world was coming to. And, incidentally – being a Scot – I marvelled at the incomprehensible English who fill half the West End theatres and cinemas with American smash hits just at the very time we need every dollar we can beg, borrow or steal. For when you come to think of it all that Margot Fonteyn and Moira Shearer are doing in New York is dancing themselves almost to death to earn dollars to pay Danny Kaye and Harpo Marx.

But by this time I was in Fleet Street and I got down among the divorcees and the bankrupts outside the Law Courts and went off to buy myself a pair of shoes. And then, dry-shod, I strode past Dr Johnson in the ruins of St Clement Danes and had a mild and bitter in the Rainbow where Belloc and Chesterton used to talk about such trifles in the age of gold. Then when I came out I ran into my ancient crony Con O'Leary, the most Irish Irishman that ever lived and a writer who learned the trade from the leprechauns. A broth of a boy indeed.

There was still one trifle left to cheer me up, however. Outside St Dunstan, where his comrades of the craft had just been remembering Robert Lynd, I saw a sign which told me a thing I never knew before – that MacDonald the Rector is also the Rural Dean of the City of London. No wonder Izaak Walton worshipped there. Finally, as I came through the Temple I noticed, as I do every day, that Oliver Goldsmith's grave is still missing. Will no one tell us where it is? And so in my new shoes and much merrier than when I set forth from Selfridge's I got to my desk at last to find somebody had sent me a new pen with which I sat down and wrote this.

Trifling, I call it.

What a Man Was My First Boss!
News Chronicle, 12 January 1952

When I was throwing away some old calendars the other night, I came across an entry which reminded me that if he had not died suddenly during the First World War, my earliest employer would have been ninety years of age today. And as he was a very great influence in my life – he colours my mind even now – I hope you will bear with me while I pay a tribute to his memory, even if you call me a sentimental old josser for doing so. He was an interesting chap and through him you may get a glimpse of that strange vanished era which seems farther away from us now than the days of Good

Queen Bess. For, as we all know, Shakespeare, Donne and Drake are much nearer to us in word and spirit than Pinero, Hall Caine and Lord Charles Beresford.

In the second decade of this tormented century, when I was a freckled urchin in a chemist's shop in Wick, my employer was the most remarkable man in the town. In fact, he was in many ways the most remarkable man I have ever met, although since then, like Ulysses, I have seen many men and cities. His name was William Gow Miller, and his rosy cheeks and friendly eyes shone with benevolence and good cheer. He wore queer-coloured suits, fancy waistcoats, flowing ties with blue and white dots on them, romantic feathered hats with green and vermilion cords and ribbons and he always carried a yellow silver-headed cane which, with a flick of the wrist, he could turn into a rapier.

There was a strange timeless look about him. As he strolled – for he could not be said to have walked – down the street he looked like one of the Cheeryble brothers dressed in Beau Brummel's fanciest suit. Every now and then he would emerge from the dispensary in green knickerbockers buttoned at the knees, which, with his corded hat and yellow stick, gave him the look of a Tirolean yodeller. On such occasions he brightened up and glorified the dull grey northern town.

He loved Chianti, smoked perfumed cigars, carried little muslin sachets of lavender in his pockets, took cocaine like Sherlock Holmes by the needle, and adored Mr Asquith, whom he resembled when he was hatless among his jars and bottles. Though he died a bachelor he worshipped in a vague antiseptic sort of way a superb but disdainful siren who ran a hotel and wore feather boas all the year round. Nothing ever came of this, though she must have spent a fortune on sedatives and cosmetics making up to him. He lived with his sisters, two aged, arid but affectionate spinsters in a bleak house beside an even bleaker burn at the back of beyond.

For all that, his knowledge of the world, like Mr Weller's knowledge of London, was extensive and peculiar. Unlike Mr Weller's, it was expensive as well. For he lived a double life. From October to July he pounded away at his pills and powders and mixed his liniments and lotions in that queer *quant. suff.*, three-time-a-day-after-food world in which druggists live among their spirit lamps, sealing wax, orris root and alembics. But when summer came, he lived in a different world, on the Riviera, in the Engadine, in Madeira or the Costa Brava. Then he was the English milord in panama and white suit, a leisured sybarite dawdling from one luxurious resort to another, and living deliriously beyond his means. Early in August, when his annual supplies of castor oil and copaiba were safely delivered in big fat barrels, he went on to the Continent – he called it the *Conteenong* – leaving the shop in the charge of a Welsh student, myself and an English lad who was afterwards devoured by a lioness in the Mountains of the Moon. He was away for two months, but every day we would get a glossy postcard from places like Bordighera and Seville. And now and then a packet of snapshots would arrive showing him in a barouche on the Promenade des Anglais, on a camel in front of the Sphinx, in a gondola at Torcello, sipping a Pernod in the Cannebiere, standing on Vesuvius with a wisp of smoke behind him or knee-deep in the water at Viareggio, with a cross to mark the spot where Shelley's body was burnt.

Then one day in October he would be back so brown that his teeth shone like snow and everybody would feel happier. He brought little odds and ends for all of us; bright-coloured little things that brought a whiff of magic and romance into our icy little lives. For weeks he would potter about with his Chianti flasks and his new pictures, some of which were considered by the local bailies to be distinctly naughty. How he would have done today I cannot imagine. For he was a *fin de siècle* character and was lucky enough to live in his own good time. God bless him, wherever he is with his funny waistcoats and his crazy hats. How Sir Max would have adored him!

Me and My Pen
News Chronicle, 12 April 1952

A very unusual and, in its way, alarming thing happened to me on Thursday morning when I sat down to write this piece. I found I had nothing to write it with. As there were no newspapers to be produced for Friday I thought it would be a good thing to stay at home for a change and do my work in the garden among the brisk orange-billed blackbirds. I rigged up a wicker-work table on the sunny side of the house and, with a glass of Beaujolais to lend warmth and colour to my fancy, I sat me down beside a bed of dying daffodils to write 'something for the paper'.

This is always a great moment in an essay writer's life. It is what the bullfighters call the moment of truth when the writer, however exalted or humble he may be, is left alone with the stubborn bull of his imagination and something must be done about it. And when the essay is for a newspaper the moment cannot be shirked or postponed, for the crowd is, as it were, already in the arena, and no matter how miserable the Fleet Street matador may be or how wild and intractable the bull, the show must go on. But the most daring and accomplished of matadors, even the great Manolete himself, could do little without their swords.

When I squared up for the kill, so to speak, I looked round for my *espada* – my faithful fountain pen which has tamed many a recalcitrant bull in its time – but it was nowhere to be found. I hunted high and low, even in such unlikely places as the coal shed and the clock, but there was no sign of it. In the end I gave up the search and hoped I had left it in the office among the old Hansards and the invitations to visit book clubs and open bazaars. Now this was a serious matter for me as I can no longer write with a lead pencil as I did when I was an honest reporter. And though I can tap out 'Annie Laurie' and 'Some Enchanted Evening' on the piano with one finger I have never been able to master the complicated contraption which the French call the writing machine.

There were plenty of things in my head when I sat down beside the daffodils, and I had even arranged some of them in decent order. I meant to write about the old lady who died in her shoes because she would wear them on the wrong feet. This, it seemed to me, was an admirable subject for a short, moralizing, but not too serious disquisition on queer habits and customs. But when I found that my pen was missing I could not write a line. I was flummoxed.

My wife has a much more magnificent pen than mine, a glittering sylph with a jewelled hood and gold waistcoat as if it were dressed by Dior, far too opulent an aristocrat to mix with my poor snub-nosed manual labourer with its broken cap and leaky joints. I tried to make a start with this bauble but it was all in vain. I called my spirits from the vasty deep but they would not come. So I just sat and stared at the paper, and all my fancies fled like a flock of starlings when a car backfires. This tyrant custom, which brought down Othello, is a terrible thing and it baffled me as well. In the end I took a cab to Fleet Street to get my pen, which cost me the price of at least two new pens and half a hundred pencils.

I had to do it, for without my pen I am as tongue-tied as Lord Balfour is said to have been at a banquet when he wore Court dress and had no lapels to hang on to when he got up to speak. I am pernickety, too, about my ink. It must be blue, the lighter blue the better, and even then I can only write on white paper. Call me a creature of habit if you will, like the old lady who could only walk with her shoes on the wrong feet. I can't help it. I am, as Descartes said, because I think I am. And as nobody else can think *me* for *me* I must put up with it and put my best foot foremost even if my shoes are on the wrong feet.

Me and my old pen must make the best of it till the day comes when I lay it up for the last time and leave the bulls to bellow in some younger head. Whoever that head may belong to I hope he will use a pen, too, and leave the writing machines to the lost souls who write about Antofogastas and Consols. It is the only way of writing for the likes of them.

•

WILLIAM BARKLEY

William Barkley (1898–1968) was born in Galashiels, Scotland, and spent his youth in Dunfermline. He was educated at Lenzie Academy and Glasgow University where he took a First in Greek and Latin. He was due to join the army when his headmaster decided he should be kept back for academic reasons. In 1917 he came south from the Glasgow office of the *Daily Express* to write about tennis, but when the parliamentary correspondent died a few years later he took his place. Thus began a forty-year career in the reporters' gallery.

He was well respected by politicians of all parties, a man of great wit but of enormous modesty. He also wrote speeches for Beaverbrook. His column was a very personalized political commentary; one year, when bored at a Labour Party Conference, he broke off from political discussion to offer readers his tips for baking bread. He took down notes in Gregg's shorthand; he hated writing, preferring to compose as he dictated to a copy-taker. He could reel off whole speeches from a Budget debate, and would often linger on to hear a debate. He was an advocate of simplified spelling (along with George Bernard Shaw and Pitman) and even wrote a book about it: *A Last Word* (1961). After Beaverbrook died in 1964, he never wrote another article. His son, Richard Barkley, joined the *Daily Express* in 1963.

I Like Ernest Bevin – His Tongue is So Rough

Daily Express, 10 April 1945

Encouraged by a reader – I say, what a fine reader! – who says my middle name is Horse-sense, I make the following shattering pronouncement: we did not destroy in succession the Spanish Armada, Napoleon, the Kaiser and Hitler in order to create a beautiful new world.

We did these things, of course, with some assistance from other people, in order to maintain our existence, to live at all. The first and best and only completely justifiable war aim is – survival.

So I like the publicity which the current *Readers' Digest* gives to a *New York Times* editorial of which a sample para. is:

> It is preposterous to say that by winning this war, regardless of anything that may come afterwards, we shall not have accomplished a great and good purpose, commensurate with whatever cost it may entail.

For over there as here it seems that the patent medicine sellers of politics think the war is lost when won unless their particular cure-all is universally applied. It would not do for the temperance reformers to say that the war was justified in making us all teetotallers or for the *Daily Mail* to say it was fought in vain unless we eat brown bread instead of white.

In just that category I put Harold Laski, who says the war was in vain unless all Europe goes Socialist, and Mr Ernest Bevin, who seems to think this war was fought in part at least to secure that we should travel to work – and plenty of it, full employment under his direction – in a state-owned puff-puff.

I like Ernest Bevin. His tongue is so rough. He is at least cut out of English oak, with all the knots and gnarls. When he does not talk sense he talks nonsense. Never anything in between. You know where you are with a man like that.

When he said in his weekend speech that before the war the Tories 'preferred' to keep millions of people unemployed, I put that in the nonsense class of sayings.

When he said that the Tories failed to prepare for the war, which is true, Bracken recalls that Bevin was just as bad saying the war might never take place. On this issue there will not be a halfpennyworth to choose between the parties. It should not be an election issue at all.

Bevin was, of course, better than the rest of his party. It was he who drove pacifist Lansbury out of the leadership by denouncing him for 'hawking his conscience'. For Bevin had a remarkable warning that the war was coming all right.

At one of his international transport workers' meetings in the year 1929, Bevin sat in a café with a German and a French colleague.

Bevin was shocked to hear the German say to the French comrade with a smile: 'We shall be friends for ten years and then we shall fight you.' In 1929, note.

Then when Hitler came to power a small number of Bevin's German colleagues fought and fell. But a far greater number threw in their fortunes at once with Hitler. This is what hurt him most.

Ever since Hitler came to power the Socialist leaders here have been questing in vain for their lost German brethren. All through the war they have hoped for a German freedom movement or an uprising of the Social Democrat trade unionists.

But there has not been one. These Germans all went after the pied piper of Munich. My fear is that they may suddenly reappear in large numbers and bamboozle the British Socialists now that the war is won.

If they reappear and are welcomed in time for the election, then quite a small bus will be big enough to carry all the Socialist MPs back to Westminster.

The election, of course, is almost upon us. This Coalition Cabinet cannot continue sitting cheek by jowl all week and biting one another's necks each weekend.

Will it break up before Whitsun, when the Socialists are to hold their conference? I do not know. But it ought to. There is no reason why the Tories should await the convenience of their opponents.

And what will the election be about? State puff-puffs? Oh, not at all. It will be to elect a Parliament to make and impose the peace and to take the first steps back to normality.

Now I myself at age forty-six have only a shadowy recollection of normal times, because they came to an end in the year 1911 on Germany's first threat of war.

It was an era of insignificant taxes, value for money, no passports, steady employment and reasonable assurance that one would reap the fruits of one's labours. So I am told. I don't remember.

All I know is you pay 6*d.* today for as much ice cream for your child as you bought for yourself as a child in 1911 for one halfpenny. Certainly if a child were back on the 1911 ice cream level he would think the beautiful new world was here.

And the menace is gone. It is finished. It has vanished. Germany is destroyed. Her wicked industry is broken and flattened. For the first time in the average adult memory in this country we can make our individual plans without taking Germany into account.

Our nation is poorer. We have lost much real property. A great part of that power which comes of investment in foreign countries is gone.

But who fears the future if we are free at last to attend to our own affairs? If our Cabinets for a change can look homeward and not for ever be absorbed in Europe?

I think much of our 'tween-war drift and indecision arose from being petrified by these Germans.

So many of our public men acted like rabbits paralysed by the baleful glare of the Teutonic stoat. What glorious news! That animal now does not petrify but putrefy. What a subject for rejoicing that the long night – thirty-three years long – is past!

For my part I have no doubt that active and prosperous days will come for us all once we give the machines a little time to retool and turn over to the products of peace.

I think the current adulation of state monopoly among some of our highbrows comes largely from a number of our rabbits not realizing that it is the stoat that is dead.

The citizen-soldier, throwing off his uniform with delight, will not tolerate conditions in which he cannot get a job unless he has a green card from the Labour Exchange.

But then a little Englishman with only one eye – he lost the other in a factory accident – can put this philosophy into three sentences. He is Major Procter, Conservative MP for Accrington. He says with great effect to working-men audiences: 'The Socialists want to nationalize the means of production. What are first means of production? Your hands.'

A neat bit of rhetoric, and true as rhetoric can be.

So Sorry! You Can't Phone Me
Daily Express, 17 February 1948

I have been directed by the government to live in the centre of London. That is to say, the government refuses to restore my pre-war late trains. Also it bans my petrol. So I have to move my bed and board alongside my work. I don't complain. I like it.

The petrol ban exhibits the official mind at its crudest. I was given all the coupons I required for petrol to take me from my house to their House (of Commons). Yes, but I had to pay for petrol, car tax, insurance, repairs: all told £200 a year.

This had to be found out of taxed money, equivalent to near £400 a year, wholly and necessarily spent in getting to and from my work, and not a penny of tax relief given me.

It is almost improper to reveal all this. Hardly fair that ministers and certain high officials, shielded from the facts of life by limousines and shovers, should be told how the taxpayers live who keep their pots boiling, and ensure their bite and sup.

Then, provided I paid, paid, paid, I could at any time phone for a taxi to burn up the same petrol to convey heavy luggage to the station or for heavy shopping a mile away, while my own car stood idle in the garage.

On 2 November I wrote setting out these facts to the London Petroleum Officer, asking for six gallons a month for these shopping and incidental purposes.

On 8 January I had a printed answer regretting that my application for extra business petrol (an application I had never made) must be regretfully refused. I wondered why it was necessary to increase these petroleum staffs by 560 in order to take two months and six days to answer 'No' to the wrong letters.

But nothing worries me for long. So here I am with a rented house, in town, on the MPs' doorstep, breathing metropolitan glory and rejoicing with Sam Johnson that in London one is always near one's burrow.

I find that in the centre of London I live in the handiest circumstances of a village community. Pillar-box ten yards, newspaper shop fifty yards. Thirty yards away a plumber. He says: 'We do everything about a house.'

Already he has raked out an old grate, mended a step, cleaned the drains, cut keys for (I hope) impregnable locks, and advised this, recommended that. What instant and on-the-spot service one gets from the myriad diversity of the little shops!

The big companies moved, too. The electric company got ten days' notice. It shook its head gravely. In eight days it promised at least a breakfast griller. Next day, with a cry of triumph, it announced the catch of the latest type of cooker.

On the stroke of the appointed hour electricians arrived from all quarters. Two jolly men heaved the cooker on to its site and smacked up its connections. Another measured me for tariff, another connected the current, a third tested all points. Time for the whole transaction by the old gold chronometer of my ancestors – twenty-five minutes.

The gas company rolled up to connect the refrigerator and a pipe for a gas-ignited coke fire. What speed, what smiling attention and efficiency on the very day I had to report at the other House the company's impending nationalization.

Here I was all set for immediate necessities in record time save for the installation of a telephone. I had given them a fortnight's notice, and as nothing seemed to happen I banged twopence in a call-box and was told to ring again next day.

Into that box next day went a cheerful wight who staggered out a doleful dump. For this is the fatal intelligence I received, that provided the Treasury does not stop capital expenditure I may, with maximum priority, have a telephone in my house – by the late autumn!

It astonishes me that the whole telephone system did not fuse at the blast of hot air which involuntarily escaped my lips at this death-knell to my hopes. For a reporter without a telephone is a pianist without hands or a songster without lungs. It is total disaster. The Post Office is most polite. But all it has to sell is 'Sorry'.

This house is in a district which was largely requisitioned during the war and then bomb-blasted. It was all de-requisitioned a year ago.

Since then hordes of men have been at work 'making good', and the properties are just being restored to private occupation. That was twelve months' notice. Now hundreds of new residents are taking possession, and apparently the idea is only now being considered that they may want some telephonic communication.

To this state system we are now handing electricity and gas, and in moments of supreme lunacy the same plan is talked of for steel production.

> Thou hast conquered, O ruddy Teuton!
> Old England grows planned at thy breath!

If a private telephone company had shown in these years how much more serviceable it was to its customers no one would talk of state-controlling the other services now. That is how good causes go by default.

Meanwhile I can communicate, but cannot be communicated with. It suits me, but it will not suit my employer. He ought to fire me for getting in such a jam. That event will cause a serious gap in my balance of payments.

The borough treasurer who has welcomed me so courteously will have to whistle for his rates. Viscount Gage, Earl Winterton, and half the peerage who have leased me this house will have to suffer financial disequilibrium in consequence of my inability to pay the rent.

And all for the lack of a telephone wire.

O tempora! O mores! O Morrison!

You've Said It, Mr Attlee!
Daily Express, 9 March 1948

We shall never get good government from this or any other government while the Chancellor is rolling in money.

The only way to induce efficiency and to release large numbers of people for productive jobs by cutting down the swollen staffs is for MPs to cut off the supply at the tap. That means that Parliament should tell the Chancellor to cut the taxes.

I had hardly written this last week – I say written, not printed, for the first part was itself cut for space – when I received a quite unexpected reinforcement in my campaign. It was the Prime Minister himself.

I took down his words and ran all the way to the telephone to dictate them. And then they were cut for space too! In these small newspapers I don't see how we are going to educate the people, the Prime Minister and I.

Try again. Here is Mr Attlee's recipe for removing the passengers and pruning the staffs of the fighting services.

'The only way,' said Mr Attlee, 'is to ration the services in regard to money, cut down the money and say "You must make do with that," and then get pressure on them to get results.

'Any officer in any of the services,' said Mr Attlee, 'will produce officers and men and say that every single one is doing a vitally important job and that we cannot get rid of him. The only way to do it is to ration them.' (*Hansard*, 1 March, col. 155)

Rarely have I heard such undiluted wisdom. The words ring such a bell of truth that I feel sure Mr Attlee will never limit their application to the fighting services only.

Look further now, my good Prime Minister! Try the same cure on the Ministry of Town and Country Planning for a start. Then on the Ministry of Works and the Ministry of Supply and the Central Office of Information.

Test it on the hospitals section of the Ministry of Health. I have a detailed account of a voluntary hospital which is being nationalized. The department – or it may be the local government – was shocked to find that the matron supervised the linen. In spite of protests she was at once given a staff to look after the linen.

More shocks on the discovery that the secretary did not have a motor car. At once he was provided with a motor car, although he insisted he had done the job twenty years without one.

And so forth. This is public ownership and control. It is part of the business which I once called empire building, in which every petty establishment swells itself at our expense in order to get its roots deeper.

The only way is for the Prime Minister, with the support of Parliament, to go to the money main; cut down the Chancellor's money and say: 'You must make do with that.'

The idea that public ownership is efficient would arouse laughter in a Siamese white elephant. I can quite see that it may be comfortable for the staffs. But as the system becomes widespread this is going to bring less satisfaction, because every individual is for most of his life a customer.

When the nationalized railwayman gets less efficient attention in respect of his coal and gas and electricity; and the electrician gets less and dearer transport, coal and hospitals – and so on, with everybody else corresponding – they will at the very least want to raise a few questions in Parliament.

But Mr Morrison has seen to that. The Socialist MPs are just waking up to what is being done. The system is not public control at all. It is board monopoly.

The Post Office in comparison offers many safeguards. It is conducted by an elected minister who is responsible to Parliament. But the government was not agreeable to repeating that set-up in nationalizing the other industries.

'Every experienced MP knows,' says Mr Morrison, 'that one of the greatest criticisms of state departments, very unfairly made, is that they are afraid to take risks and are slower in moving than they ought to be.

'There is some truth in that for the reason that a state department is accountable directly for everything it does to the House of Commons, and may be apprehensive of making a mistake and of questions being asked in Parliament.'

So your coal and gas and transport and electricity are not to be state departments within the meaning of questions being asked in Parliament. For while Mr Morrison says that questions slow them down, everybody knows that questions smarten them up.

Wait a minute! It occurs to me here am I three weeks in the centre of London without a telephone in my house and no question yet asked of the Postmaster-General in Parliament!

I receive many helpful suggestions.

Here is one which does not ask to be confidential. In the woman's interest I will leave it so.

'There are people in this road and two others round the corner who have been on the list for phones for well over two years. I moved in here one Saturday, and on Monday morning the phone was in. This is how. My husband got on to head office from a call-box and said: "My wife is a midwife and must have a phone at once." Anyone more unlike one you could not imagine. I am a pianist and used to being called by the BBC any old time. Get the girlfriend to say you're a midwife. All the best.'

Excuse me. I feel rather sick. The old profit motive seems pure and clean in comparison with some aspects of this splendid new era.

•

MAX LERNER

Maxwell Alan Lerner (1902–92) was born Mikhail Lerner, in Ivenitz, Minsk, Russia. His family emigrated to the United States in 1907 and lived in New York City and also in New Haven, Connecticut. Lerner received a BA in English literature, social theory and economics from Yale in 1923, but stayed on a further year to study law. He obtained his AM from Washington

University in St Louis and a PhD at the Robert Brookings Graduate School of Economics and Government. From 1927 to 1932 he was assistant editor, and subsequently managing editor, of the *Encyclopaedia of Social Sciences*, and for the next four years he taught social sciences at Sarah Lawrence College. By the late 1930s he was teaching political science at Williams College, doing some lecturing at Harvard, and writing for the *Nation*. His career as a columnist began in 1943 when he joined *PM*, the New York evening paper, where he also served as editorial director and radio commentator. In 1948 he took his column to the *New York Star* for a year before joining the *New York Post*. He remained there for many years and his column was syndicated through the New York Post and Los Angeles Times Syndicate. In 1948 he became Professor of American Civilization at Brandeis University and he later served as dean of its graduate school for a couple of years. Apart from his teaching and column-writing, he was a prolific author.

The Ghost of Leo Frank

PM, November 23, 1943

This is an old story, but it is one of the saddest and most ironic that I know. Besides, it has just been given a fresh twist.

Leo Frank was a young New Yorker who went down to Atlanta to work in his uncle's pencil factory – as secretary of the firm and manager of the plant. In 1913 a young girl called Mary Phagan, who worked in the factory, was found murdered.

Suspicion turned to Leo Frank. There was practically no direct evidence. But the people of Atlanta were sure he had done it, and they clamored for revenge. Was he not a 'foreigner' from the North? Had he not brought with him newfangled Northern notions, and had he not come as a Northerner and a Jew to prey on Southern girls? The decades of Southern bitterness somehow got twisted with the centuries-old myths of Jewish diabolism and blood-guilt.

The result was trial by mob. Frank never had a chance. The whole structure of legal justice was too frail to stand up under the torrential passions that the case unloosed. There was, as we look back at it now, a sickening sense of fatality about the whole thing.

The trial began on July 28, 1913, in Atlanta, with Judge Roan on the bench, with the courtroom packed with a hostile crowd, and an even larger hostile crowd outside. Toward the end the judge had on one occasion to suspend court for a day, after conferring with the chief of police and the commanding officer of the militia. On the day the judge charged the jury, the prosecutor received a thunderous ovation as he entered the courtroom. When the jurors were being polled, the crowd roared its approval after each answer. The judge advised Frank and his lawyer to stay away from the court, fearing what would happen if there was an acquittal or disagreement.

The verdict was guilty and the sentence was death.

There followed a series of unsuccessful appeals, on the ground that the mob-dominated trial had been a farce. But the Georgia Supreme Court upheld the lower court. The Federal District Court refused to intervene, saying it could not retry the facts of the case, and that the judicial forms had been complied with. The case was finally appealed

to the US Supreme Court, with the famous lawyer Louis Marshall arguing the appeal
for Frank.

In a long and learned majority opinion by Justice Pitney, the court said it was too
bad, but it could do nothing. Only two justices dissented – Oliver Wendell Holmes and
Charles Evans Hughes.

The case gave Holmes the occasion to write one of his most brilliant and militant
dissenting opinions. He wrote:

> This is not a matter for polite presumptions; we must look facts in the face. Any judge
> who has sat with juries knows that in spite of forms they are extremely likely to be
> impregnated by the environing atmosphere . . . We think the presumption overwhelming
> that the jury responded to the passions of the mob . . . It is our duty to declare lynch
> law as little valid when practiced by a regularly drawn jury as when administered by one
> elected by a mob intent on death.

Meanwhile Frank sat in jail and waited. And people outside were saying more and
more loudly that justice was slow, and that lawyers could buy any man's way out of a
noose.

After the Supreme Court had said nothing could be done, the only resort was an
appeal to the governor for clemency. On his last day in office, at the end of June 1915,
the governor commuted the death sentence to life. It took political courage, but he did
it. The mob was cheated of its victim. But he remained within its grasp.

Frank didn't have long to wait. While he was being guarded at one of the prison
farms in Georgia, the inevitable party of masked men drove up in the mid of night,
drove Frank by car the long distance to Marietta where Mary Phagan had lived, and
strung him up by the inevitable rope to the inevitable tree.

Leo Frank died an agonized death on that mid-August night in 1915. And being dead,
he cannot enjoy a sequel to his story which is the cream of the jest.

For only last week an old Southern lawyer called Arthur Powell published a book of
memoirs. He had been a judge of the Appeals Court, he was a friend of Judge Roan
who presided at the Frank trial, he was a friend of Governor Slaton, and he knew the
case thoroughly from the inside.

'I am one of the few people who know,' he writes in his book, 'that Leo Frank was
innocent . . . I know who killed Mary Phagan.' It seems further that Powell sat beside
his friend Judge Roan when the latter was getting ready to charge the jury. Roan told
his friend that 'this man's innocence is proved to a mathematical certainty'.

And so they knew all the time. The judge knew, and his friend knew. The governor
knew too: Powell says that the governor told his friends that he would have granted
Frank a pardon, 'but he believed that in a very short while the truth would come out.'

They knew all the time that an evil thing was happening. And they did nothing.

I wonder where the ghost of Leo Frank is now. I'd like to send him a copy of the
book.

The Epic of Model T
PM, April 9, 1947

At the turn of the century, in Detroit, an American mechanic who had spent most of his nearly forty years tinkering with machines made a decision in whose shadow we have all lived since. He broke with the men in his company who saw the newly emerging automobile as a luxury product to be made at high prices and high profits for the few. He decided on the mass-production of a car for the many, at low cost and with a slim margin of profit per unit on a large volume of production. Out of that decision came the epic of the Model T Ford, what has been called 'the Tin Lizzie Revolution,' which transformed American production methods and set a new cultural pattern for an America on wheels.

Henry Ford has never been one of my heroes. He was – on all the things that matter in our world of values – too ignorant, too gullible, too much of a social primitive. But now that his death gives us a chance to assess his total impact, it would be stupid to allow the memory of Ford's racist and reactionary views to distort our perspective on his achievements as a technician and an industrialist.

Ford's talent as a mechanic was in line with the great American tradition of the tool-makers and inventors – a tradition which includes Whitney and McCormick, the Wright brothers and Edison. In that field they were greater than he. But where he went beyond them was in his genius for going straight to the jugular on the question of how capitalist enterprise was to be organized.

His core-idea was mass-production. From that everything else in his economic methods flowed. To get mass-production you had to have a single and simple model with replaceable parts: hence Model T, imperishable and omnipresent; so standardized that you could get it in any color provided it was black, and could fix it in its frequent breakdowns with parts bought at the corner store or the crossroads garage. Also to get mass-production, you had to have a high-speed production belt-line, where a man did a single operation and had to keep up with the tempo set by the gods of the machine. And to get men to do this, you had to pay them high wages (remember Ford's $5 a day when the prevailing rate was $2.34), even though this meant a slimmer rate of profit on a large volume.

Mass-production, standardization, high-speed belt-line, high wages, large volume: these were the elements of the economic concept summed up in Model T. For a time, in the years just before and just after World War I, they seemed just as indestructible and irresistible as Model T. There was the general feeling in the twenties that the problems of the prosperous economy and the good society had been solved by this 'New Capitalism.' The men who felt this were as naïve in their way as Ford in his. The Great Depression wrote the epitaph of their hopes. For it proved that what one man might decide in a moment of insight was not the way of business enterprise as a whole. Businessmen *ought* to see that with high wages and low prices, they can do a bigger volume and get their products sold for a greater total profit. But as recent events have shown, their impulse when left to themselves and when given power over prices is to boost prices and profits per unit, even if it dries up the golden well.

Thus, even in economic terms, Ford's philosophy was the light that failed in the history of capitalism. When Model T came to an end in 1927, and Ford came out with a smoother, slicker and better-looking car, he lost his dominance and distinction in the automobile age. The others had caught up with him, and he no longer had the genius to strike out on new lines and forge ahead of them.

Yet we cannot help looking back at the Age of the Tin Lizzie in an elegiac mood. There was something about her that caught the affection of the American people. She was crotchety and exasperating. There were others more beautiful than she. But there was an indomitable quality about her that made her not just another car but something of a folk heroine in the American mind.

The rest of Ford's story is too shabby and stupid to have even the quality of tragedy. In our culture we make heroes of the men who sit on top of a heap of money, and we pay attention not only to what they say in their field of competence, but to their wisdom on every other question in the world. Henry Ford was one of the victims of this strain in us.

He came to see himself as a prophet on everything. His 'Peace Ship' to Europe was a fantastic failure, yet what he brought back with him was even worse – the forged Protocols of the Elders of Zion, and the conviction that the root of all evils was 'the international Jew,' who was at once a Communist and an international banker. His *Dearborn Independent* was largely the work of W. J. Cameron, and by 1926 Ford had to retract everything it had said about Jews; yet its work had been done, and the sewer of filth pouring out of it had poisoned enough minds from Argentina to China to make Ford a hero of the fascists. On another front, under the tutelage of Harry Bennett, he became a violent enemy of trade unions.

This was Ford, brilliant in technology, a genius in organization, his mind a jungle of fear and ignorance and prejudice in social affairs. Can we perhaps find in him a mirror of the American problem today?

The Atmosphere of Decay
New York Post, April 5, 1950

I think we have been standing too close to the Senator McCarthy fiasco and the case of Owen Lattimore to see their full social and moral meaning. To be sure, the Battle of the Secret Files has its legal aspects, and the maneuvers of McCarthy, Bridges and Wherry have their political aspects.

And there is, of course, the underlying issue of whether Americans who love their country are to have their lives blasted because a voice has whispered in the night to a politically desperate senator, saying: 'You have nothing to lose but your political obscurity and your fading chances of re-election. You have the nation's headlines to gain.'

To call McCarthyism* a fascist atmosphere would be descriptive enough, but I am

---

* Lerner came up with the term 'McCarthyism' for this column at around the same time that Herbert Block used it in a cartoon.

tired to death of the worn-out epithets of 'communist' and 'fascist' being bandied about. What is more striking is the smell of moral decay about the whole business. When desperate men get desperate enough, as the totalitarian experience both on the Right and the Left shows, they give us a glimpse into the cloacal depths of what is mean and destructive in man. The atmosphere surrounding McCarthyism is this atmosphere of decay.

See what elements go into forming it? There is, to start with, the brassy verbal violence that McCarthy, Bridges and Wherry have succumbed to. When McCarthy tells the President to 'put up or shut up,' those who have grown accustomed to political invective in America have to remind themselves that the Presidential office is still the symbol of our democracy. McCarthy has aimed at dragging into the gutter with himself not only the President but the Presidency.

There has been about many of his statements a kind of verbal hoodlumism that must take any historical student back to the brass-knuckle polemics of the parliamentary struggles in the Weimar Republic, or the hysterical language that Communists love to use.

Then there is the well-known use of the tactic of the Big Lie. One thing McCarthy has shown is that his talents as a student of propaganda are not to be underestimated. True, he has overreached himself and blundered badly on several scores. But he knows the core lesson of recent propaganda history – to make stentorous use of what little material you have and, if necessary, of nothing.

A striking element in the pattern is the unscrupulous shifting of ground.

You start with a charge that there are fifty-seven or eighty-one or some other magical number of card-carrying Communists or their equivalent in the State Department. You make public a handful of names, and when you have been blasted into inglorious retreat on each of them, you stake everything on one name – that of Owen Lattimore as a 'Russian master spy.'

When that too evaporates, you say that the question of whether or not he is a master spy is unimportant – that your real point is that he has shaped State Department policy in the Far East. When the secret Lattimore Report is finally published, it says little that John K. Fairbank or Harold Isaacs or Walter Lippmann or other students of Far Eastern policy would not say – or that I have not said myself.

What is important here is not just McCarthy's shifting of premises, his evasiveness, his cowardice in wrapping his moral nakedness in the cloak of senatorial immunity. What is important is the contempt he shows for the processes of the mind.

There remains to speak of the elements that remind me of the dreary and ever-present fanatic fringe in America. I have had to wade through mountains of pamphlets and literature by men like Gerald Smith, Joseph Kamp, Merwin Hart. I find in McCarthy's stuff the same obsession with cloud cuckooland conspiracies, mysterious spies, nefarious networks. And, most important, I suspect that the avalanche of mail McCarthy is reported to be getting comes from the people whom Smith and Kamp and Hart had stirred up.

There is a hate layer of opinion and emotion in America. There will be other McCarthys to come who will be hailed as its heroes.

Any Old Time
New York Post, December 4, 1952

When I first started writing for daily newspapers, almost a decade ago, I was told that a four- or five-a-week column would set a stiff pace. You never know (my mentors said wisely) when you will have a stomach ache or get into a crash or stop for one drink too many or get absorbed with a girl or just forget. So have a few 'barrel' pieces ready, they said, the kind the editor marks AOT – Any Old Time – and files away with a sigh of security.

I did it a few times, but it never really worked. Whenever I was one ahead, it would be only a few days before I would get lazy and consume my substance. The rainy-day column would be hauled out and used on the sunniest of days, when I was able-bodied and sound of mind and wind, and could have written something. Then I'd be back where I started.

As a result, I have been a day-to-day, hand-to-mouth wastrel. This has meant some close calls. Often I have found myself in some small Southern or Midwestern town, after a lecture at the college or the local forum, followed by the routine entertainment. Say it's midnight, and the local telegraph office has been closed since sundown, and the only open one is fifty miles away, and you have two hours before deadline for filing and you have left your notes at home, and you haven't an idea in your head. That's when you review your wasted life and wish you had put an AOT away in the editor's safe.

It's even worse abroad. Say you have been to a Paris cellar café and have found a ravishing girl who insists on talking about Sartre to you and in a language that requires your concentration, and you take her to an all-night joint that has good scrambled eggs, and you are about to surrender yourself to existentialism – and then you recall the home office, and you leave her to write something for the mail plane. It doesn't contribute to Franco–American friendship.

Some years ago I got a scare. The boys on the desk had a copy of my page printed up, with a big blank space where my column was supposed to be, and in the center of it a tiny notice that the space was reserved for me but my copy had not shown up. For a moment it shook me. But when I discovered the hoax, I grew cynical about all threats.

Yet I should like to say, with modest boastfulness, that in almost ten years – during which I calculate the dismaying total of at least 2,000 columns – I can't remember missing a deadline. Maybe it's because I'm such a healthy ox, or maybe there is some Puritan in the marrow of my conscience.

The question remains: Why the compulsion to wait for the last moment? I think the world is divided into two categories of people: those who arrive at the railroad station an hour and a half ahead of time and wave the train in, and those who dash up the platform and board it on the run, as in spy movies. Nature or nurture put me somehow into the second class.

No doubt this is something neurotic – the fag end of the romantic tradition about living dangerously on margins. Maybe the psychiatrists have a name for the disease – some kind of 'deadline compulsion.' I'm afraid to ask one of them, lest I be turned over to the American Psychoanalytic Association as Exhibit A. I should then have to admit to them that I'm this way about everything – catching planes, coming upstairs to dinner, walking into a classroom or lecture hall, applying for passports or visas, showing up for radio shows. No doubt, if I ever reach the heavenly gates I'll just manage to get in under the ropes before they close.

Let me say, in my defense, that too much leeway is degenerating to any craftsman. If I start a column with hours to spare, it sprawls over the terrain. Maybe I need a deadline to give me moorings – at one end, anyway. Like the sonnet form, or the rondel, it sets a frame for your work. If you never had to think about a budget you would enjoy spending less than you do. The deadline is my budget – it gives a finality to my waywardness.

PS: I had hoped to consign this column for reserve stock, as an AOT. But it never worked out that way until the deadline – which is now.

•

I. F. STONE

Isador Feinstein Stone (1907–89) was born in Philadelphia as plain Isador Feinstein, and altered his name in 1938. His teenage years were spent in Haddonfield, New Jersey. At high school he founded a newspaper, the *Progressive*, with a friend. While majoring in philosophy at the University of Philadelphia, he also worked part-time for the *Courier Post* in Camden, New Jersey, and the *Philadelphia Inquirer*. He failed to complete his degree, but instead joined the *Courier Post* as a reporter in 1927. He was an editorial writer, briefly for the *Philadelphia Record*, then for the *New York Post* from 1933 to 1939. In 1938 he began his association with the *Nation*, first as an associate editor and subsequently, from 1940 to 1946, as its Washington editor. At roughly the same time he wrote columns for various New York papers: the *Post*, *PM*, the *New York Star* and the *New York Daily Compass*. His thinking went vigorously against the grain of the McCarthyite period and rather than chafe under the collar of the mainstream press he chose to launch his own paper, *I.F. Stone's Weekly*, in 1952. The paper became *I.F. Stone's Bi-Weekly* in 1967 and Stone left in 1971. From that date until his death he was a contributing editor to the *New York Review of Books*.

If Only John F. Kennedy Were in Hans Christian Andersen
I. F. Stone's Weekly, January 30, 1961

The new President and the lovely new young First Lady are as charming as any prince and princess out of a childhood book of fairy tales. How could one's heart help but warm to them and to wish them well? There is a divinity that doth hedge presidents as well as kings, and there must be few of us who do not hope deep down that by some magic this new monarch's wand will wave away our ills. The primitive superstition close beneath the surface of our selves suffuses the beginning of a new reign or Administration with an almost religious festivity; the bands play, the troops march; past errors are wiped away, the country is reborn for a fresh start.

Eight years ago the country could place its reliance on the father image of an old soldier. Now our talisman is a youthful St George, who can slay the dragon or charm him away. The mood was deepened by the brisk but elevated tone, the brief but comprehensive sweep, of his Inaugural Message, above all by the unmistakable zest of his 'I do not shrink from this responsibility – I welcome it.' And there he was – the eager beaver – at the White House early and on time next morning, fresh after only a few hours sleep, a young man determined to make good in a new job. He didn't even take his Sunday off. This young man should go far. After a part-time President, away on sick leave or vacation much of the time, this *was* a change.

In the euphoric post-inaugural atmosphere sober reflection seems sacrilegious. Right and left, there is applause for the Inaugural Address. How could it please such diverse people? The secret lies both in the new President and in ourselves. The Inaugural Message had something in it for everybody. At one point it seemed to promise a step up in the cold war, at another an intensified search for peace. At one point there was cheer for those who want greater arms expenditure – 'only when our arms are sufficient beyond doubt' (more billions?) 'can we be certain beyond doubt that they will never be employed.' But the very next paragraph offered cheer to the advocates of disarmament – 'both sides overburdened by the cost of modern weapons, both rightly alarmed by the steady spread of the deadly atom, yet both racing to alter that uncertain balance of terror that stays the hand of mankind's final war.' But how can arms be made sufficient beyond doubt when both sides are racing to alter an uncertain balance of terror? Logically these propositions cancel each other out. But each of us assumes that the proposition with which we disagree was put in as eyewash for our adversaries. So wishful thinking shuts off the inner ear, and it does not register what we do not wish to hear.

A little sleight-of-hand, a certain modicum of chicanery, are inseparable from the governance of men. Mr Kennedy was after all the nominee of the Democratic Party; he was not elected by acclamation at a convention of idealists and pacifists; he must keep very disparate elements happy, though perhaps only happily deceived, if he is to achieve a sufficient common denominator in the party and the country for effective action. He is a President, not a dictator, and any man as either is still a prisoner of the habitual; men can only be moved a little way beyond the familiar. Mr Kennedy gives every indication of being the greatest master of manipulative politics since FDR, no mean man at razzle-dazzle. It is a necessary quality, and we must be patient. But in being patient there is no reason to shut our eyes to realities. Mr Kennedy, for all his activism, seems to be a rather cautious, perhaps even conventional man. He will grow; he reads; he can be reached; he has potentials of sympathy and of vision. But at the outset of his Administration the key posts are occupied by much the same types representing much the same forces as under Mr Eisenhower. Mr Kennedy as a politician in his dealings with Congress, the military bureaucracy and the moneyed powers of the country instinctively looks for the winning combination, the line of least resistance. This is not good enough to cope with an increasingly unstable world, long and ludicrously outgrown its nation-state diapers, menaced by the religious fanaticism of competing, oversimplified and delusive ideologies. Only unconventional measures can possibly get mankind away from the brink.

To see how little signs there are of these unconventional measures one has only to ask what was the meaning of Mr Kennedy's declaration that 'we shall pay any price . . . to assure the survival and the success of liberty.' Does this mean that we are prepared to pay the price of giving up sugar, banana or oil interests in Latin America to show our neighbors how they can end poverty within the framework of a free society? Above all are we ready to pay the price of adopting those wide measures of social reconstruction to replace the arms race and save liberty from the garrison state? Or will we find ourselves ultimately asked to bear the burden of piling up more arms in the fallacious search for that new delusion, a balanced nuclear deterrent?

•

WILLIAM CONNOR

Sir William Neil Connor (1909–67) was the son of an Ulster-born civil servant and was educated at Glendale Grammar School, Wood Green, north London. He worked as an advertising copywriter for J. Walter Thompson before joining the *Daily Mirror* in 1935 on the same day as Hugh Cudlipp and Peter Wilson. Immediately, he was asked by the paper's editorial director, Guy Bartholomew, 'Can you write a column? . . . Start now!' Under the pseudonym 'Cassandra' he wrote a hard-hitting column which appeared three times a week. He maintained this output until March 1942 when the government threatened to close the *Mirror* over a Zec cartoon for which Connor had suggested the caption. He joined the army and served under Cudlipp in the British Army Newspaper Unit, producing the *Union Jack* for the British troops in Italy. In September 1946 he resumed his *Mirror* column with the memorable opening phrase: 'As I was saying before I was interrupted, it is a powerful hard thing to please all the people all the time . . .' He ranged far and wide in terms of subject-matter, including political commentary, interviews straightforward (with John F. Kennedy) and eccentric (with Senator Joseph McCarthy at his dentist), diatribes against personalities (his notorious attack on Liberace, for which he was successfully sued for libel) and against facial hair; reflections on the use of the Christmas card as a weapon; gardening, building bonfires, and his failure as a domestic handyman.

On Hangovers
Daily Mirror, c. 1937

> *'He found that he was suffering from what he (counsel) said was vulgarly and commonly known as a "hangover".'*
> *'A what?' asked Mr Justice Hawke.*
> *'I am just as ignorant as your Lordship,' replied counsel.*
> *Mr Justice Hawke then severely rebuked people who laughed at this.*
>
> – Court report

May I hasten to help his Lordship! A hangover is when your tongue tastes like a tram-driver's glove.

When your boots seem to be steaming and your eyes burn in their sockets like hot gooseberries.

Your stomach spins slowly on its axis and your head gently swells and contracts like a jelly in the tideway.

Voices sound far off and your hands tremble like those of a centenarian condemned to death.

Slight movements make you sweat, even as you shiver from the deadly cold that is within you.

Bright lights hurt the eyes, and jeering, gibbering people from the night before seem to whisper in your ears, and then fade with mocking horrible laughter into silence.

The fingernails are brittle and your skin hangs on you like an old second-hand suit.

Your feet appear to be swollen, and walking is like wading through a swamp of lumpy, thick custard.

Your throat is cracked and parched like the bottom of an old saucepan that has boiled dry. The next moment the symptoms change, and your mouth is stuffed with warm cotton wool.

When you brush your hair you are certain that there is no top to your skull, and your brain stands naked and throbbing in the stabbing air.

Your back aches and feels as though someone is nailing a placard to your shoulder-blades.

Knee joints have turned to dish water and eyelids are made of sheets of lead lined with sandpaper.

When you lean on a table it sways gently and you know for certain that you are at sea.

Should you step off a kerb you stumble, for it is a yard deep and the gutter yawns like a wide, quaking trench.

You have no sense of touch and your fingertips feel with all the acuteness of decayed firewood smeared with putty.

The nostrils pulsate and smell the evil air.

You believe that you are in a horrible dream but when you wake up you know that it will all be true.

Your teeth have been filed to stumps and are about to be unscrewed one by one from your aching jaw.

You want to sleep, but when you close your eyes you are dizzy, and you heel over like a waterlogged barrel crammed with old, sodden cabbage stalks in the Grand Junction Canal.

When you read your eyes follow each letter to try to spell the words, but in vain – no message reaches your empty, sullen brain.

Should you look at a simple thing like a tree, it will appear that the bark is gradually crawling upwards.

Lights flash and crackle before you and innumerable little brown dwarfs start tapping just below the base of your skull with tiny, dainty hammers made of compressed rubber . . .

O Death, where is thy sting!

The Woman Who Hangs Today*
Daily Mirror, 13 July 1955

It's a fine day for haymaking. A fine day for fishing. A fine day for lolling in the sunshine. And if you feel that way – and I mourn to say that millions of you do – it's a fine day for a hanging.

IF YOU READ THIS BEFORE NINE O'CLOCK THIS MORNING, the last dreadful and obscene preparations for hanging Ruth Ellis will be moving up to their fierce and sickening climax. The public hangman and his assistant will have been slipped into the prison at about four o'clock yesterday afternoon.

There, from what is grotesquely called 'some vantage point' and unobserved by Ruth Ellis, they will have spied upon her when she was at exercise 'to form an impression of the physique of the prisoner'.

A bag of sand will have been filled to the same weight as the condemned woman and it will have been left hanging overnight to stretch the rope.

IF YOU READ THIS AT NINE O'CLOCK, then – short of a miracle – you and I and every man and woman in the land with head to think and heart to feel will, in full responsibility, blot this woman out.

The hands that place the white hood over her head will not be our hands. But the guilt – and guilt there is in all this abominable business – will belong to us as much as to the wretched executioner paid and trained to do the job in accordance with the savage public will.

IF YOU READ THIS AFTER NINE O'CLOCK, the murderess, Ruth Ellis, will have gone.

The one thing that brings stature and dignity to mankind and raises us above the beasts of the field will have been denied her – pity and the hope of ultimate redemption.

The medical officer will go to the pit under the trap door to see that life is extinct. Then in the barbarous wickedness of this ceremony, rejected by nearly all civilized peoples, the body will be left to hang for one hour.

IF YOU READ THESE WORDS OF MINE AT MIDDAY the grave will have been dug while there are no prisoners around and the chaplain will have read the burial service after he and all of us have come so freshly from disobeying the sixth commandment which says 'Thou shalt not kill.'

The secrecy of it all shows that if compassion is not in us, then at least we still retain the dregs of shame. The medieval notice of execution will have been posted on the prison gates and the usual squalid handful of louts and rubbernecks who attend these legalized killings will have had their own private obscene delights.

Two Royal Commissions have protested against these horrible events. Every Home Secretary in recent years has testified to the agonies of his task, and the revulsion he has felt towards his duty. None has ever claimed that executions prevent murder.

---

* Ruth Ellis, who murdered her lover, was the last woman to be hanged in Britain.

Yet they go on and still Parliament has neither the resolve nor the conviction, nor the wit, nor the decency to put an end to these atrocious affairs.

When I write about capital punishment, as I have often done, I get some praise and usually more abuse. In this case I have been reviled as being 'a sucker for a pretty face'.

Well, I am a sucker for a pretty face. And I am a sucker for all human faces because I hope I am a sucker for all humanity, good or bad. But I prefer the face not to be lolling because of a judicially broken neck.

Yes, it is a fine day.

Oscar Wilde, when he was in Reading Gaol, spoke with melancholy of 'that little tent of blue which prisoners call the sky'.

The tent of blue should be dark and sad at the thing we have done this day.

Camden Goods

Daily Mirror, 24 September 1956

Many years ago I had a Museum telephone number which ended with the number 56. The Camden Town Goods Station had a telephone number in those days which ended with the numerals 57.

The result was that I was continually rung up at all hours of the day and night – especially the night – and asked the most peculiar questions, such as what I proposed to do with forty-seven sheets of corrugated asbestos cement in Siding Seventeen.

At first I suffered the telephonic tortures of the damned, but after a while I used to lie awake longing to be rung up at three in the morning and be mistaken for Camden Goods.

A hoarse voice would get on and say, ' 'Arry?'

'Yus.'

'Twenty-seven rolls of netting wire. Sling 'em on Platform Three as usual?'

'Nooaw. Bung 'em out to Tufnell Park. Gunnight.'

I got to know and love these men.

We did enormous business together. In the wee small hours I shifted tons of stuff all over London. Especially I loved the crates full of pigeons.

The Voice would get on and shout: 'What abaht these bloomin' pigeons, 'Arry?'

' 'Ow many baskets?'

'Sevving.'

'Open five and let 'em fly 'ome. Sling the other two over to 'Arrods termorrer.'

'Oke.'

'Oke.'

I would deal in anything. Eggs. Plasterboard. Tiles. Dried milk. Gravel. Kettles. Cement. Pails. Tomato ketchup. Anything.

One memorable night the Voice and I did fine business with a crated pipe-organ.

'Thatchew, 'Arry?'

'Yus.'

'Gotter bloomin' organ 'ere. Wherejer wannit?'

' 'Old'ard till I git the ledger. 'Ow many tons?'
'Levving!'
'Oke. Gottit. Write this dahn. 'Ackney Gasworks, 'Ackney.'
'Cripes! Wodder they want wiv a church organ?'
'Test the pipes wiv the gas, you big stoopid.'
'Oke.'
'Oke.'
Aaah, those Camden Town nights!

The Thing in the Hall
Daily Mirror, 13 October 1960

In the hall there is the Thing.

My hall.

The Thing is in the same line of business as Dr Jekyll and Mr Hyde, the Abominable Snowman and what they are doing at Cape Canaveral.

It is about three and a half feet high, two feet wide, nearly a yard deep, gleaming white and looks more like a refrigerator than a boiler – which it is.

The Thing has been the greatest spreader of alarm and despondency I have ever bought, with the possible exception of a certain television set which reported great TV occasions, like the coronation, with nothing more than a thin, bitter, horizontal line across its sneering face.

This particular telly (which even its despairing manufacturers called 'a rogue-elephant set') had nothing on the Thing.

The Thing makes hot water and is stuffed with British Thermal Units, electric eyes, thermostats, switches, and feeds on what smells like low-grade sump oil mixed with ground-up pterodactyls.

It sits there silent and aseptic like one of those operating theatre cabinets full of long knives and oval trays for swabs they mean to leave inside you.

Then, without warning, the Thing erupts.

There is the sudden Kerrrrrrrr-*ump!* of a 2,000-pound bomb going off in the middle distance followed by a deep, guttural roar.

If you have the radio set switched on it twitches and if you have the telly on, the blood runs from its electronic face.

Milk turns sour and even strong, tyrannical men within earshot who have won prizes in weight-lifting contests lock up their daughters.

If you listen carefully I swear you will hear a faint, menacing metallic voice doing the Cape Canaveral count down . . . 'Seven . . . Six . . . Five . . . Four . . . Three . . . Two . . . One . . . *Fire!*'

The house trembles and you expect to see the Thing rise slowly from its launching pad and then, as the blast-off reaches its mighty crescendo, roar off into the night via the first and second floors and the tiled roof.

The cat, normally a confident, insolent animal by the name of Bulgy, happened to be passing when the Thing first exploded into action. So did Bulgy with a vertical take-off from Runway Four. He is now a trembling psychiatric case who fears to pass the Thing by day or night.

The sound it makes is a deep, catastrophic rumble of impending doom.

You get it in the boiler-rooms of sinking battleships with men dying of scalding steam.

You get it in organ lofts behind the thirty-two-foot diapason pipe which is pumping out poison gas.

You get it when you are entombed after an earthquake and the local gas main bursts into flame.

Windowpanes splinter and old walls crack, and spiders with deep, bass voices emerge. Then, as suddenly as it began, the Thing stops.

The silence is an explosion in reverse, and even more unbearable than the hideous grumble of intolerable profundity.

You long to hear something.

A baby screaming with terror.

A tocsin. A shrieking owl.

A prayer for the dead.

The slam of a dungeon door.

The sigh of doomed men.

But the Thing says nowt.

It crouches there in the hall with its thunderous tongue torn out.

Waiting . . . waiting . . . waiting.

What can I do with the Thing?

There is only one recourse.

I will entomb the Thing.

I will have the hall exorcized.

And then, and only then, will Bulgy and I get a decent night's rest.

Daily Mirror, 18 December 1960

In response to overwhelming public demand for morbid details of the final interment of the Thing in the Hall, I have decided to succumb to my worst instincts and release details of the last sombre and affecting scenes.

Mourners and revellers alike who have been following the story of my fight against an electrically operated, oil-burning hot-water boiler will recall when I first installed it in the hall this box of thermal pain regularly exploded with a *kerrrrrrump!* that shook the plaster off the ceiling.

This was followed by the diapason roar of a distant avalanche abruptly cut off when a million tons of snow were roaring down the side of Mont Blanc. The worst part was wondering in the deathly hush that followed at three in the morning, how the snow stopped and whether it rolled back upwards on to the summit again.

The secret decision to bury the Thing alive in a tomb of brick, acoustic tiles and walls of fibreglass was taken in Highgate Cemetery in the rain, just behind Karl Marx's grave. Dark glasses were obligatory, the muttered password was 'Jingle Bells' and sodden plimsolls were worn.

When at last we had the brute cornered, grunting, spitting and slavering like a trussed wild boar, and the last stones were being cemented in, a scholarly mourner with a sense of history remarked: 'Not since Tutankhamen was entombed in his golden coffin in Egypt near the last resting place of Rameses VI has there been an event of comparable significance. Surely it would be fitting that alongside the Thing we placed certain symbolic articles of the year 1960 that would add a topical note to man's triumphant contempt for the machine and a memorial to the heroic spirit of the Owner who, with courage and splendid vision, finally managed to put a sock in it.'

I was compelled to agree.

Through the last aperture and down into the hole were lowered the unsurrendered portion of a day-return ticket from King's Cross to Finsbury Park via the Copenhagen and Gasworks Tunnels – the squalid and pathetic symbol in the sixties of man's suffering on the Golgotha of British Railways.

The Thing evidently spotted this grimy passport to travelling pain and strained at its bolts and spewed up like Moby Dick. 'Thar she blows!' remarked one nautically minded pallbearer.

My cats, who had had the daylights scared out of them when the Thing was at large and first terrorized the whole house with its hideous rumblings and its favourite party imitation of Vesuvius blowing its top, arched their backs and screamed.

The wind sighed and the rain beat down upon the windows.

A pair of filthy mud-enslimed wellingtons were stuffed into the steaming catafalque, and a deaf mute from the Exeter region of Devonshire coughed hoarsely and sneezed.

From the heated sepulchre came a snuffling and a snoring, but it was muffled, distant stuff like a mild influenza case in a coal mine heard from pit-head level.

Someone keened and blubbered:

> 'Strew on your roses, roses
> And never a spray of yew.
>   In quiet it reposes,
>   Ah would that I did, too!'

The Thing lay still.

The head mourner tested the casing with a stethoscope. There were no heartbeats. Respiration had ceased. But it still lived with its tongue torn out and its eardrums pierced.

The soft sweet silence tiptoed down upon us with engulfing, swaddling calm.

The clocks nervously hammered away with their thunderous ticking. A tap dripped and sploshed with noisy, liquid joy.

The cats clumped and stamped across the carpet like the guards at foot-drill on the square at the depot at Caterham.

A fly roared up on to the picture rail noisier than a Boeing 707 jet, and a stray, tipsy coroner, who had just stumbled in, prayed earnestly for silence – on the grounds that he could not hear the sound of his toe-nails growing.

The Thing was in.

The Thing was down.

The Thing was out.

•

JOSEPH AND STEWART ALSOP

The brothers Joseph Wright Alsop (1910–89) and Stewart Alsop (1914–74) were born in Avon, Connecticut, to a well-connected family who were related to the Roosevelts. They both attended Groton prep school and Joseph went to Harvard (graduating cum laude in 1932) while Stewart went to Yale, obtaining a BA in 1936. Joseph's first job was as a reporter for the *New York Herald Tribune*, and after a few years he was sent to Washington to cover the White House. In 1937 he collaborated with Robert E. Kintner on a nationally syndicated political column called 'The Capitol Parade'. Stewart, meanwhile, had joined the publishing firm of Doubleday, Doran. During the Second World War Joseph, who had been turned down by the US Army on medical grounds, served first in the navy, then with the Flying Tigers in Burma, while Stewart, who was also turned down by the US Army on medical grounds, managed to enlist in the British Army, later transferring to the US Army as an OSS (intelligence) operative and working with the resistance in occupied France. After the war, when Joseph resumed his Washington column, he asked Stewart to join him. The column, called 'Matter of Fact', ran from 1948 until 1974, although Stewart left in 1958 to become political editor of the *Saturday Evening Post*. Democrats by inclination, the Alsops provided sharp analysis of domestic politics and foreign affairs. Some of their columns were collected in *The Reporter's Trade* (1958).

'Matter of Fact'
New York Herald Tribune, January 2, 1950

Washington

If you want to know where we stand at this macabre half-century mark, you will be interested in a debate that is now troubling the highest level of the government. The issue is, very simply, whether to launch an effort comparable to the wartime Manhattan District Project, in order to produce what is referred to as the 'super-bomb.'

This is the weapon, with approximately 1,000 times the destructive force of the bomb that fell on Hiroshima, that Senator Ed Johnson of Colorado recently described to his television audience. Its power will derive from the nuclear explosion of hydrogen. It will have the estimated capability of devastating, in one detonation, an area of sixty to a hundred square miles. Its theoretical feasibility is well established.

Indeed, none of those now arguing the problem doubts for a moment that this hideous weapon will be built eventually. That will be taken care of by the ordinary work of the Atomic Energy Commission – for it is the peculiar triumph of our time that we are already very close to achieving the weapons of ultimate destruction. The question is, rather, whether to appropriate the money and mobilize the man power to build such a bomb in perhaps two, or three or four years.

Interestingly enough, the same issue was first debated immediately after the war, before the Atomic Energy Commission was set up. The theoretical possibility of a hydrogen bomb was as well understood then as now. A great effort to produce one was urged in certain quarters. President Truman then referred the problem, for study and recommendation, to Dr Vannevar Bush and President Conant of Harvard.

As reported by competent authority, Bush and Conant found, first, that the problem of building a hydrogen bomb was quite as big, complex and difficult as the original problem of building the Hiroshima bomb. By the same token, they also found that the project would demand the same overriding priorities, the same mobilization of resources and man power that made possible the success of the Manhattan District.

At that time, there was no question about our monopoly of the uranium-plutonium bomb. The power-for-dollar return on the investment did not appear to justify a vast peacetime effort to produce a hydrogen bomb. Conant and Bush returned an adverse report.

When the Atomic Energy Commission was organized, therefore, its primary task was to continue and expand the Manhattan District's work. As a matter of course, studies and experiments looking to the eventual construction of a hydrogen bomb were also undertaken. Good progress has been made, by ordinary standards. Yet no rapid success can be achieved by the present sort of effort, if only because huge, highly experimental and immensely costly installations must probably be built for the later stages of the work.

In this situation, the explosion of the Soviet atomic bomb last September inevitably led to the present debate among the policymakers. As soon as Marshal Lavrenti Beria broke the American 'monopoly' of the uranium-plutonium bomb, the desirability of a great special effort to hasten production of a hydrogen bomb began naturally to be urged.

The arguments of the proponents of this special effort are too obvious to need setting down. The case of the opponents is more complex.

Some, like David E. Lilienthal, who has no taste for being a merchant of death, have been visibly influenced by moral revulsion. In the main, however, the opposition has based its case on the arguments originally advanced by Conant and Bush. It is pointed out that a bomb 1,000 times more destructive than the Hiroshima model is far from being 1,000 times more useful. And it is asserted that the strength to be gained from possessing a hydrogen bomb will not be proportional to the anticipated outlay to build it. In short, it is argued that there are more fruitful ways to invest the same resources in the national defense.

Policy planners, war planners and governmental scientific advisers are to be found on both sides of the argument, although most soldiers are 'pros,' and there is a higher proportion of scientists among the 'cons.' Discussion and study of the problem have now reached the highest level, and a policy decision will presumably be made before long.

Thus dustily and obscurely, the issues of life and death are settled nowadays – dingy committee rooms are the scenes of the debate; harassed officials are the disputants; all the proceedings are highly classified; yet the whole future hangs, perhaps, upon the outcome. It will no doubt cause irritation, it may probably provoke denials, to bring the present debate out of its native darkness. Yet this must be done, since deeper issues are involved, which have been far too long concealed from the country.

'Matter of Fact'

New York Herald Tribune, February 19, 1951

Washington

The other day a new experience – a visit from the FBI – came to these reporters. It was a surprisingly sociable, indeed a downright genial, meeting. The two agents representing the bureau were decent, intelligent young men. They neither blustered nor talked nonsense. A shrewd but friendly inquisition merged, almost insensibly, into a friendly parting. Nothing could have been more painless.

In the background of this jolly chat, however, lurking, as it were, behind the curtain of amiability that enclosed the conversation, there were one or two things that were decidedly disagreeable to think about.

To be specific, the misdeed being investigated was no sinister subversive activity. It was the publication of the proof that the Soviet atomic explosion was the planned explosion of a workable atomic bomb, and the disclosure of the best estimates available of the stock of atomic bombs accumulated by the Kremlin since the seismographs picked up the earth tremor in central Siberia. This was the crime that led President Truman to order a 'security investigation.' It would have been more fitting to investigate why the leaders of this nation failed to impart such vital information to the American people on their own initiative.

The twenty to thirty bombs now in the possession of the Kremlin, the hundred or more atomic bombs the Kremlin will have in another eighteen months, are not all pretty baubles by Fabergé. Their mere existence intimately, directly and deeply affects the world position of the United States, the future of the free world, the individual future of every American citizen. Their existence, in short, is one of the three or four salient facts that must influence every decision of national policy.

In Russia, no doubt, such knowledge may be closely guarded. But ours is a free society, whose masters are the people of the United States. The great decisions of national policy are made by the people, and not by the President or the Secretary of State, or any other temporary office-holder. In order to decide wisely, the people must be informed. And it is the most sacred trust, the most important single duty of the highest public servants to inform their masters, the people, so that the decision of the people may be wise.

As Winston Churchill brilliantly proved, facts which are matters of life and death can always be presented honestly to the people, even in circumstances of great delicacy and danger, without giving aid and comfort to the enemy. Suppression of such facts is not a sign of prudence. It is a sign of leadership that is feeble, or dishonest, or both.

If the leaders wish to represent a disastrous program of disarmament as 'cutting fat without muscle'; if they desire to bemuse the people about the meaning of such a great event as the Soviet atomic explosion; if they are pretending that the chances 'were never better for peace' with Korea just around the corner, it is only natural for everything to be classified except the toilet paper. Such is the rule that has been followed in Washington, more or less consistently, for the last two years.

In these circumstances, it becomes the duty of every self-respecting reporter to dig out, not any facts which are properly secret, but the essential facts which affect the national posture and welfare. It is a risky business; for reporters and editors cannot know what is known to Presidents and Secretaries of State – exactly how to present these vital facts so that no harm is done. But if the press lets itself be transformed into a mere machine for transmitting the doctored handouts of shabby politicians, the press has abdicated its chief function.

There are other points besides the foregoing that are raised by the recent visit of the young men from the FBI. A whole chapter might be written on the shocking but increasing use of these 'security investigations,' not only as a weapon to muzzle the press, but as a weapon of intra-departmental bureaucratic war.

Another chapter might be devoted to the methods used – the broadside inquiry which in these reporters' experience at least never hits the target; the wholesale harassment of innocent men on the method of 'who knows whom'; the unashamed official practice of the very same guilt-by-association which is considered so shocking when indulged in by Sen. Joseph R. McCarthy. Something more might even be said about the scrupulosity of the FBI as compared with the State Department's special agents, who have done things in the last two years that must have made Secretary of State Acheson's great master, Mr Justice Holmes, turn in his honored grave.

But there is no space here to go slumming in these purlieus of the American Government. The point here is very simple indeed. In a free society, secrecy is not security. National ignorance is the shortest road to national annihilation. And this 'security investigation' caused by the publication of information most vital to the national future shows how great is the confusion and the danger.

•

COMPTON MACKENZIE

Sir Compton Mackenzie (1883–1972) was born in West Hartlepool and was educated at St Paul's School and Magdalen College, Oxford, where he read modern history. He published the influential novel *Sinister Street* in 1913 and 1914, and later wrote a six-volume novel, *The Four Winds of Love* (1937–45). During the First World War he served as a lieutenant in the Royal Marines, was sent to the Dardanelles, and was invalided in 1915. He was posted to Athens and in 1917 was made director of the Aegean Intelligence Service. Thereafter, Mackenzie wrote numerous books, including the novel *Whisky Galore* (1947), and held various posts, including literary critic of the *Daily Mail* from 1931 to 1935, Rector of Glasgow University, editor of the *Gramophone* from 1923 to 1961, and President of the Siamese Cat Club. He also wrote a ten-volume autobiography, *My Life and Times: Ten Octaves* (1963–71), and in the mid-1950s he contributed a weekly column called 'Sidelight' to the *Spectator*.

'Sidelight'

Spectator, 5 November 1954

That tribute to Oscar Wilde's talk from Sir Max Beerbohm printed in last week's 'Sidelight' set me thinking about that well-loved figure now in his eighty-third year.

I first met Max at Oxford fifty years ago. Robbie Ross brought him to breakfast with me one morning at 43 High Street where I had collected half a dozen awestruck undergraduates to help me pass him bacon and eggs and marmalade. And what I remember of Max at that breakfast party is not his conversation but his cuffs. We all thought he was bored and perhaps a little contemptuous of us after his dazzling compeers at Oxford in the nineties. It never occurred to us that what we considered this elderly man almost thirty-two years old might be feeling shy in the society of undergraduates.

So, nothing can be recorded of that breakfast-party except Max's cuffs, fastened tightly round the wrist and encroaching on the hand.

When I visited Max at Rapallo in September 1913, he was no longer wearing such cuffs; perhaps he had discovered that Hall Caine wore similar cuffs. However, he had grown a moustache almost as heavy as those with which dragoons armed themselves in the eighties. It is a Savile tradition that when Max first came into the club with it, member after member kept exclaiming: 'Hullo! Max! I hardly recognized you since you've grown that moustache.'

At last Max anticipated this exclamation by saying to Edmund Gosse: 'Hullo, Gosse, I hardly recognized you since I've grown this moustache.'

Max himself was aware of his military aspect, for when sending me some prints of a snapshot taken of him and me on his white terrace, he wrote that the title would be 'A Major of the Volunteers in Conversation with a Faun'. Photography was occupying much of his attention at this date, and it was photography which had first enabled him to carry through with the most scrupulous ingenuity an enchanting trick at the expense of Bernard Shaw. There had recently appeared a number of the *Bookman* devoted to Shaw, and such special numbers were usually illustrated with photographs of the hero at different periods of his life. Max had cut out each reproduction of an early aspect of Shaw and with a very fine nib had slightly altered every one of them. Thus if there was a photograph of Shaw in knickerbockers, Max would slightly prolong these knicker-bockers till the wearer of them looked something worse than merely absurd. He would exaggerate Shaw's eyebrows in one, bulbify his nose in another, give him spots in a third, and thus turn every single portrait not into a caricature but into a very slight distortion of the original which was more ludicrous than any caricature.

But this was only the beginning of an elaborate joke. After the portraits in the magazine had been thus treated they were cut out, pasted on cardboard, and sent to a photographer in Genoa, who rephotographed them and printed them off with the faded appearance of portraits in a family album of thirty or forty years earlier. No sign was any longer perceptible of Max's elfin pen. The effect was of genuine photographs in which Shaw's clothes were even uglier than the clothes of anybody else when he was a young man, that Shaw's nose at the age of twenty-four testified to many hours spent in tap-rooms, that in fact Shaw if he ever intended to be a famous man should never have allowed himself to approach within a hundred yards of a camera. And not even yet was the joke finished. These apparently genuine contemporary photographs were now sent one by one at intervals to various friends in America and England with a request to mail them back to Shaw himself in Adelphi Terrace accompanied by a letter from some mythical devotee saying that he had come across the enclosed photograph of Mr Bernard Shaw in an antique shop in Buffalo or had discovered it on a boarding-house mantelpiece in Bloomsbury, and begging the original to be so kind as to sign it and return it to the sender in the stamped addressed envelope enclosed.

Max had played a joke of the same kind on Herbert Trench, who used to take himself very seriously. He suddenly put into my hands Trench's poem 'Apollo and the Seaman', saying, 'You know this, don't you?' or something like that, and I murmured something vaguely and turned over the pages. The poem is a longish one – a dialogue between the God Apollo and a seaman who talks rather like Coleridge's Ancient Mariner. Then I looked harder at the page. I had not remembered that Trench had made his seaman talk like one of W. W. Jacobs's bargees.

> Apollo: In what green forest inlet lay
>   Her cradle and her keel?
>
> Seaman: I think some arm of the sea-gods
>   Framed us 'er stormy frame,
>   And ribbed and beamed and staunchioned 'er,
>   And gave 'er strength a name.
>
>   Never, Sir Traveller, 'ave you seen
>   A sight the 'alf as fine
>   As when she 'ove up from the East
>   On our 'orizon-line!

I turned more pages.

> By no man's 'and unfurled was 'eaven!
> . . . That was the pit of 'ell!

'Curious,' I said, 'I never remembered that Trench made the seaman drop all his aspirates.'

Max smiled.

'I took them out myself with a penknife very carefully, put in an apostrophe, and then sent the book to Trench, saying I had not seen this edition before.'

'He must have thought he'd gone mad.'

'He was a little offended about it,' Max admitted, in that tone whose gentle suavity of utterance is familiar to so many thousands of listeners.

Most of the two or three days at Rapallo were passed on a big white terrace, behind which the hills sloped up in boscages of olives and cypresses to some remote hills beyond in that dear and familiar landscape which welcomes us to the *riviera di levante*. In one angle of the terrace was a diminutive room which would just hold Max standing up to draw on a sloping desk his examples of the pretensions, follies and absurdities of our epoch. Above the door was a pale blue porcelain tile on which was enamelled in white, 'The Study'. When perhaps I was looking a little awed by what to me was a sacred place, I remember that Max dismissed his drawing with a kind of impatience, blew as it were the diminutive study off the terrace like a plume of thistledown and said that if only he could write with as little effort as he could draw . . . after which we returned to our chairs on the terrace and to drinking the sweet wines of Sicily that appeared at intervals all through those sunny September days.

The visit came to an end, as so many other jolly things came to an end in 1913, and soon I was travelling southward down through the dusky Maremma with a delightful sense of security about the future, remembering my host's encouraging comments on the first volume of *Sinister Street* which had been published at the beginning of that month, and had in fact been the cause of my visit because Max found it so much easier to tell somebody what he thought about his book than to write a letter about it. And that is what I feel myself nowadays.

•

LANGSTON HUGHES

James Langston Hughes (1902–67) was born in Joplin, Missouri, and was brought up in Lawrence, Kansas. He attended high school in Cleveland, Ohio, where he wrote poetry for the school magazine. After a year in Mexico and a spell at Columbia University, he worked his passage to West Africa and Europe, where he did various menial jobs, before returning to the United States and attending Lincoln University, from which he graduated in 1929. During his time at Columbia, he became involved in the Harlem Renaissance and started writing poetry and short stories. In the 1930s he championed black theatre and covered the Spanish Civil War for the *Baltimore Afro-American*. From 1942 to 1965 he wrote a satirical column for the *Chicago Defender*, a black weekly paper, in which he created the character Jesse B. Semple (later renamed 'Simple'). From the viewpoint of a poor though defiant black, Simple would address the issues of racism and black social mores in dialogues with his more affluent and accommodating friend Boyd. Hughes wrote more than fifty books and, apart from his weekly column, contributed numerous articles to magazines.

Income Tax

From *Simple Speaks His Mind* (1950)

' "Taxation without representation is tyranny," so the books say. I don't see why Negroes down South should pay taxes a-tall. You know Buddy Jones' brother, what was wounded in the 92nd in Italy, don't you? Well, he was telling me about how bad them rednecks treated him when he was in the army in Mississippi. He said he don't never want to see no parts of the South again. He were born and raised in Yonkers and not used to such stuff. Now his nerves is shattered. He can't even stand a Southern accent no more.'

'Jim Crow* shock,' I said. 'I guess it can be as bad as shell shock.'

'It can be worse,' said Simple. 'Jim Crow happens to men every day down South, whereas a man's not in a battle every day. Buddy's brother has been out of the army three years and he's still sore about Mississippi.'

'What happened to him down there?'

'I will tell it to you like it was told to me,' said Simple. 'You know Buddy's brother is a taxicab driver, don't you? Well, the other day he was telling me he was driving his cab downtown on Broadway last week when a white man hailed him, got in, and then said in one of them slow Dixie drawls, "Bouy, tek me ovah to Fefty-ninth Street and Fefth Avahnue."

'Buddy's brother told him, "I ain't gonna take you nowhere. Get outta my cab – and quick!"

'The white man didn't know what was the matter so he says, "Why?"

'Buddy's brother said, "Because I don't like Southerners, that's why! You treated me so mean when I was in the army down South that I don't never want to see none of you-all no more. And I *sure* don't like to hear you talk. It goes all through me. I spent eighteen months in hell in Mississippi."

'The white man got red in the face, also mad, and called a cop to make Buddy's brother drive him where he wanted to go. The cop was one of New York's finest, a great big Irishman. The copper listened to the man, then he listened to Buddy's brother. Setting right there in his taxi at Forty-eighth and Broadway, Buddy's brother told that cop all about Mississippi, how he was Jim Crowed on the train on the way down going to drill for Uncle Sam, how he was Jim Crowed in camp, also how, whenever he had a furlough, him and his colored buddies had to wait and *wait* and WAIT at the camp gate for a bus to get to town because they filled the busses up with white soldiers and the colored soldiers just had to stand behind and wait. Sometimes on payday if there were a big crowd of white soldiers, the colored GIs would never get to town at all.

' "Officer, I'm telling you," Buddy's brother said, "that Mississippi is something! Down South they don't have no nice polices like you. Down South all them white cops want to do is beat a Negro's head, cuss you, and call you names. They do not protect Americans if they are black. They lynched a man five miles down the road from our camp one night and left him hanging there for three days as a warning, so they said, to us Northern Negroes to know how to act in the South, particularly if from New York."

'Meanwhile the Southern white man who was trying to get the cop to make Buddy's brother drive him over to Fifth Avenue was getting redder and redder. He said, "You New York Negras need to learn how to act."

' "Shut up!" says the cop. "This man is talking."

---

* Jim Crow, originally a minstrel act, was the epithet given to the segregation laws in the US South, 1877–1954.

'Buddy's brother talked on. "Officer," he says, "it were so bad in that army camp that I will tell you a story of something that happened to me. They had us colored troops quartered way down at one end of the camp, six miles back from the gate, up against the levee. One day they sent me to do some yard work up in the white part of the camp. My bladder was always weak, so I had to go to the latrine no sooner than I got there. Everything is separated in Mississippi, even latrines, with signs up WHITE and COLORED. But there wasn't any COLORED latrine anywhere around, so I started to go in one marked WHITE.

' "A cracker MP yelled at me, '*Halt!*'

' "When I didn't halt – because I couldn't – he drew his gun on me and cocked it. He threatened to shoot me if I went in that WHITE latrine.

' "Well, he made me so mad, I walked all the way back to my barracks and got a gun myself. I came back and I walked up to that Southern MP. I said, *Neither you nor me will never see no Germans nor Japs if you try to stop me from going in this latrine this morning.*

' "That white MP didn't try to stop me. He just turned pale, and I went in. But by that time, officer, I was so mad I decided to set down and stay awhile. So I did. With my gun on my lap, I just sat – and every time a Southerner came in, I cocked the trigger. Ain't nobody said a word. They just looked at me and walked out. I stayed there as long as I wanted to – black as I am – in that WHITE latrine. Down in Mississippi a colored soldier has to have a gun even to go to the toilet! So, officer, that is why I do not want to ride this man – because he is one of them that wouldn't even let me go in their latrines down South, do you understand?"

' "Understand?" says the cop. "Of course, I understand. Be jeezus! It's like that exactly that the damned English did the Irish. Faith, you do not have to haul him . . . Stranger, get yerself another cab. Scram, now! Quick – before I run you in."

'That white man hauled tail! And Buddy's brother drove off saluting that cop – and blowing his horn for New York City.'

•

JIMMY CANNON

James Joseph Victor Cannon (1910–73) was born on the Lower West Side of New York, the son of a city clerk who was also a Tammany Hall representative. Cannon was what he himself called an 'FBI' (full-blooded Irish). He went to a Jesuit school for a year and pored over books in the public library, but otherwise had no education to speak of. At the age of fourteen he started as an office boy on the *New York Daily News* on the night shift. One night when the paper was short of rewrite men, he was asked to write a 300-word story. This caught the attention of the city editor, who made him a city-side reporter. When he covered the Lindbergh kidnapping trial, he was recruited to the *New York American* by Damon Runyon, who encouraged him to become a sportswriter. In 1936 he became a sports columnist and during the Second World War he was a war correspondent for *Stars and Stripes* in Europe. From 1946 to 1960 he wrote a six-days-a-week general column, called 'Jimmy Cannon Says', for the *New York Post*, and later for the *Journal-American*. It was widely syndicated. One of his specialties was to compile 'nobody-asked-me-but' lists of aphoristic observations and opinions on all subjects.

'Jimmy Cannon Says'
Winter on the West Side
From *Who Struck John?* (1956)

We resented the winter on the West Side when I was a boy. The tenements were draughty. The wind blew out the flames of the jets on the landings and the halls smelled of gas. It seemed that a winter couldn't pass without a family being asphyxiated by the fumes from coal stoves.

We wore rubber boots in the winter. We didn't wait for snow but were told to put them on when it rained. They felt clammy and loose and were difficult to walk in except when it snowed. Walking was always fine in the snow. We were afraid of the boots.

It was a superstition that rubber boots would make you blind if you wore them on dry days. As long as they were wet, your vision couldn't be damaged. So we took them off as soon as we got into the house. It didn't make any difference whether you wore boots on the street or in the house. If it was dry, you felt your eyes getting sore.

We didn't like the way the night came with a dark swiftness. Soon as the store lights went on, our parents began to lean out the window to call us upstairs. We always said upstairs even if we lived on the first floor. There was a boy who lived in the basement of a house where his father was the janitor. He said upstairs when he talked about where he lived.

The men were crankier in the winter. There were more domestic quarrels. The men drank more because they worked harder and longer. We were a neighborhood of truck drivers and dock workers. On snowy days the horses slipped and fell.

The driver would first cover the head of the fallen horse with a blanket and speak to him with a soft kindness. That surprised me. The drivers never seemed to like their horses until they had fallen. Some of them didn't bother to give their horses names. I remember asking a neighbor what he called his big handsome gray horse.

'I call him nothing,' he replied.

'How do you make him do what you want him to do?' I asked.

'He's a good horse,' the man said. 'He just does it.'

I haven't figured it out yet. But it seemed wrong not to give a good horse a name. My old man owned horses.

They all had names. But they never caused any small talk with their achievements. I thought of them as marvelous animals. It distressed me to find out they didn't do anything spectacular except fall. Dogs made gossip and even cats and once in a while a parrot. But the horses only fell down and sickened with a disease called the glanders. That's all they did.

The horses in my neighborhood had no personality except when they were lying on their sides in the winter with their wild sad eyes covered by a blanket. Ashes were spread for footing and they usually heaved themselves up. Sometimes they broke legs and then they were shot.

No one grieved about their deaths. There was no mourning at all except if the driver owned his own rig he would tell how much his horse had cost at a mysterious place referred to as the Sale. People felt bad when other animals died but no one cared about the horses. There is a dead horse on the streets of my childhood when I think about the old neighborhood but there is no sadness connected with it.

Guys in my neighborhood loved bikes more than they did horses. They hired the bikes for a quarter an hour on Sunday if they couldn't afford to own one. The rented bikes were the ugliest machines I ever saw. The nickel handles were tarnished and covered with black tape. The paint peeled on the frame and the thin wire spokes.

It was a big deal to own a bike in my neighborhood. The guys who had them hated the winter. Most of them wrapped their bikes in burlap bags and put them in the woodshed on the first cold evening. But there were others who rode them even when there was snow on the ground.

There never was a girl too modest or shy to ride on the handlebars of a bike. The girls who weren't asked said it was disgraceful for a girl to ride on the handlebars and show her legs that way. But they were the lonely girls who weren't invited and spite made them say it. They all seemed beautiful, the girls who rode on the handlebars, every one of them. It seems it was impossible for a girl to be plain or homely riding on a bike. But that was in the summertime. The girls didn't ride on the handlebars in the winter.

You showed a girl you cared for her in a winter way when the bike was laid up in the woodshed. You washed her face with snow. They pretended they didn't like it and screamed a lot and threatened to tell your father. You had to fight their brothers if they caught you doing it. But the same girls who rode on the handlebars were the ones who had their faces washed with snow.

They never made trouble for the guy who washed their faces with snow. It was the ones who didn't who told on us. They would tell the brothers and our parents. We'd catch hell then. It seemed to snow a lot more then but it never snowed enough. I remember the sad mornings when I'd awaken and be disappointed because the day was bright and clear. That didn't make the truck drivers sad. They hated snow.

The kids didn't like winter either. But snow wasn't winter. Snow was another season.

'Jimmy Cannon Says'
The Liars
From *Who Struck John?* (1956)

Political publicity agents, who are the dumbest of the species, consider themselves sculptors of characters. As a class they are stolid men with crippled imaginations and their minds are nests of clichés. Now, in a presidential year, we may expect many photographs of candidates standing in shallow streams in hip boots, holding fly rods in their hands. Proof that an office chaser is a fisherman should cause the voter to renounce the party because this has long been the sport of the indolent, the surreptitious tippler and the braggart.

Men old enough to make a pass at the presidency are not spry enough to go up and pinch hit or run the hundred or play a quarter in the line. Tennis is associated with juveniles in musical comedies who establish themselves as worthless bums by strolling through the drawing room of a country home with racquets under arms. Indian wrestling was Henry Wallace's hobby and a candidate would be better off advocating dealing seconds at the bridge table. Poker is Harry Truman's and a guy depending on public confidence must cross the street and look the other way if a basketball is to roll into the camera's focus.

May I suggest horseshoe throwing as a hobby, which is a pastime associated with tranquil hours and doesn't create an atmosphere of corporation executives as golf might. It is the country man's time killer and offers a memory of old dobbin in the stable and lowing kine drifting across a sweet meadow and the pig grunting happily in his slop and the chickens before they are pot pies.

Scandal has never blemished hicks' pool. It is a contest for the impoverished and the rich may do it, too. It is the farmer's fun and promotes a love of the land, and even city people can understand the simplicity of its rules. Villains are not found in barnyards, and according to national myth, the rube is the purest of all men, and strongly motivated by common sense. It takes more skill than fishing for perch with a cork and a worm and indicates a man's physical soundness more than sitting in a grandstand watching a game of baseball.

The fisherman as a symbol of homely decency has long been a fabrication which remains unchallenged. The fascination of fishing has eluded me. It is an excuse for getting loaded in the daytime without building a reputation for drinking before the sun goes down. If they would concede this, I would grant fishermen the respect I withhold.

Many a man needs a drink before breakfast but, if a fellow sprinkles his orange juice with gin, they denounce him as strictly a rumor. Should he fall down dead drunk in a nightclub, disgusting all those concerned with him, such repulsive behavior becomes an office gag and in time is related as a humorous incident. But a guy picking himself up with a slap of whiskey before the coffee is believed to be a sinister guzzler who has sacrificed his honor to his vice. Sympathetic am I with fishermen who use the absurd sport as an opportunity to get bagged without sacrificing prestige in the community.

But the fisherman, who claims he is elated by the act of fishing, puzzles me. Nagging wives may send a guy out in a rowboat in the rain but I'll accept no other excuses. I will not hold still for fishing as an ally of reflection because a guy can think better if he disconnects the plug of the television set and refuses to answer the phone.

The fisherman is the most flagrant of liars. In any other sport he would be expelled from the lodge for exaggeration that would disgrace even a golfer. They are a mendacious breed and the falsehood is accepted as a gay little joke, but such lies are not tolerated in any other type of game. The whole literature of fishing is based on the one that got away and a man is expected to make up his adventure and substitute fantasy for reality. What the hell kind of a President is that?

The narration of their silly little slanders of the truth annoys me but it delights fishermen who make themselves the liar's ally with their attentiveness. They pretend to be transfixed because they realize that, should they contradict the liar, they will not be able to tell their fiction when their turn comes. In any other adult the pattern of falsehood would indicate mental unbalance. The man who inhabits an hallucination must despise the world where he lives.

The fishermen, if you measure their attitude by logic, loathe the world and their lives must be barren and miserable. If not, why would they dwell in mirages which are a suburb of lunacy?

The guy who doesn't fish finds the fisherman an awful blow-off who acts as though a trout were a sabre-toothed tiger, hunted down with a boy's buck shot rifle. The talk of fishermen bores all others and a fisherman is only entertained when he is lying about himself. So if I were a party press agent I'd be rustling up another hobby for the boss. Fishermen aren't sportsmen. They're just fishermen.

'Jimmy Cannon Says'
Guaranteed to Happen on New Year's Eve
From *Who Struck John?* (1956)

A wife will walk out of the party just as the midnight toast is about to be given.

There will be a guy trying to put a long-distance telephone call through all night.

One of the dames will weep and her husband will insist she is grieving for an old boyfriend.

If there's a new rug on the floor, a cigarette will burn a hole in it.

There will be a guy who does an imitation of Bing Crosby.

If you go to a nightclub, a waiter will spill food on you.

People who plan to have a quiet time at home will take on heavy loads.

A girl at the party will tell you people always tell her she resembles Katharine Hepburn.

The television will flicker as midnight approaches. A guy will try to fix it and manage to get a blank screen.

At least one girl will insist on playing a torch record over and over again.

If you go to the theater, you'll spend midnight on a street corner.

A guy will discover a girl he has known for a long time but hasn't really noticed.

The elevator man in the apartment house will fall asleep and guests will pile up in the hall with the hostess raging around in a sleepy temper.

There will be a guy with an untied bow tie who will ask the prettiest girl at the party to tie it for him.

A guest will follow the hostess into the kitchen and the host will be right behind him.

One girl will spend most of the evening looking for a lost earring.

An entertainer who is getting a fortune to perform will be drowned out by the tumult of drunks who paid cover charges to hear him.

At least one guy will go home with the wrong overcoat.

A man will make a resolution at midnight and break it before he gets to bed.

A guy who resembles Andrew Volstead* will keep reminding his wife she has taken one drink too many.

The last person to leave your house will announce, 'I've never been up this late in my life.'

---

* The man responsible for the Volstead Act, i.e. Prohibition.

There will be a guy who tries to recite Kipling.

The wrong guy will get the check in a nightclub because the guy who was supposed to take it passed out.

Animosity will develop between married couples because one of the wives shows off expensive Christmas gifts.

A pest who is on the wagon will annoy the hostess to get her to make fresh coffee.

The neighbors who howl up a storm every other night but New Year's Eve will beef about the noise of the party you give.

The baby-sitter won't show and at least one couple will take a child to a party.

At a party where the women decided to come in slacks at least one girl will come in a flamboyant evening gown.

One guy will beat a dish pan starting at midnight and never stop until it is taken away from him.

There will be a guy who will challenge people to Indian wrestling as soon as he gets enough coal on the fire.

There will be a dame who turns away from a guy at midnight and you'll know he's through.

There will be a guy among the guests who will appoint himself bartender and serve himself the stiffest drinks.

At least one of your old girls will show up with another guy.

You'll feel tension between a couple and try to placate them but they'll leave.

At least one guy will leave with a girl he didn't bring.

Chances are the most disliked girl at the party will sit on the floor and the guys will sit in a circle around her.

No matter how crowded the dance floor is in a nightclub there will be people who will try to do the mambo.

Guys who hate one another will make it a point to be hearty when they say Happy New Year.

One of the guests will bring a tin horn to your place and blow it.

The party that makes the most trouble for a nightclub waiter will leave a small tip or none at all.

The people next door will drop by just when you're ready to fold and have chased the last guests.

An elderly messenger boy will deliver a telegram and be invited to stay.

A husband will be embarrassed because his wife makes a fuss over a celebrity in a nightclub.

There will be a college kid and his date leaning against one another at the worst table in the joint and every middle-aged person who sees them will be thrilled.

A couple will go into a clinch and never break until the party's over.

Most of us won't admire ourselves in the morning.

•

HENRY FAIRLIE

Henry Fairlie (1924–90) was born in Scotland. One of six sons of a farmer who moved to London and became news editor of the *Evening Standard*, Fairlie was educated at Highgate School and Corpus Christi College, Oxford, where he read modern history. During the Second World War he did not qualify for military service owing to a heart condition, but instead followed his father into newspapers, working for the *Manchester Evening News* (in the parliamentary lobby), the *Glasgow Herald* and the *Observer*. He joined *The Times* in 1950 to write obituaries and leaders, and his obituary of Churchill appeared without alteration upon the statesman's death, wrapped around the paper – the first time the paper appeared without classified advertisements on its outside pages. In 1955 Fairlie joined the *Spectator* to write its weekly 'Political Commentary' column under the pseudonym 'Trimmer'. Once his identity had become known, however, the column appeared under his own name. After a couple of years he went free-lance and wrote articles for the *Daily Mail*, the *Observer, Encounter, Time and Tide, Punch*, the *Daily Express* and the *Sunday Telegraph*. In 1966, faced with a legal bill arising from a libel action and with various other debts, he left Britain for Washington, DC, leaving behind a wife and three children. There he lived for the next twenty years, writing predominantly about American politics for the *New Republic*, the *Baltimore Sun* and the *New York Times*, as well as for the British press. In 1980 he started a weekly column for his old paper, *The Times*. The two columns which follow are taken from his time as the *Spectator*'s political commentator. One of them is the column in which he defined 'the Establishment', a term which, as he says, he had already coined and mentioned fleetingly in a couple of previous columns.

'Political Commentary'
Spectator, 22 April 1955

Let's face it. Two people could not have looked friendlier than Mr R. A. Butler and Mr Harold Macmillan as they sat side by side on the Treasury bench, Marlborough and Eton joined. What were they finding to joke about with such deliberate *bonhomie*? That old Harrovian away in Syracuse? No, not in good taste. We distrust each other? Ha! Ha! What an idea! And both of them, as they laughed, felt surreptitiously for the stilettos which Conservative politicians keep on the end of their watch-chains. Suddenly, an hour or so later, as Mr Butler wound up his Budget speech, one realized the cause of their merriment. They had been exchanging mottoes from last year's Christmas crackers. A motto a year seems to have become Mr Butler's slogan, and, after 'Invest in success', what are we offered this year? 'Liberating the human spirit.' If this did not come from a Christmas cracker, the only possible alternative is that the new Economic Secretary to the Treasury, who is rather hot on the human spirit, took it down from one of those tear-off calendars which one always assumes are manufactured by Raphael Tuck & Sons. Mr Butler trying to find the 'human touch' is one of the painfully embarrassing spectacles of the present political scene. Fortunately for him, his reputation does not depend on these contortions of the soul. He has, since 1945, shown himself to be one of the shrewdest politicians of the day.

His Budget would seem to be a good election Budget just because it is, in its general trend, much the same Budget as he might have produced if there were not going to be an election at all. He cannot be charged with trying to bribe the electors: the tax concessions are too small and too carefully distributed to uphold that accusation. (Mr Morrison, however, has already made it clear that the Labour Party will try to make it. Mr Morrison, who from the ghostly seclusion of Nuffield College no doubt finds it difficult to recall the days when he was a master at bribing the electors of London!) Such concessions as have been made offer relief to a wide selection of the population: not so much that they will begin to suspect that they are being 'had', but enough to make them feel that it is worthwhile turning out on polling day. What Mr Butler has done, over the past three and a half years, by a thoroughly consistent economic and fiscal policy, is take reasonable risks in an effort to loosen the economy. He has taken that risk again, and because it coincides with a general election, he is open to the charge of producing an election Budget. But – and this is not rationalizing after the event, because I made the point in this column in February – the obvious and possibly the only sequel to last year's stand-still Budget was that this year's should offer some concession to the taxpayer. Mr Butler's past policy surely suggests clearly his preference to use the other fiscal measures which he hinted at in his speech, in order to meet any threatening crisis, rather than the weapon of taxation.

To mix the metaphors most commonly used about Budgets, he holds the reins with the bank rate and holds a carrot in front of the horse at the same time, in the hope that it will gallop faster without ever getting out of hand. The Labour Party, certainly, whatever its public attitude, is genuinely worried by the Budget. It provides a fillip for the taxpayer without in any way seriously damaging Mr Butler's and the Conservative government's well-earned reputation for good housekeeping. Moreover, the benefits will appeal particularly to the class which, quite wrongly, has come to be regarded as identical with the floating voters, but which nevertheless does hold a key position in many marginal constituencies. It is going to need a very small swing indeed – only thirty-five seats have to change hands – in order to give the Conservatives a majority of about one hundred over the Labour Party. It is far too early yet to make prophecies – though the bets are already being laid – but Mr Butler may well have ensured by his economic policy generally and by this Budget that those who have been rather surprised to find that Conservative policies have not hurt them – and may in fact have benefited them – will take the trouble to cast their votes. Elections are won by the party which can pull out the last few per cent of voters, and the Labour Party shows no sign of offering as much inducement to them as the Conservatives.

At election time every party has to be saved from its friends, and a native generosity tempts me to try and save the Conservatives from Sir David Eccles. Solely by coincidence, I believe, on the very day that Mr Attlee announced the date of the last general election, a special article by Sir David Eccles appeared in *The Times*. It was a plea for drastic cuts in expenditure, including the social services. It called for a tough economic policy. Sir David Eccles heard a good deal about that article from Mr Butler and other Conservative leaders, but he was able to plead misadventure in his defence. This time the excuse will seem rather lame. With graceful aplomb, Sir David Eccles has announced that 'We are all working class now.' I do not know how many of the readers of the *Spectator* have seen Sir David Eccles, but there is not a man from whom such a remark could be more damaging. As impeccable in his investments as in his tailoring and his taste, he smiles condescension on those who unhappily have been less fortunate than he. He lives in a charming house in the side-streets of Westminster. It is a converted public house and one admires what I believe the twenties called 'chi-chi' as one passes into his dining room through a door of frosted glass which still has the words 'Saloon Bar' inscribed on it. The rooms are decorated in those refined pastel shades which reporters try to describe when at a royal function; and on the wall are a series of Rowlandsons and other eighteenth-century watercolours, the hallmark of safe good taste. 'All working class now.' It is this sort of thing which preserves the popular legend that Conservatives are perfidious hypocrites.

'Political Commentary'

Spectator, 23 September 1955

Those who – like that admirable Cassandra of democracy, Mr Christopher Hollis – claim that Parliament nowadays does very little that is useful, should reflect on what would have happened this week if the House of Commons had been sitting. On Monday either the Prime Minister or the Foreign Secretary would have had to answer a private-notice question about the Maclean–Burgess affair. Their answers would almost certainly have been unsatisfactory, and some Member would have moved the adjournment of the House on a definite matter of urgent public importance. The Speaker would have had no alternative but to accept the motion – clearly the Foreign Office's admission that Maclean and Burgess were Soviet agents is both a 'definite' matter and one of 'urgent public importance', and it would have been raised at the earliest possible moment (another qualification which has to be fulfilled if the adjournment of the House is to be moved). He would then have asked if forty Members were prepared to support the motion for the adjournment, and there can be no doubt that forty members would have risen in their places. Consequently, at 7.30 that evening the House would have interrupted its normal proceedings and debated the remarkable statement which the Foreign Office had made to the press the day before. The result might have been as important as the result of the adjournment debate on the Savidge case in 1929, which led to an inquiry into police powers.

The government has escaped this sort of immediate, searching inquiry, which can be conducted *only* by the House of Commons, and which the House does, in fact, conduct very effectively. It has now all the time that it could ask to prepare its positions. But I do not think that, when Parliament reassembles, it will be allowed to fog the issue. I am not in a position this week – since this column has to be written before the White Paper is published – to comment on the details of the scandal. But one aspect of it seems to me to deserve immediate comment. I have several times suggested that what I call the 'Establishment' in this country is today more powerful than ever before. By the 'Establishment' I do not mean only the centres of official power – though they are certainly part of it – but rather the whole matrix of official and social relations within which power is exercised. The exercise of power in Britain (more specifically, in England) cannot be understood unless it is recognized that it is exercised socially. Anyone who has at any point been close to the exercise of power will know what I mean when I say that the 'Establishment' can be seen at work in the activities of, not only the Prime

Minister, the Archbishop of Canterbury and the Earl Marshal, but of such lesser mortals as the chairman of the Arts Council, the director-general of the BBC, and even the editor of the *Times Literary Supplement*, not to mention divinities like Lady Violet Bonham Carter.

Somewhere near the heart of the pattern of social relationships which so powerfully controls the exercise of power in this country is the Foreign Office. By its traditions and its methods of recruitment the Foreign Office makes it inevitable that the members of the Foreign Service will be men (and the Foreign Service is one of the bastions of masculine English society) who, to use a phrase which has been used a lot in the past few days, 'know all the right people'. At the time of the disappearance of Maclean and Burgess, 'the right people' moved into action. Lady Violet Bonham Carter was the most active and the most open. A study of her activities during the past twenty years would reveal how power in this country can still be exercised by someone who has, politically, been stripped of it. But Lady Violet Bonham Carter was not alone. No one whose job it was to be interested in the Burgess–Maclean affair from the very beginning will forget the subtle but powerful pressures which were brought to bear by those who belonged to the same stratum as the two missing men. From those who were expecting Maclean to dinner on the very night on which he disappeared, to those who just happened to have been charmed by his very remarkable father, the representatives of the 'Establishment' moved in, and how effectively they worked may be traced in the columns of the more respectable newspapers at the time, especially of *The Times* and of the *Observer*.

I heard recently a story which illuminates many of the ways in which the 'Establishment' now works. Mr Maurice Edelman, the Labour Member of Parliament, was asked some time ago by an American magazine to write an article about Princess Margaret which could be published to celebrate her twenty-fifth birthday. (That Labour Members of Parliament should be assumed to know about the royal family seems to me to be an amusing comment on contemporary British society in itself.) Mr Edelman wrote his article, which contained a sentence which was in no way disrespectful but which might be construed as a criticism of Princess Margaret. Then, being Mr Edelman, he submitted his article to the lady-in-waiting of Princess Margaret. The next that he heard about it was when he was called to Mr Attlee's room in the House of Commons. There, in front of Mr Attlee, was the offending article. Mr Attlee told Mr Edelman that he might have expected many other members of the Labour Party to write such an article, but not him, and he requested that it should not be published. Mr Edelman's article has not appeared. Many things are interesting about this story – not least the delightful picture of Mr Attlee in his most headmasterly mood ('I had hoped, Edelman, to make you a prefect, but now, well, you know . . .') – but the more one considers it, the more one realizes that the events which occurred did not depend on any formal relationships, but on subtle social relationships.

That was the 'Establishment' at work.

•

LEO A. LERNER

Leo Alfred Lerner (1907–65) was born in Chicago, Illinois. In the 1950s he wrote his twice-weekly 'First Column' for the *Chicago North Side Newspapers*, of which he was editor-owner. He was also a Wisconsin farmer and a civic leader in Chicago. The columnist and author Carl Sandburg described him thus: '[I am] satisfied Leo Lerner is Diogenes without a lantern and satisfied that Diogenes might have done better with a telephone. Like Diogenes, he asks questions, he wants to know . . . He knows it is good luck and a privilege to write a column and print it in a paper he himself owns. He knows it is a trust and a responsibility he ought never to violate or betray. This isn't easy. So he never hesitates at getting a chuckle or laugh out of the grotesques and monkeyshines of the endless human procession.'

'First Column'
Malice Toward None

From *The Itch of Opinion* (1956)

Oh, I think I know people. Don't tell me about people. They don't all like columns about travel and walks in the woods and life on the farm. Some of them want to know what I'm thinking, and to them thinking is thinking only when it's about politics, about money in the pocket, or about peace and war.

Because people are people, bless their souls, and this column appears only twice a week, sometimes I don't know which set of people to try to please, those who want to read about what the eyes see or those who would read about what the brain thinks.

So I must tell the awful truth here and say that I write only to please myself and express myself and my opinions, and since today is a day on which I have just seen the first stirrings of the new spring in the North country, that is what I am going to write about.

After driving nearly 4,000 miles through the Southland, coming North had the feeling of chasing the spring. From the deep lands of the stately banana and the tousled coconut palm and the scarlet hibiscus, we came through the land of the newer and younger green life – the first needle-like greens of the cypress, the new bright growth on the slash pines, the dark shiny leaves and heavily perfumed magnolia blossoms.

I began to think we were in a kind of pursuit as we came toward Chicago. At any moment I thought we would run out of green and the trees would be bare with winter. But this was not so. There were the new shoots on the peach and apple trees of the middle states, the verdant live oaks with their venerable beards of Spanish moss, the water lilies and the blue hyacinths in the canals and swamps.

One night as the sun was going down we 'discovered' along the Mississippi that the lacy growth in the tops of the willows and maples and red oaks is really pink, a pink for which an artist who painted it would be condemned as unrealistic. He might even be shot at sunrise, twelve hours before he could prove he had been right, since in the dawn's early light his betters could claim that the horizon and the treetops were a merciless orange.

We did not run out of pink, nor out of orange, and especially not out of green. It was a hopeful sign of the season that the green did not fade, so we went on up to the North country, to what seemed to be the source of wonder of the new season, the source of spring.

And here, at the source of spring, I found new wonders, wonders of color and smell and feel and mystery.

Take the mystery of the quaking aspen. In the summer the aspen flies the pure-colored deep green, the perfect-shaped leaf and the traditional tremble of hill and mountain country. But now, at the source of spring, I found the tiny new leaves of the quaking aspen a tan-pink gray stuck together with an invisible mucus, smelling like musk and quaking ever so slightly, as if learning a technique for growing up.

There is mystery in color, in the sun's tricks with the foliage, in the spread of things, as why the wild strawberry grows halfway up a hill in inexplicable patches and why the dark pointed cedars pick foolish spots to grow in. There is wonder in the rich berry color of the apple blossoms before they turn pink and puzzlement in why young oaks have such large leaves and old oaks such small ones.

My eyes and mind were filled with the color of clusters of wild plum, the tight pink buds of the flowering crab, the snowy cherry blossoms, and the now white, now green aspect of the apple.

A mind needs these things. It needs an injection of open space and the green dip of hills and far horizons. It needs to see the proliferation of the shag bark hickory with its pointed golden buds breaking into little bold umbrellas of new leaf. It needs the toleration of seeing the prickly ash throw its first tender leaves that look like peppermint candy. This is like feeling the innocence of a villain when he is asleep; you feel there may be something good about him.

There is a tender tameness about the source of spring. I saw a fat robin hopping in a meadow, and he did not fly away when he saw me.

At the edge of the road there was a cottontail rabbit, the most skittish of the woods animals. He waited until I was very near, and then he did not run, but merely hopped to the nearest exit in the wild raspberry canes.

In nature the old and the broken have their spring, too. An ancient elm, all its trunks bent or mutilated by the winter winds, given up often for dead, was uttering young leaves and slim new branches.

On a new bough stood a brilliant young red-wing blackbird, preening in the soft breeze, showing off its vermilion spots and ocher trim, like an ad for a do-it-yourself paint job. He seemed to be patronizing the tree, as though saying, 'Grandpa and I are friends, and I won't have anybody saying he's through.'

On a country lane, green and turning, shaded by wild plum and willow, there were two birds that from a distance looked like young doves. They took to wing leisurely as we approached, and revealed the fluttering white stripes and soft blue bellies of the jay.

The bees were positively phlegmatic in the orchard. They squatted indifferently on the apple blossoms, full of sweet disposition. A beaver loudly slapping his wet tail startled me at the edge of a swamp and stood there looking at me, seeming to wonder if I belonged in his world.

The radio said that day that a big atomic bomb had been exploded on the Yucca Flats. I wondered which was the real world, the peaceful world of nature or the violent world of man.

We seem to live in two worlds, on a quixotic double standard, but I was grateful that it is sometimes possible to escape from one world into the other and to behold the places where there is no doubt and no violence, only the good Lord's benevolent intentions, malice toward none, charity and beauty for all.

'First Column'
The Filchsnapper Saga *(An Imaginary History)*
From *The Itch of Opinion* (1956)

It was just after the time when the American Legion condemned the Girl Scouts. A congressman from Dreadful Gulch, Filchsnapper by name, moved to abolish Lions International and Rotary International.

He gave a simple reason, and since conditions were becoming simpler and simpler, nobody who had anything to say said anything. His reason was (simply) that any organization that had the word 'international' in its title was subversive.

The Filchsnapper Bill, as it was called, passed by a vote of 435 to 0 in the House, and 96 to 0 in the Senate.

There were several senators who mildly protested in a kind of joking way so that they could say, if challenged, 'I was only kidding the guilt-by-association section of the bill.' This provided (simply) that anybody who had ever had anything to do with a Lion or a Rotarian, any commerce or intercourse, was automatically guilty of favoring internationalism and was subject to a fine of $10,000, not to mention five years in jail.

The day after the Filchsnapper Bill was passed, International Harvester changed its name to National Harvester, and the International League, not being able to change its name to the National League, switched (simply) to the Anti-Communist Baseball Association. The International College of Surgeons discreetly became the Dreadful Gulch Surgical Seminar.

Filchsnapper, a hero of some proportions by then, was besieged with ideas for patriotic legislation. A scientist, anxious to establish his loyalty, proposed that all colors be removed from the rainbow but red, white and blue. Filchsnapper nearly introduced this one when his chief investigator discovered the red in red, white and blue and suggested an investigation instead.

Filchsnapper promptly announced that he was going to find out who was responsible, darkly hinting at treason in high places. A subpoena was issued for a Betsy Ross of Philadelphia, who, it was rumored, would plead the Fifth Amendment, not realizing that it had been abolished.

There had been a rather interesting debate on the Fifth Amendment before it was suspended. Lawyers, representing the criminal element, said they preferred to keep the Fifth Amendment, and Congress, with some sympathy, declared that it was all right as long as it applied only to thieves and murderers, but that it had to go when invoked by political nonconformists.

A political nonconformist was defined as anybody who voted against Herbert Hoover in 1932, hoped that Russia defeated the Nazis on the Eastern Front in 1945, played

Scrabble with more than four-letter words, or had mental reservations when taking the oath of allegiance to Chiang Kai-shek.

This definition took in quite a lot of people, but Filchsnapper, a kindly man of deep patriotic conviction, worked out a legal plan for confession, atonement and rehabilitation of former traitors. The rehabilitation camps buzzed with excitement. People who had formerly read books, listened to Edward R. Murrow, believed in the TVA [Tennessee Valley Authority], subscribed to the *New York Times*, favored medical insurance, or approved of the United Nations came in droves to be purified.

Gerald L. K. Smith, the Commissioner of Rehabilitation, made former Socialists creep for several miles to teach them what creeping Socialism was really like. This was accepted with considerable humility by the repentant.

Words like 'world-wide,' 'international,' 'universal,' and even the prefix 'inter' were seldom used without suspicion. There was quite a to-do when it was realized that Christianity was a foreign idea, developed by a man who had never visited the United States nor spoken in the American language (English having been abolished).

Filchsnapper himself was eventually indicted, charged with being a former Christian and, surprisingly enough, a former member of Lions International and Rotary International. In his defense, he testified that he had seldom put anything in the collection plate at church and that anyway he did not live according to Christian principles even on Sundays. For this latter plea he was able to command a considerable number of witnesses.

This availed him nothing. Under the new law taking away his citizenship for supporting anything foreign or international, he was declared deportable. He pleaded that his progenitors came to North America on the *Mayflower*, so he was deported to England.

The State Department having been abolished because its existence implied commerce with foreign countries, it was not possible to negotiate his deportation. He was (simply) dropped at dawn on the Devon coast by one of the boats in our National Fish Patrol, organized to prevent foreign trout from entering American waters.

An incorrigible patriot, Filchsnapper was quoted in the British press as saying, 'If I had a chance, I would do it all again.'

In the meantime, back at the capital, all isms having been abolished except nationalism and infantilism, there was an Era of Total Security.

There were very few people left at large, but those who were enjoyed (the simple) life, completely free of the moral or intellectual considerations that used to be so baffling in the olden days of freedom.

'First Column'
Step on the Gas
From *The Itch of Opinion* (1956)

There are some people who always know what time it is. A Yale University test says intelligent people always know what time it is within fifteen minutes without a watch.

There was even a candidate for office who once ran on the slogan, 'Vote for the Man Who Knows What Time It Is.'

This meant, of course, that he was up-to-date in his thinking. Needless to say, he lost the election.

Knowing what time it is makes me uneasy. It makes me want to run instead of walk, to act instead of think, to flail instead of consider.

I admire a watch as much as I do a car or a television set, yet I must confess that I don't look at my watch very often for fear of paying too much attention to what time it is.

But you can't avoid knowing what time it is any more. The time follows you. It looms up in big signs on street corners. The minute hand wags its finger at you from barbershops and undertaking parlors. Time for a haircut, time for . . . well, you know what I mean. It's later than we think.

Nevertheless, something inside of me is always fighting against knowing what time it is. To sit on the edge of the guaranteed correct time is like sitting on the edge of a volcano or perching on the bowsprit of a ship in the teeth of a gale.

There are some old things I haven't done yet.

When I was in college I was reading a book by Tolstoy called *War and Peace* when somebody reminded me of the correct time. I put down the book and ran off to the print shop where I was working. I have to finish that book. Will the clock let me?

As a lad of ten, I took zither lessons. I was getting to the point where I might have been the Anton Karas of my day, but I didn't have time to practice. The clock was like a whip. School, delivering papers, homework, baseball in the schoolyard, religious school, errands. It didn't bother me, then, that I didn't learn to play the zither; it bothers me now.

Now the ticking clock tells me I am going further and further away from the days of my childhood. Leaning into the wind of time (a virtue, according to the professors at Yale) is a snare and a delusion. I yearn to go back and pick up some little things I dropped along the way.

I didn't learn to ice skate or to ride a bicycle. My Daisy rifle didn't work, so I returned it to VL&A and got my money back. Never bought another. Today I would look silly with a Daisy air rifle, I suppose, but can I help it, if I wish I could shoot one?

The sunny days of childhood and those lost opportunities are not the only things I yearn for. I yearn also for the later yesterdays. I want to read more Proust and more Thomas Hardy. I want to hear more Mozart and Beethoven. I want to probe Walter Pater and Thomas Aquinas. Like John Keats, I want to look into Chapman's Homer and at the Elgin marbles. Will the clock let me? I don't think so. The clock says there is work to be done. The clock says there is no time.

I was driving South on Michigan Avenue Tuesday when my car was halted by the traffic. In front of me there was a huge electric sign advertising liquor. But that wasn't all. On one side there was a brilliancy that blinked 'Sept. 21,' and on the other side there was another brilliancy that blinked '12:20.'

It is 12:20 on Sept. 21, I said to myself. My initials are on my cuff links, but who am I? Shouldn't a fellow know who he is, before many more blinks of the electric calendar? And where am I going? And who's going with me? The whole blinking human race? The clock changes to 12:21.

12:22. The electric clock ebbs life away, while you sit helplessly and stare at it, caught in the traffic, caught in the intricate machinery of the clock, caught in the big free outdoor insane asylum, where the clocks are faster than you are.

The middle of the sign says, 'Say Seagram's and Be Sure.' Sure of what? The taste of whiskey? The purity of the ingredients and the integrity of the maker? Or the fact that Sept. 21, 12:23 p.m. is pretty late, pretty damn late?

The man behind me is honking his horn. He has seen the clock, no doubt. He thinks he's late. His head is out of his window. 'Hey, slowpoke, move along,' he yells at me.

He's right. The middle of Michigan Avenue is a terrible place to dream.

12:24 said the clock. I stepped on the gas.

•

FLANN O'BRIEN

Brian O'Nolan (1911–66), who wrote novels under the pseudonym of Flann O'Brien, was born in County Tyrone. From 1939 until his death he wrote a daily satirical column called 'The Cruiskeen Lawn' under the name 'Myles na Gopaleen' for the *Irish Times*, a conservative Anglo-Irish newspaper. At first, this appeared in Irish, then in English on alternate days, and later predominantly in English. Myles shared with J. B. Morton (the 'Beachcomber' columnist of the *Daily Express*) an understanding of the essential ludicrousness of the courtroom; he also had a scorn for bores and for the self-righteous wisdom of 'The Plain People of Ireland'. As the years went by, the column became darker in spirit and more fierce in its indignation.

Excerpts from 'The Cruiskeen Lawn'
The Best of Myles; A Selection from Cruiskeen Lawn (1968)

Do not for that singular interval, one moment, think that I have been overlooking this new Intoxicating Liquor Bill. I am arranging to have an amendment tabled because it appears that there is absolutely nothing else you can do with amendment.

My idea is to have the hours altered so that public houses will be permitted to open only between two and five in the morning. This means that if you are a drinking man you'll have to be in earnest about it.

Picture the result. A rustle is heard in the warm dark bedroom that has been lulled for hours with gentle breathing. Two naked feet are tenderly lowered to the floor and a shaky hand starts foraging blindly for matches. Then there is a further sleepy noise as another person half-wakens and rolls round.

'John! What's the matter?'

'Nothing.'

'But where are you going?'

'Out for a pint.'

'But *John*! It's half two.'

'Don't care what time it is.'

'But it's pouring rain. You'll get your death of cold.'

'I tell you I'm going out for a pint. Don't be trying to make a ridiculous scene. All over Dublin thousands of men are getting up just now. I haven't had a drink for twenty-four hours.'

'But John, there are four stouts in the scullery. Beside the oat-meal bag.'

'Don't care what's in the scullery behind the oat-meal bag.'

'O John.'

And then dirty theatrical snivelling sobbing begins as the piqued and perished pint-lover draws dressing-gowns and coats over his shivering body and passes out gingerly to the stairs.

Then the scene in the pub. Visibility is poor because a large quantity of poisonous fog has been let in by somebody and is lying on the air like layers of brawn. Standing at the counter is a row of dishevelled and shivering customers, drawn of face, quaking with the cold. Into their unlaced shoes is draped, concertina-wise, pyjama in all its striped variety. Here and there you can discern the raw wind-whipped shanks of the inveterate night-shirt wearer. And the curate behind the bar has opened his face into so enormous a yawn that the tears can be heard dripping into the pint he is pulling. Not a word is heard, nothing but chilly savage silence. The sullen clock ticks on. Then 'Time, please, time. Time for bed, gentlemen.' And as you well know, by five in the morning, the heavy rain of two-thirty has managed to grow into a roaring downpour.

The Plain People of Ireland: Is all this serious?

Myself: Certainly it's serious, why wouldn't it be serious, you don't think I'd try to make jokes about anything so funny as the licensing laws, why would I bring turf to Newcastlewest?

The Plain People of Ireland: If you're serious so, it's only a trick to get more drink for newspapermen.

Myself: Nonsense. Newspapermen couldn't hold any more than they have at present.

The Plain People of Ireland: O faith now, that's enough. That's enough about that crowd. Remember well, many's a county council meeting, fluther-eyed note-takers couldn't get the half of it, stuff that days was spent thinkin' out.

Myself: Hic!

The Plain People of Ireland: Faith indeed that was loud enough, well you may talk about putting down drink. Putting down is right.

Myself: Ut's only mey undajaschin, d'yeh ondherstawnd.

I can see even another domestic aspect of this new order. It is after midnight. The man of the house is crouched miserably over the dying fire.

'John! Look at the time! Are you not coming to bed?'

'No. I'm waiting for the pubs to open.'

While it is possible for our judges, by mere dint of swotting, to familiarize themselves with positive (or statute) law, there is ample evidence every day even in attenuated newspaper reports, that our jurists are weak in what is called case law. They know little or nothing about the grandiose dicta of decent Irishmen like Palles C. B., Bray J. or Madden J.

In the old days when it was a question of finding what was the meaning of the Malicious Damage Act of 1861, we old circuit men found ourselves in a very tortuous maze of juridical obscurantism. Take Section 17: 'Whosoever shall unlawfully and maliciously set fire to any stack of corn, grain, pulse, tares, hay, straw, haulm, stubble, or of any cultivated vegetable produce, or of furze, gorse, heath, fern, turf, peat, coals, charcoal, wood or bark, or any stack of wood or bark . . . shall be liable . . . to be kept in penal servitude for life . . .' Now in *Rex v. Woodward* it was a question of setting fire to a stack of barley, produce not covered *expliciter* in the section. In the case quoted, the offence was held indictable within the section, the court taking judicial notice that 'barley is corn or grain, and that beans are pulse'. Moreover, 'a stack of the flax-plant with the seed or grain in it, is a stack of grain'. (*Reg. v. McKeever*, IR 5 CL 86; 5 ILTR 41. On the other hand 'rushes and sedge are not straw within 7 Will. 4 & 1 Vict. c. 89; *Reg. v. Baldock*, 2 Cox CC 55.)' Furthermore, 'a quantity of straw if packed or erected on a vehicle which is capable of being moved is not a stack of straw' (*Reg. v. Price*, I.C. & P. 729). Also, a hay-cock has been held not to be a stack of hay, *per* Fitzgerald J.

Under Section 15, which deals with malicious damage to agricultural machinery, an attempt was made to obtain compensation for damage to a plough. Held by Johnson J. that a plough is not a 'machine' or 'engine' within the meaning of the statute, a contrary decision in HM courts notwithstanding. Incidentally, I notice it stated in the textbooks, in relation to the Shops Acts 1912, that 'the waiters who attend upon the resident guests in an hotel are not shop assistants within the Act' (*Gordon Hotels v. London CC*). I concur. They're just waiters.

Twinfeet J., of course, has made many strange pronouncements in the Court of Voluntary Jurisdiction. In an action brought under the Marine Hereditaments (Compensation) Act 1901, a man who lived in an old boat located on a hill sought damages from another man who had been (as alleged) negligent in the management of a dinghy on a trolly (which he was bringing to the railway station) so as to cause the dinghy to collide with the old houseboat. The defence was that the latter structure, being rated to the poor rate, could not be a boat, vessel or ship and that the dinghy, being a land-borne wheeled article, was not a dinghy but a velocipede. Twinfeet J. inquired whether it was suggested that a small paddle-steamer was a farmcart but the defence submitted that inasmuch as a paddle-steamer could not be hauled by a horse, mule, pony, jennet, donkey or ass, it could not be a farmcart within the meaning of the Farmcarts Act and must in fact be a paddle-steamer. The plaintiffs contended that they were the aggrieved parties in a naval collision and entitled to recover damages and compensation from the defendants, who had been negligent in the management of sea-going craft, which was their property and under their care and management. The defendants pleaded alternatively that the 'houseboat' was 'wreckage' within the meaning of the Wreckage Act.

Twinfeet J., in the course of a long judgment, said that he could find nothing in the Act or indeed in any statute regulating matters of admiralty which made water an essential element in a collision between boats; he was satisfied that the owners of the dinghy had been negligent in the navigation of the dinghy *Marcella* at the junction of

Market Street and Dawson Hill. He assessed damages at £4 and excused the jury from
service for a year on the ground that they had been at sea for four days.

———————

I cannot stand or understand the sort of typographical shouting that goes on in that
hierofrantic sheet, my income tax form, and it would not surprise me in the least to
learn that yours is the same. This sort of thing: 'If you are a MARRIED MAN and your
wife is living with you . . .' I think it is very bad taste using those heavy black caps, as
the convict said to the trial judges (*pace* Hanna J. and this thoughtful letter to Ireland's
premier finest most tunisian-minded newspaper, the *Irish Times*, all uncover, please). 'If
you are a MARRIED MAN.' Undoubtedly there is some dreadful sneer intended here,
some recondite official indecency that could be understood only in the underworld of
please attach file, have your papers please, please speak, can you discharge file please, I
am directed to say that the matter is under consideration.

'If you are a MARRIED MAN and your wife is living with you.' These hidden baroque-rats
have the cool cheek (warm cheek for some reason is considered rare) to suggest that it
is the exceptional thing in Ireland for a married man to have his wife living with him.
One expects the formula to go on like this: 'If, however, you are a MARRIED MAN and
have your wife parked out in Shankill so that you will not be embarrassed by her
fearful appearance, ludicrous "conversation" and appalling clothes, give her address and
telephone number.' Yes. But read the thing again. 'If you are a MARRIED MAN and your
wife is living with you . . .' Supposing your wife is living with and you are not a married
man (or even a MARRIED MAN), what then? What subtle poor oak rat's distinction is
being made here?

If I understand English, a wife is what a woman becomes after she is married and
no account of equivocal chat can convince me that anybody other than a married man
can have a wife. (I am assuming all the time that cab-horses, cows and cats are not
regarded as being in receipt of (mark that lovely phrase, 'in receipt of') a taxable income.
Why then the 'if you are a MARRIED MAN' when the word 'wife' follows on at once?
Why not say 'If you have a wife living with you . . .'? It would be too simple, I suppose.
Incidentally, what is the legal meaning of 'living'? Supposing I am a MARRIED MAN and
my wife is dying with me? Yes, I see it. The cold official brain thinks of everything.
They must insist on this word 'living'. Leave it out, they will say, or even change it to
'If you are living with your wife' and you will have all sorts of unprincipled persons
claiming relief in respect of a wife who is (sure enough) sitting in the drawing room,
very well preserved woman considering she died in 1924. Can you beat that for ghoulish
circumspection? (It just occurs to me that there must have been a lot of official jargon
in our jails in the ould days, have your file please, please attach file, is file with you
please. Why this eternal tender supplication 'please'?)

On the next page of the form I see CLAIM IN RESPECT OF PERSONAL ALLOWANCE
TO A MARRIED MAN, 'HOUSEKEEPER', CHILDREN, DEPENDENT RELATIVES, AND LIFE
ASSURANCE PREMIUMS. Why this sneering sophistication of putting my housekeeper into
inverted commas? The woman has a blameless character and makes that indigenous
culinary complication, an Irish stew, that you would get up out off yoor bad en tha
maddle off tha neight fur tay eet a wee bet off ut, d'yeh ondherstond me. Is a dependent

relative what happens when you are unwise enough to say: I seen you with the man that you were speaking to whom? And why cannot I get relief in respect of dependent absolutes? The wife's mother, for instance?

I will not harrow you with the dreadful mess that this form assumes you to be in 'if you are an UNMARRIED PERSON'. Earlier it was a question of a MARRIED MAN; if you happen to be unmarried, you are only a PERSON, which I consider insulting and sinister. Furthermore, I see no provision for the situation where you are a MARRIED WOMAN and (decently enough) support your husband. Listen to this: 'If you are an UNMARRIED PERSON having living with you . . . your mother.' What gaucherie! Unmarried persons in Ireland do not have their mothers living with them, they live with their mothers.

Small wonder faith that nobody likes this wretched form. Small wonder every bank, insurance office and big business firm in the country is tearing down and building up its walls rather than pay. Please speak. Bah!

Two attitudes are admissible in relation to roads: one, that there are not enough roads in this country and that more should be provided; two, that all existing roads should be ploughed up and wheat sown.

In relation to proposal No. 1, competent engineers have informed me that new roads could be most economically provided side by side with existing roads; this for the reason that road-making machinery can be readily and cheaply transported and operated on the existing roads. It must be borne in mind, however, that once a duplicate road has been constructed beside an existing road, the second road can itself be used as the 'base' for the construction of a third road; thus there is no considerable engineering difficulty in constructing an indefinite number of new roads provided they are located parallel and together. Hollows in the terrain can, of course be filled in with cement and eminences removed by mechanical excavators. It must be added, however – and I have the authority of an agricultural expert for saying this – that the construction of a large number of new roads in the manner suggested would tend to diminish tillage activities. Generally speaking, then, the proposal is feasible but open to objection by sectional interests.

Very well. Now as to proposal number two. The cultivation of wheat on roadways is not, I am advised, impossible; it would be, however, difficult and a successful crop could not be expected save at the cost of great skill and diligence in husbandry. Roadways of some centuries standing could not, of course, be dug or ploughed in the ordinary way. Excavation, whether by mechanical means or with pick and shovel, would be necessary. Arable soil would scarcely be reached at a lesser depth than three feet and thus a considerable quantity of material would have to be excavated to secure an arable trench of even moderate width. The disposal of this material presents a problem. Assuming that a stretch of roadway fifty miles long is to be prepared for wheat, it would be necessary to remove the material by motor lorry, starting from the remote extremity; this for the reason that since the roadway is disappearing, traffic must be confined to the portion still intact at any moment. Fleets of fast horse carts could, of course, be used for less ambitious undertakings but mechanical transport is essential for long hauls.

There is, however, another alternative. The excavated material could be stacked on the roadside at both sides of the trench. It is true that this plan would curtail the area available for cultivation to a strip two or three feet in width, but this cannot be avoided without permitting the excavated material to *encroach upon the adjoining fields*, thus diminishing what is called the agricultural potential. Since this is (for obvious reasons) to be avoided at all costs, it is possible that on a very narrow road, where abnormally deep excavation would be called for, the excavated material would have to be erected in the nature of a wall on each side of the trench, and the trench would only be of diminutive lateral dimension – possibly as little as six inches. These crude rubble walls would, of course, obstruct sunlight and even rain, and to that extent growth in the trench-bed would be retarded. Moreover, where excavation had to be brought in such a trench to a depth of four or five feet, the side-walls would be a corresponding height above ground level, so that the wheat, even if it attained normal height, would be about three feet below the level of the walls. In a trench six inches wide it would be impossible to save such wheat unless special machinery could be devised for the purpose. Whether such machinery could be devised and economically manufactured and marketed would depend on the number of very narrow wheat trenches in the country having high side-walls.

All these considerations must be weighed by every thoughtful Irishman.

•

JOSEPH CHASE ALLEN

Joseph Chase Allen (1892–1981) was born in Martha's Vineyard, Massachusetts, the son of a fisherman. He attended school in Vineyard Haven, then was absent for seventeen years, serving in the army, working for a shoe company in New Bedford, then as a trolley-car motorman, and in a toy factory. He contributed a poem anonymously to the *New Bedford Standard* and when it was published he identified himself and was invited to write for the paper on a regular basis. In 1925 he joined the *Vineyard Gazette* as a reporter and advertising solicitor, and before long he had added staff poet and columnist to his duties. As 'The Wheelhouse Loafer', he wrote a weekly longshore log called 'With the Fishermen', which took the form of a poem followed by a fisherman's tale, for over fifty-five years. He was also 'Oracle' of *Yankee* magazine for thirty years.

Those Navy-trained Ducks
Vineyard Gazette, May 1950

Commenting on the uselessness
    Of gilt and idle show,
The words come back to memory
    Of Cap'n Dan'l Snow.

Who spoke about the pollock
    With his blue and silver hide,

But not too hot a morsel
  When you tackle him inside.

And Cap'n Snow, he used to say:
  'There's people just like that.
They look like ready money,
  But their hearts are bone and fat.

Of small account as citizens,
  As sailormen or cooks,
In spite of all their furbelows
  And all their handsome looks!'

Then somebody would always say,
  'But Cap'n, you'll agree
That pollock, dried and salted,
  Is a banquet from the sea!

'Tis white, 'tis clean, 'tis tasty,
  And 'tis nourishing as well.
A man could be contented
  With salt pollock for a spell.'

And then old Snow would chuckle:
  'Yes, indeed, my lad, you're right!
Maybe these human critters
  Should be salted down a mite.

'Because the fault of both of 'em,
  The fish and human flesh –
Is simply that the critters are
  Too everlasting fresh!'

So maybe that's the remedy
  For troubles here below.
It ties with the philosophy
  Of Cap'n Daniel Snow!

According to long-established custom, we sailed, as we always do, to gam with our constituents and perform certain acts of mercy, as has become a tradition. The wind, which had boxed the compass for days, had settled in the sou'west, and it was just about heavy enough to lift a bandanna handkerchief. The sun poured down red hot and it really seemed as if winter had gone to looward.

From long habit, and in accordance with certain instincts of ours, we swayed up the mains'l and started the old mill to rolling, and so, carrying a medium bone in our teeth, we stood out of the harbor.

The day previous hadn't been fit for the devil to be abroad, and that's the solemn truth. It had been cold, with a sharp wind, a running sea, and rain, the latter not merely falling, no, we would say it dropped with all the shock and devastating effect of a bursting levee or tidal wave. But this – it was just like a summer morning!

The laughing gulls fished in the tide, chuckling to each other. Occasional loons sculled about, submerging now and then just for fun, and then coming up to look about and rejoice with the rest of nature. The shags, miserable critters that they are, decorated every spile in the West Chop dock, with shoulders hunched and their cussed pterodactyl beaks cockbilled in all directions, and saying absolutely nothing. A shag never shows any interest in his own kind or anything else, in public.

The rip on Middle Ground Shoal lay like a layer of pale green sherbet in the midst of darker water, shot through with light streaks of foam and twisting, twisting its way westerly to disappear in the distance, all the time singing its song, which was old when Old Cap'n Gosnold showed up here centuries ago.

Out on the skyline we could see the procession of draggers, moving in and out, with a few hove-to, lifting their nets. It was grand.

We hated to swing off the course; life was altogether too wonderful to go looking for misery, but off to larboard lay the green-painted marine monstrosity that Deuty Jones calls a dragger, nodding to her mooring like an old horse asleep at a hitching post. And we knew from long and lurid experience that death and disaster might well await aboard that floating coffin.

Deuty used to be a deckhand in a sawmill in the valley of the broad Missouri, and he finds ways and means of getting into trouble such as no man ever found before. It has been our weekly chore for years to haul his helpless carcass from the dripping jaws of catastrophe, and there are narrow-minded people who would criticize us if we failed to slack our sheets and go to his assistance.

The sight that met our astonished gaze as we shot up under his lee quarter, was unnerving to say the least. Deuty lost a leg off at the knee, the larboard one, years ago before we ever knew him. We have always mistrusted that it happened while he was freighting a deckload of red liquor, and that he slid under the saw or something of the kind. In consequence of which he carries a jury leg to port, and he was jumping and hopping and squirming about the deck, trying to ram his arms down the back of his neck and all the while letting go with war whoops that sounded like the long pig celebration of the Fijis.

We could continue to describe in detail the passage that followed; how we had to actually run the critter down, heave him flat and sit on his head to hold him still while we tried to discover his trouble and do something about it. But we will simply explain that the coot had set a trap to catch mice which had boarded him, and he had filled a wire trap full. Then he had sat down on a trawl tub and opened the trap, figuring that his cats – he has five – would grab the mice and finish the job.

The darned fool didn't have sense enough to realize that the mice could see the cats, and that they wouldn't co-operate at all in his scheme. No, instead, they came out of the trap and headed right into Deuty's pockets, down his neck and up his sleeves stowing away all over the critter!

We darned nigh wrecked the critter saving his life, and we still think that the heft of the mice got back into the fo'castle all safe. We then proceeded, as they say in the navy, wondering what the Lord could have been thinking of when he constructed this cussed human radish.

We made Menemsha Creek, with the tide bubbling out and running like the mill-tail of Sheol. But it was smooth and pleasant for all that and we swung like a button on a hen-house door to make the Dutcher Dock where Cap'n Herb Flanders hailed us from the caplog. Herb deals in the necessities of life in this spot, such as gasoline and chocolate bars and bass jigs and ice cream, and darned few craft run in and out of Menemsha Creek without stopping to take on something from Herb. A couple of bass rods leaned against the building, and a couple of pilgrims leaned also, having been fishing all night probably, which is one of the characteristics of striped bass addicts.

Cap'n Ernest Mayhew, who holds forth farther up the channel, was lacing in lobster-pot funnels and singing 'Sweet Adeline.' A two-foot winter gull sat on a dock spile alongside, and every time Ernest passed him the critter would try to gnaw a chunk out of his jumper. 'Begging for a hand-out,' explained Ernest. 'He will eat salt herring faster than I can haul 'em off the stick, and I haven't yet found out how many he can carry. Last time I tried, he gobbled fourteen and I quit.'

Cap'n Chet Stearns, who runs the local lobster palace and owns the only tame swordfish north of Hatteras, was fitting out for the season, and mighty busy. Chet has to clear his gangways, paint and red-lead, and polish his brightwork and rig his galley, and in between times he has to tend his swordfish which comes up in his private swordfish pool and begs for attention.

So Chet would reeve off the peak halliards on one of his venetian blinds, for example, and then Gus, the fish, would slap his tail and Chet would have to go and give him a herring, or swat a fly that had lit on his back fin where the critter couldn't reach it! We have advised Chet ten thousand times to beach the darned fish and carve him into cutlets.

Bill Seward, who runs the seagoing grocery, was practically rigged for the season. Bill had his gangway rigged and was pipe-claying the man-ropes. Aft of him we could see the lockers filled with cabin stores, and the harness-casks with their hoops polished as bright as gold. Bill is soaked chock to his tonsils with the lore of blue water, and he has tried all ways to rig a poop deck in his grocery, but it doesn't work. Short of that, however, he runs her man-of-war style and we honestly believe that if anyone should spit on his deck Bill would have him chipping paint for a week!

We shoved off, running down wind for the Bass Creek Meeting House, which is a shipyard, believe it or not, on the edge of an estuary where the ducks swim in navy formation and quack in the Continental Code. There are people who don't believe this, but the ducks are there for all hands to behold at any time.

It is here that Cap'n Erford Burt builds flaming frigates which he models after the ducks – which leave no wake at all when they travel – and here, on this day and date, he and Cap'n Link Thurber were having a launching.

It was funny. There slid the boat down the ways into the basin. Not a new craft, but a refitted one. Out of the creek swam the ducks, with the drake in the lead, his tail cocked just so and quacking out orders. They swam into the basin and formed up in line-abreast, at the dead-slow signal, and waited for the boat to take the water. 'They think it's another duck,' opined Link, but we don't know. It is impossible to determine whether they are applauding or making fun when they sound off, and sometimes we wonder if the Russians or the Democrats or both have influenced the fowl.

We dropped our peak at the yards of the Colby Corvette, Concrete, Coal Barge and Corncrib Company and things were being done. Cap'n Albert Allen straightened up from a job and lit his pipe, which promptly went out. 'Man and boy,' he said, 'I have hewn keels, shaped covering-boards and scribed gar-boards from Belfast to Bombay, but never before have I known a shipbuilder to be asked to bear a hand at so many different jobs!'

We peaked our eyebrows in unspoken inquiry, and Albert continued: 'I thought that we had hit the limit some time ago when we built brigs, dredged the harbors to lay 'em in, constructed the breakwaters, moles, and moorings for 'em, and even, by Godfrey, crated up cussed elephants to load 'em with! But no, that's not the end by a long dart! No, now comes Bill, who says that natural granite rock is getting too expensive, and besides, the people who break it up don't use good judgement in the breaking. So, says he, we will henceforth make our own, ye gods, and make it in assorted sizes and weights! And I – I, by Judas – am elected to build the forms!'

Cap'n Joe Andrews, ballast specialist, who talks just like the OPA [Office of Price Administration] agents used to, hauled his 200-pound carcass out of the bilges of a brig, squirming through a hatchway about six inches square. No one else can do it!

'I have told Albert ten thousand times that we would eventually come to this,' says he. 'It stands to reason that it had to be done. There was once a time when a pile of rocks or earth might be expected to stand indefinitely. But today, with earth tremors and other forces quickening and increasing the vibrations, there must be pattern and design in stowing ballast of any variety. I am working now on the idea of a dovetail pattern of ballast rock, which will lock together into a solid wall. I doubt if explosives would stir it.'

Bunk, the water-line artist, was not impressed. He stood at the bench, heaving the kinks out of a coil of red boot-topping that had somehow fouled. 'Dovetails, fantails, wholesales or retails, 'tis all the same to me,' says Bunk. 'They build something to go overboard – dory, dolphin or drydock, and they say, "Put a waterline on her!" just like that. So I put her on, true as a tail-shaft, quarters to cutwater, and what do they do? Shove her overboard and load her down until nobody ever sees my work at all! Blow me down, I might as well use a hose and a straw broom!'

We gammed Cap'n Bill Colby in the after cabin. Bill was talking over fifteen telephones and pushing a battery of buttons. He knocked off and snapped the lock of his cigar box when we came over the gangway. Bill is as close-hauled as the devil with his cigars, anyhow.

'What's this business about manufacturing rocks?' says we. 'Albert is spilling his wind. You ought to relieve his mind.'

'There is really nothing to it,' says Bill, speaking in his best high-school-principal manner. 'Science, which is to say, our own laboratories, has long since isolated the component parts and elements of which the natural rock formation is composed. Why go to the trouble and expense of mining when we can simply heave these elements together, mix them up, and produce a cut stone, even a polished one, if we require it?'

We went over the gangway in a dizzy frame of mind. We feel that we know what all this is leading up to. For years Bill has maintained that he could produce a separate and independent planet if anyone should want it. We figure that the day has arrived.

We came to the wind with a soft flutter of canvas off the shop of Orin Norton, the village blacksmith of Edgartown. All was calm and pleasant, but it did look odd and uncertain to see his spreading chestnut tree hung full of squash blossoms. Orin claims that no man can blacksmith successfully without a spreading chestnut tree, but he raises every cussed thing but chestnuts on his! Yes, anything from orange blossoms to kedge anchors, ye gods!

Orin was blacksmithing something that looked suspiciously like armament. Not too heavy, but deadly in appearance. It isn't always that he will let us in on what he is up to, but he loosened a mite when we inquired.

'Yes,' says he, 'there is too cussed much talk of strife in the air and I aim to be prepared for the worst. This is a rocket gun, capable of wiping out half an army if it gets within a couple of miles' distance. Two men can handle it easy, and one could do darned good execution if he had to. What do you think of her?'

Well, we had already decided that we didn't want anything to do with the business end of the thing; for the rest, we wouldn't know. Orin was welding on handles and trunions and pivots and gadgets, and was still at it when we left. It looked and sounded bad, but after thinking it all over, be cussed and be blowed if we were at all certain that he took us wholly into his confidence. Because it could as well as not be a patent apple-picker!

Manuel, the old sculpin, was in his shipyard, laying down a new brig, a slim and fast-looking craft, for use in the short seas of the quahaug beds and the like. Manuel was in fine form, working his plane on a plank and taking off seven-foot shavings with a full turn to every inch, which is no mean achievement. As always when the atmosphere of the yard is favorable, he began to spin us a yarn, this one about the tar and feathering of Parson Samuel Burgess, which happened back in 1700 or so when Manuel was a boy, or, anyhow, very young. Well he got to going in good shape when Cap'n George Golart came over the gangway, and wanted to know if Manuel couldn't remember the details of the burial of Cap'n Darius Coffin.

It was always claimed that he was headed up in a cask of rum and that the bearers bored a hole in the cask and drained it off before performing the final, sad rites. We got some of the details about both incidents, but not the complete history of either. Some pilgrim once called Manuel a walking encyclopedia, and Manuel hove a jack-plane at him with such good aim that it took his scalp-lock off chock down to the hide. 'You're a cockeyed liar,' says Manuel, 'I never walked or rode one of the cussed things.'

All the same, he knows the entire anatomy of more than a hundred family skeletons, and he is apt as not to drag out fragments for dissection at any time. We have always claimed that if he charged admission to these discourses, he would be a wealthy man, but he won't. 'Hell's bells,' says he, 'a man has to do something free to draw trade.' We suppose he is right at that.

Pursuant to our time-honored custom, we pulled the dory across Muskeget Channel from our Skiff's Island office, and landed on the edge of the Pocha marsh, bound for the Chappaquiddick ferry landing after our weekly mail. The hour was eight bells, midnight, which is the time we usually choose, when the panthers have all fed and are quiet, and the Scourge of Chappaquiddick is at a disadvantage.

We refer to Whistelpitcher, that fiend in human form, who has made life a burden to everyone and everything on Chappaquiddick Island for lo, these many years.

The crazy critter stood in the shadows of a pine thicket, alongside of what appeared to be an oil drum, and holding a bag in his hand. 'This is the appointed hour, Loafer!' says he. 'I have perfected my atom bomb and you will come to the wind right here and back your blasted tops'ls, or I'll drop her into this drum and wipe you off the map!'

He chuckled and wove about in the darkness as he spoke, and we knew that he was certain that he had us lee-bowed. For years he has resented our efforts to enlighten the world through the *Gazette* columns and has tried in all sorts of underhanded ways to scuttle us.

'Let her go!' says we, 'a man can't die younger, and besides you will go up or go out along with us and that will be a darned good thing!'

'Good guard!' says Whistelpitcher. 'I never thought of that! Just forget the whole thing, will you, Loafer, I was only fooling, anyway.'

'Fair enough,' says we, 'but what are you going to do with the bomb? If you bury it, a rabbit is liable to dig it up and explode it, and if you heave it overboard a net is liable to pick it up. It looks to us as if you've just got to hang on to it from now on in order to avoid disaster!'

•

LEON GELLERT

Leon Gellert (1892–1977) was born in Walkerville, South Australia, and was a schoolteacher before the First World War. He was wounded at Gallipoli, and after the war taught in Sydney and published poetry. He was a columnist and book reviewer for the *Sydney Morning Herald*, and he later wrote a column for the *Daily Telegraph*.

Money! Money! Money!
From *Week After Week* (1953)

I have to report a domestic upheaval of a magnitude so unprecedented as to threaten the very foundations of our modest household. The whole trouble, which began on a Saturday morning, arose over a question of money.

I was sitting on the roof attending to a few leakages, as is my habit after every immoderate shower of rain, when the postman's whistle below announced the arrival of the day's mail. Two seconds later I saw A Certain Party returning from the letter-box with a solitary envelope in her hand.

'That will be from the Water and Sewerage Board in answer to my sharp rebuke about their last account,' I called out.

She made no reply but hurried into the house. In my haste to join her I somehow missed my footing and fell backwards off the roof in the customary manner.

'Do you know what we ought to do?' she said brightly, as I limped inside, dabbing at the wound in my head with a bloodstained handkerchief. 'We ought to take a ticket in the lottery.'

'Six thousand pounds wouldn't go far these days,' I said. 'And for that matter neither would 12,000 or even 30,000. Major prizes in the State lottery are hardly worth collecting.'

'I'm not talking about little local gambles, I'm talking about the really big stuff,' she said, flourishing a letter.

'Poppy Squeamish writes to tell me that a man up her way won £50,000 in some consultation outside the State.'

'Far too much money for one person,' I said. 'A sum like that needs very astute handling. A false step might lead to disaster. What on earth could you possibly do with £50,000 at your time of life?'

'Well, firstly,' she said, starting to count on her fingers, 'I'd settle up with all the tradesmen – they've been very patient during the last years. After that I'd pay off the remaining instalments on the coffee percolator, the vacuum cleaner, the floor polisher and the lawn-mower. And Mr Pocock, the bank manager, who has been an absolute dear, surely deserves . . .'

I winced at the name.

'Let us,' I said, holding up a finger, 'put aside, for the moment, superficial matters of ordinary routine and get down to the real substance. Self-interest should not be allowed to take charge of the situation altogether. It should be remembered that there are those, near and dear to you, who perhaps might be grateful for some share, however small, in your good fortune.'

'To begin with,' she said dreamily, 'I should like to do something for Miss Pittance's veins. She can hardly walk, poor thing, and six months or so in a rest-home would make a new woman of her. Then I would have a shot at curing Mrs Jargon's chronic rheumatism. I'd pack her off to some dry place like –'

'Like Bourke?' I said. 'You might as well go the whole hog.'

'No,' she said. 'I was thinking rather of Arizona.'

'Have you gone stark staring mad?' I said. 'Do you realize what Mrs Jargon's little trip is going to set you back – and in dollars, too, if you can get them?'

'I reckon on about twenty grand,' she said, 'but what of it!'

'Go on,' I said. 'Go on. But remember you've only got 50,000 to play with!'

'Then,' she continued, 'I would set Agatha Worms up in a small frock shop at the Cross. She's always been at a loose end, poor child, and a position with responsibility might go a long way towards pulling her together. I should be able to pick up quite a bargain for about £5,000.'

'Things have come to a pretty pass,' I said heatedly, 'when, with funds already getting dangerously low, you flagrantly squander £5,000 on a parasitic ne'er-do-well like Agatha Worms. Why, the woman will be bankrupt inside six weeks! *You'll* be bankrupt! We'll *all* be bankrupt! I've never heard of such a wicked misuse of money. But don't mind me! Tip it into the gutter. Throw it down the drain!'

'After that,' A Certain Party went on, entirely ignoring my protests, 'I intend buying a nice little seaside cottage for old Mr and Mrs Hellish. With furnishings it shouldn't run me into more than £6,000 at the outside, but I'd be willing to go as far as £10,000. The dear old things have always been extraordinarily good to me.'

This was indeed the last straw. And I think that my loss of control was excusable in the circumstances.

'Look!' I shouted, rising to my feet. 'If you permit so much as a penny's worth to pass into the possession of the Hellish couple, I'm through! Do you hear? I check out! Why, Humphrey Hellish did his best to have me blackballed at the Burran Avenue Rheumatic Society! And as for his wife, she's nothing but a venomous old spider!'

'I shouldn't have to remind you,' A Certain Party said calmly, 'that, after all, it is my money I'm spending, not yours. You seem to forget that it was you who advised an attitude of benevolence in the first place.'

'That may be so,' I almost hissed at her, 'but there is a difference between benevolence and sheer insanity. Surely you don't expect me to stand mutely by while you dissipate £50,000 on a bunch of wastrels!'

Having said my say, I strode angrily to the door. But before I reached it she called me back.

'Instead of ranting and raving like a crack-brained Bedlamite,' she said, 'perhaps you could calm yourself and be good enough to tell me what *you* would do with £50,000 if *you* won it.'

'The answer to that is quite simple,' I replied. 'I would let it be known to all and sundry that I intended disposing of a certain sum to certain deserving cases. But at the same time I would make it clear that no consideration would be given to anybody who solicited me for any portion of it. Such a precaution keeps beggars at bay and yet preserves in them a proper attitude of hopeful reverence.'

'What a dirty trick!' she said. 'You ought to be ashamed of yourself! But tell me about your actual benefactions.'

'When it comes to honest charity,' I said, 'I don't think I could do better than lend a helping hand to my dear friend Martin Slime. Say a cheque for £500.'

'What!' she shrieked. 'Two hundred pounds for that disgusting old Casanova!'

'I said £500,' I corrected.

'But you owe him 300 already,' she said. 'So you're not being overwhelmingly generous. Nevertheless, I want to say this: if you give him a farthing more than is owing to him, I pack up and leave the house. Of all the repulsive types!'

'Martin's not such a bad old stick,' I pleaded. 'And he's done me many a good turn in his time. I admit he's made many a pass at a petticoat in days gone by, but he's settled down now.'

'Yes, and I could tell you a few truths about him if I cared to unseal these lips,' she said witheringly. 'That man holds nothing sacred. I could never understand what you saw in him. If Martin Slime gets a skerrick more than his due, I'm off, and that's final!'

She stamped out of the room in high fury and we didn't speak to each other for the rest of the day.

Just before midnight I popped my head into her room. She was reading in bed.

'Will you listen to a proposition?' I said.

'What is it?' she snapped.

'If I decide to chop Martin Slime down to a hundred pounds will you agree to cutting out the Hellishes?'

'Nothing doing!' she barked and went on with her reading.

'Well, would you consider reviewing the case of Agatha Worms?' I begged.

But she wouldn't listen. By noon on Sunday the situation had worsened to an alarming degree. It looked very much like the end.

At supper time I determined to bring matters to a head.

'It looks,' I said, breaking the ice with a cough, 'as though we are fast arriving at a crisis in our lives. I think that, before it is too late, we should make every effort to come to terms. I have yet another suggestion to make.'

'Go ahead,' she said haughtily.

'Would it not be possible,' I said very quietly, 'for both of us to abstain from taking any tickets in any £50,000 lottery. It seems this is the only course by which we can hope to escape catastrophe. The risks are too great.'

'Then, why the devil didn't you say so before!' she exclaimed. 'It's all okay by me. I'm willing to keep out if you are. But mind, no sneaky business! You know the sort of furtive tricks you get up to. I don't know if I ought to trust you.'

'Honour bright,' I said.

And so the situation was saved.

But it was a narrow squeak.

•

PETER FLEMING

Peter Fleming (1907–71), the brother of James Bond creator Ian Fleming, was educated at Eton and Christ Church, Oxford, where he was awarded a First in English. In 1931 he joined the *Spectator* as assistant literary editor and soon afterwards he began undertaking special foreign assignments for *The Times*. From 1936 until the outbreak of the Second World War, Fleming was on the staff of *The Times* and covered the Sino-Japanese War for the paper. During the Second World War he served in the Grenadier Guards, achieving the rank of full colonel and receiving an OBE. Throughout the 1950s and 1960s he wrote 'Fourth Leaders' for *The Times* as well as a column for the *Spectator*. Always signed 'Strix', its character was flexible: sometimes it was a notebook column, sometimes an essay column; sometimes it appeared in the middle of the magazine, sometimes as an endpaper.

The Man We Killed

From *Goodbye to the Bombay Bowler* (1961)

One of us is a Cabinet Minister. One of us died of drink last month. One is an earl. One committed suicide many years ago. One, I think, is an expert on Russia. One is an admiral. Some I have forgotten altogether. Several others must be dead.

The man we killed was called Mr Jackson. He was a master at our private school towards the end of the First War. I do not remember him as clearly as I should; one reason for this is that he did not last long.

I suppose he was about twenty-five. He had reddish hair which stood up over his forehead in a quiff. He wore spectacles with metal rims and a blazer with a crest on the breast pocket. He was very short-sighted and we believed him to make matters worse by not cleaning his spectacles. He had a plaintive, rather common voice and a lolloping gait. He took the Sixth Form in (I think) Greek; I am ashamed that I cannot remember his subject with certainty.

Mr Jackson was, I suppose, fairly typical of the sort of material with which headmasters have to make up their staffs in the closing stages of a major war. All I can recall about his previous career is that it had taken him to Singapore, where, he told us, the natives played football in bare feet. He had served as a special constable during disturbances in the city, and was easily encouraged to relate his memories of those stirring times. They were not sensational; once Mr Jackson had been on duty all night and it had rained without stopping.

It would be interesting to know how many hours or days or weeks in the school year are lost to learning by boys inducing masters to embark on martial or other reminiscences. In my time at Eton there was a French master – and he really *looked* like a French master – called M. Larsonnier, who had served with the French contingent which helped to sack Peking after the Boxer Rebellion. If you could only get him started, he had a splendid set-piece. 'Who was ze first into ze Forbidden City? It was I! Who was ze first into ze Winter Palace? It was I! Who was ze first into ze Empress Dowager's bedroom? It was I!' 'And who' (we would wittily chime in) 'was ze first into ze Empress Dowager's *bed*?' I imagine that less time is wasted in this way at girls' schools.

Mr Jackson never had a chance. It was not merely that he had no authority and was easily gulled; schoolmasters of this more or less helpless kind generally arouse in their tormentors a sort of mercy or tolerance, based perhaps on the feeling that if they are handled too barbarously they will be replaced by some sterner fellow and there will be no more cakes and ale.

But for some reason we actively disliked Mr Jackson, who had a cocksure manner and a grating personality, and we gave him the full treatment. Our school was near the coast, and soon after he arrived, Mr Jackson, jaded no doubt by the enervating climate of the tropics, was heard to speak in appreciative terms of the sea-breezes which stole into his bedroom. We took the first opportunity of wedging a bloater under the springs of his mattress.

'Good morning, sir. Lovely fresh breeze this morning, isn't there? You'd never think we were a mile from the sea, would you, sir?'

Mr Jackson would concur in a baffled way.

At length masters with adjacent bedrooms were impelled to investigate, and the putrescent bloater was removed.

'Good morning, sir. Did you see that perfectly beastly case in the paper, sir? No, sir, not *that* one; after all, there's nothing specially *unpatriotic* about murder. We meant the case where a man was fined for hoarding food. I do think that sort of thing is absolutely *rotten* when there's a war on, don't you, sir? Apparently he used to hide it in his bedroom . . .'

And so on. Our worst excesses are lost in oblivion, but my recollection is that we kept up a relentless pressure and that Mr Jackson ceased to be cocksure and became jumpy, irritable and maladjusted.

In the only incident I remember clearly, indeed vividly, I played the leading part. Mr Jackson was the sort of master who impels boys, once they have established an ascendancy over him, to see how much further they can go, and one day I decided to take a grass-snake into his class.

We wore, in the summer, grey sweaters and grey flannel shorts. I put the grass-snake, which was about three feet long but used to being handled, in my pocket and kept my hand over it as a precaution. It had had a feed a few days before and at first observed a perfect decorum.

After a bit I became over-confident and relaxed my vigilance. The snake got its head up my sleeve and began to climb up my arm. Readers who have been in this particular situation will know that, once a serpent has started climbing up your arm under your sleeve, it matters little how much of the serpent is left in your pocket; you cannot get it back into the pocket by using the arm it is climbing up, and you cannot bring your other hand into play against it without taking your sweater off, which – leaving snakes and schoolmasters out of it – I defy anyone to do with one hand in his pocket.

Being at the top of the class, I sat directly underneath Mr Jackson's beaky nose. I was in a quandary. Seventy-five per cent of the snake had not yet passed the start-line and was still in my pocket. I decided to try to stabilize this situation and gripped it convulsively round what, if it had been me, would have corresponded to its chest.

The snake cannot be blamed for failing to understand my motives. It felt thwarted, and began to hiss. Human beings, when they hiss, hiss outwards; a grass-snake makes a sound exactly like a human being drawing his breath sharply inwards while the stitches are being taken out of a wound.

'Strix,' asked Mr Jackson, peering down at me, 'are you in pain?'

'No, sir,' I said. I thought it prudent to let go of the snake. It stopped hissing but went on climbing.

My urgent duty now was to prevent it doing what, if left to itself, it would do, which was to make a bid for freedom by wriggling out through the collar of my sweater. By this time, the snake's rear echelon having left my pocket, I had both hands free and was easily able, by clasping them to my throat in a rather precious manner, to deny it egress. The snake turned south, towards my midriff.

It now had room to manoeuvre and was moving well; there was nothing to do but to grab it before it escaped from my sweater. I clasped one hand to my stomach and got it round the neck. It started hissing again.

'What *is* the matter?' asked Mr Jackson irritably. 'Is something hurting you?' My bosom was heaving convulsively, on account of the snake.

I said that as a matter of fact I didn't feel very well and stumbled from the room, clutching my midriff as though I had been partially disembowelled.

I wish I could believe that a childish prank, which he never knew had been perpetrated, was the worst we did to Mr Jackson; but I am afraid it was not. When after a mild influenza epidemic we heard that he had died I doubt if I was alone among my fellow-pupils in feeling a vague sense of guilt. I will not say that we actually *killed* him; but I have always had an uneasy feeling that we hounded him into his grave.

The Last of the Houlihans
From *Goodbye to the Bombay Bowler* (1961)

Browsing through the back numbers of a learned periodical, I was forcibly struck by the assurance, the hawk-like precision, with which scholars swoop down upon their chosen subjects. How delicate, how complex and yet how unerring must be the mental processes which cause a man to write a paper on 'The Revolving Book-case in China', or 'The Banana in Chinese Literature'. How compulsive must be the urge which drove a Miss Annabelle Hahn to follow up her study of 'The Vocabulary in Hittite' with a gripping sequel, 'More about the Vocabulary in Hittite'! One cannot help envying these dedicated specialists; but one cannot, at the same time, help wishing that their themes did not so often lie far beyond the frontiers of one's own curiosity.

I, for instance, would very much like to read a learned treatise on the Houlihans of Southwark; for it is to this family (I discovered from a general knowledge quiz in a newspaper) that we owe the word 'hooligan'. Etymologically, there is nothing particularly surprising about this derivation; what is rather odd is that the Houlihans – described by the newspaper as a riotous and by Mr Eric Partridge* as a rumbustious Irish family – flourished in the 1890s. It seems probable that several of what may be called the founder-members of this vigorous clan are alive today; it is almost certain that some of their children are still with us.

In my twisted mind this raises several interesting human problems. It is no mean distinction to have enriched the English vocabulary with your own patronymic – and not only the English language: this word is often on the lips of Russian statesmen. Are the contemporary Houlihans aware of the immortality which their exertions gained for them less than seventy years ago? Do they boast about it? Or do they hush it up? Do they try and live up to their reputation, or do they try to live it down? Are they still rumbustious, or are they now churchwardens? If only scholars would stop writing about revolving book-cases in China and get down to a bit of field research in matters of this kind, we should all be even more deeply in their debt than we are at present.

---

* *Origins* (Routledge and Kegan Paul).

Of the individuals whose names are embodied in our language most owe their niche in the dictionary to the artefacts which they invented or designed. Quisling is an outstanding modern exception to this rule, but he is by no means the only foreigner. I shall never understand what an ohm is, but I have a reasonably clear picture of Ohm himself — a huge, fat, pasty-faced man who wore bedsocks and kept canaries, quite different from the tall, gangling, eccentric Fahrenheit with his whinnying laugh, and from Ampère, chubby, uxorious, content, a keen but unsuccessful weekend fisherman. I have on the other hand no clear impression of Banting, who evolved a slimming cure and who must be indignant at the mutilation of his name to form a now obsolescent verb.

I see Macadam as austere, Davenport (who made desks) as bustling and pretentious, Hansom as cloaked, nocturnal, given to gas-lit dissipations. There are no mysteries about Shrapnel, General Henry (1761–1842), a tall, upright, slightly unpopular figure. Gatling looked exactly like Kipling, and his puttees were always coming down. It's no good telling me that Sir Hiram S. Maxim invented that machine-gun; the real Maxim was some kind of hateful foreigner, with a small black imperial. The dictionary pretends that there was no such person as Baron Howitzer, but I know better; Count Zeppelin was descended from him, on the distaff side.

How puny were the contributions made to our vocabulary by these artefact-mongers! How limited in scope and application are the words they bequeathed to us, and how inevitably they will become *obs*.! Hansom and Gatling have gone, Macadam and Shrapnel are on their way out; who, today, can recall hearing the name of Fahrenheit mentioned in polite conversations? The face that launched a thousand ships will be remembered for ever; can the same be said of the bosom whose owner gave her name to many millions of inflatable life-jackets? The day will come when Wellington boots and cardigans will be as outdated as buskins and doublets; and though Captain Boycott and Dr Bowdler may stay the course, both are somewhat specialized terms and neither, I think, has been transplanted into Russian.

But the Hooligans (Gooligans to Mr Khrushchev, who through no fault of his own cannot pronounce his hs) have surely come to stay, as the Vandals, more numerous and more terrible, have stayed for 1,500 years. If the Vandals had not left us their name, we should have had to invent a word to do all the duties it has discharged; for it has been in regular employment. How did we manage before that rumbustious Irish family broke loose in Southwark? It can hardly be argued that there was no hooliganism before 1890. Very well, then; what the devil did we call it?

I suspect that bad words take root more quickly and more deeply than good words. I shall not get, and do not court, immortality. But it *would* be rather nice to think that perhaps, in the better-class dictionaries of the twenty-second century, some such entry as this may appear:

STRIGGLE, v.t. To deal in trivialities at regular intervals; to be tiresomely facetious; (*mus.*) to drone or pipe in a monotonous manner.

[*Jane:* Oh, do stop striggling about class-warfare. Sir J. Osborne: *The Wren Goes To It*, 1981. From *Strix*, a minor literary hack, *c.* 20 AD.]

But I suppose it's too much to hope for.

•

RED SMITH

Walter Wellesley Smith (1905–82) was born in Green Bay, Wisconsin, the son of a wholesale and retail grocer. His parents were bookish and his older brother Art went into newspapers and became a rewrite man. Red Smith took a year off between high school and university, then, as he put it, 'scuffled my way through Notre Dame', doing a general arts course and majoring in journalism. In the summer of 1927 he got a job as a cub reporter on the *Milwaukee Sentinel*, later becoming a sports reporter on the *St Louis Star-Times* and a columnist on the *Philadelphia Record* in the late 1930s. From 1945 until the late 1960s he wrote a daily sports column, called 'Views of Sports', for the *New York Herald Tribune*. He subsequently joined the *New York Times* and won a Pulitzer Prize for distinguished journalism in 1976.

'Views of Sports'
Connie Mack's Inevitable Day
New York Herald Tribune, 1952
From *The Red Smith Reader* (1982)

In the winter of 1883 a skinny young cobbler's assistant who hated cobbling shoved his catcher's glove into his pocket – it was a kid glove, skin-tight, with the fingers cut off – and went out through the snows of New England and got a job as a professional baseball player with Meriden, of the Connecticut State League. He knew then, of course, that the career he was starting would have to end some day.

Throughout his sixty-seven years in baseball, Connie Mack has been aware that the day of departure must inevitably arrive. So has everybody else. But those who have known him have known also that when the time did come, it would come as a shock. It came yesterday. It was a shock.

A shock, but not a surprise, for it is not exactly a secret that Connie will be eighty-eight years old on December 23. The only surprise regarding his retirement as manager of the Athletics stems from the appointment of Jimmy Dykes as his successor instead of Connie's son Earle. For years Connie insisted that Earle, and Earle alone, would succeed him, and certainly Earle fancied himself for the job over a good many years.

Only a week ago there was a story out of Philadelphia suggesting that Dykes was through with the Athletics, and it quoted Connie thus: 'I hope Jimmy finds something good, real good.'

So now Jimmy has found something, but how good it is remains to be seen. He is manager of a bad ball team with a barren farm system and a financial future that is a topic of wide speculation, because Earle Mack and his brother, Roy, went in hock to buy the club.

Seems as though there's always got to be a catch in it when Dykes takes a new job with the A's. Sold to the White Sox in 1932, he returned to the A's as coach in December

1948, and Connie welcomed him thus at the winter meetings in Chicago: 'Jimmy, I'm afraid we can't pay you enough money.'

'Keeeripes!' Jimmy wailed. 'Do we have to start in where we left off sixteen years ago?'

But it isn't Jimmy Dykes whose name is uppermost in mind today. It is Connie Mack and the shocking, indigestible knowledge that from now on when the Athletics go out to play, the old man won't be sitting in the dugout erect on his little rubber cushion, his scorecard held stiffly over his bony knees, his Adam's apple jiggling above that high hard collar (he still buys them by the dozen from a firm in St Louis).

For one who traveled with Connie Mack for ten seasons, it would require at least ten years to tell about this glorious old guy who has been baseball's high priest and patriarch, one of its keenest minds, its priceless ambassador, one of its sharpest businessmen, certainly its most indestructible myth.

The plaster saint that they made of him in his old age, the prissy figurehead whose strongest expletive was 'Goodness gracious!' – that was pure myth. The man was a ballplayer in the days when baseball was a roughneck's game, and he did all right in the game. He was not a roughneck and not profane by habit, but on occasion he could cuss like any honest mule-skinner. Yes, and when he was younger he played the horses and drank liquor.

He could be as tough as rawhide and as gentle as a mother, reasonable and obstinate beyond reason, and courtly and benevolent and fierce. He was kindhearted and hardfisted, drove a close bargain, and was suckered in a hundred deals. He was generous and thoughtful and autocratic and shy and independent and altogether completely lovable.

There was a day when the Athletics, having broken training camp in Anaheim, California, and having left there Lena Blackburne, one of the coaches, with a leg infection, started out of San Francisco for an exhibition game. It was a nippy morning and somebody asked Connie if he wanted the auto window closed against the chill.

'Dammitohell!' Connie exploded. 'I'm all right, don't worry about me! Everybody's always fussing about me. Mrs Mack says: "Con, wear your rubbers. Con, put on your overcoat." So I put on my coat and rubbers and go out to buy medicine for her!

'And that Blackburne!' He was getting madder and madder. 'It's "Boss, are you warm enough? Boss, are you comfortable? Boss, you better come inside and rest." And where is Blackburne? Lying down there in Anaheim on his tail, dammit!'

It may have been that same day that he nearly broke a rookie's heart by telling him he was going back to the minors and then, a couple of hours later, changed his mind and kept the kid, explaining apologetically: 'At my age a man's got a right to do what he wants to do once, anyhow.' (The rookie opened the season with the Athletics and was a bum and had to go back, after all.)

One day Wally Moses, who was a holdout, burst from the room where he'd been haggling with the boss and tore out of training camp on the run, his face as white as paper. Another day Connie confided that in all his years of baseball there'd been two unpleasant tasks he'd never got used to: sending a young fellow back to the minors, and arguing with a ballplayer over salary.

He meant it when he said that, and whatever he'd said that other time to Moses, he meant that, too. There never was another like Connie. There never will be.

The Brakes Got Drunk

New York Herald Tribune, 1953
From *The Red Smith Reader* (1982)

Laguna del Maule, Chile

This typewriter is being beaten with fingers whose knuckles are bleeding and nails broken after hand-to-fin struggles with trout exactly the size, shape and disposition of Tony Galento. Up here in the Andes fishing is a more perilous game than Russian roulette. If you survive the mountain road, there are rainbow in Lake Maule ready and willing to eat you for bait. Nothing is impossible to fish that live a mile and a half up in the sky.

Lake Maule perches on the Chilean–Argentine border about twenty kilometers and 2,000 feet above the sparse grove of maytenus trees at timberline where camp had been pitched the evening before. The last drop of fluid had drained out of the brakes of the old Chevrolet truck during the journey to campsite, and there are no filling stations along the narrow, twisting shelf that serves, more or less, as a road.

Herman, the driver, halted trucks that passed camp occasionally with construction crews working on a dam at the lake. They told him oil would ruin the brakes, but said wine could serve as an emergency fluid.

'Because it contains alcohol, eh?' said Captain Warren Smith, of Panagra. 'We can do better than that. Where's the Vat 69?'

The Chevrolet scrambled up to the lake with a boiling radiator and a full brake cylinder, not the best truck in Chile, but by all odds the happiest.

Maule straddles a pass in mountains entirely devoid of vegetation. They are bare peaks of volcanic rock crumbling into gray dust under the wind that blows eternally up this gorge from the west, making even these midsummer days uncomfortably cold. A little way out from the shore there is a belt of seaweed just under the surface where the trout lie and feed on a small pink crawfish called *pancora*. This shellfish diet gives the rainbows their majestic size, but it is the barren landscape that gives them their evil temperament. In all this desolation they brood.

Captain Smith and his North American burden rode by outboard to the east end of the lake, where snow touched the Chilean mountains rising from the water's edge and Argentine mountains showed just beyond. They started casting over the weed beds, using a smallish bronze-finish spoon of scarlet and orange. Almost immediately there was a grunt from the captain and a wild splash. Something dark and shiny and altogether implausible came out of the water and returned. It looked like a trout, but not like the sort of trout people ordinarily see when their eyes are open.

'You go on fishing,' Captain Smith said. 'I'll be a while with this fellow.'

His rod was a bow and his line hissed through the water. The fish was in and out of the lake, in and out, and then it was in the boat flopping on a gaff, a pink-striped brute of black and silver. 'He'll hit about nine pounds,' the captain said calmly.

Thereafter the captain caught fish and his companion caught backlashes and weeds. So intense, however, is the dislike these trout have for people that even the least proficient angler is bound to be under attack.

Between backlashes, a distant relative of Primo Carnera [world heavyweight boxing champion 1933–4] sprang up for a look at the latest New York styles in outdoor apparel, made a face of hideous disapproval, and spat out the spoon.

Another grabbed the same spoon and went into a terrifying rage. Four times in quick succession he stood up on his tail, snarling and shaking his head and cursing horribly. On the fourth jump he snapped the leader.

Then Captain Smith had one that broke the leader and departed. Then it happened again to the amateur, but not before the whirling reel handle had smashed fingernails and stripped skin off awkward knuckles.

By now half the population of the lake had taken a passion for collecting hardware. Six leaders were snapped and six spoons confiscated by force before it was decided that the fifteen-pound test nylon was faulty. There's an awful lot of trout in Maule going around with their faces full of painted metal with nylon streamers. Maybe the style will catch on, like nose rings in the cannibal islands.

With the spoon tied directly to the casting line, anybody could catch fish. Practically anybody did. The outboard would take the boat upwind to the lee of a point or island; then the wind would drift it swiftly over the weed beds. Duck and geese and tern and grebe swam on the water. Except for one other fishing party, the place belonged to them and the fish.

'Let's take one more drift,' the captain suggested, 'and call it a day.'

Half a moment later his companion screamed. The reel handle was snatched from his grasp and the drag sang. A trout leaped, fell back on his side. He looked six feet long. He dived, wrenching off line. The boat drifted on, but he wouldn't come along. Twice the captain ran the boat upwind, cautiously undoing knots the fish had tied around weeds. At length the sullen beast came aboard.

He was a good twelve pounds, broad-shouldered, magnificently colored, and splendidly deep, like Jane Russell.

The Round Jack Nicklaus Forgot

New York Times, 1978
From *The Red Smith Reader* (1982)

Jack Nicklaus's golf is better than his memory. When he came charging home in the Inverrary Classic last weekend, picking up four strokes on Grier Jones, three on Jerry Pate and Andy Bean, and two on Hale Irwin with five birdies in the last five holes, he was asked whether he had ever put on such a finish before. 'I can't imagine any other time,' he said. 'It was the most remarkable thing I've ever seen in my life,' said Lee Trevino, comparing it with Reggie Jackson's three home runs in the last World Series game and Leon Spinks' victory over Muhammad Ali. Well, it was remarkable but it wasn't unprecedented.

Fifteen years ago, Nicklaus and Arnold Palmer represented the United States in the World Cup competition at Saint-Nom-la-Bretèche near Versailles in France. If Jack has forgotten his performance there, perhaps he wanted to forget it. Maybe he deliberately put it out of his mind as too outrageously theatrical to bear remembering.

The things he did on the very first hole were downright scandalous. The hole was a legitimate par 5 for club members but a trifle short for a pro with Jack's power, measuring somewhere between 450 and 500 yards. In his four rounds, Jack played it eagle, eagle, eagle, birdie, and that was just for openers.

Bretèche may have been a trifle shorter than Inverrary's 7,127 yards, but this was no exhibition on a pitch-and-putt course, and the opposition was at least as distinguished as the field Nicklaus encountered last week. The World Cup, now twenty-five years old, is a movable feast that leaps from continent to continent, usually playing national capitals, matching two-man teams from virtually every land where the game is known. Though it hasn't the prestige of the United States or British Open, it is probably the closest thing there is to a world championship.

In 1963, Saint-Nom-la-Bretèche was a comparatively new course built on land that had been the royal farm when Louis XIV was top banana. The clubhouse, once the royal cow barn, was a splendid building of ivy-covered stone set in a terraced stableyard ablaze with roses, snapdragons, chrysanthemums and pansies.

The galleries had a touch of quality seldom associated with, say, Maple Moor in Westchester County. Among those who followed the play were two former kings and one former vice-president – Leopold of Belgium, the Duke of Windsor and Richard M. Nixon.

Before play started, Prince Michel de Bourbon-Parme, the club president, dispatched ten dozen fresh eggs to a nearby convent. This, he explained, was an ancient custom in the Ile de France. Anyone planning an outdoor binge like a wedding or garden party sent eggs to the poor and this assured him of good weather. The standard fee was one dozen eggs, but the Prince had laid it on to guarantee a week of sunshine.

Morning of the opening round found the Prince glowering through a clammy fog. 'So,' he said, 'I am sending to the sisters to get back my eggs.'

Soggy turf made the course play long for little guys, but not for Nicklaus. His second shot on the opening hole was twenty feet from the pin, and he ran down the putt for his first eagle 3. After that he had five birdies and three bogeys for a 67. Palmer's 69 gave the pair a tie for first place with Al Balding and Stan Leonard of Canada.

Prince Michel changed his mind about reclaiming the eggs, but the weather didn't relent. Day by day the fog thickened, until the green hills and yellow bunkers were all but blotted out. Realizing that if a hitter like Nicklaus tried to fire a tee shot into that soup the ball would never be seen again, officials postponed the final round for twenty-four hours.

It didn't help much. Next day a gray soufflé garnished the fairways. The climate dripped sullenly from the trees. Windsor and Leopold showed up as they had for each earlier round, but the weather reduced the gallery to a minimum. Reluctantly, the committee decided to cut the final round to nine holes. At this point Nicklaus and

Palmer were tied with Spain's Ramon Sota and Sebastian Miguel for the team trophy, with Nicklaus and Gary Player all square in individual competition.

Automobiles were driven out past the first green, where they made a U-turn and parked with headlights on. From the tee, lights were blurred but visible, giving the players a target. For the first time in four rounds, Nicklaus needed four shots to get down. Then he got serious.

With that birdie for a start, he played the next five holes as follows: 3–3–3–3–3. When he walked toward the seventh tee, a spectator asked: 'What are you going to do for an encore?'

'Try to finish,' Jack said.

On the first six holes he had taken 19 shots. On the last three he took 13 for a 32. It won.

•

BILL VAUGHAN

William Edward Vaughan (1915–77) was born in St Louis, Missouri, and educated at St Louis University, where he received a BA in journalism in 1936. From 1936 to 1939 he was a reporter for the Springfield *Leader and Press*, in Massachusetts, and from 1939 until his death he was attached to the *Kansas City Star*. During the Second World War he served in the US Army Air Forces, and in 1945 he emerged as a columnist. He wrote one column, initially called 'Starbeams', and another one, 'Senator Soper Says', which was distributed by the North American Newspaper Alliance. His main column was syndicated under the heading 'Vaughan at Large' by the Bell–McClure Syndicate. His columns were collected in *Bird Thou Never Wert* (1962), *Half the Battle* (1963) and *Sorry I Stirred It* (1964).

'Vaughan at Large'
A Case History . . .
From *Bird Thou Never Wert* (1962)

Editor
The *Kansas City Star*
Kansas City, Mo.

Dear Sir:

As per our agreement of June 1 (please enclose attached voucher with your check) we have made a time-motion study of the 'columnist' you mentioned.

Frankly, we feel here at Tuckerman and Associates that this is a case almost without parallel in the annals of efficiency engineering. How one man can spend so much theoretically on-shift time performing acts which seem to have no relation to his duties is beyond our comprehension.

Straightening out paper clips, for example. We timed subject on June 7 and he spent a total of 27 minutes straightening out paper clips. What bearing does this have on the production of his 'column'? Not only is this activity time-wasting, but it renders the paper clips inoperable, a fact which even the subject knows, as on the same day (June 7) he spent an additional 18 minutes trying to rebend a paper clip which he had straightened.

The straightened paper clips are used by the subject under surveillance to clean his pipes, of which he seems to have an inexhaustible supply in the lower left-hand drawer of his desk. He also has a considerable supply of pipe cleaners which are useless for pipe-cleaning purposes because he has made them all into little animals.

Which is why he has to use the paper clips.

The pipes took up 97.6 minutes on the day checked. This doesn't include the time spent smoking them. It includes only the time spent cleaning them, knocking them against the desk (disturbing to other employees), looking at them, filling them, searching through other people's desks for matches, etc.

Another time-consuming activity of subject is his letter-opener drill. On June 12 he devoted a full 63.8 minutes to the letter opener. If the .7 minute devoted to actually opening letters with it is subtracted, this still leaves 63.1 minutes of simply fooling around.

Here are some of the things he does with the letter opener: puts it up his sleeve like a stiletto and practices fast draws; scratches his back; balances it on finger; taps out rhythm of 'Keep Your Sunny Side Up' (disturbing to other employees); reads 'Made in USA' on blade; cleans pipes; scratches ankle; cleans fingernails.

On June 16, subject made four trips across office to insult editorial writers. The question may well arise as to whether duties of 'columnist' include insulting editorial writers. Moreover, each trip required an average of 63 steps, while most direct route (assuming trips were necessary) should consume no more than 50.

Visits to water cooler on average day: 18.

It is also our thinking that subject's efficiency would be improved if he learned how to use the typewriter. His apparent inability to make the machine work properly causes a definite erosion of man-hours. Typically, on June 13, he spent 29 minutes looking inside his typewriter and poking at it with that letter opener.

Other activities, to which a total of 2.3 hours were devoted, include wiping his glasses, apparently sleeping, arguing baseball with sports writers, kicking the candy bar machine, eating candy bar, reading candy bar wrapper, sharpening pencil, doing crossword puzzle (incorrectly), moving his car from 1-hour parking zone, wadding up paper and trying fancy hook shots into wastebasket, staring out window, putting coat on and off.

The steps that should be taken to correct this situation are obvious.

Yours sincerely,
Sidney B. Tuckerman
Tuckerman and Associates

PS Time spent actually writing 'column': 14.3 minutes.

'Vaughan at Large'
Write Your Own . . .

From *Bird Thou Never Wert* (1962)

The type of columnist I have always wanted to be is the kind that writes under some headline such as 'Little Tales of the Big Town' or 'Vignettes of Life.' This type of columnist strolls the streets and encounters more interesting copy in one ordinary block than I would at a five-alarm fire.

Panhandlers approach him with pathetic tales; he overhears hilarious remarks; he spies little kiddies in delightful antics. All he needs to do to work up a column is to take a saunter in the nice fresh air – and it's all done, except for the minor task of getting it down on paper.

Somehow the system never works out for me. If anything odd ever actually happens on the streets it doesn't happen while I am around.

Anyway, I don't think it makes much difference, as even when I do see something I can't seem to make much out of it.

The other day, for example, I was passing a big downtown bank when my attention was attracted to a shoelace vendor in the corner. He was standing with his nose about two inches from the bronze plate on which the great financial institution's deposits were listed.

And he was carefully pointing to each with his right forefinger, counting the zeros.

Think what O. O. McIntyre could have done with that. This fellow had been president of the bank once, you see, but had been caught embezzling, had served his time in prison and now was selling shoelaces in front of the bank which he once had headed. They wouldn't let him in the door, of course. He was a fiscal Phil Nolan, a man without a bank.

But, lovingly, the way dear old Nolan used to count the stars in the flag, rejoicing over every one that was added, this man counted the zeros in the bank's deposits.

For a follow-up column he could report that the old shoestring peddler had collapsed and that they carried him into the bank to breathe his last, which he did in peace and joy as he looked around him at the gleaming marble and the tearful faces of the vice-presidents and assistant cashiers gathered around his prostrate form.

'Don't cry, boys,' he whispered just before the end. 'I'm going to the great Clearing House in the sky.'

And when a few of the men who had known him in the old days went to his pitiful room they found that he had furnished it like a bank. On his table was a little, round, wet sponge, and checkbooks, and a rubber stamp which said 'Overdrawn.'

I lack the McIntyre touch, however. For a moment I thought of treating it Winchell style: 'Attention *New York Mirror* – isn't the old shoestring peddler who counts the zeros in front of a Kansas City bank really Judge Crater?'

Then there are lots of columnists who could give it a gentle, philosophical twist: 'The sun was shining and the wind was whipping the dresses of the pretty girls as I saw the old man on the corner counting the zeros on the bronze plaque which listed the deposits of a great bank. So intent was he on his chore that he did not notice Your Observer as I stopped to watch him.

'And as I watched a great feeling of peace came over me. Wasn't this old man happier, perhaps, than the financier who sat inside in his swivel chair? To the old man the millions had reality; they could be touched with his fingers – and how beautifully they sparkled in the noonday glare.

'But to the cold-hearted men inside, the millions meant nothing. They were just a symbol, an abstraction.

'And that led Your Observer, as he continued his stroll, to recall the words of Phlebitis the Elder, who said of happiness –'

But, no, again I'm not up to it.

All I can do, it seems, is just to report that I saw an old shoestring salesman in front of a bank, counting the bronze zeros.

Write your own column.

The Election: Some Sobering Afterthoughts . . .
From *Bird Thou Never Wert* (1962)

The results of last Tuesday's election showed clearly that when the issues are stirring enough to arouse the average American voter to apathy, he will not be denied. Early in the campaign it became evident that certain factors had to be considered, and although there were those who thought we had given them too much consideration, this mandate at the polls indicates quite the opposite.

In spite of what anybody says.

With all but a few scattered precincts in, a pattern begins to emerge. It shows, or should show, to the most stubborn partisan and the least-informed observer, that the party which receives the most votes for its candidates, on the national, state or local level, will win.

Incidentally, it occurs to us that more attention should be paid to these scattered precincts. They are an interesting political phenomenon. Some scattered precincts vote very early. Almost as soon as the polls close, the man on the radio says, 'A few scattered precincts show . . .'

Then, after the election is all over, he says that a few scattered precincts are still out.

As a matter of fact, the total elimination of scattered precincts might not be a bad idea. If we could all get behind a drive to unscatter our precincts, it would be a worthwhile endeavor. Cities all over American are afflicted with two things – sprawling suburbs and scattered precincts. That's the sort of thing that makes us lose prestige abroad.

Be that as it may, we can say that never has there been an election of such proportions. People who voted really got out and voted, and they voted for the party or man of their choice. Whether those who didn't vote would have voted for the man or party of their choice is something we may never know.

The big thing now is to close ranks and get behind the administration. Nothing is worse for an administration than to have open ranks behind it.

Summing up, the election turned out just as those who thought it would turn out that way thought it would.

'Vaughan at Large'
The Humidity/Stupidity Index . . .
From *Half the Battle* (1963)

Friends, I know that there are worse problems in the world. I read the papers. But it's hard to concentrate on the big worries when you have a small one going for you at the same time.

The thing that happens is that you carry an umbrella to work on a rainy morning and when you leave that afternoon the weather has cleared and you walk off and forget the umbrella.

The next day your wife says, threateningly, 'Don't forget the umbrella, Sam.'

It is a bright day, full of sunshine and heat shimmering off the asphalt. That afternoon you have the problem of carrying the umbrella home on the bus without looking like some species of filbert.

Bus stop humorists are unable to resist the sight of a man carrying an umbrella when the nearest rain cloud is hovering over Intermittent, ND.

'Well, Mr Chamberlain,' they will say, 'does it look like peace in our time?'

If it's a raincoat you are involved with you can wrap it up and stick it in a paper sack or some such. But how are you going to wrap an umbrella so it looks like anything but an umbrella?

You can, of course, sit as far away from the umbrella as you can and pretend that it doesn't belong to you. But this can be tricky.

I tried it one time and an acquaintance sat down next to me and said, 'Is that your umbrella?'

'Why, uh, no,' I said. 'I just found it.'

And he said, 'Oh,' rather suspiciously, so when I got to the stop near my house I had to take the umbrella and, because the acquaintance was watching me (a fellow I never really liked), I had to turn it in to the bus driver and tell him that I seemed to have found this umbrella.

Then, the next morning, I had to call the lost-and-found department of the bus company and ask them if anybody had found my umbrella.

'No, sir,' the man said after he had gone away from the phone for a while to see about it. 'We got a left shoe and a trombone but no umbrella.'

'I happen to know better,' I said. 'My umbrella was found yesterday on bus No. 18975 and turned in to the driver.'

'How come you're so sure?'

'Because I found it myself.'

Click!

A half hour later I had my wife call and by this time they had found the umbrella and asked her to describe it, which she did.

'When did you say your husband lost the umbrella?' the man asked her.

'Yesterday.'

'What was your husband doing carrying an umbrella yesterday?' the man wanted to know. 'The sun shone all day.'

'Because he is a nut,' said my wife.

'Is he the same one who called a while ago and said he found his own umbrella and gave it to the driver?'

'I'm afraid so,' said my wife.

'You poor thing,' said the man.

I finally got the umbrella back. But not that day because it was raining too hard to go to the lost-and-found place. I had to wait until the next day, when the sun was shining.

I got it home by running it down one leg of my pants, with the handle hooked over my belt. There were only a few people on the bus but I had to stand up all the way home because of the umbrella in my pants leg.

The same acquaintance got on and asked why I didn't sit down next to him and I told him, 'No, sir, I got in enough trouble sitting next to you a couple of days ago.'

He went and sat behind the driver, and when I got off I'm pretty sure I heard one of them say to the other, 'That nut looks like he's got an umbrella in there somewhere.'

•

MEYER BERGER

Meyer Berger (1898–1959) was born on the Lower East Side of Manhattan, the son of poor Czech immigrants. He was a paper boy at the age of eight, a newspaper night messenger for the New York *World* at eleven, and at thirteen he left school for a full-time job on the paper. During the First World War he was turned down by the army because of poor eyesight, but he cunningly memorized the eye chart and re-applied. This time he was accepted and sent as an infantry sergeant to France, where he won the Purple Heart and Silver Star. After the war he became a Brooklyn police reporter for his old paper and subsequently the chief rewrite man for the Standard News Association in Brooklyn. He moved to the *New York Times* in 1928, where he combined rewrite and reporting assignments, covering the trials of Al Capone and Dutch Schultz. He spent a year as a writer on the *New Yorker*, but decided that he preferred newspaper work and returned to the *Times*. He started writing 'About New York', a local human interest column, in 1939, but a year later travelled to London as a war correspondent. Illness caused him to return home, although he toured Europe and North Africa for the *Times* in 1945. After the Second World War he wrote special news features, winning the Pulitzer Prize for local reporting in 1950 with his account of how a crazed veteran had run amok in New Jersey and killed thirteen people. In 1953 he revived his 'About New York' column and continued writing it until his death six years later. A selection of these columns was published as *Meyer Berger's New York* (1960).

'About New York'
New York Times, May 31, 1954

Teddy May has walked and crawled through Manhattan's 560 miles of sewers for fifty-one years, but tomorrow he must be done with them for ever.

There will be a little party for him in the Sewer Department office, and they will make him honorary Sewer Commissioner. Teddy will fidget, blush, scrub at his white thatch and go quietly into retirement – only because, at eighty, the city says he must.

Borough engineers who have known him will be sad when he goes, because for all their formal knowledge and schooling, they know less about the system, in some ways, than he does. Teddy has had a minimum of schooling but loves sewers as other men love warmer and more easily understood creations.

Teddy, christened Edward Patrick May after he was born on West Forty-seventh Street down by the river on May 5, 1874, made the first comprehensive Manhattan sewer survey for Chief Engineer Harris Loomis in 1903. His affection for the system started then.

He is a small man, and he could get into small pipe. He got to know every foot of the sewer network, even the amazing brick sewers put down before 1850 that now carry skyscraper waste though they were designed for one- and two-story buildings.

Mr May knows some fifty underground streams – where they are trapped into the sewers and where they trickle and course around them, stubbornly burbling on under countless tons of asphalt and concrete, in approximately the same beds they followed when the island was lush green.

Teddy has testified on sewers in the high courts for more than forty years, and his evidence has always held up. He has recovered murder weapons and robbery loot from catch basins. He has cleared the system of a rash of alligators. Dropped in by harassed parents when the reptiles were tiny pets, they grew amazingly.

The job has called for shrewd detective work. So many years ago that Teddy forgets the date completely, General Grant's daughter, a guest at the King's Hotel in Forty-third Street, west of Fifth Avenue, lost in the plumbing a ring presented by the Japanese Emperor when she was married in the White House.

Lloyd's had the trinket insured. The hotel superintendent swore he had searched plumbing traps but hadn't found it. Mr May had Lloyd's make an inexpensive duplicate of the ring and, in the presence of detectives and a Lloyd's man, proved it could not be flushed away.

The police got the ring back from the superintendent.

One October Saturday three years ago Teddy saw his men collapsing, one by one, in the Liberty Street sewer as if felled by an invisible hand. One of the men died. Teddy traced the cause of death to a cleaning establishment. It had used an odorless acid to clean its vats, and the acid fog from it was lethal.

Those are things to talk about now – those and countless others. And Teddy May will talk about them as he does of his boyhood when Times Square was a dark spot, when pigs, steers and mustangs were herded from barges down Eleventh Avenue.

If the city thinks, though, that it can break Teddy May of the sewer-walking habit after more than fifty years, it could be wrong. Teddy says, 'You don't need keys to get into a sewer.'

'About New York'

New York Times, December 25, 1957

On Christmas Eve the city glowed. Last night it was truly the City of Light. It wore its Christmas jewels – millions of rubies and emeralds, golden tiaras, blue gems, azure and sapphire and turquoise, all softly bright.

Fifth Avenue was an Avenue of Light from the Plaza to Washington Square. At the north end, just beyond the park's roped golden beads of road lights, the Christmas trees shimmered like cloth-of-gold and the trees and window boxes in the Plaza Hotel were spangled with a deep mysterious blue.

The great Fifth Avenue shops had their windows outlined with Christmas lights, like giant jeweled buckles. Hotel marquees in the side streets were rimmed with red and white and blue and green. At 666 Fifth Avenue, Santa Claus and his elves clawed their way up the spotlighted façade and thousands stood to watch.

In Rockefeller Center the sixty-five-foot tree from the White Mountains bathed the area all about it with wondrous glow, and the path to it was lined with tributary trees, cone-shaped and man-made that bloomed in pale green with inner lighting.

Angels in samite descended from white cloud in the Lord & Taylor windows. The Tree of Light that reaches from roof to sidewalk was radiant on massed, upturned faces. Carols sweetened the night and the throngs nodded, unconsciously keeping time.

The Library's façade and its lions were pale and the lions wore their giant neck wreaths, studded with electric gems. Below the shops, in Madison Square Park, a lone tree stood in the darkness, a happy beacon; then comparative loneliness and unlighted windows to a point below Fourteenth Street.

Lower Fifth Avenue was a fairyland of light, gem-studded at the First Presbyterian Church, at the Church of the Ascension, the Hotel Grosvenor, at No. 1 and at No. 2. Christmas candles burned in the little old houses and in the skyscraper apartment houses.

Unsold Christmas trees cast great blocks of shadow in Paddy's market in Ninth Avenue. Chestnut venders' carts gave off their charcoal-fire glow. The waterfront on Hudson River lay dark, but candles and trees sent cheery beams through even the meanest, blackened tenement windows.

The city's own tree was gem-bedecked on City Hall lawn. Trees sent their colored mass out of darkness at St Paul's and at Old Trinity. Down on South Street the tugs wore their running lights like Christmas rubies and emeralds. Great freighters had small lighted trees at top mast and the reflections danced and spread on the black tide.

The wide spread of windows in the Al Smith Houses showed thousands of golden panes, with blazing jewels on some levels; whole windows trimmed with colored glimmer facing East River. So up all the east shore, a glory of holiday glow, wondrous, probably without parallel anywhere else on earth.

Jeweled trees on hospital lawns and hospital terraces. A huge jeweled tree in front of the Mayor's home in old Gracie Mansion, on the front of Doctors Hospital. Eighty-sixth Street from First Avenue to Lexington was arched with golden lights and red Christmas bells, which is Yorkville's traditional canopy at Yuletide.

Park Avenue was a row of lighted mall trees from the Nineties to Thirty-fourth Street. Trees glowed in Park Avenue and in Fifth Avenue lobbies and Christmas candles spread gold on rich window draperies. From the park's west end a watcher could see the effulgence rewritten on the dark lake mirrors.

One Hundred and Twenty-fifth Street in Harlem, where poverty stalks, did not show its poverty last night. Looped ropes of light made a golden canopy over the pavement from Madison Avenue, west to St Nicholas. To the south around Columbia University subdued Christmas lighting gleamed like spangles and sequins against nocturnal velvet.

This was Christmas Eve in New York. This was the city dressed in richest stones and trinkets. This was the city trying to match the gems from her endless treasure chest against the winking and sparkling brilliants in heaven's vault. This was a city bathed in Christmas peace, breathing carols into the night. This was the City Magnificent.

•

PAUL JENNINGS

Paul Jennings (1918–89) was educated at King Henry VIII School, Coventry, and Douai School. While he was serving as a lieutenant in the Royal Signals, his first humorous article was published in *Lilliput* in 1943, and by the end of the war he had established a reputation as a free-lance contributor to *Punch* and the *Spectator*. After the war he worked briefly for the Central Office of Information and as an advertising copywriter before joining the *Observer*, for which he wrote his 'Oddly Enough' column from 1949 to 1966.

'Oddly Enough'
The Boy's Got Talent
Observer, February 1958

GENTLEMAN (31), wide knowledge ancient history, especially ancient Egypt, comparative religion, rationalism, very experienced public orator and lecturer, author of daring thesis on the origin of world civilization, artist, fluent Spanish, many years commercial experience, seeks position where this unusual combination of talents could be used.

The Times personal column, 3 Feb.

Well, it's pure imagination of course, but the picture I have is this: when Lucas Pickering's young wife bore him their only child in 1927 there was plenty of head-shaking among their neighbours in the little grey weaving town of Bragdyke. Some of them resented the slight fair-haired girl whom this tall, solitary, deep-eyed man, apparently a confirmed bachelor at fifty-one, had unexpectedly brought back as his bride from a rationalist congress in London. Others, discovering that Elsie Pickering was not a London hussy but a quiet, shy girl ('Aye, a gradely lass to be wed to thon old atheist'), pitied her.

Most of the townspeople were used to the sight of Pickering on his stand outside the Corn Exchange every Saturday night, rain or fine, declaiming passionately from Herbert Spencer, Bradlaugh or Ingersoll to a few curious bystanders or giggling adolescents. He was respected as a solid craftsman (after many years as a ring-doubler and two-end winder he was now overlooker in the cheese-winding department), and Lucas Pickering's credit was as good as the next man's. But undoubtedly he did not fit into the cheerful Bragdyke life of pub and club and the annual performance of the *Messiah*. 'Happen it'll be a lonely life for the child' was the verdict.

In some ways this was true. But Herbert Renan Pickering, who grew up a slight though healthy boy, was adored by his father. Together the two would go for long walks on the moors. Gazing down at the town, from which the sound of church bells floated up, Lucas would exclaim 'Eh, the daft fools, there they go worshipping their gaseous vertebrate. That's what Haeckel called their God, lad, the gaseous vertebrate – but thou aren't listening.'

'Oh yes, dad, I am,' said Herbert, looking up with a start from his sketch-book. For it was clear the boy was an artist. A rich local lady (and church worker), Miss Thwaite-thwaite of the Manor House, swallowing her dislike of Pickering, told him 'that boy's got talent'. With her generous help Herbert became an art student.

The exciting turmoil of post-war London was a fertilizing influence on the dreamy eighteen-year-old from Bragdyke. He was particularly influenced by the history of art classes given by kindly old Professor Tonkins, and spent many hours in the Egyptian Room at the British Museum, in a trance before the glories of this hieratic art. On holidays in Bragdyke he would try to explain to his father. 'Well, dad, it depends what you mean by religion. Now when Amenhotep IV founded his religion of the sun . . .' But he loyally accompanied Lucas to rationalist meetings in the dales, himself becoming a very experienced public orator.

Suddenly there was tragedy. Lucas caught a chill at an open-air meeting and was dead within a week. Herbert abandoned his art studies and went into commerce to help his mother. He got a job with Jarkins, Clanger and Pobjoy, Importers and Exporters, hoping to be sent to their Cairo branch. But because of Middle Eastern politics he found himself a trainee in the Buenos Aires office of JCP. He tried hard, learning fluent Spanish, studying Company Law. But his heart was not in it, and one day his boss, Mr McCluskey, a tough old South America hand who spent all his leisure drinking whisky in the English Club and had no time for artists, came unexpectedly into the office and found Herbert writing in a large exercise book. 'Well, Mr McCluskey, it's a kind of thesis on the origins of world civilization. I . . .' The result was a blistering letter to head office, and, eventually, this advertisement.

Meanwhile, in the dark, rich, oak-panelled City offices of Wilbye, Morley and Bateson, Sherry Importers, Travers Morley, Old Etonian head of the firm, is saying angrily: 'Can't we keep a manager on our *fonda* for six months? Here's a letter from that young puppy Henderson. He's resigned and goin' to be a *Jesuit*, if you please. Carter, before him, went off to learn bullfightin'. Can't understand why these young fellers get bowled over by Spain nowadays. I was there meself, turn of the century – enjoyed it, larked with the gels after the fiesta an' all that – but none of this rot about *hispanidad* and dignity. We want a chap immune to all that, philosophy of his own, able to talk to the Marquis – he's a dotty old scholar, mummies an' that in his castle, but our vineyards *are* on his land; a chap able to harangue the *obreros* in their own lingo if there's any trouble – but, above all, immune to all this Spanish-civilization stuff – yes, Simpson, what is it?'

Well, you know what Simpson, the head clerk, is excitedly bringing in.

'Oddly Enough'
200 Bdrms, 7 Bthrms
Observer, May 1964

As always in the tall, high, sad bathroom of a big old English hotel, I feel a faint air of trespass. Everything is too large and bare; the huge gaunt bath with its brass taps from which gush torrents of startling power, unknown in any human bathroom, as if for some industrial process, the grudging cane-seated chair and the cork mat on the worn brown linoleum (as though one were having a bath in the Home Office) – all these seem to be mysterious, oversize, symbolic objects, not for actual use.

Above all, there is absolutely no sign of any previous or present human life. Although one's bathroom at home is, by its very function, a solitary place, it is nevertheless one of the most human rooms in the house, with its familiar toothbrushes, its little pink useless bottles and tubes, its sense of faces and souls having been renewed a thousand times here (and, in *our* bathroom, its five small odd shoes, its plastic buses and helicopters, its sodden teddy bear and pieces of comics).

But here there is nothing. The bathroom is in a back part of the hotel, looking out on to an unrecognizable part of the town (or it would if one were ten feet high and could look out of the window). I go to it past an open door showing a room with a dowdy settee in it; radio music sounds, it seems inhabited yet looks too humble to be a hotel room. Two women in overalls are speaking a foreign language and laughing softly round a corner. There is an impression of bundles, piles, trays, *stocktaking*. I have somehow got behind the scenes; this is an anteroom, a scenery store, a disused temple. They know I am here, but they make no comment.

(Why do I never see anyone coming from these bathrooms? Am I the only one in this party of journalists that hasn't got a private bathroom? Where *are* all the others, why has it gone so quiet? Who is this man with a creased face and thinning hair, coming out of his room with a secretive look? What is my room number, which is the way back? Who am I? Will they take my clothes away, switch the rooms round, while I am naked in the bath?)

It predates all smart, specially designed bathrooms. It is just a room with a bath and a lavatory in it. The claw feet of the bath are visible. It is the bathroom of one's childhood, of something even farther off, of an E. Nesbit child's childhood (although no child bathes here, only older, soberly rich businessmen seven feet long, doffing serious good underwear). There is a low moaning of wind as in childhood bathrooms (we are high up, in an outcrop of the hotel), it moans under the door . . .

The door; ah yes, of course, the bolt, before I start. It is out of alignment with the socket, and will go in only when I simultaneously lift the great Victorian cream door by the handle. Then I have to use both hands to shove it home. At the last shove the bit with the knob comes off. I am locked in, like the famous three old ladies.

I fight off a feeling that the hotel has done this on purpose, it was a special trick rusty bolt, they are taking my clothes away now, waiting to see what I will do. Somehow it would be a surrender to shout out. What words would I use? *Help!* would be absurdly dramatic. Yet if I played it down with *Hi!* or *Oi!* or something equally informal, passers-by would think I was calling to a wife, or was an eccentric of some kind, they would creep away saying, there's a man shouting in the bathroom, let's not get involved. It would have to be something formal, a *dignified* shout. *Holloa! I say there! Er, I SAY, ARE YOU THERE? HULLOAH!* . . .

Perhaps I can attract attention by running the overflow, they would eventually look up from the kitchens at the perpetual dribble (but no, I hear it going down an internal drain); or by clanking SOS in Morse on the chain (but the frightful roaring gushing from the immense high cistern would drown it). Ha, inspiration! I will tear out letters from toilet paper and spell out a message under the door. After some thought I reject appeals like LET ME OUT or SEND ENGINEER in favour of the simple statement BOLT IS BROKEN. But when I lay out the letters on the floor the moaning draught blows them about even there, so what would it be like where the draught is concentrated under the door, suppose someone came by and found the words BOOB RENT SILK, or LOB NO BRISKET or even O STINKER BLOB?

Suddenly I hear the two foreign women coming, talking and laughing. 'Holloa!' I shout. 'The bolt is broken. Please send an engineer.' It sounds absurdly like a phrase-book sentence, I am half tempted to go on *that bolt is rusty. It is too much. Tell him to come quickly. I shall inform the police* . . .

To the male voice which presently arrives I shout, 'Will you please bring me a short steel rod not more than a quarter of an inch wide.' This is presently pushed under the door and I push the bolt back from the other side, which is fortunately open (they never thought of that). I feel I have won, and I do not attempt to explain the paper letters and shreds all over the floor.

•

HARRY GOLDEN

Harry Golden (1902–81) was born to immigrant parents on the Lower East Side of New York, where his father was an editor of the *Jewish Daily Forward*. He studied literature at City College in New York, although he did not complete his degree. He did a spell in Federal prison for mail fraud before working as a reporter for the *New York Post* and the *New York Daily Mirror*. In 1939 he moved to the South as a salesman, eventually settling in North Carolina, where in 1941 he started his own small-circulation paper, the *Carolina Israelite*, one of only a couple of liberal titles in the South. He wrote most of the paper, including a column which was later handled by the Bell–McClure Syndicate. A dedicated integrationist, he wrote in a satirical vein, promoting such schemes as the Vertical Negro Plan, the White Baby Plan and the Out of Order Plan. He even produced a plan to eradicate anti-Semitism, urging that all Jews convert to Christianity so that Christians would feel impelled to start their own Anti-Defamation League and try to dissuade Jews from converting.

Excerpts from *You're Entitle'* (1962)

The Invisible Negro

In a small West Texas town the school board was faced with a unique problem: the town's oldest Negro boy had become eligible to enter high school, but the nearest school available to him was in a city about forty miles away. Since his family could not afford to pay for his transportation, they had asked the board to pay his way for the daily trip. And therein lay the problem. The State statutes could only provide a school bus. But again the board was stymied. There had to be a minimum of seven students before a bus could be furnished. The board took its problem to the town's lawyer.

The answer he finally gave them was fairly simple. He told them that there was nothing that kept the board from exercising its judgement and discretion in deciding who was and who was not a Negro. The board, being fairly smart, caught on fast. Quite hastily the members agreed that this colored boy (whose skin was very dark) was not a Negro.

On the boy's high school entrance paper the space for 'race' was discreetly left blank, so that no questions from outside the town were ever asked. Apparently few, if any, were asked in town either. He went all the way through high school there, and graduated with the 'other whites.'

The boy is practicing law in Illinois today. Apparently he was not prepared to risk practicing his profession in Texas – as an invisible Negro.

What is a Jewess?

A minority often begins to believe the propaganda used against it. It begins to absorb the phrases of its opponents.

One of these big deals is 'Jewess.'

Now what is a Jewess?

Strangely the suffix '-ess' is used only for the Negro and the Jew.

'Jewess' is actually an anti-Semitic term. It has been used for centuries, but gained popular usage with the genteel anti-Semites toward the end of the nineteenth century.

When one thinks of the promiscuous heroines of literature, they are either poor like Miss Forever Amber or rich like Miss Constant Nymph or sophisticated like Brett or soulful like Sophie or selfish like Emma Bovary. But the Jewish girl in the novel of promiscuity winds up playing the third act in a sadistic daydream. She is voluptuous and ripe and dark and electrically attractive, like poor Rebecca of Sir Walter Scott's *Ivanhoe*. People want to drag her through the streets by her hair. They'd love that, wouldn't they? And all because a high social status group has always stereotyped a low social status group as somehow being sexually primitive.

Thus 'Jewess' and 'Negress' – like lioness and tigress.

Anna Magnani says, 'I am an Italian,' and Vivien Leigh says, 'I am English' and the chairman of the Woman's Guild at Christ and Holy Trinity says, 'I am an Episcopalian.' No one says, 'I am an Italianess,' 'I am an Englishess' or 'I am an Episcopalianess.'

Why Tom Waring is Mad at Me

Tom Waring, a Southern gentleman of the old school, is the editor of the Charleston *News and Courier*. Every so often he runs a piece about me which he headlines, 'Golden Fights Dixie,' or 'Golden, Go Back to the Garment District.' Tom Waring is a die-hard segregationist and he wants to fight me because I am a die-hard integrationist. Up until a few weeks ago, I thought this political difference was the root of our disagreement.

But I have changed my mind. I doubt seriously that the integration issue is what bothers Tom Waring about me. My intuition about our real differences is a little tortuous to describe but I shall attempt it anyway.

One of the local tycoons recently returned from a trip around Europe. This man is a world traveler and he told me that in former years when he told government officials or foreign businessmen that he was from Charlotte, one of them was sure to say, 'That Charleston is a delightful city,' or, 'My wife has relatives in South Carolina.' Whereupon this world traveler wearily but without fail had to go into a long explanation that Charlotte is in North Carolina and has nothing to do with Charleston, which is in South Carolina.

But now, says this world traveler, the shoe is on the other foot. In Madrid, Berlin, Minneapolis or Tokyo, when someone says he's from Charleston, someone is sure to volunteer, 'Charleston? Isn't that where Harry Golden lives?'

This sad state of affairs has been filtering back to Tom Waring and has inspired his vituperation. He has nightmares that perhaps I really do live in Charleston and he wants me back in the garment district of Charlotte.

Tom: Stop worrying. I am home.

No More Hong Shew Gai

A true story that grew out of the 1962 demonstrations against segregation in restaurants along major highways leading from Baltimore.

Two young ferrows walk in Woo Lin's Chinese Restaurant on Washington-Baltimore Parkway.

Walking softly over, as the gold of dawn steals over the rice paddies, is Woo Lin, proprietor.

'Mushroom egg foo yung?' asks Woo Lin. 'Gai kew? Harr kow? Hong shew gai?'

But, before young ferrows can answer, Woo Lin notices something. Young ferrows not corored pale white. Not corored yerrow. Corored blown.

Ah, thinks Woo Lin, these must be the sit-ins.

So, as Amelican lawyer for restaurant association advise, Woo Lin takes out bulky papers and reads Maryland Trespass Law. Many difficurt words. Takes rong time.

Finarry, young ferrows get bored. They walk out.

Immediatery, two more young ferrows come in. Also corored blown.

Too much, thinks Woo Lin. He pulls shutters and locks door of restaurant.

No more hong shew gai today.

The Turban Plan

You are, perhaps, familiar with my Vertical Negro Plan to end segregation (based on
the observation that segregation persists only in a seated situation, and not in the South's
supermarkets, banks, department stores or at the cashiers' desks of big utility offices).
This plan, which entails removing all the seats from classrooms and permitting white
and Negro children to stand amicably together, has been put into effect successfully by
a number of lunch counters at Southern dime stores.

Since removal of the stools of these establishments, Negro and white kids munch
hotdogs without the slightest show of emotion.

The stools, of course, will come back, gradually. Maybe at first the Negroes can just
lean against the seat in a sort of half-standing position; and by such easy stages finally
get to a sitting position without stirring up anything.

But now it's time to review several other Golden Plans.

My Potemkin Toilet Plan was suggested by my observation at a recent concert in the
civic auditorium of a large Southern city. At this concert there were few Negroes in the
segregated audience. During the intermission I counted no fewer than twenty-eight
white ladies waiting to get into the 'white' powder room (at least half of them hadn't
gained admittance at the sound of the intermission buzzer). Less than twenty yards
away, behind a post, was the 'Negro Women' powder room, empty and silent, a complete
waste.

I suggest that we build a dummy door marked 'white' and attach to it a sign,
'Temporarily out of order, use "Negro Women" door,' a system that would work very
well in the upper South – Virginia, North Carolina and Tennessee – but which might
be a bit too drastic for the Deep South.

My SRO Plan actually is an adaptation of the Golden Vertical Negro Plan.

But it is simplicity itself: In all America there isn't a movie owner who doesn't dream
of the day when he can again hang out an SRO sign – standing room only.

The Negro audience has segregated movie houses stuck in some out-of-the-way alley.
Yet here are millions of people hungry for a first-run movie.

Let the motion-picture distributors hang out the SRO sign. This is justified because
they are also going to take the seats out of the theater. While it is never comfortable to
stand through a two-hour movie, certain sacrifices are necessary in order to do this
thing gradually. The inconvenience of standing can be somewhat alleviated by installing
vertical hassocks, which need not be elaborate, modeled along the lines of the hassocks
Englishwomen use at the races. This would allow folks to lean during the movie.

Finally, I present to the world my Turban Plan: You have all heard of the Negro reporter
who, a few years ago, visited a half-dozen Southern cities wearing a turban, and how well
he was received in fancy hotels and on a basis of fellowship with leading citizens, and how
in one city a ladies' society actually sent flowers and an invitation to make a speech.

Well, I have seen this work. A Negro social worker I know often visits a white colleague for two or three days at a time.

'I felt guilty about disrupting their family routine,' he reports. 'They want to go to the movies and I see them looking at each other in embarrassment, because they know I can't go, and so I carry a turban and use it when necessary; we are all more comfortable.'

The Golden Turban Plan has many facets. It will relieve the depression in the textile industry (caused by Japanese imports), which Secretary of the Interior Luther Hodges fights so hard to control and balance. If the textile industry were to start grinding out eight million turbans for the men and eight million saris for the women, the mills would hum morning, noon and night, and the officials of the Kennedy Administration could turn their attention to the problems of Africa, Berlin and South America.

Already Negro students at the University of Texas have adopted my plan with modifications. They do not wear turbans, they simply swear to movie ushers they are Egyptians.

Keeping a straight face, three college students raise their hands and swear they are respectively Egyptian, Hawaiian and Hong Kongese.

The supreme test, however, is yet to come.

There is now a Negro literary club, numbering eighty-odd, which has adopted my suggestion to wear turbans once a week wherever they go. The turbans are expected to arrive early next fall and these four-score-and-some-odd fellows will venture forth on a Saturday night in the near future to various cafés, movies and the like. It will be very interesting. The Angles, Picts, Scots, Celts and Saxons always roll out the red carpet for one guy with a turban. Let's see if it works for eighty guys with turbans.

A Liberal's Creed

An impression persists that perhaps we liberals are trying to help 'our little brown brothers.' This is an attitude no different from that of the paternalistic segregationists who put up the bail for their favorite Negroes.

I'm reminded here of a story about Captain Alfred Dreyfus, the Jewish officer on the French general staff, who was framed by a military clique but who found some noble defenders.

Captain Dreyfus was not a particularly pleasant fellow. During a moment of frustrating conversation with Captain Dreyfus, Emile Zola said, 'You are mistaken, Captain Dreyfus; we are not doing this for *you* – we are doing this *for France*.'

•

ARTHUR KROCK

Arthur Krock (1886–1974) was born in Glasgow, Kentucky, and was brought up there and, later, in Chicago. Although he went to Princeton in 1904, he was obliged to return home owing to his family's reduced circumstances, and he completed an AA at Chicago's Lewis Institute in 1907. From 1907 to 1910 he was a general assignment reporter for the *Louisville Herald* (in Kentucky) and was night editor of the Associated Press in that city for two years. In 1910 he became the Washington correspondent for the *Louisville Times* and the following year he took on the same role for the *Louisville Courier-Journal* (the papers shared an owner). From 1915 to 1919 he was managing editor of both titles, and from 1919 to 1923 he was editor in chief of the *Louisville Times*. However, in 1923 he departed for New York to work on the *World* under its highly esteemed editor Herbert Bayard Swope and was soon promoted to be assistant to the publisher. In 1927 he was hired as an editorial writer by the *New York Times* and in 1931 he returned to Washington as the *Times* correspondent there. He would stay for the remainder of his career and in 1932 he began his 'In the Nation' column, which ran until 1966 and garnered him four Pulitzers. A conservative by disposition, Krock was a critic of Roosevelt, Truman and Kennedy, and a supporter of Eisenhower. His columns were collected in *In the Nation, 1932–1966* (1966).

'In the Nation'
Wit and Humor During a Campaign
New York Times, September 15, 1952

General Eisenhower and his advisers have come to the deliberate conclusion that the witty gibes and humorous anecdotes with which Governor Stevenson is wont to lighten the necessarily serious business of discussing grave issues may be turned against him. They hope the American people can be brought to resent these as a wisecracking approach to weighty affairs and the mark of an essentially frivolous man.

The General launched on this strategy today when he said at Fort Wayne: 'As we face the issues of the campaign I see nothing funny about them and no way to make them amusing.' And he implied this was especially true of any discussion of the Korean war, which certainly is nothing to laugh about.

Of course, Stevenson did not laugh about the Korean war. But he did say a couple of witty things in the speech in which that war was a large topic. It will be interesting to try to discover whether, for example, the people of the United States believe, or can be brought to believe, that when a presidential candidate discusses such a topic, as Stevenson did at San Francisco Sept. 9, he establishes himself as light of mind by preceding it as follows:

> I want to share with you, if I may, a letter from a California lady who knew my parents when they lived here fifty years ago. She writes that after Grover Cleveland was nominated for the Presidency in 1892, and my own grandfather was nominated for Vice President, she named her two kittens Grover Cleveland and Adlai Stevenson. Grover, she writes, couldn't stand the excitement of the campaign and died before the election. But Adlai

lived to be a very old cat. And this, my friends, is obviously for me the most comforting incident of the campaign so far.

It seems improbable the Republicans can establish, from the method used by Stevenson to get his audience 'with him' at the outset, that he is congenitally frivolous and light-minded and finds everything funny, including the deadly serious. True, people who are opposed to a presidential candidate for any reason, or are looking for reasons to be, can readily be persuaded of almost anything by his critics. And it is also true that, if the impression can be created a candidate is 'too light to be President,' this constitutes a real danger to his chances of election. Some of the political strategists who are circulating the sobriquet of 'The Little Joker' for Stevenson understand that very well, and the favorable contrast for Eisenhower that might be effected thereby.

But it would seem that, to make this impression stick with enough voters throughout the nation, who otherwise would support Stevenson, to affect the result of the election, the masterly prose and the excellent delivery to which the witticisms and anecdotes are but narrow fringes must first vanish from the Governor's oratory. Or he must grow so fond of gags and stories that he will subordinate the issues to them.

This is always a danger for a man with a strong sense of the mirthful and the ridiculous. And in the case of Stevenson the danger is increased by the fact that, through the channel of some bright young men around him who are adept at saying and writing clever things, the gag-writers of Broadway and Hollywood are deluging his headquarters with japes and quips that go fine at '21' and the Brown Derby but on the presidential stump are not so good. It seems probable that the other day, when Stevenson facetiously offered to quit telling the truth about the Republicans if they would quit telling lies about the Democrats, he had become unwisely infatuated with one from the professional gag factory.

Except for that, however, and a couple of impulsive remarks at his press conferences, Stevenson has furnished his opponents with little substantial hope that they can prove him to be but a postprandial wit at the core. His two speeches at the Chicago convention where he was nominated restored the level of political oratory in this country to that which Woodrow Wilson occupied. Throughout the campaign thus far he has kept on this level. He has been urbane at times and humorous, but not flippant. And not only is his prose style facile in presenting the complex and the profound; it is his own.

Stevenson may be trapped by his wit into saying something disastrous in the context, or something where the offensiveness kills the humor. The eminence of his opponent makes that a constant hazard. But the skill in composition and the political sagacity he has shown so far make this improbable. 'Were it not for this occasional vent [of humor],' said Lincoln in 1864, 'I should die.' And that has always been a vent for the American people, too.

It is when Stevenson's wit and anecdotes are employed to cover a weakness of position that the Republicans have their opportunity. But Eisenhower has yet to strike hard at these. The Labor Day speech at Detroit, when the Governor swallowed the CIO [Congress of Industrial Organizations] program on labor relations while asserting his independence of all groups, is one example of a shining target for courageous attack.

'In the Nation'
The Candidate's Dream That is Seldom Fulfilled
New York Times, October 2, 1952

The intensive campaigning through the country by the rival candidates for the presidency, in which Mr Truman has now joyously joined, is a strategy of electioneering that many aspirants to the White House have sought vainly to reject. Ever since William McKinley spent the campaign of 1896 rocking sedately in his porch chair at Canton, Ohio, while William Jennings Bryan, his unsuccessful opponent, was covering every whistle stop, other candidates have dreamed they could pursue the same tactics and get elected. But since 1896 only Harding and Coolidge came anywhere near fulfilling the dream.

Maybe it vanished indefinitely from the hopes of presidential candidates in 1948 when Mr Truman took to the road and retrieved what almost all politicians but himself believed to be his lost cause. At any rate, years may pass before a presidential nominee, including any future incumbent of the White House, ventures to imitate the McKinley–Harding–Coolidge strategy.

Governor Stevenson's reported new plan to forgo several political excursions among the voters, in order to prepare and deliver more 'fireside talks' like that of last Monday night, suggests that the advent of television may presage a swing back toward McKinley's stationary campaign method of 1896. Talking to the people from a quiet room, free of the noise and other distractions of crowds and exploding flash bulbs, a candidate can concentrate on his message and experience no interruption. But the experiment will be made cautiously, with 1948 in mind. And, if Stevenson is elected, the President's undoubted conclusion that the Truman whistle-stop tours were essential to the event will probably prolong the successful pressure of political managers on national candidates to spend most of their time speaking to the people at first-hand.

The record contains many entries since 1896 of presidential nominees who wanted to take McKinley for their model and were argued out of it.

In 1904 the Democrats nominated the dignified and eminent jurist of Esopus, NY, Alton B. Parker. He had warned the party convention before it balloted on the presidency that, whatever the monetary plank of the platform might say about the parity rate of silver to gold, he would advocate the maintenance of the gold standard. The idea of what was then called a 'swing around the circle' was repugnant to Parker.

And, if anyone had suggested the modern expansion that Senator Taft in 1948 derisively named 'whistle stopping,' he would have risked banishment from Esopus for himself and apoplexy for the judge.

Parker announced that, like McKinley in 1896 and 1900, he would stay at home and receive delegations with whom he would discuss the issues. He would permit certain of these discussions to be made public. But there would be no speaking tour. Before the campaign was in its final phase, however, the Democratic nominee was making speeches in New York and states near-by on industrial 'trusts' and finance. They got him into trouble because the Republicans assailed them as ignorant. But the point is that, against his will, he went campaigning.

In 1908, after his third nomination to the Democrats, Bryan decided on a total change in his tactics. McKinley had rocked on his front porch throughout two contests with Bryan and been elected. Well, Bryan would do the same. But by Aug. 20 he was engaged in what Mr Truman would concede to have been a classic whistle-stop tour.

In this same year the Republican nominee, William H. Taft, informed all concerned he would not stump the country. He did not think it seemly. His resolution lived longer than Bryan's, but on Sept. 23 he started traveling and speaking and kept it up until the returns disclosed his election.

'My private judgement,' said Woodrow Wilson to his political advisers, after the Democrats named him for President in 1912, 'is that extended speaking tours are not the most impressive method of conducting a campaign.' He would make a few addresses at strategic points. There would be no rear-platform oratory (at whistle stops). The split in the Republican Party made Wilson's election almost a mathematical certainty, yet it was not long before he totally abandoned his 'private judgement' and went on the road.

Four years later, when President Wilson's opponent was Charles Evans Hughes, he returned to his resolution of 1912. He had, he said, no intention of making a campaign tour. He would accept a few invitations to discuss public questions, but only if they came from nonpartisan organizations. But in October he changed his mind and spoke under partisan auspices in several cities, concluding the series at Buffalo and Madison Square Garden. When the President discovered that Tammany sponsored the latter engagement he talked of refusing to appear because he had not been fully consulted before it was made. But he kept it and delivered one of the most notable addresses of his career.

After that, except for Harding and Coolidge, presidential candidates have bowed to the inevitable.

'In the Nation'
If Lincoln Had Invited 'Guidance'
New York Times, January 29, 1962

President Kennedy's statement at last week's news conference that even the highest civilian officials and military officers should circulate their proposed speeches through the government for 'guidance,' as he did his State of the Union message, has happily brought to light an anonymous paper on this subject, worthy of having been inspired by Bob Newhart's idea of how Madison Avenue would have edited the Gettysburg Address. The anonymity is attributed to the continued presence of the author in the State Department's 'speech-guidance' group.

The work is a speculation of interdepartmental comments Lincoln could have received on the Address if he and it were contemporary with present times and the 'guidance' system. There is room here for only the subjoined few of these might-have-been guidelines, which seem less imaginative than they would have before the Stennis subcommittee assembled:

Comments by the State Department (1) The phrase 'brought forth on this continent,' while technically correct, implies that the United States feels it owns the entire territory. This conflicts with our hemisphere policy and should be changed to 'an area bounded on the north by 49 degrees N. latitude,' etc.

(2) The use of 'dedicate' five times is tautological, which should be corrected by the alternate use of 'apotheosize.' Since 'nation' is a popular term without basis in international law 'member state' should be substituted. On the other hand, 'our poor power' implies self-admission that the United States is not a major Power, and the Secretary has directed the staff to work on a substitution. 'The world will little note' invades the department's statutory assignment to make such evaluations; substitute 'There probably will be only a few people who will note,' etc.

(3) The requirements of international harmony call for the elimination or modification of phrases such as 'conceived in liberty,' 'created equal,' 'birth of freedom,' 'government of * * * for * * * and by the people,' etc., because a number of our member states do not believe in liberty, freedom or equality and would properly take offense. The same objection applies to the words 'under God.' Also, 'conceived,' 'brought forth' and 'new birth' are open to interpretation among some of our NATO allies as offensive references to some recent irregular goings-on in their high official and motion-picture circles.

Other Departmental Comment (1) The Department of Defense urged the elimination of 'We are now engaged in a great civil war.' The passage recalls to the people the cost of our military establishment, particularly undesirable in this budget-making period. The words should be changed to 'We have entered upon a period of civil uncertainty involving fairly high mobilization.' For the same reason 'brave men, living and dead,' 'honored dead' and so on are ill-chosen; they unnecessarily call popular attention to a by-product of war the people don't like. And 'all men are created equal' must be excised because it is highly objectionable to the air force.

(2) The Navy Department deplored the misleading impression, created by stress on land operations, that there were no engagements at sea. It proposed mention of air-sea rescue. The Department of Commerce reported it would take years to coordinate the interests of all its units so that they could be safeguarded in the Address, but meanwhile had compiled 253 suggested editorial changes. The Department of Health, Education and Welfare (joined by State) asked that the speech be postponed until it could locate all its officials with titles conveying supreme authority.

(3) The Budget Bureau proposed the Address be turned over for complete revision to a working-group from State, Defense, Treasury, Post Office, Labor and Commerce, explaining the bureau did not seek membership on the group because it could make whatever changes it chose later. Meanwhile, however, Budget counseled against figures of specific commitment such as 'Fourscore and seven years ago' – advising 'A number of years' instead – against 'we cannot hallow this ground' as in conflict with Secretary Freeman's plan, and reminded the President that only Congress can 'highly resolve' – or 'resolve' at all.

If the luck of the United States is holding, the anonymous author of this paper is still in the State Department.

•

MICHAEL FRAYN

Michael Frayn (b. 1933) was educated at Kingston Grammar School and Emmanuel College, Cambridge. In 1957 he joined the *Manchester Guardian* as a reporter and in 1959 he began to write the three-times-a-week 'Miscellany' column for the *Guardian*. From 1962 to 1968 he wrote a column for the *Observer* and thereafter he became a successful playwright while continuing to write occasional features about foreign countries for the *Observer*.

'Miscellany'
I Said, 'My Name is "Ozzy" Manders, Dean of King's'

From *On the Outskirts* (1964)

I must not tell lies.

I must not tell pointless lies.

I must not tell pointless lies at parties.

I must not tell pointless lies at parties when they are plainly going to be found out in the next ten minutes.

I must not:

1. Let it be thought that I have caught the name of anyone I am ever introduced to, because statistics show that I have never caught anyone's name until I have heard it at least twelve times.

2. Give it to be understood that I have already heard of the owner of the inaudible name, because tests show that apart from one or two obvious exceptions like William Shakespeare and Sir Harold Sidewinder I haven't heard of anyone.

3. Say I have read the man's books, or admired his architecture, or used his firm's brake-linings, or seen his agency's advertisements, or always been interested in his field of research, or know his home town, because I do hereby make a solemn and unconditional declaration, being before witnesses and in sober realization of my past wrongdoing, that I have done none of these things.

4. Say that I know any of the people he is sure I must know, or have heard of any of the names he takes to be common knowledge, because I don't and haven't, or if I do and have, I've got them all hopelessly mixed up, and when he says Appel I'm thinking of Riopelle, and when he says Buffet I'm thinking of Dubuffet, and when he says Palma I'm thinking of Palermo, and when he says syncretism I'm thinking of syndicalism, and when he says a man called 'Pop' Tuddenham who hired a barrage balloon and dressed it up to look like an elephant I'm thinking of a man called 'Tubby' Poppleton who hired a horse and dressed it up to look like the Senior Tutor.

5. Try to sustain the fiction that I have heard anything he has said to me over the noise, because I have not, and because he has heard nothing I have said, either, so that by analogy he *knows* I am lying just as surely as I know he is lying.

6. Bend my lips in an attempt to counterfeit a smile unless I am absolutely assured by the raising of a flag with the word JOKE on it that the man has made a joke and not announced that his mother has died.

7. In short, get involved in any more conversations that go: 'I've long been a great admirer of your, er . . . stuff, Mr . . . er . . . er . . .'

'*How kind of you.*'

'Oh, all kinds.'

'*No, I'm afraid some critics haven't been at all kind.*'

'The tall kind? I see. I see.'

(A long silence. I think.)

'I particularly liked your last boo . . . er, pla . . . um, one.'

'*Last what?*'

'One.'

'*One what?*'

'Um, thing you, well, did.'

'*Really? The press panned it.*'

' "The Press Bandit" – of course, it was on the tip of my tongue.'

'*Well, the Irish banned it.*'

'I mean "The Irish Bandit", of course. How stupid of me.'

'*But everyone else panned it.*'

'Oh, Elsie Pandit. You mean *Mrs* Pandit?'

'*Who – your missus panned it?*'

'No, India's Mrs Pandit.'

'*They panned it in India, too, did they?*'

'Did they? I suppose Mrs Pandit banned it.'

'*Ah. You know India, do you?*'

'No. You do, do you?'

'*No.*'

'Ah.'

'*Hm.*'

(I smile a cryptic, knowing smile. He smiles a cryptic, knowing smile. We are getting on wonderfully. Just then my wife comes up and wants to be introduced, and I have to ask the man who he is.)

Why do I do these things? Do I think the man's going to give me a fiver, or a year's free supply of his works for having heard of his name? Do I think he's going to twist my arm and kick me on the kneecap if I don't like his stuff? He doesn't *expect* me to like it. No one likes it except his wife and the editor of *Spasm* and 780 former pupils of F. R. Leavis. Anyway, I've got him mixed up with someone else, and he didn't do it, and even what he didn't do isn't what I think he did. For heaven's sake, am *I* going to strike *him* because he thinks I'm called Freen, and that I write articles for the Lord's Day Observance Society?

I must not waste my valuable talent for deceit on lies which have no conceivable purpose when I could be saving it up for lies which would show a cash return.

I must instead say, 'I'm sorry, I didn't quite catch your name.'

I must say, 'I'm sorry, I still haven't quite . . .'

I must say, 'I'm sorry – did you say "Green" or "Queen"? Ah. Queen who? Come again . . . Queen *Elizabeth*? Elizabeth what?'

I must say, 'I expect I should know, but I'm afraid I don't – what do you do? I beg
your pardon? Rain? You study it, do you – rainfall statistics and so on? No? You rain?
You mean you actually rain yourself? I see. I see.'

I must say, 'No, I *don't* see. What do you mean, you rain . . . ?'

I must . . .

I must not, on second thoughts, be pointlessly honest, either . . .

'Miscellany'
Spock's Guide to Parent Care

From *At Bay in Gear Street* (1967)

Parents are just large human beings. It's only natural for a small child to feel a little daunted
by the hard work and responsibility of coping with parents. All parents get balky from
time to time, and go through phases which worry their children, and all children get
tired and discouraged and wonder whether they're doing the right thing.

The important thing to remember is that most parents, deep down inside, want
nothing more than to be good ones. A parent may act tough and cocky, but at heart he
wants to be one of the gang. He wants to learn what's expected of him as a parent and
do it. What he needs from you above all is plenty of encouragement, and plenty of
reassurance that he's doing all right.

Every parent is different. This one flies into a fury at the sight of crayoning on the
wallpaper. That one bursts into tears. Yet another goes into a sulk and won't say anything
all afternoon. All these are perfectly normal, healthy reactions. I'd be inclined to be
suspicious of the parent who seems a little too good to be true. He or she may be
deprived of emotional experience for lack of opportunity. I think I'd ask myself in this
case if I was drawing on the wallpaper enough.

They aren't as fragile as they look. Handle them confidently. Many parents look as though
they'll have a nervous breakdown if you bang your toy on the table just once more.
Don't worry – nine times out of ten they won't.

Don't be afraid to insist on your own standards. There's been a great swing away from the
overpermissiveness which used to be the fashion, when a parent's every whim was
regarded as sacred. Nowadays we've come to realize that on the whole people don't
have any very clear ideas about manners or morals until they become parents, when
they hastily start to make them up as they go along. They're secretly very grateful for a
little firm but tactful guidance.

I don't mean by this that you should squash the parents' own spontaneous efforts to
help. But what they eventually learn to think right and proper will be decided very
largely by the way you act anyhow.

Play is education, too. All the time you are with your parents you are educating them in
tolerance and self-discipline. Playing games and romping with them is specially useful.
It's not only great fun for them – it's helping to form their characters. Various games,

such as hitting your little brother, and then bursting into tears before he does, train their powers of detection and judgement. Jumping on their stomachs after meals and finding reasons to get them up in the middle of the night develop their resistance to hardship, and generate a sense of righteousness which will enable them to face cheating their colleagues next day with an easy conscience.

Temper tantrums. Almost all parents have temper tantrums from time to time. You have to remember that between the ages of twenty and sixty parents are going through a difficult phase of their development. They have got to a stage in their exploration of the world at which they find it is rather smaller than they thought. They are discovering the surprising limitations of their personality, and learning to be dependent. It's natural enough for them to want to explode at times.

It's no use arguing with a parent who's in this sort of state. The best thing is just to let him cool off. But you might try to distract him and offer him a graceful way out by suggesting something that's fun to do, like taking it out on your little brother instead.

Go easy on kidding. Most parents enjoy a joke. If you get hold of a good one, try it on them twenty or thirty times, just to show them what it's like being on the receiving end of the family's sense of humour. But I think I'd give it a rest after that, in case it causes nightmares.

Jealousy. Most parents are worried, though they probably wouldn't admit it, that they're not really good enough, and that other parents are better at the job than they are. In one parent it will take the form of worrying that his children are not as pretty, or as well behaved, or as intelligent as other people's. Another will try to resolve his fears by telling himself that other parents don't really look after their children properly.

A parent showing symptoms of jealousy needs lots of love and reassurance. Once in a while it might help to beat the boy next door in a clean fight, or win that scholarship. But you can't do this too often without the risk of spoiling the parent. Once a parent gets the idea that he can just sulk and you'll win a scholarship for him he'll lead you a terrible dance.

Be friendly but firm. In general, don't give your parents too much chance to argue. Just quietly get on with whatever you want to do, perhaps chatting amiably to distract their attention. The chances are they won't even notice, or that when they do it will be too late for them to feel like making a fuss.

Parents can sometimes drive a small child almost to distraction by dawdling about in shops, or talking to friends. It doesn't really help to keep nagging, or to try dragging them along by brute force. If I were you I'd hop cheerfully about from foot to foot, and say in a firm, friendly voice: 'I want to go to the lavatory.' If that doesn't work, you could try turning white, and saying you're going to be sick.

Remember you're helping them to grow up. It's your job to help your parents grow up into mature responsible old-age pensioners, self-confident, armed with a workable code of morals and manners, and too exhausted in mind and body to make trouble for anyone else. If you keep in mind that you're training your children's grandparents you won't go far wrong.

•

RICHARD L. STROUT

Richard Lee Strout (1898–1990) was born in Cohoes, New York, but was brought up in Brooklyn. After two years at Dartmouth and a spell in the US Army, he entered Harvard University, where he obtained an AB in 1919 and an MA in economics and political science in 1923, while writing for the *Harvard Crimson* and *Harvard Advocate*. He went abroad to England, where he became a reporter for the Sheffield *Independent*, and on his return to the United States he worked briefly at the *Boston Globe* before joining the *Christian Science Monitor* as a reporter and copy-editor. In 1925 he moved to the paper's Washington bureau and for the next sixty years he was a Washington correspondent. From 1943 to 1983 he was also the writer of the liberal commentary column 'TRB from Washington', which was published in the *New Republic* and syndicated to sixty papers. He still had time left over to write occasional pieces for *Reader's Digest* and the *New Yorker*.

'TRB from Washington'
Predictions
New Republic, December 11, 1965

We got as far as our first 'We predict,' in a year-end political forecast, when we checked ourself. We fished out our folder marked 'Predictions.' It took us completely off the track.

'There is no cause for worry. The high tide of prosperity will continue.' Andrew W. Mellon said that right before the 1929 smash.

'The economic condition of the world seems on the verge of a great forward movement,' Bernard Baruch told Bruce Barton in an interview in the *American* magazine for June 1929.

Poor old Hoover. 'I can observe little on the horizon today to give us undue or great concern,' he said, as the bottom dropped out.

But that's old stuff. Let's look at the yellowed clippings of a later date, the FDR–Landon presidential race of 1936. You recall: Landon carried two states, Maine and Vermont. Our favorite predictor here was columnist David Lawrence: 'Landon to win in Pennsylvania by 250,000,' he wrote in the *Boston Transcript*, October 22. 'New York for Landon,' is another headline on a Lawrence column. Others were in there pitching, too: 'California swings to Landon with rest of West Coast,' said a correspondent of the *New York Sun*, October 31. 'Kiplinger Sure President Vote Will Be Close,' according to headline, October 22, in the *Boston Herald*. And the *New York Herald Tribune* published what it described as 'a new type of presidential forecast' by Rogers C. Dunn, a voting research expert: 'Landon To Win 33 States, New Forecast Shows.'

Well, we were all younger then. We were, perhaps, more sure of ourselves. But a prediction that blows up in your face can be a humiliating matter. We know. Let's pass hurriedly over Dewey's 'victory' against Truman in 1948. This column (we blush to say) was so confident of a Dewey win that we went to press on it. We still recall our conflicting emotions that Wednesday morning: exhilaration over Truman's victory and mortification over our forthcoming reference to President-elect Dewey. All we can say is that the public loves this kind of thing. Nothing rejoices a reader more than to point out with a smirk, to some hardworking columnist, a little slip he has made like naming the wrong president.

Hum, hum. Here's a nice column by Stewart Alsop, June 2, 1951, beginning: 'Secretary of State Dean Acheson cannot conceivably remain in office very much longer.' And here's the 'Newsgram' page of the *US News & World Report*, February 13, 1953, 'A Look Ahead': 'Eisenhower will be a strong president, a leader.' Even at that early hour of the new Administration, something led us to file that away.

The *Boston Globe*, September 15, 1955, had a piece: 'Why Ike Won't Run Again.' Seems he had promised Mamie he wouldn't.

In 1957 the Soviets lofted Sputnik into space. In a way it resembled 1929. There was the same awful jolt to confidence and the same official rush to cover up. 'The satellite is a nice scientific trick,' said Charles Wilson, ex-Secretary of Defense. 'Nobody is going to drop anything down on you from a satellite while you are asleep, so don't worry about it.'

Senator Goldwater also refused to get excited 'just because the Russians have lobbed a basketball into space that goes beep, beep, beep.'

Clarence Randall, Ike's special adviser on foreign economic policy: 'The satellite is a silly bauble. I am personally very gratified that our nation was not first.'

General Eisenhower mildly protested that it 'does not raise my apprehensions, not one iota.'

Our most notable modern prophet is Defense Secretary McNamara. His field: Vietnam. 'The corner has been definitely turned toward victory' (May 1963). 'The major part of the US military task can be completed by the end of 1965' (October 1963). 'We have every reason to believe that plans will be successful in 1964' (December 1963). 'The US hopes to withdraw most of its troops from South Vietnam before the end of 1965' (February 1964). We read, with mixed feelings, his latest effort last week: 'We have stopped losing the war.'

So where were we when we got interrupted? Oh, we were just going to offer a few speculations, *not* predictions. Chief of these is that the dominant political issue next year will be Vietnam.

There certainly is a sour mood in this capital today. Draft calls and casualties are going up, and administration officials are beginning to educate the public to the idea that it's going to be a long war. The man in the street somehow can't understand it. How can a country as rich as the US, he asks, be thwarted in a silly little war? Surely there must be some easy way out.

This is what politicians call a 'gut' issue. It affects everybody. It touches a naked nerve. The issue seems likely to grow – and it is eleven months to the midterm election. Republicans have been desperately looking for an issue: inflation?, centralized government?, Johnson the dictator? People don't get roused over such matters, not when the economy is booming. But a dirty war in Asia, with your boy in it, that is another matter.

House Minority Leader Gerald Ford of Michigan says he is resisting 'increasing pressure' to break sharply with the Administration. Senator Dirksen and Richard Nixon want to extend bombing. Many Democrats go along. Mr Johnson is in a cleft stick. If he tries to negotiate it will be a sign of 'softness.' If casualties mount, it will be because he did not use air power, or the Bomb.

Republicans insist they will not make this a political issue. But we can't believe they will keep Vietnam out of politics any more than they kept Korea out of politics.

Of course we are better mannered and less excitable today. Leopards have changed their spots, and politicians are less anxious to get elected. Just the same we predict – but no, not this week.

'TRB from Washington'
TRB Remembers
New Republic, July 28, 1973

We're going on vacation and would like to leave some thoughts. We've seen some sad things in Washington in our time: the day they buried FDR, and the Negro woman sobbed in the crowd on Pennsylvania Avenue and made us all sob, too; the day they brought back Jack Kennedy's body and we watched the fountain playing behind the White House, a steady stream, something that you could put your hand through, something without substance, but never ending – like democracy.

We've seen stirring things, too: the night we waited under the portico of the White House and watched the grim-faced members of the isolationist Senate Foreign Relations Committee go in and come out after Pearl Harbor, in preparation for the speech next day.

Way back we remember the tear gas hissing out of the canisters when they drove the bonus veterans out from Hooverville on Pennsylvania Avenue, and a soldier had to come up and lead us down from the second floor of a half-demolished skeleton structure because we were blinded.

We can remember (or think we can) when Albert Fall came into the marble caucus room of the Senate in the Teapot Dome scandal, all shrunken and collapsed; the formerly arrogant Secretary of the Interior who scorned the Walsh committee the first time he came.

We can remember Borah standing in front of the lion house at the zoo one fall day and how leonine *he* looked (like John L. Lewis), and we gave him a lift in our Model T.

Wry things, too: Calvin Coolidge with an Indian headdress on; any speech in the Senate by J. Ham Lewis; the circus midget climbing into the inadequate lap of J. Pierpont Morgan as a publicity stunt, and he thinking it was a little girl.

Yes and recently, LBJ. What a character he was! – as indigenous a folk figure as little fox terrier Harry Truman; how we interviewed him one time when he was majority leader, and he said nobody was going to treat him like a child-in-arms! And by golly, in an instant he was bounding out of his chair behind his enormous desk in a palatial room that looked like the Sistine Chapel with floating nymphs painted on the ceiling, bounding out of the chair and striding up and down the carpet with arms bent, indignantly rocking an imaginary baby.

The pay in Washington ain't much, but the show's swell. After a while, though, things begin to repeat. James McCartney writing in the current *Columbia Journalism Review* wonders how the press let the White House story on Watergate go so long. Well, here is the comment of a great reporter, the late Thomas L. Stokes ('Chip Off My Shoulder') looking back at the time he served in the White House pressroom: 'The irony of it all to me – the amazing disclosures that came later – was that we newspapermen at the White House sat, all the time, at the outer gate, so to speak, and had known nothing.' Watergate? – no; Teapot Dome of course. McCartney and Stokes agree that the worst place to find out the scandals of an Administration is in the White House pressroom: 'the world of Ronald Ziegler,' as McCartney puts it, 'of the handout, the announcement, the statement, the official view.'

Things repeat themselves in other ways. The Supreme Court has just taken another crack, five to four, at deciding what's 'obscenity,' already causing a Virginia sheriff to discover that the girls in *Playboy* aren't clothed and opening up a probable new chaos of 'contemporary community standards.' Dear me, we've seen it all before; who's this grim figure stalking about the Senate, offering to show lascivious foreign imports and asking permission to read aloud to his colleagues, in secret session, excerpts from the new novel by D. H. Lawrence, *Lady Chatterley's Lover*? Why, tall, dignified, humorless Reed Smoot, to be sure, demanding to save the public morals and inspiring my favorite of all editorial captions, 'Smite Smut, Smoot!'

Here's another issue coming up now, so repetitive that I have a file on it, 'executive privilege.' Yes, the Constitution would practically fall apart if President Nixon invited a Senate committee to the White House to tell what he knows about Watergate, let alone if he went himself to Congress to testify.

Well, old Abe didn't talk much about executive privilege. They set up a committee to watch him in 1861, a group of suspicious, hate-ridden superpatriots ('Radical Republicans' they called them) – the Joint Committee on the Conduct of the War. They felt they knew how to run the war better than he did. But he didn't appeal to separation of powers. There was talk of his impeachment. He didn't retreat inside the White House.

One time, according to Carl Sandburg's *Lincoln: The War Years* (Vol. 2), the committee met in secret session to consider Mrs Lincoln's loyalty. Suddenly, as they sat, the orderly came in with 'a half-frightened expression' and, before he could speak, there at the foot of the committee table 'standing solitary, his hat in his hand, his form towering, Abraham Lincoln stood.' Sandburg says that Lincoln came voluntarily, took oath of family loyalty, and departed.

The story may be apocryphal but there's no question that Lincoln met with the committee many times. In *Lincoln Day by Day*, an authoritative chronology issued here in 1960, the President is shown to have conferred personally with the committee ten times, 1861–4. He didn't fear loss of dignity or constitutional collapse by dealing directly with a committee of Congress.

That's the difference between then and now; it's what we've been mulling over in these prevacation musings. The new tone is monarchical; it varies from the bizarre to the berserk. At one minute it's the light-opera uniforms the President proposed for his

White House palace guard. At the next it's the sinister suggestion that the people are 'children' and that the critics are subversive.

A sympathetic White House witness, under oath, quotes the President's dismay at discovering what practically everyone else already knew: 'I have racked my brain. I have searched my mind. Were there any clues I should have seen that should have tipped me off?' Well, the answer is yes. Furthermore for the first time in history we've had a quasi-conspiracy to grab an election. And for the first time in history we've had burglars on the White House payroll.

●

JAMES RESTON

James 'Scotty' Reston was born in 1909 in Clydebank, Scotland, and attended the Vale of Leven Academy in Dunbartonshire before emigrating to the United States with his parents in 1920. The family settled in Dayton, Ohio, and after graduating from high school Reston spent a year editing a General Motors in-house publication before studying journalism at the University of Illinois. He received his BS in 1932, then worked as a sportswriter and sports publicist. He began his first column, 'A New Yorker at Large', for the Associated Press Feature Service in 1934, and from 1937 to 1939 he was again a sportswriter, for AP in London. When the Second World War broke out, he covered the blitz for the *New York Times*, and in 1941 he moved to Washington, DC, for the paper. He received a Pulitzer Prize for national reporting in 1945, for his coverage of the Dunbarton Oaks Conference. He turned down the editorship of the *Washington Post* in 1953 and instead became Washington bureau chief of the *Times*, and in 1957 he won his second Pulitzer. In 1960 he started a thrice-weekly column called 'Washington' and in 1963 he retired from his administrative responsibilities. While holding other senior executive titles on the paper, he continued writing his column until 1989. He has also been owner of the *Vineyard Gazette* since 1968.

Funny People, the Americans
New York Times, October 7, 1956

Fiery Run, Virginia

The American voters are funny people: They don't listen. Once every four years they are courted and coaxed by presidents and would-be presidents, by Democrats and Republicans, by commentators, reformers, Socialists, teetotalers, vegetarians and Prohibitionists, but they don't listen.

They have more radios and television sets, more loudspeakers and hearing aids than all the rest of the people in the world, but they don't listen. They talk more politics, they start more arguments, they attend more rallies, they watch more political forums, they tune in on more 'press conferences' than all the other peoples in all the other elections in Christendom, but they don't listen.

The American voters are funny people: They don't read. They buy more newspapers and subscribe to more magazines than the British, the French, the Germans and the Italians, but they don't read them. They line their shelves with them, they start fires with them, they make hats for their children with them, they pack dishes in them, but they don't read.

For their special benefit, the presses turn out scores of political books, pamphlets, charts, cartoons, histories and biographies, but they don't read them.

Armies of correspondents interview politicians and taxi-drivers, housewives and bartenders, farmers and trade-union leaders, political-science professors and editors, mayors, sheriffs, county clerks and policemen – all for the special benefit of the voters – but they don't read.

Serious novelists take time out from their life's work, Harvard historians and economists are excused from classes, distinguished magazine writers and college professors get a leave of absence – all to write speeches designed to persuade the American voters – but they don't read what is written.

They are told that the future of the Republic depends on the reelection of Everett McKinley Dirksen of Pekin, Illinois, as United States senator; they pay no attention. Billboards are purchased in the working-class district of Portland, Oregon, to convince the laborers that a vote for Wayne Morse is a vote for slavery; they won't look at them.

Brochures are printed by the ton and circulated in Cos Cob, Connecticut, to prove that the President and Senator Prescott Bush of Connecticut are 'tools of Wall Street . . . instruments of big business . . . hard-hearted men who love General Motors and hate Joe Smith'; nobody sees them.

The American voters are funny people: They don't vote. They present themselves to the world as the most successful Republic in history – a model of democracy, the most responsible and best-educated people on earth – but they don't go to the polls. They are critical of the British, the French, the Italians, the Belgians, the Dutch, the Indians, the Japanese, the Germans – all of whom have a higher percentage on election day than we have – but they don't vote.

The farmers swear by the Republican Party but go fishing on election day. The industrial workers complain to their long-suffering wives about the Republican Administration but forget to register. The white-collar slaves proclaim their superiority, condemn their fate, and whine about inflation and discrimination, but they don't vote.

They complain. They criticize. They condemn. They philosophize. But when the contention ends, when the people they like and the people they don't like have had their say and the great day comes around, they don't vote.

The American voters are funny people: They don't care. They are told that the Russians have slipped into the Middle East for the first time in 200 years, that the Chinese Communists are quietly building a vast empire in the Pacific, and that the British and French empires are breaking up before their very eyes, but they don't care.

They are told that the Secretary of State has outraged every major-league statesman in the world and is now working on the bush-leaguers; they pay no attention. The President is portrayed to them as a man with nothing but a smile and a prayer; they won't believe it. The Democratic nominee is condemned as an egghead with nothing but brains; they're not interested.

The English tell them their Constitution is unworkable; the French criticize their logic and their cooking; the Communists foretell their inevitable destruction; the Socialists predict their economic collapse; the moralists wail about their children; and they don't give a damn.

They don't listen. They don't read. They don't care. But that's all right. They don't need to; never did need to. They get along. And think of the nonsense they miss every four years.

'Washington'
The Imprudent Man's Tax Deductions
New York Times, July 8, 1962

Fiery Run, Virginia

Secretary of the Treasury Dillon has been working on a new tax law, and is going around asking for suggestions about how to close the biggest tax loopholes. Actually, there are only three ways to get rid of the biggest loophole of all – the 27½ percent deduction for depletion and depreciation of oil and gas wells.

The first is to get rid of Texas, which may be difficult. The second is to shoot Senator Robert Kerr of Oklahoma, which is illegal. And the third is to apply the principle of tax deductions for depletion to all natural resources.

Part 1 of Section 611 of Title 26 of the Internal Revenue Code deals with 'natural resources' and is based on the idea that if you have a natural resource which is used up or 'depleted' with the passage of time, you are entitled to a tax deduction.

Mr Dillon's mistake has been in trying to persuade Texas and Senator Kerr to give up this bonanza. They want to be paid for the oil they sell and paid again for not still having what they have sold. What Mr Dillon could do, however, is to apply the depletion principle across the board.

Take pretty girls. Nobody would deny, certainly not Senator Kerr, that they are a 'natural resource.' Also, feminine beauty, like oil, is a wasting asset. Nothing depletes a gal more than having a flock of kids, yet the present law does not apply to her. This is clearly an injustice. Section 611 of the Internal Revenue Code says: 'There shall be allowed as a deduction in computing taxable income a reasonable allowance for depletion and for depreciation . . . according to the peculiar conditions in each case.'

Admittedly, it might be difficult to calculate the value of depleted beauty, especially since there would indeed be 'peculiar conditions in each case.' Some women, for example, depreciate fast and would therefore be entitled to a quick write-off or depreciation allowance.

Also, if oil wells are entitled to a depletion allowance, what about prizefighters? Nothing depletes a man quicker than a hard punch in the nose. It takes longer to bring in a good heavyweight than a good oil well, and the supply of natural prizefighters is short.

Thus, the American prizefighter is at a disadvantage. He has no protection, like glass and carpet manufacturers, from foreign competition. Ingemar Johansson, the Swedish meteor, has a tax haven in Switzerland and got out of this country with more dubious foreign-aid funds than Chiang Kai-shek. But the poor American pug is stuck. He blooms and fades like the morning glory, and while Section 611 of the tax code protects the 'operating mineral interest' of lead and zinc – the Senate Majority Leader, Mike Mansfield, comes from a lead and zinc state – nobody protects the 'operating mineral interest' of bone and gristle.

Novelists are another American natural resource with a high depletion rate. They deplete themselves gathering enough experience to write a novel, and then deplete themselves further in the writing. The Treasury Department recognized this fact for General Eisenhower when they let him consider his memoirs as a life work and write them off as a capital gain. But most novelists shoot their whole story in a single volume and usually end up without either capital or gain.

Secretary Dillon ought to put these points to Senator Kerr. He cannot remove the depletion allowance in the tax structure without removing Senator Kerr, who has almost as many oil wells in and around Oklahoma as he has votes. But Secretary Dillon might be able to appeal to the senator's sense of humor, if not to his sense of justice.

If this cannot be done, Mr Dillon is in trouble. For he cannot recommend a general tax cut without tax reform, and he cannot get a fair tax reform without doing something about the biggest tax loophole of the lot. In fact, the oil and gas depletion allowance has become the symbol of tax inequality, and Senator Kerr the personification of the problem. His political influence is not depleted but enhanced with the passing of time, so Mr Dillon has to find a new approach, no matter how silly.

'Washington'
Washington's Brains and Feet
New York Times, February 15, 1963

President Kennedy is a puzzle. One day he pleads with the country to sacrifice, and the next he pleads with it to accept a tax cut. One day he venerates brains, and the next he tries to popularize walking.

Trying to popularize walking in America is like trying to popularize Prohibition in Kentucky. Asking a citizen to walk instead of ride in America is like asking a Frenchman to drink milk instead of wine. And the last French premier who did *that*, Pierre Mendès-France, was booted out of office.

President Kennedy himself is a living symbol of the dangers of exercise. So long as he concentrated on history, literature and politics, he was all right. But the minute he picked up a spade and started digging a hole for an Arbor Day tree in Canada, his back buckled and he's been a rocking-chair case ever since.

There are great advantages to the sedentary life, particularly around the White House. President Franklin D. Roosevelt survived and succeeded in office at least partly because he was a victim of polio. He wasn't always mounting his horses or airplanes or promoting fifty-mile hikes. He had to sit still and think, and he survived four presidential elections and lived sixty-three years seventy-two days, whereas Theodore Roosevelt, the champion of the strenuous life, only got through one and a half terms and died at sixty.

This is very dubious advice, living on Metrecal and hiking for publicity into the Blue Ridge mountains. Look at President Taft. When they sprung him from Yale in the class of 1878, the average weight of his classmates was 151 pounds. Taft weighed in on graduation day at 225 and kept going up from there to around 300. Meanwhile, he endured long sentences in the War Department, the Philippines, Cuba, the presidency, Yale Law School and the Supreme Court before he finally died here in Washington at the age of seventy-two. In contrast, Calvin Coolidge, that skinny symbol of austerity, died at sixty, probably because after he left the White House, he took up the reckless and strenuous craft of writing a newspaper column.

The political implications of this walking binge could be even more serious than the physical. President Kennedy survived the anti-Catholic vote in the election of 1960, but the anti-walking vote in America is infinitely larger.

For example, as soon as the President started urging people to take to the hills, an anti-exercise organization in Washington, previously partial to President Kennedy, held an emergency protest meeting here in Hall's saloon. The name of the organization is Athletics Anonymous. It is composed of men who have previously suffered from exercise, most of them heart cases, and it works roughly on the same principle as Alcoholics Anonymous. Only in Athletics Anonymous, when a member hears about somebody who begins to get a compulsion to walk or ride a horse, or run around the Lincoln Memorial, he goes to the poor fellow, puts a drink in his hand, and talks him into staying home.

Bobby Kennedy, of course, is the villain of this whole silly business. Bobby is an athletic delinquent. He bats his kids over volleyball nets from birth just to toughen them up, and it was no surprise that he was the first New Frontiersman to hike the fifty miles. He should study the life of Winston Churchill, the greatest man of the age. Winnie trifled with exercise in Africa during his youth and later built brick walls, but later he reformed and most of the time thereafter preferred smoking and drinking to hiking.

What this capital needs is not the fifty-mile hike but the fifty-minute 'think.' It could easily be arranged. The National Security Council, for example, could have been summoned to think for fifty minutes before doing or saying anything.

Even Theodore Roosevelt, who is being blamed for the official hiking craze, wasn't all 'Rough Rider.' He made his daughter Alice learn something new out of a book every night before she went to bed, and tell him what it was at breakfast every morning, no matter how late she was out the night before. The device worked too. She has been following his advice ever since, and bless her, she was seventy-nine this week and is the most interesting lady in Washington.

•

ALEXANDER MACDONALD

Alexander Macdonald (1915–73) was born in Sydney and educated at a Catholic seminary in Scotland. At the age of sixteen he returned to his father who was a gold miner in Queensland. He joined ABC in Sydney as a continuity writer. He wrote humorous scripts for comedians such as Jack Davey and Roy Rene as well as a weekly radio review for *Smith's Weekly*, and he also wrote humorous columns for the *Daily Telegraph* and *Sunday Telegraph*, the *Sydney Morning Herald* and the *Daily Mirror*.

The Great Bank Robbery

From *Don't Frighten the Horses* (1961)

Stand up the boy who's been tampering with my cheque-book during my absence!

It is an extraordinary thing that I cannot leave this country for more than a fortnight without something comparable to the Great Wall Street Crash happening to my bank account.

Heaven knows, I'm not responsible, but every time I return from abroad, I can count on a reception committee of at least one.

He is always there; a sombre, solitary figure, wearing deep mourning, waiting on the wharf or at the airport, and carrying something at the end of a ten-foot pole.

It is my bank manager, and the article attached to the end of the ten-foot pole is my Statement of Account, emblazoned in scarlet from margin to margin.

The procedure never varies. He looks at me with the big, reproachful eyes of a consumptive Basset hound. 'So you've done it again,' he says.

Any boon companions who happen to be present immediately melt away, and we are left alone with our grief. We invariably finish up back in his office. The drink cabinet remains locked throughout the interview, despite all my subtle efforts to coax it open.

I have tried to be rational, but as everybody knows, bank managers are quite devoid of logic. Last week, once again, I put the usual, incontestable argument: 'How can I possibly have spent all this money when I've been out of the country?' I asked.

Mr Dalwhinnie favoured me with a sad smile. (I think I mentioned that I resigned from my last bank – run by a Mr Crankshafte – some months ago. Mr Crankshafte arranged it.)

'It is my opinion, Macdonald,' said Mr Dalwhinnie, 'that even if you were deprived of cheque-book and pen, and imprisoned in a sealed room, you would still manage to run up an overdraft.

'Indeed, I sometimes suspect you could probably materialize cheques from beyond the tomb. It is a disquieting thought.'

'You look pale, Mr Dalwhinnie,' I said. 'A shot of brandy is what you need. Where do you keep it?'

'What I need,' said Mr Dalwhinnie, 'is an explanation of how you've come to be £43/6/8 in the red in a matter of two weeks.'

'That 6/8 sounds very bogus to me,' I said, gravely. 'I never write cheques for amounts like 6/8. It makes the account look so untidy.'

'Untidy! cried Mr Dalwhinnie, waving my statement under my nose. 'Why, economically speaking, this is a positive pigsty.'

I winced. 'Please cover it up,' I said. 'The glare hurts my eyes. And, coming back to that 6/8: Have you considered the possibility there might be a master forger nibbling at my account?'

'I'll soon scotch that notion for you,' said Mr Dalwhinnie, rising. 'I'll show you your own cheques!'

'Please don't bother,' I said. 'And, talking about Scotch, would I be wrong in assuming that this little cupboard over here contains – '

'Come away from there!' said Mr Dalwhinnie, sharply. 'This is not a social gathering. Tell me, what are you going to do about that £43/6/8?'

I pondered. Followers of these chronicles must by now be aware that behind this sloping forehead lurks one of the keenest financial brains in the country, capable of lightning manipulations. (Readers of last Thursday's Pounds Shillings and Pence page may recall, for example, the significant headline – 'Watkins Consolidated Ltd is Floating' – an operation, let me say with a modest bow, which would have been quite impossible if I hadn't lent them my waterwings.)

Finally, the solution came to me in a flash of inspiration. 'I shall write you a cheque for £43/6/8 on my No. 2 account,' I said.

Mr Dalwhinnie darted me the sort of look Lord Chatterley probably gave Lady Chatterley when she got back from the Gamekeepers' Picnic. 'Don't tell me you also belong to another bank!' he barked, his eyes ablaze with jealousy.

I reassured him. 'No, I mean my No. 2 account here,' I said.

'But, confound it, man, you haven't got a No. 2 account here!'

'Then I'll open one,' I said, 'with one pound, cash, deposit. I'll give you the pound now. In the circumstances I'm sure you wouldn't mind extending me an overdraft of £42/6/8. The usual collateral, of course – my centuries-old recipe for Peking Duck, hand-printed on pig-hide.'

Mr Dalwhinnie leaned slowly forward until his head was resting on his blotting-pad. I could see he was thinking it over. Meantime, I was going through my pockets, and without much success.

'Too bad about the deposit,' I said. 'I seem to have left my wallet at home. Could you see your way clear to lending me a quid till next Thursday? Personal loan, of course, with no interest attached.' (We financial wizards have got to be careful about small details such as this.)

Without lifting his head Mr Dalwhinnie pointed in the direction of the door. 'Go,' he said. 'Go, and do not come back, ever.'

'But what about the £43/6/8?' I asked.

'Pay it off, if, and how you can,' said Mr Dalwhinnie. 'Preferably by post. Not in person. And now, go.'

I went. I cannot bear to watch a grown-up banker cry.

The Pub and I

From *Don't Frighten the Horses* (1961)

The sweetest pipe-dream ever extracted from the poppy-pod recently took shape in the frosty paw of Mr Arthur Lown, a sixty-five-year-old English pub-keeper who lobbed here last week aboard *Stratheden*.

Barely giving the opium fumes time to clear, this benevolent Boniface – who insists on being addressed as Uncle Arthur – issued a series of visionary utterances, the likes of which have seldom been equalled outside the Book of Revelation.

The main Vision Splendid in Uncle Arthur's Ode to Joy is a Cosy, Comfy Pub in the Olde Englyshe Style, which he proposes to establish here – God and the licensing authorities willing.

'There is no friendly atmosphere in the hotels out here,' said Uncle Arthur – adding, in his kindly, avuncular way – 'Probably because none of your pubs are more than a hundred years old . . .'

Before exploring any further into the Secret World of Uncle Arthur, I really must check him on this last point. No pubs over a hundred years old! Bless your innocence, Uncle – there are several pubs I know in NSW which are at least *five* hundred years old – and they've got the cobwebs to prove it, along with the hot and cold running rats, the wallpaper of greater antiquity than the Bayeux Tapestry, decorated with the delicate stipplings imprinted by the swatting of countless generations of beetles and flies.

As for the atmosphere of the average beer salon – I can think of no place more positively *reeking* of atmosphere . . . except, maybe, the torture chamber adjoining the Bloody Tower. Atmosphere, Uncle? Our pubs are lousy with atmosphere.

Eyes still agleam with Faith, Hope and Prophecy, Uncle Arthur went on to describe his ideal of the Perfect Pub: 'The first requirement of a good pub,' he said, 'is comfortable furniture and good service.'

Oh, Uncle. Here, if you like, is a gratuitous insult flung in the very teeth of Australian Pubbery. Comfortable furniture? What, pray, could be more relaxing than a nice, shiny tile wall to lean on? Why, in the more sybaritic pubs they have even installed those marvellous new tin chairs, over which the laughter-loving customers slop libations of beer.

And as for cuisine . . . Uncle, you just haven't been around much yet. Ah, those magic menus of Murwillumbah, and all points north, south, east and west! Those tantalizing breakfasts of gutta percha swimming in glue – in surroundings where the hygiene is such that the head chef, in person, runs a feather duster over the meat loaf at least twice a week.

Uncle Arthur's most startling statement, however, was one which sent me helter-skelter to my favourite hostelry, to fling the imputation back in his face.

'In England,' said Uncle A., 'it helps to run a pub with your wife, who can be a hostess and a mother to all the customers. This does not seem to be the case over here.'

As I said, this slur on our incidence of Pubbish Mumship sent me scuttling around to the Pig and Whistle (you drink like a pig and then whistle).

There, presiding over her chicklings, as usual, was the huge, bombazined matriarch we all refer to, tenderly, as Drip-tray Dora, always ready with some friendly quip, such as 'Haven't youse had enough?' or 'Drink up, sport, it's closing time any tick of the clock . . .'

Proffering my florin, I said: 'Scotch, please.'

'Anything with it?' said Dora.

'Yes, indeed,' I said. 'One little teeny privilege, Ma'am.'

'Eh?' said Dora.

Leaning over the bar, and taking her tiny hoof of a hand in mine, I said, shyly – 'From now on, Madonna, may I call you mater?'

Dora picked up a dishclout. 'What do you mean?' she said suspiciously.

'I want you to be a mother to me,' I said. 'Ah, Dora – let me be your Sonny Boy!' . . .

Well, Uncle, that's the last thing I remember. I am at present in Ward 3, just up the road from the Martin Place clock, suffering from an ailment known as Barmaid's Backhander.

Dr Mac's Seasonal Sermon to Partygoers
From *Don't Frighten the Horses* (1961)

We are now approaching the season of the year when the bird is in the bag, the beer is in the fridge and grog-blossoms are in full bloom.

It's the season when every boy's thoughts turn, not a little anxiously, towards the state of Old Man Liver.

(He don't say nuthin' – he gives no warnin' – he grins and bears it – till one fine mornin' – dat ol' Man Liver, he just quits playin' along.)

Meanwhile, speaking with all the bumptious superiority of one who is pledged to drink nothing but buttermilk and creaming soda during the next fortnight, allow me to give you weaklings (who don't possess my iron willpower) a short sermon on the Perils of Partygoing.

(No sneaking out, in the bleachers, there! Back to your pews, sirrahs!)

Text: *The Seven Deadly Gins:* The partygoer's commonest weakness is a form of hallucination in which he imagines he is consuming one drink for everybody else's four. Thus, at the end of seven Martinis he deludes himself that he's only had two, and so on, and so on – until the Sandman finally arrives, armed with the usual blunt instrument.

(I witnessed a classic case of this one morning back in 1937, when I was making a light breakfast on champagne – at 9d. a glass – with Mr Peter Finch. After breakfast Finch – who had about seven or eight under his belt – declared, 'Ah, there's nothing like a couple of champagnes to fix a man up for the day.' At which he stepped from his stool and, with the consummate dignity of a born actor, fell flat on his face.)

Dr Mac's Counter-ploy – the Mock Middy: Borrowing the principle used by a give-up-smoking agency – which recommends puffing at a plastic dummy cigarette and making believe that you're actually smoking – I have devised a foolproof gimmick for those who Don't Trust Themselves at Parties (and we are legion).

It consists of a middy glass filled with solid amber and topped with a layer of meerschaum (to simulate foam) which you take along to the party under your coat.

Produce your mock middy and pretend to sip from it – with every evidence of lip-smacking relish. *And remember – it's all in the mind!* Simply make *believe* that it's beer. Soon you will find yourself actually *enjoying* the natural hop flavour of the solid amber. You'll wonder what you ever saw in *real* beer. '*Liquid* beer? Ugh!' you'll say. 'How did I ever drink it?'

(I am assuming, of course, that you are a congenital idiot, with a file a foot thick at the Reception House.)

Dr Mac's Counsel to Hopeless Cases: Not many of you, alas, will have the strength of character to employ the mock middy system this season. So, for you unfortunates who will almost certainly be greeting Christmas Day with a bleached scowl, allow me to offer one or two time-hallowed words of advice:

On Waking Up: The first thing you will be aware of, once the priceless boon of consciousness has been restored to you, will be the metallic thudding of gay gong-notes somewhere behind the ears. Do not panic. These are the Christmas chimes from the neighbouring church, wishing you jollity, joy and goodwill.

On Making Breakfast: Don't!

On Getting Dressed: Choose, first, a shirt with no buttons. In your condition, what with the church bells and a curious, humming noise in the frontal lobe of the skull (this last is quite imaginary – ignore it), shirt buttons will assume the magnitude of manhole covers and each buttonhole, the abstract unreality of a slit in a marshmallow.

The greatest hazard, however, is that exhausting operation, the Putting on of the Shoes. There are some reckless fools who court instant insanity by sitting on the edge of the bed and *bending forward* to perform this feat . . . with the result, of course, that the head falls off and rolls under the bed.

Correct procedure is to *step* into the shoes from an upright posture. If the shoes are too tight-fitting to be stepped into, go barefooted for the rest of the day.

But now, at last, you are prepared to face the world!

No, not yet. There is still one little chore to be attended to. Go to the cupboard under the stairs where you keep the radiator, the vacuum-cleaner and last month's unpaid bills, and take out your shotgun.

And now off you go, at a trembling jog-trot, to the Wee Kirk around the corner.

Steady now, lad – you need a keen eye and a cool head for this job! Line the bell-ringer up in your sights. *Bang!* You've potted him!

(Shove the cadaver up the A flat organ pipe. It won't be discovered for weeks.)

Your task is done. You may now face the residue of the year with a clear conscience.

•

RALPH McGILL

Ralph McGill (1898–1969) was born in Soddy, Tennessee, and was educated at Vanderbilt University. He cut his teeth as a reporter on the *Nashville Banner*, covering politics, crime and sport. In 1929 he joined the *Atlanta Constitution* as sports editor. He wrote a daily column for the paper from 1929 to 1969, which became renowned for its civilized treatment of the race question. He was also given the title of executive editor in 1938 and in 1968 he became the paper's publisher.

A Free Man Killed By White Slaves

Atlanta Constitution, April 5, 1968

White slaves killed Dr Martin Luther King Jr in Memphis. At the moment the trigger man fired, Martin Luther King was the free man. The white killer (or killers) was a slave to fear, a slave to his own sense of inferiority, a slave to hatred, a slave to all the bloody instincts that surge in a brain when a human being decides to become a beast. In the wake of this disaster in Memphis, a great many such slaves must consider if they wish to continue serving their masters of fear, hate, inferiority and beastliness. It is something of an irony that Dr King was free and was hated by so many slaves. It is perhaps too much to hope, but much of the violent reaction to this bloody murder could be blunted if in every city and town there would now be a resolve to remove what remains of injustice and racial prejudice from schools, from training and job opportunities, from housing and community life in general.

Dr King's voice was the last one arguing for non-violence. The young militants respected him enough to pledge him they would accept his leadership in the summer ahead.

And now?

The old ghost of John Brown whispers out of the by-gone years. He was a white man and a violent one. He was hanged after his foolish foray at Harper's Ferry, Virginia, in the autumn of 1859. Brown was the martyr. His death was a catalyst. His soul became a cutting edge that broke hearts and walls as the great war came on with a rush. One frets with that memory.

There are other effects of martyrdoms.

Dr King would not want his death to be an emotion that brought on what he had all his life opposed – violence and death. Atlanta's Mayor, Ivan Allen, who drove his car through a rain-swept city to the home of Dr King and took the stunned wife to the airport where she learned that death had come in Memphis, was another symbol of the South. He, too, was a free man. He was not a slave to hate and far. His city is not a slave city bound by such terrible chains as held the killers in Memphis.

That city, which allowed a strike of Negro garbage workers to grow into a protest against all the many remaining forms of racist prejudice, did not meet a necessary test. And so Memphis became the site of a slave uprising where death and hate opposed freedom.

The Memphis killer and his associates have done their own race a grave and hideous injustice. They have made it possible for blind violence to be loosed. They have elevated the beast in man. They may have imperiled the negotiations that, hopefully, may be arranged to end the war in Vietnam. The slave beast does not reason. The beast, unless chained, is only a beast.

The white South – the white population in all the country – must now give an answer. If injustice and inequity, if racist prejudices and discriminations now become the targets of all decent men and women, Dr King's death may bring about what he sought for himself, his people and country.

If this does not happen, then slaves who serve masters of hatred, fear and evil will have to be put down mercilessly and immediately.

Out of martyrdom must come the right answer.

A Church, a School
Atlanta Constitution, February 5, 1969

Dynamite in great quantity ripped a beautiful temple of worship in Atlanta. It followed hard on the heels of a like destruction of a handsome high school at Clinton, Tennessee. The same rabid, mad-dog minds were, without question, behind both. They are also the source of previous bombings in Florida, Alabama and South Carolina. The school-house and the church were the targets of diseased, hate-filled minds.

Let us face the facts. This is a harvest. It is the crop of things.

It is the harvest of defiance of courts and the encouragement of citizens to defy law on the part of many Southern politicians. It will be the acme of irony, for example, if any one of four or five Southern governors deplore this bombing. It will be grimly humorous if certain attorneys-general issue statements of regret. And it will be quite a job for some editors, columnists and commentators, who have been saying that our courts have no jurisdiction and that the people should refuse to accept their authority, now to deplore. It is not possible to preach lawlessness and restrict it.

To be sure, none said go bomb a Jewish temple or a school. But let it be understood that when leadership in high places in any degree fails to support constituted authority, it opens the gates to those who wish to take law into their hands.

There will be, to be sure, the customary act of the careful drawing aside of skirts on the part of those in high places. 'How awful!' they will exclaim. 'How terrible. Something must be done.'

But the record stands. The extremists of the citizens' councils, the political leaders who in terms violent and inflammatory have repudiated their oaths and stood against due process of law have helped unloose this flood of hate and bombing.

This too is a harvest of those so-called Christian ministers who have chosen to preach hate instead of compassion. Let them now find pious words and raise their hands in deploring the bombing of a synagogue.

You do not preach and encourage hatred for the Negro and hope to restrict it to that field. It is an old, old story. It is one repeated over and over again in history. When the wolves of hate are loosed on one people, then no one is safe.

Hate and lawlessness by those who lead release the yellow rats and encourage the crazed and neurotic who print and distribute the hate pamphlets – who shrieked that Franklin Roosevelt was a Jew – who denounce the Supreme Court as being Communist and controlled by Jewish influences.

This series of bombings is the harvest, too, of something else.

One of those connected with the bombing telephoned a news service early Sunday morning to say the job would be done. It was to be committed, he said, by the Confederate Underground.

The Confederacy and the men who led it are revered by millions. Its leaders returned to the Union and urged that the future be committed to building a stronger America. This was particularly true of General Robert E. Lee. Time after time he urged his students at Washington University to forget the war between the states and to help build a greater and stronger union.

For too many years now we have seen the Confederate flag and the emotions of that great war become the property of men not fit to tie the shoes of those who fought it. Some of these have been merely childish and immature. Others have perverted and commercialized the flag by making the Stars and Bars, and the Confederacy itself, a symbol of hate and bombings.

For a long time now it has been needful for all Americans to stand up and be counted on the side of law and the due process of law – even when to do so goes against personal beliefs and emotions. It is late. But there is yet time.

•

VERMONT ROYSTER

Vermont Royster was born in 1914 in Raleigh, North Carolina, and spent several years in Chapel Hill. He attended the University of North Carolina, where he majored in classical languages and worked on the *Daily Tar Heel*. After graduating in 1935 he moved to New York City, and within a year he had joined the Dow Jones News Service and been sent to the *Wall Street Journal*'s Washington bureau to cover the Department of Agriculture. He was later assigned to report on the Supreme Court, and after serving with the Navy Reserves in the Second World War he returned to the *Journal*. In 1946 he was made Washington bureau chief, but before long moved back to New York as an associate editor to write editorials. In 1951 he became senior associate editor and received a Pulitzer Prize for editorial writing; from 1958 to 1971 he was editor of the paper. After his retirement he settled down into writing a weekly column, 'Review and Outlook', for which he received a second Pulitzer in 1984.

What Indignation?

Wall Street Journal, October 16, 1964

It's been a couple of hundred years since the English went to war because they were scandalized, and half a century since a French government quaked over a little matter of lying and forgery in high places.

Since the Dreyfus affair and the War of Jenkin's Ear there's been no dearth of scandals, some of which have made loud uproars and consumed reams of newsprint, but it's a rare thing nowadays when they have any more political consequences than the titillation of the public. The French have had Cabinet officers chasing nymphets, the British have had Foreign Office officials chasing not only Communists but each other, and of course there was the delightful Profumo affair which the staid English seem to have accepted with relief because it at least involved opposite sexes.

Meanwhile, we've had our own passing scandals. Nothing lately has quite touched Teapot Dome, in which some wheeler-dealing Cabinet officers tried to steal the country blind, or the juicy morsels provided by the extramarital activity of Warren Harding.

Both of these things contributed to history's low opinion of Mr Harding, and a couple of jail sentences did come out of the Teapot tempest. But for all the national attention to these scandals, there's no evidence that very many people were scandalized enough to rebuke anybody via the ballot box.

So it's been ever since. At the time there was much outcry over the blatant immorality of Harry Hopkins's political doctrine of 'spend and spend, tax and tax, elect and elect.' It never hurt Mr Hopkins, who continued as the gray eminence at the White House, played a major role in the wartime deals with the Russians which afterwards gave so much trouble, and was the posthumous subject of an adoring biography that won a Pulitzer Prize.

To be sure, other public servants, including gray eminences, haven't been quite so lucky. A crony of President Truman's went to jail for a felony and a close adviser of President Eisenhower lost his job for slipping on a rug. Again, however, there's no evidence that any of these scandals, for all that they had their noisy day, had any appreciable effect on the political fortunes of the political leaders upon whom the scandals breathed.

Herewith, then, a minority report. The substance of it is a suspicion that a recent Washington scandal, involving the nocturnal peccadilloes of President Johnson's close friend and confidant, won't have much of any political effect. It's a nasty business, all right, and because it involves sexual mores it will probably raise more noise than Billie Sol Estes and Bobby Baker combined. Any way you look at it the halo on Lyndon Johnson's head as the great moral crusader against the wickedness of Barry Goldwater will doubtless be tarnished. But the question is whether the American people will get indignant about the right thing, which is not what happened one night at a YMCA but an attitude toward moral standards in public life of which this case is but one hapless example. The question, indeed, is whether the American people any longer have the capacity to get really indignant about anything.

Whatever you may think about a man's sexual habits, there are other immoralities more worthy of public censure. Yet only a few years ago a man high in the councils of state was convicted of perjury in a treason case and the widespread reaction, especially among those who lay claim to intellectual leadership, was that even if he was guilty the act ought not to be too terribly condemned because, after all, that was a time when 'everybody' was being kind to Communists. In rather wide circles there was less indignation over the thought of a man's betraying his country than over his betraying his wife.

And where, really, was the public indignation over Billie Sol or Lyndon's Bobby Baker? Billie himself got convicted of various misdemeanors, but there was no great demand for a thorough airing of the circumstances that made those misdemeanors possible. As for Bobby Baker, only a few Republican congressman seemed interested in finding out what happened. At any rate, the Democrats tried quietly to quash the matter and if that caused any outrage among the electorate it certainly wasn't an uproar.

Even over the highest offices people are pretty tolerant, and you don't have to go back to Warren Harding. A man who spent all his life on the public payroll can end up several times a millionaire and the fairly common reaction is that that just shows how smart he is.

More subtle moral questions make no dent at all. People go to the polls and vote for a man for senator for no other discernible reason than that he's the brother of, or was once a secretary to, a national hero. A governor of a state can be under indictment for using his party power to defraud the public; the prosecutor may put the ex-governor in jail but the public asks no accounting from the man's political party.

This phenomenon, if that's the word for it, is one that can't all be blamed on Lyndon Johnson. Senator Goldwater can fulminate about the moral and ethical climate of Washington, and be right, but it's doubtful if it will get him very far in the present climate of the country. Why blame it all on politicians when the president of a huge national union can milk the Treasury, stand convicted in two courts, and arouse no indignation among the majority of the union's members? The prevailing view of the members seems to be they'd have done the same thing if they'd had the chance, and anyway didn't Jimmy [Hoffa] do a lot of good things for his followers?

A lonesome judge can get indignant about whiskey-drinking parties for teenagers, preliminary to manslaughter, but not the suburban parents. Mobs – without regard for race or creed – can disturb the public order, smash shop windows, and bash heads, and respectable people will lament police brutality because the mobs acted in a good cause. And among most of those we trust to teach our young, 'Puritan ethics' are as laughably outmoded as McGuffey's Readers.

So we wonder if this latest bit of scandal will prove of such great political moment. No doubt the poor fellow is going to be giggled at, even pilloried, for his human failing. This want of charity will miss the point, which is not whether men sometimes succumb to weaknesses of spirit or flesh – there but for some kind of grace perhaps go we all – but what it means to government and society when immorality of all kinds is shrugged off as accepted behavior among those we thrust to honor and trust.

Personally, I'd like to think that morality and ethics in government officials could still be a telling issue in any campaign. But neither the record nor the times give much hope that it will be.

Blessed Ignorance
Wall Street Journal, August 23, 1965

One among the pleasures of a vacation is the privilege of not reading the newspapers from first day's beginning to last day's end. From someone who's spent a lifetime putting things in newspapers this will perhaps sound like rank heresy. And when you add to not reading the newspapers a firmness in not listening to any news on the radio, the confession will certainly earn you black marks among those who think 'keeping informed about world affairs' is somehow a moral obligation ranking slightly ahead of obeying the ten commandments. Nothing will earn you such looks of surprise from such people as being asked your opinion on the Los Angeles riots and answering them with the query, What riots? When it further develops that you are totally ignorant of what's been going on lately in Vietnam, of the situation in the Dominican Republic, of the moves to save the UN from its financial crisis or, worse, of the rationing of air-conditioning in New York City, the surprise of those who formerly thought well of you turns to consternation.

It gets a bit embarrassing. You expect one of your literary-minded friends to remind you of Oliver Wendell Holmes's remark that a man avoids sharing the action and passion of his time at the peril of being judged not to have lived. You even feel awkward under the glances of kinder friends who seem to be excusing you for this retreat from life on the ground that, after all, you are getting along in years.

Of course the retreat was only temporary, and the lack of interest in 'news' somewhat deceptive. It's just hard to explain to friends that at times some news is more important than others, which means that sometimes some things are more important than the latest dispatch from Saigon.

Robert Manry, that fellow journalist who fled the sedentary copy desk where he read all the Saigon dispatches, can hardly be accused of escaping life's perils by sailing the Atlantic alone in what was little more than a pram. But for some two months' time what happened in Los Angeles was only of abstract interest compared to the happenings within the four-mile circle of his horizon aboard the *Tinkerbelle*. Within that circle his problems were tangible, ones that he could confront with his own efforts. What could he do about Los Angeles, or Saigon? What, in all truth, did he or the world suffer from his two months' ignorance of disasters at the antipodes?

So it often is with the rest of us, and more times than we are willing to admit. On a beach or a mountain top you will be vitally interested in the weather. If you time the radio to catch the weather report and cut out the breathless bulletins about what President Johnson said to Hanoi, you aren't fleeing life. You're gaining a sense of proportion. It's not too different, really, in the workaday lives of most of us. Mr Manry will find when he returns to Cleveland that for all the burst of excitement over his adventures the world he left will be centered exactly where he left it. The concerns of that world will be the traffic on Euclid Avenue, the pollution of Lake Erie, or the PTA at Shaker Heights. The dollar crisis and NATO will rank somewhat after.

The cliché is that this is all one world. In real life there are as many worlds as there are inhabitants of it, and each man's world is very small indeed. This is true even at the vortex; in Vietnam a Marine's world is bounded by the boondocks, and the Congo is as unreal as outer space. Outer space, in turn, is briefly two men's world, but who will listen to an astronaut more than a curious hour amid the pressing problems of the household or the shop? Yet every housewife, so it says in the advertisement, must read the complete news report of the world's daily disasters. Tune in every hour on the hour, the announcer declaims, or you won't know about the latest riot. And if you don't, how can you be a good citizen? Maybe so. But fresh from a surcease from incessant news, you might begin to wonder.

A little trick in this business, returning from a vacation, is to read the accumulated papers backwards. Working from the present to past, many earlier stories can be skipped because events have outmoded them. This leads to the rueful corollary – rueful at least, for a news-gatherer – that many of the stories could have been skipped in the first place. The suspicion grows that 'keeping informed' is not only frequently time-wasting but often futile. Knowing that Singapore has seceded from Malaysia, and agreeing that it's a sad business, what do you propose to do about it?

If all this sounds like praise for ignorance, it isn't – quite. Some people need all the news they can get about the balance of payments, the shortage of water or the fighting in Vietnam. All of us need to know something about all of these things, not lest we be vegetables but because some or all of these things may impinge upon the little world that is our own. Bad news, if it gives timely warning for remedies, is good news. But it is also true that the world can be too much with us. The tragedies, the disasters, the horrors are real enough; perhaps the greatest horror is that they are, somewhere, daily occurrences. They always have been and there's no relief in sight.

It does not follow, though, that there is a virtue in pounding ourselves with each of them every minute of every day. Nor that it's a disgrace for a housewife wrestling with diapers not to read the *New York Times* from cover to cover. And there's certainly something to be said for a holiday not merely from the cares of the office but the woes of the world.

In this business you have to admire David Lawrence for his unflagging indignation at the way the world is governed, Walter Lippmann for his inexhaustible passions at how it ought to be governed, Joseph Alsop for his matter-of-fact gloom about future battlefields, and James Reston for his middle-aged energy in helicoptering over present ones. All the same, there's something to be said for that copy-desk editor from Cleveland who turned the Atlantic into Walden Pond and for two months let the world go by in blessed ignorance.

•

THE EARL OF ARRAN

Arthur Kattendyke Strange David Archibald Gore (1910–83), 8th Earl of Arran, became a columnist after a career as a diplomat and civil servant. He was attaché to the British Legation in Berne in 1941, then at the British Embassy in Lisbon (1942–3), and thereafter returned to England, where he worked in the Ministry of Information for the remainder of the war and in the Central Office of Information from 1945 to 1949. In 1958 he succeeded his brother to the title and became an active member of the House of Lords: he was passionate about homosexual rights, three times introducing a Sexual Offences Bill, and about the need to protect badgers. He became a director of the Daily Mail and General Trust for several years in the sixties, but was best known for his weekly column in the London *Evening News* (sometimes billed as 'The Earl You Love to Hate'), which ran from 1960 until 1978, when he suffered a stroke – an event he claimed was the result of his daily intake of a half-bottle of champagne before lunch. 'He was an irrepressible personality always bubbling over with controversy,' explained his former editor Lou Kirby. 'From week to week it was impossible to predict which target he would choose next – and they ranged from the Swiss to the IRA.'

Excerpts from 'The Earl of Arran'
Lord Arran Writes (1964)

The Eighth Earl

I am constantly being mistaken for a pub. I ring up and order something from a shop and when I say who I am, they say, 'Manager's name, please.'

Often, too, I get letters addressed to 'The Earl of Arran' in quotation marks. And on one glorious occasion I got a crate of whisky at wholesale prices because they thought I was in the trade. Actually, I am told that there are quite a lot of pubs dotted over the country which bear my name. Can someone please tell me where they are? I think I should be entitled to at least a free drink on the house.

I have several surnames. I am Arran, Sudley, Saunders of the Deeps – rather pretty that one – and Sir Arthur Gore. This offers great possibilities, of which I take full advantage. One day I am Lord Arran, the next Lord Saunders, and sometimes – though not very often – plain Mr Gore.

I wake up each morning and say to myself, 'Who shall I be today? I feel rather Sir Arthurish.' Each name has a different character. Saunders is a rather raffish fellow, vaguely beatnik, who would like to smoke reefers if he dared. Sir Arthur is a sporting squire, swashbuckling, port-drinking and, I'm afraid, rather naughty. Sudley is the courtesy name which with infinite generosity I have lent my elder son. I don't know him at all, but he seems a nice fellow.

Arran is just me.

But, of course, the use of these various names tends to lead to confusion and sometimes annoyance.

My wife gets shirty when she rings up my office and is told that Lord Arran is not in but she can speak to Lord Saunders if she likes.

In restaurants, too, I am regarded with suspicion. And when it comes to signing cheques with different names, shop assistants either think that I have gone mad or that I am trying to defraud them. One day someone is going to fetch the police and I shall collect enormous damages.

Meanwhile, I gaily pursue my quadruple life. What is the point of having a lot of legal aliases if you don't have fun with them?

I will now reveal that I also have five Christian names. *Arthur Kattendyke Strange David Archibald.* Kattendyke was my mother's maiden name – I am half Dutch. The other four are family names. And instead of being known by any one of the five, I have a ridiculous nickname, 'Boofy', which acquaintances who do not know me well sometimes spell 'Buffet' or 'Boosy'.

I had the best and kindest parents in the world. But they should not have given me all these names. I calculate that I have spent a whole week of my life putting my signature to legal and official documents. Think what I might have done with that week.

And what made it worse is that when I came of age my father got mixed up and put the Strange before the Kattendyke. From then on I too got confused. There are 120 possible permutations. Now it is all quite easy. I just sign 'Arran' and that is that. I reckon that the one-word signature is a peer's best perk.

In case you should think my number of Christian names a record, I give you a lady related to the Earls of Dysart and mentioned in the Peerage. She was christened Lyona Decima Veronica Esyth Undine Cyssa Hylda Rowena Viola Adela Thyra Ursula Ysabel Blanche Lelias Dysart Plantagenet.

She married a man called Charles Stone.

With Knobs On

Just how vulgar can I get? I have surprised even myself with my coat of arms which I am going to fly above my house in Technicolor. After all, they do it at Belvoir and Windsor, so why shouldn't I? True, those are somewhat larger buildings than my suburban villa. But is not every Englishman's home his castle?

As the television compères say about the gowns at the dance competitions, I wish you could see the colours of the coat of arms. There are three crosses and a horizontal stripe in gold on a brilliant scarlet background. In heraldic terms this is 'Gules a Fess between three Crosses crosslet fitchy Or'.

The only trouble is that the flag clashes with the colour of (a) my house, (b) my face. The former is red-brick, the latter brick-red.

Up till a year or so ago I had never seen a coronet in my life, though, thanks to my coat of arms, I do know what mine ought to look like. It has eight balls and eight strawberry leaves between them.

Leaving out the barons who hardly count anyway the curious thing is that the higher your rank the fewer balls you have. A baron has six enormous ones. A viscount sixteen little tiddlers. But when you get into the earl category, your balls decrease in number and you have strawberry leaves as well. A marquis has four balls and four strawberry leaves. A duke has no balls at all.

These are solemn thoughts, and I ask you to give them your earnest consideration.

Anyhow, I thought it might be rather fun to try a coronet on. Dammit, I *am* a peer. So I rang up quite a lot of shops, but none of them seemed to have one for sale or hire. Not often asked for, they said.

Eventually I found a rather dignified establishment. Yes, they had an earl's coronet, second-hand, 6⅞ (I wondered who his dead Lordship might be and what he had died of). But most peers owned family coronets or had them specially made like a bowler hat. Price: £60. My head is 7⅜, I don't need a coronet, and I haven't got £60. So I said no thank you.

Then I went to a theatrical costumier's. They had one for hire, but they were deeply suspicious. Was I going to a fancy dress ball? I said no.

'Amateur theatricals?'

'No.'

'Where then' – with infinite sarcasm – 'do you propose to wear it?'

'In my bath.'

The Bravest Sight in Europe

A few years back I horribly mistimed my arrival at the State Opening of Parliament. I had got up at six o'clock to take my younger son to the bus stop, en route for work. Then I went back to bed. This was fatal. When I woke up it was 9.45 and I had to be in the House of Lords – thirty miles away – by 10.45.

I never give up, so I jumped to it. By 10.40 I was in Regent's Park, where I parked in a 'Residents Only' street. Then I shot underground like the White Rabbit and emerged, breathless, at Westminster. It was eleven o'clock. A lightning change into my robes and there I was in the ante-chamber. Diving under the arms of a tremendous Life Guardsman, I burst into the Chamber itself.

I stood alone. Before me were ranged Her Majesty's judges, awful in black, a sea of bishops shimmering in their white lawn, and 400 of my fellow-peers. I was face to face with the might and majesty of Britain. It was as though I stood before some great heavenly tribunal. I expected them suddenly to rise to their feet and with one great shout pronounce me guilty.

Scarlet in robe and face, I bowed to the still empty throne and charged the scrum. The weakest point seemed to be the bench of dukes, and rising above the jolly jibes of their graces I literally forced my way to the back. There I found myself jammed up against the bar of the House. Behind it were members of the House of Commons. Compared with our parakeet brilliance they looked like a lot of old crows.

But they were most kind. 'Thank God, he's a small chap,' said one. 'At least we can see over his head.'

You should not think that because I write about my own little adventures on this day that I am lacking in respect for the dignity of the scene. It is a truly splendid occasion.

There is a moment when, the Sovereign having bidden us be seated, we await the arrival of the Commons, led by the Speaker. The House is completely still. In it are the great men of our time – statesmen, soldiers, judges, diplomatists, men who have given their country service. One feels privileged to be with them. The silence wears on and one looks around. The colours are stupendous. The peers in their scarlet and ermine, the peeresses – many of them are very beautiful women – with diamonds on their hair and on their arms and necks, the heralds like court cards in some oriental pack, the foreign ambassadors in black and gold slashed by the ribbons of their countries' orders. And on the throne, over and above us all, there sits the head of the British Commonwealth of Nations, and Defender of the Faith. The Commons arrive. In a high, clear voice the Gracious Speech is read aloud to us. And then we go away.

I declare that the State Opening of Parliament is the bravest sight in Europe.

Non-Hon.

I haven't figured in this year's Honours List nor in any other year's list. I can't think why. Is there something wrong with me? Sometime ago I said to Mr Harold Macmillan that I could not see the point of honours. 'After all,' I said, 'you can't eat them.'

'No,' he said, 'and you can't shoot them either.'

That disposed of honours as far as we were concerned.

Bow How

But if royalty were within medal-pinning distance of you, would you know how to bow? If you do, you are one in a hundred. Most people get it all wrong. They bow with their bodies, sticking their behinds in the air and making themselves look ridiculous. Mayors seem particularly prone to this. A correct bow is with the head only. The body should remain absolutely upright. If you are very grand and self-confident you bow as soon as you or they come into the room. Then you do not need to do it when you shake hands. But I would not recommend this. It calls for considerable nerve.

The most beautiful bow I ever saw was by an equerry who had an unexpected visit from one of the royal dukes before breakfast. Summoned from his bed, he came down in a blue silk dressing-gown. Though he had had no warning, he was immaculate. Not a hair was out of place. I can only assume that he slept in a hair-net. The duke was awaiting him in the drawing room. Sir Henry bowed from the door – coolly, neatly, wonderfully. 'Sir,' he said, 'this is quite delightful.'

Bow Wow!

Bowing was, literally, my father's undoing on one occasion in his youth. Soon after Edward VII became king, my father, at that time a subaltern in the Blues and stationed at Windsor, received an invitation to dine at the castle. His brother officers told him that he had better take plenty of cash with him. The King always gambled after dinner, they said, and the stakes were high. So my father cashed a cheque for fifty sovereigns and stuffed them into a cartouche box attached to his uniform. They were a tight fit. In fact, he need not have bothered. There was no gambling; instead, a charming lady entertained the company by singing some charming ballads.

When the moment came to take leave, my father did his neat and formal bow. He knew how these things should be done. But this elegant gesture was too much for the overstrained cartouche box. It burst and a shower of gold cascades on to the floor.

'What a lot of money!' said Queen Alexandra.

Everyone, including the royal family, went down on his hands and knees. Rugs were rolled up and sofas upturned. But it proved an expensive evening for my father. He started out with fifty sovereigns; he went home with thirty-seven.

⅞ of a Top Peer

Meanwhile his son must be content with fame of a different order. I wrote a letter to *The Times* about the telephone service, and though it is not going to be printed *it has received the Editor's personal attention*. I can't tell you what he said in reply, because he has expressly forbidden me to do so, but I am deeply moved. No doubt the Editor – Sir William Haley is his name – was equally moved. Imagine the scene that night in the Haley household.

Enter the Editor.

Lady H.: 'Good evening, Sir William.'

Sir William: 'Good evening, Lady H.'

Lady H.: 'Have you had an interesting day, Sir William?'

Sir William: 'Yes, Lady H.: but of course my position carries with it grave responsibilities.'

Lady H.: 'What in particular is worrying you tonight?'

Sir William: 'I have received a letter from Lord Arran and I have decided not to print it for reasons which I cannot divulge to you.'

Lady H.: 'I quite understand, Sir William. Time for your Benger's.'

More seriously on the subject of *The Times*, someone even more godlike than Sir William Haley said to me some years ago that he reckoned that over the last thirty years *The Times* had done Britain less good than any other single newspaper.

I agree.

But let us be fair. William John at least showed originality. You will remember he allowed his music critic to liken the noise made by the Beatles to the songs of Mahler. Anyone acquainted with the awful sombreness of the Austrian composer will not easily see the resemblance. Horror comics are not the same as Edgar Allan Poe. Still it is an idea, and of course it stems from Old Bill's dedication to 'swing'. Not for nothing is he the boss of the Comets (or isn't he? People insist that this is a different Mr Haley but I don't want to believe it).

The other night I dreamt that at last year's Jazz Festival Old Bill was voted the 'most with it' trumpeter of 1963 after his rendering of 'Halier than Thou' with that tremendous crescendo: 'Haley, Haley, Haley, yea, YEA, YEA.' But in my dream I remember saying to myself: 'How I wish he would stick to music and retire from journalism.'

When it comes to his editorship of *The Times* I say:

'Haley, Haley, Haley – nay, NAY, NAY!'

Flirtation Polka

I have only one claim to fame – I once danced with Queen Mary. This is something rather exceptional, because for the last thirty years of her life she did not dance at all in London so far as I know, even at court balls. She used, however, to take an active part in the annual Ghillies Ball at Balmoral. It was there that I met her – in a sort of Paul Jones called the 'Flirtation Polka'. That same evening she also danced with my host's chauffeur.

I hate the phrase 'great lady', but that is what she was – the greatest of them all. When troubles come to the royal family, as they come to all families from time to time, one finds oneself thinking: 'If only Queen Mary were alive!'

Wrong Door

Here is another royal story. Many years ago my father went to a shooting party in Suffolk. King Edward VII was one of the guests. Mistaking his bathroom, my father opened a door and came upon the monarch majestically enthroned. Kings, it appears, do not lock the door.

'Go away, young man!' shouted the King. 'Go away, go away!'

My father suspected that in that ghastly second he had not been recognized. Showing therefore his customary ingenuity he quickly changed his blue suit to a brown one. He was rewarded when the King rounded on the luckless Sir Harry Stonor, resplendent in a blue pin-stripe, and called him an impertinent jackanapes.

Oh dear, how much I owe to my father. He taught me to laugh when I was quite young and I have never stopped laughing since.

To my mother I owe even more. But that is not a thing one writes about.

Neutral Ardour

Every now and then I think about the Foreign Office. This throws me into a rage. It isn't just that I don't like our diplomats. It's the fact that they're so utterly un-English, so unlike you and me. Here are two examples of their humourlessness. In 1942 we in the Lisbon Embassy were electrified to receive a circular initialled by the ambassador, which read:

'Members of HM Mission are asked to note that they may not have intercourse with neutrals.'

This was both stupid and annoying. Some of us were quite happily married, and it had not occurred to my wife to take a Portuguese lover or to me a Swiss mistress. I raised the matter with the ambassador. I was told to shut up. I did not shut up.

Then, again, eighteen months earlier, when the Battle of Britain was at its height, the British Legation in Berne received a telegram. Telegrams meant something in those black days. Any one of them might announce the invasion of Britain. With anxious hearts we decoded the message.

It read: 'HM Missions are reminded that only those with the rank of First Secretary and above are entitled to (a) carpets (b) roll-top desks in their rooms.'

We almost died of laughter and relief. If the Office could still send us messages like this, things at home could not be so very bad. I would like to think that the telegram was deliberately and subtly sent in order to raise our morale. But knowing the people concerned, I must say that I think this unlikely.

PS Will the lady called Mimi, who keeps on sending me saucy postcards addressed to the House of Lords, asking me if I have forgotten her, please stop it at once? They are left on a table in the Princes' Chamber and they upset the Bishops.

•

WILLIAM CALDWELL

William Anthony Caldwell (1906–86) was born in Butler, Pennsylvania, and grew up in Titusville, where his father was managing editor of the *Herald*. He had no college education, but instead joined the *Bergen Record* in Bergen County, New Jersey, as a sportswriter (it was subsequently renamed the *Hackensack Record*). Later he was put in charge of the editorial page and produced the daily 'Simeon Stylites' column. He wrote some 12,000 columns for the paper and received a Pulitzer Prize in 1971. When he retired the following year and moved to Martha's Vineyard, he continued to write a Sunday column for the *Record* and began an editorial page column for the weekly *Vineyard Gazette*.

'Simeon Stylites'
The Potbelly Revisited
From *In the Record* (1971)

The morning after this latest of the snows we judged it might be shrewd to get in to work early. So to catch the 5:23 out of Midland Park the compleat neurotic got up at 4:15, and foundered over to the queer little station with time to spare for making the acquaintance of the potbellied stove. Before the other 5:23 commuter came in we had a precious few minutes alone with the stove. Our boyhood on the farm came back to us. Only a moment; a moment of strength, of romance, of glamour – of youth! (Conrad) And the best we can say for boyhood on a farm is, you can have it. (Caldwell)

Lord, it was cold!

The Susquehanna's potbellied stove is an Estate Hot Blast Smoke-Consuming. Across its cast-iron top is graven the legend: 'If You Like Me Tell Others About It.' It is whitewashed, about the size of a small fiend; it burns bituminous coal; it stands on a square of zinc over near the wall of the station agent's office, which has a heavily barred opening down at floor level. That's how the agent keeps warm. It looks like an ingenious way to let people goggle at alligators in a zoo.

Keeps warm?

The potbellied stove at the farm was, as we remember it, more elegant than the Susquehanna's. It was lower – no bigger than a well-born hobgoblin – and heavier in the paunch. It was glossy black, had brilliant brass ornaments like a 1912 Ford, burned hard coal, and had isinglass windows, delicately crazed. This was so that our sainted grandmother could peer over her spectacles into its depths 179 times a day and say humph.

But that icy morning in the Susquehanna station we took judicial notice of one thing in common between the two potbellied stoves in our life. Each emitted about as much heat as would an adult mouse.

For all one commuter knows, the Susquehanna potbelly does duly heat up later in the day, and if this is the case it is herewith granted a severance from the following generalization, which will be stated in the form of a law: That the charm of ancient institutions varies in geometric proportion to one's distance from them in space and time.

We'd drag in the stove from the barn in the fall and attach its pipe to a hole in the wall and stoke it up, and, since the flue was choked with swifts' nests or leaves or the remains of feeble-minded guinea hens, the house would be filled with smoke and spectral figures and humphs. But after a while the obstruction in the chimney would burn out with a hollow roar. Then we'd open the doors and windows to disperse the fumes, the water in the bedroom bowls and pitchers would freeze over, we'd close the doors and windows, the water would stay frozen, and we'd settle down miserably for another old-fashioned winter.

Out in the kitchen was a vast gray grease-bespattered stove that was always warm because, humph, the victual had to be cooked and there was no known way of convincing a slab of salt pork that it was warmed through if it wasn't. The kitchen was comfortable. But it took a later culture, which doesn't have to live in the kitchen, to establish that living in the kitchen is gracious. On the farm, one lived in the room where the potbellied stove was. Manners, the old minesweeper used to say, was manners, humph, and she wouldn't have you boys sitting out there in the dark a-tittering.

So into the room where the potbellied stove was she'd take the only operational kerosene lamp in the house, and she'd pull a chair up close to its bleak flanks and peer under her spectacles at the day before yesterday's issue of the Elmira *Star-Gazette*. Every once in a while she would lower the paper and impart culture. It said here that a man she called that sniveling hypocrite Wilson had made another speech. We could take a hint. We would say humph and try not to titter, and after an hour or so of this we'd ask if we might be excused and go to bed.

The best room in the house was not, of course, the room where the potbellied stove was. In the parlor were kept the Bible, the sofa, the platform rocker, the Victrola and records (to be played only on feast days), the hams and apples and honey and sides of bacon. It was the freezer. Through it we'd run barefooted to the stairs, then up them to our room, and then we'd commit ourselves to the icy sheets, in agony, with a sob. She often heard us in our anguish, and would call up through the grilled register in the floor that we were just as warm up here as she was down there. This was nothing but the truth. As we were saying of boyhood on the farm, you can have it.

'Simeon Stylites'
Who Let This Bum into the House?
From *In the Record* (1971)

It's embarrassing, and I suppose the lapse is attributable to my bad habit of having birthdays so often, but doggoned if I would ever have recognized this barrel-chested, bullet-headed, bemedaled goon that's lumbering around introducing himself as my government.

He's a government that has interests separate from mine, as in southeast Asia, which – for reasons he is not disposed to divulge – he will not explain. He is the law. For my own good he will sick his spies on me, tap my telephone, arrest me without a warrant, lock me in preventive custody, and charge me if I squawk with doing irreparable damage to the national security.

His powers are hereditary, like crown jewels, and so are the mistakes which he has established as loyalty tests. If you would die in defense of the mistakes made by this government's great-great-granddaddy you're loyal. If not you are engaged in treason.

He is stupid. In the suppression proceedings against the *New York Times* and the *Washington Post* the government said its classification of secret documents is absolute and final, the ultimate wisdom, and when Judge Gurfein looked at the documents and said fiddlesticks, the government said that naturally the classifications will be reviewed and revised. He is vain. When the appeals judges asked what injury has been done by the publication of the Pentagon papers so far the United States Attorney in New York replied that the government's rights as author of a literary work had been infringed.

Who the blazes is this blubbery impostor? Even now that he has introduced himself I do not recognize him.

Lay the mistake to an unsystematic upbringing among wild-eyed Middle Western conservatives, and it still seems to me that the concept of government as a person having rights and privileges arrogated to itself for private reasons of its own is a novel and ominous concept. As I was given to understand the relationship, government was the creature of a contract between you and me. It was what we agreed it was. Its powers were limited and transient.

And its capacity to do harm was carefully divided among three jealous and competing branches having built-in incentives to keep each other sawed down to size.

Get a scholar to tell you when that tripartite system fell apart – maybe in the thirties and forties, when FDR made the judicial branch an annex of the executive department, maybe in the sixties, when LBJ went to war without asking the legislative for a declaration or even telling Congress and the people what he was doing and they were paying for in blood and money.

But perish it did, and in its place here's the Big Brother government, the jealous author government, the keyhole-peeping government, this parvenu monarch that said in two circuit courts last week he'd be glad to sit down with the press and renegotiate its freedom under the First Amendment.

I do not love this stranger.

The multiplying cases of *de facto* censorship are important not only because they involve the freedom to know on which the purity of democracy depends but because they test the competence of this new government to control the flow of information for reasons of its own on mere allegation, not proof, of clear and present danger.

No matter how the Supreme Court decides the cases, even if the *Times* and the *Washington Post* and umpteen other defendant newspapers prevail, the First Amendment has been badly damaged as of now, and – worse – the government has established its power to stalk into the newspaper shop and stop the presses.

Where does that end?

They're saying in some of the cities that this is likely to be another long, hot summer. Unemployment, which the Detroit 1967 riot investigations found to be the detonator in any explosive situation, is up in the cities – to forty percent among black teenagers. Dope addiction is up. Hope is down.

So much can be reported safely. But go one more step, and listen for the footfall on the stairs.

Now suppose some busybody newspaper team finds the city – the state, government – is buying gas and mace, tanks, field artillery. And suppose that in good conscience, toward the prevention of bloodshed and havoc or toward the investment of tax money in humane and efficacious ways of reducing tension – suppose the newspaper writes the story and prepares to publish it.

There's the footfall, and here's the chief of police with a temporary restraining order forbidding publication of the copy and supporting documents such as bonding ordinances and city council resolutions. Publication of this inflammatory stuff would endanger relations, prevent the deployment of forces according to secret plan, in a word confront the government with irreparable damage to its interests.

Farfetched? I wish it were. I wish it were melodramatic and fanciful to suppose the day might come, once we grant this monster standing and a soul of its own, when government could prevent the publication of contract awards and no-show job appointments and shakedown and graft and the other absolute corruptions to which absolute power is subject. But unless we toss that swaggering bum out of here it may be later than you think.

●

PATRICK CAMPBELL

Patrick Campbell (1913–80), 3rd Baron Glenavy, was born in Dublin and educated at Rossall, 'a public school in Lancashire where high tides blocked the drains and the headmaster beat tall, pale students with billiard cues'. He managed to stick one year at Pembroke College, Oxford, which was followed by two grim years in Germany and a thrilling six-month sojourn in Paris before he joined the *Irish Times*. He served in the Irish Marine Service during the Second World War and thereafter wrote his first column, 'The Irishman's Diary', for the *Irish Times*. In 1947 he moved to London, where he wrote a weekly column for the *Sunday Dispatch* for thirteen years and contributed numerous articles to *Lilliput*, where he was assistant editor from

1947 to 1953. Starting in 1961, he was for many years a columnist for the *Sunday Times*, and he charmed television viewers with his stutter on the BBC's *Call My Bluff* from 1962 to 1979.

The Home of the Mole Wrench

From *35 Years on the Job* (1973)

'And now,' he said passionately, 'now do you know what They've gone and done to me?'

The capital 'T' was unmistakably there, indicating that he could be speaking only of the government.

'They,' he said, 'have sent me this.'

He held up, between finger and thumb, the familiar brown envelope. Through its transparent window gleamed the thin red line of the Final Demand.

'Pay it quickly,' I advised him. 'After March nineteen they'll be slapping you into a concentration camp on the Isle of Man if you're five minutes in arrears.'

He made an impatient gesture. 'Never mind that,' he said. 'Just look at it.'

I took the envelope from him, also employing finger and thumb. 'You never know where these things have been,' I said.

'That,' he said with conviction, 'has been somewhere indescribably beastly. Just look.'

I looked. Stamped on the envelope, just below On Her Majesty's Service, was the injunction, 'Ship through Newport (Mon) the Home of the Mole Wrench.'

'You're right,' I said in a low voice. 'It's absolutely filthy.'

'But what are they trying to do to me?' he cried. 'Even if I do pay the thing, do I really have to ship it to them through Newport (Mon) – '

'The Home of the Mole Wrench,' we said together.

'I see it,' he said after a moment, 'as an obscenely Welsh secret ceremony, carried out at dead of night on the far side of some bestial slag heap – '

'The word has been passed around all day,' I suggested, 'from Dai to Dai – '

'We're wrenching tonight, boy bach. Same time, same place, whateffer.'

'And then Dai and Dai and Trefor Whateffor – '

'Just a moment,' he said. 'I'm handling this. At midnight – exceedingly heavy rain, of course – the whole male population of Newport (Mon) is gathered behind the slag heap – '

'And then there's about an hour of choral work – "Land of Our Fathers" – that sort of thing – '

'Possibly,' he said impatiently. 'Very possibly. And then the lads begin to get a bit restive. Some hothead calls out, "Well, then, whateffer – are we wrenching or not, boy bachs?" '

'It's a pity we're so short on Welsh dialect,' I said, 'whateffer.'

'But, of course,' he went on quickly, 'they're waiting for Mordreth, the Queen of the Bardic Druids, Newport (Mon) Branch, who is bringing the Mole. She arrives. The lads form a circle around her, let lash with "Land of Our Fathers" again, then Mordreth holds the Mole high in the air, there's a great cry of "Wrench – Wrench!" '

'Whateffer!'

'And Mordreth wrenches, doing the poor little animal in.'

'That,' I said, 'is the Mole Wrench.'

I couldn't get this ludicrous business out of my head for several days afterwards, and indeed went so far as to look up Inland Revenue in the telephone book, without finding the courage, however, actually to ring them. Well, you know what they're like. Once they've got you out in the open they'll have you, for sure.

Suddenly, then, I could stand it no longer, slotted in a couple of purple hearts, waited for the buzz, and then rang.

'Good morning, I want to make an inquiry.'

'Yes, sir. In connection with – ?'

'Well, this friend of mine got a final demand and stamped on the envelope was the order, "Ship through Newport (Mon) the Home of the Mole Wrench". We were wondering what a Mole Wrench was.'

Absolute silence, and then the nervous female voice saying, 'I'll put you through to the press office.'

The press officer cleared the matter in a flash. He himself had been using a mole wrench for years – a device which can be clamped on to a pipe and screwed tight – and it must have been the Post Office who had stamped the envelope because the Revenue *never* did that kind of thing.

I thanked him, soberly, regretting the loss of a dream.

Ironmonger's Lassitude

From *35 Years on the Job* (1973)

During my years of residence in a basement apartment off Notting Hill Gate, which we called Campden Hill, I got a big hole in the wall above the mantlepiece, as a result of trying to put into it a nail or a hook sufficiently robust to support rather a pretty looking-glass, with a stripped pine frame.

Thanks to gimcrack construction this particular piece of wall seemed to be about an inch thick and made of papier-mâché. Three Rawlplugs, each of increasing size, had been inserted into the hole, which was also getting bigger, and then at the first pressure of the screw the Rawlplugs had simply disappeared into the wall, falling into some bottomless cavity behind it.

I put this problem to a professional handyman and he solved it instantly. 'Y'll want one of y'toggle screws on that,' he said. Handymen often personalize equipment in this way. 'Take a bit of y'four be two scantlin',' and 'countersink y'coach-bolt, see?'

I asked him what my toggle screw was. It turned out to be a kind of butterfly nut that could be collapsed to pass through the hole in the wall and miraculously opened up the other side. 'She'll hold a grand pianner,' the handyman promised, and said that she could be obtained at Carters.

I was glad he'd mentioned Carters. It was ideally placed, at the far end of Tottenham Court Road, for a writer trying to get away from writing in Campden Hill. At least an hour to get there and if Carters was the same as other ironmongers at least another hour to make the purchase. It was possible, of course, that a toggle screw could have been found at the ironmonger's round the corner, but I didn't want to take a chance on it, with so much work to do.

Carters turned out not only to be ideally placed, but absolutely ideal in itself, a very cathedral among ironmongers with five or six different entrances and dozens of long counters and elderly men in caps leaning against them in a way that suggested they'd been there for ever. Of assistants, as is usual in ironmongers' shops, there was no sign.

I joined a small group at what looked like the nuts, bolts and toggle screws counter, and prepared to slip off into ironmonger's lassitude. A telephone at the end of the counter shrilled endlessly. No one even looked at it. It was possible to imagine another telephone in another ironmonger's shop on the other side of London with its receiver lying on the counter, calling Carters hour after hour after hour. It was also possible to imagine handymen all over London, drooping in telephone boxes, getting the engaged signal hour after hour from Carters and from whomsoever the other ironmonger might be. A splendid buttress against the rigours of work.

Ten minutes later nothing had changed, except that we'd been joined by a youth in an apron, carrying one of those hydraulic mechanisms that automatically close doors. He put it on the counter, but watched it warily, as though it might be about to spring into the air.

The oldest customer of all joined him in his vigil for five or six minutes. At the end of it he said, 'Y'washer gorn?' The youth nodded in lack-lustre fashion. 'Ah fought so,' said the old man, with no appearance of triumph. We all listened to the telephone again.

The following year an assistant appeared, a bent, grey-haired man of about seventy in a brown overall coat. He carried a piece of metal of unimaginable purpose with a short length of pipe sticking out of it. He put it on the counter in front of the washer expert and they both looked at it for a long time without speaking. Then the assistant said, 'That's y'five-sixteenths.'

The washer expert inclined himself very slightly, to look at the thing from another angle. 'Ah wus lookin',' he said, after a long interval, 'fer inch an'a quaw'er.'

The assistant said, 'Ar,' so tonelessly that it was a mere expulsion of breath. They resumed their study of the object without further interchange.

Time, even for a writer getting away from work, was getting on. 'Excuse me,' I said to the assistant, 'am I at the right counter for toggle screws?'

He spoke with astonishing heat. 'Jus' a minit, guv,' he said. 'Ah'm servin' this gent 'ere.' He glared at me for an instant, and then returned to his previous condition of semi-consciousness. His moment of passion, however, had one beneficial effect. Without looking at it, he picked up the telephone receiver and laid it on the counter, where it continued to buzz rather than to shrill.

After another week a man who had the head of a hammer in one hand and the shaft in the other said to me, 'Toggle screws ain't 'ere, mate. Rahnd the corner.' He pointed with the shaft of the hammer, not quite achieving the horizontal.

I thanked him, but it was plain that the stripped pine mirror would not be mounted with a toggle screw today. At least, however, the morning's work was safely over.

The time was twelve-fifteen. I was steaming into the haven of lunch.

•

KAYS GARY

Kays Gary was born in 1920 in Fallston, North Carolina. His father was a school principal and his mother a teacher, and they instilled in him a love of reading. He went to college in Mars Hill and then to the University of North Carolina at Chapel Hill, where he obtained a degree in journalism in 1942. After serving in the US Army's Military Police until 1945, he joined the Shelby *Daily Star*, where he gained experience as sports editor and columnist, county courthouse reporter, feature writer, correspondent for the *Charlotte Observer* and news announcer for the local radio station owned by his paper. In 1952 he was hired by the *Charlotte Observer*, where he was recognized as a reporter and feature writer of distinction, and in 1956 the paper entered him for the national Ernie Pyle contest, which he won. That same year he began writing a three-times-a-week personal column for the *Charlotte Observer*. After six months, owing to enthusiastic reader response, he graduated to writing his column five days a week. Apart from a brief period in 1968 when he attempted to perform the role of PR man for a North Carolina mountain development company only to discover that he did not like it, he was a columnist with the same paper, commenting on all subjects from national politics to local whimsy.

Front Porches
Charlotte Observer, August 29, 1965

Nobody builds front porches anymore, and I think the Communists are behind this.

That must have been old Joe Stalin's last major assault on the American Way, and he sure struck a blow.

They quit building porches on houses in about 1950 and by 1953 when Old Joe died very few people were sitting on the porches that were left.

Now the builders say the Communists haven't got a thing to do with it.

They say that people quit building front porches to save money, because of a desire for privacy and laziness, because of now-available air-conditioned comfort inside, because of set-back lines leaving houses too far from the street and because of the drift from downtown living where there's activity to watch from a porch.

Now this is just a round-about way of skirting the brass tacks fact that somebody put 'em up to it.

And that is just what Old Joe wanted. Oh, he was a smart one, all right.

I can see him sitting up there in the Kremlin chewing on his mustache and trying to think up some way to break up America, which would mean breaking up the community, which would mean breaking up the family.

'Dadgumovitch,' he growled to his secretary, 'I'm done thunk out, Comrade Dishova. What in the Helsinki we gonna do? Ain't you got no idears?'

And Comrade Dishova, who is scratching herself while reading a 1936 copy of the *Saturday Evening Post*, hands him the magazine so she can scratch with both hands.

'Here, oh, Peasant Cock o' the Walk,' says she, 'lookit this here capitalistic rag and maybe you'll think up sump'n 'nother.'

Old Joe thumbs through the magazine, stops, studies one page long and hard and leaps to his feet.

'Wowski! Hotdogovitch!' he yells. 'I done got it!'

His hands, trembling with excitement, rip out a Norman Rockwell picture of Maple Avenue, Centerville, USA, showing a typical residential street scene.

Mamas and papas and grandmas are sitting on front porches.

Teenage sweethearts are sitting in swings.

Kids are playing on the sidewalks all up and down the street in front of the porches.

A fat man is helping a skinny neighbor fix his lawn mower.

People on the porches are waving to sidewalk strollers and people passing in automobiles.

In the foreground a lady carrying a chocolate cake is handing it over to a front porch family and you get the idea that soon there'll be lemonade and an informal party as a part of daily life on the Street.

'The front porchski!' growls Old Joe. 'Get ridda them things and we'll bust up the American Way.'

So he called the Central Committee into all-night session and they hashed over the idea in detail.

Obviously the Americans were all a big family.

Everywhere else in the world people built walls or fences around the houses and the point was privacy, divorce from involvement with whatever went on next door.

Unlike any other people these Americans built porches not thirty feet from the street so they could see and be seen by everybody. Everybody had a bad habit of being involved with everybody and everything on the street – joys and sorrows, triumphs and failures.

Obviously, too, the porch held the family together, so the Central Committee decided on a tactic.

Create the desire for privacy, for backyard patios. Make 'em status symbols. Make Americans want to get behind hedges and fences, away from meddlesome neighbors. Talk about the value of the building dollar and ways to stretch it by eliminating – porches.

Then grandma can go to the old folks home. With no swings for evening courtin' watch young lovers hit the road.

Get rid of the porches, in short, and create a community of suspect strangers who are up to no-telling-what behind the house on a patio sheltered by fast-growing vines.

Divide, by gumski, and conquer and build boulevards for ghosts so that men fear to walk their own streets.

Well, it took 'em fifteen years but they did it. The American Scene remains in scattered small towns and in isolated city areas like Charlotte's Dilworth.

The builders say they haven't had a request in years to build a porch. They figure the desire for porches disappeared for the same reasons other styles disappeared.

Poor fellows.

They just don't realize that it had to be a Communist plot.

The Cherubs Aren't Singing
Charlotte Observer, September 10, 1974

The honeymoon is over.

There was sweet pathos about it while it lasted. Bruised and hungry hearts picked up a stronger beat. The long, dry thirst for nourishment in the faith of our fathers seemed about to end.

And now.

The honeymoon is over and the faith of our fathers has turned to Monday dust.

This commentary is not my professional duty. Mine is to let the sunshine in, to play the flute so that cherubs sing at heathen fests. But this commentary I claim as a right after twenty-eight years as a newsman, almost fifty-four years as a citizen imbued from childhood with the idea that my country is the last best hope for consummating the second sentence of the Lord's Prayer.

And now.

President Ford has granted, in advance, a full pardon to former President Nixon for any and all federal crimes he may have committed.

I am outraged and no riptide of 'What about Chappaquidick?' will change that.

The man just pardoned faced evidence, rather than speculation, that cold sober he directed crimes against the Constitution, assaults against principles established as the bedrock of this country and compounded deceit against the people who gave him the most precious gift in their power. He is pardoned.

Who can declare, ever again, that in America every man stands equal before the law?

Who can, ever again, be shocked at the breakdown of law and order when its chief apostle has profaned its trust?

Who can, ever again, demand that punishment be swift and sure in the name of Justice?

What do we tell the Boy Scouts? The bright young faces in classrooms? Our youth errant in their defiance of our claimed morality?

What do we say to those guilty of crimes of momentary passion? To the deprived, sub-intellects who assault and rob, taking what they cannot earn? What do we say to those whom we have caged, segregated from contact with our pious persons?

Shall we say that the right to lie, to cheat, to steal belongs only to those whose mastery of deceit can first carry them to the highest places?

What shall we say to deserters whose only crime was fear? Or to thousands of young whose conscience told them 'Thou shalt not kill' is a law stronger than that of Selective Service?

Recall it, now.

We cheered or added prayerful 'Amens' when our President said that to grant amnesty to these would bring dishonor to those who fought so gallantly, some dying, in Vietnam.

Now a President, pardoned in advance for high crimes and misdemeanors, voices no such anguish for dishonor brought thus to the tombs of Washington, of Jefferson, of Lincoln.

He is in anguish, we are told. The act of mercy was extended to relieve it.

Yet that anguish has never penetrated the heart of a man to the extent of publicly acknowledging other than 'mistakes.'

Richard Nixon has never and will never ask the American people's forgiveness, and it is to be strongly suspected that in that twisted person writhes the suspicion that he does not need to. That in this, the ninth or tenth or twentieth-whatever crisis of Richard Nixon, the seed of his justification may still be alive in the hearts of many.

If this be true it is time for the funeral of the great American experiment. It is time, indeed, for the benediction.

Certainly there are ambivalent feelings in the most partisan hearts about what the law should have done to Richard Nixon.

It is to no man's credit to wish for him a sentence in jail as received by other mere mortals for lesser crimes.

Yet the pardoning seems to have done more than save him from jail. Instead, it places truth behind bars, buries it in a dungeon, stifles it to the point that rumor and distortion may yet someday bring a resurrection of the politics of pious infidels. That is the risk of it and the tragedy of it.

Though it is a documented matter of history more than thirty years after the fact there are those in Germany who consider the genocide of World War II a fairy tale. It is one way of burying guilt and keeping alive the promise that Hitler's Germany may rise again.

And now.

President Ford, most would likely agree, acted in good conscience. Richard Nixon was a close friend. For more than sixty percent of us, he was more than a friend. He was, if you please, a 'return to honor and decency,' to 'old-fashioned values.' For that reason many find condemnation of Richard Nixon a condemnation of self and cannot, just as he cannot, bring themselves to do it.

But I must and for the record.

No matter what the Dow-Jones does today I can hear no cherubs sing.

Loving Trash

Charlotte Observer, December 27, 1977

There's a mountain to be moved.

It's a paper mountain atop my desk with ragged, paper-clipped peaks, yellowed valleys and curling pink slips cascading down to the edges of an overflowing ashtray.

My desk. Scorpio's shrine, Capricorn's nightmare and it was ever thus. But once each year comes resolve with delivery of the new desk calendars.

Last year I struggled for hours to clean it. It was, to be sure, an emotional struggle because when it was done my priority pile of papers had simply been shifted from the left to the right side of the desk and the 'things to remember' pile had been spread in a leftward-leaning semicircle.

Ultimately, challenged by the do-it-now command of the new calendar, I finally scrapped it and decided to use 1976 all over again. With minor mental computations, I figured, it would serve another year and it did. True, on some occasions I was a day late for appointments, but all in all things worked out pretty much as always. True, also, I was one of the few to miss 1977 altogether but gained the distinction of living 1976 twice. I am told, by the news in review, there was not a lot of difference.

But now here we are again, a new desk calendar waiting and a mountain to be moved, at least shifted, again, and the first item I pick up is a Christmas card which reads: 'All We Need Is Love!'

Strange it never had the impact on Dec. 20 it suddenly acquired on Dec. 26. The immediate day-after reaction is, 'So what are we going to do with all this Christmas stuff?'

Well, what we will do with it is to exchange it for something else or wear it or play with it for awhile until we get bored with it or it goes out of style which may be next week or the week after that.

Love, on the other hand . . .

There seems to be so little time for it.

Things get in the way. We have to buy them or trade them or sell them and create a want for them at which point they become a necessity.

We have to get wide lapels and throw them away for narrow lapels or vice versa. If the hems are down they have to go up or in the middle or some place except where they are. We have to figure a way to make denim as dear as silk, beads and scarves as indispensable as bread and meat, something in sex that nobody ever knew before. If we can just afford that right thing on wheels or the thing with the right label or the things that will be better than the things most others have . . .

Well!

Then, by all that's holy, we will at last explore the dimensions of love.

And that is why I cannot clean my desk.

These mountains of papers all tell me, in one way or another, that love is alive in the human heart.

They are letters that have come all year long from people telling me about other people who are quiet royalty in the business of loving.

They tell me of individuals and neighborhood groups, heroic in small ways in dispensing love and concern.

They tell me about their laugh-a-minute Aunt Hattie, their Uncle Ben and his six toes or the antics of their children.

They are letters in response to needs of others. They are letters expressing thanks, even praise for a job I am paid to do.

All these papers, individually, have been free admission tickets to the greatest show on earth — the human family. Individually, they represent gifts of time for intimate sharing. Individually, they carry 13-cent stamps from somebody's earnings. And they have not yet received an adequate reply.

To anybody else my desk is heaped with trash. To me it is heaped with little bits of people and to sweep them into the can would be total rejection.

So I have moved them around a little. I have puffed away some dust. I have even installed a new 1978 desk calendar. It's easy to find. It's right under the Christmas card with the legend, 'All We Need Is Love.'

•

LUCIUS BEEBE

Lucius Beebe (1902–66) was born into a wealthy family in Wakefield, Massachusetts, and was expelled from several private schools. His journalistic career began on a New England tabloid for which he penned scurrilous gossip items before this activity earned his expulsion from Yale. Instead, he went to Harvard where he wrote for the *Crimson*, attacking compulsory chapel at Yale, and graduated in 1927. He remained there another year to study poetry. In 1929 he joined the *New York Herald Tribune* and remained on its staff for the next twenty-one years, eventually contributing a Manhattan society column called 'This is New York' (which ran until 1952). During this time Beebe, who was homosexual, visited Virginia City, Nevada, with his partner, Charles Clegg, and in 1950 they decided to settle there, re-launching the *Territorial Enterprise*, the old weekly newspaper which had once employed Mark Twain. For the next six years, Beebe used the paper to stir up one row after another, while cutting a dash in his eccentric Western costume – he stood six foot tall and weighed 220 pounds. Although the paper attained the highest paid circulation of any weekly paper west of the Missouri, Beebe and Clegg tired of their routine and decided to sell it. Thereafter, they lived in both Nevada and California.

In 1960 Beebe joined the *San Francisco Chronicle* as a columnist. He refused to join the American Newspaper Guild, the union which the paper's staff members were obliged to belong to, and turned himself into a Nevada corporation so as to evade this rule. Beebe regarded modern newspapers as anaemic in character and in thrall to liberal shibboleths, whereas his column declared itself an enemy of lawyers and anti-smoking campaigners, air travel, organized religion, materialism, the interfering and financially feckless Federal government, welfarism and debased currency. However, the column also celebrated his own Lucullan tendencies: he enjoyed caviar, champagne and cigars. He had to undergo five kidney stone operations and boasted that his liver had expanded 'to ducal dimensions'. He owned several Rolls-Royces in his lifetime, a Thunderbird every other year, and invariably travelled to England aboard the *Queen Mary*. He also wrote numerous books about America's railroads and owned a private railroad car. Once, when he arrived by such means in New York, he invited the writer Wolcott Gibbs to visit him in his temporary abode. He greeted Gibbs from the platform of his private car, resplendent in morning dress, brandishing a glass of champagne, and uttering the cry: 'Welcome to Walden Pond.'

'If anything is worth doing, it is worth doing in style,' he once told fellow *Chronicle* columnist Herb Caen. 'And on your own terms and nobody's God damned else's. I like people who never give a passing thought to public opinion or the suffrage of society, not who deliberately antagonize it, but simply are unaware that it exists. I'd like my obit to say: "Everything he did was made to measure. He never got an idea off the rack." '

A Pioneer Passenger

From *The Lucius Beebe Reader* (1967)

I first flew, if memory doesn't betray me, as a paid passenger in a two-seater Wright biplane with a barnstorming lady aviator named Ruth Law at the Wakefield–Reading Fair of my boyhood at approximately the age of twelve.

Aviators then had to pay dolts like myself to ride with them and I collected an unbelievable five dollars for riding out front with Miss Law whose attire was a pair of riding breeches, goggles and a motoring cap turned backward so the visor covered her neck. A pair of propellers made of wood at the back end of the machine were activated by chain gears from a motor conveniently situated where it would flatten the plane's occupants like waffles in the event of a crash landing.

I was enchanted with flying and with Miss Law and would have gone on with her gladly to the Rockingham and even the Rochester Fair if an account of my daring hadn't appeared in the *Wakefield Daily Item* and so apprised my family of my folly. I was then handcuffed to a heavy item of furniture until the Fair was over.

By the time I achieved the ivied halls of Harvard passengers were no longer being paid to fly, but themselves paid a modest fee to ride in open cockpit planes. A drinking acquaintance of mine named Bradley Fisk evolved the theory that flying was a sovereign remedy for hangovers, which everyone had in depth in those days, and we used to go over to Boston airport and take a restorative flight over the Charles river basin after which, revitalized, we would repair to Honest Parker Shannon's groggery hard by the *Boston Herald* in Avery Street and start all over again.

An Excess of Zeal

From *The Lucius Beebe Reader* (1967)

As a fourth-generation Boston banker myself, I only escaped permanent enslavement in a cashier's cage when I discovered, and actively practiced the discovery, that a copy spindle was ideally suited to impaling to the counter the hand of a depositor outstretched in an attempt to withdraw funds. While applauding my sentiments to the hilt, the management felt I was carrying institutional loyalty to extremes and I was released to seek employment elsewhere.

The Wisdom of Polonius

From *The Lucius Beebe Reader* (1967)

In May 1922, I first took passage to cross the Atlantic in the Cunard steamship *Aquitania*, then at the apex of its celebrity as a luxury vessel of the type spoken of in the public prints as 'an ocean greyhound.' As a youth traveling alone, I was assigned, as was the custom of the time at capacity sailings, to share a stateroom with another gentleman, whose identity was revealed as that of Claude Graham-White.

At this remove the name may mean little except to students of aviation, but Graham-

White was a flying pioneer of impressive dimensions, so valued by the English Government as an expert and consultant that he was paid an annual sum, reported to be $25,000, never to set foot in an airplane. He was a handsome, sophisticated and urbane viveur in whose debt I shall always stand for many kindly offices of worldliness.

Learning, conversationally, that I was an undergraduate at New Haven and that this was my first trip abroad, my roommate was quietly amused and remarked: 'I think you will learn more that will be useful to you in life in six days aboard a Cunard steamship than in a semester at any university in the world.'

Claude Graham-White couldn't have been more right. Others may sit at the feet of Yale or Oxford or the Sorbonne as their alma mater, but although I am a graduate elsewhere and have latinate documents to attest to it, I own to being a graduate first and foremost of transatlantic travel and the University of Cunard.

A good deal of gin has flowed under the bridgework since Claude Graham-White instructed me in some of the basic facts of life: gentlemen wear shawl collar dinner jackets, peaked lapels are for musicians (this was 1922); only show-offs drink more than one bottle of champagne at breakfast; the most costly cognac on the wine list isn't always the best; don't ask for Maine lobster on an east–west passage or English channel sole going from west to east; tip the carver at Simpson's no more than threepence.

Don't get in fist fights with Frenchmen, which is insulting, strike them with your walking stick; try not to use the words 'bottom' or 'bum' in polite English society; they mean something else. When the King of Spain asks you to have a drink in the Ritz Bar, which he will probably do if you're a regular, it's more polite not to order a King's Death, which is what he himself will be drinking, but to call it a Royal Highball.

Nearly forty years afterward these instructions may, to some, seem vaguely frivolous. In 1922 they were the wisdom of Polonius.

A Curmudgeon's Stewardship

From *The Lucius Beebe Reader* (1967)

It so happens, fortuitously, that this column will appear on the sixty-first birthday of its vagrant and often, no doubt, fallible conductor, and at the same time marks approximately four decades of editorial activity on four different newspapers, a period largely enlivened by reciprocal insult, bad feeling and the exchange of metaphorical dead cats and decayed vegetable matter.

This is neither the space nor, contrary to the hopes of many readers, the occasion for an *apologia pro vita sua* but it may well be the occasion for a brief account of editorial stewardship which has endured and maintained continuity since the first outraged subscriber to the *Boston Telegram* in 1922 called on the managing editor at 99 Portland Street and demanded the dismissal of the Boy Beebe and that instanter as an affront to God and public morality. I think I had submitted an irreverent report of a temperance meeting in Tremont Temple.

The powerful boot of the m.e., a tough and temperamental fellow named Leo Taffe (whose temper was uncertain until after the fifth drink of the morning which he had not yet had), was applied in the appropriate place. The editorial rooms of the long since defunct *Telegram* were on the fifth floor achieved by a steel and cement stairwell down which a descending body ricocheted in gratifying manner. On the sidewalk outside, the prostrate and barely recognizable advocate of temperance was collared by Murph the cop as an undesirable early morning drunk and thrown in the tank.

'The thinnest skinned sons of bitches in the world,' Mr Taffe remarked, replacing the bottle of rye that occupied the file drawer in his desk marked 'City Hall Contacts, Confidential,' 'are reformers and liberals. All they want of a newspaper is everything their own way and the suppression of all opposition. The anointed can't take it.'

Over the years it has been my almost unexceptional experience that Mr Taffe was so right. The identifying hallmark of the true, deep-dyed liberal, the dedicated sorehead and witless do-gooder is intolerance of any opinions but his own and the clamorous demand that the voice of heresy be unequivocally stilled. The discovery has been a source of inspiration throughout a professional lifetime predicated on the realization that combat is part of the human condition and that combat against the dedicated forces of spurious benevolence in the world is the most satisfying of human occupations.

The risk of being detested by mannerless inferiority is not just the calculated risk of the practicing journalist of any discernible integrity; it is his vindication.

The commentator motivated by any sense of responsibility to his readers, his employer or to himself cannot be simply an unctuous playback for the golden opinions the human race has come to form of itself through the simple but defective device of believing its own publicity. To do so is a profound disservice to a completely inconsequential placental mammal who, through his innate capacity for murdering other animals, has contrived to dominate a molecule of galactic dust floating on the outer perimeter of a sea of time. The human race has always paid the highest going price to its priests to tell it it was immortal and its press agents and secular comforters to tell it it was consequential. Both are, however, mendacious and often hilariously disproved by the headlines in an adjacent column.

'A newspaperman mistakes his calling,' said Raymond Moley, strictly an old pro himself, 'when he enters a popularity contest.'

The measure of a true professional on this basis is not his friends but the enemies he has acquired and should cherish as his justification for existing at all.

Of a winter's evening, before a blazing fire of letters to my employer demanding my dismissal and suppression instanter as an enemy of the people, I warm myself with the recollection of creeps, humanitarians and other shysters whose disapproval I have incurred.

As I have suggested before in these columns, the disfavor of envious inferiority is a boutonnière that can be worn by a gentleman all day without fading.

Be a Patriot! Light Up!
From *The Lucius Beebe Reader* (1967)

In the years of my youth, a period approximating, as it now seems, the Custer massacre, cigarettes were not a highly regarded article of commerce. Their use generally was restricted to the lower orders of society, pimps, racetrack touts, congressmen and the like, and certainly none was ever smoked in my father's house by any member of the family, although now and then guests asked if they might be excused to go into the garden and smoke a cigar after dinner.

Smoking in the presence of ladies was unthinkable and there was still a statute on the local Boston law books against smoking pipes on the public street, pipes being associated with the Irish and not to be tolerated in the presence of gentlefolk.

There were, to be sure, exceptions to the rule. My friend Edwin Arlington Robinson was notoriously a smoker of Sweet Caporals, but he was a recognized and widely acclaimed poet and was accorded the tolerance usually extended to genius. A bleak and craggy Down Easter, he had been a mighty skirmisher with the bottle in earlier times and cigarettes were regarded as a sort of tapering off. Most other men of letters of the time smoked pipes, and cigars were, of course, the universal hallmark of manhood and symbol of prestige according to their quality and cost.

Nor was this prejudice against cigarettes a parochial one confined to Puritan New England. As evidence of bad morale among the ship's company in the sinking of the *Titanic*, witnesses attested that in the lifeboats many stewards and other members of the crew lit cigarettes in the presence of ladies, not to mention the Grim Reaper and the greatest catastrophe of modern times. It was, incidentally, the most serious evidence of misconduct ever made against the company's servants on that ill-starred vessel.

Tobacco in those days wasn't especially big business, certainly nothing to attract the hostility of a predatory Federal Government bent on taxing out of existence every possible source of revenue except the billion dollar union racket, some of whose components are wealthier by far than the industries they seek to impoverish by extortion.

Now the wowsers, do-gooders and reforming trash generally, including 'medical authorities' from mail order schools of osteopathy with nothing better to occupy their childish minds, are grinding out a sustained barrage of anti-cigarette propaganda. The Surgeon General of the US, presumably a handy fellow in the realm of gunshot wounds, has appointed the usual committee to investigate the potentialities for lung cancer, and publicity-mad politicians of the more debased order are rallying to denounce the sinful cigarette as a smoke screen for the evasion of more potentially dangerous issues.

To date the principal source of this septic fright talk about lung cancer has been England, where socialized medicine has reduced the once haughty practitioners of Harley Street to a confraternity of seedy pensioners dependent on the favors of a Ministry of Health that is a shining example of bureaucratic incompetence, corruption and political expediency.

The massed forces of bigotry, superstition and infected politics are ganging up on tobacco in general and cigarettes in particular with an ultimate view to their total prohibition. And don't think for a minute this cretin babbling about lung cancer isn't going to cost you and me money. Tobacco taxes last year yielded $3.2 billions in state and Federal revenue, and any least dime's abatement in this sum is going to be compensated by some other confiscatory rooking of the taxpayer to support the nest of boodling elected mendicants in Washington, DC.

The time for all men of independence and integrity to start smoking is right now.

I doubt if I have smoked ten cigarettes in the last ten years but I am going to re-establish a habit I neither admire nor take pleasure in as a patriotic duty.

The cold war that is waged every minute of the day and night between the voters and taxpayers of the United States and the government at Washington is getting hot with a meddlesome, impertinent and paternalistic hierarchy of shiftless time-servers trying to move in once more on the personal liberties of those of us who maintain them with their front feet in the public hog trough.

For thirteen long years I fought the good fight along with 160,000,000 other American patriots allied against the infamies of Prohibition. I've got scars on my liver to show for it.

I'm not too old to enlist again in the unceasing battle that all Americans have to fight all the time against the enemy that is Washington, your enemy, my enemy and everybody's enemy, the Federal Government of the United States in all its bureaucratic infamy. May I offer you a light?

The Infamy of Jury Awards
From *The Lucius Beebe Reader* (1967)

Perhaps the most unmitigatedly asinine aspect of the American legal structure, and to rate such a superlative you have to be far gone in idiocy, is that which permits juries to award damages with no control over the outrageous sums demanded and often granted for the most trifling of causes.

Professional litigants, trading on the maudlin sentimentality of juries in which women are permitted to sit and represented by cry artist shysters on a contingency basis, make a handsome living blackmailing corporate and individual defendants for sums simply dreamed out of thin air which are often awarded without hesitation by juries unable to count that high and who have to spell out the figures with their lips when they read them.

Recently a laborer was awarded half a million dollars by a jury of sniveling illiterates for the loss of his legs in an accident that was a standard occupational hazard of his calling.

Almost as outrageous a sum was a short time back awarded by a jury to a housewife who claimed she had been disfigured and her 'beauty' ruined by defective cosmetics. It may be doubted if even the personal pulchritude of Semiramis or Helen of Troy was worth $334,000.

That the cosmetic industry is the world's most monstrous over-all swindle and might well be eliminated from the cosmic scheme of things along with the packaging industry and the legal profession isn't in question. No woman's beauty, unless she is a professional prostitute, has any cash value worth mentioning.

Next to damages for alleged and in ninety-nine cases out of a hundred totally imaginary physical harm, the libel racket is the most shocking of all indictments of a system which permits juries to determine the amount of cash damages. Most libel is altogether imaginary. In perhaps one case in a thousand it is conceivable that a professional man's standing and reputation can be harmed by contrived defamation.

To state for the record that a surgeon of fair repute is secretly in the pay of the local undertaker could conceivably do hurt to his gainful practice. For a politician or public officeholder to claim libel against his good name, which is completely non-extant, is simply hilarious.

When a Chicago newspaper at the turn of the century alleged that Theodore Roosevelt was a rumbum and an alcoholic, an enlightened court awarded him damages of less than a dollar. Most reasonable men would account such personal characterization as purely honorific.

If potential damage awards for libel were limited by statute to a reasonable sum, say four bits, the nation's courts would be less littered with this sort of trash.

To entrust a jury empaneled from the shiftless unemployed whom the sheriff's officers are able to dragoon into service with the awarding of money damages is simply a travesty of the justice the courts so noisily maintain is their stock in trade.

If actual damage can be proved and is available to redress in cash, the sum should be entrusted to a responsible magistrate presumably trained in the law and not available, as are the witless housewives and small tradesmen of juries, to the breast-beating of legal hamfatters retained on a contingency fee basis. There is, of course, risk even here, but it implies some chance of justice by placing it in the hands of only one man who may be a scoundrel instead of twelve who are certain to be.

What Was Wrong with 1905?

From *The Lucius Beebe Reader* (1967)

Now and then some dolt rises up in meeting in the columns of the inquiring reporter or letters to the editor with the horrid pronouncement that, if elected, Senator Goldwater 'will set the country back fifty years.' Were it indeed possible by some superlatively benevolent tinkering of the time machine to turn back the clock and replace the scattered pages of the calendar, it would be to restore an infinitely better world than anybody now alive is likely ever to see again.

Envision, if you will, a world where the most hideous manifestations of contemporary barbarism were mercifully unknown, one which was innocent of even intimations of jet travel, radio commentators, television comedians, mendacious opinion polls, the graduated income tax, women in trousers, nuclear fission, sports shirts, television dinners, peace marchers, sit-ins, plastics, condominium apartments, parking meters, Hollywood diets, beatniks, tailfins, the 30-cent dollar, Bobby Kennedy, the Rev. Billy Graham, zippers on men's pants, Hilton hotels and once a day mail delivery.

I am aware that a hanker for the irrevocably vanished past, the *temps jadis* of the poet, has existed in all ages and that a dim view has been taken of it by the deluded gulls in the community who subscribe to the illusion of progress. Somewhere in the *Iliad* Homer complains bitterly of contemporary degenerate times and looks backward to a more heroic age when warriors were bashing in the heads of the opposition with rocks no man of today can even lift. To look backward in admiration and affection is supposed by partisans of the truly dreadful here and now to be an index of insufficiency, an inability to cope with the changing condition of life which has confronted every generation of recorded time.

It seems to me that Senator Goldwater could do a lot worse than promise to turn back the clock to the first decade of the century which now appears to most people to have been a radiant time of ineffable serenity, prosperity and abundance. At least it lacked the disasters, say, of women's suffrage, the universal motor car, credit cards, international airports, repudiation of the national currency, tranquillizers, freedom riders, digit dialing and the one-ounce Martini.

Suttee for Vice-Presidents

From *The Lucius Beebe Reader* (1967)

The end result that it didn't take either a Merlin or J. P. Morgan to foresee, namely, that the Asiatic adventure to which the Johnson government has committed the nation was an unmitigated blunder is presently being unfolded.

The whole sorry Vietnam excursion was a major error, not of course from the political and idiot humanitarian viewpoints that dominate the thinking of the bleeding hearts and the beard and sandal set, but from reasons of plain economics. It was and increasingly is a war the United States cannot afford. The potential profit was less than nothing, the advantage ephemeral or altogether chimerical and the cost, to a nation already tottering on the verge of bankruptcy, astronomical.

Notwithstanding the daily reassurances from interested parties to the contrary, your Uncle Sam is up the spout, stone broke and financially in the hands of the Morris Plan. I know, I know there are more motor cars per capita than anywhere else on earth and personal income is at all-time highs. The motor cars are largely defective, most of them aren't paid for, and the personal income is in depreciated paper or shinplasters whose value has been on a steady toboggan since Roosevelt II assured universal bankruptcy by repudiating the national currency.

And yet with a confrontation with the taxpayers (who in the end pay for all military adventures whether justified or as spectacularly reckless as the current one) in the immediate offing, the Johnson Administration, which means President Johnson since there is no opposition, still wants to play politics as usual and evade the perfectly obvious fact of life that it can't have its cake and eat it too. It can't have both the war that is its own unappreciated dream child and the Great Society.

President Johnson has got himself out not merely on a limb with his Asiatic adventure, but on the horns of an ugly dilemma of economics which, as is usual in a democracy, he will ask the American taxpayer to resolve for him. He will demand in the name of a variety of holy pretexts that his military imbroglio in Vietnam be financed in its every aspect of waste and costliness and at the same time that the already gasping economy maintain him and Sargent Shriver and all the rest of a mendicant Administration in the fullest flower of profligate spending for their own political advantage.

If there is any lesson to be learned from this unsavory imposture it may well be that when an American President dies or is assassinated in office, his Vice-President without any evasion and in the national interest should be required to commit suttee.

•

CHARMIAN CLIFT

Charmian Clift (1923–69) was born in Kiama, New South Wales. She did not receive much in the way of formal education, but her parents instilled in her a love of books. At the age of twenty she decided that she wanted to be a writer and in 1946 she joined the staff of the Melbourne *Argus*, where she met the war correspondent George Johnston, marrying him the following year. Together they wrote a novel, *High Valley*, which won a prize from the *Sydney Morning Herald*. In 1951 they moved to London and in 1954 to Greece, where they remained for the next decade. During this time Clift wrote several novels: *Mermaid Singing, Peel Me a Lotus, Walk to the Paradise Gardens* and *Honour's Mimic*. In late 1964 Clift and her husband returned to Australia and almost immediately she began a weekly column for the *Sydney Morning Herald*, which also appeared in the *Melbourne Herald*. For the next four and a half years until her death she wrote a column characterized by lyrical charm, literary allusion, common sense and humility. She often went against the tide of public opinion, not to mention the editorial line of the Fairfax press, her own publishers, especially over the issue of conscription of Australians to fight in Vietnam.

On Being Unable to Write an Article
Sydney Morning Herald, 2 December 1965

It has been more than a year now that I have been writing these pieces every week. And this week, as every week, I have come smack bang up against crisis. Annihilation even. Because I know myself to be completely incapable of writing an article. This is the most terrible feeling, of panic and desolation, of terror, of the most awful loss. I have compared notes with other writers about this chronic recurring paralysis of the talent and find that it is common. Everyone gets it. I suppose that ought to help, but in the grip of the paralysis it doesn't seem to be of any consolation at all.

There are, scattered about me at this moment, a litter of – press-*cuttings* I was going to say, only they look like desperate press-*fearings* – any one of which could be elaborated into an article.

There is one, for instance, about the clubs with the poker machines being embarrassed by the difficulty of spending their gains. One could let loose on that. But not today, somehow. There is another that records a 1904 Ford advertisement that boasts with lovely simplicity 'it gets you there and it brings you back'. And that's all it boasts about. Some time or other I would like to base an article on that. But not today. And there is a cute one from Qantas (or about Qantas, rather) who have started up a whole series of advertisements in America in which the Big Sell is an archaic or Sentimental Bloke slang, like 'dekko' and 'bonzer' and 'tucker' and 'shebang' and – God help us – 'bobby dazzler'. I would like to do something on that, but today I think oh well – they also sponsor the making of some very good films. One wonders. But then one wonders so often.

There is also a perfectly grisly one about the RSL [Returned Services League] where an official stated (in words that carried the deepest moral conviction considering the poker machines: the RSL club just up the way from my place covers a whole block and has the squat rich solidity of a Mayan temple) that rather than bring the bodies of dead soldiers home it would be better to spend that money sending more soldiers away. He said that soldiers killed in action should be buried in the nearest war cemetery because bringing them home would 'cause many upsets'.

Well, for goodness sake, let's not upset anybody, and I would have to be very upsetting indeed if I wrote an article on this particular subject.

On the other hand I could write about the current trend in the pop song, which seems to be returning directly to the nursery rhyme. Inky Dinky Spiders and Roses are Red Dilly Dilly and everything. But the very thought of writing about the infantile implications of all this quite honestly makes me sick.

I asked my son, who often helps me out in these recurring crises, what I should write about, and he looked up vaguely from a Ruy Lopez (Steinitz Defence Deferred) involvement which was engaging his attention and said, briefly: 'Chess.'

I thought about this for a while, and indeed some fairly wild ideas began to beat about in my brain, echoes of the sort of delirious and dizzy conversations that are tossed about among the young men who gather around that old chess board. 'How the Bishop was Rooked.' 'The Blackest Knight in the Castle.' 'How to Identify Losing Gambits, by Napoleon, Hitler, and Barry GoldH$_2$0.' But I think it is their subject, rather than mine, and I shall leave them to write their chess articles themselves.

The awful thing about having to write an article today is that there are so many other things I should like to be doing.

Like setting off on a trip that would take me to and through all the Australia that I have never seen – the very trip that I have been promising myself ever since I came home – the very trip that in a sort of a way brought me home, since it seemed uncivil, to say the least, to be on such intimate terms with so many other countries when my acquaintance with my own was limited to two cities and one small country town. But like the Steinitz Defence, or hope, the Trip is always being deferred – for the most excellent of reasons, naturally (I hate excellent reasons: they ring like the death-knell of possibility).

Or, accepting deferment of an introduction to the land I would so very much like to meet, I would like to go shopping. Not desperation shopping (which is my usual type of shopping, because I just have to have stockings or another set of underwear or something suitable to wear to some dinner or lunch or gathering to which I've been invited and although my daughter has just the thing, unfortunately I'm bigger than she is and, wiggle and wriggle hopefully as I might, the wretched garment looks as though it belongs to somebody else even if it is just the thing: it isn't just the thing for me).

No, the sort of shopping I would like to indulge in is the leisurely kind, rather like Nicole and Rosemary in *Tender is the Night*, who drifted all one afternoon along the boulevards of Paris, and Rosemary bought two dresses and two hats and four pairs of shoes, and Nicole bought coloured beads and a guest bed and a dozen bathing suits and a travelling chess set (how chess does crop up, to be sure) and chamois leather jackets in singing colours and a rubber alligator and lots of other beautiful and impractical things.

I am certain one could do this sort of thing in Australia. I am an avid reader of the shopping columns, which are very enticing, and I know I could drift with the best of them if only I had the money and the time. I don't think one actually needs to buy anything – it's the drifting and looking and trying on that is important, spiritually, I mean.

Or, most of all, I would like to be sitting around that new and splendidly monastic table and benches with George Johnston, talking and talking and talking for hours at a stretch (we talked for thirteen hours straight once and came up with an idea that turned into a novel called *My Brother Jack*) and drinking very cold beer and inventing plots for novels and plays and stories.

We invented a philosopher once and made him acceptable to everybody, and I rather wish now I'd written this article about that, because it is a very moral and instructive story. I will write it one day, only George Johnston has written it already as a short story and it would look as though I was pinching from him (actually, we are allowed to do that between ourselves, but not often, and only from necessity).

Well, then, since I can't sit around the table and talk to George Johnston because George Johnston is in hospital and hospitals aren't conducive to our particular sort of talking and don't have cold beer and wouldn't allow thirteen hours for working out an idea, and since I can't do anything else I want to do today because I have to write this article, I can think about all the things I ought to do, and seek a sort of moral refuge in them.

I ought to take the washing in from the line.

I ought to unpack the groceries.

I ought to have a real archaeological exploration of the midden accumulating in the rooms of my children, since nobody has two socks of the same colour or underwear or Students' Passes for buses or anything.

I ought to give up smoking, but my doctor knew I had to write this article today and has given me a period of grace which lasts until I go to bed tonight.

At least that gives me something to write about next week (it all reminds me of Laurence Sterne, who was always promising a chapter on 'Chambermaids and Buttonholes': I think my article on Giving Up Smoking might turn out to be one of those – deferred again).

What I should be doing, of course, is writing this article.

Democracy Laid Low

Sydney Morning Herald, 16 May 1968

This column almost didn't get written because I am sick. And not, alas, romantically sick, although I have taken to the sofa and piled myself around and about with all the most brilliant and beautiful Cretan and Macedonian rugs and cushions I own, and installed my kitten Jeoffrey since I don't have a 'my dog Flush'.

But what is the use of trying to play Elizabeth Barrett when your hair is clinging to your face in sweaty rats' tails and your skin is as clammy as wet dough and your mouth is dried out and peeling with fever and you feel so bruised and aching that even the kitten's little weight is much too much: besides, the kitten wants to play and you don't? And anyway who would relish the entertainment of distinguished literary gentlemen (even if any were likely to call) with a streaming nose and a mucky bubbling chest and the embarrassing suspicion that you might not, in any case, actually smell very good?

So in this condition my head isn't clear enough or my resolution strong enough to tackle the subject I had in mind. I had intended, this week, to write a follow-up on a piece I did a couple of weeks ago on the question of the restoration of democracy in Greece. Or, rather, I wanted to write about the response to that piece, which to my mind was quite curious.

Now it would not have surprised me at all if whole numbers of Australian Greeks had written to attack me, rebuke me, castigate me, or even instruct me – poor ignorant woman that I am – on the complicated machinery of the Greek political system and the desirability of the present regime. In fact I half expected something like that.

But what happened was that the only attacks, rebukes, castigations and instructions came from Australians. Australian Australians I mean, born and bred in democracy, schooled in democracy, sworn to uphold the principles of democracy, individual liberty, constitutional government, freedom of speech and the right of dissent until death do them part from such notions. Sworn, in fact, to choose death rather than part from such notions.

Curiouser and curiouser. What on earth can they mean? Do they mean, these irate democrats who rebuke me, that democracy is the prerogative of the affluent and complacent and much too good for poor foreigners? Or do they mean they are afraid their affluence and complacence might stand in jeopardy unless buttressed against Communism by fascism? Or are they really saying that they thoroughly approve of fascism anyway? Anywhere? Here, for instance?

But I feel much too sick to nut it out so I will save it for another time, although I loved the outraged letter from the gentlemen who asked me if I belonged to any organization for the restoration of democracy in Russia. No sir, I don't, knowing the complete futility of attempting to restore what never was, but I don't belong to any organization for the restoration of serfdom either, so you can be easy about my Slavic activities.

Anyway, presently my activities are confined to a little desultory reading and watching the goggle-box as well as I can through the peculiar still-life arrangements that have accumulated on the kitchen table since my sickness.

(I must explain here that in sickness I am cunning, and install myself in a public part of the house, partly so that I won't miss out on anything interesting – which I can't bear – partly so that I can still supervise activities to a certain extent, and partly so that I am under everybody's noses and they can't forget about me or how sick I am and how necessary it is to pay me little attentions. There are disadvantages to this policy, of course, because some of the things I don't miss out on I would gladly not know about, and being sick I am at the mercy of anyone and everyone who feels like exerting a little authority over my helplessness. Why do people think that because you are sick you must also of necessity be either infantile or imbecile?)

However, I was watching this television programme out of bleary eyes that have grown piggy and dim (I know, because I took one look in the mirror and burst into tears and made them piggier than ever), and it was all about present scientific investigations into the workings of the human brain, and weighty prognostications as to the possible future application of the discoveries being made. The prognostications were horrific.

For instance it was suggested, on the basis of these discoveries, that in future the faculty of memory could be so greatly enlarged and enhanced that schools would be literally unnecessary. You would take a learning pill instead. It was also suggested that the success or competitive drive could be so stimulated that any fairly bright child, by a course of drug treatment, could be success-oriented and examination-oriented to an extent that would satisfy the most ruthlessly ambitious parents (who, I suppose, would be responsible for ordering the drug treatment). It was suggested that a quarrelling or nagging spouse could be made docile and tractable to order (whose order?). It was suggested that the instinct of aggression could be manipulated at will. Ah, but whose will? Who would have the choosing of the meek and the violent? How many Frankensteins are these bland scientific gentlemen blandly creating? And what will happen if they get loose?

The only experiment that to me was not fraught with the utmost peril was one in which man is practising the control of his own brain rhythms. I haven't read anything on brain rhythms since W. Grey Walter's *Living Brain* was published in 1953, but I was a bit hooked on the subject for a while, and it was fascinating to see on the box this girl student actually turning on alpha rhythms on request. Alpha, as I understand it, is the rhythm that scans for pattern, and we all fall into types according to its activity – visual types, non-visual types and the big bulk of in-betweeners. What they didn't say was whether alpha is the only one they can control yet. And I was thinking that it would be marvellous if, instead of being controlled by somebody else, we could each control our very own selves. Literal self-control, and the dignity of being able to handle one's anxieties and fears and frustrations all by oneself in one's very own head, instead of shrieking for help from the nearest psychiatrist.

Or maybe that is fraught with peril too.

Anyway, it's all a long way off, and the clever scientific gentlemen have a lot of experimenting still to do before we become supermen or zombies either.

In the meantime, and quite personally, I wonder, when they are all so clever and can do such marvellous things, why they can't take a few minutes off one day to whip up some little old preventive drug for common ordinary miserable stinking aching sweating smelly influenza?

•

JIM COMSTOCK

Jim Comstock was born in 1910 and was educated at Marshall University, Virginia, and held many jobs (farm boy, factory worker, schoolteacher, printer and navy decoder) before going into the newspaper business with Bronson McClung, a former English pupil of Comstock's, as his co-publisher. Together they created the *News-Leader* after the Second World War, and in 1956 they started the *West Virginia Hillbilly* – 'a newspaper for people who can't read, edited by an editor who can't write'. It foundered after a couple of years, but was relaunched in December 1959. The back page of the *Hillbilly* was given over to a column called 'The Comstock Load'.

'The Comstock Load'
A Stickler for the Truth
From *Best of 'Hillbilly'* (1968)

One time Uncle Noah went to the barn to milk and saw one hundred quail sitting on a rafter. He went back to the house and got his shotgun and killed ninety-nine of them. The neighbors asked him how he got so many, and he told them when he shot he just moved the gun along from left to right. This is called a slathering shot. Then they asked him why he didn't say he killed all hundred of them, and he said damned if he'd tell a lie for one quail.

'The Comstock Load'
God Made Something That Wouldn't Split To Split Something That Should Be Split
From *Best of 'Hillbilly'* (1968)

I went out fence-rail hunting the other day, and found just what I wanted. The find was at a deserted farm up on Hinkle Mountain and I figured that the rails there, some still in the worm, some scattered by wind or hunter, were my age and more, which means a pretty well-seasoned rail. I need to fence off the back of the museum, and I thought what could be nicer than rails, split a half century ago, but good for maybe another fifty, all to give the idea of age and at the same time save me some money? Very fitting thing for a museum. And all I have to do is to call the Forestry Service, which has merged the farm with the Monongahela Forest, and get permission, and get me a truck and start picking out the better ones.

Rail fences bring back a lot of memories to me, some good, some very bad. I grew up when the rail fence was going out and the wire fence was coming in. Or at least was coming in on Hinkle Mountain. I remember my father, when a fence was to be built, getting out the Jim Brown fence catalogue. He would look it over longingly and then would cut some chestnut trees, section them off in ten-foot lengths and split them into rails. Jim Brown was the patron saint of farmers of my early days. I don't know what has happened to the company, maybe merged by now with Anaconda or some other wire people, or maybe didn't weather the depression. I was through high school and in college before my dad got to the point where he bought his fence in a roll instead of cutting it from our chestnut stand.

Perhaps it would be good in running for office, to say that I was a rail splitter. But I wasn't actually. My job was to carry the rails, split fresh, chestnutty smelling, and really too heavy for child labor laws of today, to the creeping worm and put them on, one end on and one to be placed on. I worked with my brother at this, or with the neighbors if it were a line fence between our farm and another. We joined forces, the neighbors and we, at such times. My dad, no poet he, said good neighbors make good fences. Chestnut was used because it split easy, and stayed long. It was indeed an unhappy thing when the Communists, or whoever it was, unleashed the chestnut blight. What a wood! It housed us, kept us warm, it kept us fed, it kept us kids in schoolbook money, it solved the game imbalance, it made very excellent cradles and the nicest coffins.

I don't suppose my dad ever checked the record to see how many rails Abe Lincoln could do in a day, but he said if you couldn't do one hundred in a day, you weren't much of a rail splitter. He did most of the splitting, and kept ahead of the rail layers or fence builders. Every time he raised the ax and let it go, or the big maul that drove in the wedge, the air would release from his lungs in a loud hickkkkkkkk-like noise. I remember I always wanted to ask him if he was aware of this noise, but I never did. Iron wedges were used to open the log, and after that dogwood wedges were used. My dad said that there was a sermon there. God made something that wouldn't split to split that which should be split, he said. And then he said that dogwood wouldn't make much of a fence, but then you could hardly make a fence without dogwood. He said that people were that way. I remember now that his philosophy didn't cut much ice then. I wanted to find a big flat rock and play like I was God too, looking down upon the harassed and rapidly depopulating city of ants.

My dad called the iron and dogwood wedges just that – 'wedges.' I learned later the wooden wedge wasn't a wedge at all, but a 'glut'. I think back in that time that a rail fence was a farmer's hallmark of distinction, and I know I had to do a lot of extra work when I let my fence get out of line. And the rails were precious, too, a thing that was impressed upon me when my mother made her annual breathless runs to the school house to get me excused to hurry home and get the rails moved out of the path of the forest fire which invariably got into our fence rows. Something that the Forest Service has now made a thing of the past.

As I grew older on the farm, the fences grew straighter and took up less space. My dad became anti-worm, and started using posts with hay-bale wire tied side-strips to hold the rails together. He didn't like to scythe the triangles that the mowing machines couldn't get to, and he didn't like the fact that a puff of wind could make a bit of a mess of a rail fence for several panels. The neighbors and the hunters from town didn't like it, because good worm fences made good hunting, they said. But my dad didn't care. He only hunted when a neighbor got sick and needed squirrel broth and he never asked about the season. He just took his gun and went out, and soon we'd hear the gun, and he'd be back with squirrel. The game warden heard it once and was waiting for my dad when he emerged from the woods. But that's another story. And the end of this. It's funny how far back a few thoughts can take one.

'The Comstock Load'
They Don't Like Bad News in Puzzle Hole

From *Best of 'Hillbilly'* (1968)

Now, if you have never been to Puzzle Hole, you really haven't seen West Virginia. Where? Did you ask where? Webster County. And I would have thought everybody had heard of Puzzle Hole.

'I ain't a-skeered if you ain't a-feared,' this fellow said to me once. That's the way they talk. Or used to. Maybe things are different now. It's been years since I was in Puzzle Hole, but things do change. Roads do it mostly. Roads bring school buses and the first thing you know nobody's saying they ain't a-skeered if you ain't a-feared, if you see what I mean. But I don't think they'd change there. Too much, too soon, I think.

'Let's go gigging fer pints,' a man said to me, and I said to him that surely gigging is against the law. He said they had their own law in Puzzle Hole and when a man wanted to gig he gigged. Gigged for pints. Pints? You haven't heard of that either? Sunfish.

I went there once, four, five, maybe six years ago, and I saw all the men were gone. I said to a woman I knew, 'Where's the men folks?' And she told me, and what she told me is the index to Puzzle Hole. They'd all gone over the hill and up the hollow, a good two miles there and a two good miles back, to get a load of cabbage that the government was a-giving. It was surplus and they went for it, seeing as to how it was free, don't you see? But never seeing that a patch of cabbage – in planting and harvesting too and hoeing in between – wouldn't take the time it took for all to go over to Diana and pack back a trifling bit on their backs. But that's Puzzle Hole.

An old woman – woman up in years, mind you – married a young boy over in Puzzle Hole once and the news didn't cause nothing but a belling. What did the man tell me once who knew them best? 'Two axe handles betwix the eyes.' Betwix, he said, like one of them. 'Why, if all the brains there was rendered there wouldn't be enough to grease the hinges of a pair of speck-tickles,' he told me.

But the best they tell on Puzzle Hole people is on the fellow who had the stroke and went to bed and stayed for more than twenty years. He told how he was crawling under the wire fence that the rich man from Charleston had stretched around his game preserve, when he had his stroke. 'I just remember rizin' up when it went through me like electricity,' he said. They didn't tell him that they knew what was wrong and it wasn't a stroke. It was just an electric fence that the Charleston man had put around his game preserve. I asked them why they didn't tell him and they told me it was this way. 'We just never like to be bearers of bad news to nobody,' they said.

'The Comstock Load'
Snake-handling

From *Best of 'Hillbilly'* (1968)

The only thing that can equal the negative aspects of the cult of snake-handlers is the legislation that is now being enacted against it. The House has voted the practise illegal and punishable by fine, and it is now up to the Senate to pass or not to pass. I hope they don't pass it because there is great inconsistency in a legislature that one day will officially recognize the Eastern Orthodox Church as a major faith in the state and on another day take the ikons away from others.

One step below snake-handling, to my way of thinking, is meddling with religion and trying to limit its way of worship. I agree that snakes should be taken away from such people, but education, not legislation, is the way. Legislation only drives this practise farther up the hollow and on over the hill, and puts it down with moonshining and cockfighting. I would bet you a flock of subscriptions that few, if any, high school graduates are found among rattlesnake worshippers. It would be a sight better for the legislature to seek means of keeping students in school instead of kicking against the thorns in this fashion. A cult of religious fanatics who have the nerve to fraternize with rattlesnakes certainly isn't going to be scared by any deputy sheriff, and people of this mold thrive on persecution. The Apostle Paul, who, I'll bet, wishes he had never said 'ye shall take up serpents,' was a pretty steadfast man and his followers know how firmly he would press toward the mark of the calling.

If the House had voted against the snake-handling bill, it would never again be possible for them ever to deprive any man of religious freedom of any kind. I don't mean that they *would* ever vote to take away a man's crucifix, his rosary or his Bible. But now that they have taken his snakes, they jolly well *could*.

There is nothing to me as repulsive as snake-handling as a form of religious worship, except, as I said, a law that prohibits it. The cult will lose its faithful adherents when schools open themselves to the children of the faithful by eliminating the high cost of school through class rings, expensive garb for class proms, and charges for extra-curricular activities. Education, not legislation, will eliminate snake worship. Or most any other evil.

•

CASEY MOTSISI

Karabo Moses Casey Motsisi was born to a poor family in South Africa, and educated at Madibane High in Western (Native) Township. He sold sweets in trains to help pay his school fees and was arrested as an unlicensed trader and made to do menial chores at the railway police station. He went to Pretoria Normal College, where he co-edited the school magazine, the *Normalite*. Pressed by the school authorities to reveal the identity of a pseudonymous contributor, he refused and was dismissed from the school. He joined the magazine *Drum* as tea-boy and messenger in 1955. He soon became a copy-boy and his first contribution to the magazine, 'If Bugs Were Men', gave rise to a column called 'Bug-Talk', in which the bugs (i.e. non-whites) ruminated on the idiocies of 'humans'. His later column, called 'On the Beat', related the Kid's adventures in the shebeens (illicit drinking parlours) of the townships. He wrote the column from 1958 to 1962, then he worked for a Soweto newspaper, the *World*, resuming his 'On the Beat' column for *Drum* in 1974. He was still working for *Drum* when he died in 1977.

'Bug-Talk'
Boycott Bugs
Drum, c. 1957–8

'I'm going to lead a movement,' a twenty-one-year-old bug confessed to another who was about to dig its teeth into the pinkish flesh of a magnate in the comfortable Johannesburg suburb of Parktown. 'A movement? What kind of a movement?' the other bug barked back, mad at the appetite-flagging interruption. 'A movement to boycott bugging all rich people.'

'Then all your bugging will be restricted to the locations and townships. You must bug people irrespective of race, colour or creed. Variety is the blood of life, and besides, I understand that there is tension in the south-west areas of Johannesburg. Inborn savagery or ethnic grouping trouble, I believe.'

'Variety or no variety, I still say I don't like the taste of this bloke's blood. Has a funny taste.' The other bug dug its teeth into the pinkish skin, swallowed the blood tastingly, and remarked: 'Now that you mention it, his blood does taste sort of – I can't find the word – copperish.'

'Copperish! That's the word. Remember the night they had to call a doctor for him in the middle of our sipping session. I overheard the doctor say he has duodenal alphabets.'

'Ulcers,' the other bug, which had the memory of a veteran Special Branch cop, corrected.

'Alc . . . Alpg . . . whatever you call it. What with his high blood pressure on top of it, his blood is bound to be affected.'

'I don't see what that's got to do with the fact that he's rich.'

But the boycott-crazy bug only became infuriated with its friend's rank simplicity. 'Man, I've reached the conclusion that all people who have too much coppers get high blood pressure, and then their blood gets that copperish taste. They eat too much, grow fat, then they get all these illnesses through lack of something to do.

'Why, the only time when this blighter's not eating is when he's looking for something to eat – or when he's asleep. This kind of blood is not good for my constitution. Just look how thin I am! Have you ever noticed how big bugs that bug poor people are? They drink rich, wholesome blood because poor people are lean – and you know yourself that the nearer the bone the sweeter the blood.

'Boycott the bloated blighters, that's what I say. Tomorrow I'm moving down to the locations. I'm declaring this place a High Blood Pressure Spot.'

'Include me in,' the other bug said.

'We'd better not be too successful, though, if we don't want to stir up too much opposition.'

'On the Beat'
Kid Hangover
Drum, May 1958

One of my pet hates is going to a midnite party – you know those riotous money-making affairs which begin on Friday and follow through right up to the impossible hours on Sunday.

But I guess I'll have to go to this here midnite party 'cause the bizarro who's throwing it happens to be my pal with the name of Kid Hangover. And besides I reckon he'll need the boodle he charges guests since he's been out of a job for a mile of a time and spending the better part of it in the jailhouse on account he didn't square up with the maintenance of his two bambinos – not that he's wedded.

It's about eight bells, and the bright Saturday moon makes me feel somewhat romantic and adventurous. I leave my Sophiatown shanty and head for Western, which is the place where this here midnite party is participating.

When I reach Western I find the place spilling over with humans, and I reckon Kid Hangover is going to make himself a good screw. There's enough booze to keep Mr Khruschev blotto for weeks on end.

I go to the back of the house, where there's a tent pitched for 'rockagers' who now and again want to shake a leg.

Benches are supplied for those who are tired or can't get partners, and those – like myself – who want to battle with the bottles.

A busty young girl in jeans slides a disc on the battered gramophone, and some rockagers begin to dance while the Elvis of Presley accuses each and everyone of being 'Nothing but a Hound Dog.'

Kid Hangover walks in and pats me on the back, then asks if I have been attended to. I put on my best midnite party manners and howl: 'Waddya mean attended to. You crazy? Shake a leg boy and give me half-a-dozen beers. I'm thirsty!' I pay him thirty-six bob of hard-earned pennies. As it is I don't need all those beers but there are janes around, and a guy's got to make an impression.

In fact, I don't need beer at all – sissy stuff – and I could do with some hooch. But I know that midnite party hooch is always 'doctored' with methylated spirits calculated to knock the hair off your chest, after which the boys can get at your pockets undisturbed, to say nothing of the five-day-long hangover.

I can see that I've made an impression all right 'cause no sooner have I opened the first bottle – without spilling a drop thank you – than I'm being surrounded by a batch of gum-chewing cherries all breathing down my neck and telling me that if there were more guys like me life wouldn't be the touch and go affair it is.

The girls howl for some more, and I oblige. This time we switch over to vodka.

In the wee small hours of the morning I find myself under one of the benches. Needless to say my boodle is all gone – whole week's pay. All I have between me and starvation is my hangover. That vodka must have been over-doctored. I brush myself and criss-cross home.

Three weeks later Kid Hangover corners me at a bus stop and tells me that he went and lost all his money at the races and it's about time he paid some more maintenance for his bambinos. Can't I loan him five quid?

This, I tell myself, is moral blackmail since he knows I have money on account it's payday. I give him three begrudgingly, and remind him that I'm not his father.

Now here I am twiddling my thumbs and wondering when Kid Hangover is going to throw another midnite party – which I won't attend – so's he can pay me back the three quid I loaned him so's I can pay Aunt Peggy for the 'straights' I got on tick the month before.

•

ROSS CAMPBELL

Ross Mackay Campbell (1910–82) was born in Kalgoorlie, Western Australia, and educated at Melbourne University and at Oxford University as a Rhodes Scholar. Back in Australia, he worked for the Sydney *Daily Telegraph* until the Second World War, during which he served in the RAAF. After the war he joined the *Sydney Morning Herald* as a feature-writer. He later moved over to Consolidated Press, writing for the *Daily Telegraph*, the *Sunday Telegraph*, the *Australian Women's Weekly* and *Bulletin*.

The Garbage Code
From *Daddy, Are You Married?* (1963)

Women have a strangely stubborn objection to carrying garbage tins. An instance of it came to my notice last week. Our neighbour Rhonda Waffle, whose husband was away on a business trip, came in looking very miserable.

'I miss Albert terribly,' she said. 'If I have to carry the garbage tin to the front gate again I'll scream.'

She is typical of the many women who believe one of the main functions of a husband is to carry the garbage tin out.

Certainly the job has to be done by someone. The only way to get out of it, in our district, is to produce for the garbage men a doctor's certificate that everyone in the house has general paralysis of the insane. In that case their hearts are touched and they come inside the gate to get the tin.

We are not in this privileged class, so I have to carry the tin out. My wife's inflexibility in the matter was shown the other night, when I stayed out late with some fellow-workers.

She knew that when I came home I would probably forget to put out the tin. But did she put it out herself? No; that would have been a breach of the Garbage Code.

In the early morning darkness the garbage collectors descended on the street, sounding as usual like a team of howling dervishes. Although I was in a low state after my night out, the harsh rules of the Code demanded that I perform the grimmest of all garbage duties – the pre-dawn dash. I staggered to the gate with the tin just in time.

Later, brooding on the unfairness of the system, I tackled my wife about it. 'Our garbage is something that we have made together,' I said. 'Isn't it fair that we should both help to dispose of it?'

She replied sharply: 'That's not the way you talked before we were married. You didn't tell me: "We could make wonderful garbage together!" Oh no.'

True. But in those days I did not know so much about garbage.

Daddy, Are You Married?

From *Daddy, Are You Married?* (1963)

'Daddy, are you married?'

Little Nell asked me the question while I was shaving.

'Yes,' I said. 'I'm married to Mummy. We've been married a long time.'

'Before I were born?'

'Yes. Before you were born.'

She went away satisfied. Perhaps the answer took a weight off her mind.

A minute later Lancelot came in.

'Daddy, why was Davy Crockett killed?' he said.

Davy Crockett has had such a build-up from his publicity men that children find it hard to believe he was mortal.

'He was killed fighting baddies,' I said. 'He was always fighting somebody. But this time he took on too many at once.'

'Oh.'

In the course of a day I have to answer questions on a wide range of subjects. The main thing is to be patient and tactful. As a help to beginners, I've listed here a few recent questions, and the way I handled them:

Q: *Were there pigs in the war?*

A: Yes. They didn't take part in the fighting. They were grown so their meat could be given to American soldiers. Their meat is called pork.

Q: *Have we ever won the lottery?*

A: No. You'd soon know if we did. We'd have lots and lots of money. We'd buy a lovely electric dish-washer, so I wouldn't have to dry up any more. Mummy would have her picture in the papers, hugging Rhonda Waffle.

Q: *Why don't we win the lottery?*

A: Because of our stinking luck. Probably we haven't bought enough tickets, either. People who win the lottery have usually been buying tickets for fifty years.

Q: *Do they let you go to the toilet at your office?*

A: Yes. I just have to put my hand up and ask the editor. He's quite decent about it, as long as you don't go too often.

Q: *What colour is a burglar's hair?*

A: It comes in different colours. Some burglars have black hair. Some have red hair. Old burglars, near the retiring age, have white hair.

Q: *Was Mummy living in the olden days?*

A: No. She doesn't even go back to the First World War. But there were ladies like her in the olden days.

Q: *Who?*

A: Helen of Troy, Cleopatra, Diane de Poitiers, Florence Nightingale . . .

That went down well with the audience. As I said, it's just a matter of being tactful.

Bargain Wives

From *Daddy, Are You Married?* (1963)

A judge has awarded a man £375 damages for the loss of his wife. 'Not much, is it?' said my wife. She was reading the paper.

'It depends on what condition she was in,' I said. 'She might have been a bit of a bomb, you know.'

'But look at the cost of replacing her! If he hired a housekeeper the £375 would be gone inside six months.'

I thought about it for a minute. The valuation of wives is a tricky subject.

'I don't think you can estimate a wife's value by the cost of replacement,' I said. 'Probably the husband has had this wife for several years. Even if she has been carefully looked after she's not the same as a new one.'

'You can't look at it that way! The Bible says the price of a good woman is above rubies.'

'I don't know what Ruby's price was. But the courts usually value wives at a reasonable figure.'

'What would you say I'm worth?' she asked.

I had to admit that I didn't know. I've had no training in wife-valuing. Judges can do it, but it's their business.

'A man should be able to find out the correct value of his wife,' I said. 'I don't see why a judge shouldn't start a radio session like the one where they value cars. "Ring Judge Dingwattle tonight for a free spot-valuation of your wife." You know what I mean?'

'Women are more interested in the value of husbands,' she said. 'They depreciate fast as a rule.'

I ignored this comment.

'The judge would talk like this,' I continued. 'Now, Mr Hoggett, of Pymble, you say you have a 1955 wife in good order, useful for heavy work, bonnet slightly dented, one owner, insured till next January. The 1955 model was a reliable one. This wife should be good for years of trouble-free service. I'd say she was worth every penny of £650.'

'She sounds a bargain to me,' said my wife.

'And now, Mr Smith, of Darlinghurst. Your wife is a small 1959 sports model, practically unmarked, with smart lines, but noisy and a little hard to control. This is not the family type of wife, but there is always a demand for them. I would estimate her at £550–£570 if she has a radio.'

My wife was looking at me coolly.

'1947 husband,' she said, 'two tones of grey, tartan seat-covers, large boot, body slightly battered . . .'

I did not pursue the subject further.

•

RUSSELL BAKER

Russell Wayne Baker was born in 1925 in Morrisonville, Virginia. He was five when his stonemason father died, and he was brought up by his mother in New Jersey and Maryland. He was educated at Johns Hopkins University, where he edited the campus newspaper, and after obtaining an AB in 1947 he joined the *Baltimore Sun* as a crime reporter and rewrite man. In 1953 he was sent to London, as bureau chief, and the next year returned to the United States and became the paper's Washington correspondent. However, in late 1954 he left the *Sun* to join the *New York Times* as a Senate reporter (Jack Kennedy, then a young senator, was practically his office boy and would obligingly fetch the texts of amendments for him from the Senate floor). In 1962 James Reston gave him a thrice-weekly editorial page column, called 'Observer', which has always mixed commentary and humour, and is syndicated to around 500 papers. He won the Pulitzer Prize for commentary in 1979 and a 1983 Pulitzer for biography, for an autobiographical book, *Growing Up* (1982).

The Great Forgetting [1973]
From *So This Is Depravity* (1980)

What the country needs now at the end of the Vietnam war is not amnesty but amnesia.

It is time to put the whole thing up in the attic, to store it away up there with the snapshot of Granddaddy as a young man, foot up on the running board of his Model T Ford. Up there where we keep the old Blue Eagle (NRA [National Rifle Association], kiddies) window decal, the 1945 newspaper with the headline about Roosevelt's death, the stamp collection we started that year we had the mumps and couldn't leave the house. The Vietnam war ought to go up there very first thing in the morning, so we can start forgetting about it right away. The sooner the better.

What a protest that's going to produce, what an overpoweringly reasoned lecture of right thought, summoning Freud, history, Founding Fathers, 'The Star-Spangled Banner,' Joseph Pulitzer and the memory of Heinrich Himmler, among others, to prove that forgetting is bad for you, particularly if you are a heavily muscled superpower half mesmerized between Cotton Mather and Krafft-Ebing.

The great forgetting wouldn't be for ever, though. The attic isn't for things we want to forget for ever. Things get put up there because we don't know what else to do with them this year, or because they are in the way right now, or because we want to get them out of our lives for a while without throwing them away.

Later, when we have changed and become different people, we will go up there and examine this or that on the chance that it will tell us something about who we were once, what sort of times we lived through, what kind of people we have become.

Granddaddy's snapshot is up there for that reason. Years ago, it just looked dully and depressingly old-fashioned – that straw boater, those sleeve garters, that Model T – but we didn't want to throw it out. Later, we sensed – being too young to *know* it then – we might want to come back to it when we ourselves were twice as old as Granddaddy was when the snapshot was taken, come back to it and try to grasp something about time, change, youth and the grave.

This is why we now need a great national forgetting. Nobody knows what to make of Vietnam right now, and it is in our way. We try to get back into the old American habit of liking ourselves again, and we keep stumbling over Vietnam.

Politicians keep shoving it into our shins. People with axes to grind keep using it to win this argument or clinch that. There is evidence that office seekers intend to use it for the next generation, as politicians after the Civil War used to 'wave the bloody shirt,' whenever it is in a politician's interests to bring out the absolute worst in us.

We need time to forget, to let it yellow in the attic, to get on with tomorrow's things. And how will we win this time? It will cost everyone something.

It will cost both the hawks and the doves a concession on amnesty. So let it be. Let there be amnesty for the draft runners, deserters and refusers who went to jail, if that will bring us the quiet that helps forgetting.

There must be amnesty too for Lieutenant Calley, and an end of accusations against war criminals. Fair is fair. If justice is to be suspended in the higher need for amnesia, it must be justice equally suspended for all sides, or there will be no justice, and certainly no quiet.

The doves will also have to grant the government's points about the morality of the war and the excellence of its conduct. Until they do, the government will never give us quiet.

Let all doves who look to the future shout out loud, therefore, the following declarations: to wit, that there was good and just reason for the war, that the government fought it honorably, that President Nixon was always right about how to end the war while almost everybody else was consistently wrong and that this is really peace with honor, and plenty of it, which he has brought us. A hard dose for doves, assuredly, but worth the swallowing if this government, and other governments to come, quiet down about the war for simple lack of someone to argue with, and let us have sweet forgetfulness.

And what of the dead and the wounded? Shall they be forgotten with the rest? The question can only be answered with another. Are they honored in this endless ugly snarling about whether or not they died to no purpose, or are they simply forgotten in the gratifying emotional binges Americans experience in the uproar?

Later we shall be able to come back to them and make more sense of their deaths and mutilations, but we must age before we can do that, and become different people. We must put more time between this business and the people we are to become, so that those people can come back to it, some remote day in the attic, with the maturity and detachment to grasp what it was about, this war that made them older and perhaps wiser.

Caesar's Puerile Wars
From *So This Is Depravity* (1980)

Among treasures recently uncovered by Italian workmen excavating for a new disco-thèque in Rome is an essay entitled 'How I Spent My Summer Vacation,' written by Julius Caesar at the start of his junior year in Cato the Elder High School. At the request of the Italian Government and the classics faculty of Oxford University, I have translated it from the Latin into English. The text reads as follows:

These things thus being so which also, from the nones to the ides, the impediments having been abandoned, Caesar constituted on the rostrum to exhort his comrades to joy. 'No more lessons, no more parchment scrolls, no more teacher's dirty looks,' Caesar hortated.

Ten days having subsided, of which the maximum was the first Sunday, Caesar, of whom the parents having to a villa in Capri passed from the injurious sun of Rome to that lambent insular quiescence. Which, therefore, Caesar, being abandoned solely to the urbans of the Rome, he gave himself illicit custody of his father's chariot and hied it through the Roman routes and streets in quest of frumentum.

Between those all which conjoined with Caesar in the paternal chariot, thus to harass the maximally beautiful feminine youth of the city and to make the ejection of empty wine jugs on to the lawns of quaestors, censors, tribunes and matrons, were Cassius and Marc Antony.

Brutus noble was superior to the omnibus, however, of others between Caesar's cohorts. That one opposed his stance to the puerile search for frumentum, stating which things thusly: primary, that harassings of femininity from a moving chariot and ejectings of empty wine jugs had not been predicted by the Cumae Sibyl. Fourthly, that Caesar was a reckless driver which would wreak ire, not only of the gods, but also of Caesar's father, by the arrogance of which he burned the iron from the paternal chariot wheels.

The which made much risibility itself between Cassius, Marc Antony and Caesar. 'Friends, Romans, countrymen,' said Brutus, 'evince respect to the public thing unless you will have forgotten to obviate too long our patience, O Catiline.'

These things having been exhorted, Marc Antony asked Caesar to lend him his ear and declared into it, 'Brutus is a sissy. For two denariuses I'd whip his gluteus maximus.'

Caesar's ear whence, by forced march, having been manumitted to Cassius, this one, his lips having been juxtaposed to the lobe, uttered, 'Brutus thinks too much about the public thing. Such schoolboys are stuffy.'

Twelve nights having marched, Caesar and his amiables having collected a six-pack of Falernian wine and three frumentums from South Tiber Girls' Latin School, these made strategems to effectuate nocturnal sport on Capitoline Hill.

To which speeding full of equitation, the chariot encountered an opposing chariot adjoined in much agitation, having debauched from the superior route without attention to the whiffletree connection.

After brusque externalization from Caesar's chariot in a shower of frumentum, Caesar,

Cassius and Marc Antony, their wounds being inferior, hurled themselves furioso with epithet upon the two passengers of the intersecting chariot shattered in regard to the right wheel.

'Tacit your puerile abuse,' said the younger of those there two. 'You are speaking to Cato the Younger and this one here of us two is Pliny the Elder.'

Thus which then Caesar being aware, without days of wrath and being recognized by Cassius and Marc Antony as the without whom none, Caesar sent pleas to Cato the Younger and Pliny the Elder lest they make him under arrest for driving a chariot without a license.

Of which indeed it would have been made, the more thus also by which that inspection of Caesar's chariot would have unopened the essence of a can of paint, revealing his juvenilian strategy to paint a graffito on the statue of Romulus and Remus. By high fortune joined the dispute Cicero, having been awakened from his oration by the crash.

'How long, O Julius, will you continue to abut our patience?' asked Cicero. Then was Caesar full of dolor, by which he made the oath to work hard all summer and respect the public thing, whomever would Cicero lend him the money to repair the two ruinous chariots before his father got back from Capri.

'I shall make it thus to be so which,' said Cicero, 'because of the respect I support for your old genitor.'

Thus came Caesar to toil his summer vacation in labored makings and to ponder the glory of the public thing, of which the which is such that there is no posse to improve it, although Caesar is determined to study hard this year so he can grow up and improve it anyhow, whichever is of what.

The New York Experience

From *So This Is Depravity* (1980)

Our friend Winokur, who is ill at ease in New York, arrived from Iowa for a visit recently and immediately noticed two cucumbers on the sidewalk in front of our house. Apparently he had never seen cucumbers on a sidewalk before.

'Should I bring in these cucumbers?' he asked. We all smiled at his rustic simplicity and advised him to let sidewalk cucumbers lie. 'Why are there cucumbers in front of your house?' he asked.

Nobody tried to answer that. We are New Yorkers. In New York different things turn up lying in front of your house. Sometimes they are cucumbers. Who knows why? Who cares? 'This is New York, Winokur,' I said. 'Enjoy it, and don't get bogged down in cucumbers.'

We gave him a potion to calm his anxiety and bedded him down on the first floor. Having stayed with us in the past, he refuses to sleep upstairs for fear of being crushed by objects falling off the Emperor, the forty-six-story apartment building across the street. The last time he visited, the Emperor shed an entire window of thick plate glass and crushed a car in front of our house. We assured him that the Emperor was always doing that sort of thing, that nobody had been killed yet and that when somebody was, the police would do something about it, since this was the high-rent district and in New York the upper-income folks got action from the law.

Winokur was not reassured. In Iowa, I gather, they don't have buildings that litter. He insisted on the downstairs sofa, but we had scarcely snuggled down for the night when he was upstairs rapping at the bedroom door.

'It sounds like somebody's stealing hubcaps out front,' he said. Why did he think law-abiding New Yorkers went to bed at night, if not to allow hubcap thieves the right to work in privacy? Winokur was unhappy with this explanation. 'Why don't you go to the window and look?' he suggested.

He was clearly uneasy about going to the window himself, and sensibly so, since you can never tell when the Emperor will send some plate glass sailing out from the thirty-fifth floor, across the street and right into the window where you are investigating a hubcap theft.

So I went to the window. Sure enough, a man was removing the rear hubcaps from a red sedan parked under the Emperor. He was a short, elegantly dressed man with a mustache, and his work was being admired by a large, heavy, well-dressed woman, obviously his wife or companion. I described all this to Winokur.

'Why is a well-dressed man removing hubcaps at midnight?' he asked. 'Why is a well-dressed woman watching?'

'Why are there two cucumbers lying on the sidewalk in front of my house?' I explained.

Dissatisfied, Winokur came to the window. 'The elegantly dressed man is now putting both hubcaps on the wall at the base of the Emperor,' he whispered. 'And now, he and the well-dressed stout woman are walking away.'

'This is New York,' I said.

'Somebody is going to come along and see those hubcaps and take them,' said Winokur.

'Not necessarily,' I said. 'One night when I parked my car out there somebody came along, lifted the hood, stole the radiator hose and didn't even touch the hubcaps.'

'Something very funny is going on here,' said Winokur. 'Fancy-dress couple take off hubcaps. Leave hubcaps where they're sure to be stolen. Obviously, they don't need the hubcaps, they don't want the hubcaps, they just want the hubcaps to be stolen.'

Predictably enough, the loose hubcaps were spotted by two very civilized-looking men who seemed to be out for a stroll. They stopped, discussed the hubcaps and, picking them up, walked away with them, one hubcap per stroller. They didn't look like men who really needed hubcaps.

Winokur's Midwestern sense of decency was so offended that he threw up the window and shouted, 'Put those hubcaps down.' They didn't, of course. Winokur was baffled by this example of white-collar street crime, which was not at all mysterious to a New Yorker.

The man who removed the hubcaps, I explained, hated the owner of the red sedan for having a free parking place at the curb while he had none. In fact, he regarded that curb space as his very own and had taken vengeance, possibly at his wife's urging, by promoting the theft of his enemy's hubcaps.

'Ridiculous,' said Winokur.

'This is New York,' I said.

I sent him out for the papers next morning. 'Somebody has stolen the cucumbers,' he said, returning, 'and now there's a slice of pizza lying where the cucumbers were yesterday.' Life must be very strange in Iowa.

•

PETE HAMILL

Pete Hamill was born in 1935 in Brooklyn, New York, and started adult life as a sheetmetal worker in the Brooklyn Navy Yard. After serving in the navy for a couple of years he attended Pratt Institute and Mexico City College. He worked in advertising for a year or so, then joined the *New York Post* as a reporter in 1960. He spent a year as a contributing editor of the *Saturday Evening Post* (1964–5) and in 1965 began writing a political column of distinctly liberal bent for the *New York Post*. He kept this up, with a couple of breaks, until 1974. He has subsequently been a columnist for the *New York Daily News*, the *Village Voice* and *Newsday*, and is currently editor of the *New York Daily News*.

Free Willie
New York Post, December 23, 1969

Dear Governor Rockefeller:

We, the undersigned, feel that the time has come to let Willie Sutton out of jail. He is now sixty-eight years old and has spent thirty-seven years of his life in various prisons. He is suffering from hardening of the arteries and needs cardiovascular surgery; he might not live another year. The state parole board has turned down his latest appeal, and he cannot legally appear before another board until August, 1971. That might be too late.

We know what Willie did, but then he never made any secret of it. He held up banks, he once said, 'because that's where the money is.' When asked for an occupation, he once told a judge: 'It was of an illegal nature. It was bank robbing.' There were times when he was less than co-operative with authorities, but this was at least based upon principle.

Willie Sutton was one of the best bank robbers who ever lived. He planned his jobs with care and precision and posed at various times as a policeman, a bank guard, a postman and a window wiper to gain access to the banks. In his extracurricular activities he was always a gentleman, a suave dresser, an expert on psychology, Irish history and chess, and a gallant with women. He had an aversion to steam-table food, to be sure, and three times broke out of jail. And when they put him away the last time, in 1952, he was locked in Attica, that most gloomy of all New York fortresses.

We remember Arnold Schuster, too. This young man turned in Willie Sutton in 1952 and – eighteen days later – was murdered on a Brooklyn street. This vicious act, according to Joe Valachi, was committed at the whim of Albert Anastasia. Willie Sutton knew nothing about it. In all the years he spent sticking up banks, he never once committed an act of violence. He carried guns, but they were more props than anything else. In fact, when he was arrested for the last time, Brooklyn detectives spent an hour with him before discovering that he was carrying a .32-caliber automatic. There is no known record of violent activity by Willie while he has been in jail.

The point is this: Willie Sutton has paid for his crimes with most of the years of his adult life. He is now an old man. If he were set free, there is little chance that he would stroll into Chase Manhattan with a pistol looking for some walking-around money; if anything, the lecture circuit would provide him all the money he would ever need; you might even make him a consultant to the poverty program, since nobody knows more about the instinct toward larceny than Willie Sutton.

If state prisons are anything, they must be institutions which go beyond punishment. There is much lip service to this concept these days; acknowledging that this man had paid for his crimes would be a chance to show it. If Willie Sutton had been a GE [General Electric] board member or a former water commissioner, instead of the son of an Irish blacksmith, he would be on the street now. There are some of us today, looking at the mortgage interest rates, who feel that it is the banks that are sticking up us.

This is frankly an appeal for mercy and human feeling. Willie Sutton should be able to sit and watch the ducks in Prospect Park one more time, or go to Nathan's for a hot dog, or call up some old girl for a drink. As governor, you have the right to overturn the decision of the parole board. Letting Willie out won't gain you a vote, but it would be a hell of a thing if the old bank robber could take a look at the Christmas tree in Rockefeller Center for one last time.

Respectfully yours, The Free Willie Sutton Committee (John Scanlon, Charles Monaghan, Joe Flaherty, Joel Oppenheimer, Pete Hamill. In formation.)

No Sad Songs

New York Post, December 30, 1970

Mendel Rivers will be safely tucked into the earth today, accompanied by the usual gushy salutes and the familiar lying rhetoric of death. There is a convention, rigidly adhered to by politicians and editorial writers, that says one must speak only about the nobility and goodness of the dead, no matter how rotten, dangerous or disgusting they were in the flesh; it's as if death and its attendant mysteries could suddenly cleanse a man's history.

Richard Nixon's eulogy of Rivers is a masterpiece of the genre and seems taken from unused drafts of his celebration of Everett Dirksen, on the occasion of that old fake's demise. 'I have lost a friend,' Nixon tells us. '. . . South Carolina has lost one of the most distinguished men in her history and America has lost a patriot.' In two sentences Nixon thus manages to demolish all previous ideas of human friendship, genuine distinction and true patriotism.

The truth was that Rivers was a common drunk and a nasty, willful, power-dazed man who obtained great power in Washington because of the vile anachronism of the seniority system. As chairman of the House Armed Services Committee, he knelt before the admirals, generals and defense contractors for more than five years. He was such a great patriot that he managed to avoid military service through all his sixty-five years.

But it was Rivers' sense of his personal mission that was the worst thing about his tenure. He once told his fellow Representatives that his committee was 'the only voice, the official voice, that the military has in the House of Representatives.' Even granting that Rivers might have been half in the bag, this was an astonishing description of the committee's function. Representatives are elected by civilians to represent civilians; under our system of government the military is controlled by civilians; and for a civilian like Rivers to say that a committee of the legislative branch is a mere press agent for a section of the executive branch is to say that the Constitution is dishwater.

Under Rivers, no questions of importance were ever asked of the military. In fact, it was while he was chairman that the military moved more strongly than ever before toward becoming a separate national entity, not answerable to civilians, like the army in a banana republic. If Rivers had been scrutinizing the military, instead of blowing kazoos at its parades, there would have been no military 'intelligence' units gathering information about American civilians, their loyalty or lack of it. We found out about that little caper without Rivers' help; God knows what else is going on deep in the Pentagon, among those people who refer to the *Washington Post* as *Pravda* and the *New York Times* as *Izvestia*.

Rivers gained personal rewards from his position, although most were ceremonial rather than financial. There were hundreds of foreign junkets paid for by us. And the air force would fly him home to Charleston, at taxpayers' expense, whenever he cared to go. But the best of all was for Rivers to sit around with his cronies, belting down the sauce, saying things like: 'I've made a lot of millionaires in my time, and I'm going to make a lot more.'

A lot of that kind of money went to the Congressional district which elected him to sixteen straight terms. Visiting Charleston today is like flying into one of Ron Cobb's cartoons of the Pentagon: Jets scream through the air every five minutes; civilians salute each other; highways are marked with as many military installations as there are Stuckey signs. In the three-county Charleston area, employees at military installations will earn $329,600,000 this year – almost thirty-five percent of the area's buying power. No wonder they named a highway after Ole Mendel.

But the people who really loved Rivers were all those sleek generals and admirals, all those procurement officers who bought tons of military junk from arms manufacturers and retired the following year to go to work for the people they'd just rewarded with contracts. Rivers never questioned any of this; after all, it was all to make America the toughest honcho in the saloon.

Rivers is now supposed to be succeeded by Representative F. Edward Hebert (D-La.), at sixty-nine another aging hero; he says that we would have won in Vietnam five years ago if those damn civilians had only let the military do what Hebert and Rivers had suggested: Kill everybody. In other words, he is another agent of the military, taking over a committee whose basic function should be to police the military. It's as if David Rockefeller became chairman of a banking committee. If there were ever a case for destroying the seniority system, this is it. Meanwhile, there should be no sad songs for the passing of Mendel Rivers. He's gone, and we're better off without him.

•

HERB CAEN

Herb Caen (1916–97) was born in Sacramento, California. He was educated at Sacramento Junior College and from 1932 to 1936 he was a reporter for the *Sacramento Union*. He moved to San Francisco, the city he later dubbed 'Baghdad-by-the-Bay', where he started his column in 1938. It appeared in the *San Francisco Chronicle* until 1950, then in the *San Francisco Examiner* until 1958, and thereafter in the *Chronicle* again until Caen's death. Known as the 'three dot column' because of the marks that separated it into sections, it appeared three times a week under the heading 'It's New to Me' and combined gossip, sketches, whimsy and reflections on San Francisco lore. Caen's column was syndicated through Chronicle Features and in 1993 he was awarded the lifetime achievement award by the National Society of Newspaper Columnists.

'It's New to Me'
Black Friday
San Francisco Chronicle, November 24, 1963

After the first newsflash on the radio there wasn't much reality to Friday. The morning had started out cold and gray, and the young ladies of Montgomery St, on the way to their first coffee break, were wrapped in their own arms (and thoughts) and saying 'Brrrrr' in exaggerated tones. A few people were chattering about something known as the Big Game. The saloons were getting ready for a big night. The inevitable cliché expert, in the office hallway, was heard to say, 'Thank God it's Friday.' At that point Dallas was still most renowned as the home of Neiman-Marcus, a fancy department store; the fact that Adlai Stevenson had been spat upon in Dallas was still remembered by only a few. Dallas. 'Big D,' they call it. D as in Death.

The radio was playing a thin, insipid record by an English dance band – the kind of music you listen to unconsciously, if at all – when the first bulletin was announced. Like all such things, it had a fictional ring. The announcer sounded stunned and confused, and for a moment you felt sorry for him. His careful training in voice and diction went out the window, and he stumbled over the words. 'There is a report – a bulletin – there is word from Dallas that . . .' You snatched fleetingly at the hope that it was only an unconfirmed rumor as you spun the dial through the networks.

Slowly a stillness crept over the city. A paralysis was setting in as a million minds focused on a city in Texas. Cars pulled over and parked – it seemed impossible to drive and listen at the same time. The only sign of life on the Bay was a gray army transport inching past Fort Mason; no flags shown on her, and she seemed like a ghost ship. I picked up my telephone. No dial tone.

Now there was a steady flow of radio bulletins, the announcers sounding breathless, as though they had just been slugged in the stomach. 'He is at least gravely injured –' ABC quoted a Secret Service man as saying the President was dead, 'but this is unconfirmed, we repeat, this is unconfirmed.' But all the while a lump was forming in your throat, and your heart was sick. NBC had the President dead, while ABC said, 'He is still alive, we repeat –' Flash: Two priests entered the hospital. You found yourself praying for the first time in years. Oh, God.

Your thoughts rambled in the most confused way as the news tickers clattered in the background. You remembered Arthur Godfrey sobbing on the air as he described FDR's funeral, and the peculiar, choked phrase, 'God bless his gaudy guts.' And 'the drums are playing slowly, ohhh sooo slowwwly.' You remembered France, 1945, and the first announcement of FDR's death – tears glistening on the stubbly cheeks of combat GIs. Zangara firing at Roosevelt and killing Mayor Anton Cermak of Chicago; just the other day Westbrook Pegler, that paragon of journalists, had said again, 'Zangara killed the wrong man.'

You sat by a window and stared out at the empty street, your mind still as cloudy as the skies. Odd, nagging thought: Gavin Arthur, grandson of the twenty-first President of the United States, had refused to vote for Jack Kennedy in 1960, although he is a Democrat. Arthur, the expert on horoscopes, had cast one whose signs, he said, indicated only one thing: the thirty-fifth President would die in office. You smiled condescendingly at him – then. There was a brief, terrible silence on the radio. And then the announcer, clearing his throat, said the simple words you could scarcely bear to listen to.

'John Fitzgerald Kennedy, the thirty-fifth President of the United States, is dead.' There was a brief interlude of recorded classical music that sounded like Beethoven and then the 'Star-Spangled Banner' came on. The great Flag on the Telephone Building was slowly lowered to half-staff, where it rippled briefly in the cold air and then sagged.

And so you cried. You cried for the young man and his wife and his family. You cried because you hadn't realized how much the young man meant to you. You cried for every stupid joke you had ever listened to about him, and you cried for the fatuous faces of the people who had told them. You cried for the Nation, and the despoilers of it, for the haters and the witch-hunters, the violent, the misbegotten, the deluded. You cried because all the people around you were crying, in their impotence, their frustration, their blind grief.

By early afternoon the city had collected itself slightly. The sun tried to force its way through the overcast, but it was a feeble effort. Downtown, the Salvation Army bells were ringing on the street corners – mournfully. A cable car rattled over distant tracks, sounding like firecrackers far away. Now the radio announcers had regained their aplomb, and a few commercials were creeping back on. One senator said, 'Words are of no use at a time like this,' but other politicians had their statements prepared. A San Mateo lady I know took her son in to the dentist, and said, 'Isn't it terrible?' 'Oh, I don't know,' said the dentist. 'I didn't like him or his politics.' She managed to walk out into the hallway before she became ill.

The President is dead. Long live the President.

'It's New to Me'
The Troubled Summer
San Francisco Chronicle, July 17, 1966

It should be, as always, the most fruitful and self-indulgent time of the year, and at first glance it is. The tourists smothering the cable cars and laughing-screaming down the hills. Freeways jammed with the chrome-hard bumper crop of the Affluent Society. Even the Giants are doing well and could win it all. Then why is there so little joy in this joyous season?

The answer is so obvious nobody wants to talk about it – yet it is always at the back of your mind and on the tip of your tongue. The answer is in the almost constant drone of planes heading westward, the servicemen on the street corners, the gray carriers sliding past the Embarcadero toward the Gate, decks crowded with planes whose wings are folded as though in prayer. The answer is in caskets, casualty lists, napalm and inflation – in the war that is not a war in pursuit of a victory that has no name. The answer is in presidential popularity polls that climb higher every time more bombs are dropped, and in bumper strips reading 'Escalate! Get It Over With and Get Out!' (How appropriate that the popular American philosophers of the day are those who write for automobiles.)

By unspoken assent, the big game at dinner parties these nights is to see how long you can converse without mentioning the Word. Anything else is an OK subject – especially religion (nothing controversial *there* any longer) and politics, as long as it is kept on the state level (God is alive and in the White House). Even LSD, that bore, is acceptable if you can think of something brighter to say than 'I'd like to try it, but only under strict supervision, of course, as a scientific experiment.' Travel is a safe topic ('I never fly tourist class because who wants to meet a lot of tourists?'), and so are the redwoods and pollution, although conservation, like a lot of other worthy causes, seldom makes conversation. Civil rights is out – nothing left to say – and Berkeley buttons are in (the latest: 'KCC – Kill a Commie for Christ').

But after the martinis, the wines, the coffee and cognacs, the pressure becomes too intense. At last, somebody snaps – the man who has been sitting grimly through the small talk ('Have you read *The International Nomads*? Heaven!'). He pounds the table in agony: 'Jesus, if we could only find a way out of that goddam –' Shocked silence. Reproving glances all around. But the delicate, artificial spell has been shattered. The game hostess begins falteringly: 'How do you think the Brundage collection compares with –' and it is too late. Pandora's box is open. 'Frankly,' speaks up an advertising man, 'I thought Steinbeck's reply to Yevtushenko was pitiful – hell, it sounded as though McNamara had dictated it.' 'McNamara – you mean that guy with Stacomb on his hair?' 'You should be so smart.' 'How does he explain the Edsel? The Edsel of wars, that's what we've got.' The dinner table is roaring.

Amazing, the expertise that falls out once the Word has been spoken. Hans Morgenthau, Bernard Fall and Jean Lacouture are quoted. 'The awful geography lesson,' as H. V. Kaltenborn once called it, goes on: Da Nang, Hue, Mekong Delta, Annam, 'Did you know that the Chinese once occupied all of Vietnam?' A former naval person speaks up: 'We are the most powerful country in the world, so we have to use our power. What good is it otherwise? Crush 'em! We will impose a Pax Americana on the world.' A bespectacled psychiatrist murmurs: 'The military mind is a pathological mind.' A visiting European actress shrills: 'The Americans are hypocrites. Why, if the Russians were doing what we were doing –' A stockbroker shrugs: 'So it's good for business.' 'The hell it is,' roars a prominent manufacturer. 'I've got military orders I don't even want. Who needs this damn war? If I were young again, I'd grow a beard and demonstrate. I'm *rabid* on this subject.' Magazine writer: 'The first casualty of this was Humphrey – I wouldn't vote for him for dog catcher.' The hostess, desperately: 'What can we do? I mean, if you were the President, what would *you* do?' The psychiatrist again, again with his $50-an-hour murmur: 'He is so Oriental about saving face – I wonder how he feels about hara-kari?' Naval person: 'I agree with LeMay – bomb 'em back to the Stone Age.' Psychiatrist: 'You, sir, are a madman.' Naval person: 'I, sir, am an American' . . .

Midnight, the party dying in a flurry of wraps, hugs, pecks on cheeks, 'marvelous dinner,' apologies, 'wonderful time,' coldness, grunted apologies, growled acceptances. A last dying sentence down the stairs: 'Can anybody remember why we went to Vietnam in the first place?' End of a summer night: a wet fog on the Bay and the misty lights of a ship heading toward – but we don't talk about that, do we?

•

ART BUCHWALD

Art Buchwald was born in 1925 in Mount Vernon, New York. He was only five when his mother died and his hard-pressed father was obliged to put him into foster homes. During the Second World War he lied about his age and joined the Marines, serving in the Pacific. He attended the University of Southern California after the war, and in 1948 moved to Paris to become a nightclub reporter on the European edition of the *New York Herald Tribune*. In 1962 he returned to the United States, settling in Washington, DC, to write a satirical column for the *Tribune* called 'Capitol Punishment'. He switched to the *Washington Post* and the Los Angeles Times Syndicate in the early 1970s, appearing simply under the heading 'Art Buchwald'. His columns have been exhaustively collected in book form.

The New New (sic) Nixon
From *I Never Danced at the White House* (1971)

We've had an Old Nixon and a New Nixon, and one Monday night on nationwide television we saw a New New Nixon. How the New New Nixon came to be President is a very interesting story.

Back in January, 1972, the New Nixon was engaged in working out the details of the Vietnam cease-fire and solving difficult problems with Red China and the Soviet Union. Because the duties of the presidency consumed so much of his time, he turned over his reelection campaign to the Old Nixon, who at the time was unemployed and needed the work.

On June 17, while the New Nixon was in Florida resting up from his trip to Moscow, he received word of the Watergate break-in. He was appalled at this senseless, illegal action and was shocked to learn that employees of the Committee to Reelect the President were involved.

The first thing he did was to call the Old Nixon and order an immediate investigation to find out who was responsible.

The Old Nixon promised the President that he would leave no stone unturned in rooting out the people who were involved in this sordid affair.

As the weeks went by, the *Washington Post* and other newspapers started writing that people in the White House were involved in the Watergate. The President called in the Old Nixon and asked him what he knew about it.

The Old Nixon replied, 'It is rotten journalism, hearsay and mudslinging at its worst. I have talked to John Dean III, Charles Colson, John Mitchell, Jeb Magruder, H. R. Haldeman and John Ehrlichman, and they have assured me that no one in a position of any responsibility had anything to do with the Watergate. I also have seen Pat Gray's FBI files and everyone is clean.'

The New Nixon breathed a sign of relief, but he gave further instructions to the Old Nixon. 'I don't want a whitewash. The chips must fall where they may.'

'Yes, sir.'

On March 21 the President received new information implicating members of his own White House family. This information shocked and appalled the New Nixon because the White House was a sacred trust.

He called in the Old Nixon and demanded his resignation.

'I'm not going to be the scapegoat,' the Old Nixon shouted. 'If I go, I'm going to involve a lot of other people. This whole Watergate mess wasn't my idea, and I'm going to name names.'

The New Nixon told the Old Nixon he could stay on. Then the New Nixon went to Camp David to think about what he should do. He knew he had to get rid of the Old Nixon. However, he was hoping to save Ehrlichman and Haldeman.

But the pressure was too great, and a group of highly influential Republicans flew in secretly to see him. They told him not only would he have to get rid of the Old Nixon, Kleindienst, John Dean III, Ehrlichman and Haldeman, but he would also have to go himself.

The New Nixon couldn't believe it. 'I haven't been accused of anything.'

One of the Republican leaders said, 'In matters as sensitive as guarding the integrity of our democratic process, it is essential that the public have total confidence in the President of the United States. While you are probably innocent, you were in the White House when all this took place.'

'But who will replace me?'

The door opened and in walked the New New Nixon. 'I'm sorry about this, Dick,' the New New Nixon said, 'but the country comes first.'

The New New Nixon sat down in the President's chair and started dictating the speech he gave that Monday night.

As the New Nixon left the room, the New New Nixon told a friend, 'This is the most difficult decision I've ever had to make.'

A Great Honor

From *I Never Danced at the White House* (1971)

The worst thing that can happen to any public official in this country is to be mentioned for a top appointment in the government and not get it.

It isn't just the rejection of the job that is hard to swallow – it is that while he is under consideration, the candidate is being subjected to exhaustive investigation by everyone from the FBI to the *Harvard Law Review*, and his reputation can be destroyed for ever.

The Supreme Court nomination circus that President Nixon put on is a perfect example of how dangerous it is to be mentioned for one of the highest positions in the land.

Take the case of Judge Chilblain Clamchowder. Judge Clamchowder, who had been appointed to the Fifth Circuit Traffic Court for the work he had done in carrying Tornado County for President Nixon in 1968, found himself listed as one of the 'leading' candidates for a Supreme Court seat.

Judge Clamchowder told me in his chambers, 'I knew they had just thrown in my name as a smoke screen, and at first I was flattered to see my name in the newspapers.

'But then the Eastern Establishment press started coming down here and asking about me, and my life has become pure hell.

'They talked to my second wife, who said I had cheated not only on her, but also on my Bar exam. Even if it's true, it's something you don't like to read about in the newspapers.'

Judge Clamchowder continued: 'Then some Democratic senators found out I hadn't paid my income tax for the past five years, and they tried to make a big deal of it just to embarrass the Nixon Administration. They made it sound as if I was the first Supreme Court Justice nominee who had ever cheated on his taxes.

'To make matters worse, the FBI discovered that I was a major stockholder in the firm that prints all the traffic tickets for Tornado County. So I had to get rid of the stock at a great financial sacrifice.

'Then Jack Anderson found out about a Christmas party I had last year in my chambers for the meter maids, and while only two of them took off their clothes, he made it sound like an orgy. So now my third wife is suing me for divorce, and it's gonna be damn expensive, particularly since I don't have an interest in the printing firm any more.

'The American Civil Liberties Union then dug up the fact that I had donated $1,000 to buy dynamite to blow up all the school buses in Tornado County, and that made the newspaper headlines. Now I believe this was a personal matter and had nothing to do with whether a person would make a good Supreme Court justice or not.

'Finally, some smart-aleck law professor discovered that since I've been ruling on traffic offenses, I have been reversed by higher courts 768 times.

'He also claimed that I had fixed the tickets of forty-five members of my country club. It turns out I had only fixed forty tickets since I've been on the traffic court, but the media doesn't seem to be concerned with accuracy as long as it's a good story.

'The American Bar Association rated me as "less mediocre," and this certainly hasn't helped me keep any decorum in the courtroom.'

'From what I can tell, Judge,' I said, 'you might have done better by not being mentioned as a possible Supreme Court Justice.'

'Frankly,' he replied, 'if it wasn't for the honor, I would just as soon forget it.'

How Not to Write a Book
From *I Never Danced at the White House* (1971)

There are many great places where you *can't* write a book, but as far as I'm concerned, none compares to Martha's Vineyard.

This is how I manage *not* to write a book, and I pass it on to fledgling authors as well as old-timers who have vowed to produce a great work of art this summer.

The first thing you need is lots of paper, carbon, a solid typewriter, preferably electric, and a quiet spot in the house overlooking the water.

You get up at six o'clock in the morning and go for a dip in the sea; then you come back and make yourself a hearty breakfast.

By seven a.m. you are ready to begin Page 1, Chapter 1. You insert a piece of paper in the typewriter and start to type 'It was the best of times . . .' Suddenly you look out the window and you see a sea gull diving for a fish. This is not an ordinary sea gull. It seems to have a broken wing, and you get up from the desk to observe it on the off chance that somewhere in the book you may want to insert a scene of a sea gull with a broken wing trying to dive for a fish. (It would make a great shot when the book is sold to the movies and the lovers are in bed.)

It is now eight a.m., and the sounds of people getting up distract you. There is no sense trying to work with everyone crashing around the house. So you write a letter to your editor telling him how well the book is going and that you're even more optimistic about this one than the last one which the publisher never advertised.

It is now nine o'clock in the morning, and you go into the kitchen and scream at your wife. 'How am I going to get any work done around here if the kids are making all that racket? It doesn't mean anything in this family that I have to make a living.'

Your wife kicks all the kids out of the house, and you go back to your desk. It suddenly occurs to you that your agent may also want to see a copy of the book, so you tear out the paper and start over with an original and two carbons: 'It was the best of times . . .'

You look out the window again, and you see a sailboat in trouble. You take your binoculars and study the situation carefully. If it gets worse, you may have to call the Coast Guard. But after a half hour of struggling they seem to have things under control.

By this time you remember you were supposed to receive a check from the *Saturday Review*, so you walk down to the post office, pause at the drugstore for newspapers, and stop at the hardware store for rubber cement to repair your daughter's raft.

You're back to your desk at one p.m. when you remember you haven't had lunch. So you fix yourself a tuna fish sandwich and read the newspapers.

It is now 2:30 p.m., and you are about to hit the keys when Bill Styron calls. He announces they have just received a load of lobsters at Menemsha, and he's driving over to get some before they're all gone. Well, you say to yourself, you can always write a book on the Vineyard, but how often can you get fresh lobster?

So you agree to go with Styron for just an hour.

Two hours later, with the thought of fresh lobster as inspiration, you sit down at the typewriter. The doorbell rings, and Norma Brustein is standing there in her tennis togs, looking for a fourth for doubles.

You don't want to hurt Norma's feelings, so you get your racket and for the next hour play a fierce game of tennis, which is the only opportunity you have had all day of taking your mind off your book.

It is now six o'clock, and the kids are back in the house, so there is no sense trying to get work done any more for *that* day.

So you put the cover on the typewriter with a secure feeling that no matter how ambitious you are about working, there will always be somebody on the Vineyard ready and eager to save you.

•

MAX HARRIS

Maxwell Henley Harris was born in 1921 in Adelaide, South Australia. Educated at St Peter's College and the University of Adelaide, he became a poet and literary journalist. He was founder and joint editor of *Angry Penguins* (1940), founder of *Ern Malley's Journal* and of the Reed and Harris Publishing Company in Melbourne. In the 1940s Harris and others launched 'Australia's first modern example of the political opinion newspaper', called *Tomorrow*. His poetry appears in several anthologies of Australian verse. A debunker and an iconoclast, he was a founder member of the staff of the *Australian*, Rupert Murdoch's weekly, and wrote a column for that paper for over a decade.

It's About That Flamin' New Year Honours' List, Ma'am
From *The Angry Eye* (1974)

Dear Your 'Royal Highness':

One of your humblest liege subjects makes bold enough to address himself to you on behalf of the loyal but bemused citizenry of Browser's Gully, a roughneck and tiny part of your domain.

We have a problem akin to that of the late Samuel Johnson (not on the Honours' List, I believe) who could well have been a philosopher, but that cheerfulness kept breaking through.

We members of the Browser's Gully Euchre Club and Buffalo Lodge could out-Menzies Menzies if only we could understand the way you bestow your New Year favours on those subjects who happen to please you! You are not the only one who moves in a mysterious way your wonders to perform, but need you be all that mysterious!

I am grateful that Sir Alex Downer's chauffeur has found favour in your eye and been honoured, presumably for his services to the transport industry. I've seen him in that Rolls-Royce with the plates AUST 1 choofing around London, and right posh he looks, too.

Now, we peasants are perfectly content to pull the fetlock and acknowledge that men are not all equal. A bloke called George Orwell (not on the Honours' List, I believe) proved that to our complete satisfaction. But how less equal are we?

Like, I mean we all know that Sir Alex Downer (gosh, how I love all those English trees he planted in the Adelaide Hills after rooting out all the scrubby Australian natives) is of more import than an ordinary Aussie citizen, and that his chauffeur bears a great public responsibility chauffing him around.

But how many Aussie citizens equal Sir Alex Downer? This is the hub of the matter. The High Commissioner's chauffeur has certainly served public transport well in his Rolls-Royce; yet a Sydney taxi-driver, often in a clapped-out Holden, safely transports a hundred citizens a day. I never heard of a Sydney taxi-driver being made a Member of What British Empire.

Then there's this matter of the public service lady steno-secretaries. We can't work out what makes them (and country post-mistresses) so special in your regal eye. This year, you honoured a great swatch of them for doing steno-secretarial work. Well, what else, bless me, does a steno-secretary do but steno?

As humble subjects, could we point out that it's Miss Thelma Bloggs, steno-secretary to a bloke in the Flinders Street rag trade, who works like a drain to keep the old economy buoyant, plus 10,000 like her. Go on, Your Majesty, be a devil – give 'em *all* a Damehood. Like Sir Robert Menzies told us, you believe in scrupulous fairness to all your subjects.

As it is you quite rightly honoured the lady who works the switchboard at Government House. But, your Royal Majestyhood – have you ever copped the way those girls serve the community at the Sydney Telephone Exchange? Flat out all day long I do assure you. Next year, give 'em *all* a guernsey. They'd be that grateful.

While on the subject of making suggestions for next year, there's the matter of the big weight-for-age events. That is racing parlance, Your Majesty, and I am referring of course to the subject of Knight Hoods.

Out here at Browser's Gully, our collective eyes popped when we saw that among the few Knight Hoods bestowed in this modest realm to begin the new decade, you decided to give one to a nicotine pusher from Sydney and another to an alcohol pusher from Melbourne.

The Prime Minister is too well-bred to have said anything, I know, but I reckon he wasn't all that pleased with you about this. He was about to bring in new legislation to make nicotine pushers label their products as not too healthy, and you gave one of the boss-cocky pushers of the weed a Knight Hood.

I know they call them company directors, and when their operation gets pretty big then it's not the same.

Size makes the difference, let's be reasonable about that.

And there's a guy pushing pot and speed round the Cross who's getting pretty close to the tycoon class, I hear tell. Ted Noffs will give you his name. (When's the old Ted going to cop a Knight Hood, by the way?) He might be worth considering for the big money next year.

I do apologize for taking up your time with these insignificant colonial puzzlements. But you'll understand. After all, I did see you passing by, and yet.

I remain,

Yours by the bootstraps,

Snowy Harris

•

PETER SIMPLE (MICHAEL WHARTON)

Michael Wharton was born in 1913 and educated at Bradford Grammar School and Lincoln College, Oxford. After serving in the army during the Second World War, he worked for ten years as a scriptwriter and producer for the BBC. He joined the *Daily Telegraph* in 1956 and subsequently wrote his five-days-a-week 'Peter Simple' column for the *Sunday Telegraph* and the *Daily Telegraph*, in which he satirized liberal progressives. For the first few years, Wharton co-wrote the column with another *Daily Telegraph* journalist, the late Colin Welch.

'The Way of the World'
1955–7

Excerpts from *The Stretchford Chronicles: 25 Years of Peter Simple* (1980)

Dylan as I Knew Him
By Ronald Dace

'Lend me another ninepence and make it up to seven-and-six – lovely, pocket-splitting, beer-belching, girl-giggling seven-and-six.' Dylan didn't seem to be addressing anyone in particular, but I am proud to say I was the first to get my hand to my pocket.

I shall never forget that first meeting in the 'Bag of Nails' in 1937. Dylan Thomas was in tremendous form, as he drank pint after pint and told us wonderful, revolting stories of Welsh life, full of lechery and vomit.

By the end of the evening I had managed to lend him £12 15s. 3d., had suggested he should take my girlfriend to Brighton for the weekend, and had had one and a half pints of beer (I counted them carefully) spilled over my new tweed suit.

I still have that sacred beer-stained suit. I have treasured it, unworn and uncleaned, ever since.

During the wonderful weeks that followed I haunted the 'Bag of Nails'. Every now and then, to my disgust, Dylan would disappear and write poetry. I grudged every moment of the time when he wasn't borrowing my money, taking my girlfriends away from me, or pouring beer or worse down my neck.

I don't want to boast. But I honestly believe I had more of these attentions from him than anybody.

Vividly I remember the last time I met the Swansea genius. 'Look what the great, black, yellow-blinking, whisper-twitching nightmare-tomcat has brought in,' yelled Dylan as I entered the pub one evening. He promptly spilled a glass of light ale down my neck.

'Go on, Dylan,' I murmured. I was loving every minute.

'All right. I will. Why don't you go and take a seagull-screaming, tram-ticket-swallowing, split-and-bandaged coffin-black running jump at yourself, and leave me alone?'

These words of purest poetry, the last Dylan ever spoke to me, are graven on my heart for ever. That is why I have been talking, thinking and writing about him ever since.

Sophistry

'We do not talk about the tastes of the mob; we talk about what ordinary people like. What some regard as the herd, we regard as the human family.'

These noble words were spoken by Sir Robert Fraser, Director-General of the ITA [Independent Television Authority]. The Greeks called this sort of statement 'making the worse cause appear the better' – in other words, sophistry.

You know that people are being fed, day in and day out, on a diet of paper and shadows, a thin and wretched soup of clichés and stereotypes, boiled up from the sweepings of the human mind. So you tell them it is wholesome, nourishing food, plain perhaps, but to the taste of all ordinary people.

You know that people are being taught to live in a half-dead world where advertisements have taken the place of art and entertainment; that they are being encouraged to hate and despise taste and intelligence, the love of beauty and the sense of order.

So you tell them they are the human family, ordinary decent low-brow people, laughing to scorn, with great roars of wholesome laughter from their warm, loving human hearts, the desiccated highbrow, with his dead books and paintings, for ever lecturing them in high-pitched tones about the values and standards of civilization.

1964

A Barefaced Lie

Frank Harris, as everyone knows, was a bounder and social climber of the first order. In his so-called autobiography, *My Life and Loves*, he boasts of his invariable success. I am glad to say that there was at least one occasion when he was not successful.

One day in 1907 I was in the library at Simpleham when Venables, the butler, announced: 'A Mr Francis Harris to see you, sir.' I looked at the man's card with distaste.

It was of large size, engraved with florid vulgarity, gold-edged, and bore the inscription: 'Frank Harris, Genius and Lover of Women.'

A loud booming, whiffling noise was coming from the ante-room and there was a smell of pomade and expensive cigar-smoke. 'I do not know Mr Harris,' I said with freezing hauteur. 'Nor, on the evidence I now have about his character and antecedents, do I wish to know him. Kindly convey that message to him, Venables, and ask him to leave Simpleham at once. If he refuses you may eject him, using the maximum of force. If necessary, get Bennett, Dodds and Hargreaves to help you.'

In the event, Venables exceeded his instructions, stuffing Harris up a chimney in the unused East Wing, from which he had to be removed by block and tackle.

Needless to say there is not a word about this incident in Harris's autobiography. Instead there is a long, boastful account of a weekend at Simpleham in 1909, when King Edward is said to have been a guest – a typical absurdity, since I always made a point of cutting that monarch whenever I saw him.

A Great Debate

Moving the second reading of the Discrimination (All Purposes) Bill, Mr A. Grudge (Lab., Stretchford North) said that if Britain were to maintain her standing in the eyes of the non-aligned world and move rapidly forward into the Space Age, it was essential to stamp out all vestiges of discrimination whether on grounds of race, sex, religion, age, moral character, intelligence or anything else.

It was intolerable, to give a few examples, that one-armed Pakistani women were excluded from the Oxford Boat Race crew; that magistrates, in open court, publicly discriminated between honest people and so-called criminals; that Calvinistic Methodist children of low intelligence were excluded from the higher grades of the Civil Service.

We must build a Britain in which everyone pulled together. If we could not make everyone alike (and personally he hoped that science would soon make this possible), at least we should treat them alike.

Sir Rufus Grunt (C., Natterhurst) said that he hoped the Bill would deal with the possibility of flogging everyone, not merely violent criminals, periodically. A good sound tanning never did anyone any harm; if he might say so, he was himself a living proof of this. If he could not get anyone else to flog him, he flogged himself every day.

Miss Edith Sandpiper (Lab., Shuffham) complained of sex discrimination in such places as men's Turkish baths, which deliberately excluded women. She herself, as a test case, had recently entered a men's Turkish bath in London. At sight of her all the customers fled and one of the attendants fainted (laughter).

Sir Rufus Grunt: They thought she was a Turk (laughter).

Mr A. Grudge: That is a perfect example of the sort of racial discrimination we are trying to deal with. How would the Hon. Member, if he were a Turk, like to have such offensive remarks made about him? (Labour cries of 'Cyprus!' 'Suez!' 'Smethwick!' etc. etc.)

Wing-Cdr H. J. Wolfram-Jones (C., Nerdley) said that the problem of discrimination was closely bound up with juvenile delinquency, road accidents, old-age pensions, the 11-plus examination, steel nationalization, alcoholism, indecent films and the present flood of printed filth. He believed that unless this country devoted itself to the ideal of service it would perish, as the Roman Empire perished. But he did not think more motorways and shorter licensing hours were necessarily the answer.

The debate continues.

1965

Romance

Rumours that Mrs Dutt-Pauker, the fifty-three-year-old Hampstead thinker, is thinking of marrying for the third time have caused surprise and some bitterness in left-wing circles. Surprise, because she has the reputation of being faithful to her second husband's memory; bitterness, because of her impressive financial resources, which, meant for all mankind, may now go to benefit one man.

By inheritance, by thirty-five years of progressive thinking, by a left-wing flair for the stock market and by sheer forward-looking greed, she has built up a considerable fortune. As well as her large house in Hampstead, she has a country house in Dorset, Beria Garth, another in Wales, Glyn Stalin, and another in the West of Ireland, Leninmore.

Her first husband, whom she met and married during the Spanish Civil War, had to be accidentally liquidated in Barcelona in 1937; at the same time her name became linked with that of Walter Ulbricht, then working in Catalonia, with whom she shared a romantic passion for the techniques of terrorism. Though love faded, as love will, they have always remained good friends. He still sends her a coloured picture postcard of the Berlin Wall every May Day.

But the love of her life was her second husband, bespectacled, four foot ten Ernst Dutt-Pauker, a typical swashbuckling Highlander, stalwart of the Siege of Madrid, hero of a thousand purges, friend of Bela Kun, Yagoda, Beria and Gerö, and at one time motoring correspondent of the *Daily Worker*.

His study in Mrs Dutt-Pauker's Hampstead house is still kept just as he left it at his death: on his desk a half-completed plan for a people's re-educational labour camp on Exmoor lies next to the stuffed head of Marshal Tukhachevski and a silver-mounted upper set of Marx's false teeth.

Can any individual man, however bold and resolute, many people are asking, take over, as well as Mrs Dutt-Pauker herself, this glorious but overpowering heritage of progressivism? Isn't there rather a case here for a people's collective, an object lesson in the building of Socialism?

1975

Among the Squatters
By Doreen Gaggs

I've just been talking to some of the big group of squatters who've occupied Hokewell Manor, a large Regency house in its own grounds which formerly belonged to the proud-lineaged Lestrange-Haggard family but is now encircled by the Stretchford Conurbation.

The squat was organized by the Department of Theoretical and Applied Squatting at Stretchford University, part of Dr Pixie Dutt-Pauker's prestigious Department of Social Protestology. The squatters were supplied by Rentacrowd, the mammoth mob-supplying consortium, which has a section dealing with orders for small, specialized groups, human, semi-automated or mixed.

Hokewell Manor was just about to be opened by the Corporation Welfare Department as a centre for homeless families, so the squatters moved in just in the nick of time.

'I mean like we're here to make a statement about the plight of the homeless in an alienated society,' said Jim, the leader, a gentle, raucous-voiced nineteen-year-old who's had a varied career (after leaving university he tried to go back there but found it too alienated).

'I mean like we're here to make a statement about the plight of the homeless in an alienated society,' put in Jim, a raucous, gentle-voiced knee-length-haired eighteen-year-old. All the men squatters are called Jim and all the girls are called Jill. As there are about fifty of them this might make for confusion in some circumstances. But here, in this relaxed, infectious, youthful atmosphere of protest, it somehow doesn't seem to matter.

'I mean like we're here to make a statement about the plight of the homeless in an alienated society,' explained Jill, a fair-haired, rather jerky girl who plays a microbiotic guitar and is trying to recycle baked bean tins all over the place. 'It's ecology,' she added.

'As this house was just due to open it's all properly painted and wired for electricity and that, so it seems just the right place for our statement,' said another squatter, Jill, a dark-haired girl with staring eyes who is recycling saucepans and takes a lot of interest in the environment.

Twenty-year-old Jim, another 'drop-out' from university who has played the bicycle-wheel in a West Indian steel-band and is recycling door-knobs, and fifty-five-year-old Jill, a recycled student who believes even ecology to be alienated, both told me as I left, speaking in unison, that they were all there to make a statement about the plight of the homeless in an alienated society.

Whatever you may think of these dedicated youngsters you've got to admit they are ready to defy conformity and think for themselves.

Norman the Good

12 March 2015

One of our national characteristics which still persists in the age of Socialist Monarchy is a love of dogs. So it is only natural that King Norman and his family should keep one. Indeed if it were not for this he would long ago have been overthrown by a Council Palace Revolution.

The royal fox-terrier, Spot, is an elderly, obese, balding and malodorous animal of indeterminate sex, but makes up for this in popular estimation by its greed and its habit of biting Princess Tracey, the younger and more unpopular of Queen Doreen's daughters, whenever it sees her.

Spot also gains popularity for the Socialist Royal Family on ceremonial occasions (as an economy measure, it also has to do duty as mascot for the Royal Socialist Anti-Nuclear Air Force) by being able, on the order 'Die for the Socialist King', to roll over ponderously on its back, slowly waving its paws in the air like a monstrous beetle.

It is too infirm to get on its feet again and has to be helped by Brass-Stair-Rod-in-Waiting, who is invariably bitten for his pains, to the delighted cheers of the crowd.

Republicans, of whom there are a few even in Good King Norman's Golden Days, are putting out rumours that Spot has in fact been 'put to sleep' and its carcase sold to a Chinese restaurant, and that the creature shown in photographs of the Socialist Royal Family is a stuffed replica.

The other day, to scotch these rumours, King Normal asked Duke Len of Erdington, the black sheep of the Socialist Royal Family, to take Spot for a walk in the Council Palace Garden of Plastic Gnomes at Bevindon, which is of course open to the public.

Instead the Duke made straight for a nearby public house, the Quantity Surveyors' Arms, where his close friend Miss Gwenda Briggs, twenty-one, works as a barmaid. There he not only drank several bottles of light ale himself but gave some to Spot. The dog lapped it up greedily, then instantly went into a coma.

The Duke laughingly carried the animal back to the Council Palace, where the Queen Gran, thinking it was dead, upbraided him and repeatedly struck him with her iron-tipped outsize handbag. She was mollified only when Spot, suddenly regaining consciousness, bit the Duke, King Norman, Queen Doreen, Prince Barry, Princess Shirley, her husband Duke Ron of Brownhills, and Baby Cindy in rapid succession.

That Sunday the French newspapers carried a headline: 'LE DUC D'ERDINGTON, MOUTON NOIR ALCOHOLIQUE DE LA FAMILLE ROYALE SOCIA-LISTE D'ANGLETERRE, EST-IL SADISTE?'

•

SIDNEY ZION

Sidney Zion was born in 1933 in Passaic, New Jersey. His father was a dentist and his mother was a business executive. He was educated at the University of Pennsylvania and Yale Law School, and practised law as an assistant US attorney when Bobby Kennedy was Attorney General. In 1963 he joined the *New York Post* as an investigative reporter and from 1965 to 1970 he was a reporter for the *New York Times*. He left to set up a magazine, *Scanlan's Monthly*, which lasted for about a year. Subsequently, while working as a free-lance journalist, he broke the story of the Pentagon Papers on a radio show, which so enraged the rest of the press that he found himself blacklisted for several years and was obliged to practise law again. It was during this time that he became a columnist for the *Soho Weekly News*, covering national and Middle Eastern politics, New York, and sports. Rather than take a salary, he took five per cent of the paper's stock and when it was sold several years later he received a $50,000 windfall. In 1977 he returned to the *New York Times* as a contract writer for its Sunday magazine. Next, he wrote a column for the *New York Post*, and after that wrote for *New York* magazine. He was fired from there in 1980 and opened a restaurant called Broadway Joe's, which was a magnet to journalists, policemen and firemen. That lasted for about a year and thereafter he settled down to writing books. Since 1994 he has written a column for the *New York Daily News*, which now appears twice a week. He has published a collection of his early columns, *Read All About It! The Collected Adventures of a Maverick Reporter* (1982), and a collection of journalism including his columns for the *New York Observer*, called *Trust Your Mother But Cut the Cards* (1993).

Death of a Jewish Godfather
Soho Weekly News, March 17, 1977

Doc Stacher died in bed the other day at the Munich Sheraton next to a twenty-two-year-old blonde, a circumstance that surely would have brought forth memories of John Garfield, except that nobody seemed to note Doc's passing, much less the blonde. When Garfield called it a career under similar conditions some twenty-five years ago, the tabloids fell over their own headlines trying to top the story every day, until one exhausted editor suggested the banner 'John Garfield Still Dead.' And to think that two weeks after his demise I have to tell you who Doc Stacher was.

In the twenties, Stacher was one of the two largest importers of bootleg hooch in the United States, the other being his partner and boon companion, Longy Zwillman. Longy and Doc ran as an entry out of Newark, which they also ran, and while Zwillman was the more famous, Doc was known in underworld and police circles as the brainier, no mean comment since Longy had one of the finest noodles in the business.

'Longy went to night school while Doc went to nightclubs,' Manny Manishor, the venerable Broadway oddsmaker, recalled at Gallagher's one cocktail hour last week. As usual, Manny was on the nose. Stacher was what the girls at the Board of Education would call a 'functional illiterate,' which is to say that he couldn't read a menu, but who needs menus when you can buy steak for the house? Dutch Goldberg, who invented the Combination at a convention assembled in Atlantic City in 1929, credited the Doc with the best legal mind in the country, and this was a country that had Justice Holmes, not to mention Bill Fallon, the Great Mouthpiece. But Goldberg knew exactly what the mob was doing against the statutes, and if Doc Stacher was house counsel we have only to look at how few of the big dogs went to the can to understand how little reading skills had to do with Blackstone.

After Repeal, Longy and Doc picked up substantial points in the legitimate liquor business and plenty of other legal entities, even as they sat in the top echelons of the Combination, which was rapidly growing into the Syndicate. It's a toss-up whether the Mafia mavens or the B'nai B'rith are more embarrassed by the names that dominated the rackets from the twenties through the fifties, but facts are facts and let the vowels fall where they may. So: Arnold Rothstein, Waxey Gordon, Dutch Schultz, Lepke Buchalter, Gurrah Shapiro, Meyer Lansky, Bugsy Siegel, Moe Dalitz, Nig Rosen, Boo Hoff, Tootsie Herbert, Isador (Kid Cann) Blumenfield, Hymie Siegel, the Detroit Purple Gang, Murder, Inc. – and of course Stacher, Zwillman and the Godfather himself, Dutch Goldberg.

Alas, all but Dalitz, Nig, Kid Cann and Meyer have gone to the Maker from this select Hit Parade, though this is by no means to imply that others of the brothers have no say-so in the Syndicate and is surely not to say that Lansky and the survivors are out to pasture. That, however, is another tale, and we have room only to praise poor Doc, still warm in his final resting place in Israel. To die in Munich and be buried in Israel – well, there must be a story goes with it, though just what Doc was doing in Germany is a mystery to me. There was always talk that he ran a string of whorehouses there, but the only thing I know for sure about him and the Nazis is that he and Longy used to like breaking their heads whenever they put on the brown shirts in those Bund rallies outside Newark. Lansky did the same in Yorkville, which is one reason I found it nice to shake hands with both of them one afternoon in Tel Aviv about five years ago.

Stacher, whose intimates called him 'Gedalia,' and whose Diaspora name was Joseph, went up to the homeland in 1964, though not entirely out of a spirit of *aliyah*. The Feds had him convicted on a tax rap and gave him the option of Israel or durance vile. The Israeli Government welcomed him, or at least gave him no trouble, which is hardly the way they treated Meyer when he showed up in 1970. The US wanted Meyer back as fervently as once they wanted Doc out, and in what became known in Israel as the 'Phantoms for Lansky Detente,' Meyer was booted back to Miami, where the government was unable to do a thing to him.

They were never able to do much to Doc, either, which is why, when I met them by chance in the lobby of the Tel Aviv Sheraton that day, I was caused to blurt: 'Gentlemen, it's like meeting Ruth and Gehrig.' Maybe Gedalia didn't live as good as the sluggers, but a lot longer and you have to admit he died better.

•

ARTHUR MARSHALL

(Charles) Arthur (Bertram) Marshall (1910–89) was educated at Oundle School and Christ's College, Cambridge. From 1931 to 1954 he was a schoolmaster and housemaster at Oundle. Thereafter, he had jobs as a private secretary to Lord Rothschild (1954–8) and as a TV script editor (1958–64). In 1935 he started broadcasting on the BBC and contributing to the *New Statesman*, for which he later wrote a humorous column from 1976 until his death.

'Musings from Myrtlebank'
In Gratitude
From *I'll Let You Know* (1981)

How odd is the extraordinary variety of the persons who, not always for a very apparent reason, catch the public imagination and remain for ever of interest. Crippen, for example, a shoddy and inefficient little murderer. Mata Hari, both a bad dancer and a doubtful spy. Some achieve it mainly by an early death. I always maintain that if Lawrence of Arabia and Isadora Duncan were still living in querulous retirement as OAPs in a run-down private hotel in Bognor, nobody would give them a second thought. Sometimes inactivity does the trick. The reputation of E. M. Forster, who was already to some minds rather too highly rated, increased to giant proportions with every silent year that passed. The matchless Lunts, ever modest, have claimed that they only became really famous the moment they gave up acting and nobody could see them any more. It pains me to couple the name of W. Somerset Maugham with that of Crippen but he, too, is one of whom the public will never let go. Biographers will, till kingdom come, be having a go at him and digging here, ferreting there.

The latest offering by Frederic Raphael has just been published by Thames and Hudson at £3.95. The book's illustrations, strangely inept here and there, reveal the shape of facial things to come – the sad, serious orphan boy and the gloomy scholar of King's School, Canterbury. Mr Raphael's is a conscientious attempt at a fair biography but the text reveals little that was not already widely enough known and carries with it less than hearty appreciation of both Mr Maugham and his works. That face would be glummer still.

As I said, it pains me because he was a friend. I was lucky enough to stay with him and his companion, Gerald Haxton, at the Villa Mauresque at Cap Ferrat a number of times in the thirties and, though Gerald was dead by then, also after the war. Beyond displaying extreme pleasure at his jokes, which were more frequent and funnier than some may imagine, I had little to offer either socially or intellectually and he must have found me a bore but he was far too polite and kind to show it. If I had things to say, I was, anyhow, in those days far too shy to say them. Willie, as I was soon allowed to call him, had great charm and beautiful manners but he could be chilling and one didn't risk a bromide in his presence. The villa was large and comfortable. The food was perfect. There were bathing and tennis and trips in the yacht. There was a wonderful garden and guests had a whale of a time. I suppose that in the climate of today I ought to be feeling ashamed of enjoying such privilege and hedonistic activities. Well I am not.

Some quirk in his character made him not greatly mind when people behaved badly. He expected them to, for he had no high opinion of human nature and when events supported his view he was not really displeased. Gerald Haxton could be relied on to provide him, periodically, with stimulating jolts. One day at the villa there was what was, for me, a lunch party of an impressive kind for among the guests were G. B. Stern, Elizabeth ('German Garden') Russell and H. G. Wells. Elizabeth Russell, living nearby in France, had written a book of enormous charm and humour, *The Enchanted April*, and it was fascinating to meet her. She was indeed enchanting. She told us that she never attempted to conform to summer time or French hours or ever to alter her clocks ('I'm very hungry. You see, it's half past three by my inside'). When Willie wasn't looking, Gerald, who had a problem, darted to the drinks table and briskly lowered half a tumbler of neat gin. We went into lunch, somewhat formally, and sat down. Willie, searching about for something with which to start conversational balls rolling, said genially, 'I've just had a h-h-hot bath' (when writing of him, it is essential to indicate the stammer). Gerald, semi-tipsy, gave a snort of disgust at this banality, leaned forward and said loudly and clearly, 'And did you masturbate?' A terrible silence fell as we scooped up our avocados. But Willie had been asked a question, and questions must be answered, if with difficulty. There were some anguished facial contortions and finger snappings, which sometimes helped, and then came 'As it h-h-h-happens, n-n-n-n-no.' We ate on.

At less formal and more relaxed meals, interesting matters emerged, among them the usual behaviour of his brother Frederick, the Lord Chancellor. 'I've always sent him tickets for my first nights, and first editions of my b-b-b-books, but he's never even acknowledged one of them or let it be known, even by mistake, that he'd seen the play or read the book. Isn't he a sh-sh-sh-shameful fellow!' He knew well how sometimes to use the stammer to the best advantage. During the thirties, many of the famous, Gladys Cooper among them, were bursting into advertising and making large sums (it was always said that the royal family had to do a deal with the proprietors of Pond's Cream when Princess Marina, impoverished and cheerfully and profitably exposing her beautiful face to the soft smoothness of Pond's, became engaged to Prince George). Willie said that he had been approached several times to advertise this or that. Why, then, had he refused? 'To put it bluntly, they've never offered me enough money. I've never done it before and virginity is v-v-v-valuable.' Very occasionally past regrets surfaced. 'Through diffidence or shyness, I've missed a number of chances of sexual congress, even when they were handed to me on a plate.' The combination of the slight pomposity of 'sexual congress' with the slang of 'on a plate' was very characteristic. The age, sex and nationality of the plate-profferers were not produced. He never liked his novels or plays or short stories to be referred to too directly, but an oblique reference, when talking of something else, did not come amiss.

He was immensely kind to the young writers who sent their work to him and asked for advice. He came down to lunch one day, exhausted. 'I've spent the entire m-m-morning telling polite fibs to people I d-d-don't know. I can't h-h-help putting myself in their shoes. When I was young, nobody ever b-b-bothered to encourage me. I only wish the silly b-b-buggers wouldn't write so much.' In Cambridge, at a party for some intelligent undergraduates in King's, he became nervous. 'D-d-d-don't leave me,' he whispered, and so I hung about. A highish-minded young man came up and asked him whether he had allowed his stories to be made into films because he 'approved of the cinema as a medium', or some such. Willie became flustered and unhappy. 'Oh, no. I don't give a d-d-d-damn about that sort of thing. I just did it for the m-m-m-m-money.' The undergraduate, looking slightly shocked, walked away. 'I felt I h-h-h-had to tell him the t-t-truth.'

In London, at lunch at the Dorchester, he had just received a fan letter from T. S. Eliot, who had also sent him, and it was January, two dozen red roses ('I feel not unlike an elderly t-t-tart'). Recently, Willie had been to Buckingham Palace to receive from the Queen the considerable honour of the CH. Of course one congratulated him but, though not ungrateful, he was unimpressed. 'But don't you see what the CH means for somebody like me? It means "well done, but . . .".' He was, of course, referring to the possibility of the OM, which some, including myself, might consider that he had deserved, an opinion strengthened by a glance at the names of some of the recipients over the last fifty years. But enormous commercial success consorts ill with the OM. Those aiming at this distinction must be careful not to bring too much enjoyment to too many people.

'Musings from Myrtlebank'
Stop It at Once

From *I'll Let You Know* (1981)

Life at a boys' public school a half century ago was a little short on scheduled enjoyments but at the house, one of twelve, that I was in, the housemaster did treat us all, at pleasantly recurring intervals, to sensational moral lectures of a prolonged and fascinating nature. We found them totally electrifying for he was a brilliant speaker, had obviously conscientiously prepared his material, and was quite unaware that, to young people, he was a hilarious figure. Every so often after evening prayers he would stand up and, speaking without notes, let fly. As a new boy, I couldn't always understand why he was so concerned and what had gone wrong. Had somebody, perhaps, said 'Drat' or been rude to Matron or left some gristle or smiled at a boy older or younger (you couldn't smile at a boy in another house at all, and, as I was by nature an inane smiler, I was at constant risk)? But as time went on I began to get the hang of the affair and the gist of the matter and hung upon the housemaster's words, later in the day to be so splendidly mimicked by wags as we disrobed, shrieking, for bed, and cackled ourselves into the Land of Nod.

One of the most memorable pi-jaws, delivered during a power-cut but with flickering candle-light rendering it even more, so to speak, electrifying than usual, began with the striking phrase 'This house is a midden', followed by a dramatic pause while the dimmer boys tried to work out just what a midden was and, if so, what might be the matter with it. On another occasion we were told that 'the trouble' lay neither at the top of the house, where the prefects were, nor at the bottom of the house, but in the very middle of it, and a most pious boy (later a distinguished academic and now high up, and highly respected, in the church), anxiously totting up on the house list, found that out of sixty-three boys he was the thirty-second, precisely in the middle and therefore at the very seat of the bother and deplorably culpable.

Other pleasantly recurring treats, also of a mainly moral kind, were the regular weekend visits to the school of the then Bishop of London, dear old, kindly old, indubitably wonky old Winnington Ingram, much loved by all. He preached, of course, in our chapel on Sunday and, after pronouncing the Blessing at the altar, swung round and dextrously extracted from his billowing canonicals a large gold watch and had a dekko at 'the enemy'. And indeed he was operating on a tight time schedule for as soon as the service was over he repaired to our Natural History Museum which stood close by and there, unsuitably seated among pressed grasses and cases of spreadeagled moths and the skeleton of a singularly unattractive horse, he received any boy who cared to call on him solo, and very many did, for a little moral uplift and spiritual encouragement at two minutes flat a head, though the more personable boys could usually count on a few seconds longer. A warm, soft and somewhat clinging handshake concluded the interview. Then he was up and away to a nourishing repast with the headmaster at School House, whence a boy had once written home, 'We had beef for lunch today. The headmaster calved.' And after that, at 2.30, three school prefects appeared to make up a four at tennis with the bishop, a lively player who liked to win and whose wild rushes to the net with a loud screech of 'Mine, partner!' seemed to be in no way slowed down by the fact that he always played in enormous elastic-sided brown boots.

When this delightful cleric was not at Oundle, the newspapers kept us in touch with his doings and activities, one of which was to protest. If there was anything morally unworthy going on and ideal stuff for protesting about, there was the bishop, piping up too. He took against, for some not very clear reason, a play called *The Sacred Flame*. Doubtless the word 'sacred' upset him as the flame part meant love, of course, and the illicit love in the play was far from sacred. So protest he did, to the great profit of the newspapers and even more so of Gladys Cooper, who played the lead, and of Somerset Maugham, who had written it. Boosted by the bishop, the theatre was jammed for months with titillated playgoers and envious theatre managers pressed free seats on him, hoping that he might unearth something and be inspired to protest about *Rose Marie* or *Peter Pan* or *Where the Rainbow Ends* or *George and Margaret*.

And now, bless me, here he is again after all these years, popping up as fresh as paint and hot on the track of filth, his wails and strictures now resurrected in Edward Bristow's admirable *Vice and Vigilance* (Gill and Macmillan, £12), a fine panorama of the various purity movements in Britain. I hadn't fully realized how good the bishop's track record was. In the whole thirty-eight years of his London incumbency, he never once missed a meeting of the Public Morality Council's subcommittee on brothels, the air thick with tch tchs. He kept the Home Secretary on his toes ('I took him in twenty-one filthy books', and followed them up with a cartload of saucy magazines, light reading that was probably an agreeable change from the official boxes). He spoke out, rather unfairly, against plump ladies in flesh-coloured tights displaying themselves, with not a follicle of pubic hair in sight, in music-hall *tableaux vivants*. In 1934 he announced in the Lords, muddle-headed to the last, that he would like to make a fire of all contraceptives 'and dance round it' (in those brown boots, again).

We remember Macaulay's verdict that there is no spectacle so ridiculous as the British public in one of its periodic fits of morality. Last century's fit was a longish one. There was an agitation to clothe (what with? Bloomers? Jock-straps?) some nude statues in the Strand. Sellers of obscene toothpick cases were ruthlessly tracked down and 'spoken to'. Purity workers, armed with lanterns, lurked at the doors of brothels to identify the customers, subsequently writing up their names on walls. Then the ladies were invited to leave their work awhile and come to church (male salvationists were warned 'never to kneel down with women at midnight meetings, especially behind a pew'). Tea was served, nosegays were handed out by the Bible Flower Mission, and, as soon as dawn broke, there was a group photograph ('Smile, please'), followed by breakfast.

Everybody got very worried and panicky about white-slave traffic and crateloads of drugged and insensible womanhood getting shipped abroad. Abductors, clutching hypodermic syringes, were said to haunt the most unlikely places (Barnet, Banbury, Finsbury Park) waiting to pounce and whizz servant-girls off to Buenos Aires. Beasts in human shape were alleged to rig themselves up as clergymen and, with attractive offers, lure maidens to the capital ('Dear child, you're going to love the British Museum'). The West Ham area was apparently an unexpectedly fruitful supplier of moon-faced girls ripe for Marseilles, and even as late as 1913 the 5,000 girls of London's telephone exchanges were given official warnings to watch out for drugged chocolates. Just the one violet cream or strawberry surprise and everything might go black.

•

CHARLES McCABE

Charles Raymond McCabe (1915–83) was born in Hell's Kitchen, New York. His parents were Irish immigrants and he was brought up in Harlem and educated at Catholic schools before starting his journalistic career as a police reporter for the *New York American* in 1937. He subsequently worked in public relations, and during the Second World War was a war correspondent for the United Press. He was also managing editor for the *Puerto Rico World Journal.* In 1955 he went to San Francisco and worked as a reporter and feature writer until 1959, when the *Chronicle* invited him to write an irreverent sports column called 'The Fearless Spectator'. He performed this task for five years, then resigned. After a break of about a year he came back to the *Chronicle* to write a five-days-a-week general interest column called 'Charles McCabe Himself'. He wrote a column, with only a couple of short breaks, for twenty-two years, turning out more than three million words, and at the time of his death he was six columns ahead.

His passions included Montaigne, Dr Johnson, Horace Walpole, Oscar Wilde, Gucci loafers and Rainier Ale (The Green Death); while his hates included Richard Nixon, Ronald Reagan, Jimmy Carter, lawyers, women's libbers, IRA supporters, psychiatrists and 'hiss' – the word he used for American beer because his editors would not let him call it 'piss'. He was fascinated by the female sex, although he never took to the institution of marriage, despite four attempts. He was a serious drinker and periodically sought to purge himself by going on the wagon.

A colleague once wrote that McCabe was the only Catholic he knew who went to confession in public and got paid for it. 'His daily trips to the confessional,' wrote the man who edited

McCabe's columns, 'began early in the morning in his Telegraph Hill apartment when he rose to type out the column which had been gestating in his head since the previous day. He then bathed, shaved, dressed and sallied forth to his favorite North Beach bar (for many years it was Gino & Carlo's on Green Street) . . . His bar stool was his office. He read the papers and his mail and collected ideas for future columns all the while sipping at the Green Death with a chaser of ice water (five ales during the morning was his quota). Come lunchtime he was off to a favorite restaurant for his first real meal of the day, then home to read and ruminate about the next day's column.'

'Charles McCabe Himself'
Biddytalk
From *The Charles McCabe Reader* (1984)

Oh, isn't life a terrible thing, thank God.   Dylan Thomas

I don't know whether my sainted mother ever uttered the above words exactly, but I can hear them now in her accents. The words reek of her and her friends. They describe with total and deadly accuracy a good part of her life and that of her friends.

I call it biddytalk, because it is the idle roadside gossip of the Irish housewife. Since New York didn't have any countrysides, like the old country, this talk was limited to the airwells of the tenements we lived in. These were called areaways and the ladies eased themselves on their elbows and shouted out the windows of the well, to the neighboring ladies, who did the same.

The period lasted an hour or so in the morning, after the old man had gone to work and the kids shoved off to school and the young ones had been pacified by some milk or orange juice.

This was my mother's Happy Hour. The chief subjects were men, of course, and other calamities, like fires and arrests.

Arrests were big news. 'Did you hear that Jimmy's son got pinched for goin' into Woolworth's and treatin' himself to a hammer and some nails?' This was a real bulletin, for Jimmy was the son of the Tammany district leader, and thus royalty.

My mother was everybody's rabbi since she was in good with old Jimmy, the street captain of the organization. She opined, 'Ah, his father will have him out before you can say "Shut up".'

This was one of the few unkind things you might hear, because when anybody was in *real* trouble, the biddies all showed their essentially generous hearts. What infuriated them was gossip that could not be confirmed. Most of it centered around what happened to their men at Dan Ford's saloon, up the street on Columbus Avenue. There, and at the men's club, the men could get away from the women and children after dinner.

'I hear Biddy Clancy has got ahold of a new possible. A fireman it is this time. The woman's a menace, wagging that black tongue around in Dan Ford's. A good man would shut her up, by the Grace of God.'

The ladies hated that saloon, which they were only allowed to enter on weekends and holidays.

'I hear Tom Ryan is going to see Dr Goldfarb.' That meant that Ryan had the clap or something worse, for that's what Goldfarb specialized in. And it meant that bad times were in for Mrs Ryan for a couple of weeks. 'Ah, she had it comin', with her nose higher than the roof of a church.' Or, 'I wonder what she did to deserve it.'

This kind of black talk, and some of it was a lot blacker than this, served to pacify the ladies. When they went out to shop at Dan Reeves' or the German butcher shop after their session, they were sated but happy, and greeted each other as if they were members of some kind of Middle European court or something.

Before I went to my first grade of school, I used to hide myself behind a sofa or some other bit of furniture, and listen rapturously to this daily badmouthing. 'Who's dead,' was the way most of those sessions started. My mother, while making her neighborhood rounds, found out who had fallen off the hooks in the preceding twenty-four hours.

After that, the form was: 'Ah, he was a wonderful man, I wonder who will take care of the family now.' And then came an airwell threnody on the deceased's faults, which would have had him whirling in his casket. If life wasn't a terrible thing, the biddies would have been bereft.

'Charles McCabe Himself'
On Ex-es
From *The Charles McCabe Reader* (1984)

> My wife made good soup, but I miss her just the same.   Cannibal Chieftain

Casualties of even the most awful marriages must, I would think, still at times agree with the cannibal's little *pensée*. After all there must have been something, even if only such an ignoble consideration as self or pelf, that persuaded the couple to enter the contract in the first place. There must have been a moment of glory for each or both, however brief.

There are lady cannibal chieftains, too. They may, in fact, exceed the lads, in marriage and less formalized arrangements. Yet these lovely predators must have a memory, however fugitive, of some good, even if only bestial sex, that was once thought to inhere in the union.

For my part I've been lucky enough, on the whole, to have given the truly predatory lady cannibals a miss. This is not to say that in even the most demure of mates there is not just a smidgeon of the carnivore.

I am sure that each and every one of the ladies with whom I resided for any length of time were in agreement, when it was over, that I had been good soup. Nor do I doubt that there are times when they miss me.

As my old friend Jim Knox used to say, 'They may not like us, kid, but they aren't about to forget us.'

The thing I miss most as a bachelor is the talk, damn it. Those long, rhapsodic voyages into self that passed for passionate exploration of each other. These came at the beginning of the arrangement. You never forget them.

You meet a number. You *know*. Then, if you are like me, you embark on a conversation that lasts anywhere from ten hours to long months, occasionally interrupted by sleep. You are filled with the wonder of finding the Echo to your Narcissus. Except that your Echo has love returned. You think.

You discover that you use funny words in the same way. Ultimately you develop a private language. I know at least four of these tongues, into which I could easily relapse if one of my former affinities should heave into view.

Whenever I hear the word refined pronounced 'rafeened' my heart still takes a slight bounce because it reminds me of someone once dear. She is now again very dear in memory.

I have always liked women who walked well. Most of those I liked best carried books or pipes on their heads when young. A fine carriage in a woman, on Montgomery Street or Fifth Avenue, brings back the good times, old boy. I think proud bearing in a woman is so seductive because it is a challenge.

In sexist terms, which I still happen to like and use, the well-borne woman is a citadel crying to be taken, a redoubt, and a test. When a woman slouches, and so many of them do nothing but in these liberated days, it is as if she had given away her spirit.

The favorite of my ex-es is still around, somewhere. I proposed to her in a ginmill about seventy-five yards from Claridge's hotel in London. I opened the joint at eleven a.m., ordered my first pint of the day, and stuck my head in the *Times*.

She arrived in a few minutes, said she was feeling ever so crapulent after a large party at the Mirabelle the night before. She ordered a pint, and asked that a double gin be put in it as a float. As we clinked mugs for the first sip of the day together I said, out of a clear sky, and out of my own head: 'I'm going to nail you, old girl.'

She replied, in that staccato English voice I never tired of hearing, 'I shouldn't be a bit surprised.'

In the end, I'm sure, we both made good soup. And, speaking only for the party of the first part, I miss her just the same.

'Charles McCabe Himself'
Lolling

From *The Charles McCabe Reader* (1984)

How I love the sound of that word – lolling! This is perhaps because there is no word in this language that my mother more delighted in using. Not that she liked it. She detested the word and what it connoted.

My mother had a formidable lexicon of contempt, most of it rooted in the Puritan ethic. Simply put, it went something like this: If you weren't working with your hands, you were doing the work of the devil. I was usually doing the work of the devil.

'Is it all you can do, loll about?' she would demand. When that good lady's patience was at a total end, she would heighten the accusation, 'Ah, there he is, lolling about with a book!' Lolling about with a book wasn't quite as bad as having lascivious relations with girls; but it ranked right up there with breaking and entering.

The dictionary before me says the word loll perhaps comes from the Dutch, meaning to sit over the fire. It is defined as 'to lie lazily about, to lounge, sprawl, to dangle . . . to let hang out.'

I should say a major part of my life has been spent lolling, or hanging out. I truly understood the moral background of my mother's opposition to this sort of thing, since I was brought up on the word bum. A bum was what my father was, and what I was destined to be. My mother's life was given her to save me from bumhood, with the co-operation of various dour clerics. To this day I cannot tell the difference between saving somebody from being a bum, and steering him toward glorious bumhood. If you want non-bums, forget the word bums, or something like that.

I knew that I was made to loll, as other people were made to fuss, and fidget, and build bridges and that sort of stuff. As I've grown older, I've managed to get over the feeling that lolling is somehow wrong. Lolling is the way that I live, the way that I was made to live, and there's an end to it.

One of those tediously sagacious Chinese remarked, in some dynasty or other: 'Only those who take leisurely what the people of the world are busy about can be busy about what the people of the world take leisurely.'

We are really just on the brink of the Age of Leisure. Us lollers have something to tell the future. We are closer to the nature of things than the movers and shakers, who tend to move and shake in ways that beat the hell out of the world around us.

Our first lesson is a simple one: Practically nothing ever comes out of trying. I cannot think of anything in my life worth preserving which came from what is called sustained effort. A lot of things, including a couple of marriages, were ruined by the application of this boring principle. Hanging loose in situations where social pressures dictated strenuous effort would have mightily mitigated the old vicissitudes.

Every good idea I have had in my life has come to me when I was both mentally and physically lolling. Thinking about absolutely nothing, walking through the park, or putting away a morning ale – suddenly, out of the ancient and empty air, a notion came. Unbidden, almost unsought; but usually most welcome.

Being undisciplined, like everything else, requires a discipline. You have got to figure out the conditions under which your lolling is productive.

I have several procedures. One is staring blankly at a page of the *Times*, whether of London, or New York, or Los Angeles, with a bottle of ale in front of me. If this is continued long enough, everything you want to know comes to you.

This is usually nothing more than the lede for the piece you are going to write tomorrow; but it may involve such transcendent ideas as what you are going to do with your money, or how you are going to get out of your current high passion. If you do nothing long enough, everything somehow gets done. This is what lolling is all about.

•

JOHN GOULD

John Gould was born in 1908 in Boston, Massachusetts, and spent most of his childhood in Freeport, Maine. He received an AB from Bowdoin College in 1931, then worked for the *Brunswick Record* for the next eight years. From 1945 to 1951 he was owner and publisher of the *Lisbon Enterprise*, in Lisbon Falls, Maine. He contributed a feature to the *Boston Sunday Post* from 1954 to 1974, joining the *Baltimore Sun* in 1975. While he has also farmed, owned a florist and greenhouse business, and worked as a professional guide, he has contributed a weekly rural affairs column to the *Christian Science Monitor* since 1952.

High Frequency Tingle
(Or, Front-door Frisk)

From *The Shag Bag* (1972)

In the promise of things to come, there is an ultrasonic gadget to be attached to a front door, and everybody who comes in will be cleaned slick as a whistle just by passing through. Just step into the activation and zip! – you're immaculate. If this comes to pass, and it probably will, the bath and laundry may disappear from the domestic scene, and both our bodies and our clothing will be vibrated tastefully every time we step in or out.

I guess this will be mostly for the cities – I don't see its becoming popular with us country people right away. As a happy participant in the present arrangement I suppose I would resist a change, but I wonder if this ultrasonic wave will work through a farmer's clothes, particularly in winter with some spruce pitch on the outside. I'd as soon expect to find an apple worm in a cannonball. I speak for myself, but I'm supposed to be typical. Starting with long-handled underwear and a couple of sweatshirts, I'd come in from the woodlot with three or four woolen shirts, a mackinaw, and a pea jacket with overalls. That's quite a rig to vibrate. I don't mean that I work in all this. Up in the woods I'm probably layered down to the underwear, and I have that open at the neck even on cold days. We don't see much of formal society up in the woods, and don't try to keep our neckties straight and our cuffs shot. A limber ax handle and a chilly day work together. Cutting your own wood warms you right up to lugging out the ashes.

But come evensong and the lowering sun fades behind yonder knoll, and the air hangs brisk with the coming night, I lay my tools under a snatch of tops, rearrange my winter garb one by one, haul on my mittens, and wend my weary way homeward o'er the plod, as the poet puts it. This walk home is usually into the bitter north wind, which is pronounced wind, and I have icicles on my eyeballs when I get to the door. Not only the things I wear, but my whole manly physique, would be poorly served now by an electronic nettoyage, or as I often call it, a non-tubly lavender.

In the very first place, I am in no mood now for a brisk and quick going over. Instead, my approach to freshening up calls for sitting on the kitchen rocker for about twenty minutes, while I pant. The dog and the cat help me do this. The cat comes and leaps up to express concern, and the dog lays his head on my knee to show sympathy over my fatigue. They get stroked and patted, and this calms me down a good deal. By the time I feel strong enough to take off my boots and the three pairs of woolen socks, the animals have settled into a deep sleep and it always seems a shame to dislodge them. But I get my boots and socks off, and then after an appropriate rest I am able to grasp the kitchen table and the corner of the cupboard and pull myself to a standing position, after which I work carefully toward the bath.

In my earlier days I really did use a wooden tub that I lifted off a shed nail and arranged in front of the kitchen range, which was never so bad as many have supposed, but we have long since had sophisticated plumbing and I have a real tub in which I can lie back and feel the art of living slowly returning to my exhausted fibers. I permit my nose to resemble a periscope, and because of where they are my knees stick up, too. In this fashion I entertain myself for quite some time, and I would be the first to doubt if an electronic shot at the doorway could really replace this luxury. While I am lolling in the tub my laundress hangs up whatever raiment I may effectively utilize again without immediate cleansing and she heaves the others in the machine, so that a rich melody of detergent and spruce gum mingles throughout the dwelling with the cozy aroma of my personal ablutions – anybody can see that this homey touch will never be replaced by a high-frequency tingle at the front door.

I will point out, although it is not an essential part of this narrative, that upon rising from my bath and throwing on some informal garb that will see me through to bedtime, I am ready for nourishment, and apply myself to the fried ham, turnips, squash, potatoes, boiled onions, succotash, hot biscuits and the two kinds of pie that are my reward for working in the woods all day.

Against all this, the technocrats would offer me a noiseless vibration, and even if it might clean me, I doubt if it would give my appetite the hearty nudge that comes from soap and water. If 'twould make me as pure as a newly opened Bermuda lily, I'd rather do it my way. And I have spoken only of working in the woodlot. What about cleaning out hen-houses, and so forth and so on? Have they tried anything like that on their invisible and soundless front-door frisk?

•

AUBERON WAUGH

Auberon Waugh, the son of the novelist Evelyn Waugh, was born in 1939 and educated at Downside School and Christ Church, Oxford. He served in Cyprus with the Royal Horse Guards in 1958 but was sent home an invalid after managing to shoot himself with a tank-mounted Lewis machine-gun – he had been holding the barrel and using it to hoist himself up on to the turret when bullets sprayed his torso. However, he made a full recovery and in 1960 he joined the staff of the *Daily Telegraph*. In 1963 he became a columnist for the *Catholic Herald* and the following year joined the Mirror Group as a special writer. He has written numerous columns for different publications over the years: the fortnightly 'Auberon Waugh's Diary' for *Private Eye* from 1970 to 1986, the weekly 'First Person' for the *New Statesman* in the 1970s, followed by 'Another Voice' for the *Spectator* from 1976 to 1995. From 1990 he has been writing 'The Way of the World' column for the *Daily Telegraph* and from 1996 a weekly column for the *Sunday Telegraph* as well. In addition to all this, he has been a frequent book reviewer and editor of the *Literary Review* since 1986. His columns are grounded in his extensive reading of newspapers as well as books, yet they usually have an absurdist bent to them. He is perhaps the closest that Britain has come to producing an H. L. Mencken.

'First Person'
Not to Worry

New Statesman, 29 March 1974

Commenting on the attempt to kidnap Princess Anne, Mr Colin S. Harvey of 20A
Berkeley Square, Bristol, wrote to *The Times* on Saturday 23 March, urging the restoration
of the death penalty with these words: 'We worry too much about murderers and
hijackers and their kind, and too little about their victims.'

Many people will have allowed this little pearl to roll away unexamined. It is remarkably
similar to the one produced by twenty backbench debaters, forty leader-writers and the
9,000 letters that are written to the newspapers every time the subject comes up for a
ritual airing. The same elegant paradox is there – on the one hand, the helpless, innocent
victim, on the other, the callous miscreant. But there is a subtle difference in Mr Colin
S. Harvey's approach. He does not accuse any specific group of this error – the
Hampstead softies, so-called intellectuals or Communist agents inside the teaching
profession. He does not even employ the immensely subtle trick of rhetoric: 'Are some
of us, perhaps, not – ah – in danger of worrying too much –?' No, he makes the bald
statement that 'we' – Mr Colin S. Harvey and I – worry too much about one class and
too little about another.

My first reaction on being accused of anything is always to deny it hotly and see if I
can lie my way out of it afterwards. However, since Mr Harvey was not present to hear
my lame excuses and feeble attempts to laugh it off, I found myself alone with his
terrible accusation. All the books in my library were full of learned arguments and other
people's advice, but essentially I was alone with my soul. The more I examined my
conscience, the more I discovered that if I was completely honest with myself, I didn't
in point of fact worry in the slightest little bit either about murderers, hijackers and
their kind or about their victims.

This seemed to put me beyond the pale of civilized discussion. Everybody must
surely worry about one or the other, and really civilized people worry about both. That
is plainly the correct answer. But worry is not something which can be summoned out
of the void in response to some notion of social propriety. It either happens or it
doesn't.

Of course, I am not so inhuman or un-British as to have no opinion on the death
penalty. The death penalty is a universal leveller in the sense that where one has no
other apparent basis for communication with a fellow citizen, having exhausted the
weather, one can always listen to his opinion on the death penalty. Listening to thousands
of conversations on the subject, one could easily fall into the popular error of supposing
that since so very many people derive comfort, if not actually pleasure, from the thought
of murderers being hanged, and since, in the natural course of things, the process
involves distress and inconvenience to so few, then it might be promoting the greatest
happiness for the greatest number to have an occasional hanging. It might even be a
good idea to have it done on television, which would give pleasure to the disregarded
minority of sadists who can find few lawful outlets for their propensity while also

confronting the 'normal' majority of pro-hangers with the consequences of their choice.

But my own views are more austere, and more boring: hanging or any form of judicial killing is a self-evident atrocity; such an atrocity following the original atrocity of murder does not wipe it out, but merely adds up to two atrocities; to deter a conjectural atrocity in the future by committing an actual one now is illogical and absurd, not to say wrong.

That, then, is where I stand. That is the noise I make whenever the subject comes up. But can I honestly say I worry about it? If, like sorrow at the Jew's funeral, everything can be priced, I will pay £35 to prevent the reintroduction of capital punishment – as against £2,000 to prevent amputation of one of my legs, and £25,000, perhaps, to prevent one of my children dying.

Some will be shocked by this. Warmer-hearted people will want to pay more – £50 or even £100 – to prevent hanging. Obviously, the plight of an innocent man who faces execution for a crime he did not commit – and I don't doubt that there have been many – is quite exceptionally poignant and distressing. If one knew about such a case, one would have a clear moral obligation to do whatever one could to prevent it happening. But life is full of dangers. As I write this, I would not be at all surprised to learn that an old-age pensioner is being squashed by a juggernaut in Liverpool. If I had known, I would certainly have warned her not to cross the road at this stage. But it is no good pretending that when I read in tomorrow's newspaper that my worst fears for this unfortunate lady have been confirmed, I shall be in the slightest bit worried. And, compared with the risk of being killed on the road, or suddenly learning that you have cancer, the risk of being murdered or unjustly executed for murder is not a particularly high one.

Let us take the argument a stage further. If Princess Anne, instead of being driven happily around in a horse box, were now lying stiff and cold in Westminster Hall while a tearful nation filed past her coffin, I would certainly choose my company very carefully before uttering whatever jests seemed appropriate to the occasion. But I would not be any sadder about it than I am for the lady who might have been run over in Liverpool. Above all, I wouldn't *worry*.

All of which may seem a roundabout way of making the obvious point that there is a limit to the Christ-like obligation of the private citizen to take the sufferings of the world on his own shoulders. To say, in politics, that charity begins at home is often a polite way of saying that the voter is a selfish brute who doesn't give twopence for the underdeveloped nations. But my point is that political debate in this country is rapidly losing its power even to appease the selfishness of the voter through its inability to distinguish between opinions and motives.

Only politicians are prepared to go to war over whether one should eat a boiled egg from the big end or the little end, although circumstances may be created – as in Ulster – where private citizens can be persuaded to follow them. These circumstances do not yet exist in England. The Tories faced the country in 1970 on a programme of enforcing law and order, staying East of Suez and allowing industrial lame ducks to drop out of the race through the rigours of competition. They were elected because of the rising cost of living. Mr Wilson, who offered the country a most exciting and varied programme, was returned in 1974 for exactly the same reason. It is easy for that tiny minority in

England which worries about how we should all eat our eggs to suppose that a general election gives them a mandate to make us all eat them from the end they have chosen. This is a sad and rather comic misunderstanding, but one which will no doubt be cleared up in time.

'First Person'
The Great Savings Swindle
New Statesman, 25 October 1974

Searching for a birth certificate this week in a neglected corner of the house, I came upon a Post Office Savings book in my name whose last entry – a withdrawal of £1 – is dated 21 April 1954. In those days I did not possess a calculator, but I now see that the account (No. 124 at Stinchcombe post office in Gloucestershire) is two shillings in credit, and has been for the last twenty years. I shall probably never know how I came to overlook this sum at the age of fourteen when it would have bought ten Players Medium or six Mars bars. Nowadays I couldn't buy a single cigarette, since shops have stopped selling them singly, and only one Mars bar for the money. Moreover, the Mars bar of 1954 was a great deal bigger than the one today. Its size was brilliantly calculated to make any child feel slightly sick if he ate a whole one himself. Today I could probably eat three of the new ones, if I had a mind to, without any problem.

As a child, one knew instinctively that Post Office Savings were a fraud. Like obligatory offerings in the church box, they were a sort of Morality Tax, a system of confiscation by grown-ups apparently in the interests of character improvement but almost certainly dictated by envy of our simple pleasures and jealousy of our youth. Among the lies told to encourage this form of thrift (or promote this form of theft) was a preposterous statement which I believed until half an hour ago when I began to think about it, that a penny invested at compound interest in Julius Caesar's time would now be worth the world's weight in gold. Quite apart from the fact that since the world is not made of gold your thrift would simply have resulted in a bad debt, it must be obvious to the meanest intelligence that the other party to the deal would rat on it long before. There is no remotely secure way of investing money at the present time – or so I have been told – where interest is greater than the rate of inflation. A penny invested now at compound interest would be worth infinitely less than a hundredth part of a grain of sand in 2,000 years' time – always assuming, as life insurance brochures stipulate, that current trends are maintained.

This unexpected windfall of two shillings in the Post Office Savings Bank in fact represents my entire investment portfolio, the sum total of my stake in the usury system. It promises 2½ per cent per annum interest, and I spent a happy hour with my computer working out the compound interest on two shillings for twenty years at 2½ per cent before coming up with the amount of 40.332135 old pence, being the principal plus accrued interest. It was the work of a second to convert this into 16.805056 new pence, still not enough to buy three of the new, small Mars bars at 6p each. Whereas, as I never tire of pointing out, I could have bought six of the large ones for my original two shillings in 1954.

In fact, it looks as if I may never get this interest, as I see I should have been sending the book to head office on the anniversary of my opening the account (29 July 1953) every year for the past twenty years in order to have the interest entered in it. Probably this is intended as a protection against would-be Julius Caesars, but it seems a little hard on small savers like myself who can only hope for two fifths of a penny by way of interest this year. I only want my Mars bars back.

Post Office Savings have always been the most notorious of the many methods employed by government to rob the poor of their savings. The amazing thing is that the poor have never twigged. Interest rates have gone up but so, of course, has the general level of inflation, and it is truer today than ever before that anyone who saves money is losing it. Yet from his earliest days every citizens is subjected to a barrage of propaganda from parents and teachers as well as from politicians and crooks, all urging him to save money. Between them, inflation, hire purchase and personal taxation have removed every rational argument which ever existed for saving and we are left with nothing but irrational, atavistic terrors as our individual inducement to the one activity which holds the entire economy together.

It was Len Murray who produced what is surely the most significant quotation on the subject, when talking to Michael Leapman of *The Times*. 'We've got to stop worrying about inflation and learn to love it,' he said. Obviously, this pronouncement holds the key to everything that has been puzzling the rest of the world about Britain's attitude to inflation. The great problem is where to start. Children must be taught the simple proposition that saving equals waste. No doubt teachers can illustrate this with ingenious coloured charts but parents, too, can play their part by confiscating any pocket money which has not been spent by bed-time. The only thing which nobody can hope to do at the present time is to make any financial provision for his old age.

Logically, perhaps, I should welcome Mrs Castle's catastrophic increase in social security payments for the self-employed next April. The idea of her scheme is apparently to provide a pension which will be related to the cost of living around the year 2000 – just when I shall be applying for it. But a certain peasant caution creeps into my calculations, derived, no doubt, from the biblical injunction: 'O put not your trust in princes nor in any child of man; for there is no help in them.' I can see it will be very nice for Mrs Castle and her successors in office to receive my huge payments until the year 2000; but also that it will be rather less agreeable for them when it comes to paying out. And it is a feature of government that it can simply pass a law whenever it likes to rid itself of these tiresome obligations.

My own policy has been to shower my poor wife with useless but possibly saleable objects – ancient Greek coins, china boxes, harpsichords with the innards removed – and encourage her to cultivate the vegetable garden. We now have fourteen hundredweight of potatoes in store against the hard winter and enough bric-à-brac to stock the entire Portobello Road for a month against our old age.

'Another Voice'
The Nilsen Millennium
Spectator, 2 March 1985

Somewhere along the line, Dennis Nilsen seems to have got it all wrong. His father, a Norwegian soldier stationed in Scotland, moved off at the end of the war leaving his mother to cope with three children, of whom Dennis was the youngest. From his earliest years, his memories are those of a client of the welfare state. By the time he had moved on from two forms of government employment – in the army and the police force – to a third, in the Manpower Services Commission, he had emerged as such a boring and unpleasant person that nobody could bear to spend time in his company. He was a homosexualist, of course, but even with the opportunities available to him for making new acquaintances of similar persuasion through his post in the Charing Cross Road Job Centre, people found him so stupendously boring that nobody would spend more than an evening in his company. Like so many social and emotional cripples he drifted into left-wing politics and became branch organizer of the Civil Service Union, but even there his boring self-righteousness failed to secure the warmth and comradeship which he sought. So he was reduced to seeking the company of corpses as being the only people who would not walk out on him.

Other people, in the same sort of predicament, became prison visitors, but Nilsen kept his corpses under the floor-boards, retrieving them from time to time to sit them in an armchair and harangue them with his boring left-wing opinions, his grudges and grievances and the catalogue of his self-pity. Then, when the natural processes of decomposition made the corpses unacceptable company, even by his own undemanding standards, he boiled their heads, put them down the lavatory, and started looking around for a new companion. In this way he disposed of fifteen young men in the course of five years, before being brought to book as a result of blocked drains in the house where he lived.

Nilsen obviously provides an extreme example of what used fashionably to be called urban alienation – the loneliness which rootless town-dwellers suffer who are too boring, too unpleasant or too unattractive in other ways to make friends. He also, perhaps, offers a paradigm for the relationship between personal inadequacies, left-wing views and bureaucratic sadism. Although I have no particular reason to suppose that Nilsen was such a sadist as one is liable to meet in the course of any dealings with a government ministry or local authority, a glance at his face assures me that he almost certainly belonged to that group. I have often speculated about the private lives of people behind desks who spend their working hours making things difficult for other people. It would be tempting to think they all have corpses under their floor-boards and return home, of an evening, to harangue them. But Nilsen, as I say, is an extreme example. His problem was loneliness, and the traditional solution to that is within the marriage bond. No man is so boring, or so unpleasant or so unattractive that he cannot find an equally boring, unpleasant or unattractive woman to be his life's companion if he sets his mind to it and I have no doubt that the same must be true in the homosexual world. But Nilsen's only attempt at a homosexual marriage ended in mutual disgust; obviously he is better off in prison.

The latest edition of *Social Trends* (HMSO £19.95) reveals a dramatic increase in the number of people living alone – from eleven per cent of the population in 1961 to twenty-four per cent in 1983. Add to this the proportion of people living in one-parent families, which has doubled from two and a half per cent in 1961 to five per cent in 1983, and one sees that the institution of the family is under serious attack.

Where abortion and contraception are freely available, the dramatic rise in illegitimate births – from six per cent of live births in 1961 to sixteen per cent in 1983 – must be seen either as a deliberate flight from the institution of marriage or, more probably, a logical response to government incentives. Under the ghastly Mrs Williams's education system, children of the poor are no longer taught the old-fashioned disciplines of plasticine modelling, or how to make the longest plasticine worm. Apart from Reasons for Not Smoking, they are more or less exclusively taught How to Claim their Welfare Benefits. The first lesson in this course is to have a baby and become a single parent. There are now a million or so of them. Add to them the four and a quarter million now living completely alone, and one is plainly just beginning to be allowed a glimpse into the Nilsen millennium.

•

GEORGE FRAZIER

George Frazier (1911–74) was born in Boston and educated at Harvard University, where he received his AB in 1933. Although he came from a modest background, he affected the dress, demeanour and manners of a high-born Bostonian. He was a free-lance journalist at first, then entertainment editor of *Life* magazine from 1941 to 1946, and when he had just turned fifty he started a daily column. He was a daily columnist for the *Boston Herald* from 1961 to 1965, then for the *Boston Globe* from 1970 to 1974, and also a monthly columnist for *Esquire* magazine from 1967 to 1974. He was fired from the *Globe* in 1971, partly for lambasting as amateurish some young *Globe* reporters who had appeared on a public television show, and partly for writing too many columns from New York. A couple of radio talk show hosts hired a plane and trailed a banner with the words '*GLOBE* FEARS FREEDOM AND FIRED FRAZIER' over a sports stadium during a New England Patriots game, and soon afterwards the *Globe* relented and invited him back. Bostonian smugness was one of his targets, but others included Richard Nixon and the high-profile feminists. He referred to Gloria Steinem, a former Playboy Club waitress, as 'Bunny', and named Susan Brownmiller 'the goose girl' – she had broken her foot kicking a man who had goosed her in New York and then written about it in *Village Voice*. He was a proud curmudgeon: when voted worst 'male chauvinist' by a group of Boston feminists, he had the muzzle they awarded him bronzed and then hung it above his mantelpiece. In one of the columns below, he managed to offend the citizens of Dallas, New Orleans and Miami in one throw. He also once reported a Yankees–Red Sox baseball game in Latin, primarily for the pleasure of rendering the technical term 'designated hitter' in the ancient language. His columns ranged from vicious mockery to lyrical reverie, and he interspersed his essay columns with acerbic list columns, such as his popular 'Another Man's Poison' feature.

Excerpts from 'Another Man's Poison'
Boston Herald, October 1961–December 1963

WEEI's Priscilla Fortesque's praise for a play is my cue to pass it up.

If you're interested in going to, say Brookline or Needham by way of Buffalo, then take one of those gypsy taxis at Logan Airport.

I'm plenty perplexed by a Chicago escort service that bills itself as 'the oldest escort service.' Does that mean that all the competing services provide younger escorts than does this one?

I'd be deeply disappointed if I were ever to draw Betty White as a blind date.

Joey Bishop's television series will bring back reading.

One of the best-looking shirts I've seen is the new broad-striped Brooks button-down in Scottish broadcloth. But I'd gladly pay $14, instead of the $13.50 asked for it, if they would remove the damn breast pocket.

Such sadness as is spun in the classified columns – such as in this ad from the *Bar Harbor Times* of April 26: 'House Lot, 90 by 150 ft, centrally located in town, $650; also, engagement ring, worn only short time, priced reasonably for quick sale. Tel. AT 8-46-4639.'

If you think I'm not clairvoyant in my distaste for those cornpone double first names, then may you christen your son Billy Sol.

I'd feel a lot less sinful if Pat Boone would swear, start a rumble, steal a car, get a divorce or something.

Did ever any sports team have to bear with a sillier name than the Houston Colt .45s?

'Sonny' strikes me as an absurd nickname for a grown man, but somehow I can't visualize myself telling Charles Liston so.

Why do manufacturers persist in making swimming trunks with metal buckles when it is generally acknowledged that bright objects attract sharks.

I never know what kind of airplane I'm on.

You must admit that most dogs you see riding in cars look a lot more intelligent than the drivers.

Bobby Whatever-his-name-is won't make me jealous if he avails himself of the appalling offer extended by that idiot child who does 'I Wanna Be Bobby's Girl.'

I'm absolutely fascinated by the fact that the Mexican restaurant at 1430 Commonwealth Avenue is called Concannon & Sennett's.

I'd rather be caught in a downpour than have to watch those Weather Girls on Channel 7.

Combination hair and clothes brushes that fold flat for traveling make an unusual Christmas gift for the man who has everything, including dandruff and lint.

Tell the truth now – don't you really think that Pat Brown and California deserve each other?

You're kind of bright if you know what an & is called.

I've never found a Christmas gift suggestion for men in the *New Yorker* that I wouldn't be embarrassed to own.

Even if I could make out the words, I'd like the Rooftop Singers' recording of 'Walk Right In.'

On the other hand, however, if I ever catch my sons singing that 'My Dad,' I'll put them up for adoption.

Don't you think the Peace Corps should have a department devoted to teaching English to Rock 'n' Roll singing groups?

To show you what influence I wield, the madrigal called 'Bobby's Girl' is still a best-selling record.

The opposition to fluoridation seems to be as sensible as suicide.

Just what the hell am I supposed to do when I see a sign reading 'Caution– Falling Rock'?

I waste an awful lot of time looking for a golf ball that doesn't have exactly 360 dimples.

Everything considered, I think it's just as well that Beethoven and Brahms can't hear Steve Lawrence and his roommate being referred to as 'Mr and Mrs Music.'

I have the funniest feeling that when an announcer insists that some drink must be tasted to be appreciated, he's afraid I'm so stupid I might bathe my feet in it by mistake.

Do you think it's possible that my abstinence has anything to do with the per capita consumption of alcohol's being so much less than it was in Prohibition?

Who Are Those Guys?

Boston Globe, January 27, 1972

New Orleans – Where in God's name do they dig up those Dallas Cowboy camp followers, those loud and blowzy men and, one assumes, women, in ridiculous royal blue ten-gallon hats who, boozy glasses in hand, have been reeling through the hotel lobbies and the streets of the French Quarter these past few days and nights? Where, for God's sake, where?

But the answer is obvious. They dig them up in Dallas, of course, which fact immediately absolves the boors of any responsibility for their uncivilized behavior.

After all, these people – these louts, these drunkards, these all-but-illiterates – are products of their environment – of Dallas.

Dallas – the Big D. Dallas – cradle of Neiman-Marcus, that monument to execrable taste. Dallas, such a bloody awful place – not because John F. Kennedy was assassinated there, but because, only a few hours afterward, the city's music lovers – music lovers? – flocked to the opera in black tie. Dallas, ugh city of America.

But if the Dallas Cowboy partisans are not to be held accountable for their conduct, what is Carol Channing's excuse? Carol Channing, who, at half-time at Super Bowl VI this bitter cold afternoon in the Sugar Bowl, was so stupendously forgettable. And yet, ineffably untalented as she is, it is not she, but the National Football League, that must be blamed for her opportunity to defile this sacred rite of our wintertimes. But the hell with Miss Carol Channing, star of stage, television and the department of how to lose friends and make one want to throw up. And, while we are about it, the hell with those horrors, those fans, who came here from Dallas to observe the Cowboys, who deserve better. Not that people from Miami were any bargains either, but they, too, are victims of their ambivalence. Dallas, Texas and Miami, Florida, and if you can name another American city that is worse than either of those two, you are much more widely traveled than I – widely and, also, wastefully.

Yet Super Bowl VI was great fun, largely, I think, because New Orleans is a city of such special character, a city of one frolic after another, of many, many fêtes. And then, too, of course, there is the football fever that afflicts the whole state. Louisiana may be corrupt and illiterate, but no one can claim that it has ever neglected the care and feeding of football. It is the home of LSU (stand up and take off your hat, for this was Gaynell Tinsley's college, his and Billy Cannon's and an honor roll of others); of Southern (ave Isaiah Robertson); of McNeese State (such a wondrous wee football power); of Southwestern Louisiana (up on your feet again, for this is where Chris Cagle went before he was a son of slum and gravy, long before he stumbled drunkenly down a subway stairs to his death); Tulane (Greetings, Tommy Mason and Richie Pettibone); and, naturally, Grambling (and we'll never get to sit down if we hail its heroes) – Grambling, the practically all-black college where football is taken so gravely that, a few years ago, when Tiny Gaspar was beaten out for his first-string tackle job by Charles Roundtree, he followed Roundtree into the cafeteria and shot him. Blessings on thee, Tiny, for greater desire to be in the starting lineup has no man.

So, corrupt and ignorant and fearful of black priapism though many Louisianans are – for all the state's US senators' arrogance of ignorance, notwithstanding a district attorney under Federal indictment, despite an attorney general likely to go to prison, for all the in-direct-apostolic-succession-to-James Michael Curley-preposterousness of a sheriff's being re-elected while in jail – for all such dishonorable public servants, Louisiana is the state for the Super Bowl, and New Orleans the city. (Still, one must not give the impression that the state is entirely a fool's paradise – as, indeed, what state could be that has, or has had, such treasures as Vida Blue, Walker Percy, Truman Capote, T. Harry Williams, Louis Armstrong and Tennessee Williams, towering people like that.) Forget, too, about such blights of New Orleans as its two really terrible daily papers, the *Times Picayune* and the *States Item*; forget about the owner of the Saints, John Mecom Jr, who recently appointed a former astronaut as the team's general manager. Think, instead, of the admirable people and things – Clay Shaw, that figure of massive dignity; Mayor Moon Landrieu, who defied Jim Garrison by appointing Shaw to an important city position; and, for ever and always, the tone of the town, the charm, the exuberance.

The days and nights immediately preceding yesterday's football game were a madhouse, the hotels so jammed that overflow visitors had to take accommodations on the two steamers that docked here or in hotels and motels in towns like Biloxi on the Mississippi Gulf Coast. The hustlers were doing so thrivingly that a cabdriver told me last night that in three days he had made almost $500 in gratuities from girls whose services he had recommended to raunchy passengers. In this city it was show time twenty-four hours a day, and not only because of the Super Bowl either, for in hotel ballrooms around town the Mardi Gras was doing the gavotte as a kind of preview.

But ultimately, like as of around 1:30 p.m. yesterday, the moment of truth arrived with the Cowboys prevailing 24–3 over a presumptuous team from Miami. The Dolphins? Who are those guys anyway? The temperature was 31 degrees and the sun was dazzling out of a cloudless blue sky as the game started. There was – naturally – the usual nonsense attendant upon such extravaganzas. I do grant that it is better to have one's daughter become a cheerleader or a drum majorette than to have her on heroin. But how much better? Moreover, there was Al Hirt, of whom the nicest thing that can be said is that he doesn't really harm anyone. And if there was that abomination of desolation named Carol Channing, there was also Ella Fitzgerald.

But what one will remember out of today was, say, Calvin Hill as he summoned up Saturday afternoon in the Yale Bowl, Calvin Hill and Roger Staubauch and Walt Garrison and, of course and by all means, a poignant black man named Duane Thomas, who during the past week has been the butt of sportswriters' gibes because of his refusal to talk to them. Personally, I'd say that it showed good taste on his part, and you would, too, if you knew some of the sportswriters I do. If my information is correct, Duane Thomas lost his mother and father within six months of each other, was divorced by his wife, and is now suffering the agony of seeing his twenty-seven-year-old brother about to die. Small wonder he didn't feel like talking. But when it counted, as it did today, he played football. Oh, he played it so beautifully, so exquisitely, so devastatingly. I do wish that the Dallas Cowboy camp followers could have kept their mouths shut, too. Duane Thomas is a man, Dallas Cowboy fans are idiots.

The Bush

Boston Globe, January 19, 1973

Used car dealers who do their own commercials.
Fraternities, sororities and girls who get 'pinned.'
As well as the damn fools who 'pin' them.
Wits who call fat men 'Tiny' and short men 'Stretch.'
Anyone who has his own bowling ball.
Men who wear short-sleeved business shirts, ankle socks, plastic hat covers,
        suits with flaps on the coat pockets.
Or, damn it, double knits!
Anyone who ever sang along with Mitch.
Anyone with a boat on top of his car.
Men who speak of 'the missus.'
Anyone described as 'a card' or 'the life of the party.'
Women who wear hair curlers in public.
Women who wear hair curlers in private.
Richard Milhous Nixon and family.
Anything described as 'wholesome.'

People who make their own wine.

Men who speak of having gone to 'State' or 'the university.'

Any father who refers to his son as 'Junior.'

Any son who lets father refer to his son as 'Junior.'

People who know the words of 'The Star Spangled Banner.'

Or 'The Pledge of Allegiance.'

People who put ketchup on everything.

Men who marry Zsa Zsa Gabor.

One Man's Secret Diary
Boston Globe, March 13, 1974

Sunday – Early morning train to Marblehead for brunch. About to light cigarette when see No Smoking sign. Ask conductor if forward car same. Smirking, says, 'Correct.' I furious, say, 'No need to be so gleeful,' and he say, 'Damn right I'm gleeful,' and I say, 'No damn right to be gleeful. You exceeding authority. You pain in —' He fling arms in air, scream, 'Any more lip and I throw you off train.' By now whole car out of seats and staring. Woman with *Globe* open to Bruce McCabe piece on me tell conductor, 'Stay away from him. I just read about him. He's dangerous.'

I stand up and point with finger. 'It's you who should be thrown off, madam.' She move back as if I going to strike her. She say to conductor, 'It says here he's insane. Conceited, rude, stays up all night, drunk from morning to night.' I glare at her. 'Make that early morning you crone. I go to bed at ten a.m.,' I say. Conductor say, 'Don't worry, lady. I know about him. He's the one who hates white socks.' He bend down, draw up pant leg, shows white sock. Ankle not bad. 'You insulting me, boy,' he says to me. 'Oh, God,' I say wearily, 'with people like you no wonder trains vanishing. If you any good, you'd be on Super Chief.' He reaches toward me. 'Out!' he yells. 'You're getting out at the next stop.'

Just then get big flash. 'Oh, yeah?' I say darkly. 'Oh, yeah,' say he, and his hand touches my shoulder. I sweep away, raise coat and shirtsleeves, point to hospital band on wrist. 'Read that,' say I. He reads aloud to whole car, 'George Frazier 31005. Doctor C. Hatem.' He frowns, reads again. 'Just what the hell is this supposed to mean?'

'I'll tell you what it means, Casey Jones,' say I. 'This band from Mt Auburn hospital means I'm out on pass so I can be fitted for yachting cap in Marblehead. It means all I ask is tall ship and star to steer her by. It means I very sick man and if you throw me off train I may have attack and die.' Conductor back away. 'Yeah? What's wrong with you?' 'Inverted clavicle,' say I. 'You know what inverted clavicle is? Well, you'd better learn, 'cause the court will ask you when they try you for murder-two.' He shake head, glance at other people. 'Sorry, this man seriously ill. Better not excite him.' I say, 'OK, now you take off those white socks.' 'Why,' says he. 'Why?' say I, 'because they're making me even more seriously ill.'

Red-letter day. Great brunch. Eggs Benedict. Fresh orange juice. Smoked like chimney.

Confession of an Ex-addict
Boston Globe, March 29, 1974

The grace notes embellishing the cessation from smoking take the oddest turns, even to the point of enabling the abstainer suddenly to see a whole city in a different light, from a fresh perspective. But before I get into that, I would like a word about an affliction that can be a lot more unseemly than smoking itself. This is the tendency of the reformed to proselytize, to bring the wayward into the fold, and, in the process, make a bloody bore of himself. The way I see it, a man wants to smoke, that's his affair and he'll get no sermon from me. On the other hand, there does seem a certain justification for the reformed sinner to provide *obiter dicta* anent his entering estate of grace. So much for that.

I was talking about the different light in which a sudden abstainer from smoking may look at a whole city. God knows I hate Boston – no Bogart in pursuit of the bird on the tube when it is a real dark night of the soul; no even passable food in the hours before dawn, and, far from the least, the statute against smoking in Boston movie theaters. I don't suppose that over the years I ever saw a film in Boston without leaving my seat several times to go out and have a cigarette. As a result, I regarded all theater-owners as my natural enemies, nor can I recall ever having seen a movie in Boston that I enjoyed without reservation. Now, in retrospect, I all of a sudden realized the distorted vision, the erroneous sense of values, that can be imposed by such a special interest as an addiction to smoking. And not only that, either, but the other day, for the first time in a lifetime spent half in the sky I was able to sit up forward (that is the non-smoking section) in a plane. Parenthetically, this particular aircraft, as my luck would have it, deplaned at the other end. The what skies of Eastern?

Yet there's an addendum to all this, which is that the reformed smoker who is forever avoiding occasions of sin lest he backslide better take another look at the game plan – either that or reconcile himself to a truly lousy life, a life on the edge of terror. Personally, I can't imagine living in the constant fear of falling if I should catch the aroma of somebody else's cigarette or, upon seeing someone smoking on a movie or television screen, of being seduced into going and doing likewise. The exquisite part of extirpating an addiction through hypnosis – the part that makes it work – is that one has put such temptations behind him.

The problem of smoking or drinking or fear of flying has been eliminated, and no more any need for exerting one's willpower, of forever being en garde against one's personal devil. As for switching to a pipe or to little cigars, or Tiparillos or whatever they're euphemistically called, God forbid! The beauty of hypnosis is that it removes any peril of the addict's looking like that ridiculous little figure known as the Winchester Man or like some untalented author on the dust jacket of some eighth-rate novel.

There is also, of course, the little matter of personal freedom. One thing I respect is a person's right to his vices, so far be it for me ever to carry on as a doctor of animal husbandry named Joyce something-or-other did upon finding herself seated by necessity in the 'smoking permitted' section on a plane. When the man in the next seat ignored her order to put out his cigarette, she dumped her tray, which was laden with lunch, in his lap. A jury obviously partial to personal freedom found quite substantially for the man. As for cabs that forbid fares to smoke, the hell with them, especially now that I'm an abstainer and not disadvantaged. Let the damn drivers find some line of endeavor that will preclude their presuming to interfere with the freedom of others. People who, because they don't indulge, refuse to keep cigarettes or alcohol in the house should be taken out behind the barn and shot between the eyes. One of the most admirable things to me about Robert Coughlan, with whom I was on *Life*, is not that he reportedly received almost half a million dollars for editing the Rose Kennedy thing, but that at *Life* editorial luncheons he would invariably be the first guest to order a drink and thereby court abstemious Henry Luce's displeasure. I defend every person's right to get smashed provided he keeps his hands off the sweet gentle wife. You want to smoke, you go right ahead and smoke.

Me? I'm going to keep sitting it out – as I have been for 336 hours.

•

MIKE ROYKO

Mike Royko (1932–97) was born in Chicago. His parents owned several bars in the Polish district on the Northwest Side, and by the age of fifteen Royko was adept at serving drinks and passing on bribes to minor public officials. He was a regular truant and dropped out of high school at sixteen, yet while working full-time, as a department store clerk and as a theatre usher, he returned to school and obtained his high school diploma. In 1952 he joined the air force and was sent to Korea as a radio operator. Having secured a transfer to Chicago's O'Hare Field, where he was supposed to become a military policeman, he falsely claimed to have been a reporter for the *Chicago Daily News* and offered to edit the base newspaper, although no such publication had previously existed. He spent three days in a public library boning up on newspapers, then went to work, writing a column for the paper as well as editing it. He quickly discovered the potential for a columnist to cause trouble. In his first column he criticized the officers' wives for failing to match the smart dress code followed by air force personnel. When a deputation of angry wives burst into his office demanding to see the writer, Royko said the culprit had gone on permanent leave. In another column he revealed that the base's star softball pitcher had been kept on beyond the period of his enlistment just so that he could play in a tournament. As a result, the personnel responsible for this improper Sergeant Bilko-like arrangement were transferred elsewhere and the paper was closed.

On completing his military service, Royko joined a group of Chicago suburban weeklies and then worked as a reporter for the City News Bureau, before landing a job on the paper he had earlier lied about working for, the *Chicago Daily News*. He was a reporter on the police and city hall beats, but before long graduated to being a daily columnist. A scathing critic of urban machine-politics, he also wrote powerfully about racism, crime, the counter-culture and the quiddities of urban life. Occasionally, he would adopt the persona of Slats Grobnik, a character from the Polish neighbourhood where Royko was raised. In 1978 when the *Daily News* closed he joined the *Chicago Sun-Times*, but resigned in 1984 when Rupert Murdoch acquired the paper. For four days, while the *Sun-Times* sued him in an effort to prevent him joining the *Chicago Tribune*, his column was published in both papers. In 1970 he wrote a column about the four stray cats his son had brought home, threatening to feed one to a friend's pet piranhas unless a parent phoned to offer the cat a home – his appeal was addressed to children: 'Because if somebody doesn't, little children, it will be snap, snap, gobble, gobble, gobble, right down to his curly tail.' He won a Pulitzer Prize for his column in 1972 and the Damon Runyon Award in 1995. He still had the ability to provoke as well as enlighten and entertain – twice in March 1996 Hispanics marched on the *Tribune*'s offices to complain about a column in which he had averred that the best thing to have come out of Mexico this century is tequila. He published a biography of the ex-Mayor of Chicago, Richard J. Daley, as well as several collections of columns.

Daley Dissected

From *I May Be Wrong, But I Doubt It* (1968)

Chicago is crawling with visiting writers all asking the same questions: What is Mayor Daley really like? Who is this chubby-cheeked man in City Hall who munches cookies with LBJ and is courted by Bobby? And whom will he support for the nomination?

It is a strain for local newsmen, being interviewed by visiting writers, especially the scholarly ones. They always ask if the mayor has charisma. In the mayor's neighborhood, they could get punched for talking dirty.

To assist visitors, I have prepared a primer on the mayor. Most of it isn't new to Chicagoans, but it might help others appreciate our most famous citizen.

It is needed because some visitors get confused by the many popular versions of what Mayor Daley is really like.

There is the Mayor Daley his most ardent admirers describe.

This mayor, legend has it, first appeared during the Chicago Fire of 1871. He doused the fire with one hand and milked Mrs O'Leary's cow with the other. Before the ashes cooled, he hired Frank Lloyd Wright to redesign the city, dug Lake Michigan to cool it, organized the White Sox, and set aside land for two airports in case airplanes were ever invented.

More restrained admirers say he is simply the greatest mayor Chicago ever had, which is like singling out the best player the New York Mets ever had.

The best way to view Mayor Daley is in pieces. At least that's what Republicans say.

His Early Years: The key to Daley's success is the fact he was born in a magical old neighborhood called Bridgeport. It has produced Chicago's last three mayors, their rule spanning thirty-seven years. All this political clout means nearly every family has got somebody on a government payroll. In the East, some families register a newborn son at Harvard or Yale. In Bridgeport, they sign him on with the city water department.

The mayor's father was a sheet metal worker. As a kid, Daley worked in the stockyards. This convinced him there are better things than work, so he got into politics.

He showed talent. He did what he was told, never got caught associating with newspapermen, reformers or other low types, never squealed on anybody, wore fat-Max ties, baggy suits and broad-brimmed hats just like his peers and went to church on Sunday.

His only flaws were that he didn't smoke cigars or wear diamond rings, but the party overlooked this because he had been to college. During the late thirties and early forties, he served in the Legislature and came out clean, which hasn't happened too often. In the late forties, he ran for sheriff and lost. He didn't like the way that felt and it hasn't happened again.

Rise to Power: In 1955, the Democrats had a serious problem. The mayor was Martin Kennelly, a businessman and a reformer. The Democrats had put him in because there had been so much scandal they had needed a reform candidate to beat off the Republicans.

But Kennelly betrayed the Democrats by actually trying to reform things. Outraged, they dumped him for Daley, who was then the county clerk. He wasn't well known to the public, but he had power in party circles. Kennelly bravely fought Daley in the primary, but he was exposed as a reformer and the voters kicked him out.

As Mayor: Daley likes to build big things. He likes high-rises, expressways, parking garages, municipal buildings and anything else that requires a ribbon-cutting ceremony and can be financed through Federal funds.

He isn't that enthusiastic about small things, such as people. Daley does not like civil rights demonstrators, rebellious community organizations, critics of the mediocre school system, critics of any kind or people who argue with him.

Daley the Public Figure: Until he became mayor, Daley was known as a quiet, behind-the-scenes politician. When he started making speeches, it was clear why he had been quiet. He has since developed two much-improved styles of oratory: a controlled mumble for TV and an excited gabble for political rallies.

He has simple tastes. Nobody catches him chatting about literature, music or French cooking. He likes White Sox games, fishing and parades. He has led more parades than anyone since Rome fell apart. Hardly a Saturday passes when the mayor isn't hoofing down the middle of State Street with thousands of city workers behind him. It has been estimated he has paraded the distance from Chicago to Minsk.

Daley the Politician: He is old-fashioned. Other city machines took up civil service and got in other bad habits. They fell apart. The old-fashioned Daley organization controls about 60,000 patronage jobs. It has thousands of others in unions, private industry, utilities, at racetracks.

Loafing or getting lost in a bar won't get a guy fired, but failing to get the vote out will. Besides patronage, the organization offers something for everyone: There are welfare checks for the obedient poor, big projects for contractors, rezoning for real estate men, prestige appointments for the socially important, promotions for the right cops and firemen.

Nepotism is big. Half the top officeholders are sons of former officeholders. Even the crime syndicate has its men in government. Everyone can join in if they do what they are told. It is truly democratic in a dictatorial sort of way.

Whom will he support for the nomination? The mayor will consider which candidate is the wisest, the noblest, the most inspiring, the best qualified. Then he will pick the one with the best chance of winning. In his parades, the politicians always march up front. No matter how pretty they sound, the flute players walk behind the horses.

Chicago Mourns . . . But Not Too Much

From I May Be Wrong But I Doubt It (1968)

The country mourned over the weekend. People looked into their hearts.

This is what it is like in Chicago when people go into mourning and look into their hearts.

It was hot Saturday night, so Nathan Ross and his sister walked to the lake. On the way back, they stopped to rest. Ross has deformed feet and he's fifty-eight, so he tires easily.

While they were sitting on a front porch on Lawrence Avenue, a man ran up to Ross. His sister says she doesn't know who he was or why he did it. The man shot Ross in the head and killed him. Then he ran away. Just like that.

Maurice Lee, twenty-six, took a walk, too. He was walking with his wife when a gang of kids jumped him. He struggled, and one of them shot him in the head. Mrs Lee went home a widow.

A man stood in front of a judge and was told he must never hit his son that hard again or next time he'd go to jail. The nine-year-old boy had stolen a can of shoe polish. His father taught him right from wrong by splitting his head so it took ten stitches to close and by whipping open cuts in his back.

LaMar McCoy figured that if Bonnie and Clyde and Jesse James could do it, he could do it. He got a gun and went looking for money, just like a folk hero.

He went in a restaurant and drew on a woman cashier. She pulled out a gun and shot him in the head. She was lucky. Sometimes the robber is shot. More often, the storekeeper is. But with millions of guns around, the battle never ends.

Thomas Daniel, a gas station attendant, was just cleaning his gun. The doctors say he will survive despite the large hole it made in his abdomen.

In the case of Guy Bibbs, somebody insulted somebody else in a tavern on Pulaski Road. The details will all come out later when an inquest is held into Bibbs's death.

Abder Rayyan wasn't bothering anybody. He was in his grocery store when two men came in and shot him in the head. The police figure they were mad at him because he's a Jordanian and it was their way of avenging Senator Kennedy's death. Just like in the better westerns they have probably seen.

And somebody broke into Mrs Sophie McElvenny's apartment on Lake Shore Drive and strangled her. She was a widow and a cripple.

John Hicks was quarreling with a friend over how to raise dogs. The friend finally settled the argument by stabbing Hicks in the heart.

Jim McPherson was stabbed eleven times, but he was lucky enough to survive. As far as anyone can tell, he was just walking near the lake on the Far North Side when half a dozen large young men felt like killing him.

At about the same hour, the County Morgue got the bodies of a man named Driver and a woman named Young. They didn't know each other and had nothing in common, except their respective mates had stabbed them to death during domestic quarrels. It is cheaper, in the long run, to hire divorce lawyers.

In a park in the suburb of Chicago Heights, some teenagers got angry about something.

Insults, the police say. Scott Cross died at the age of eighteen of a knife wound.

If she's lucky Margaret White will live. The police came by her street just in time to grab the man who was standing over her with a bloody brick in his hand.

By police standards, it was a fairly quiet weekend in Chicago.

There were only five murders with guns, and three or four with knives, plus a strangulation.

Of course, there were hundreds of other people put into hospitals by fists and feet, bottles and bats.

There were the assaults on the nervous systems. People on North Burling couldn't sleep much after some punks tossed homemade bombs on their porches, shattering dozens of windows. Nobody knows why. Just for fun, probably.

There were the wife beaters and children beaters, the street-corner brawls, the dozens of people who settled quarrels by slugging someone else.

We can't even begin to list all of those. I'm paid to write a daily column, not a daily book.

The Welcome Wagon Didn't Come
From *I May Be Wrong But I Doubt It* (1968)

Buying a house is a risky business. Just ask Alice and Charlie Roberts.

About five months ago they went house hunting because their neighborhood was getting too tough and they wanted a house of their own. Part of the American dream.

A real estate man took them to the Southwest Side, to a neighborhood of winding streets, big back yards, two-story brick houses, trees, grass.

The house was empty because the former owner had lost it to a VA foreclosure. It looked like a good buy, $19,500, six rooms.

The Roberts looked at the local school and saw white and Negro kids. That was OK because they didn't mind an integrated neighborhood.

They closed the deal and moved in. Now, five months later, Mrs Roberts wishes she had never seen the place.

There's nothing wrong with the house. It's the neighborhood that bothers Mrs Roberts.

What she and Charlie didn't know about the neighborhood was that it is not integrated; it is all white, but the Roberts are Negroes. The school fooled them. The Negro children they saw are bused in.

If they had known that, Mrs Roberts said, they would have gone straight back to Sixty-third and Blackstone, the Rangers and all.

That way she wouldn't be spending her days cooped up in a house with the drapes always closed and the children seldom outside; and her nights waiting for bricks to again crash through the windows or the garage to again burn.

She can laugh now, though, when she recalls her surprise on moving day. 'When we got here, there were already a couple of police cars outside and people all outside their houses. A lady was screaming for us to stay off her lawn. In December, can you imagine? I told Charlie, "Let's go back." But we had bought it so we moved in.'

A few nights later the first brick came through the picture window and a police car was stationed outside. Then a rock came through the back window. Later, during the blizzard, someone poured gasoline on the garage and tried to set it afire.

And all the while, there was the Sign, which read: NEXT HOUSE.

It is on the front porch of the house next door, directing prowlers with rocks or gasoline to the right house.

The sign was put up by John J. Bowden, a gaunt undertaker who works for the Egan Funeral Home, 3700 W. Sixty-third Street.

Bowden says he put up the sign because he feared someone might make a mistake a throw a brick through his window. 'It is self-protection,' said Bowden, who has ignored pleas of police and city officials to take it down.

The sign is a symbol of the neighborliness that has greeted the Roberts.

They were in the house one day when several men came in and said they wanted to buy the house, warning of the discomfort that goes with being a Negro in a white neighborhood. Then came phone calls, cold, unfriendly.

The man from the corner stomped over and warned Mrs Roberts that his kids had always played on their sidewalk and that nothing had better happen to them. She promised him that her children, ages four, five (twins), seven and nine, would not be violent to anyone.

Another man quit his bowling league, saying he was afraid to leave his wife at home with a Negro family in the neighborhood.

And there were the mean remarks to her children by other children in school and the glares of the neighbors when she went out.

Mrs Roberts says she has tried to be a good neighbor. Or at least an inoffensive one.

Deliverymen were confused by the Sign and delivered the Bowdens' Christmas packages to her. Mrs Roberts told them the sign was for people bearing rocks or bombs, not gifts.

She stopped shopping at the local supermarket and went to a distant Negro store because her presence offended the other customers. 'They stared at me like I was some sort of freak.'

She does not let her children out to play, so as not to terrify the neighbor who cherishes his sidewalk rights. They come straight home from school and stay inside or use the back yard. Maybe this summer they'll go out in front, she says, but she is not looking forward to it.

The Roberts even got rid of their dog because when it was in the yard it barked, which offended the neighbors. The kids cried, but their mutt went.

Mrs Roberts says she does not want to be treated like a close relative. When she collapsed from nervousness and was hospitalized for a few days, she didn't expect any get-well cards and didn't get any.

But she would like her kids to be able to use their sidewalk and people to stop staring at her and her house.

'I'd really like to leave, but Charlie says he thinks we'll stay, so that means we'll stay. It doesn't bother him as much because he works two jobs and isn't here that much.'

Then she laughed:

'Maybe I'll take the advice of a friend of mine. She said I should put up a sign just like the one next door except with the arrow pointing at them.'

•

JOHN LEONARD

John Leonard was born in 1939 in Washington, DC. He was educated at Harvard and the University of California at Berkeley, where he received a BA in 1962. His first experience of journalism was as an intern at the *National Review* (1959–60). He worked in radio and publicity before joining the *New York Times*, where he was first a book reviewer, then book review editor. From 1977 to 1983 he was the *Times*' cultural critic and wrote a column called 'Private Lives'. A collection of his columns was published as *Private Lives in the Imperial City* (1979), and he has published several other books.

To Dance or Not to Dance

From *Private Lives in the Imperial City* (1979)

My sidekick is transferring names and numbers from an old, broken-down telephone book to a new, squeaky-clean telephone book. I am not. I am on top of the orgone box, sucking cyanide from a peach pit, reading the Egyptian *Book of the Dead*. It is clear to me this weekend that the sixties are dead. Their license has expired. Back to back, Bella Abzug and Muhammad Ali went down to defeat. I am considering the ontological consequences of this fact. Perhaps we should remove the sixties from our telephone book.

According to my sidekick, we will not, for the time being, remove the name of a psychiatrist of her acquaintance from our telephone book. Why is this? Psychiatry, I explain, is a fifties category – brains washed while you wait, symbolic parricide, the whole syzygy. True man, I point out, has no condition but himself.

Besides, haven't we a viable relationship? That is, she relates to me and I relate to her and neither of us relates to John Travolta. That the sixties should have died giving birth to John Travolta is probably H. R. Haldeman's fault.

My sidekick is firm. She will not remove the name of the psychiatrist from the telephone book until she can bring herself to appear in public on a dance floor. Only then will she consider herself to be a healthy, functioning adult.

I grok that I must be careful. As Valéry observed, 'Every word is a bottomless pit.' There was, in the mountains last summer, an incident. One night in one of those joints that specialize in loud music and low-calorie beer, out on a toot with the extended family, my sidekick refused to go on to the floor to dance with me or anybody else. She does not believe herself to be an adequate dancer. She did not intend to embarrass herself in front of friends and strangers. And later she was furious at her own behavior.

This lapse from sociability didn't bother me at the time. For one thing, I dance like an oil rig myself, all elbows and pumping action. For another, Ginger Rogers never lit my Bunsen burner. (Cyd Charisse is a separate story.) For a third, if my sidekick were perfect, she wouldn't need me. My many imperfections would offend her. I thought we had agreed to regard each other as Navajo rugs: the occasional flaw was a signature, saying that we were made by hand and not by a machine.

Just because I wasn't bothered, though, doesn't mean the matter wasn't serious. I do not monopolize the available seriousness, a one-man Oberammergau. Other people's seriousness can be cabalistic, druidical, Republican, Spinks-like, dangerous. They, too, have cuds to chew. My sidekick has been brooding for months about a smudge on her self-esteem.

My job, of course, is to fix it up, make it right. I put the *Book of the Dead* in the refrigerator. I give her some coffee beans to play with. Listen, I say, I went, just like every other stumblebum, to all those dances in all those fetid high school gyms where, after practicing with our mothers, we were supposed in our stocking feet to do the hop. I waltzed in broken boxes. Wherever I stepped, I seemed to break the wing of a defenseless bird. Even the varsity letter sewn to my jacket was a lie; I was a track manager, a clerk of sweat.

And in college, there were mixers. Half boy, half dysthymic stork, I cluttered and sulked and went back to my cell to count, as if they were rosary beads, my pimples, and read *Tonio Kröger*, which, although I missed the main point, made it perfectly clear that the athlete who could dance would always get the girl and that the artist who lost her would after years and years and years still feel rotten about it; and as bitter time ran out on my club-footed youth I thought: Can you imagine Kafka or Nabokov doing the frug? Or Stephen Dedalus? Or Freud's wolfman? Or Handel's *Messiah*? Or Kant's categorical imperative? Or the Elgin marbles and the general theory of relativity?

My sidekick admits that she cannot imagine any of this.

And so – I go on, gathering confidence – I was, like you, a child of the fifties. But I cherished my reaction formations and my hostilities, my estrangement and *Gestimmtheit*. Repress, regress: I would indulge the syn of my own drome. Let them tickle and writhe and square a polka and quadrille for oil and *danse macabre*. I was autonomous, and therefore I could take myself seriously.

Then came the sixties. In a series of seedy discothèques, to which I went only in the company of Erving Goffman and other dramaturgists, I found that people were dancing without looking at one another. It was possible to make a fool of oneself and be unnoticed. Narcissism was liberating. Energy did not require talent; it was self-authenticating. To be sure, a partner or two complained that a key was needed to unlock my knees, that I lacked *soul* – but I have always believed, with Descartes, that my soul, if I have one, is in my pineal gland, not in my pelvis or anywhere else south of the tropic of my belly button. I could dance, while at the same time maintaining my autonomy, the *crux criticorum*.

The point – I tell my almost perfect sidekick – is that after the Norman O. Browning of the sixties, nobody cares anymore what any of us do on the dance floors of seedy discothèques or in the privacy of our own refrigerators. Everybody surfs, and nobody watches.

She has, with the coffee beans, fashioned a syzygy that looks like a noose. Listen, she says, her freckles flaring: Has it ever occurred to the Elgin marbles or the categorical imperative that I might want to be better at something than you are?

Well, no this hadn't occurred to me. Maybe I missed the point of the sixties after all.

•

JAMES J. KILPATRICK

James Jackson Kilpatrick was born in Oklahoma City in 1920 and became a copyboy at the *Oklahoma City Times* at the age of thirteen and edited his high school paper. He received a BJ from the University of Missouri in 1941. While at college he worked in summer vacations for the *City Times* and during termtime as a staff photographer for the public relations office at the women's school in Columbia, Missouri. After graduation he joined the *Richmond* [Virginia] *News Leader* as a reporter. In 1949 he was made its chief editorial writer and in 1951, at the age of thirty, its editor. Although he came out against racial integration at the time of the controversial 1954 Supreme Court decision in *Brown v. Board of Education*, he was subsequently a vigorous opponent of racial discrimination. In 1964 the Washington Star Syndicate tried to lure him to Washington as a columnist, but he preferred to accept an offer from *Newsday*, the Long Island paper, to write a column while continuing to edit his paper in Richmond. However, in 1966 he decided to go with the Washington Star Syndicate and move to Washington, DC. His later column, called 'A Conservative View', was handled by the Universal Press Syndicate and was bought by 450 papers. Kilpatrick was noted for a fluent prose style, rich in metaphor, and offered not only political commentary but also ruminations about Virginia wildlife and weather. In the late 1980s Kilpatrick and his wife moved to Charleston, South Carolina, and he now writes two weekly columns, 'Covering the Courts' and 'The Writer's Art'.

America's Heart Beats Steadily
Newsday, October 23, 1968

On the Road

The dateline for this copy is simply 'On the Road,' which is where most of us roving pundits will be until the election winds up on the night of Nov. 5. After weeks in Washington, the road is a wonderful place to be.

You discover, soon enough, that it is useless to try to report on what Nixon said in Kansas City, or Humphrey avowed in St Louis. The AP does it better and faster; and so far as substantive comments are concerned, the candidates say pretty much the same thing wherever they go. What counts in this point-to-point scramble is a fresh and humbling impression of this great big beautiful land.

Deskbound in Washington, with his nose snubbed tight against the passing hour, a man tends to forget what lies beyond the Potomac. He forgets the physical image – the vast reaches of prairie America, the flat land, the straight roads, the sculptured silos soaring above the fertile fields. He forgets the western sunrise, red-orange, the burning sky slashed with distant rain. Imprisoned in Megalopolis, he loses sight of the spacious vistas that remain.

Yet it is not so much the physical America that lifts the sagging spirit. It is the stimulation of new faces, different accents, unfamiliar newspapers, local concerns. The itinerant reporter finds his way to strange city rooms; he trades ritual gossip with fraternity brothers he had not known before. Mostly we talk of politics: How's Mike Monroney doing in Oklahoma? Will Tom Curtis make it to the Senate in Missouri? What's the pitch in downstate Illinois?

You stand at the edge of crowds, picking up conversations where you can. You listen to cabdrivers, barbers, room clerks, porters. You listen to speeches – Lord knows you listen to speeches – but what you are listening for, really, is the heartbeat of your country.

How beats the heart? Steadily, I think. Powerfully. This isn't a sick country. Oh, you could bring in a diagnosis based upon a few exhibitionist hippies; you could dwell on the miseries of ghetto life, inflation, crime rates. But such a diagnosis would err if it failed to give greater account to the healthy vitality one senses across the land.

The greatest discontent I have encountered in recent days provides its own odd commentary on our affluent society: It lies in the difficulty that employers experience in finding men and women to fill jobs that go begging.

I digress to remark the encouraging prospects for capable Negroes. Everywhere a man travels these days, he runs into Negroes in jobs that used to be closed to them, in department stores, banks, airline counters, business offices. I am familiar with statistics that show that Negroes, as a group, are falling behind in their struggle toward income parity with whites, but out on the road the statistics take on a doubtful look.

My intuitive stethoscope may be out of kilter, but I sense less of the much-publicized 'mood of rebellion' than I had expected. My guess is that Hubert Humphrey will close fast in this race, and that George Wallace's actual support in the polling booths, as distinguished from his vocal support in the noisy halls, will fall short of what the Alabamian is expecting. This election is not a shoo-in for Richard Nixon. There isn't that much brooding demand for a change.

You look at faces, you eavesdrop in restaurants, you marvel at the traffic that begins to flow in firefly streams by 6:30 in the mornings. And something is wrong if your heart doesn't swell with love for this country and for the free election process that absorbs its people this autumn.

Advice for Apoplectic Liberals
Newsday, November 14, 1980

Washington

My brothers and sisters of the liberal press are having apoplexy these days – apoplexy or deep depression, take your choice. Ten days have passed since Hallelujah Tuesday, and most of them are still in shock. But I too have been apoplectic in my own time and would offer reassurance. They will recover.

James Reston, Tom Wicker, Carl Rowan, the *Washington Post*, the *New York Times*, the *New Republic*, the *Nation* – all of them are down with the spavins and heaves. In the garden of liberalism they see only crabgrass and thistles. Civil liberties will vanish. Women will be relegated to the kitchen. Blacks, if permitted to speak at all, will be reduced to crying massuh, massuh, massuh. It is all too awful to behold.

Let me see, I seem to recall that conservatives have been through similar spasms in days gone by. After all, it has been twenty-six years since the Republicans gained control of the Senate, and twenty-six years of spasms add up to a quarter-century of acid stomach. Conservatives groaned with the election of John Kennedy in 1960. They wept at Barry Goldwater's defeat in 1964. We had our own conniption fits in 1976. Will the liberal commentators, tossing on their bed of pain, recall our misery in 1974? That was when the Democrats gained forty-nine seats in the House. We felt worse then than they possibly could feel now.

But as Congress came back to town for its lame-duck session, the Republican mood was positively euphoric. Howard Baker's feet finally touched ground at 3:42 last Friday afternoon. Bob Dole, who will take over the chairmanship of the Senate Finance Committee, was filled with charity: He offered to appoint the outgoing Russell Long as 'honorary chairman, without perquisites.'

At Senate Judiciary, Strom Thurmond was asked about staff changes as the Republicans succeed the Democrats. 'We will treat the Democrats,' purred the contented South Carolinian, 'with the same courtesy and kindness they always have extended to us.' With those gentle words, Democratic staffers fainted in windrows and had to be carried away. Judiciary's staff will have two Republican appointees for every one named by Democrats.

Disconsolate liberals have much to be disconsolate about. The incoming conservative tide is not likely to affect such bulwarks as Social Security or the Civil Rights Act. Neither the Department of Energy nor the Department of Education will be instantly swept away. But the beaches of liberalism will be strewn next year with legislative flotsam.

For example: That relic of the New Deal known as the Davis-Bacon Act will be repealed or greatly modified. This is the law that requires payment of prevailing union wages on any federally aided contract for public works, even though actual wage rates in a given area may be much lower. Even the General Accounting Office, not exactly a branch of the Chamber of Commerce, has urged its repeal.

Second example: Conservatives will do something about the minimum wage, which has operated with terrible cruelty upon teenagers, especially black teenagers. A two-tiered structure will give them some hope of gainful employment.

Such prospects may account for gloom on the liberal left, but they are seen as rays of sunshine by the conservative right. A new President! New committee chairmen! New staffs! A wholesale housecleaning in executive offices! To be sure, the Republicans' jubilation ought to be tempered. They have won a victory and lost their excuses. They must now take on the burden of forming a government and governing – but that is a burden that can cheerfully be borne.

So cry your eyes out, Scotty Reston! And take heart, my despondent brothers. As critics of the new regime, you guys will now have all the fun.

Thankful for Freedom . . .
Newsday, November 25, 1980

Scrabble, Va.

Ours is a small county here in the Blue Ridge Mountains – only 5,200 people, more or less – and nothing much ever happens. But this past Sunday was different. We had both a baptism and a funeral at our church, just an hour or so apart. Nobody could remember when that had happened before, and coming just before Thanksgiving the two events set off some reflections.

We buried Norman Sims, age sixty-three, and we christened Bethany Meade, age six months. In the Christian faith, as our parson remarked, it wasn't an end and a beginning, but rather a beginning and a beginning. Even so, it was a day for looking backward and forward.

Norm was born during the presidency of Woodrow Wilson, just as World War I was ending. You think about all the changes he observed during his lifetime, and most of them, of course, are obvious. Our country more than doubled in population. We progressed in a thousand technological ways. We landed men on the moon and sent a satellite to look at Saturn. We saw profound changes in the scope of government, and we experienced all kinds of social changes also.

One thing remained constant. It is, if you please, the one constant factor in the American equation: Freedom. Norm lived in a free country, and with God's grace, Bethany Meade will be equally blessed. Balanced against this intangible asset of freedom, nothing else amounts to much – the computers, the transistors, the jet planes and all the rest. At Thanksgiving, we ordinarily give thanks for the harvest and for the material benefits we enjoy. This year I am suddenly minded to say a word of thanks for something else.

We seldom think upon these things. Freedom is a quality we take for granted. When it seems to be infringed, we gripe. Otherwise it's just there. A few weeks ago we voted – half of us voted, anyhow – for a free government. We could read different opinions about that election in a free press. When a couple of hundred persons came to our little church on Sunday to say hail to Bethany at noon and farewell to Norm at one o'clock, we were exercising freedom of religion. On Monday we went freely back to work in a free marketplace, or we dwelt in the security of our homes and farms.

Elsewhere in the world, hundreds of millions of human beings have no awareness of a free society. Over most of the Asian continent, personal freedom – the kind of freedom we take for granted – is simply unknown. Born in the Soviet Union, Bethany becomes a ward of the state; here, a child of God.

Driving home from church the other afternoon, after the services had ended, we could think upon our inheritance. Here were the roadside stands, vending apples and cider and handmade baskets: We are free to work as we please. The road went winding up the mountains: We are free to travel. In the pastures of Rappahannock County, black cattle were feeding: We were free to own our land, to farm it, to build upon it. We drove by our local high school; we mailed some letters at the Sperryville post office; we caught a newscast on the radio. The hallmarks of a free society were everywhere stamped upon our hills.

Now, at Thanksgiving time, I would voice both thanks and prayers – thanks for what we have enjoyed all these years, prayers that our children preserve it. With any kind of luck, Bethany will live longer than Norm Sims lived, to 2050 or 2060 or thereabouts. It's hard to think in terms of such distant dates. She will see still further technological changes, more marvelous than those that have gone before. But it will take more than luck – it will take vigilance, and understanding, and hard work – to hold on to the ideas of personal liberty in a free society.

Politically speaking, we can ask with the psalmist, Whence cometh our help? It comes from traditions and values at least as old as Magna Carta. Norm Sims knew this. And Bethany Meade will know it, too.

•

JAMES CAMERON

(Mark) James (Walter) Cameron (1911–85) was born in Battersea, London, and was educated in France before becoming an office boy on *Red Star Weekly*, a title owned by the Dundee publishers, D. C. Thomson. In 1938 he joined the *Scottish Daily Express* and within a year had moved to the *Daily Express* in Fleet Street, where he worked as a sub-editor until the end of the Second World War (he had been pronounced unfit for military service because of a heart condition). Thereafter, he became a foreign correspondent, though he resigned from Beaverbrook Newspapers in 1950 when the *Evening Standard* attacked John Strachey, the Labour Minister. A brief spell with *Picture Post* came to an end when the magazine's proprietor, Sir Edward Hulton, refused to publish Cameron's dispatches from Korea (the magazine's editor, Tom Hopkinson, was sacked and Cameron resigned in support). He spent several years reporting foreign wars and other events for the *News Chronicle* and, following its closure, for television. From 1974 to 1984 he wrote a general interest column for the *Guardian* (producing roughly 400 columns during this period).

A Sudden Month of Fundays
Guardian, 10 May 1976

I got a bit of news last week that took weeks off my life. Four, to be exact. It came to pass that for some damnfool official purpose I had to have my birth date verified from the Registrar General's records, and the certificate shows that I was born on 17 July of a year that I need not specify except to say it was the year in which King George V was crowned and some joker pinched the 'Mona Lisa' from the Louvre.

That is all very well. Except for the fact that for my entire life up until this moment I have supposed that I was shown the light of day on 17 *June*. This trifling statistic, admittedly of no great importance to the chronology of man, is nevertheless recorded on every official paper, minute, chronicle and file that bureaucracy has accumulated about me over three score years, it is endorsed on every one of my sixteen passports, it is enshrined in mouldering stacks of *dokumenti* in dozens of countries, it is a date hallowed by the years and accepted without question by one and all – except, it now seems, the Registrar General. As a revelation it hardly ranks with Watergate, or Joanna Southcott's Box, and at my time of life I cannot see one month making much odds to my prospects of making the *Guinness Book of Records* as the oldest boy wonder in the world. It is none the less an odd feeling to be officially that much younger than one had for so long believed. There is a curious, meaningless mystery about it.

How, for example, could my parents have believed to the end of their days that they had had their firstborn in June, and not July? It is not the sort of mistake that one would expect a mother to make. It is true that I sprang a bit untimely from the womb, a trace premature, perhaps a little foolishly impatient to join the human race, but my parents would presumably have been aware of this. Unless of course my arrival was so inconspicuous that nobody even noticed for a month. This theory does not square with the family legend that I howled horribly and virtually without a break for the first year of my life, and that in fact we were required to move house at the instance of our exhausted neighbour. I still find it difficult to believe that my father and mother would have waited four solid weeks before trotting along to the East Battersea sub-district of the Wandsworth region of South London to get me on the index, and then to have falsified the entry. There could hardly have been the conventional reason for this, since they had already been married for three or four years, or so I have been reliably told. Could the above-mentioned coronation have had something to do with it? This happy event is recorded as having taken place just five days after my supposed début, that is to say on 22 June. Could it be that my parents were thrown into such transports of royalist fervour that I wholly slipped from their minds for a full month? It does not sound in the least like my old man. But if so, some infantile anti-monarchical resentment on my part could explain a lot.

Anyhow, that is the technical situation. The question is what to do about it now. To put the record straight I should have to correct about a million dossiers all over the world, arousing suspicion wherever I went, and doubtless getting myself blacklisted by all the barmy little bureaucracies that take these things seriously. It hardly seems worth it for a simple month. I think the answer is to keep the whole thing quiet, a harmless secret between me and the Registrar General. Certain personal adjustments will have to be made. I shall have to come to terms with being not a Gemini but a Cancer, which I could have done without. I shall have to wait another month for my old-age pension, but that will make little difference since I am told I'm not getting it anyway: to pay one's compulsory £2.41 a week for absolutely nothing is the cherished privilege of the self-employed.

Some questions about this June–July business still haunt me. Why didn't my astrologer in India spot the discrepancy? Why have I been kidded for so long? Could it be that I was some changeling, possibly of noble blood, the truth of whose birth had to be obfuscated in this way? Can my parents have both had a simultaneous attack of amnesia? Was I, in fact, *ever born at all*?

Meanwhile, what shall I do with my borrowed time? It is like the beginning of one of those Edwardian novels in which some stricken fellow steps out into Harley Street having been told that he has but a month to live. I have been told I have an *extra* month to live. So, anyone for tennis?

Unless, of course, the Registrar General has boobed. It was, after all, quite a time ago.

A Pain in the Neck
Guardian, 28 January 1985

There are two wholly exact and irreversible punctuation marks in everyone's life that can be exactly defined: the day you are born and the day you die. No one has any control whatever of the first, and only a troubled minority claim the right to decide on the second.

For some people, indeed many, there comes a third chapter heading, always uninvited. Using the punctuation mark analogy again, it could be described as the semi-colon situation, suggesting something tentative between the opening phrase and the full stop. Most writers use the device when they cannot make up their minds whether they have finished with one thought, or whether it needs a sort of PS, a compromise.

Clinging to this whimsy, I would suggest that this semi-colon arrives when the customer is told on absolute authority that he, or she, is ill of a condition once considered grave, but that in this enlightened world is unlikely to send him to kingdom come today or tomorrow, or next week, or even with luck this year, and which can be postponed by accepting some tiresome and painful disciplines. In a word – which is unfortunately not mine – it is the moment of truth.

At least for himself; he will of course continue to lie to everyone else.

We may stop being coy about it. A man learns quite suddenly, though after a fairly long suspicion, that he has an established malignancy in this or that part of him. The doctors have hedged and fiddled about with the definition, since the thing can be described in arcane technical terms that they, usually correctly, assume are unintelligible to the layman. Eventually, however, they are obliged to come clean, or cleanish, and tell the poor sod that this or that part of him has got cancer and has got to be fixed, or else. If the patient is lucky this has happened somewhere that can be chopped off and forgotten. But the chances are, since cancer is cruelly crafty, it usually takes over some awkward and inaccessible organ that the unlucky customer cannot readily do without. Both cases are fairly determinable: you chop it off or you leave it to the painkillers.

Sometimes, fortunately, there is a third option: the thing can grab you somewhere that is fairly accessible but nevertheless essential, requiring much complicated and expensive machinery and demanding a fair chunk out of the customer's daily life, and a lot of hitherto inexperienced pain.

Some people flatly refuse to accept it. This bloke didn't; he realized what was up from the start; indeed he provided the hospital with much of his own diagnosis. Privately, of course, he continued to kid himself, and others, insisting on calling his little trouble by the name of its zodiacal mate: I got a touch of Capricorn.

This provided the additional satisfaction of leaving the questioners uneasy or bothered: should we have known of this Capricorn business? Sure you should; if you had worked in the South Pacific you would have seen it all the time. Just call it, as this chap does, a tropical disease.

Remember Arthur Clough. 'Thou shalt not kill, but needst not strive, officiously to keep alive.' However, the customer cannot so strive, officiously or otherwise. The others must strive; he must submit.

Once the chips, as they say, are down, there is something quite soothing about this submission. From now on the buck is passed to the experts. If it doesn't work it is not his fault. Or – dare we say – not entirely. The medics talk a lot about the 'will to live'. This particular customer didn't have too much of that. In his trade he had seen a fair amount of death, mostly violent. The process itself was clearly unpleasant, but the end product seemed restful enough. Indeed, as the psychological depression (which he had been warned was to be a clinical part of this illness) deepened, the end product came to seem quite desirable. The electric rays and lasers and things did not do anything about that.

When alone at night this chap would frequently grizzle and weep to himself, but only because it hurt. It did not do the least good, but it got something off his chest. Not, unfortunately, off his throat.

Family and friends had to be considered. As this customer quickly realized, few of us are beloved enough to be missed for more than a couple of days or so. Meanwhile their reaction is either embarrassment or resentment. Initially everyone feels that the selfish bastard has cooked up the situation to attract consideration or create a drama. Some are even frank enough to ask one to hurry it up a bit.

Useless for him to say that this wasn't his idea, that the scenario came from total strangers whose concern was wholly clinical, and sometimes not especially even that. It will be blamed on him, as everything is blamed on him.

This patient's regard for the National Health Service had always been totally steadfast; it had saved his life before. He began to invent fantasies – which was higher on Mrs Thatcher's hit list: him or the NHS? He mused on this for hours in the radiotherapy machine; it passed the time well.

Regarding this situation objectively, forgetting personal pain and fear, this unimportant personal crisis had come at a strange time. This customer (and it is becoming affected and pedantic to disguise his identity now) has lived for almost two score years with the dread of my wife and children being caught up in the Holocaust that was made possible by my generation, in my generation, and probably for my generation, and for which I have always felt an absurd and wholly illogical responsibility, if only for the silly reason that I personally witnessed the explosion of atom bombs, and did nothing about it, and could do nothing except protest, tiresomely and uselessly, and finally boringly.

Paradoxically, and I suppose romantically, I hoped that I would be there again, with them, to share the real thing, hands in hands. I still refuse to surrender that, which means the obligation of getting well. I can truthfully think of no other reason.

Before the hospital business even began, the doctors, who had done this often before, said that an inescapable concomitant of this treatment was depression, a lowering of the spirits inexperienced before. I said: You should have known me years ago. They said: You don't know nothing yet, and they were right.

Anyhow, we shall see.

Before you slip, inconspicuously and guiltily, out of the room, let me tell you about my operation . . .

•

EUGENE J. McCARTHY

Eugene Joseph McCarthy was born in 1916 in Watkins, Minnesota. He was educated at St John's University, where he received his BA in 1935, and at the University of Minnesota, where he received his MA in 1941. He taught at various high schools and at St John's, before serving as a civilian code breaker for US Military Intelligence (1943–4). From 1949 to 1958 he represented Minnesota in the US House of Representatives, and from 1958 to 1970 he was a US senator. In 1968 he was the Democratic candidate for President and he ran again in 1970, but as an independent. He was Adlai Stevenson Professor of Political Science at the New School for Social Research (1973–4) and has subsequently concentrated on writing books. His column, one of the most elegant by a politician, started in the *Washington Star* in 1977 and has been syndicated ever since.

Why the Best Isn't Good Enough
Washington Star, January 1, 1978

The search is on for the most wanted man. The search is not being conducted by the FBI, but for the FBI – to find its new director. The procedure reportedly followed by the Administration is to have the Attorney General recommend ten possible appointees. From among the ten, the President, after due consideration and reflection, will make his choice.

This method is an application of recent FBI practises. Many years ago, the bureau used to name someone as the most wanted man – and possibly someone else as the second most wanted man. Whether the first was wanted more or wanted first, and the other less or later, was never clear from the language. More recently, for reasons not given, the most wanted are thrown into a group, usually designated as the ten most wanted. The conclusion is that these ten are wanted, either collectively or individually, more than any other persons. Catching any one of them is a mark of special credit, for each one must be most wanted.

We can safely anticipate that the President's choice of a new FBI director will be declared superlative – the best of the ten. It will be difficult to make him an absolute best, because we already have been told, and more or less have accepted, that Judge Frank Johnson, who had to turn down an appointment to head the bureau because of ill health, was the best man for the job. So what we will be getting this time is the best of the ten second-best.

In recent administrations, it has become the general practise to appoint none but the best. The old saying that 'a good man is hard to find' seems to be outmoded. Beginning with Dwight Eisenhower, Presidents have accepted only the superlative 'best,' not being content even with appointing better persons than those who had served in previous Administrations. If Thomas Marshall (Vice-President in Woodrow Wilson's Administration) were in politics today, he would not dare to say that what America needs is a good five-cent cigar. He would be forced to say that what America needs is 'the best' five-cent cigar.

In this modern spirit, President Carter wrote of his approach to the presidency in a book called *Why Not the Best?* Consistent with that theme, the President has labeled nearly every one of his choices 'the best' – the best Vice-President, the best director of OMB, Judge Johnson the best head of the FBI, and so forth.

One of President Nixon's favorite words was 'greatest.' President Johnson spoke modestly of establishing 'The Great Society.' The move from great to greatest is easy. Members of the Kennedy Administration, when referred to as 'the best and the brightest,' accepted the adjectives with modesty.

In the same spirit, when special committees are set up today, whether by government or by business, they are called blue-ribbon committees. Blue, of course, is the color of the ribbon given to winners of first place in horse shows. It would be a pleasant relief, and would be more honest, to have a President occasionally designate a committee as a red-ribbon committee (second place) or a yellow-ribbon committee (third place) or a green-ribbon committee (fourth place) or a brown-ribbon committee (just for coming).

I do not recall President Truman's ever having appointed a search committee, certainly not a blue-ribbon committee. There was never a great talent search during his Administration, with the President waiting anxiously for the select list to be submitted to him, and with the country standing by like the faithful waiting for white smoke from the Vatican announcing that a new pope had been chosen.

President Truman kept his judgements and credits well within the limits of the positive degree. He seldom ventured into the comparative, and never into the superlative. He did make distinctions in his judgement of persons, but the positive was all that he needed. 'Good' was the commanding adjective. Some persons he described as simply good – a good man or a good woman. Some he described as 'damn good.' (That was high praise.) On the other hand, he thought that some persons were 'no good' and that others were 'no damn good.' It was good language, well spoken.

•

PEREGRINE WORSTHORNE

Peregrine Gerard Worsthorne was born in London in 1923. His father was a Belgian, Colonel Koch de Gooreynd. His parents divorced and his mother subsequently married Sir Montagu Norman, the Governor of the Bank of England, and eventually became Baroness Norman. Worsthorne (his father had changed his surname by deed poll in 1922) was educated at Stowe;

at Peterhouse, Cambridge; and at Magdalen College, Oxford. During the Second World War he served in the army and in 1946 he joined the *Glasgow Herald* as a sub-editor. He moved to *The Times* in 1948 and stayed there until 1953 when he joined the *Daily Telegraph*. When the *Sunday Telegraph* was launched in 1961 he was made its deputy editor. He stayed with the paper and eventually became its editor (1986–9). He started his column for the paper back in the 1960s and throughout most of its history it took the form of an elegant and paradoxical political commentary. In later years it became more personal in its concerns and perhaps less followed than it had been before. However, in early 1997 the column was peremptorily dropped by the *Sunday Telegraph*'s editor, Dominic Lawson. Since then Worsthorne has been writing columns for the *Daily Telegraph* and the *Spectator*, once again as political commentary, which have all the sparkle and cogency of his earlier work. Some of his columns were collected in *Peregrinations* (1980) and he has also published a highly entertaining autobiography, *Tricks of Memory* (1993). He was knighted in 1991.

Why Eurosceptics Should Be at Least as Worried about Westminster's Sleaze as New Labour's Voters

Spectator, 5 April 1997

The disadvantage of bandwagons is that they attract the wrong kind of passenger. This has been the fate of the Conservative Party in recent years. Because it has for so long been seen as unstoppable and a safe bet to pass the winning post first time and time again, every dubious political careerist in the land was eager to climb on board, with results that are likely to become ever more apparent with each new edition of the *Sun*. How could it be otherwise? For those attracted to politics largely by the prospect of glittering prizes are bound to hanker more to be on the winning side than on the right side, particularly at times like these when even idealists can be forgiven for finding it difficult to tell one from t'other.

Initially, of course, Thatcherite Conservatism was indeed a great cause as well as a winning one, no less attractive to the idealist than to the careerist. But as time went on and what had begun as a moral crusade and an adventurous exercise in intellectual pioneering settled down into becoming little more than a vehicle for an easy ride, the supply of careerists increased and then, on the principle that birds of a feather flock together, increased still further, while the supply of idealists, more and more put off by the company they found themselves keeping, first dwindled and then disappeared.

Of course, none of this necessarily results in sleaze. Not all careerists are sleazy, any more than all idealists are unbribable. But it is surely fair to say that a party in power for a very long time, which is pretty well bound over the years to have accumulated more than its fair share of careerists, is likely to be more prone to sleaze than a party out of power for years, which is pretty well certain to have accumulated more than its fair share of idealists. In short, if it is true that rats proper are more prone to leave ships which are sinking than those which are riding high, so are their human variety more prone to joining political bandwagons which are going at full throttle than those which are slowing down or even grinding to a halt.

In time, of course, if the Labour Party wins not only this election but the one after and the one after that, a surfeit of careerists more interested in what they can get out of politics than what they can put into them will become its problem to the same degree that it is now the Conservatives'. But that is not likely to happen at once. At least for one parliamentary term a sleaze-mongering media is likely to find slender pickings. For however much it may suit New Labour's opponents to paint the Blairites as being themselves from the word go careerists of the worst possible kind, prepared to jettison all their principles to be on the winning side, this charge strikes me as grotesquely unfair. At the time they cast in their lot with Labour, that party looked more like a hearse than a bandwagon. That they did not join the Labour Party out of any idealistic faith in Socialism, so much has now become obvious. But that is not at all the same thing as having joined it opportunistically only to further their careers.

A more likely parallel, it seems to me, would be with the generation of young men who came to prominence in the Tory Party after Labour's landslide victory in 1945 – the Macleods, Heaths, Maudlings and even Enoch Powell. With the exception of the last, not one joined because he believed in true-blue Toryism, i.e. in what the pre-war party had stood for since time immemorial. They recognized, as did their patron, R. A. Butler, that true-blue, semi-feudal Toryism was unelectable, that the Conservative Party's only hope was to adapt to the post-war *zeitgeist*, i.e. to aspects of Socialism. Hence the adoption of the Middle Way – Harold Macmillan's phrase – which involved accepting the welfare state, planning, cosseting trade unions and anti-colonialism.

To old-guard Tories like the late Lord Salisbury, this seemed a betrayal of principles. But to those young men themselves, the Butlerites, it seemed like a rebirth of principle – giving new life to the old Tory ideals of paternalism and *noblesse oblige*. Opportunistic yes, but not cynical. Building up a new Middle Way Conservative bandwagon, which is what the Butlerites succeeded in doing, is quite different from joining one. Sleaze starts developing not when a party wants power very much, but when it starts taking it for granted. Eventually, in the last years of Macmillan, that did happen to the Middle Way Conservatives, as it has now happened to the far right Conservatives and in time, as I say, may happen no less fatally to the Blairites. But it has not happened yet.

This is Labour's signal advantage and, in these non-ideological times, when no profound issue divides the parties, arguably its most decisive one. For in policy terms it is unlikely to matter vitally who wins the election. Neither party is promising to do anything which the other could not live with. Equally difficult to assess is the respective quality of the two front-bench ministerial teams. No, there is only one area where the difference between the parties seems to me to stand out like a very sore thumb, and that is in their respective capacities to make the air around Westminster smell a bit sweeter.

Eurosceptics should be the first to realize why this is so vitally important. It is vitally important because if the British people are to be persuaded, in the course of the next Parliament, to fight to the last ditch to defend rule from Westminster, there must be something there worth defending, something there which inspires admiration and devotion. As it is, the British people are increasingly distancing themselves from Westminster, not so much in disgust as in indifference. Just when Parliament needs to show itself at its best, it is showing itself at its worst. Of course the sleaze scandals are petty and paltry, more demeaning than shocking, but that only deepens the indifference.

An Augean stables is at least worth cleansing. Faced by nothing worse than a bad smell, people can't be bothered. They just pass by, holding their noses.

To believe, as I do, that New Labour might sweeten the atmosphere at Westminster is not to credit them with superhuman rectitude. Any party halfway healthy could do the same. As I say, the sleaze is petty and paltry, and what condemns the Tory Party is not so much the prevalence of it in its ranks as the incapacity of those in charge to do anything about it. Yet something must be done about it, if Westminster is to be seen as worth defending. Making the British hate Brussels, that the Tories can be relied upon to do, but New Labour is the more likely to restore their faith in Westminster.

•

MURRAY KEMPTON

James Murray Kempton (1918–97) was born in Baltimore, Maryland. He majored in history and science at Johns Hopkins University, where he obtained a BA in 1939. He worked as a welfare investigator for a year, then became organizer for both the Non-Communist American Youth Conference in New York and the International Ladies Garment Workers. In 1941 he served as publicity director for the American Labor Party and the following year became a labour reporter for the *New York Post*. He spent two years during the Second World War covering the Pacific theatre, and a year (1946–7) reporting for the *Wilmington Star*, in North Carolina, before returning to the *Post* as assistant to its resident labour columnist. In 1949 he became labour columnist, but over the next decade his scope widened to include political commentary and reportage (especially of the civil rights movement in the South) and sports. This column continued until 1963, when he moved to the *New Republic* for eighteen months, and thereafter it appeared in the *New York World-Telegram and Sun*, until its closure in 1966. Another stint on the *Post*, until 1969, was followed by a period at the *New York Review of Books*. In 1981 he began a new column for *Newsday*, and in 1985 received a Pulitzer Prize for commentary. An elegant writer of immense range and knowledge, his gift was in being able to produce spare prose that was accessible to a variety of readerships.

He Went All the Way
New York Post, September 22, 1958

Mose Wright, making a formation no white man in his county really believed he would dare to make, stood on his tiptoes to the full limit of his sixty-four years and his five feet three inches yesterday, pointed his black, workworn finger straight at the huge and stormy head of J. W. Milam and swore that this was the man who dragged fourteen-year-old Emmett Louis Till out of his cottonfield cabin the night the boy was murdered.

'There he is,' said Mose Wright. He was a black pigmy standing up to a white ox. J. W. Milam leaned forward, crooking a cigarette in a hand that seemed as large as Mose Wright's whole chest, and his eyes were coals of hatred.

Mose Wright took all their blast straight in his face, and then, for good measure, turned and pointed that still unshaking finger at Roy Bryant, the man he says joined

Milam on the night-ride to seize young Till for the crime of whistling suggestively at Bryant's wife in a store three miles away and three nights before.

'And there's Mr Bryant,' said Mose Wright and sat down hard against the chair-back with a lurch which told better than anything else the cost in strength to him of the thing he had done. He was a field Negro who had dared try to send two white men to the gas chamber for murdering a Negro.

He sat in a court where District Attorney Gerald Chatham, who is on his side, steadily addressed him as Uncle Mose and conversed with him in a kind of pidgin cotton-picker's dialect, saying 'axed' for 'asked' as Mose Wright did and talking about the 'undertaker man.'

Once Chatham called him 'Old Man Mose,' but this was the kindly, contemptuous tolerance of the genteel; after twenty-one minutes of this, Mose Wright was turned over to Defense Counsel Sidney Carlton and now the manner was that of an overseer with a field hand.

Sidney Carlton roared at Mose Wright as though he were the defendant, and every time Carlton raised his voice like the lash of a whip, J. W. Milam would permit himself a cold smile.

And then Mose Wright did the bravest thing a Delta Negro can do; he stopped saying 'sir.' Every time Carlton came back to the attack, Mose Wright pushed himself back against his chair and said, 'That's right,' and the absence of the 'sir' was almost like a spit in the eye.

When he had come to the end of the hardest half-hour in the hardest life possible for a human being in these United States, Mose Wright's story was shaken; yet he still clutched its foundations. Against Carlton's voice and Milam's eyes and the incredulity of an all-white jury, he sat alone and refused to bow.

If it had not been for him, we would not have had this trial. It will be a miracle if he wins his case; yet it is a kind of miracle that, all on account of Mose Wright, the State of Mississippi is earnestly striving here in this courtroom to convict two white men for murdering a Negro boy so obscure that they do not appear to have even known his name.

He testified yesterday that, as Milam left his house with Emmett Till on the night of August 28, he asked Mose Wright whether he knew anyone in the raiding party. 'No, sir, I said I don't know nobody.'

Then Milam asked him how old he was, and Mose Wright said sixty-four and Milam said, 'If you knew any of us, you won't live to be sixty-five.'

And, after the darkened car drove off, with his great-nephew, Mose Wright drove his hysterical wife over to Sumner and put her on the train to Chicago, from which she has written him every day since to cut and run and get out of town. The next day, all by himself, Mose Wright drove into nearby Greenwood and told his story in the sheriff's office.

It was a pathetic errand; it seems a sort of marvel that anything was done at all. Sheriff George Smith drove out to Money around 2 p.m. that afternoon and found Roy Bryant sleeping behind his store. They were good friends and they talked as friends about this little boy whose name Smith himself had not bothered to find out.

Smith reported that Roy had said that he had gone down the road and taken the little boy out of 'Preacher's' cabin, and brought him back to the store and, when his wife said it wasn't the right boy, told him to go home.

Sheriff Smith didn't even take Bryant's statement down. When he testified to it yesterday, the defense interposed the straight-faced objection that this was after all the conversation of two friends and that the state shouldn't embarrass the sheriff by making him repeat it in court. Yet, just the same, Sheriff Smith arrested Roy Bryant for kidnaping that night.

When the body supposed to be Emmett Till's was found in the river, a deputy sheriff drove Mose Wright up to identify it. There was no inquest. Night before last, the prosecution fished up a picture of the body which had been in the Greenwood police files since the night it was brought in, but there was no sign the sheriff knew anything about it, and its discovery was announced as a coup for the state. But, with that apathy and incompetence, Mose Wright almost alone has brought the kidnapers of his nephew to trial.

The country in which he toiled and which he is now resigned to leaving will never be the same for what he has done. Today the state will put on the stand three other field Negroes to tell how they saw Milam and Bryant near the murder scene. They came in scared; one disappeared while the sheriff's deputies were looking for him. They, like Mose Wright, are reluctant heroes; unlike him, they have to be dragged to the test.

They will be belted and flayed as he was yesterday, but they will walk out with the memory of having been human beings for just a little while. Whatever the result, there is a kind of majesty in the spectacle of the State of Mississippi honestly trying to convict two white men on the word of four Negroes.

And we owe that sight to Mose Wright, who was condemned to bow all his life, and had enough left to raise his head and look the enemy in those terrible eyes when he was sixty-four.

The Fruit of Islam
New York World-Telegram, February 23, 1965

And now that Malcolm X is dead, it is odd how sad some of us who knew him find ourselves and how pitiful, for all his dignity, he seems to have been all through our memory.

We knew him first and best as the preacher of the eternal separation of black and white; there is a theory that near the end he was struggling unevenly toward some idea of community. But I do not think he changed much with time; he lived with America for thirty-nine years and, whether from love or hate, I should doubt he really knew until the day he died.

Yet he was always a man of Harlem; he never entered white New York, except as ambassador from an independent, hostile nation. Never, that is, except the last night of his life, when he came to us as a refugee. He spent Saturday night at the New York Hilton because he did not feel safe in Harlem. That night he was a fugitive from black men; his dignity must have commended him to go back among them Sunday and now he is dead.

Until the end, Malcolm X preached that Negroes must arm themselves against us, the enemy. And now he has been assassinated by armed Negroes at a meeting from which white people were barred.

It was his conviction that his father had been murdered by white men and thrown under a streetcar. Now his widow will have someday to explain to her youngest daughter Lomumbah that her father was shot down by Negroes.

The journalists always suspected that he was their creation, and in a way he was. He had both an exotic presence and considerable native wit; he came to New York at a time when he perfectly suited the demands of electronic journalism. There have been very few public men whose message fit so snug and yet so lively into a two-minute segment of a news broadcast.

That gift would have made him notorious under any circumstances; but he had something else. I do not know a Negro so completely adjusted that some part of him did not respond to what Malcolm X was saying, just as I do not know a Negro so entirely alienated that some part of him does not respond to what Martin Luther King, Jr, is saying. Just by his insistence, Malcolm X created himself a nation to which every Negro owed a small allegiance. As Jimmy Hicks said yesterday, this *was* an assassination, for Mr Malcolm was a head of state.

And yet he had a strange, trusting side. The longest I had ever talked to him was in Miami the night before the Cassius Clay—Sonny Liston fight where Mr Malcolm had gone as Clay's spiritual prop. I remember his saying that, if you found a good white man, he was usually a Southerner, and how innocent that notion seemed to me as a hybrid Southerner. I tried to disabuse him and failed, and then the subject turned to Cassius and I said I hoped he wouldn't be immobilized by fear of Liston.

'To be a Muslim,' Malcolm X replied, 'is to know no fear.'

And there he seemed to me correct, insofar as any white man can judge whether a Negro is correct about other Negroes; there was a quietness, a containment and a dignity about the young men around him that made you believe that Mr Malcolm and they had been given a community and rescued from fear.

He lost that community when he was expelled from the Nation of Islam and it must have taken an immense amount of character to carry on as well as he did. Now what can we believe but that he was killed by young men very like the ones who used to surround him, and whom he had helped liberate from fear?

I do not think that, until now, I have ever really known what a terrible thing a ghetto is.

Ralph Ginzburg: Panderer
New York World-Telegram, March 16, 1966

With all sympathy to Ralph Ginzburg, who will go to prison for five years as a pornographer, it should be said of him, almost with admiration, that he has a far broader and more sensitive instinct for profiting by appeal to the baser passions than the Supreme Court imagines. He is really a dangerous, though not indictable, man.

Eighteen months or so ago, there came to my office a postcard which, if memory serves, bore no more than a sentence saying approximately:

> If you have ever had the experience of distortion by *Time* magazine, please write and tell us about it at the address below.

The address below was *Fact*, followed by a post office box address.

Now, the man who conceived this postcard could have sent me a page from *Fanny Hill* day after day and never have come close to the depths beyond decent expression that he had plumbed within me by the mere mention of *Time* magazine. My hatred of *Time* is my one unbridled lust. If the pornographic impulse is an obsession with the contemplation of a debased object, then I have a dirty mind about *Time*.

For example, I could not imagine myself participating in an obscene telephone call except in response to a polite inquiry from a gently nurtured young lady identifying herself as a *Time* researcher. Young men from *Time* are the only ones I meet on a story whom I automatically identify as enemies rather than as colleagues. As a slaughterhouse of moral integrity, *Time* is the Verdun of the young. Its agents greet you, be you Gus Hall or Robert Shelton, with the announcement that they are on your side against their bosses. This, for some reason, is supposed to make you believe in their honesty.

I remember hearing a Kluxer in Little Rock call a young man from *Time* a liar because he had gotten an interview on the plea that the North needed to know the Klan's side of the story and then the Kluxer had read the result. I do know what special places in hell are reserved for editors who will encourage innocent youth thus to place itself at a moral disadvantage to a member of the Ku Klux Klan.

But let me cease this public surrender to thoughts of which I am ashamed by saying that, if I were conscripted to execute the Central Committee of the Chinese Communist Party, I would trust myself to do the job with solemnity and sorrow, yet I would machine-gun the entire board of editors of *Time* in a fit of laughter. That is the only orgy with any appeal to my fantasies.

So this postcard had no need to identify itself as to source; it acted upon me as a note from a sailor would have upon Hart Crane in a bar near the Navy Yard. Say *Time* to me and tell me to answer with a letter in a tree in Lafayette Park and I would run slavering through a hundred vice cops to get there. Still I forgot to answer, being as indolent in this, my last sex mania, as I am in all things.

Then the months went by and I discovered that Ralph Ginzburg, with his special genius, had found my perversion. He had started *Fact* and had decided to lead its first issue with some comments on *Time*.

Ginzburg's first cover was emblazoned with something like: 'What *Time* did to me' and a list of victims detailing their experience. The authors included James Gould Cozzens, Bertrand Russell, David Merrick, P. G. Wodehouse, Dwight MacDonald, Mary McCarthy, John Osborne, Eric Bentley, Tallulah Bankhead, Senator John McClellan, Conrad Aiken and Igor Stravinsky.

Now this is an extraordinary author's list for a new magazine. It is possible that some of these people would not write their children unless a stamped self-addressed envelope were sent in advance; being professionals, they work only for pay. Yet Ginzburg got them all for free and writing from the inmost reaches of the heart, just for a postcard offering them a shot at *Time*. Now there's a man who knows how to exploit perversions.

●

JOHN JUNOR

Sir John Junor (1919–97) was born in Blake Isle, Ross and Cromarty, and educated at Glasgow University, where he received an MA in English. During the Second World War he was a lieutenant in the Royal Navy Volunteer Reserve. He stood unsuccessfully as a Liberal parliamentary candidate in 1945, 1948 and 1951. He was assistant editor of the *Daily Express* from 1951 to 1953, then deputy editor of the *Evening Standard* (1953–4), but he came into his own as editor of the *Sunday Express*, a post which he held from 1954 to 1986. He was knighted in 1980. From 1973 to 1989 he was that paper's principal editorial page columnist and developed a uniquely cheeky style which made it difficult to tell when he was being genuinely indignant from when he was being simply mischievous. From 1990 until his death he wrote a similar column for the *Mail on Sunday*. A selection of his columns, *The Best of JJ*, was published in 1981, but the hardback had to be withdrawn after a review by fellow columnist Alan Watkins inadvertently provoked a libel action. Watkins cited a paragraph as an example of Junor's cunning use of words so as to avoid being sued for libel. The victim, who had not seen the original piece, did, however, see the review and Junor duly received a writ. He also wrote an entertaining autobiography, *Listening for a Midnight Tram* (1990).

Excerpts from *The Best of JJ* (1981)
28 August 1977

Nice isn't it, to come back from holiday and find a quarrel with an old friend settled?

On 16 May last year I published in this column an item which caused the Rt Hon. Sir James Harold Wilson to blow a gasket.

In it I wondered aloud why Sir Harold seemed so obsessed with the idea that the scandal then surrounding Mr Jeremy Thorpe might be the work of South African agents.

By hot hand came a letter from Sir Harold's solicitors, describing the item as 'grossly defamatory of our client' and demanding an unreserved apology and statement in open court; the removal of the libel from all back numbers of the *Sunday Express* in our possession and indeed from all back numbers in public libraries.

I am happy to report that the matter between Sir Harold and myself has now been settled.

Has there been a statement in open court? No. Has the item been removed from all back numbers? No.

Instead, Sir Harold has taken out of court a sum of money in full settlement for the defamation of his good name.

How much was his good name worth? £105.

Isn't it lucky I didn't libel Marcia too? It might have cost another fiver.

2 October 1977

I do not even know his name. He is a man in a cloth cap I sometimes stand next to in a bus queue.

But that morning he was clearly excited, and wanted to talk. He began telling me about the second-hand caravan he had bought; how he had paid £300 for it; how he had parked it in his garden; how he was going to use it to take his wife and thirteen-year-old daughter on holiday.

His daughter would love that, he said. She had been born with a heart condition. She had spent most of her little life in and out of hospital. Even now she could only sleep propped up on pillows.

That was months ago. Last week I met him again. This time I initiated the conversation. How was the caravan? The caravan, he explained, did not matter any more. His daughter, his only child, had died just before they were due to go on holiday.

There are times when one thanks God for one's own good luck. There are also times when one is humbled beyond measure by the courage with which other people face up to personal and total disaster.

22 October 1978

When twenty-one-year-old Rhodesian Mr John Gardner looks into a mirror the reflection he sees is as black as the ten of clubs. Politically he is a supporter of Mr Joshua Nkomo.

So on both counts he is, at least in the eyes of Dr Owen, flawless. Isn't it a hoot then that had it not been for the personal panic-stricken intervention of the Minister, Mrs Judith Hart, Mr Gardner would have been deprived of the place provided for him at Keele University by the British taxpayer under the Overseas Development Ministry's Rhodesian African Training Programme?

Not because he is black. But because he is not black enough.

For Mr Gardner's paternal grandfather was Scottish. And therefore he is classified not as black but as coloured.

And Rhodesian coloureds, like Rhodesian Asians, like Rhodesian whites, are not eligible for any help.

Don't you call that racial discrimination?

And even if you don't, isn't it almost beyond belief that a black man may be deprived of help just because one-quarter of his blood may have started life behind a pair of visiting trews from Auchtermuchty?

2 November 1980

As I watched Mr Michael Foot on TV the other night I remembered the first time I saw that stick on which he leaned.

It was 1964. I had gone to visit Lord Beaverbrook in the South of France. Mr Foot, then painfully recovering from the car crash which caused his present limp, was already there as a house guest.

It was clear that Beaverbrook was dying. And that the end could come suddenly. I wanted an obituary of him ready to be published in the *Sunday Express*. Michael Foot, as a long-time associate of Beaverbrook, was clearly the best man to do it.

He and I walked along the cliff edge at Cap d'Ail. I asked him if he was prepared to take on the task. I promised him that if he did so no one would know about it until Lord Beaverbrook died. I offered him a considerable amount of money.

I still remember how Michael Foot ground the ferrule of his walking stick into the turf of the cliff top. Then he said: 'No, I cannot, I love that old man and I would not want to write anything which might mean I wished to hasten his death.'

I do not know many good things about Michael Foot. But at least a chap cannot be all bad who is loyal to the man who has been his boss.

1 March 1981

I can understand the jealous anger of Mrs Jean Harris, the fifty-seven-year-old upper-class headmistress who murdered her sixty-nine-year-old lover, Dr Herman Tarnower.

But it is the dead man, whose last words, as she entered his bedroom and began to blaze away with her gun, were: 'Good God Jean, don't you realize it's the middle of the night?', who intrigues me.

He was the author of an internationally famous diet known as the Scarsdale diet and which consists largely of grapefruit and carrots.

He was also during the period of his affair with Mrs Harris having it off with thirty-five other women – some not much more than half her age.

Thirty-five women at the age of sixty-nine? Some of them still in their twenties?

And on grapefruit and carrots?

Isn't it a mercy for what was left of the flower of American maidenhood that no one ever introduced the old lecher to haggis and whisky?

29 March 1981

The son of Jewish immigrants, Manny Shinwell, was brought up in poverty in the East End of London at a time when the destitute had to scavenge the dustbins for food.

As a boy if he had a farthing to spend he felt rich beyond measure. He had almost no schooling of any kind. At the age of eight, when poverty temporarily prevented his parents maintaining a home together, he was separated from his mother and dispatched by rail with a label round his neck to live with his father wherever his father could find work. He became an ardent Socialist and served a prison sentence for his views.

Last week, Manny, now aged ninety-six, attended a press party to launch his new book *Lead With The Left* – a warm compassionate story which I urge you to buy.

One man who took the trouble to attend was former Tory Prime Minister Lord Home. That fact in itself is an indication of the esteem in which Manny is held. And rightly.

Even at his advanced age, he would still punch in the nose anyone who spoke ill of Britain.

Isn't it extraordinary that he who started with so little should have been so true, while others who started with so much should have so consistently betrayed us?

7 June 1981

Yet another toddler has been savaged to death by Alsatians.

The dogs, of course, have been put down. They always are. When it is too late to bring the child back to life.

Wouldn't it be a better idea to put down the people who persist in keeping such dogs?

14 June 1981

The apology given by British Caledonian Airways to the anonymous vicar who, when his DC-10 was delayed by a mechanical fault, was given overnight accommodation in a Hong Kong brothel, could not be more complete or more contrite.

They explain that the incident would never have happened had the fault not coincided with a Chinese festival which meant that all the airline's normal hotels were full.

Just one thing puzzles me.

None of the lassies at the reception desk so much as flickered a slit-eye at the vicar.

It is true that his bed was circular in shape. But that might have been a quirk of modern fashion.

It is also true that the walls were lined with mirrors. But might not that have been to help him with his shaving?

How then, since presumably he had no previous experience, did he know he was in a brothel?

Is it just possible that, having placed his long-johns over a chair and his dentures in a tooth mug, the reverend gentleman made the fundamental mistake of ringing room service for a hot water bottle.

21 June 1981

Last Sunday afternoon I saw a brown and white spaniel jump into the sea from a jetty at Cowes on the Isle of Wight.

At first I thought it was simply trying to retrieve a stick or a ball. But it quickly became evident that the dog had another purpose. It struck out in the direction of the mainland.

A cross-Solent ferry was entering Cowes. It missed the dog by feet. The dog still kept swimming.

I slipped my mooring and went in pursuit. A dinghy tried in vain to catch the dog and a Royal Yacht Squadron launch came out from the shore.

The dog was by that time almost all in. When it was brought ashore, it staggered for about ten minutes exhausted and full of water.

Why should it have acted as it did? It transpired that the spaniel owner's main home was in Shoreham, that he was about to go abroad on holiday and the dog was to be placed in kennels on the Isle of Wight.

Did the spaniel decide that he did not like the idea of kennels? Was he making a frantic effort to reach his own home?

For Shoreham some forty-six miles away was exactly where he was pointing.

I do not know.

But I sometimes think that we humans, who regard ourselves as masters of the world, are not alone among God's creatures in having feelings.

•

WILLIAM SAFIRE

William L. Safire was born in New York City in 1929. He attended Syracuse University, but was unable to complete his degree owing to insufficient funds. He became a gofer for Tex McCrary, who wrote a column called 'New York Close-Up' for the *New York Herald Tribune*. After a couple of years in Europe and the Middle East working for radio and television, Safire served in the US Army. In the mid-fifties he again worked with McCrary, producing his TV show and joining his public relations firm. In 1960 he set up his own PR company and started working for the Republican Party. He was a speechwriter for Richard Nixon and together with Pat Buchanan ghosted a newspaper column for Nixon. He began his own commentary column for the *New York Times*, 'Essay', in 1973, and he has also written another column, 'On Language', for the *New York Times Magazine*. He won the Pulitzer Prize for commentary in 1978 for his coverage of the Lance affair.

'Essay'
Of Two Cities
New York Times, March 25, 1974

If you want to compare New York City with Washington, DC, as a symbol of civilization or a center of power, a good place to stand is the corner of Fifth Avenue and Fifty-ninth Street.

There, amidst the traffic's din (score one for Washington) you can see New York's Plaza Hotel, sixty-seven years old and going strong, a tribute to the marriage of free enterprise and good taste.

In Washington, by way of contrast, the equally famous Willard Hotel – the work of the same architect, Henry Hardenbergh, at about the same time – stands empty and desolate, thanks to some arrogant goo-goos and timorous bureaucrats.

A decade ago, a grandiose Pennsylvania Avenue plan was bruited about in the nation's capital, which blighted any renovation prospects for the historic Willard; now, with Caesarism on the wane, the city fathers want to preserve the hotel, but the owners are not sure enough of the bureaucracy's steadfastness to invest several million dollars in turning the Willard into another Plaza Hotel. (Score one for New York.)

Still on the corner of Fifty-ninth and Fifth, one can be impressed by the equestrian statue of General William Tecumseh Sherman, his horse being led by the winged figure of the goddess of victory. (Visitors from Atlanta often say, 'Isn't that like a Yankee to ride while the lady walks?')

As a work of art, the Sherman statue is not much; the sculptor, Augustus Saint-Gaudens, did far better for Washington with 'Grief,' a small classic of a woman in a hooded cloak, located in Rock Creek Cemetery. John Galsworthy placed one of his *Forsyte Saga* characters in front of the mysterious memorial and wrote: 'It was the best thing he had come across in America; the one that gave him the most pleasure, in spite of all the water he had seen at Niagara and those skyscrapers in New York.' One for Washington.

Scraping the sky, of course, is a hallmark and a glory of New York; when Boston put up the tallest tower in New England, Fate treated the city like Icarus and made the windows fall out.

No such presumption could take place in Washington: the Capitol dome stands a nicely proportionate 130 feet and no commercial structure can look down upon it. Only the obelisk to Washington towers over the Capitol, as the executive one-ups the legislative, and the result is a city built to the scale of people rather than giants.

The Federal city's bursting into cherry blossoms this week while the trees in Manhattan's side streets still hang lifeless on the crutches that hold them up. Washington is graced with an Italianate spring and New York suddenly lurches into summer, tempting Washington columnists to wax lyric about their gardens, yet John Kennedy added a necessary astringency to the assessment of the government town: 'Filled with Southern efficiency and Northern charm.'

New York is still the communications capital, but Washington has become the news capital; listen to the way Walter Cronkite on CBS News rushes through the names of the reporters who will be giving the Washington stories and lingers on the names and datelines of stories from anywhere else.

Local television announcers in Washington are most often black, dress conservatively, and maintain a certain dignity; their counterparts in New York are most often white, dress flashily, and try to maintain an aura of youthful irreverence.

New York has had a subway for seventy years, and riders grimly tolerate it; Washington is finally digging itself up to have a subway of its own. New York talks about the stock market; Washington rarely does, because there can be no economic recession in the nation's capital; if hard times hit, the bureaucracy will grow ever faster.

New York is too diverse to have a 'mood'; the life of the mind is livelier there, the social crosscurrents swifter, the intellectual fashions more demanding of conformity but of shorter duration. One-industry Washington's mood, on the other hand, is discernible: Right now, muscular Christians are tearing apart toothless lions in the arena, and the crowd is titillated by the roars of the martyred beasts.

Standing on the corner, watching a pothole grow in the street that leads to Bergdorf's and Tiffany's, a former New Yorker gets the feeling that the big town is a university, a tumultiversity, while Washington is a well-endowed college on the make.

An affection for both is not a sign of fickleness. Both places of learning are 'at the center,' because the symbol of our civilization at this stage of its development, and the center of power in our time, is not a city but a state of mind.

Thank God for the shuttle.

'Essay'
Cover-up Scorecard
New York Times, September 10, 1979

Washington

Philip Heymann, chief of the Criminal Division of the Department of Justice – who boasts of his experience as a special prosecutor investigating Republicans – has been leading the Carter Administration fight to prevent the appointment of special prosecutors to investigate Democrats.

The thin-skinned ex-Harvard professor has been derogating the Ethics in Government Act, which mandates court-appointed independent prosecutors to handle charges against high officials. Mr Heymann wishes us to believe he can do better. His record:

1. *The Vesco bribe accusation.* A fugitive financier paid $10,000 to a crony of Hamilton Jordan's to get President Carter to intercede in his behalf. When a Carter aide made the approach, President Carter – instead of blowing the whistle on an apparent bribe – wrote his Attorney General a note directing him to see the possible fixer.

Because it could not ignore columnist Jack Anderson's revelations, Justice grudgingly convened a grand jury. After eleven months, the grand jury foreman went public with charges of 'cover-up.' He was disgusted with Justice's foot-dragging to protect the White House.

In a meeting called to allay suspicion that Justice prosecutors were obstructing the grand jury, Mr Heymann admitted that he considered the sworn testimony of a key White House aide to have been untruthful.

When this admission was accurately reported by Edward Pound of the *New York Times*, Mr Heymann issued an artful statement claiming he had never actually used the word 'perjury' in connection with Mr Carter's aide. With the narrow denial, Mr Heymann tried to placate the White House and mislead the public, but the truth is that the chief criminal law enforcement officer of the US led several witnesses to believe that a special assistant to the President had lied under oath.

2. *The Lance case.* Exactly two years ago – in September 1977 – Justice was handed the evidence of Lance wrongdoing by the SEC and Treasury's Comptroller of the Currency. Result: The Treasury Secretary fell from favor, the SEC [Securities and Exchange Commission] enforcement chief's career has been blocked, and all the Justice officials forced to work on the case have fled.

The indictment was returned in May of this year, breaking little new ground. The politically embarrassing trial is not scheduled until late January of next year, and is likely to be postponed further, until after the early primaries. The venue will be most favorable to the President's friend.

3. *Koreagate.* This case hinged on the ability to convict former Congressman Otto Passman of taking over $200,000 in bribes, and then to turn him into a witness against a dozen other congressmen. But Mr Heymann's Criminal Division – to the amazement of the District of Columbia judge – permitted the bribery charge to be tied to an income tax charge, which automatically enabled Mr Passman to change the venue to his hometown in Louisiana.

As predicted here, Mr Passman was promptly acquitted, and – thanks to the ineptitude of Mr Heymann's 'Public Integrity Division' – twelve bribe-takers now sit safely in Congress.

4. *The Marston affair.* When corrupt Congressman Joshua Eilberg called President Carter to demand that he fire the Republican prosecutor who was closing in on him, the President told Justice to do just that. Mr Heymann has suppressed the FBI report on this suspected obstruction of justice. Inquiring Congressman Bob Walker (R.-Pa.) is told only that the President has been 'exonerated,' but the embarrassing report must remain secret because it 'contains information that is inextricably intertwined with other current criminal investigations.'

5. *The Carter warehouse-money laundry.* Only when prodded in this space to 'follow the tangent' did Mr Heymann permit Lance investigators to follow leads into questionable fund raising by the Carter family. The Ethics in Government Act was circumvented, because cover-uppers at Justice did not want a panel of judges to pick an aggressive, independent prosecutor; under pressure the Carter men chose amiable Paul Curran, and sought at first to restrict his powers, with his acquiescence. Press agitation stopped that nonsense, and now the probe is ambling along. (The long delay in the related Lance case, however, means that no heat is being applied to Lance to induce him to co-operate in the Carter warehouse case.)

6. *The Jordan cocaine charge.* Last year, when Presidential Drug Adviser Peter Bourne was caught fraudulently prescribing drugs, he told newsmen that illicit drug use was

frequent among Carter staffers. But Philip Heymann decided not to send a single FBI investigator to question Mr Bourne; his apparent crime was shrugged off.

Were it not for the new Ethics in Government Act, that is exactly how Mr Heymann would be handling the accusations of cocaine use against the President's Chief of Staff. DC drug sleuths conduct well-publicized busts against newsletter writers, but have no inclination to follow the white stuff into the White House.

The record of the Carter Department of Political Justice has been a series of grudging investigations, unconscionable foot-dragging, suspicious ineptitude and self-righteous posing. No wonder Philip Heymann resists the appointment of special prosecutors now required by law: They might even investigate, prosecute and convict a Democratic public official.

•

JIM MURRAY

Jim Murray was born in 1919 in Hartford, Connecticut, and was educated at Trinity College. He was briefly a reporter for the *New Haven Register* before moving to Los Angeles, where he reported for the *Examiner* from 1944 to 1948. After ten years as Los Angeles correspondent for *Time* magazine, he was one of the founders of *Sports Illustrated*. He has been a sports columnist for the *Los Angeles Times* since 1961.

A Matter of Blind Faith
Los Angeles Times, March 16, 1978

For years, I have had a secret ambition in life. It's simple. Some guys want to climb the Matterhorn. Others want to shoot 69. Some want to corner the market. Me? All I want to do is see a hockey goal.

I guess I've been watching the sport off and on for thirty years. And I've never seen a goal. If they don't light that red light, I'm in trouble. My compliments to the guy who lights it. He must be part hawk. When I see a 4–3 hockey game, I take it on blind faith there were seven goals scored. I didn't see any of them.

I mean, look! I have seen home runs in baseball, bombs in pro football. I can dig a service ace in tennis. I can catch a layup in basketball, a short KO punch in boxing. But, when eleven players get around the net in hockey with two linesmen thrown in for good measure, that puck might as well be white.

You know what I think? I don't think goals are *scored* at all. They bounce off pipes, ricochet off skates, slide in by themselves. They usually award a goal and two assists when this happens. Some guys get assists who haven't touched the puck in hours. If I were a hockey player, I'd just kind of skulk around the net, skating back and forth till a crowd collected, and, the minute I saw the light start to go around, I'd throw my hands and stick up in the air and act like I did it.

I was there the night Phil Esposito set the record for most goals – or most points – or both – in a season. Know how he did it? He *slid* into the net. The puck was somewhere on him. It was a kind of like a catcher making a tag with his gloved hand in baseball. But it was kind of disappointing. Like Babe Ruth *bunting* a home run, if you know what I mean.

I think the eleven-inch touchdown is the most uninteresting play in football, next to the shovel pass. But, in hockey, that's all you get. I keep going to games hoping to see the midcourt slap shots go in the crease. They never do. They hit the goalie, the glass, the pipes or the wall. Laid end to end, all the hockey goals in one season wouldn't reach to the blue line.

I mean, what does a goal look like? What color is it? What does it sound like? Is it bigger than a breadbox? Does it even exist? Or was hockey really invented by Lewis Carroll?

I figured if anyone knew what a hockey goal looked like it would be Gary Simmons. Gary Simmons is the backup goalie on the Los Angeles Kings and, the other night in Boston, the Bruins scored nine goals against him. This is not a record, but the light is on so much you need sunglasses in the crease when this happens. When you get nine goals scored against you in one night, you ought to be able to describe a goal right down to the mole on its neck.

On the other hand, maybe Gary's problem is that he, too, has no idea what one looks like. And therefore can't stop it.

Goals, Garry says, are like viruses. You can't see them, but when you get hit by them you know they're there. Plenty of goals have been scored in the NHL by guys trying to stop them. Many a goal has caromed off the skate – or the eye – of a defenseman trying to block it. As a result, a goalie can't trust anybody. He has eleven men to watch – twelve if the opposite goalie's out of the net for a late-period flurry. I say twelve, because a goalie can't even rely on himself. Many a goalie has carried in a goal himself by mistake.

Like me, Gary takes goals on blind faith – with the accent on blind. 'In the first place, you're screened off from most goals,' he says. 'You can hear the puck coming but you can't always see it.'

A puck, of course, is just a giant tiddlywink. It is designed for stealth, just one inch high, three inches across, and the color of skate shoes. The game is almost incomprehensible on TV, like a fox hunt on skates, in that you can't see the quarry.

'Fully half of the goals are scored in scrambles in front of the net, or on deflections or on funny bounces,' says Simmons, in an opinion shared by the starting goalie, Rogie Vachon.

The other night, I sat near center ice at the Forum and dutifully tried to watch the puck as the Kings and the Penguins played. I was determined to see a goal.

I felt as if I were on a snipe hunt. The score was 3–2 late in the third period. According to the scoreboard, that is. You couldn't prove it by me.

With about two minutes left, I sneaked a look at my program to see which of the bewildering series of lines was on the ice. A great roar went up. The light went on. Next to me the official scorer, John Bealey, was shouting into a telephone. 'Score by No. 19!

Assist by 17 and 7!' He turned to me. 'Did you see that?! A breakaway by Butch Goring! He deaked the goalie right out of his skates! A great goal!'

I took his word for it. I sighed, and just put it down with the others in my book, *My Life at Center Ice, Or, Great Goals I Never Saw.*

Just Once, I'd Like to See . . .
Los Angeles Times, December 15, 1981

Well, it's that time of year again, chestnuts roasting on an open fire, rump a pum pum, jingle bells, all that jazz. I think I'll send along a letter to my old friend St Nick and see what falls down the chimney for me.

Dear Santa,

Listen, old sport, I really don't need any soap on a rope or ties with a picture of Maui on them this year. In fact, I got one Christmas present already. There was this guy playing for Miami who scored a touchdown and, when he went into his funky dance and spiked the ball, he sprained a ligament or something. Way to go, Santa! It's a nice start, but if you're making a list and checking it twice, here are some other things I'd like to find under the Christmas tree.

– If it could be arranged, I'd like to see a World Series where it's the bottom of the ninth, the visiting team is ahead by two runs, but the bases are loaded and there's two out. What I would like is for the batter to hit a high fly to center field. The runners go and are crossing the plate as the center fielder puts up his glove to make a nonchalant one-handed catch. You guessed it! He drops the ball! I want it to pop right out of his mitt and just lie there. He has just nonchalanted away the world championship. I ask this not for myself but for an old-time ballplayer friend of mine who gets tears in his eyes every time he sees a guy one-hand a routine fly ball and he cries out, 'John McGraw would have him on a bus to Peoria by morning!'

– Just once, when one of those tennis brats throws a tantrum, I would like to have the guy sitting in the chair be the ex-light-heavyweight champion of Brazil or the Third Fleet or something and have him come down and say to the player, 'What was that you called me again?' And then, he'd unload the best one–two he's thrown since he won the Olympics in Helsinki. A punch to the snoot can do wonders for a guy's manners. All I ask is the incident be caught by a camera as it will be the most popular piece of film since *Bambi*.

– You know those guys who throw their arms in the air and do a little dance over their fallen victim, the quarterback they've just sacked, or the receiver they tossed out of bounds into a snowbank? Well, I would like for them to go home and have a fight with their wives. If possible, I'd like to have tapes of it to play when I'm feeling down.

– The next time two heavyweight contenders get in a phony publicity scuffle at the contract-signing ceremony, arrange for one of them to break a knuckle on a microphone. If a bystander gets hurt in the scuffle, have him turn out to be the son of the godfather of the local Mafia.

– The next time a school gets caught cheating in recruiting or staging phantom classes for athletes, don't tell them they can't play in the Rose Bowl or the NCAA [National Collegiate Athletic Association] tournament the next few years. Tell them they can't have a team at all for the next two years. You'll only have to do that once.

    – Put a time clock on golfers lining up a putt or studying an approach. Let no golfer ever walk ahead of his ball. If he does, penalize him a stroke for offsides when he walks up to a green from a ball 100 or even forty yards out. Give him three minutes to get the ball in the hole from any point on the green.

    – Let baseball have split seasons and wild cards and mini-playoffs, it might just as well get under the red light the same as all those other sports. Integrity's nice, but it gets lousy Nielsens.

    And, if you can't give me any of those things, you old humbug, how about a new Cadillac? Or, give the Rams back Jack Reynolds, Vince Ferragamo, Bob Brudzinski and Fred Dryer, and all is forgiven.

●

FERDINAND MOUNT

Sir Ferdinand Mount, Bt, was born in 1939 and educated at Eton and Christ Church, Oxford. Over the years he has worked for the *Sunday Telegraph*, the *Daily Sketch*, the *National Review*, the *Daily Mail* and *The Times*. He has also written columns for the *Spectator* (1977–82; 1985–7), the *Standard* (1980–82) and the *Daily Telegraph* (1984–90). Since 1991 he has been editor of the *Times Literary Supplement* and he now writes a weekly political column for the *Sunday Times*. Apart from his journalism, he has worked for the Conservative Research Department and was head of the Prime Minister's Policy Unit (1982–3).

'Political Commentary'
The Lovable Old Menace
Spectator, 8 November 1980

He voted for Silkin . . . he *didn't* . . . well, he said he was going to . . . he wouldn't say he had unless he had, would he? . . . said he was in the navy with him . . . Silkin wasn't in the navy, was he?

    There's nothing like a PLP [Parliamentary Labour Party] ballot to bring the roses back to the cheeks. After the result of the first round, Michael Foot looked pink with pleasure. He and his aide de camp, Neil Kinnock, were grinning all over their faces as they barged their way through the mêlée outside Committee Room Ten. A curious crowd scene this, halfway between the Storming of the Winter Palace and waiting for opening time at the Coach and Horses.

    For about half an hour afterwards, the Left was euphoric. There were 112 votes for Healey, 153 against Healey. Ergo, Foot must win. Then the two eliminated candidates, John Silkin and Peter Shore, began publicly to anatomize their votes. According to Mr Silkin's friends, between eight and seventeen of his votes might go to Mr Healey. Mr

Shore's votes were always thought to be an assortment. So if Mr Healey could gather a dozen from each, he would still squeak home. There might also be one or two Labour MPs who, after the sentimental luxury of voting for Mr Foot first time, would begin to brood on his age and chances of winning the election when it came to the final choice. By the end of the evening, in the engine-room of the Left they were talking less about Mr Foot winning on the second round than about him running close enough to justify a challenge in the electoral college next spring, at which they confidently expect him to wipe the floor with Mr Healey.

Still, Mr Foot is doing remarkably well with his new suit and his haircut. Which makes all the more poignant the sight of poor Mr Shore with *his* haircut, scuppered by his dear old friend, but still wishing him all the best and throwing him his support. One haircut might be a coincidence; two suggests competition.

We need some of that modern investigative journalism here. Official spokesmen for the candidates may tell you that 'this was just the normal autumn trim, the candidate has been going to Trudgers of Hampstead the first week in November for thirty years'. A *New Statesman* analysis of the clippings would probably reveal no more than 0.3 per cent deviancy from the median score on the Samson-Belfrage Scale. But with so timely a trim, one cannot help suspecting the hand of the PR men.

After all, the Conservative Party's retiring Svengali, Mr Gordon Reece, is said to have taken Mrs Thatcher's voice down an octave, shifted her hair from the colour of New Zealand butter to that of ripe wheat, and taken the frills off her frocks. In comparison, the most that Mr Will Camp, handler to Mr Shore, would have had to do would be to drop the faintest of hints, '. . . the hair, Peter, perhaps a little . . . well . . .' Or it may be that old Mr Trudger himself made the suggestion: 'Just a fraction shorter this year, sir? I remember when Mr Kingsley Martin used to sit in that same chair, sir, hair just like yours he had, a fine head but a rather dry scalp.'

Such modest preparations for the leader's mantle are touching, not shocking. Labour politicians – and most Tory ones too – remain disarmingly innocent about the arts of self-promotion. This innocence, comes, I suppose, partly from a snobbish distaste for anything which smacks of America in general and Madison Avenue in particular. Indeed, there is no surer way to get laughed out of consideration at Westminster than to be caught energetically promoting yourself. British politics retains what is usually thought of as a public-school aversion to 'side'. Unfortunately, British politics retains also a public-school aversion to sustained thought.

For behind the struggle for power in the Labour Party – which at the moment is understandably absorbing the energies of Left and Right alike – there is a terrible mental deadness, which has existed for years now. Everyone goes on saying how the social democrats haven't had an interesting thought since Tony Crosland in his heyday; what is less often said – because the Left's zest for conspiracy is so conspicuous – is how dead behind the eyes the Left is too. If you have not read the statements in the *Guardian* by Mr Foot, Mr Shore and Mr Silkin, don't. It may be unfair to judge too much from a hurried 1,000-word essay on What I Would Do If Elected Leader – that at any rate was Mr Healey's excuse for declining to put pen to paper. Yet you glimpsed great gaping spaces, full of dust and draughts, under the planks in their platforms.

But doesn't Mr Benn have all sorts of exciting new plans for workers' control and co-operatives? Isn't there an Alternative Strategy? Is not the Left a ferment of ideas? Not really. The Left is a ferment of slogans, but not of coherent arguments. If a Benn government were to come to power, it would have no more real grasp of how its new structures would work than the Attlee Government had of how old-fashioned nationalization was to be organized. Now as then, the trouble is that you would not know the full extent of their ignorance until ten years later when some latter-day Manny Shinwell revealed all. There is little sign that Mr Benn and his friends have really learned any lessons from the failure of his first batch of co-operatives.

These shortcomings, it will be said, have nothing much to do with getting elected, which is perfectly true. But any incoming Labour Government, whoever leads it, is likely to be even worse prepared to implement its manifesto than its predecessors. This is not entirely bad news. Mr Healey, if elected, would have two chances to water down or cut out extreme proposals – when the manifesto was being drawn up and when the government began trying to translate its election commitments into action.

On the other hand, if Mr Foot were to become Prime Minister, although he might prove a veritable Robespierre for guillotining Bills and trampling on opposition in Parliament, he might well also lack the executive stamina to carry through some complicated and impractical schemes against the opposition of the government machine. That is less comforting than it sounds. For the slower the pace at which the Left proceeds, the better its chances of holding the Labour Party together until it has completed the irreversible process of 'making Socialism'.

A Left-wing leader of the Labour Party who is too explicit or who forces the pace too obviously might risk destroying the precious asset of a single legitimate party of the working class. At Blackpool, Mr Benn – who I stubbornly continue to think is not very bright – showed total indifference to this danger for the sake of a few cheers from the constituency delegates whose adoration he could already count on. That is why the interests of the Left and the interests of Mr Benn are not necessarily the same thing, though they might be in the end.

No such caveats apply to Mr Foot. For the moment, the Left could wish for no more ideal leader, as long as he can achieve power by peaceful means – and I doubt whether challenging Mr Healey in the electoral college would count as peaceful. Indeed, that might be the one provocation that could offer the Right the excuse for a split in the immediate future.

It is precisely Mr Foot's lack of executive capacity, his impatience with the dreary details of the business that make him so dangerous. His endearing vacuousness gives his opponents so little to get a grip on, so little excuse to take umbrage, let alone to force a split in the party. While he rants and maunders and fidgets and grins, all manner of dirty work may proceed unhindered.

I missed his triumph in the Employment debate last Wednesday. When I read it up in *Hansard* later it was the same story: three good jokes, a continuous blast of indignation, and not much else. Between 1974 and 1976, he piloted through the House of Commons some of the most illiberal legislation of the century, while adding to his reputation for charm and wit and winning new friends as a responsible and unifying force. With each year that passes, he becomes even more widely loved and even more of a menace.

•

JILL TWEEDIE

Jill Tweedie (1934–93) was educated at eight girls' schools and a Swiss finishing school, then went to stay with relatives in Canada, where, at the age of eighteen, she married a Hungarian count, Bela Cziraky. She was desperately unhappy in the marriage which ended when her husband disappeared, taking the children with him. She did not see the children until years afterwards. Subsequently, she had a child by an American hippie carpenter, Robert D'Ancona. Then in 1973 she married the journalist Alan Brien and they remained together for twenty years. In the early 1960s she wrote features for *Town* magazine and she was working for the *Sunday Telegraph* when she was hired as a columnist by the *Guardian* in 1969. She was a socialist and a feminist, and her column, which ran in various guises until 1988, was politically engaged, passionate and often very funny. Sometimes it took the form of letters from a fainthearted feminist, a housewife, writing to a more purist friend about the difficulty of putting feminist precepts into practice. (These later formed the basis of a situation comedy starring Lynn Redgrave.) She was an active campaigner for equal rights, for better treatment of women in maternity units and for the outlawing of rape within marriage. She won Woman Journalist of the Year in the 1971 IPC National Press Awards; and won another award, from Granada TV's *What the Papers Say*, in 1972. Following her death from cancer, her editor for many years, Peter Preston, paid tribute: 'She was truly sympathetic, changing over the years from a journalist who wrote about the world because she was A Woman into a writer who made a woman's feelings and insights the point of everything. She came and went (to the new *Indy*) and came again. Sometimes it was great, for she was also a brilliant reporter; sometimes she was hunting for a theme and voice. But she was always terrific fun and always alive to the feelings of others, so that the office buzzed when she arrived. Jill was a star.' She published an autobiography, *Eating Children* (1993), and some of her columns were collected as *Letters from a Fainthearted Feminist* (1982).

Guardian, 26 June 1980

I visited a relation in hospital last week. An old lady lay in the next bed, her white hair a thick thatch around her face, the sheet rucked up to expose one white and spindly thigh. As I approached, she extended a thin hand and tried, ineffectually, to draw her curtain around her. A nurse bustled up, pulled back the curtain and straightened the sheet.

'This is Martha,' said the nurse, nodding at me. 'Say hullo, Martha.' Martha looked at me and said, very softly, 'How do you do?' 'That's it,' said the nurse and bustled off. Quite without thought, picking up the cues from that exchange, from the old lady's thatch of hair, her helplessness, her semi-nudity and the use of her first name, I assumed she was . . . what? Senile, wandering into second childhood? Not, anyway, entirely like you and me.

My relative knew better. Fresh from the outside world, she had begun to talk to the old lady. They had introduced themselves. She was Mrs Y, a widow who lived with her sister, who had had a fall, who was worried that she might never return to her pretty house in Wimbledon, that she might have to sell some good paintings and antique furniture to pay for help. The catalogue of Mrs Y's anxieties went on and, as the personal details mounted up, the old lady fleshed out for me, became an individual, grew again to full stature.

Now I could well imagine her, hair neatly coiffed, old bones discreetly clothed, dispensing tea in her ordered sitting room. Do sit down, Mr X. Thank you, Mrs Y. Once again, she was herself, an elderly widow ensconced in a dignified manner in her own home, giving and receiving courtesies and respect, an adult among other adults. How, then, had thoughts of 'poor old Martha' come to pass, so quickly?

People, when they are ill and frightened, easily discard their normal personalities and revert, in pain or in bewilderment, to the vulnerabilities of childhood. Other people, like nurses, who must feed, bathe and otherwise tend them, are doing what mothers do for children and it is, thus, not surprising that they easily regard their charges as children and address them in those terms, employing first names or nicknames and all the shooing sort of jollities that mothers use: come along now, tut tut, can't have this, we must, we mustn't, good girl, naughty boy, just another mouthful for mummy.

Nevertheless there is a wide gap between ordinary maternal kindness and the sort of nursery intimacies so often considered normal among nurses. And it is, to my mind, a dangerous gap, contributing not only to the trepidation with which many people regard a stay in hospital but even to their slower recovery.

Older women, in particular, whose sense of identity is often built upon the privacy of their homes and families, dreadfully fear this stripping of themselves. Bad enough that familiar surroundings and routine have vanished overnight, bad enough that they feel physically ill, worse that they no longer appear to merit the small signs of adult status upon which they have come to rely.

I remember, once, sitting by a friend's hospital bed when a nurse walked into the centre of the ward and said, with hockey-sticks jollity, 'Anyone here want their bums washed?' Who, among us, is so secure as to claim, in the necessary ringing tones, that facility? I remember, as a patient myself, another nurse asking us all, loudly, who hadn't had a bowel movement that day. And yet another, who popped her head through the ward door to shout 'Anyone here with a specimen of their poo?' As one woman – and we ranged in age from eight to eighty – we blushed at the infantile word and the notoriety publicly thrust upon one of us.

Now, most of the women in any ward at any one time have long been forced to come to terms with the physical vagaries of their bodies. Child-bearing itself is not the most private of functions and nine months of pre-natal examinations, not to mention birth itself, are hardly calculated to retain, intact, the veils of modesty. Later, child-rearing does away with any remaining squeamishness about bodily functions or disfunctions.

Yet there is a world of difference between accepting with good grace one's own and one's children's physical upheavals and having them revealed, willy nilly, for strangers to see or hear. That sort of revelation confuses, belittles and often deeply upsets the carefully cherished standards of personal modesty upon which is based much of our selves.

How often, in maternity and other wards, have I heard women plead for the curtains to be drawn before a bed bath, an injection, or some other treatment administered by nurses who seem habitually surprised at such eccentric fastidiousness. How often have I seen other patients embarrassed by their neighbours' embarrassment. How often do patients sit, every day, on cold bed pans, unable to do what they long to do for fear that a thin curtain is not concealment enough.

Most of us become accustomed, in hospital, to gauging just how ill another person is by their relinquishment of all natural modesty and, yet, how much does this relinquishment – in public view – lower our own poor spirits and poor health?

Hospitals, today, are far better places than they used to be. Gone are most of the pernickety boarding-school attitudes to visiting, smoking and disciplined tidiness at the expense of humanity. But there lingers on that occupational hazard of nursing, the curious lack of regard for patients' modesty, privacy and individuality, three things at least as essential to a swift recovery as the generous doling-out of sleeping pills at the close of day.

When I was last in hospital, in a maternity ward, the matron appeared with the Registrar of Births, explained the registration procedure to the respectably married mothers and, loudly, informed me that I could not participate at this point due to the fact that my child was illegitimate.

As in so many examples of this kind of ward-wide publicity, I was not ashamed of the fact itself – as many others are not ashamed of their physical needs. But I, like them, was upset because forced to share what I might have chosen to keep to myself. The abrogation of choice has many repercussions, particularly for invalids who must, to some psychological extent, conserve choice to conserve the identity that helps them to cure themselves.

Nurses, by virtue of their work, quickly become inured to and, even, dismissive of the often pathetic and seemingly unimportant ways in which their patients assert individuality. Mrs This, Miss That, Mr The-Next, curtains drawn or curtains open, what matter?

All I know is that even a receptionist in a doctor's waiting room who declaims my first name as well as my surname to the waiting crowd causes me to feel very slightly diminished. Or am I unduly sensitive?

Guardian, 29 November 1983

As the world sinks deeper into madness, I put my faith in simple things, like making soup and tidying drawers and letting the air out of radiators. Here, at least, there is sanity, order and control. Here, I am She Who Must Be Obeyed.

That is the theory. Unfortunately for me, the practice is quite other. Take a simple thing like clothes. How peaceful to think of clothes, how nice to wear them with authority, turning one's mind away from the insane ranks of missiles springing up across Europe like some new Black Forest and towards the mirror wherein one's image stands obedient, clad à la mode in biddable garments. The problem is, mine are not biddable.

They, too, have slipped beyond my control, refusing to behave as garments are supposed to behave. There they flaunt themselves in shop windows and fashion magazines and on other people and butter wouldn't melt in their mouths. But just let me push across the counter and take delivery of them and they rise up against me with a life of their own. Sartorial anarchy reigns.

I bought a pair of short lace-up boots the other day. Sturdy, sage-green, comfortable. I set out in them. Before I had reached the end of the street the centre flanges had worked their way down my instep under the laces and extruded themselves, so that my feet looked like two small green beasts, tongues flapping, ravenous for food. At the same time my nylon slip had crawled up my legs and lodged itself round my hips, creating a curious pannier effect, while underneath a pair of lacy cami-knicks were busily turning on their axis, corkscrewing my legs into a drunkard's lurch. Defeated, I was forced to shuffle home again, plucking at myself as I went like a person with St Vitus' itch. The clothes had won.

In my experience the clothes always win. When I first dress, they do what they are told. When I regard myself, standing still, they are as good as gold. When I move, all hell breaks loose. Before the mirror, I arrange a string of beads around my neck in two graceful loops. Most tasteful. Halfway downstairs the top loop begins its slow journey upwards. As I emerge from the front door it leaps to clutch my throat and garrotte me. I am forced to fight free, face reddening dangerously, veins standing out, panting for air. Scarves have the same lethal habits. Gently they lie cowled at my neck, ends tucked in or swinging free. Minutes later they have a stranglehold on my jugular and brain cells begin to die for lack of oxygen. Recently I bought one of those new coats that are so fashionable now, half-poncho, half horse-blanket. I draped its weight over my shoulders, from whence it descended in satisfactory folds. But the moment I began to move it heaved itself backwards. I toppled, choking, and regained my balance, shoving it forwards. It lunged at my neckline again, cutting off breath. People on the street were beginning to stare at me, a woman at war with her coat, struggling for very life against wave upon wave of wool. Eventually, gasping, I gave in. The coat was victorious.

My clothes are not always out to kill. Sometimes they are content to embarrass me to death or simply overheat me into torpor. I'm very fond of the layered look as it appears in glossy photographs upon ice-maiden model girls. A chemise topped by a V-necked sweater topped by a sleeveless waistcoat over a skirt with an underskirt above another layer of boots and leg-warmers and tights and shawls over all tied in with three belts. Charming in pictures. Doubtless thoroughly practical if you move in Eskimo circles, doing the social round of igloos. But on me, in central heating, all charm goes up in steam as I mop my brow and quietly roast from done to overdone in my self-inflicted oven. How do other women manage, I ask myself. What did the designers have in mind? Perhaps, being mostly Japanese, they are in a plot to drive us all into residence at Greenham Common, the only place I know in England where such layering serves a purpose.

Other embarrassments are legion. Half my shoes stay firmly rooted to the ground as my heels rise, so that I look like a child clattering about in her mummy's footwear. The other half swaddle my feet so I hobble on bound stumps, a left-over Empress of China.

Leg-warmers, chic and sportive on other women, do nothing for me. Either they move up-leg and balloon out my trousers, transforming me into a 1920s flapper on a Swiss ski-slope, or they inch down-leg and spread out round my ankles like woolly hooves. My shawls do not stay in place, demurely framing my shoulders, they lash out around them as I pass and hook inanimate objects to them, so that soon I look like a travelling tinker hung about with merchandise for sale. Crushed linen, on me, does not look expensive. It just looks crushed. When I thrust my socked toes into boots, the thrust jams the socks backwards, shrinking the boots two sizes and causing me day-long pain. If I buy a pretty blouse, it turns out to be indecently transparent and I must wear vests underneath or frighten the horses. Rings on my fingers turn green or give rise to disfiguring rashes. Earrings make my ears resemble the pendulous lobes of the Ubangis, chic in Africa, death in Kentish Town. I am constricted to one tattered handbag – if I get two I am doomed for ever to be scrabbling within, unable to find the vital accessory left behind in the other one. On me, tops inevitably part company with bottoms, revealing expanses of immodest flesh. On me, dark glasses do not shade my eyes from the sun, they cut it off completely and leave me stumbling in the country of the blind. On me, cosmetics wander, leaving my lips for a journey down my chin, deserting my lashes to settle on my cheeks, emigrating from my eyelids into my eyes.

One day last week, I thought I'd won the battle. Opaque blouse, long waistcoat anchored firmly into no-nonsense skirt, padded jacket – all withdrawn from one wardrobe. As I arrived at my destination my hostess sniffed the air. A month ago I had treated the wood for worm and now the very wardrobe that housed my clothes was getting its own back. Everything I wore exuded powerful waves of Eau de Rentokil. The worms had turned.

•

JIMMY BRESLIN

Jimmy Breslin was born in 1929 in Jamaica, New York. While studying at Long Island University from 1948 to 1950 he worked as a copy-boy for the *Long Island Press* and he left college without a degree to become a sportswriter for the Newspaper Enterprise Association. He moved to the *New York Journal-American*, then free-lanced for three years. In 1963 he started writing a sports column for the *New York Herald Tribune*, but soon expanded into general commentary. He later moved to the *New York Post* for a year (1968–9), before abandoning his column to write books. In 1976 he came back as a columnist in the *New York Daily News*, where he stayed until he joined *Newsday* in 1987. He won a Pulitzer Prize for commentary in 1986. His gritty, observational columns have principally been about life in New York, although he occasionally reported from abroad. Two of the following columns demonstrate his scorn for public officials who treat the little man with contempt, Governor Hugh Carey and Mayor Ed Koch, and there is also a series of excerpts from his annual turn, 'People I'm Not Talking To This Year'.

Society Carey
New York Daily News, February 1981

There arrived in this office yesterday, and thus prominently, this message that came whizzing through the communications satellite and joined the flood of worldwide news:

CABLES

H CAREY DRYDENS 08200: ELEVEN-PERSON CAREY GROUP ARRIVED HERE HONG-KONG SATURDAY EVENING FROM TOKYO. DUE LUNAR NEW YEAR'S HOLIDAYS NIGHT-CLUBS ETC. CLOSED UNTIL TODAY. CAREY STAYING AMERICAN INTERNATIONAL UNDERWRITERS' GUEST HOUSE AND MOST OTHERS AT MANDARIN HOTEL. ABOUT DLRS 80 MINIMUM. PLANNED MEETINGS TODAY LEAVE TUESDAY ABOUT NOON. TOKYO ANSWER SEPARATELY. RGDS. ANDERSON-HKG UPI.

Beautiful. We in New York are privileged to have the most marvelous representation by the government for which we pay. Let these other states have governors who slobber around state fairs and supermarket openings. Look at Connecticut. The governor who just died, Ella Grasso, was a dear woman, but she sold the state plane and helicopter and drove around in a Citation. Our governor in New York is different. Our governor is Society Carey. For the last several days, Society Carey and a party of ten, paid for by tax funds out of the money you work for each week, have been sweeping across the Orient.

The object of the trip is to let Society Carey see the Orient, which he never has, and to let the Orient see Society Carey, which it never has. In that way, a whole new part of the world will know that we in New York have a governor, which we have, and his name is Society Carey.

There are many thousands living without heat in Brooklyn who say that they never knew they had a governor until newspapers ran pictures of Society Carey looking out of a helicopter in Japan. But these people living in the cold in Brooklyn are not Society Carey's kind of people, and you can be sure that he will keep the same distance from them that he always has, and that is quite a lot of distance. Tokyo is not that far.

We in New York could be proud of the first picture of Society Carey, the one showing him in a helicopter, because that let all of Tokyo know how our governor lives in New York. Society Carey has a great big million-dollar helicopter that he rides all over New York while we take subways, if you can get on them, and he also has two planes, one of which is so big it can barely fit on a runway, and he uses it every night to go back to Albany from Manhattan and it costs only $750 a night to do this.

The Society Carey party in the Orient includes three advance men. An advance man is a traveling doorman. He sees to it that the right luggage is in each hotel room and that cars are available and helicopters ready on the pad, and that, always, doors are held open for Society Carey. The luggage is much more important than you think. As someone from the governor's office in New York was pointing out yesterday, this trip to the Orient involves dramatic climatic changes. The trip started in Albany, where the temperature drops to the low teens, and went through Hawaii, in the high seventies, to Tokyo, which was in the forties, and on to Hong Kong, which is in the sixties. But this is weather in the winter and is highly unreliable.

Why, here one morning you could have Society Carey arising in Hawaii and the temperature could be in the high seventies. Moreover, if Society Carey ever put on a heavy Albany suit and went out into the street, he most certainly would boil like a cabbage. By noon in Honolulu, Society Carey would keel over. Yet on the other hand, if Society Carey ventured out in his truly tropical suit, his tea planter's white, he might be out and about the whole town and have the temperature suddenly plummet many degrees. Here would be Society Carey in the middle of Honololu, being attacked by chilblains.

So here is what the three advance men have been doing each day on Society Carey's trip through the Orient: One advance man stands outside the hotel each morning for a half-hour in order to fully acclimate himself to the temperature. Then the first advance man makes a policy decision as to the weight of the suit Society Carey will wear. This outside advance man waves his arm, in coded signal, to a second advance man, stationed inside the hotel lobby. The second advance men grabs a phone and calls up to the third advance man, who is positioned in Society Carey's suite. Upon getting the message, the third advance man pounces upon Society Carey's wardrobe and pulls out the proper suit for Society Carey to wear on this day.

Sometimes this system, which worked beautifully at hotels, had to be modified to fit a change in Society Carey's living quarters. As the UPI cable from Hong Kong indicates, Carey in Hong Kong stayed in the American International Underwriters' guest house. American International Underwriters appears to have some connection to the insurance industry. By staying there, Society Carey placed great hardship on his advance men. They had practiced long hours for hotel duty, but this method of climate control at the American International Underwriters' guest house could be done by only two advance men. And the two advance men were able to do the job, and apparently quite well. The trip has gone so smoothly for Society Carey, wearing all his suits in all the different weather, that he has not even taken a Dristan.

Society Carey's party in the Orient also includes two New York State policemen. This causes some people in New York City to say that since there have been 9,851 murders in the city in Carey's time as governor, then perhaps any loose cops should be used on Nostrand Avenue instead of Honolulu. Other people say that if Society Carey's trip to Hawaii, Japan and Hong Kong is so dangerous that he cannot make it without great protection, then perhaps he shouldn't go at all.

You must disagree with those who say such things. It is now official American policy to face up to terrorism wherever it may be. If there is terrorism on Waikiki Beach, or at the American International Underwriters in Hong Kong, then it should be fought vigorously. We in New York State have sent Society Carey and two state troopers to make sure that this national policy is carried out.

These same people squawking about the cost of sending secretaries, advance men, and two state troopers around the Orient – round-trip plane fare is $1,600, and that is only the start – are the same ones who made the most noise the other day when Society

Carey, before leaving for Hawaii and the Orient, put in an expense voucher of $6,400 that was to be paid to Dr Philip D'Arrigo. He is the dentist whose house on Shelter Island was seized by the state because it blocked the view of the water from Society Carey's family house. They had to give the house back to the dentist. This switching back and forth caused the dentist to run up bills of $6,400. As the problem was part of the governor's personal life, he sat down and, of course, asked the taxpayers to pay the $6,400. This is why Society Carey has such great style; he has fourteen million people paying for him.

Officially, Society Carey has announced that his trip, his eleven-man sweep of the Far East, has nothing to do with sightseeing. In Japan, Society Carey announced that the great Okuma Machinery works would expand its business and set up a huge production plant on Flatlands Avenue, Brooklyn. The Okuma plant would sit alongside the great new international headquarters of the Mitsubishi Corporation, which will move here on March 3. These announcements of great industries coming here are similar to those made when Society Carey took his last overseas trip, to Germany. Society Carey then announced that the main Krupp plant in Dusseldorf would move to Flushing Avenue, Maspeth, on February 16.

Society Carey's tour of the Orient does make a fool of at least some of his critics. Society Carey has maintained that the state cannot run without the services of his assistant, Robert Morgado. To prove this, Society took Morgado with him all over the Orient and he and Morgado even stopped at Morgado's home in Hawaii. And the state ran just as it always did, which proves how important both Society Carey and Morgado are to us.

Also out of this great, quite costly trip, I personally learned a lesson. Some time back, I noted that Society Carey was unique in government: he had invented the eleven-hour workweek. A person I respect and cherish called me on this. He said I had my figures wrong and should be embarrassed. I can now report to this man that, yes, he was right and I was wrong. By careful addition, I have determined that since January 1 of this year, Society Carey has worked an average of nine and a half hours each week. As this is not the eleven-hour week I said he worked, I stand corrected. Beautiful.

His Charm Offended Koch
New York Daily News, August 1982

Among atrocities committed in this city last Friday was the incarceration of Joseph Cruz, fifty-five, for the crime of attempting to live decently while being poor. Mr Cruz was rounded up on what can only be direct orders of Mayor Koch.

With his personal liberty being crunched under the feet of a half-dozen policemen and a crowd of bureaucrats bumping against one another, Mr Cruz was snatched from his living quarters on a traffic island on the East River Drive and then hurled into a mental ward at Bellevue Hospital, where he undoubtedly was filled with enough lithium to turn him into a door.

Before this outrage, Mr Cruz had demonstrated that he was one of the few who understood that boredom is Earth's greatest plague, that charm depends upon neither money nor the garments covering the body.

I discovered Mr Cruz's taste yesterday while walking in the footprints he left in this city, a personal adventure that I will relate in detail, but first we must deal with the most urgent matter: Mr Cruz's being denied the rights of a country for which he fought.

Two years ago he was thrown out of a single-room-occupancy hotel because his Veterans Administration check had arrived late. Cruz inspected the disgraceful chambers the city runs as shelters for the homeless and decided they were beneath his dignity. He became one of our street people, but a highly imaginative one.

Several months ago, he discovered a marvelous spot under the southbound East River Drive at the Sixty-first Street exit. It is a traffic island, a triangle with a low wall separating the island from the cars rushing northbound on the drive. On the open side of the triangle, cars getting off the drive roll slowly by and turn on to Sixty-first Street.

In this spot, with the roof over his head provided by the southbound lanes of the highway, Cruz set up full housekeeping, with bed, stove and chair. He washed body and clothes in a Parks Department building that is on the other side of the exit lane. He watched tens of thousands of cars race by him, and his other view was of fewer cars and young trees across the street and the Queensboro Bridge and the towering apartment houses of East Side living, which cannot be as good as Cruz's was, because he sat in the open air.

He sat in the open air, and he was different.

When Cruz's home was discovered by the brilliant Bella English of this newspaper, motorists stopped and handed Mr Cruz money, beer and encouragement. In return, they got a wave and a smile, giving the motorists perhaps their only cheer of the day. Sitting in his home, drinking his beer, reading a book, smiling as motorists yelled at him, Mr Cruz never thought of himself as an aggressor.

Oh, but he was. Mr Cruz was an embarrassment to Mayor Koch, who runs for governor and whose car went past Mr Cruz on the way to Gracie Mansion each night. For a week, there were so many calls among so many city agencies that it was apparent the bureaucracy was reflecting nervousness and anger from the mayor's office at City Hall.

'Whey are they bothering me now?' Mr Cruz said. 'I've been living on the streets for over two years and nobody cared.'

But that was before he became part of an election, Mr Cruz was warned. For in the city now we have Mayor Koch, voice braying, face muscles so tired that his mugging now comes about an eighth beat off, big-footing about the state in search of coronation but finding that he is in a fight that is quite distasteful because perhaps he could lose it.

On Friday, a psychiatrist arrived with Mr Cruz's daughter, Evelyn. Mr Cruz did exactly what any sane man would do.

As the only place where Mr Cruz could run was out on to the highway, he suddenly gave the bureaucracy all that it needed. Mr Cruz is a danger to himself and others, the psychiatrist ruled.

Mr Cruz had been living on the island for months, and there is no record of him ever endangering anything except an official reputation or so. But now the claim could be made that he was a nut who played in heavy traffic. So on Friday, on a day when several murders were committed in the city, on a day when there were so many armed robberies, here were six policemen pulling up to the traffic island to grab Mr Cruz, dismantle his living quarters, and take him to Bellevue and lithium.

Koch's office said that the mayor felt the action was 'appropriate' but that Koch most certainly had not personally ordered the action. Which is another reason why Koch soon will be known everywhere as Cop-out Koch.

Bellevue yesterday said that Mr Cruz is not allowed to leave the psychiatric ward.

Now on Friday, after Mr Cruz was placed in Bellevue and his living quarters dismantled, city workers placed twenty yellow barrels, each containing fifty-five gallons of sand, on the traffic island. The drums are the Fitch Inertial Barrier System, made in Canada. They are generally placed around highway traffic islands to soften any accidents. But the drums obviously were placed at Sixty-first Street to prevent anybody from replacing Mr Cruz as a resident.

This situation lasted until yesterday morning, when I arrived at the traffic island with my friend Desmond Crofton.

'It would make a lovely beach,' I said.

I went to Crofton's apartment on Fiftieth Street, changed into smashing beachwear, and returned to my private beach with an umbrella, beach chair, radio and book. I sat in the sun, digging my toes into the sand, and now and then looked up through the leaves of the young maple trees across the street and followed a tramway car as it slid through the sky on the way back from Roosevelt Island.

I found my beach so thoroughly delightful that I remained for quite some time, and I intended to be there with my book and umbrella, waving at motorists, until Joseph Cruz is freed from Bellevue and returned to his home.

But it never should be forgotten that the temper, whim and nastiness of the city government, certainly reflecting the desires of one man, Cop-out Koch, resulted in citizen Joseph Cruz's being taken by force of police and thrown into a mental ward on a summer weekend merely because he tried to live decently in New York.

People I'm Not Talking to This Year
New York Daily News, 1976–83

Whenever somebody does something bad to me, I write an account of it on a piece of paper and then at night transcribe the notes into a copybook and thus into my life permanently, or at least for a full year. The copybook prevents me from forgetting any feud, which is important, as it would be the worst sin of all, the sin of omission, if I failed to hold up my end of the disagreement.

Perhaps some think that if you turn the other cheek you are displaying maturity. I believe that if you turn one cheek, then you only have one left.

I live therefore in the spirit and memory of my friend Eddie Borden, who was arrested for gambling back in the times when that was considered a crime and not a means for newspapers to raise circulation, and was told by a guard that bail had just been posted for him. He walked to the last set of bars, peered through them, and saw both freedom and his most hated enemy, Eddie Walker, on the other side.

'What's he doing here?' Borden asked the guard.

'He put up bail for you,' the guard said.

'Give the bum his money back,' Borden said. He turned and walked back to the freight elevator that took people up to the cell blocks.

It is in this spirit that I go through my marvelous copybook and present my list of People I'm Not Talking To This Year:

WHISPERING MILLSTEIN – He is in a law company with GOOD-TIME CHARLIE GOLDSTEIN. Goldstein was part of the legal-government complex called Our Thing that runs this city and state just as the military-industrial complex runs the nation. Goldstein was paid more than $4 million in two years by the State Urban Development Corporation as a legal consultant. Goldstein called it a public service. When I wrote about this in my newspaper, the *Daily News*, Goldstein first had somebody from his company call my newspaper and try to put the muscle on, as would some cheap tough guy. The newspaper's lawyer, RETAINER TYLER, was careful to pass on the threats, for he is first a lawyer, and thus part of Our Thing. And now we come to Whispering Millstein. He stands at a cocktail party and says, so ominously, that he sure hopes that scruffy Breslin knows the law about slander. Of course, a lot of worried faces came up to me after the party and said, 'Say, you could get hurt.' At this point, I was supposed to quit. This is how Our Thing works in New York. It probably is the same in every state in the country. Great power. But let me tell you what I did. First, I said I was going to challenge Good-Time Charlie Goldstein and Whispering Millstein to a duel, with seconds, guns on the Palisades or swords on Park Avenue. I practiced shot and wonderful quick thrust. But then Cuomo, the incoming governor, who was not a member of Our Thing, told me to challenge them to a lawsuit. He wanted me to suck them in and then he would step out from behind me and put them all into a trash basket. I issued the challenge and stood on a street corner for days waiting for one of them to show up with lawsuit papers. They dogged it. Nobody showed and Good-Time Charlie Goldstein disappeared from 'public service' and the public funds that go with it. His man Whispering Millstein uttered no more. Nobody came to me with cocktail-party stories anymore. But that doesn't mean I forget anything. He may have quit, but I do not.

LIEUTENANT ANDREW MURPHY of the 109th Precinct – With three prisoners in front of his desk, Murphy stopped everything so he could make some cheap remark about me to somebody. I received a phone call about it as soon as one of the prisoners was allowed his phone calls. Of all the remarks made about me by all the police in New York during the last year, my notes show that Murphy uttered the lowest.

MARTY STEADMAN – He sits up all night writing ads or letters to the editor attacking me personally. Then he runs around all day with his hands in the air and crying that he never did it. Just another stool pigeon.

FAT THOMAS – He slows as he steps into the twilight of the twentieth century; perhaps he is as slow as the horses he bets on. But he still thinks that he can snarl at people as if he were some Tartar conqueror. I also was told about all the bad things he said about me on Metropolitan Avenue the other night.

STEVE BERGER — I just found a notation in my book about how Berger, a man who genuflects in front of politicians, used to sneak into the *Daily News* newspaper on behalf of Ed Koch and spread a lot of bad stories about me to the bosses. I have studied my notes on this for some time. I now emerge from the dugout to take my turn at bat.

MARK and ZEV of the Pastrami King — Shelley Chevlowe went to get sandwiches for Abe Deutscher and me and Mark and Zev treated Shelley very bad and now it is a major feud on Queen's Boulevard that cannot be handled.

BELLA ABZUG — For what she said to Ronnie Eldridge about me.

SOCIETY CAREY — Greatest of tragedies! Society Carey's helicopter gets a cough and has to be grounded. They find a smaller helicopter, which has only one pilot. Society Carey grouses. He wants two pilots. No one is available. So a state trooper puts on a baseball hat and earphones and slips in and poses as the co-pilot. Society Carey is happy. He has two pilots. The state trooper in the baseball hat is happy. He is flying in a helicopter for the first time in his life.

This is what the public pays for, and what those who know Society Carey best think of him.

Society Carey circles his desk with his new red hair and old red face and he says my name and then he says 'mongrel' and 'cur.' Of course somebody goes to the phone and calls me; Society Carey can't go into the next room without somebody calling me up. Forget about a restaurant, the waiters and customers line up at the phone booth. So I know what he thinks about me, but it's not half as bad as what I think about him. Even at the end of the world, at any Last Judgement, where everybody has to stand around and say hello like they love each other, I am going to raise my hand and say, 'If it's all the same, the one person in the whole history of the world I don't want to talk to is Society Carey.'

KOCH THE MAYOR — He made a big thing about not being able to support Mario Cuomo because of Breslin and Newfield. The first insult is that he mentioned me in the same breath with Newfield, about which I will tell you later.

Koch has done this before, too. One day in City Hall he said that Breslin and Newfield are part of the Elaine's crowd that doesn't like him. I don't know about Newfield, but I have been in Elaine's maybe three times in my life, even though Elaine and I have only the greatest memories of each other from another life, when we were young and vibrant in the weeds in the empty lot at Sutphin Boulevard and 101st Avenue in Jamaica.

I think that using Breslin's name was a way for Koch to keep himself from facing the cold, uncomfortable fact that Cuomo was here, was not going away, and was ready for one of those reasonable public discussions in front of a lot of people, the idea of which causes Koch to freeze; in the small of the night he sees Mario Cuomo answering a question.

Koch has made it harder to walk around this city. He throws his arms in the air and screams how great he is, while taxpayers step into potholes and do flips. He says the crime is going down, but the people with their heads opened believe it is still rising. I am beginning to think that if, by mouth or mannerism, you help impress on the poor of this city the idea that they have no future, then each year a few more of the young poor will go out and act as if they have no future.

I truly loved Koch at the antihandgun rally after John Lennon was shot. Because Koch's fund-raising dinner was run by his great friend David Margolis, chairman of Colt Industries. This is the company that makes the great Colt handguns that go off all over the city. Koch also took Margolis to Rome, where they visited the pope, who had been shot by a handgun. This is known as great taste.

Most people will come to realize soon that Koch is the loudest mirage we've ever had. See the next election.

MONTALVO from St Anne's Avenue – He yelled at me in the street one day. Maybe he doesn't remember it, but I do.

JAMES J. COMERFORD – The Joseph McCarthy of the Saint Patrick's Day Parade Committee. Among the thousands of charges he hurls about, never has anybody heard him utter the great truth, that the only thing he ever did for anybody Irish was to get his own name on a city payroll.

CHRISTOPHER LEHMANN-HAUPT – He gets permanent listing. Once, in his book reviews, he proclaimed that a book I wrote should not have been written. Marvelous idea! Ban books. Every time you let a German near a typewriter to do anything except repair it, he goes straight to authoritarianism. Ban books. Meanwhile in New Jersey, a local politician who became a federal judge, Lacey, took up the same cause. A reporter named Farber, who works on the paper where Lehmann-Haupt works, the *New York Times*, was writing a book on a case in Lacey's court and Lacey screamed and put Farber in jail. Immediately, I thought it would be a terrific idea for Lehmann-Haupt and the judge to hang out together, seeing as they have the same views. Then someday Lacey the Judge could put Lehmann-Haupt in jail.

DAVID GARTH – There is nothing that pleases him more than the sight of a turned back.

AL NEWMAN – He is the big bail bondsman. Once in the last year, I made a terrible mistake. I went to Sidney Krautt's party in Atlantic Beach and I forgot my copybook. When Al Newman came up to me, I knew I shouldn't have been talking to him, but I couldn't remember why. So I spoke to him. When I got home, I looked him up in my book and memorized what Al Newman once did to me and now, by rote, I know what to do if I see Al Newman on the street: cut him off with a glare.

JACK NEWFIELD – And the whole *Village Voice* newspaper with him. Each year, with these people, it is a different game. Once, Newfield put my picture in his newspaper and said I was one of the greediest people in New York. Because I wrote a book for money. Let him try to do the book, never mind get the money for it. Another time, I don't know exactly what the point was, but they put in my picture and said I was selling out the whole industry. Now this year, all of a sudden, Newfield decides to change. So here is this picture in the *Village Voice* the other day and it said underneath, 'Jimmy Breslin, real good guy this time.' No, thank you. I felt better about Newfield and his place when they were saying that I was greedy and bad. I don't believe in correcting the past by suddenly putting down five or six good words. Maybe Newfield likes me this year. But I didn't like him the year before last and last year and now for sure I'm not going to talk to him for all of this year.

DOUG IRELAND – Standing broke on the sidewalk outside a magazine. Runs inside and types them out a personal attack on me. Grabs ninety-five dollars and runs back on to the street. I'm not Frankie McPhillip, but Doug Ireland sure as hell is Gypo Nolan. Ireland edges out Marty Steadman as stool pigeon of the year.

WILLIAM SHAWN – The one worst weeper I ever came across. He is the editor of the *New Yorker* magazine. When he's not in freaking tears. In his magazine, he ran a long editorial that attacked people on newspapers who had to write about Son of Sam because he was real. One of the reasons why the killer was caught was that he had in his car window an envelope with printing familiar to police because they had received samples of his printing from me. When I called Shawn up and told him this, his immediate reaction was to weep: 'Oh, I knew something like this would happen.'

CIRCULATION WEIGHART – He was the editor of my newspaper, the *Daily News*, at a time when policewoman Cibella Borges was fired by middle-aged Irish Roman Catholics because she had posed for dirty naked pictures about a year before being sworn. Stories about Cibella infuriated cops and their friends and papers were sold. Then the police commissioner, Dead Body McGuire, snuck around to the *Daily News* with the pictures of Cibella Borges. Greatest filth! Oh, look at this dirty little naked slut! Circulation Weighart then sabotaged his own paper in order to receive a pat on the head from the police chief. Dead Body McGuire now has a job as a plant guard. Circulation Weighart is somewhere right now, but he sure isn't the editor of the *Daily News* anymore. How can these children pester Breslin?

THE ALSO RANS – Whitey Lewis; Morgenthau the Tireless – the man for whom the phrase 'No Heavy Lifting' was coined; Arthur Lonschein, who likes to write nasty letters and then smile sweetly and say he doesn't remember doing it; Joe Cannon; John O'Mara, Cusamano; Nick from the Forge Diner; Kay O'Hare; Sy Rotker; Weinstein the Judge; John Keenan – the Keenan who was a bookmaker with a loose mouth and they made him a federal judge; Superior Cohn; John Neckland; Tony from Tutto Bene – he is on this list not for a year, but for ever; Fel – soon, he'll be what he is worth mentioning, one letter; Suzanne White; Darnell Price; Joey Beglane; Podhoretz's wife; Gael Greene – the secret about her is that she has absolutely no taste; Rughead Hauptman; Bill Flanagan - one of the troubles in this country is that they sell typewriters to anyone; and, as always, Kleinstuber.

•

ANDY ROONEY

Andrew Aitken Rooney was born in 1919 in Albany, New York, and educated at Colegate University. He started his professional journalistic career during the Second World War as a correspondent for the *Stars and Stripes* and subsequently became a writer for radio and television presenters Arthur Godfrey, Garry Moore and Harry Reasoner. In 1971 he began to broadcast his own essays and TV specials as well as his weekly 'A Few Minutes with Andy Rooney' for

CBS's *60 Minutes*. He became a thrice-weekly columnist for the Tribune Company Syndicate in 1979, appearing in over 300 newspapers.

Going Newspaper Wishing
From *Word for Word* (1986)

A painting bought in 1971 at a garage sale for $12 by a Connecticut man, Andrew Rooney, was sold at auction yesterday at the Sotheby Parke Bernet Gallery for $647,000.

Rooney, who bought the dirt-covered painting because he admired the wood in the frame, put the painting in his basement. Several weeks ago, while cleaning out a storage area between the washing machine and his workbench, Rooney brushed some of the dust off the old picture and realized it was a genuine oil painting. Inspecting the grime-covered surface of the picture more carefully, he noticed a signature in the bottom right-hand corner.

The painting proved to be a rare early work by August Flambeau, the great seventeenth-century Dutch master.

Asked what he's going to do with the money, Rooney replied, 'I'm not sure. Maybe I'll spend it staying two nights in a New York City hotel.'

A homeowner's attempt to reposition a piece of flagstone in the walk leading from his home to the street led to an important discovery yesterday. Andrew Rooney, a writer, lifted the heavy stone with a pry bar and was about to shovel sand under the stone in an attempt to level it when he noticed the corner of a metal box sticking out of the ground under the walk.

Rooney dug carefully around the box and, after unearthing it, discovered that it contained more than $1 million in $5, $10 and $20 bills. He said there were also a lot of $1 bills he didn't bother to count.

Although the money appeared to be more than fifty years old, it was in perfect condition. After counting it, Rooney took his find to the local police station and turned it over to the sergeant on duty. Police officials said that if the money was not claimed in an hour and fifteen minutes, it would be turned over to Rooney.

Asked what he would do with the money, Rooney said he was thinking of turning it over to a home for tired writers.

In 1971, a local resident, Andrew Rooney, bought three acres of land in the northeast section of the state, thinking he might someday build a house there. Rooney paid $375 an acre for the land at that time.

Yesterday, the Acme International Machine Tool and Computer Corporation announced its plans to build its new $400 million headquarters complex in a two-square-mile area there. Because Rooney's three acres lie in the middle of the proposed construction site, work cannot begin until Acme can negotiate a sale price for the purchase of his land.

'I want to be fair,' Rooney said when questioned by reporters. 'I'm asking $125,000 an acre.'

*

A Circuit Court judge has ruled that more than $2 million that has been accumulating interest in a dormant savings account for more than sixty years belongs to Andrew Rooney, of this city.

The money, which was deposited there by Joshua Reynolds, a second cousin of Rooney's great-grandfather, has increased greatly in value over the years because of the accrued interest.

A bank official said that just as soon as one of the tellers was free, the money would be counted. It is estimated that, with interest, the amount will exceed $10 million.

While Rooney never knew his benefactor, the court decided he was Reynolds' closest living relative. Asked yesterday how he felt, Rooney said that he felt good. He went on to say that, even though he never knew Joshua Reynolds, he felt that if he had known him he would have liked him very much.

Because of a little-known provision in the tax law governing such funds, Rooney will receive the money tax-free.

I read these stories, but never about me.

Explaining It All for You
From *Word for Word* (1986)

Not today, but soon perhaps, I'll be explaining the war between Iraq and Iran to you. I'll tell you how the war started, what the war is about, who is fighting whom and why. I think by the time I finish my explanation, it will make a lot more sense to you than it does now. First, of course, I'll have to find out myself.

I haven't quite decided how, but I'll probably start by explaining the difference between the two countries. One of them is predominantly Moslem and I think the other may be, too. If not, it's something else. I'll make all that clear for you.

One of the big troubles with that war for most Americans is that the names of the two countries are so much alike. It isn't as though they were called France and Germany. Calling two countries France and Germany makes it a lot easier to tell them apart than calling them Iran and Iraq. Don't worry about it for now, though. Just as soon as I find out what it's all about, I'll let you know.

While I'm at it, I might as well explain what's going on in India for you.

In 1984, hundreds of Indians were killed when the Indian Army attacked the Golden Temple in Amritsar. The Golden Temple is headquarters for the Sikhs. (I'll be explaining who the Sikhs are.)

Amritsar, according to the newspapers, is in the Punjab, so naturally, I'll be telling you where and what 'the Punjab' is, too. As I understand it now, it is not a religion. The Punjab is a geographical area of India.

India, by the way, is no longer to be confused with Pakistan, although the food is a lot alike. I'll go into a detailed explanation of why Pakistan is no longer part of India and how the Sikhs in the Punjab differ from the Hindus.

If I have the time, I'll probably explain how the Hindus differ from the Sikhs, the

Moslems, the Buddhists, the Baptists, the Seventh-Day Adventists, Jehovah's Witnesses, Methodists, Jews, Shintoists, Catholics and Confucians. Most of the world's wars have begun over religious differences between people who honestly believe their religion is the only right one, so I think it's important that you understand how the religions differ from each other. A detailed explanation will be forthcoming from me very, very soon, probably.

Nor do I wish to exclude Central America. There are still a few people in the United States who don't completely understand why Nicaragua is constantly having trouble with its neighbor, Honduras. I'll be making that clear so you'll all better understand our problems there. Likewise, I'll be telling you the difference between San Salvador and El Salvador. Unless I'm very much mistaken, one of them is a city and the other a country. When I finish, there won't be any doubt in your mind.

Because there's also some doubt about which are the good guys and which are the bad guys in the guerrilla war in either El, or San, Salvador, I'll find out and let you know once and for all about that, too.

Everyone hates war, everyone says. If we're going to do something about stopping wars, we ought to do what we do with any problem. We study it and write a report. That's why I'm going to do this public service, explaining all the wars of history, just as soon as I get some free time. I'll be explaining not only the differences that brought on the war between Iran and Iraq, but I'll also be telling you the details of the Punic Wars, the Napoleonic Wars, the Crimean War and the Peloponnesian War. I'll refresh your memory about the Crusades and what the Crusaders were crusading for and why they killed so many people doing it. I'll tell you whether Attila the Hun was really all that bad a guy or not.

On a separate occasion, I'll tell you why we got into the war in Vietnam.

I won't leave one war unexplained . . . if there is an explanation for one.

•

BERNARD LEVIN

(Henry) Bernard Levin was born in 1928 and educated at Christ's Hospital, and graduated in economics at the London School of Economics, University of London. He became a journalist in 1953 and has written columns for various papers, but particularly *The Times*. Many of these have been collected in book form.

Keeping Them in Their Place . . .
The Times, 20 September 1977

The death in captivity in South Africa of John Cheekykaffir, leader of the movement among black South Africans to persuade the government to admit that they mostly have only two legs each, has given rise to a considerable amount of disquiet, controversy, criticism and kicking demonstrators in the head. It will be recalled that Cheekykaffir, who was twenty-two years old at the time of his death, was said by the Minister of Justice, Mr Sjambok-Goering, to have died of old age. Asked at a press conference how a man of twenty-two could die of old age, he said that he was himself a qualified doctor and had examined the body shortly before the murder, and it was quite clear to him that old age was the cause. 'All the signs of old age were present,' he said; 'a broken nose, torn ears, boot marks on his ribs, the lot. Anyway, the inquest decided that it was old age, which settles it.' At this, several reporters pointed out that the inquest had not been held, and the Minister explained that that had nothing to do with it. 'If we are going to wait for an inquest to be held before we announce its findings,' he said, 'our admirable and overworked police force would never have time to murder anybody at all.'

Next day, 417 leading doctors signed a statement saying that it was quite impossible for a man of twenty-two to die of old age, and the Minister was asked to comment. 'I never said he had died of old age,' snapped Mr Sjambok-Goering. 'I said quite clearly that it was a severe cold in the head.' A journalist (actually it was that horrible man Donald Woods,* who has in the past gone so far as to suggest that it is somehow improper for South African police to throw suspects out of high windows) then reminded the Minister that he had claimed to have examined Cheekykaffir himself. 'Ah, yes,' said the Minister, 'but it appears there was some confusion. The body I examined was that of another man altogether – an easy mistake to make, after all, considering that the buggers all look the same anyway. Besides, don't forget I'm not a doctor – I'm only the Minister of Justice. I don't know anything about medicine – or justice, either, come to think of it.' Woods (for it was indeed he) then pointed out that the Minister, on the previous day, had said that he was a qualified physician, whereupon the Minister smiled wearily and explained that he had been trained as a doctor, but was subsequently struck off the register.

Next day, 8,124 doctors signed a statement saying that it was impossible for a man in Cheekykaffir's excellent state of fitness to die of a cold; at the same time, both the Pope and the Archbishop of Canterbury expressed anxiety at the circumstances of Cheekykaffir's death. Once more, the Minister was asked to comment, and explained that when he had said that the cause of death was a cold he had had no direct responsibility himself, but had been relying on the report submitted to him by the governor of the prison, Mr Thug-Deadman. (When Mr Thug-Deadman was asked about this, he replied that he had had no direct responsibility himself, but had been relying on the report submitted by Colonel Proudly-Swastika, police chief of the district in which the prison lay. When the Colonel was asked about this, he replied that he had had no direct responsibility himself, but had been relying on the report submitted to him by General Jack Bootz, head of the South African security services. When the General was asked

---

* Then editor of the *East London Daily Dispatch*; he was subsequently 'banned' (that is, forbidden to work or write or associate with other people, while it became a crime for any publication to quote any of his words) for his part in exposing the truth about the torture and murder of Steve Biko by the South African police, and the subsequent cover-up by the Minister of Justice, Mr James Kruger. It is, of course, to that case that this column refers.

about this, he replied that he had had no direct responsibility himself, but had been relying on the report submitted to him by the Prime Minister, Mr van der Scoundrel. When the Prime Minister was asked about this, he replied that he had had no direct responsibility himself, but had been relying on the report submitted to him by the Minister of Justice, Mr Sjambok-Goering.)

The Minister was then asked to comment on the Pope's statement. 'The Pope is a Communist,' he replied; 'I thought everybody knew that.' 'But what about Archbishop Coggan?' he was asked; 'is he a Communist, too?' The Minister curled his lip: 'Coggan?' he said; 'don't you know his real name is Cohen?' This, as may well be supposed, entirely disposed of the matter as far as all decent and reasonable people were concerned, but it was not enough for the loathsome Woods, who asked the Minister whether an independent judicial inquiry would be set up to examine all the circumstances of Cheekykaffir's death. The Minister first suggested to Mr Woods that he would do well to have himself examined by his own doctor for signs of a serious cold in the head, as well as old age. 'Something tells me,' he went on, 'that you are in great danger of dying of one or the other quite soon. I mean, it is well known that people with colds often fall under motor cars, and the number of old people who put their heads in gas ovens without leaving a note – or indeed anything but signs of a struggle – is shockingly large.' He then went on to take the wind out of the sails of the repulsive Woods by saying that not only would an independent inquiry be set up; it actually had been. 'And what is more,' he continued triumphantly, 'it has already reported.'

The Minister informed the journalists that the members of the inquiry had been the Prime Minister (Mr van der Scoundrel), the head of South Africa's security services (General Jack Bootz), the police chief of the district in which the prison was situated (Colonel Proudly-Swastika), the governor of the prison (Mr Thug-Deadman), and himself. 'And in addition,' he added, 'the inquiry had two *ex officio* members, namely the policemen who actually murdered Cheekykaffir, and were therefore in a much better position to know what happened than any journalist.'

Asked to say how long the inquiry had taken, and what its findings had been, the Minister said that it had been set up immediately before Cheekykaffir had been arrested, and had reported the same afternoon – fully six days before he had died. 'I venture to say,' he added, 'that few countries could equal that record of swiftness and efficiency. As for its findings, the inquiry concluded unanimously that Cheekykaffir died of measles – just as I told you.'

The Minister then went on to reveal that, at the time of Cheekykaffir's death, a number of charges against him were being prepared, on which he would shortly have been prosecuted. These charges included: damage to public property, viz. several police truncheons rendered almost useless by Cheekykaffir repeatedly striking them with his kidneys; unauthorized use of electricity, viz. the substantial amounts consumed through Cheekykaffir's genitals during police questioning; and failing to report an accident, viz. falling down three flights of iron stairs at police headquarters.

Stop Press: The condition of Donald Woods was today said by the Minister of Justice to be 'critical'. Asked to comment, Mr Woods said he had never felt better in his life.

Asked to comment on Mr Woods's statement, the Minister said that he had been misreported. Mr Woods's condition was not yet critical, but was due to become so towards the end of the week.

Ah, So
The Times, 23 November 1977

As a lifelong collector of significant conjunctions, I was delighted to find the other day, in an unobtrusive paragraph, a specimen (in excellent condition) of that rare form the Apparent Contradiction. 'Americans,' it read, 'are using the post more and more, so stamp prices will not rise as fast in coming years as previously predicted.'

So. Not 'but', you notice, or 'however', or even the neutral 'and'; a full-strength 'so' links the fact that Americans are using the post more to the conclusion that the stamps they buy are cheaper than they might otherwise be.

The Apparent Contradiction will be apparent only to the British. Here, if we are told that more letters are being posted, we brace ourselves for the inevitable announcement of an increase in the price paid for posting them, and even for a massive campaign by the Post Office to persuade us to write fewer.

That is because of the well-known Post Office principle that the best way of responding to an increase in the use made by the public of any of its services is to seek ways of reducing demand rather than increasing supply. The easiest way of doing that, of course, is to raise prices; the Post Office dreams of the day when the cost of a stamp will have reached infinity and the number of customers *nil*; as the customers are well aware, satisfying progress towards achieving both these laudable intentions has been made in the last few years.

Now the Post Office is not alone in this attitude; if it were, I would hardly bother to bring the subject up. In fact, it typifies an entire range of practices and instincts in the commercial life of Britain which contrast strikingly with those of the United States, and, increasingly, the rest of the world. America practises the precept that if you are in business to make money, it helps to find out what people want and then sell it to them at a price they can afford, and also that the lower the price the more of it they will buy, and the more money you will therefore make.

How many times have you been told in a shop in this country that you cannot have the object you are seeking, not because the shopkeeper does not like your face, or because he fears that you will ill-treat it when you have got it home, or because he is too distracted by the fact that his wife has just run off with the milkman, but because 'there's no call for it'? Well, I assure you that if an American shopkeeper said that to a customer, the customer would literally be quite unable to discern any meaning in the words, and would conclude that he was being addressed in some unknown tongue.

This variety of *vice anglais* can be seen in a particularly vivid symbolic form in restaurants of the less sophisticated kind. If the menu, for instance, includes roast beef with brussels sprouts and roast lamb with peas, it may take you anything up to forty minutes to convince those in charge that you want the beef with the peas, and even at the end of that time you will as like as not be unsuccessful in your request, possibly even being told that there is no call for it.

The American attitude, when faced with an eccentric or even hitherto unknown demand, is to seek first to understand exactly what is being asked for, and to seek next a way of providing it. I have often asked in the United States for something that was either unknown there, or was known under a name that was unknown to me. The response has always been to try to elicit what I am talking about, and then to find something as close to the specification as possible.

In Germany this is taken still further; if you go into a restaurant – not just a café, but a real restaurant – and order only a bowl of soup and a glass of wine, they will not only serve it to you without demur; it will never occur to them to think your request is in any way odd. Nor, of course, is it; they are there to sell you food, and what items of food they sell you depends only and entirely on your wishes in the matter. (And I have never, to my recollection, been refused service in a restaurant or café in Germany, Austria, France or Italy if the door was open and the lights on, whatever the hour of the day or night. I could not count the number of times I have entered a British establishment, and been met only with a snarl of 'We're closed'.)

What all this amounts to, of course, is the difference between the respective attitudes to competition held in Britain and the rest of the world. It can be seen with limpid clarity in the motor car industry; the British driver having expressed a liking, by his purchases, for Japanese cars, large numbers of these are imported to meet the demand. It did not occur to the British manufacturers to meet this competition by making their product more attractive to the customer; they simply squealed 'unfair, unfair' and Mr Edmund Dell* was sent to Tokyo to beg the Japanese to export fewer cars to Britain. The Japanese are a notoriously polite people, but even they must have been hard put to it to go on bowing and smiling when what they wanted to do was to throw him down the stairs.

It's no good saying that Britain is the nice place it is precisely because we are not imbued with the spirit of competition and hustle and push and ambition and commercialism. In the first place, since we live in an internationally competitive world, we have to sell our goods and services competitively, and cannot now turn ourselves into a kind of Gandhian peasant economy, with the good men of Didsbury, Handsworth and Claygate sitting before their semi-detached doors clad in dhotis and plying spinning-wheels. In the second place, we actually have all the worst forms of envy without any of its good effects. (Indeed, another example of what I am talking about, and that perhaps the most terrible of all, can be seen in the widespread reaction to the discovery that somebody else has got, or is earning, more money than the discoverer. The response is not, as it would be in America, to strive to catch up and surpass the rival; it is not, as it would be if Britain really practised what the simple-lifers preached, a complete indifference; it is a sour determination to ensure that the other man is so penalized, weighted, taxed or even – in the case of trade unionists, for instance, putting in more

---

* Then Minister for Trade.

hours of overtime than the union specifies – actually fined, that the balance will be redressed. If you want a specific example, go and read some of the comments made about Mr Don Revie when he signed his lucrative contract with the Saudi Arabian government.)

And so – so indeed! – the American can look forward to cheaper stamps as a reward for posting more letters, while if we dared to emulate them we could expect only fewer collections and higher prices as a punishment for our temerity. It has been pointed out that if the Post Office introduced a special cut-rate postage for Christmas cards, not only would this please many people, but so many more cards would be sent that the Post Office might actually make more money than it otherwise would. But the Post Office will not heed the suggestion; and when I say 'but' I mean 'so'.

•

KHUSHWANT SINGH

Khushwant Singh was born in Hadali, Punjab, in 1915. Educated at Government College, Lahore, King's College and the Inner Temple, he practised law in Lahore before joining the Indian Ministry of External Affairs in 1947. He served as a diplomat in Canada, London and Paris. His journalistic career began in 1951 with All India Radio. His column first appeared intermittently in the *Illustrated Weekly of India* (which he edited from 1969 to 1979), under the heading 'The Editor's Page'. When he moved to the *Hindustan Times* (which he edited from 1980 to 1983), he wrote a regular Saturday column, under the heading 'With Malice Towards One And All', which has been described as 'the most widely read column in India'. Typically, a 'Malice' column was a potpourri of autobiographical reflection, topical commentary, book review and humour. He has also written a two-volume history of the Sikhs, several novels and short stories, and occasional feature articles for foreign newspapers, particularly the *New York Times*. He was a Member of Parliament from 1980 to 1986.

'With Malice Towards One and All . . .'
Hindustan Times, 1 May 1982

Amritsar

Who would have believed in 1947 that a day would come when Hindus and Sikhs would be rioting against each other? There had never been tension between these two communities during the days of the Raj. When we abolished separate electorates and declared ourselves a secular Socialist state, we assumed that we had cut off the roots of communalism and all communities would be able to live happily ever after. What went wrong?

A major contributing factor was the resurgence of fundamentalism in all our religions. 'Secularism does not mean no religion but respect for all religions,' our leaders told us. And to prove that they were men of religion (*ergo* good men) they spouted *slokas*, *shabads*, performed *havans, bhoomi poojas, ardas* at every possible function. Thus premium was put on orthodoxy which bred a sense of superiority of one's own faith over others. Fanaticism and intolerance of other communities followed as a matter of course. Therefore the first thing to do is to ban every kind of religious ritual at state or civic functions and dissuade political leaders from chanting sacred texts. Harking back to the past can be hazardous: to wit Josh Malihabadi:

> *Maazee ke dosh pe gaye thhey voh charahaney*
> *Maazee nay utha utha ke paika sau bar.*

> They went to climb up on the shoulders of the Past;
> The Past picked them up a hundred times and hurled them on the ground.

Sikh–Hindu tension has a background uniquely its own. The two communities are so close to each other that the dividing line is often invisible. Hence Sikhs who wish to emphasize Sikh separateness are driven to exaggerate or even create differences. The Bhindranwale type of fundamentalism is one manifestation of this attempt at separateness. The exaggerated abhorrence for tobacco (never alcohol) is another. Even in the heyday of Sikh political power and Maharajah Ranjit Singh's rule, no Sikh bothered about non-Sikhs smoking in the streets and bazaars around the Harimandir. Suddenly now some of them have decided that smoking, although it may be indulged in half a mile away from the temple, violates its sanctity. Having scored on fundamentalism and tobacco they have now turned to the cow. Although the *Granth Sahib* has nothing to say on the subject, there are many references to its sanctity in the writings of Guru Gobind Singh which most orthodox Sikhs regard as sacred as the *Granth*. But who is bothered about religions? If the cow serves the purpose of the Sikh separatists, they are willing to sacrifice it. I cannot think of a more diabolical perversion of religious traditions to gain political ends.

Merit or Caste?

One afternoon last week a delegation of three junior civil servants came to call on me. From their names I could tell that they were *dwijas* – twice born. They were in a high state of agitation because they had been superseded by men in lower ranks for no other reason except that promotions had been reserved for Harijans and Scheduled Tribes. 'As an instructor, I trained boys who have now been made my bosses,' said one bitterly. 'What can I do about it?' I asked. 'Give our cause publicity,' replied another and added in delightful Anglo-Punjabi: '*Fast unto death da program banaya hai.*'

The next morning a young man from Gorakhpur insisted on his right as an aggrieved citizen to speak to me. He was also in a high state of agitation. He placed a two-page representation before me and ordered: 'First read this then you will better understand what I have to say.' Obediently, I read the two pages. They were about assurances given by the government to rectify the imbalance in the administrative services between those coming from the villages and those with urban backgrounds. The representation was full of spelling and grammatical errors. No sooner had I finished reading it, the young man slapped three certificates in quick succession on my table: '*Fusht deeveezun fusht, eskool* leaving; *Fusht deeveezun fusht*, intermediate; *Fusht deeveezun fusht*, BA.' Although suitably impressed, I was also puzzled. 'What can I . . .' He interrupted me. 'They have failed me three times in the IAS *igjam*. I want that *phor rural peepil* it should *phibe* chances.' I conceded that the urban–rural imbalance had not been rectified but doubled if extending the number of times a candidate could take these competitive exams would make any appreciable difference. In any case, there was little prospect of the rules being changed immediately to enable him to take another two shots at the IAS. His eyes glowed with anger and he threatened: '*Nahin hoga to main paagal ho jaoonga.*'

The feeling of injustice is all pervasive. With justification the Harijans, scheduled castes and tribes, feel that they were discriminated against for many centuries and must now be given their legitimate share in the services. With equal justification people belonging to higher castes feel that when better qualified and more experienced men and women are denied promotion to appease lower castes they are being unfairly victimized. Rural folk feel that city dwellers have unfair advantage over them, the poor feel that their children do not get the same opportunities as the children of the rich to be able to compete with them. When a member of a minority community is not given a job, he insists that minorities are discriminated against. When a member of the majority community is denied a job, he feels Hindus' interests are sacrificed to keep Muslims, Christians and Sikhs happy. Thus personal interests are identified with community and even national interests.

I am not sure that we can do anything to obviate this general feeling of disenchantment with the state of affairs. But it is time that special privileges accorded to certain castes (except free education up to the graduation level for Harijans and tribals) were abolished. In matters of specialized education, employment and promotion only merit should count.

Dignified Exit

Dying and death are always in my mind but they never make me morbid. However, when I hear of a friend welcoming it with open arms, I get somewhat depressed. So it was last week when I got a letter from Dharam Yash Dev. Remember him? Ex-diplomat and author, he had accused Sanjay Gandhi and Adil Shaharyar (son of Mohammad Yunus) of making off with his brother's car or scooter and was later sued by Maneka for writing about it! We were, as it were, on opposite sides. But I always looked forward to his visits because he was so incorrigibly cheerful about everything. He was living in retirement in Dehra Dun and occasionally came to Delhi for hearings in Maneka's case and for treatment for some kind of cancer. He was so casual about it that I presumed it was one of the curable variety. Then Thursday before last he wrote to me from his son's house in Delhi. 'Because presently I am dogged by a terminal illness (cancer) and am beginning to feel the futility of living like shrivelled cabbage, the subject of euthanasia has been very much on my mind.' In short if the law did not forbid it, Dharam would like to end his life. I think he has every right to do so and if the law forbids it, so much the worse for the law.

It should be the fundamental right of every man to go with dignity. Minoo Masani has set up an Indian branch of the Society For the Right to Die with Dignity. There are already twenty-seven branches all over the world with many eminent writers (Arthur Koestler among them), scientists, doctors (including Christiaan Barnard), lawyers and industrialists as its members. The object of setting up a society for what would appear to be primarily a purely personal affair is to have this right legalized through an act of Parliament so that a person suffering from a terminal disease can either himself or, if he is past making this final decision, his relatives and doctors can decide that he should be allowed to depart in peace.

Another friend of my Bombay days, Colonel C. L. Proudfoot has put his thoughts on the subject in verse:

> Since the Going is inevitable
> Fear not the Time, but rather
> The Manner of departure;
> For me, the grace of a quick
> Exit, with no long-drawn agony
> Of helplessness to plague loved
> Ones, demanding time, money and
> Endless heartbreak, an object
> Of pity and despair, praying
> Mutely for the end. For me, a
> Swift clean gateway with bother
> To none, stealing silently into
> The night; quietly, without fuss
> Or fanfare; a kindness to loved
> Ones, the ultimate act of charity.

'With Malice Towards One and All . . .'
Hindustan Times, 26 September 1987

Hang Widow Burners!

I wish I had been in the shoes of Chidambaram, Minister of State (Home), when he confronted the 1,000-strong procession of Rajputs of Sikar district who claimed that nobody should interfere with the religious matters of their community. For one I would have told them that in the past it was not only the Rajputs who practised *Sati* as a religious rite but Brahmins, Kshatriyas and Jats as well. If other communities had been persuaded or frightened into abandoning this revolting custom, it was time the Rajputs of Sikar also came to their senses. I would have quoted actual incidents from Indian history. The most memorable of these was in the Punjab soon after it was annexed by the British. John Lawrence, who was Commissioner of Jalandhar-Doab, came across the practice of *Sati* and female infanticide among the Sikh Zamindars, as well as of burying lepers alive. He decided to put them down in the manner he thought would prove most effective. Since leases of land had to be renewed, he made every Sardar who sought their renewal make three vows on the *Granth Sahib: Beva nahin Jalaoonga*, (I will not burn a widow), *Beti nahin maaroonga* (I will not kill my daughter), *Korhi nahin dabbaoonga* (I will not bury a living leper). Lawrence's attitude was clear: no oath, no land.

Inevitably there was a howl of protest. Since the head of the Bedi family claiming descent from Guru Nanak was regarded as the spiritual leader of the community, he was prevailed upon to lead a delegation to Lawrence. The Bedi reminded Lawrence of the solemn undertaking given by the British on annexing their kingdom that they would not interfere with religious practices of the people and that *Sati* was one such practice sanctioned by religion. The Sahib gave him a fitting reply, 'We will abide by our promise if you abide by yours. We will not interfere with your customs if you do not interfere with ours. Your custom is to burn widows; our custom is to hang those who burn them.'

Mr Chidambaram, that is what you should have told the Rajputs of Sikar. And hang those who were party to the gory demise of the lovely, eighteen-year-old, Roop Kanwar.

HM the King

Slept the sleep of the just: eight unbroken hours of dreamless slumber. For one used to rising at four a.m. it was quite a throwback to younger days to be roused by the sun streaming through the windows and the crowing of roosters. White clouds floating on green hills, deep blue sky and distant murmur of the Wang Chu. Mahaguru Padma Sambhava was in his heaven and all was right with Bhutan.

Our first call was on His Majesty Digme Singye Wangchuk, King of Bhutan. He lives in a modest-sized villa, out of bounds for all except close members of his family. Like other Bhutanese bureaucrats he comes to the Secretariat to receive visitors and clear his files. It is a vast complex, some of it built in the thirteenth century as a monastery (*Dongon*) of blue stone. It was enlarged into a fortress (*Dzong*). In the seventeenth century the most notable builder of Bhutan, Ngawang Namgyal, added to its fortifications and, being a devout Buddhist of the Drupka school, named it the 'Fortress of the Glorious Religion'. Today it goes under the name of Tashichdozong. It was the present ruler's father, who made it the nation's chief secretariat. It is unlike any other secretariat in the world because besides departments of government, this one encompasses a huge six-storeyed temple, dormitories for monks, a school and much else. It conforms to the traditional pattern of Bhutanese architecture: sloping walls of sheer white interspersed with red beams, small latticed windows and tiled roofs. The base is stone and brick, the superstructure of blue pine. All walls are decorated with paintings of dragons, demons and deities. People who have difficulty in climbing stairs are best advised not to seek an audience with the king. You have to climb almost a hundred stairs in three different sections before you arrive somewhat out of breath outside his reception room.

I had never shaken hands with a king. Nor spoken to one. That morning I did both. And with the handsomest and the youngest (thirty-two) monarch in the world. The audience went on well over an hour. He spoke of the hazards of going too fast, of having hordes of undesirable tourists loitering inside monasteries, bribing poor Bhutanese to steal invaluable *tankhas* and idols, of the need to preserve Bhutanese cultural traditions etc. I asked him how he would contain the natural desire of his people to be involved in the administration of the state. He told me of the largely elected National Assembly and the Royal Advisory Council. 'People have to get accustomed to responsibility before they can be entrusted with power,' he said. As we got up to take our leave, he asked, 'Have you seen any Bhutanese folk dancing?'

'No', I replied, 'they are not on.'

'You will. Tomorrow at four p.m. in your hotel.'

From the palace we went to see the temple-memorial built for his father. There was a lot of coming and going of worshippers; prayer wheels churned, bells clanged and we heard mournful chanting. Buddhism practised in Bhutan has a strong admixture of Animism and Tantra. The temples are very ornate with fantastic animals around multi-armed gods and goddesses in the tight embrace of *maithuna* symbolizing life force.

What the king said of the need to preserve Bhutanese culture and tradition we saw in action that afternoon. Six kilometres from Thimphu is a 350-year-old fortress converted into a school very much like our Gurukuls. Some 360 boys ranging in age between ten and twenty study Bhutanese language and literature, painting and astrology, as well as some English. They are trained to become monks but are free to opt out and become householders.

One thing I have noticed during my travels is that in India, Pakistan, Bangladesh and Sri Lanka, common birds of all kinds are in greater abundance than in other countries. Bhutan has all the species we have, but I saw more doves and pigeons than sparrows, crows, kites or mynahs which infest our cities. Bhutan has wild animals in much greater abundance than we. The people, being Buddhists, rarely kill for sport. So tigers, panthers, leopards, bears, deer, wild boars, elephants and rhinos can be seen in the wild. Though boars damage potatoes and bears raid apple orchards, people shoo them away rather than shoot them. My security officer, Ramjar Dorji, who shamefacedly admitted that he loved shikar (including trout and Mahaseer fishing), told me that he had to secure permission to shoot a snow leopard which had become a cattle-lifter. He had to hand over its skin to the government.

Another thing I noted are Bhutan's excellent roads – narrow but well maintained. Also considerate drivers. No sooner you honked, than bus and truck drivers pulled up on the side to let you pass. Only once a bus kept hogging the road for almost half an hour. The driver was an Indian.

Encyclopaedia of Nature

It is not very often that I get excited over a book: I wade through almost one a day and forget about it within a few hours of finishing it. Books on art and natural phenomena have this great advantage that even after you have read the text, if the pictures are any good you go over them again and again. The latest addition to my shelf reserved for reliable books of reference is *Indian Wild Life, Sri Lanka and Nepal*, brought out by Insight Guides under the editorship of Samuel Israel and Toby Sinclair. It is a compendium of articles on our flora and fauna written by renowned experts (Gurung, Zafar Futehally, the Whittakers Sankhala, Billy Arjan Singh, Karanth Brijendra Singh, Seshan and the Grewals). The photographs are superb; the price extremely modest for the fare provided.

Next time you visit a bookstore, take a look at it and decide for yourself whether or not it is worth Rs. 150.

•

CALVIN TRILLIN

Calvin Trillin was born in Kansas City, Missouri, in 1935, and received an AB from Yale University in 1957. From 1960 to 1963 he was a reporter for *Time*, then he joined the staff of the *New Yorker*. In 1978 he began writing his 'Uncivil Liberties' column every third week for the *Nation*, on the strict understanding that he should be allowed to criticize its editor, Victor Navasky, if he so chose; and in 1986 he syndicated a shortened, weekly form of the column for the first time through the Cowles Syndicate. His columns have been collected in three books – *Uncivil Liberties* (1982), *With All Disrespect* (1985) and *If You Can't Say Something Nice* (1987).

My Tuxedo

Nation, January 1, 1983

I am often mistaken for the sort of person who does not own a tuxedo. Once or twice, I regret to say, this mistake has been made even though I happened to be wearing a tuxedo at the time ('My goodness, are they still renting that kind?'). More often, it is part of a general impression. 'I don't suppose you own a tuxedo . . .' people sometimes say to me, the way an English country gentleman might say to the Hasidic scholar he has met on the train, 'I don't suppose you own a shooting stick . . .' The general impression is incorrect. I do own a tuxedo. I have owned a tuxedo for nearly thirty years. The same tuxedo. If you were planning to invite me to an event at which tuxedos are required, rest assured that I would show up properly dressed.

Don't ask me for New Year's Eve. I'm busy. I go to the same party every New Year's Eve, and one reason it gives me great pleasure is that it presents me with an opportunity to wear my tuxedo. I bought the tuxedo in 1954, when I was a thrifty young undergraduate, because I had added up the number of black-tie events I would have to attend during college, divided the cost of a tuxedo by that number, and concluded that I would be better off buying a tuxedo than renting one. As you must have gathered, this was a fancy college. I am often mistaken for the sort of person who did not attend a fancy college, but that's another story.

As it turned out, there have been a number of occasions to wear the tuxedo since graduation – that possibility hadn't even figured in my tuxedo management scheme in 1954 – and every time I wear it the cost per wearing decreases. This New Year's Eve, for instance, wearing my tuxedo is going to cost me only about forty-eight cents. Try renting a tuxedo for forty-eight cents these days. Knowing that my tuxedo becomes cheaper every time I wear it may influence me in the direction of showing up in a tuxedo now and then at events where black-tie is not strictly necessary, like a hog roast or a divorce hearing or a meeting where people are planning the overthrown of the government by force and violence.

'Oh, you shouldn't have bothered,' the hostess often says, while gazing admiringly at my cummerbund.

'It's nothing, really,' I tell her. 'A matter of approximately fifty-five cents.'

When I tell people about my tuxedo ('Guess how much this tuxedo is costing me tonight. Go ahead – don't be afraid to guess. Just take a guess. How much do you think?'), they often tell me that I should be proud of being able to fit into something I bought in college. True. I would be prouder, though, if I did not have reason to believe that the pants of my tuxedo actually belong to Joe LeBeau. Joe was a college classmate of mine – a rather rotund college classmate of mine, if you must know. I have reason to believe that just before graduation, at a black-tie party for which a large room was converted into a dormitory for a number of out-of-town guests who were wearing nearly identical tuxedos, Joe LeBeau and I came away with each other's pants. That's the sort of thing that can happen at a fancy college.

When somebody who sees me in my tuxedo asks a question that leads to the subject of Joe LeBeau ('Say, are you by any chance wearing somebody else's pants, or what?'), I am often asked why I did not simply exchange his pants for my own once the mistake was discovered. Anybody who asks that never knew Joe LeBeau, for whom the phrase 'not vulnerable to reason' was invented. As an example of LeBeauesque conversation, I repeat an exchange between LeBeau and an earnest fellow from down the hall who happened to be taking the same course in modern history:

JOE LEBEAU: The French and Germans were fighting on the same side then.

EARNEST FELLOW: But that's impossible! The French hated the Germans!

JOE LEBEAU: Do you blame them?

I haven't seen Joe LeBeau since graduation – I understand he's a judge in California – but I occasionally run into other classmates who, as graduates of a fancy college, tend to be Wall Street financiers, impatient with those of us who have not just depreciated a factory or written off an airline. 'What are you up to?' they always say.

'I am amortizing my tuxedo,' I tell them. 'I am amortizing the hell out of my tuxedo.'

By exchanging such pleasantries with the rich, I realize, I continue to disappoint Harold the Committed, who continues to worry a lot about the possibility that I am not worrying enough.

'What are you doing about the finite supply of natural resources on this planet?' he said only the other day.

'I'm glad you asked, Hal the C,' I replied. 'As it happens, I have been wearing the same tuxedo now for nearly thirty years. No squandering of the earth's irreplaceable fossil fuels to produce a new tuxedo every season for me. Nobody's clear-cutting any forests to make me a tuxedo. Little children in Europe aren't starving while I leave perfectly good tuxedos on my plate.'

Harold the Committed, after reminding me that the Scottsboro Boys* didn't own

---

* Nine negro youths convicted of raping two white women; their death sentences were later overturned.

even one tuxedo among them, said that I was badly in need of attending one of his regular recommitment meetings.

'Any time but New Year's Eve,' I said. 'I'm busy on New Year's Eve.'

I can see my New Year's Eve now. I am dressing for the evening. I calculate what my tuxedo is going to cost me to wear to the same party one year hence, assuming I wear it occasionally during the intervening months – to a turkey shoot, say, or a bris. Even taking the voluminous pants off the hanger gives me pleasure. I find it a bit awkward putting on Joe LeBeau's pants, of course, but I love to start the new year by thinking of him trying to put on mine.

Investment Opportunities
Nation, March 21, 1983

Those who think that our family is a bit listless about looking after our financial affairs are apparently unaware of the sort of effort we put into the Publishers Clearing House Sweepstakes every year. We really go for it. We do our homework. We play hardball. We keep our eyes on the bottom line. We always lose.

'I think this year we should leverage our options,' I said when the Publishers Clearing House Million Dollar Sweeps entry arrived in the mail a couple of months ago.

'What does that mean?' my younger daughter, Sarah, asked.

'Your mother can explain the details,' I said. 'I'm strictly an idea man.'

I'm the one who had the idea about entering sweepstakes in the first place. Sarah, who is eleven, hasn't come up with any sound investment strategies since she got stymied trying to fill out the entry form for a drawing some beer company was holding for a new Pontiac Trans Am ('What should I put for business phone?'). It's natural for me to have a lot of ideas about these matters because I know a number of Wall Street millionaires. As it happens, every single person in the lower third of my college class – every single person, that is, except Blinko Moshler, who's a prominent lawyer in Toledo, and Dalt Durfee, who is the Deputy Undersecretary of State for Asian Economic Affairs – is a Wall Street millionaire. I occasionally run into one of them, usually at some restaurant I can't really afford. They're always talking about leveraging their options, or maybe optioning their leverages; ask my wife if you want the details.

They also talk a lot about what they're getting out of and what they're getting into. 'I just got out of the market and into shrimp boats,' one of the millionaires said when I came across a brace of them at an East Side nouvelle cuisine joint that seemed to be charging the price of a shrimp boat for three cold shrimp and a heart-shaped raspberry.

'I just got out of shrimp boats and into boxcars,' said the other one, someone I'll call Martin G. Cashflow. In his crowd, Cashflow is known for having just got out of whatever it is that everyone else is about to get into. Cashflow also happens to be one of those trendy millionaires who gets in and out of fads at the same time he's getting in and out of investments, so sometimes he's getting out of backgammon and into cattle ranches or into Sufism and out of discount plumbing supplies. Cashflow is the person who told me a long time ago that my problem was that writers are labor in a labor-intensive industry.

'I just got out of the New York State Instant Lotto and into the *Reader's Digest*

Sweepstakes,' I said. When they looked unimpressed, I assured them that I was savvy enough to have marked my entry form in a way that kept my name in the sweepstakes without obligating me to sign up at the special sweepstakes rate for a subscription to *Reader's Digest* for life plus ninety-nine years. I don't subscribe to any magazines. Some time after Cashflow told me that my problem was being labor in a labor-intensive industry, he told me that the smart money got out of magazines and into software years ago, at around the same time he got out of silver futures and into the Maharaj Ji. ('I don't think I want to get into software,' I said at the time, thinking that it had something to do with flannel pajamas. 'Kid, you *are* software,' Cashflow replied. 'That's your problem.') I figured there was nothing much I could do about writing for magazines – unless, of course, the big New Jersey Lottery number does turn out one year to be my army serial number with the last two digits reversed for good luck – but I was at least smart enough not to subscribe to any.

This year, we had a family meeting about the Publishers Clearing House Sweepstakes. We sat at the dining-room table, with sharpened pencils and clean white memo pads in front of us. 'How's the little-bitty sticker end holding up, Sarah?' I asked. In our operation, Sarah is the specialist in how to figure out which little-bitty sticker is supposed to be pasted where on the entry blank.

'Piece of cake,' Sarah said.

With Sarah trouble-shooting the little-bitty sticker end, I figured, the main decision we had facing us was which of the three superprizes we wanted – a certified check for $250,000, a $250,000 custom-built dream home or $40,000 a year for ten years.

'How do the numbers look on that one, Abigail?' I asked my older daughter.

'Ten times 40,000 is 400,000, Daddy,' Abigail said. 'Don't you remember what I told you about just adding a zero on the tens table?'

'But the question is whether we want to go for the ten-year payout or get the two-fifty up front and put that money to work for us,' I said.

'I'd rather have a Pontiac Trans Am,' Sarah said.

'OK, we'll meet again as soon as I figure out which option gives us the most leverage,' I said, trying to imagine how Martin Cashflow would end a meeting. 'I'll have my girl get back to your girl.'

'But Daddy,' Abigail said, 'we *are* your girls.'

I spent the next weeks trying to answer the questions that would allow us to eyeball a ballpark figure on the bottom line, or something like that. Is a $250,000 custom-built dream home the sort of thing Cashflow has in mind when he goes on about shelters? Aren't all $250,000 dream homes custom-built, or do some people have prefabricated dreams? In ten years, will $40,000 buy a Pontiac Trans Am? How about a Mars bar? I was thinking about such questions when Alice pointed out that entries to the Publishers Clearing House Sweepstakes had been due four days before ('You forgot to assign someone the deadline end'). I still had questions. If we decided to take the up-front cash and get it working for us, how many Instant Lotto tickets would $250,000 buy? What could 'leverage your options' possibly mean?

●

PHILLIP ADAMS

Phillip Adams was born in 1939 in Melbourne, Australia, and educated at Eltham High School. In 1954 he began reviewing films for Melbourne's Communist *Guardian* and contributing occasional items about the arts to the *Bulletin*, where he was briefly theatre critic. He moved to the *Australian* as television critic, and before long he had switched to a general column called 'Adams' Rib' (which appeared between twice and four times a week). The column generated a huge mailbag and Adams has ever since considered it a part of his role as a columnist to answer letters (sometimes as many as 10,000 a year). After Rupert Murdoch was browbeaten in a television interview by David Frost in London he decided to purge any satirists from his publications, which included the *Australian*. Adams went over to *Nation Review*, where he was given a page. However, the *Australian* received more mail about Adams than about the Vietnam War, and so it invited him back at twice his old salary to write 'Adams' Apple'. Over the years he has contributed to several Australian papers as well as to the *Financial Times*, the *Sunday Times* and the *New York Times*. After a period of being syndicated from the Melbourne *Age*, he returned to the *Australian*. He says he has always mumbled his columns into a hand-held dictating-machine, sometimes while driving 'the 300 kilometres between Sydney and my farm'. Although he has declared that 'columns are as evanescent as Kleenex tissues or leaves of Sorbent', he has published several collections and has stated that 'writing columns saves me the bother of writing novels and, even better, of writing autobiographies'. In addition to his work as a columnist, he has been a radio presenter for the Australian Broadcasting Corporation.

Australian, 25 July 1992

Whenever I hear about an off-duty policeman arresting someone in a park at night for an alleged act of moral turpitude, I can't help asking myself a question. Well, a couple of questions. Why do so many off-duty policemen lurk in parks after dark? And why do they hang around or in public loos?

Let's deal with the first question first. It would seem that a high percentage of Australian policemen are chaps of nocturnal and perhaps meditative proclivities, who like to walk through moon-dappled foliage. Perhaps they're amateur astronomers trying to spot supernovas or comets, or part-time naturalists who, inspired by the example of the ABC's Richard Morecroft, are seeking orphaned bats to mother.

Whatever the motives of their moonlit meanderings, such police invariably suffer from weak bladders. These, in turn, propel them to public lavatories where, not surprisingly, they meet men seeking sexual solace.

This raises another issue. Are the policemen we're recruiting too good-looking? Does Mr Plod now look like Robert Redford? Either they're excessively attractive or, inadvertently, they're sending out the wrong signals. Why else would perambulating policemen in parks get propositioned? Of course, being off-duty they're probably not in a uniform. So what the hell are they wearing? String singlets and excessively tight jeans? Lethal aftershave?

These are not frivolous issues. Australian policemen seem to loathe homosexuals even more than they detest Aborigines. 'Twas ever thus. So they like nothing better than trying to banish the scourge of sodomy from places of plumbing or horticulture. Thus there was a time, in Melbourne, when Russell Street had a policy of sending its prettiest policemen around the queers' beat. (It's OK, 'queer' has become politically correct. Many gay spokesmen prefer it to 'gay'.)

Mind you, being arrested could be seen as preferable to being beaten up. Some years ago I met an old school friend, one of Eltham High's sporting heroes. He was now a cop. After the mandatory nostalgia, I asked him what he and his partner were going to do, in their prowl car. 'Go around the dunnies and beat up poofters,' he said amiably. When I said that this procedure was neither sensible nor legal, both constables seemed puzzled. It was something they did regularly. A sort of sporting activity. My disapproval was, to them, utterly mystifying.

For years, nocturnal encounters in this or that park, between cops and queers, have led to a sad succession of men appearing in court, to face humiliation over something of monumental inconsequentiality. Sometimes a career is destroyed, or a marriage, because someone yields, perhaps for the first time, to temptation. To an invitation kindly extended by a policeman. Or things get a little out of hand and someone is thrown into the river Torrens, to end up on a coroner's slab.

A few months back, the Melbourne Comedy Festival ran a debate. What is more important, sex or a sense of humour? Of course, sex and humour are exactly the same thing. Or rather, should be. As Lord Chesterfield said of sexual intercourse, 'The position is ridiculous, the pleasure momentary.'

Since sex was invented, it has caused human beings almost more trouble than it's worth. Look at its tradition in British politics. There was Gladstone, that frequent prime minister, indulging in self-flagellation after visits to whores. More recently we had Profumo, whose career was destroyed by a little hanky-panky, while spanky-spanky has seen the destruction of others. The desire to be spanked seems a specifically upper-class British perversion, something to do with being raised by nannies and attending public schools. (That's why the French call it the 'malaise Anglaise'.) Then there was the sad case of Jeremy Thorpe, whose dazzling performance for the Liberals ended with a homosexual dalliance. All of which emphasizes that the best way of dealing with sex is not to take it so seriously.

While the French scoff at the English, they have the odd sexual scandal within their own Establishment. But at least they display a sense of humour. You may remember a recent French farce starring a cardinal who 'died on the job' in a Parisian brothel. Given the glum choice of demises, many of us would opt for the cardinal's method of opting out, by carking it at the climax. Trouble is, when you die in the act, and you're a VIP, there will be a lot of headlines before you can enjoy the haven of your headstone.

Not that you have to die on the job to be killed off. Look at Gary Hart. Although his sin was not so much fornication as lying about it. Ditto for the Irish bishop.

The pages of political history are littered with the victims of sexual innuendo. John Gorton, Janet Powell, Don Dunstan. Others like Bob Hawke and Paddy Ashdown (and perhaps Bill Clinton) escape the judgements of the tabloids, while a fortunate minority have actually benefited from the judgements of the courts. (Consider the profits of Jeffrey Archer.) None the less, the political toll, particularly in Britain, with ministers caught gutter-crawling or in massage parlours, suggests a lip-licking voyeurism on behalf of the mass media and a huge waste of resources on behalf of the police.

So let's go back to the opening of this column and raise the fundamental question. What business is it of the cops to arrest anyone on such sad, silly charges?

There are certain sexual activities that should clearly be of legal concern. By all means arrest the rapist and the pederast. Let us protect the child from prostitution and from some forms of incest. I'm not sure about the flasher, and certainly the streaker is now a bit of a yawn, in an era of full-frontal television and nuddy bathing. But certainly the negotiations between clients and adult prostitutes should be their business entirely, as confidential as the murmurings of guilt to a confessor. It is nothing to do with the policeman, even if, shock horror, it involves sex between members of the same gender.

Or have we learned nothing from thousands of years of history? Did we learn even less from the Fitzgerald inquiry? As long as we have such laws on the books, they will corrupt the policemen who are required or, worse still, yearn to enforce them. Only fools and fundamentalists deny that it's futile to attempt the prohibition of sex outside officially sanctioned, heterosexual double beds.

To hell with hypocrisy. To hell with convicting homosexuals for what they might do in a public loo. Particularly when a jail sentence means that they're likely to be pack-raped by heterosexuals in Pentridge, Boggo Road or Long Bay.

We talk about deregulation in Australia. Deregulation is meant to be good for us. Good for industry. Good for export. Good for telecommunications. Good for airlines. Well, if deregulation is good for banking, it's good for bonking as well. Let us deregulate sexuality, thus saving our police an awful lot of trouble. After all, we've long since dismantled most of our ludicrous censorship laws. It wasn't so long ago that Australia banned everyone from D. H. Lawrence and Mary McCarthy, along with forgettable art films from Sweden. And many of you will remember when policemen from Melbourne's Vice Squad decided Michelangelo's David was guilty of indecent exposure.

Recognizing that modern technologies have made censorship impossible, and yielding to common sense, we now have a system where, by and large, it's 'buyer beware', with the consumer required to take responsibility for what he or she reads or views.

And while we're deregulating, let's also deregulate drugs. Having proven at vast expense that US-style policies of prohibition and interdiction don't work (indeed, that they make matters immeasurably worse) let us abandon the absurdity of having legal versus illegal drugs. The legal ones are clearly more destructive, given that out of every one hundred drug-related deaths, ninety-seven are from cigarettes and grog. Yet Australia spends billions on ludicrous policies and strategies that condemn the other three per cent to lives of criminality and, worse still, to death. For as any medical authority will confess, the only serious side-effect of pure heroin is constipation.

Nothing will stop people taking drugs, irrespective of what we pronounce to be legal or not. By having bad laws about drugs we create bad results, of which bad police is one, and badly overcrowded gaols another. Let all drugs be legal and then let us try to persuade our fellow citizens to use them, all of them, more responsibly. This is slowly being achieved with cigarettes and could be achieved with alcohol, heroin and cocaine.

By getting rid of dotty, moralizing, wowserish prohibitions we would suddenly find that we had far fewer criminals. That we would need not nearly so many prisons. That the cost of customs and policing would be remarkably reduced.

I'm not suggesting that all our social problems would be solved, as if by magic, but we'd be taking a sensible step in the right direction.

As we approach the end of this long and rather unpleasant twentieth century, let us abandon the intolerance and unreality of the nineteenth century. Let us get the junkies out of the gaols, the law out of the bedroom and the off-duty policeman out of the parks. Instead of adopting British hypocrisies in sexual matters and American madness on narcotics, let us choose compassionate pragmatism.

Australian, 5 February 1944

It was frequently necessary, during history or geography at Eltham High, to draw maps of Australia. Most of us had to do this freehand, resulting in rather incontinent versions of our continent, but the privileged had plastic templates. Anticipating our Asian destiny, they were a fluorescent yellow and had little perforations in them to help in the delineation of states and territories.

The next procedure, irrespective of how you got this far, was to surround the map with a little fringe of blue, to indicate the oceans. The fringe looked a bit like the frilly paper skirt that went around birthday cakes. While it had no name, it should have been known as the lunatic fringe for it indicated that part of Australia where mad people went to sit on the beach and, worse, go swimming.

Much is made of the fact that Australians choose to live along the coastline, for whereas the sands of our great deserts are deemed hostile, the sands of our beaches are held to be attractive, welcoming, delightful.

Crap. They're as close to hell as you get on earth. And all the books on Robert Drewe, all the soaring anthems about our home being girt by sea, won't change my mind.

Let me be precise about this. I am not complaining about the landmass. Nor am I being petulant about the ocean. They are both admirable places. It's that little in-between bit we're discussing, the beach, which is neither one thing nor the other. For the beach is like purgatory. It is no man's land. This endless, rarely interrupted stretch of sand is a cruel and savage place, and hardly a day passes, particularly in summer, when we're not reminded of its dangers.

I'm dictating these notes on a day when the television news services are replete with warnings. First of all, there are bluebottles stinging people almost everywhere. Second, it's just been admitted by the Noosa Council that their sewage system is failing to remove all the viruses they're discharging into the ocean, so that you've got a good chance of catching herpes or leprosy. And I'm watching an interview with a greenie who says that Noosa is simply being candid about something that other councils obfuscate about.

Australians should know about beaches. We should have learned how dangerous they are from our experiences at Gallipoli. For while you're not all that likely to be shot at by a Turk at Torquay or masticated by a shark at Mornington, you're very likely to be nudged by a turd just about anywhere. And even if you stick to the shallows can you be absolutely certain about the froth? This is a country where piddling and paddling blur and overlap.

Australia's beaches are immense tips. Endless rubbish dumps. It's where the sea throws up its detritus and where the land tries to dispose of its effluent and rubbish. Like dandruff on the shoulders of a business suit, Australia's beaches are covered in polystyrene foam, perished thongs, the razor-sharp crystals of broken glass, not to mention discarded heroin needles. So, long before you get into the water to be munched by a grey nurse or stung by a bluebottle, you're likely to be lacerated by a shard of coke bottle or harpooned by a hypodermic. And even if you're not, the chances are that by the end of the day you'll have third-degree burns and be well on the way to a melanoma. Yet we flock to this misbegotten place, persuaded that the beach represents the kingdom of hedonism.

Meanwhile, the ocean is vomiting its flotsam and jetsam on to the sands with every turgid wave. And it's not just giving us back what we've tossed into it. The sea is regurgitating its own unpleasant muck, such as rotting seaweed. And let's face it, the sea isn't just full of human poo. It's also full of fish poo. Not only do fish poo wherever they feel like it, but there are some pretty big fish around Australia. So can you be sure that's a piece of decaying seaweed you've just stepped on? How do you know it isn't a disintegrating whale dropping? A piece of shark shit? Flounder faeces?

So a beach is where you get filth coming or going, and very often both. Your average gutter is cleaner than our golden sands.

And sand is very unpleasant material in its own right. It's highly abrasive, which is why they glue it on to pieces of paper so that you can rasp away at wood and metal with it. Yet people sit on the stuff. It gets into their crevices and threatens their genitalia. It gets between the toes where it feels like ground glass. Which, on second thoughts, it is. Let's face it, they make glass from sand, and all those broken bottles are simply returning to their original state. Being ground down to that venomous muck that we take back to the car on togs and towels and thongs, so that it rips hell out of upholstery. And it finishes up at home, all over the place, wreaking havoc on your carpet.

Sand is man's natural enemy. One grain of it in the right place at the right time might produce a pearl, but that's with oysters. And humans don't just have one tiny bit of it. They get covered in it. You show me sand and I'll show you trouble. The ancient Egyptians had terrible teeth because, despite their admirable diets, they were always getting sand in their food. And it's been causing trouble ever since. Look at the Middle East, at any bit of it. Entire countries are made out of sand there with the consequence that humans living in the region have become very, very abrasive. Sand makes you aggressive. People who have anything to do with sand are almost always trying to kill each other.

The sooner they replace all the sand with astroturf or synthetic shag carpet the better. Then, perhaps then, going to our beach will be tolerable. But as long as it's got all that sandy muck providing the line of demarcation between all the wet stuff and the hard bit that we dwell upon, I'm not going near it.

What else is wrong with the beach? Apart from being hot, uncomfortable, malodorous, dangerous and carcinogenic? Apart from it being smelly and abrasive? Well, people are always running along it, tossing sand all over the bit you've claimed. So that you get sand in your sandwiches and sand in your newspapers and sand in your clothes. And then you get foreign people doing handstands and being preposterously muscular, just reminding you how woefully out of condition you are. And you get wet dogs who can't read signs saying 'No Dogs Allowed' shaking themselves all over you. Then there are all the ugly bodies to look at which are even worse than the pretty bodies. Nowhere else are you reminded so forcibly about human mortality, about the brevity of life, as you are on a beach. Not simply because people are drowning thither and yon, or being chomped by sharks, but because you see the seven ages of person all around you, and you realize that you've already whizzed through six of the ages yourself.

Beaches suck. Show me a beach and I'll show you a great potential car park. There's only one thing that's any good about the beach and that is that they sound nice. The slip, slap, slop of the waves, particularly on piers. Quite pleasant. But you don't hear the sound any more because there's always some hoon sitting there with a ghetto blaster who refuses to accept that they are now utterly anachronistic and have been replaced by the Sony walkperson with its discreet headphones.

Then we've got the bloody seagulls. I almost forgot about the seagulls. Seagulls look all right but they are, let's face it, disgusting birds. They have harsh, shrill voices like Edna Everage's and attack anything edible with the savagery of antibodies in the bloodstream. If seagulls were much, much smaller, about the size of willy wagtails and didn't have such hard, beady, greedy little eyes (closely resembling the contestants' in *The Price is Right*) they might be all right. But they're not all right. Giving feathers a bad name, they have only two natural habitats, both equally horrible. The beach and the tip.

Nobody really likes seagulls. Not even fish. Which is why so many seagulls only have one leg. Serves them right.

So if you survive the sharks and the bluebottles and the turds and the broken glass and the syringes, you're likely to be impaled by surfboards that rocket through the waters like cruise missiles. Or else you'll be chopped to shreds by an outboard motor, which has the same effect on human flesh as a blender on cooking ingredients. I remember the times when you used to be afraid of standing on a toadfish or being stabbed by the spine of a stingray. Forget that. Most of the sea life has been killed by the effluent society, but you've every chance of being killed by a surfboard or outboard or some somersaulting windsurfer or a loony on a surf ski, those aquatic Harley Davidsons.

I used to wonder why people built backyard swimming pools, given the swimming pool is the most infuriating possession that any human being can possibly have. They are the bottomless pits into which you throw your money, blue holes with a greater appetite than black holes. But you've only got to go to the beach to see why Australians are retreating to their back gardens.

Three cheers for the Greenhouse Effect which, as I understand it, is going to put an end to beaches. The sea will rise and rise and rise until it laps the first-floor windows of Australia's waterfront homes, which only serves all those rich buggers right. While it's a pity we'll lose Venice and Bangladesh, not to mention most of the Pacific islands, so be it. At least it means that St Kilda and Elwood and Bondi and Manly and Noosa and Surfers and Glenelg and all those other ghastly places will be drowned, drowned, drowned.

As Lewis Carroll put it in *Through the Looking Glass*:

> The Walrus and the Carpenter
> Were walking close at hand:
> They wept like anything to see
> Such quantities of sand.
> 'If this were only cleared away,'
> They said, 'it would be grand!'

●

JEFFREY BERNARD

Jeffrey Bernard (1932–97) was born in London, the son of what he called 'middle-class Bohemians'. His mother was 'an opera singer who came from a working-class family with vague gypsy origins', while his father was a designer and an architect. Bernard was educated at Pangbourne ('a ghastly naval college'), where he discovered the illicit pleasures of sex, booze and the Turf. After leaving school he gravitated towards London's Soho, where he spent as much time as possible among the various eccentrics and misfits who congregated there. He worked as a navvy, a dish-washer, a professional boxer, a film editor and an actor; but in 1964 he became a journalist. He was a columnist for the *Sporting Life* and, as he describes below, was sacked in 1971 for drunkenness. He wrote a racing gossip column for *Private Eye*, bylined 'Colonel Mad', but it was in his role as 'Low Life' columnist for the *Spectator* from 1976 onwards that he made his reputation as a wry observer of his own misfortunes and misdemeanours. He would reflect upon his wayward career, his drunkenness, his failed marriages, and the activities of his fellow low-lifers ('I've met a better class of person in the gutter than I have in the drawing room'). He made a minor celebrity out of Norman Balon, London's rudest landlord, proprietor of the Coach and Horses pub in Soho's Greek Street, the prism through which he used to view the world. Readers were able to chart his deteriorating physical health over the years, principally his diabetes which led to the amputation of a leg and his fondness for alcohol which led to constant liver and kidney problems. Fellow columnist Keith Waterhouse wrote a successful stage play based on ten of Bernard's autobiographical columns, called *Jeffrey Bernard is Unwell* after the apologetic explanation for the occasional absence of his column from the *Spectator* through indisposition. Three collections of his columns have been published as books: *High Life – Low Life* (1982), *Low Life* (1986) and *More Low Life* (1989).

'Low Life'
Indisposed
From *Low Life* (1986)

At last, after years of trying, I've finally landed the Spring Double. Pneumonia *and* pleurisy. I wonder how much Ladbroke's would have laid me against getting the two? Anyway, I'm back in St Stephens Hospital where I was first shown the yellow card in December 1965. But this is the first time I've ever been in a hospital for something that wasn't self-inflicted and that makes it seem somehow a little unfair. They didn't *conscript* kamikaze pilots.

The ward I'm in is called Ellen Terry and down the corridor there's a ward called Alfred Tennyson. I tried to get moved to Benny Green or Larry Adler but they're completely filled with industrial accidents: people who've fallen into typewriters etc. There are six of us in Ellen Terry. Mr Rice opposite has a dodgy lung and he also has diarrhoea which he reports to me on in graphic detail every thirty minutes or so. I think I hate him. Next to him there lies a sheer hulk, poor Mr Collander, whose bladder is up the spout. Then there's Mr Handley, a costermonger from Fulham, who is rather delightful really and who has cancer of the lung. He quite rightly got a little crotchety with a young doctor last week who told him to give up smoking. As he said, 'A little late for that fucking advice, isn't it?' My chest man and registrar is all right though, even if he has developed the habit of draining my right lung via a needle inserted into it under my shoulder blade. Sadly, his students who play games with me preparatory to taking their finals all suffer from halitosis. A couple of them couldn't diagnose a decapitation but I gather they'll qualify.

What has been fascinating though, here in the bowels of Ellen Terry for the past three weeks, is the behaviour of the 'domestics'. Nearly all these ladies are West Indian, and by Christ what a mistake people make in thinking black is black and all the same. Africans are far more benign as a rule. But my *bête noire* is Granadian and we fell out a fortnight ago when I asked her to include a paper cup in the rubbish she was clearing away from the top of my locker. She erupted more rawly than the psoriasis in the next bed. 'I clean away shit,' she told me, 'and I clean away wine. I clear up tissues and wash glasses, but I don't touch paper cups.' Then, grabbing a handful of her own flesh, she went on, 'And this skin is black. Pure black. It's black, West Indian skin and what's more I know who my father is and I know who my mother is.' Never have I known such sudden paranoia. That evening Miss Barbados declared war too. She gave me a bowl of soup but wouldn't give me a spoon. 'I serve soup,' she said, 'but I never have anything to do with spoons.' 'Particularly white men's spoons,' she muttered under her breath.

But open warfare has existed since I became addicted to tea twenty days ago. Not a drink or a cigarette for twenty days and something had to give. (Are addicts addicted to addiction?) I must have continuous tea now. I chain-drink the stuff but I'm not allowed in the kitchen to boil the water for my tea bags and the West Indians watch me like hawks. I run dangerous gauntlets to boil water. Yes, it's quite a serious place is the Ellen Terry Ward and you don't have to behave that eccentrically to get into their bad books or get classified as I have by Sister as being a 'difficult patient'. Only the other night as they were doing their final round with the drugs trolley I asked the staff nurse in charge of the amazing vehicle, 'Do you have anything to make love last?' *Eine klein Nacht* aside, but that nurse has been off me ever since. This is a very serious place and if my friend Mr Handley doesn't start taking his impending death a little more seriously he could be in for some cold treatment. Meanwhile, the cockles of my heart have been wonderfully warmed by the amazingly kind and touching get well cards and letters I've received from readers of this column since I've been in Ellen Terry. What a nice lot you sound. And now for two weeks' convalescence. My man with the long needles has told me to do absolutely nothing when I get home. That shouldn't be too difficult.

Life History
From *Low Life* (1986)

When you get to be fifty you find yourself talking and thinking as much about death and money as you used to about sex. The nearness of one and the shortage of the other fill me with a sense of urgency, but urgency about what I'm not quite sure. I suppose it's a feeling of wanting to *cram* it all in; 'it' being just about everything. I used to leap out of bed at six a.m. and get on with the trivialities, now I wake at six a.m. and lie there smoking and thinking of these matters until it's time for an analgesic Smirnoff. (That time gets fractionally earlier which is worrying. Why is it perfectly OK abroad?) Anyway, today's heavyheartedness was provoked by good news I had last week. I'm going to start writing a column again for the *Sporting Life* after an absence of twelve years. It won't make me rich but it will be great fun. It seems that my passing out when I was guest speaker at the National Hunt dinner in 1971 has been forgiven. Incidentally, what was odd about that was that no one minded at all except for my boss and trainer, Bill Marshall, who always said to people, 'If you want a really good after-dinner speaker get Jeff. He's not boring because he doesn't say anything.' But as I say, the heavy heart within is weighty because of the memories of those days on the *Life* between Nijinsky's narrow defeat in the Arc and Mill Reef's victory in the Arc exactly one year later. In fact, just as we were swilling champagne after Mill Reef's victory it was none other than the champion trainer today, Henry Cecil, who told me I'd got the sack from the *Sporting Life*. He'd heard it on the grapevine.

But those 365-odd days were heady, great fun and eventually disastrous for me. To my astonishment the column took off like a rocket and became immensely popular. I wrote a lot about loss and I suppose the average reader could identify with that. There was a ghastly little picture of me at the top of the column, so complete and utter strangers recognized me at the races. They'd send me over bottles of bubbly in the Members Bar and trainers who befriended me and showed me the ropes, like Bill Marshall and Eddie Reavey, poured whisky down me like I was a drain. Of course I loved it. To be famous on any circuit in this life is fun and we all want to be loved, don't we? Typical was Ireland. I went to see a trainer called Con Collins one morning and he was on the blower. A maid brought me a tray on which was a bottle of gin, a bottle of whisky and a bottle of brandy. She said, 'Mister Collins will be with you in five minutes. If you need any more to drink ring the bell.' *Any more!* That was just after the first lot had been out, about 9 a.m.

At Newbury one day I won a fair bit on the first race and then started laying favourites to bookmakers and won a little bundle. Risky but beautifully adrenalin-filled days. And the race trains I loved. The restaurant cars filled with bookmakers, spivs, villains, mug punters and scallywags of all kinds of playing cards, telling amazing anecdotes about the Turf and drinking as though there was no tomorrow. In those days I think I'm right in saying that the only train in England to sell champagne was the race train to York. We drank the buffet dry by Doncaster. Well, of course, it couldn't last. The whisky was killing me and the bouts of pancreatitis became more frequent.

As I said, the end came at the National Hunt dinner at some dreadful hotel in Kensington. It was suggested that I be the guest speaker and they should have known better. I was extremely nervous, never having spoken publicly before, and I went to the *Life* offices at 6 a.m. to try and write something, couldn't and thought a jar in a Smithfield pub might get the typewriter going. I was accompanied by one of life's and the *Life*'s real eccentrics, a greyhound correspondent called Albert Bright. He used to come out with some very odd remarks and I remember him once saying, apropos of nothing, 'Yes Jeff, I had my first fuck when I was firewatching on the roof of the *Greyhound Express* during an air raid in 1941.' Anyway we got smashed in Smithfield and then continued in the Stab – the *Daily Mirror* pub – at opening time. Still no speech. From there I went to the Colony Room club and so it continued all day. I got to the hotel, fell asleep in the lobby and was taken upstairs and put to bed by the waiters. Here endeth the first lesson.

The next morning I flew to Paris for the Arc de Triomphe and Henry told me I'd been fired. The fact that I could never behave as I did in that year ever again doesn't diminish the depression at the memory of it all. Even at the end the lily demanded gilding. The whisky nudged me into a nervous breakdown and I ended up in a nut house. When I came to, there was an Irish psychiatrist sitting on my bed. Peace and saved at last, I thought. Then he opened his mouth and said, 'What d'you think will win the 2.30?' You just can't win, can you?

'Low Life'
Jaundiced

From *Low Life* (1986)

My body seems to have become more and more addicted to the Middlesex Hospital. Last Sunday I had to be admitted again to have a biopsy on a large lump which suddenly appeared in the mastoid region behind my left ear. From the post-operative pain I can only surmise that they have removed half my head, as opposed to taking a mere sample of it. It was the first time since my schooldays, which I can't anyway remember, that I'd had a general anaesthetic, and I don't like it. Added to which they gave me yet another local anaesthetic while I was out to the world. During the whole so-called trivial business I was also on an insulin drip, dextrose drip and a Hemanevrin drip. I had more tubes coming in and out of me than Piccadilly Circus. They seemed mildly surprised when, later, after a large injection of Valium as a bonus, I collapsed twice on their marble floor despoiling it with one of their school dinners. I feel sure that these things do not happen in the London Clinic.

But the day started badly enough and I was full of foreboding when, walking to the Middlesex, I found a dead cat in a plastic carrier bag on the doorstep of my local butcher's shop. It was a little sinister. Could it have been an inside job, or had some nasty person put it there as some sort of hint? Anyway, I arrived at the hospital and waited an interminable age to be seen by someone, and so was obliged to read the posh Sundays from cover to cover. You may imagine my horror when reading 'A Life in the Day of Rosie Swale' I came across the awful sentence: 'It's a brilliant feeling when my writing goes right – the greatest adrenalin booster in the world and better than any orgasm.'

Now I've never read any of Ms Swale's writing, so I can't really tell or know what it's like when it goes right, but I've always been suspicious and envious of people who actually enjoy the loathsome task. But more to the point I'm extremely worried as to the quality of her orgasms. It all sounds rather like a situation in which Jane Austen might have been writing in a ménage with Adolf Hitler. She also says: 'In the past I've relished my notoriety and sexy image, but now I've reclaimed my body and only do what I want with it. Nobody's using me again.' Oh, lucky Ms Swale. The last thing I wanted to do was reclaim my body from the last person who laid hands on it and I do so hope someone uses me again. What I wonder about is Ms Swale's unnatural happiness which suffuses her Life in the Day. Just as village idiots wear permanent grins, I feel sure that constantly happy people are not concerned, never reflect and care very little. But good luck to her. I shall continue to be propelled by angst. Nor, unlike Ms Swale, is my idea of heaven to eat, curl up in front of the fire in the arms of the man I love, listen to music and play with the dogs. I might perhaps curl up in the arms of a dog, if I had one, and play with the man I love, if Lester Piggott would permit it, but I'd never be able to concentrate on the music.

What's always puzzled me is how the *Sunday Times* finds such innocuous people to feature. Is there a section headed 'Benign' in the Yellow Pages? All these people wake up in the morning and have a cup of tea or coffee, apparently, and then think about the next chapter of their book. No one, it seems, wakes up to the spine-chilling and persistently commanding ring of the door-bell to find they've run out of both tea and coffee and are therefore unable to entertain the Inland Revenue. They always take their children to school, since they're never divorced, and then they work on their books until lunchtime instead of staring at blank paper until opening time.

One of the questions they asked me at the Middlesex before they trepanned me was, had I ever been jaundiced. I said yes, fifteen years ago. I forgot to tell them it was a chronic condition. But I've opted for this mess instead of sailing round the world, single-handed, collecting owls and doing all the other things people do in the lives-in-the-day-of; and the programme *Opinions*, which goes out on 23 November on Channel 4, in which I've said just why, should suitably disgust you if you're up at 11.15 p.m.

watching telly and not curled up with your fire, stroking your man and planning your next chapter.

But enough of this nonsense. The Middlesex's generosity with drugs is forcing me yet again to my bed.

•

FRANK GILBRETH, JR

Frank Bunker Gilbreth, Jr, was born in 1911 in Plainfield, New Jersey. The son of the inventor of time-and-motion study, he was educated at St John's College in Maryland, completing his BA at the University of Michigan in 1933. He was managing editor of the university paper, the *Michigan Daily*. He was a reporter for the *New York Herald*, then for the *Post and Courier* in Charleston, South Carolina. From 1936 to 1941 he was night editor for the Associated Press in Raleigh, North Carolina, and during the Second World War he served in the navy as an aerial photographer and an aide to Rear Admiral Frank D. Wagner in the Pacific. From 1945 to 1947 he was back with the AP in Raleigh, then he joined the Charleston *News and Courier* as an editorial writer. For forty years, from 1953 to 1993, Gilbreth wrote a daily column, 'Doing the Charleston', for the Charleston *News and Courier*, under the pseudonym 'Ashley Cooper' – after Anthony Ashley Cooper, 1st Earl of Shaftesbury, who was one of the founders of the city. However, Gilbreth also felt that it allowed him to adopt the persona of a 'fastidious, marcelled dandy . . . a fencing master, with his rapier-like thrusts against all that is evil, dull, boorish and humorless'. Lord Ashley's column, or his 'Pillar of Strength' as he called it, was a repository for nostalgic anecdote and humour, much of it furnished by his enthusiastic readers, and for reflections about the local community and – one of Gilbreth's bugbears – the historic preservation of Charleston. In all, Gilbreth wrote approximately 13,000 columns – more than five million words. With his sister, Ernestine Gilbreth Carey, he wrote two family memoirs, *Cheaper by the Dozen* (1948) and *Belles on Their Toes* (1950), which became bestsellers and were filmed in Hollywood.

Excerpts from *Ashley Cooper's Doing the Charleston* (1993)

Osceola's Beleaguered Bones
Osceola's bones are in the news again, for the umpteenth time, because of the possibility that the Charleston Museum may sell a portrait of the Indian chief to Florida for $25,000.

A column by John Pennekamp in the *Miami Herald* says that a condition of the sale should be that Osceola's bones accompany the portrait to Florida.

Mr Pennekamp quotes an unidentified out-of-state correspondent as saying, 'Osceola's remains do not historically or sentimentally belong to South Carolina.'

Well, in view of the fact that the Seminole chief's remains have rested continuously in South Carolina from the day he died until today [1961] – some 124 years – it seems to me that the remains belong historically and sentimentally to the place where they've always been – South Carolina.

Mr Pennekamp's correspondent also proceeds to make this unique argument: 'Florida should be permitted to discharge a moral debt to his (Osceola's) memory. We seized him under a flag of truce and sentenced him to ... confinement and death ... His seizure was deceitful and our consciences shouldn't rest until we make some public atonement.'

It is laudable indeed that Florida has qualms of conscience about how it treated the Indian. But I scarcely see why South Carolina should be expected to atone for Florida's past sins. South Carolina has plenty of sins of its own to atone for.

If Florida is dead set on discharging a 'moral debt to his memory,' this could be accomplished, short of swiping the bones from South Carolina. To mention one such way, Florida could send Charleston a big appropriation to build an imposing tomb over the site of Osceola's bones at Fort Moultrie.

No, this pious urge to cleanse Florida's conscience will fool no one. Florida wants these bones as a tourist attraction.

If Floridians really want Osceola to rest in peace, why do they keep stirring up the controversy about his bones? Every year or so someone down there starts the old refrain about how South Carolina should *roll dem bones*.

And Floridians seem to think it's a disgrace that Osceola's remains are in a quiet, out-of-the-way resting place. They want him to be the Loved One, in a tourist-trap Forest-Lawn type of resting place so typical of both Florida and southern California.

Mr Pennekamp himself professes to be puzzled at South Carolina's refusal to disturb the gallant Indian chief.

'The grave site, as with Fort Moultrie itself, is neglected and overgrown with weeds,' he writes, 'except for those intervals when Florida's efforts to have the body reclaimed bring about a temporary refurbishing.'

Lo, the poor Indian! Surely he would turn over in his grave today if he should see what Floridians have done to his native land.

Surely there is no more tasteless state in the United States than that land of neon signs, roadside zoos, waving pennants and shoddy developments.

Perhaps the most naturally beautiful region of our country has been turned into a commercialized, garish, vulgar happy hunting ground for ugly Americans.

Frankly we can't believe that it would serve any moral purpose or salve anyone's conscience to move the remains of a brave Indian from the majestic, natural, windswept surroundings at Fort Moultrie, to the land of the fast buck, the new-rich hideous hotel suites and the chromium cocktails bars.

Salve anyone's conscience? Ye gads, it would be a crime against nature. Any Indian in his right mind would prefer a few weeds.

What's so hateful about weeds, anyway? Some of them are downright beautiful.

But, of course the creed of modern Florida is: If you see a weed, pluck it out; if you see a tree, bulldoze it; if it's dark, hang colored lights; and if it's quiet, install a loudspeaker.

Happy hunting ground for an Indian, indeed! And what effrontery to suggest that one would be easing one's conscience to bring an Indian – dead or alive – back to such an environment!

Sure, we'll sell Florida Osceola's picture for twenty-five Gs. But for mercy sakes let his weary bones rest in peace.

Charlestonese Isn't Corncobs and Grits

I almost had what my po' old granny used to call a duck fit when I read a Washington column by Sandy Grady about Senator Fritz Hollings. Did you-all read hit, Bubba? How about you-all, Honeychile? Lawzy!

It seems that Sandy Grady – whose very name suggests a country road – said that Fritz's big trouble as a presidential candidate was his 'country' accent.

Some Gradyisms: 'Fritz is as country as a pickup truck full of corncobs . . . Hollings is a boomer who could call the cows home four counties away. Fritz has a Charleston, South Carolina, accent so thick he sounds like a grits-and-magnolia parody of a Southern politician . . . Hollings is as Southern as Moon Pies and RC Cola . . . I'm not sure how Hollings will be received in New Hampshire, where his Southern-fried accent will be as inscrutable as Sanskrit . . .'

I'm not such a dull tool that I don't grasp the humor in the above. And I'm not indignant at the supposedly hilarious slurs aimed at Senator Hollings. He's a big boy and has a tough hide – let him look after himself.

But what gets my dandruff up – as we boys used to say – is the assertion that a Charleston accent is (a) country, (b) similar to a truck full of corncobs and (c) reminiscent of grits.

The Charleston accent is euphonious, pleasing, expressive, melodious, mellifluous and dulcet. If the accent is anything in the world, it is not country! Charleston was a thriving, sophisticated metropolis before the city of Washington had ever been thought of, and while Chicago, Denver and San Francisco were peopled solely by coyotes and Red Indians.

In the early days, the city-state of Charleston furnished four signers of the Declaration of Independence. Many visitors to Charleston – especially Europeans – have called it the most civilized city in the 'New World'. The grace of our priceless collection of antebellum mansions, peopled for the most part by a charming gentry with old-school manners, is well known in discriminating circles throughout the world and by a heck of a lot of gaping tourists, too.

I'm not saying that there aren't many Southerners with country accents, but Fritz's accent is Charlestonese. And that's just about as far from country as you can get. To compare it, even humorously, with corncobs and grits is sheer, utter, maddening, coocoo ignorance.

In a few words, Charleston isn't Plains, Georgia, folks.

Nor am I intimating that Senator Hollings's accent may not be difficult for some provincial Americans to understand. But please remember that, to a Southerner, many of the accents of other regions are not only difficult to understand but quite unpleasant.

To a Southerner, for instance, the New England accent is a discordant, nasal, twangy cacophony which sounds as if baa-baa-black-sheep had been mated with an individual suffering from a miserable and perpetual summer cold. The Ivy League accent of Long

Island and Westchester County is, of course, a whining, bored, patronizing copy of the tones of an effete English dandy of two or three centuries ago.

As for the New York accent, in which *these* and *those* and *them* become *dese* and *dose* and *dem*, and *thirty* becomes *thoity*, well, what can you say except that illiterate provincialism often springs from a cosmopolitan metropolis where ignorance is bliss?

I could continue, but not without becoming abusively repetitious. I do wish, though, that some of the strict, self-imposed rules against ethic denigration could be applied to the South. I guess it's wheel-spinning to hope that other columnists would ever return to the good old days when Boston baked beans were more the butt of ethnic humor than Iowa corncobs or Charleston hominy.

How to Win a Pulitzer

If I were a Northern editor I'd picket the Pulitzer Prize judges for being unfair. Nowadays the only way to win a Pulitzer Prize for editorial writing is to:

(a) Live in the South.

(b) Work on a Southern paper. And . . .

(c) Write 'fearless' editorials saying that the South had oughta be ashamed of itself for being so stupidly backward.

They tell me that some Southern newspapers have an application list a mile long of Northern editors who are applying for jobs, so that they can move South, write editorials like that and win next year's prize. The line forms on the right, you-all. It takes a lot of naked bravery, unflinching courage and steely grit to write those editorials about the backward South. Gracious peace, the KKK may come after you the very next day and tar and feather you. Sure!

If you're lucky enough to have that happen to you, you're a virtual cinch to win a Pulitzer Prize with enough Oak Leaf Clusters to start your own private arboretum.

Not So Crazy About Ashley

Former State Senator Richard M. Jefferies, the Super-Duper of Santee Cooper, has received more payments in salaries and legal fees from public and quasi-public bodies than any other South Carolinian in history. Yes, living or dead.

He also doesn't have much use for a good many newspapermen, especially me. Goodness knows why!

A couple of weeks ago, I wrote a piece here kidding him about allegedly mixing up feet and fathoms, in discussing the depth of Charleston Harbor back in the old days.

The piece made him so mad that he cranked up a hot letter to me, saying that he hadn't mixed up feet and fathoms and asking me whether I was 'man enough' to set the record straight, without disclosing that he had asked for the correction. He sent me the letter by special messenger.

Well, sure, I was man enough. I apologized, in my usual, incomparable, hilarious, witty way. But did that satisfy the Super-Duper of Santee Cooper? No, my friends, it did not. In fact, quite the contrary.

Last week, there arrived here at the office from the Power Politician a carbon of a letter he had written about me to Sherill Poulnot, a harbor pilot here in Charleston.

Mr Jefferies, although doing me the courtesy of letting me see what he thought about me, marked his letter 'not for publication.' That's a tactic the politicians use sometimes when they want to kick a reporter in the pants, but don't want him to yelp in pain for all the public to hear.

But since I didn't ask the Super-Duper to share any confidences in me, I feel at liberty to print excerpts of the 'not for publication' letter here. Maybe that'll teach him, next time, not to entrust his top-secret communications to a blabbermouth like Lord Ashley.

I don't have to quote the whole letter. Mr Jefferies starts by saying that my article about feet and fathoms heaped 'abuses, ridicule and insult' on him.

In the calm, moderate prose which he reserves for the likes of me, the Walterboro electrician continues: 'The trouble with a large number of newspapermen is that they are the most conceited, arrogant, presuming, "better-than-thou," inconsiderate, pompous, claimants of perfection impossible to make errors, seeing only one side of every controversy, intemperate and unreasonable, bunch of people in any of the professions. This simply means that the freedom of the press is the most widely abused freedom that exists in America today.'

I could have accepted that illuminating bit of philosophy without flinching, but what really threw me into a livid rage was the intelligence that, some time ago, I lost the Super-Duper as one of my readers. I grew red in the face, my hand started to tremble and my voice got choked up when I read this crusher: 'I admit that I have discontinued reading the Ashley Cooper column because it is usually silly and has no news or cultural value, but the one on April 25 was brought to my attention and caused me to write Ashley Cooper as I did.'

Ouch! I surrender! And I wonder, since the Super-Duper is bored stiff with this Pillar of Strength, if some pal of his will call today's little effort to his attention. I certainly hope so. Honey, 'deed I do.

Secrets of a Columnist

Here's a page from Lord Ashley's top-secret handbook on how a columnist for a Southern newspaper can generate mail:

Discuss whether 'you-all' is ever used in the singular south of the Mason-Dixon line.

Explain the difference between hominy, grist and grits.

Write whimsically about cockroaches.

Comment on the merits of using 'War Between the States' instead of the 'Civil War.'

Ask whether it is all right for Southern school children to be required to sing the 'Battle Hymn of the Republic.'

Postulate that Southern hillbilly talk and certain common Southern errors in grammar are really pure Elizabethan English, as brought to the New World by the original settlers.

Complain that Yankees have brainwashed us on certain holidays – and that Southern Santas don't *have* to ride in sleighs and that Thanksgiving isn't necessarily the monopoly of descendants of Massachusetts Pilgrims.

Argue whether President Woodrow Wilson wasn't really a Southerner. And whether President Jackson was born in North or South Carolina.

Extol the merits of black-eyed peas, okra, turnip greens, rice and gravy, hominy and ditto, shrimp for breakfast and ham hocks.

Scold such authors as Erskine Caldwell and Tennessee Williams for depicting the South as either one big Tobacco Road or inbred and nutty.

Assert that the North, which for generations enjoyed lecturing the South on racial relations, now can't cope with similar problems of its own.

Gloat about all the Northern industry moving to the Sun Belt.

Compare Northern and Southern accents, and 'youze guys' with 'y'all.'

Speculate on who would have won 'the war' if there hadn't been that tragic day when Stonewall Jackson was killed, and if . . .

•

LYNN ASHBY

Lynn Ashby was born in 1938 in Dallas, Texas, and received a BJ at the University of Texas at Austin in 1961. He served in the Marine Corps and wrote a column for the *Houston Post* from 1968 until that paper closed. His columns have been collected in two books: *As Your Acknowledged Leader* (1983) and *As I Was Saying* (1984).

Stay Away

From *As I Was Saying* (1984)

After a few years of lying low, Richard Nixon is making his first, tentative feelers into the outside world.

In recent weeks he's been to New York City twice. He's signed another million-dollar book contract, and has given a few sidewalk interviews. Once again he is being addressed as Mr President. He plans trips to foreign lands. He grants interviews at his home in which he gives his advice on the economy, inflation, the state of the government.

It is clear that, step by step, Richard Nixon is carefully orchestrating himself out of his political purgatory and back into the mainstream of American life, where he has spent most of his adulthood. Perhaps, if things go well, he will return someday to the Republican National Convention where tearful crowds will give him a standing ovation and Nixon will deliver one of his give-'em-hell speeches, castigating his enemies.

Well, they may give him a standing ovation. They may call him Mr President, and they may cling to his every word of advice on matters both foreign and domestic. But not me. You can – in the immortal words of Samuel Goldwyn – include me out. I don't like Richard Nixon. I don't need Richard Nixon. And, Lord knows, I don't want Richard Nixon.

It is a personal matter. For although we never met, he lied to me. He misled me. He cheated me. He abused the power I entrusted to him. He hurt me.

Let us not forget that this is a man who cheated on his income tax and now has to pay up. His vice-presidential papers were backdated. His accountant and his papers' appraiser went before the judge. But Nixon did not. He said he knew nothing about it. You try that.

This is a man who used his elected position to line his pockets, reward his friends, and punish his enemies in ways the meanest political hack never contemplated. He tried to muzzle the press. He plotted to revoke the TV license owned by the *Washington Post*. Two *Newsday* reporters had their IRS records dragged out after writing less than flattering stories about Bebe Rebozo [real estate businessman and Nixon crony].

This is a man who preached mother, flag and apple pie while – in the taped secrecy of the Oval Office – he cursed, schemed and backstabbed. He was a corrupter, devising ways to make otherwise honest men break the law. He brought down to the gutter with him the FBI, the CIA, the IRS, the Justice Department. He ruined countless lives. When he got into trouble, he willingly threw his aides into the sea to keep his own lifeboat from swamping. A man who touted loyalty as the greatest of assets showed none when it counted.

He lied. He went before the cameras and came into my home and told me lies. Vast numbers, so many that I can't count them. He trotted out volumes of tape transcripts and told me they were the truth, when he knew they weren't. And his only reason for lying was to cover up other lies.

He used my tax money to trim trees, build walls and landscape his homes. He got the Secret Service to put down under 'security' such items as ice makers and drapes.

This is a man who brought my country down to its lowest ebb in self-esteem, and at a time when it could not afford the trip. This is the worst part of all, for he was a thief, not so much for the dollars he took, but for a theft unparalleled in our history: he stole our self-confidence. He robbed an entire nation of its faith in itself.

Now, let us remember what happened. We had gone through the civil rights riots and a series of assassinations. Then we were torn by Vietnam. There were, quite literally, riots in the streets. This had happened to others, but never in our lifetime had it happened to us, and it scared us. We were faced with the chilling possibility that we were no better – and maybe worse – than a second-rate banana republic. Maybe America was not so special, after all. Doubts began to step in, but we kept telling ourselves that while we had our problems, we were still internally sound. Strong. Honest.

Then one man, Richard Nixon, robbed us of that last remaining faith. The greatest office in the land, the one held up to every schoolchild as an example of the rewards of hard work and honesty, was shown to be no more than a platform for deceit, a power base for paranoia. At a time when we desperately needed to get back on our feet, he cut our legs out from under us.

A nation's strength is rather like the value of stock: it's worth whatever anyone thinks it's worth. All of a sudden the rest of the world didn't think US stock was worth much.

Oh, our factories still produced, our armies still marched, our farmers still fed, but our faith, our energies and, most important, our self-confidence plummeted. We haven't brought it up yet.

Richard Nixon hurt me, he hurt my family, he hurt my country in a way no foreign enemy could. It was an inside job. When the thief was caught, he denied it then and he denies it today, but only for a price. Maybe a million or so.

He is not in jail due to a little help from his friend, who promptly lost the presidency because of it. Today, Nixon lives far better than most Americans, and I'm paying for it.

Now he wants to make a comeback. Perhaps he will, because there is a mood in the land that 'he's been punished enough.' Well, as far as I'm concerned, Nixon can just stay away, because he's punished me enough, too.

The Art of Merging

From *As I Was Saying* (1984)

The most important aspect of driving on Houston freeways during rush hours is the art of merging. It can be dangerous, frightening, expensive, illegal and annoying. On the other hand, if done properly, it can be thrilling, frightening and illegal.

To get the art of merging down correctly, let us separate the drill into two distinct categories, the offensive team and the defensive team. Individually, the *merger* and the *mergee*. The merger is the motorist outside the freeway, beyond the pale, who is trying to get into the moving traffic. He or she is the new kid on the block, attempting to join the gang and swagger on down the street. But it is not that easy.

For the merger is the late arrival, and must go on to the end of the line. Of course, there is no end to the line of traffic on a Houston freeway during rush hours. It goes on for ever. So it is that the merger must somehow break in.

The city, or someone with more dollars than sense, has put up traffic lights next to the on ramps to assist the merger in his pursuit of a slight space in the line. These lights are obeyed by those who drive 55 and by cars whose engines die at that particular spot. And by no others.

Where there are no lights, there are yield signs. Yield signs are not obeyed by anyone whatsoever.

All right, that takes care of the mergers, those upstarts who wish to poke their bumpers into other people's line of trot. We now move on to the mergees, those already stacked up on the freeway, patiently awaiting the time when the dead eighteen-wheeler in Montgomery County will be towed over to the side so that traffic on the West Loop might move on. The mergees have been moving along as a body, a giant amoeba slithering across a glass slide under a microscope.

Up and down the miles, over hill and dale, this group of strangers has become a band of brothers, the sole survivors in an armored column. A spirit of kinship and camaraderie has grown up. Some even swap information over CBs, good buddy.

Then, suddenly, a new face appears, and like a young buck who must prove his machismo before being allowed to join the herd, he snorts and paws the earth as a show of courage. Others have been fighting since the Kirby Street entrance to get here, and now this new fellow wishes to slip right in. Well, he can just go back to the Kirby Street entrance and get on like everyone else.

Thus it is that we have these two mutually antagonistic groups: the mergers and the mergees. Now that they are suitably identified, let's move on to the proper role of each.

If you are in the inside or middle lanes of the freeway, then you are a simple bystander, for all the action is on the outside lane. If you are on the outside lane, I suggest you move over, since it is always the slowest lane of traffic.

But assuming you are stuck there, you are a mergee, and as such, you will see cars coming up from your right side trying to get in. As a rule, I allow one car in at each entry ramp. This is not easy to do, for once you slow down and motion for one vehicle to take its place in line in front of you, often a second car will try to slip in, too. *Do not let it!* This will mess up the entire operation. One entry ramp, one vehicle let in. It's the law.

Ah, but which vehicle do you let in? I mean you are slowly passing by a line of cars on your right, all stopped dead, all awaiting a chance to jump in. How do you select the proper stranger? I suggest you allow in any of these:

- Pretty girls.
- Ammonia trucks that have a running start.
- The 1st Armored Division on maneuvers.
- Any vehicle with dented fenders and a roll bar.

Once that vehicle is in line, tailgate it immediately or the flood is on.

Now we come to the unwritten rule of mergedom. Under no circumstances do you allow in a car that comes on the freeway from the entry ramp and whizzes down the shoulder for several hundred yards, passing all the motorists lined up in the right-hand lane.

No, sir. All the other mergers back there at the entry ramp are patiently awaiting a chance to join the flow of traffic. And so can these line bargers. Thus when you hear thunder on the right and see rocks and dirt showering around you as some car comes flying down the shoulder seeking a chance to cut in, just swerve slightly to the right. With any luck, the line crasher will have to avoid you, and should spin into the mud and stay there until a thoughtful wrecker comes by.

Now, what are the duties when you are poised on the entry ramp, waiting to get in line? First, you should be patient. Second, you should not be *too* patient. What you do is slowly creep up alongside a car to the left, one that is already in line. Then you look plaintively, sending out an unspoken plea to join the club. When you receive the proper nod or hand wave, you quickly slip in and then wave your right hand in a thank-you.

If, however, the fellow does not allow you to slip in the line, you may use any other well-known gesture of the open road.

Traffic merging during rush hours is a little-understood but highly important operation. Done properly, it speeds up the flow of vehicles and allows me to get home before sunrise.

Done improperly, i.e., not allowing my little yellow VW Beetle in front of you, it may be hazardous to your health. My nose gunner is a crack shot.

•

KEITH WATERHOUSE

Keith Waterhouse was born in 1929 in Leeds, where he was educated and did his first work as a journalist. He has written several novels, including the hugely successful *Billy Liar* (1959), which he co-wrote with Willis Hall and which has been adapted for stage – as both a straight play and a musical – and for screen. He has also written a column, for the *Daily Mirror*, from 1970 to 1986, and for the *Daily Mail*, since 1986. He was Granada Columnist of the Year and IPC Descriptive Writer of the Year in 1970, and IPC Columnist of the Year in 1973. In 1989 he wrote a stage play about a fellow columnist, *Jeffrey Bernard is Unwell.*

The Beast of Brighton
From *Mondays, Thursdays* (1976)

This week, by mutual consent, the Beast of Brighton and I decided to part company. You have heard of the Loch Ness Monster? The Beast of Brighton is its cousin once removed.

It is a strange, malevolent creature with a wickerwork hide and sinews of bamboo. When you touch the brute it creaks menacingly and breathes out evil dust-clouds through lungs of raffia. When you leave it alone it just crouches there, brooding.

But every so often, in the stillness of the evening, it stirs angrily and lets out a sort of grating shriek, like the Bridge of Tay on the night it collapsed with the resultant loss of ninety souls.

The Beast of Brighton is, in melancholy fact, an Edwardian beach-chair – a bulbous, hooded monstrosity six feet high, three and a half feet deep and, at its broadest, four feet across.

Picture a gigantic avocado pear sliced down the middle, scooped out and equipped with the seating capacity of a steam tram. That's my baby.

At one time, milk-skinned seaside belles in striped one-piece bathing suits reclined within that cavernous basketwork womb to protect themselves from the harmful rays of the sun.

Then it fell on evil days and finished up in a junk shop. Then I saw it, and it was my turn to fall on evil days.

I bought it for twelve quid in the laughable belief that it would do something for the living room of my flat.

It took two experienced removal men to squeeze it through the front door, and reinforcements were called to get it up the stairs.

There are still mysterious scratches on the paintwork consistent with King Kong having dropped in for a bite of lunch.

It did something for the living room all right. The Beast of Brighton threw an immense shadow from wall to wall like Stonehenge on Midsummer's Day.

'No,' I said after a full three seconds' appraisal. 'I don't think it really improves the living room. Let's try the hall, shall we?'

So we tried the hall. Push. Pull. Prod. Heave. Charge. Coax. Kick. Bash. Threaten.

It didn't do a lot for the hall, either. In fact, if the hall had been able to speak it would have said: 'It's either you or me, buster, and if it comes to it, I belong in the lease.'

'The bedroom?' I suggested. The men had arrived at the crack of dawn and they were already on overtime.

Swear. Sweat. Squeeze. Shove.

By nine o'clock, using every weapon we could lay our hands on including the coal-tongs, we had driven the Beast of Brighton into the bedroom and the removal men were saying they didn't have to do this for a living, there was always road-sweeping.

In the bedroom the Beast remained.

It has been there, creaking and groaning, for two years. If you can imagine sharing a billet with the Graf Zeppelin, mooning restlessly around its mooring post during the long windy nights, that is what it has been like.

I have never dared sit in it, for fear of being swallowed alive. If I have gone near it with tempting offerings such as a fortnight's laundry, it has growled ominously.

The shadow across my bed has grown bigger. Sometimes I have fancied that the Beast was expanding, imperceptibly, like a science-fiction marrow about to take over the world.

In the middle of the night when it was creaking and cursing to itself I got up and said: 'Look, you and I have come a long way together and so I can speak freely. Wouldn't you be happier on a bonfire?'

Creak.

The second-hand clothes dealer said he would be delighted to cart the Beast away for nothing, provided I got the flaming thing out into the street first.

So I called in some removal men. Not the first lot, who refused to come, but another lot. They stared at the Beast in some awe.

'We'll have to take the door off its hinges,' they said at last.

'You can pull the wall down for all I care,' I said. 'Just get it off the premises.'

I gave them the key and waltzed off singing happily to myself, secure in the belief that I had seen the last of the Beast of Brighton.

Needless to say, when I got home it was still there, looming belligerently in the corner and creaking with quiet indignation.

'We can't understand it,' the removal men said. 'How did it get here in the first place?'

I explained that it was a long story. 'What we thought was, it must have been built here. Either that, or it was craned up through the window.'

'No,' I said. 'It got in through the door.'

'In that case,' they said, 'it must have bloody well grown.'

'I know,' I said. 'That's what's worrying me.' And from the bedroom there was a sort of smug creak, and a shadow fell across the threshold.

Does anyone want to take over a nice flat, part-furnished?

The Magic City
From *Mondays, Thursdays* (1976)

I see that a vacancy has arisen for a city to accommodate 600,000 souls in the neighbourhood of Essex. I hereby apply for the job of designing it.

If I am not allowed to design it, I may as well warn you what you will get (assuming that you'll get anything, for despite Mr Heath's assumption of victory, the battle of Maplin Sands has not yet even started).

You will get pedestrian tunnels daubed with slogans. You will get fountains that do not work and promenades on which no promenading takes place. You will get rust-stained concrete, piazzas strewn with coke cans, and a sunken traffic roundabout looking like a gigantic po.

What you will not get is a city, because building cities is practically a lost art, and very few of us remember the secret.

I will pass on the recipe.

To make a city, you must first take a very large quantity of good stone from local quarries. With this as your basic ingredient you fashion a stupendous parallelogram in the Renaissance style, with Corinthian columns, pilasters, caryatids, gargoyles, balustrades and six great stained-glass windows extolling the virtues of commerce, industry, science, agriculture, herring-fishing and the fine arts.

Add marble to taste. Add a mighty organ with 1,500 pipes. Surmount this confection with a dome of copper.

You now have a town hall.

In front of your town hall you must next lay out a flagged square equal in size to a football pitch, and guarded at each corner by stone lions. This square will be dedicated, by a statue on a plinth, to the Unknown Alderman.

You have now built the centre or hub of your city. From this axis you must now cause to be constructed four broad avenues, each equipped with tram-lines. These avenues, which we shall call Corporation Street, Corn Exchange Street, Market Street and Station Road respectively, will conveniently divide your city into quarters.

We will deal with the Corn Exchange Street area first. Taking the remainder of your stone you will first of all build, of course, a corn exchange. To this you will add a number of savings banks, a building society or two, a Conservative Club, a Free Trade Hall, a Philosophical and Literary Society, a cathedral, a parish church, and chapels or tabernacles for the Methodist, Baptist, Unitarian and Four Square Gospel persuasions.

Corporation Street will be devoted to civic buildings, including a courthouse, a Department of Sanitation and a mahogany suite of rooms for the truant officer. You must also find space for an infirmary, a public library and museum, an inspectorate of weights and measures and a People's Dispensary for Sick Animals.

Station Road will obviously contain the railway station, together with a solid commercial hotel smelling of gravy. Having taken advice on wind prevalences, you may also place in this quarter your slaughterhouse and your corporation slipper baths.

Now let us build Market Street. Having run out of stone at this stage, we will construct our market hall of glass, and support it on iron pillars encrusted with dolphins. This market hall will be at the centre of a lively bazaar composed of many shops and cafés, an impressive department store, a theatre, several cinemas and an infinite number of arcades, each one of which will feature an ornamental clock whose hours are chimed by mechanical figures wearing suits of armour.

Drawing our four avenues together, like the strands of a spider's web, there will be an intricate network of back alleys, side-streets and passages. These will house a multitude of small public houses, jobbing printers, pie shops, billiard halls, barbers, engravers and die-stampers, key-cutters, sandwich bars, furtive chemists, knife grinders, fish and chip saloons, painters' sundries-men and other necessary trades.

Beyond all this, but no farther than a ten-minute tram-ride away, there will be villas and terraces, and semi-detached houses called Dunroamin'; there will be grammar schools and co-operative societies and Scout huts and municipal parks; and from every suburban hill we will be able to look down on the spires and domes and twinkling lights of our magic city.

There were such places once, you know. Manchester, Bradford, Birmingham, Leeds, Liverpool were all such magic cities before they had the guts ripped out of them. They had their faults, God knows, but if they had soot in their lungs they also had red blood in their veins, and there was such a thing as provincial pride.

These places had affectionate nicknames: Cottonopolis, Worstedopolis, Brummagen; and already that unbuilt conurbation in the wastes of Essex has a nickname too: Jet City.

That alone shows that the mould has been broken. There will be no more magic cities.

Three Wise Social Workers
Daily Mail, 24 December 1990

And it came to pass in those days, that there went out a decree from Caesar Augustus that all the world should be poll-taxed.

And all went to be poll-taxed, every one unto his own city, that he might not be taxed as if he had an second home.

And Joseph also went up from Galilee, out of the city of Nazareth, unto the city of David which is called the borough of Bethlehem, to be taxed with Mary his wife, being great with child.

And she brought forth her first-born son, and wrapped him in swaddling clothes, and hid him in an cardboard box, because there was no room for them in the hostel for homeless people.

And there were in that same borough three social workers named Ros, Kev and Glo, keeping watch over their cases by night.

And lo, their Co-ordinator came upon them saying, I want you to get down to this address and sus out what is going on, for we have had a tip-off from one of our field backup team that there may be a child at risk living in an cardboard box.

And it came to pass, as the Co-ordinator was gone away from them back to the office, that the three social workers said one to another, Let us get our skates on and see this thing which is come to pass, which our Co-ordinator hath made known to us.

And they came with haste, and found Mary, and Joseph, and the babe, lying in an cardboard box.

And that social worker which was named Ros spake unto Mary, saying, All right, love, we are taking this babe into care.

And Mary, being sore afraid, asked of the social workers wherefore they wouldst take the child of her loins into care.

And that social worker which was named Kev said, We do not have to give a reason, but just look at the poor little mite, it is blue with cold.

But Joseph protested unto the social workers, beating his breast and saying, Is it our fault there was no room in the hostel? If we hadst not been forced to journey unto Bethlehem, this babe would be tucked up in his crib in Nazareth.

And that social worker which was named Glo said, So you do not even live in the borough? There's a care order out for the kid in Nazareth, right, so you thought you'd do a runner?

Then did Mary tell the social workers how she with her husband Joseph had been commanded to come unto Bethlehem to pay their poll tax.

And the three social workers looked one upon the other and tapped their noses. And that social worker which was named Ros said unto Joseph, You're not telling us you've been living in these squalid conditions yet you've never had the nous to apply for poll-tax relief.

And that social worker which was named Kev said, Pull the other one. And that social worker which was named Glo said, Surely your social worker told you the score, about your benefit entitlements and that?

And Joseph shrugged saying, We have not a social worker.

And Ros gasped in wonder saying, I do not believe it. You have not a social worker? Who then looketh after you?

And Mary said, Just an Angel of the Lord.

Then came unto Bethlehem from the east to Jerusalem three wise men bearing gifts for the young child with Mary his mother of gold, and frankincense, and myrrh.

And Ros looked upon Glo and Glo looked upon Kev and Kev spake unto himself saying, This is getting fishier by the minute.

And Ros took out her note tablet and began to inscribe words upon it, saying to the three wise men who had come bearing gifts, Excuse me, but what are you lot on precisely?

And the three wise men replied, saying, We saw a star in the east which went before us and led us here.

Then went the three social workers into an huddle. And that social worker which was named Ros said, What do you reckon? Satanists? And that social worker which was named Kev said, Some kind of evil ring, believe you me. And that social worker which was named Glo said, If they are into myrrh-sniffing, we have cometh not an moment too soon.

Then seized they the babe, and took away its swaddling clothes, and clad it in an romper suit.

And Mary wept saying, Where are you taking him?

And Ros said, We do not have to tell you that, love, but since you ask we will probably foster him out to a very nice family named Herod which art longing for a toddler.

And Joseph said, Can we come and visit him?

And Kev said, Not unless you get a court order, mate.

And the three wise men said, Can we not give the child his gifts?

And Glo said, I should cocoa. He will get an black doll to play with from the women activists' toy bank.

Then asked Kev of Joseph, Hath this child an name?

And Joseph said, Not yet, no.

And Glo said, We will call him Rory after my bloke. Now we had better be legging it, gang.

Then leggeth it the three social workers, with the babe.

And the three wise men returned from whence they came, shaking their heads and asking one unto another. What was that all about, then?

•

ERMA BOMBECK

Erma Louise Bombeck (1927–96) was born Erma Harris in Dayton, Ohio. Her father, a city labourer, died when she was a child and she and her mother went to live with her maternal grandmother. She attended a vocational high school, where she wrote a humour column for the first time in her high school newspaper, and she worked part-time as a copy-girl at the *Dayton Journal-Herald*. While attending the University of Dayton she wrote a column for a department store periodical and did PR work for the YMCA. After obtaining a BA in English in 1949, she joined the *Dayton Journal-Herald* as a reporter – by her own admission she was 'terrible' – but before long was writing a column called 'Operation Dustrag'. In 1953 she abandoned journalism to start a family and after experiencing fertility problems went on to have a daughter and two sons. In 1964, bored with her role as a housewife, she started her column about motherhood and suburban life, 'At Wit's End', in an Ohio paper, the *Kettering-Oakwood Times*, for $3 a week. The *Dayton Journal-Herald* invited her to write her column twice weekly in 1965 and it later became thrice weekly. It has since been syndicated under various auspices, reaching some 900 newspapers throughout the 1970s and 1980s, and it has been published in several best-selling book collections. In 1971 *Life* described her as the 'Socrates of the ironing board'. Bombeck also wrote a monthly magazine column for *Good Housekeeping* from 1969 to 1975.

'At Wit's End'
No More Oatmeal Kisses

Dayton Journal-Herald, January 29, 1969

A young mother writes: 'I know you've written before about the empty-nest syndrome, that lonely period after the children are grown and gone. Right now I'm up to my eyeballs in laundry and muddy boots. The baby is teething; the boys are fighting. My husband just called and said to eat without him, and I fell off my diet. Lay it on me again, will you?'

OK. One of these days, you'll shout, 'Why don't you kids grow up and act your age!' And they will. Or, 'You guys get outside and find yourselves something to do . . . and don't slam the door!' And they won't.

You'll straighten up the boys' bedroom neat and tidy: bumper stickers discarded, bedspread tucked and smooth, toys displayed on the shelves. Hangers in the closet. Animals caged. And you'll say out loud, 'Now I want it to stay this way.' And it will.

You'll prepare a perfect dinner with a salad that hasn't been picked to death and a cake with no finger traces in the icing, and you'll say, 'Now, there's a meal for company.' And you'll eat it alone.

You'll say, 'I want complete privacy on the phone. No dancing around. No demolition crews. Silence! Do you hear?' And you'll have it.

No more plastic tablecloths stained with spaghetti. No more bedspreads to protect the sofa from damp bottoms. No more gates to stumble over at the top of the basement steps. No more clothes-pins under the sofa. No more playpens to arrange a room around.

No more anxious nights under a vaporizer tent. No more sand on the sheets or Popeye movies in the bathroom. No more iron-on patches, rubber bands for ponytails, tight boots or wet knotted shoestrings.

Imagine. A lipstick with a point on it. No baby-sitter for New Year's Eve. Washing only once a week. Seeing a steak that isn't ground. Having your teeth cleaned without a baby on your lap.

No PTA meetings. No car pools. No blaring radios. No one washing her hair at eleven o'clock at night. Having your own roll of Scotch tape.

Think about it. No more Christmas presents out of toothpicks and library paste. No more sloppy oatmeal kisses. No more tooth fairy. No giggles in the dark. No knees to heal, no responsibility.

Only a voice crying, 'Why don't you grow up?' and the silence echoing, 'I did.'

'At Wit's End'
Socks Lost in Washer

Dayton Journal-Herald, May 28, 1969

Don't tell me about the scientific advances of the twentieth century.

So men are planning a trip to the moon. So computers run every large industry in America. So body organs are being transplanted like perennials.

Big deal! You show me a washer that will launder a pair of socks and return them to you as a pair, and I'll light a firecracker.

I never had what you would call a good relationship with washers. They hate me. They either froth at the lid, walk across the utility room or just plain quit. But mostly they have a sock deficiency that defies reason.

Men don't understand this. They are too rational. My washer repairman leads the list.

'If your socks don't come out even, lady, that means you didn't put them in even,' he said flatly.

I looked at him closely. (How can you trust a repairman who looks like Barnabas on *Dark Shadows*?) 'I remembered distinctly gathering them two by two. Believe me, Noah didn't do a more complete job. I took two black ones from my son's sleeping feet, a red pair from the tennis bag, a stiff pair from his ceiling, a mud-caked pair from the glove compartment of the car and a moldy pair from two boots. You can see for yourself I have only one of each. The mates have disappeared.'

'You've got a pale blue pair that match,' he said.

'Of course we've got a pale blue pair, you cluck. We hate the pale blue pair. They come out of the washer even when we don't put them in. This washer is just plain insolent. Don't you understand that?'

'I mean no disrespect, lady,' he stammered, 'but you aren't a tippler, are you?'

'I think inside this washer is a little trap door that pulls in one sock from each pair and holds it captive. Somewhere in this machine lies a secret treasure house of mismated socks.'

'Maybe just a little cold one to get you through your ironing?'

'If we could just find it, do you know what that would mean?'

'Get hold of yourself, lady, they're probably clogging up the pump. I'll take a look.'

Exactly $12.50 later, the repairman shook his head. 'The pump is clean. Tell you what. Why don't you put the socks in a little bag and —'

'I have put them in a little bag by twos, and you know what? When I take the little bag out, every snap is in place and still there is one sock missing from every pair. I tell you I can't go on much longer like this. Not knowing where the next sock will disappear. Having the children go around with one foot bandaged all the time. What's a mother to do?'

'For starters, lady, I'd keep the bleach away from my nose. And if that didn't work, maybe you and your friend could get on the *Ed Sullivan Show*.'

I told you they didn't understand.

'At Wit's End'
My Husband the Prince of Darkness
Dayton Journal-Herald, February 20, 1973

The poet who said 'It is better to light a candle than to curse the darkness' did not know my husband.

He has dedicated his entire life to flipping off light switches, giving rise to his theory that 'It is better to break your leg in the darkness than to curse the light bills.'

By his description, our house is lit up like a pleasure boat cruising up the Potomac. He lies. Had we lived in England during the blitz, ours would have been the only house that never needed blackout curtains.

It is like living with a hamster with long arms. For example, I will turn on the bathroom light switch, and fifteen seconds later the light will flick off. From the darkness, a voice will proclaim, 'Unless you're rearranged the furniture in there, you know your way around, don't you?'

His tour through the house every evening has become rather predictable. 'Who's in the kitchen?' (*Click.*) 'Who's in the hall closet?' (*Click.*) 'Who's in the bedroom?' (*Click.*) Then we are in for his dramatic tally. 'I have just turned off thirteen lights.'

The most frustrating patch of darkness is the garage. He pulled the car in the other evening and doused the lights. I fumbled with the car door while he fumbled for the house key. Finally, he shouted, 'Are you all right?'

'Don't talk to me,' I said. 'I'm counting my steps like the blind boy in *Butterflies Are Free.*' Inside the house he inched his way through the darkness.

'It's twenty-two steps to the family-room light switch,' I said.

'I don't want the family-room light switch,' he said. 'I want to turn on the stove light. It's a smaller bulb.'

'How about a sparkler?' I asked.

'I've had enough of your smart remarks about my war against waste,' he said. 'Today I bought a lamp that illuminates the entire room. No more stumbling around. No more squinting. You and your lack of regard for money will love it!'

I followed him into the bedroom, where he proceeded to turn on the light above our bed.

Recoiling from the glare into the corner, I had the strangest sensation either Moses was going to write something on a mountain or a new supermarket was being opened.

As he lay in bed reading, and as the lids of my eyes were being broiled to medium well, I could only wonder if Thomas Edison could be named as co-defendant in a divorce suit.

'At Wit's End'
Daddy Doll Under the Bed

Dayton Journal-Herald, June 21, 1981

When I was a little kid, a father was like the light in the refrigerator. Every house had one, but no one really knew what either of them did once the door was shut.

My dad left the house every morning and always seemed glad to see everyone at night.

He opened the jar of pickles when no one else could.

He was the only one in the house who wasn't afraid to go in the basement by himself.

He cut himself shaving, but no one kissed it or got excited about it. It was understood whenever it rained, he got the car and brought it around to the door. When anyone was sick, he went out to get the prescription filled.

He kept busy enough. He set mousetraps. He cut back the roses so the thorns wouldn't clip you when you came to the front door. He oiled my skates, and they went faster. When I got my bike, he ran alongside me for at least a thousand miles until I got the hang of it.

He signed all my report cards. He put me to bed early. He took a lot of pictures but was never in them. He tightened up mother's sagging clothesline every week or so.

I was afraid of everyone else's father, but not my own. Once I made him tea. It was only sugar water, but he sat on a small chair and said it was delicious. He looked very uncomfortable.

Once I went fishing with him in a rowboat. I threw huge rocks in the water, and he threatened to throw me overboard. I wasn't sure he wouldn't, so I looked him in the eye. I finally decided he was bluffing and threw in one more. He was a bad poker player.

Whenever I played house, the mother doll had a lot to do. I never knew what to do with the daddy doll, so I had him say 'I'm going off to work now' and threw him under the bed.

When I was nine years old, my father didn't get up one morning and go to work. He went to the hospital and died the next day.

There were a lot of people in the house who brought all kinds of good food and cakes. We never had so much company before.

I went to my room and felt under the bed for the father doll. When I found him, I dusted him off and put him on my bed.

He never did anything. I didn't know his leaving would hurt so much.

I still don't know why.

'At Wit's End'
Speak 'Thermostat'

Dayton Journal-Herald, December 19, 1982

My husband has been trying to teach our children to speak 'Thermostat' for years.

They say the younger you start to teach them a foreign language, the faster they learn. This has not been the case. 'Flush' did not come easy for them. Neither did 'Lights.'

'Thermostat' is one of the last of the foreign languages to be taught to children. It comes just after 'Hang Up That Phone' and 'Shut the Door.' (Note to parents: Please do not proceed to 'Thermostat' until they are speaking 'Shut the Door' fluently.)

There are several methods of teaching 'Thermostat.' Some parents use the Berlitz concept. They put recordings beneath the pillows of children that instruct, 'A thermostat controls the furnace. When the door is open, the bad cold air wants to come in and the furnace tries very hard to heat the outdoors. God never meant for a furnace to heat America or He would never have invented snow.'

One of the first phrases a child learns about 'Thermostat' is 'My room is cold.' 'My room is cold' voluntarily triggers his motor activity. He will proceed to the thermostat and with nimble precision move the thermostat dial to 82 degrees (by sheer coincidence, the boiling point of his father).

This is followed by 'My room is hot.' However, a strange phenomenon occurs. Instead of turning the thermostat back, your child will open a window. He needs work in the language.

Our children were slow. We spent a year and a half on 'How do you spell relief? S-W-E-A-T-E-R!' We spent another two years on 'Daddy is not a rich man, and we can no longer afford three children.'

It wasn't until last week when we took them on a field trip to the meter that they seemed to comprehend what we were talking about. We showed them how the little dials twirled around on the meter and how we were charged for each little twirl. They watched our lips closely as we formed the word *Bankruptcy*.

One of them said, 'Wait a minute. Are you telling us that the colder it gets outside, the harder the furnace has to work to keep it warm inside?'

We nodded happily.

'And every time it clicks on it costs money?'

We jumped up and down excitedly.

'Why didn't you say so?'

My husband smiled. 'Do you think we can progress to "Thank You"?'

'I hate to push 'em before they're ready,' I said.

•

MICHAEL BYWATER

Michael Bywater was born in Nottinghamshire in 1953. The son of a doctor, he was educated at Nottingham High School and Corpus Christi College, Cambridge. He became a free-lance journalist in 1979 and from 1984 to 1992 was assistant editor of *Punch*, where he wrote the weekly 'Bargepole' column from 1986 to 1992. He was a diarist for *The Times* in 1992–3 and wrote a monthly column for *Cosmopolitan* from 1990 to 1995. Since 1995 he has been writing a weekly column for the *Independent on Sunday*. The purpose of 'Bargepole' was to satirize the orgy of consumerism in the 1980s.

'Bargepole'
Punch, 6 July 1990

On the principle that being thoroughly wicked and nasty is preferable to keeping one's nose clean and paying the poll tax, I feel obliged to support the Provisional IRA, but my sympathy is being badly stretched. It's not that your men shoot people and blow them up, because that's what you do if you're a Provo. To say that one would sympathize with them if only they would be less violent is like saying one would support the Pope if only he would drop all the God stuff – a position, in fact, with which I agree, but it's my column and if you don't like it you can bugger off and write your own. You'll run out of ideas within a month and the pay is derisory, but you're not going to listen to me whatever I say so I might as well keep my gob shut.

The trouble with your men is their sheer incompetence. The average Provo atrocity could nowadays be summed up as *wham, BANG, sorry, ma'am*, and that just won't do. The Carlton Club bomb is yet another example of your men's incompetence. They are stuck in the past, believing that the Carlton Club is the very centre of the British Establishment. It is nothing of the sort. That is merely newscasters' theme-park talk. The *real* Establishment is all pushy grammar school people in unsuitable shoes, and the poor old boobies of St James's are just kept on for the tourists to gawp at.

I am not even sure why your men want to strike at the 'heart' of the 'Establishment'. I suppose the idea is that we would all become terribly shocked and upset if they succeeded in blowing up a few politicians, and immediately exercise our franchise to demand a settlement of their demands. This is twisted and feral thinking, the consequence of eating green potatoes in all likelihood. First of all, if the daycent folk of Britain *were* outraged at the blowing-up of politicians, there would be nothing we could do about it at all. The government ignores our outrage until it's time for the next election, when they all start greasing up like mad. Secondly, a successful blowing-up operation would mean that there was nobody left to call an election or referendum anyway. And thirdly, nobody would be particularly outraged or upset.

That's the important point: threatening to kill politicians in order to frighten us is like someone saying to me 'If you don't leave my wife alone I will break into the Inland Revenue computer and erase your file.' Your men, I imagine, are so excited by the idea of the Great Political Struggle that they assume we are, too, instead of realizing that one of the nicest things imaginable to the thinking Briton is the thought of a ruthless, efficient and comprehensive blowing-up of politicians. We're all *Sun* readers now, and nothing excites us more than a politician meeting sudden and violent retribution, as much as anything else because we don't actually believe they exist anyway: reality and image are blurred and we'd be just as chuffed if the Thatch bit the dust as we were when they shot JR.

Your men the Provos should take my advice and go for our support. That doesn't mean they have to stop letting off bombs, merely that they have to let off *sensible* bombs. They must *immediately* stop blowing up harmless people and even politicians' spouses, who already have enough on their plates with being married to politicians. And I would suggest that they leave politicians out of it altogether. Blown-up politicians only excite us briefly because, as aforesaid, we don't think they are really real nor do we much care about them. Instead, they should concentrate on blowing up significant enemies of our happiness, and we would grow to love them and want to give them their way.

If they want to blow things up on the European mainland, they could start with the *European*, or failing that, the I M Pei pyramid in the Louvre, and follow that with blowing up whoever decided to pull down the Berlin Wall, thus destroying the last bit of Europe which hasn't become a Levi's-wearing, Budweiser-drinking, condom-wearing outpost of America. While they are at it, they could blow up whichever executives of Levi's, Budweiser, NatWest and Swatch are responsible for considering the idea of advertising their nasty products on huge television screens in discotheques.

The death list is endless. Marks and Spencer's for buying Brooks Brothers. Anyone who says 'Hi, Richard' to Richard Jobson. Art Fry for inventing Post-It Notes. Marla Maples, for humping Donald Trump then getting asked to 'act' in *Dallas*, thus setting a lousy example to all those other women who think they can open doors by opening their legs. Whoever it is who thinks Australia is exciting, so that we not only have Fosters and Castlemaine advertisements but also the ones for that horrid microwave pot noodle stuff, and endless Australian soaps and series and the preposterous Shell advertisement, all featuring common, sweating people in Akubra hats, giving totally the wrong impression of Australia which is in fact full of decent, loyal, handsome women with good muscle tone who root like rattlesnakes and can't pass a prick.

And, of course, my stinking producer friend who after years of trouble and despair culminating in two twelve-months of unrequited love has finally found happiness in the arms of his beloved, against all odds. That makes me *really* angry, and I can hardly breathe with the amount of cocaine I have had to put up my nose to cope with my grief and rage.

The trouble is, the Provos, if they follow this advice, would become so popular that they would lose. How? Simply because, if we gave in, they would stop all this exquisite public service and settle down to build grim bungies in Neath and claim EC grants, and that we cannot have, not at any price.

'Bargepole'

Punch, 24 August 1990

I crawled back into this decaying hell-hole of a 'country' last week but I shall not be staying for long. It's chaos. I can't even ring up my enemies for solace because British Telecom (it's *who* they answer to, precisely?) have disconnected my lines for payment of the bill. Payment *twice* actually: once in my absence, and once on my return, which flung them into complete confusion to the extent that joke 'engineers' in plastic trousers were dispatched into the exchange to seize my equipment and throw it away.

This won't do. The gas people can whistle for a bit – one can get by on charcoal and it's actually a relief not to have gas around the place; I can run away again next week without worrying about the house blowing up – but the telephone is essential. The only reason I returned was to try to regain the affections of the woman I love, and intermittent, crackling communications from traffic-haunted, kebab-reeking telephone kiosks fail to carry the subtext of wealth and power that bimbos of her kidney seem to require before they will, let us be frank, put out for a chap. Nor can I communicate with my primary fallback, the erudite and *vicieuse* lady from Paris, since I cannot recall her address and even the French post office has proved unable to deliver a billet-doux addressed to The Woman With The Big Hat And The Holland & Holland Handcuffs. She Hangs Out In The 14th Arrondissement, You'd Probably Catch Her At Lipp Or Les Deux Magots, Oh For God's Sake, You Know Who I Mean.

And so (it's at times like this you need an admiral, and a surgeon called Farquarson and old Bollocks the waiter, clustered around the fireside) began the adventure which led to my identifying the fabled Arsehole of the Universe. It left me scarred and I will never be able to hear *Swan Lake* without screaming, rolling my eyes, and beating an old lady to death (I always carry an old lady, next to the mug shot and the lariat). But was it worth it? That, reader, is for you to say, though if you think I give a pig's foot about your opinion you must be even more barking mad than I thought.

When you ring up British Telecom, the first thing is that they don't answer. Then you try again and they do. This is a good trick. A woman – her voice strained by snobbery and vaginismus – thanks you for calling and tells you you'll have to wait. That is something I have heard on innumerable occasions, but at least the women who usually deliver the line have the courtesy to launch immediately into insane self-justifications about finding out who they really are, having been hurt in the past, suffering from insurmountable insecurity, being already committed to dog-breathed backbenchers and finding me so physically repulsive and mentally overpowering that their flesh creeps at the very thought of my name.

British Telecom don't do this. They simply play *Swan Lake* at you while the phonecard bleeds its thin magnetic life into the slot. After a few hours of this I realized that the only way to survive was to find Mr Iain Vallance, British Telecom's profoundly unattractive 'boss', and disembowel him slowly with the Nantucket flensing knife I always carry next to the mug shot, the lariat and the old lady. That proving impractical, regular irrigation was the next best thing, and over the last week you could have seen me at all hours of the day, huddled in a pre-vandalized phone booth outside Nabeel's Tandoori, swigging raw Pimm's from the bottle and alternately cuffing and consoling a small female in an orange dress who claimed to be my daughter.

When *Swan Lake* became too much to bear, I would call the woman I love, because being snarled at is better than being ignored, and there were even times when I wanted to ring up the dark-haired beauty who ruined my life and tell her that all I asked was for us to be reunited; but fortunately anything strong enough to twist the intellect to that pitch of craven supplication is banned in this country, just like everything else is banned in this country, which is why I am leaving at Christmas *for ever*.

Presently, I got through to a woman in Accounts, who referred me to a woman in Sales, who referred me to Debt Management, who referred me to a woman in Accounts, who referred me to Customer Service, and eventually it became clear that the only thing to do was to go to Croydon, where their offices are.

And that, gentlemen, is how I discovered the legendary Arsehole of the Universe, a sort of reverse Shangri-La where you age hundreds of years in a mere lunchtime. Can I speak of the mystical Telecom eyrie, the fabled Delta Point, with its solemn procession of whining, impotent, bearded men in brown Terylene suits? Can I tell of its burger bars, car parks, building society offices? Is my pen capable of painting its atmosphere of municipal snivelling and cheeseparing rapaciousness? Have I the tongue to sing its one-way system?

No.

The telephone is still not working, the woman I love is coming to be fed this evening and I have nothing to give her but blood, toil, tears and unpaid bills, my parents are disappointed in me but none of this is why I am leaving. I simply cannot countenance remaining in a country which can harbour a place like Croydon, and, despite the evidence of self-knowledge which allows them to erect Delta Point, I have to go. Sorry about that. But I'll be in touch. You'll find me near the Panthéon. Just follow the sound of clanking chains and whistling bullwhips.

•

DAVE BARRY

Dave Barry was born in Armonk, New York, in 1947 and educated at public schools and Haverford College. He wrote for his high school and college papers, and his first job in professional journalism was as a reporter for the *Daily Local News* in West Chester, Pennsylvania. In 1975 he joined Burger Associates, a company which taught businessmen to write better prose. He began to submit his column to the *Miami Herald* as a free-lance before joining the staff of the paper in 1983, and his column has been widely syndicated. He has said that he tries to make his column read as if he had dashed it off while carpet-chewing drunk. In 1988 he won the Pulitzer Prize for commentary.

Sock It to Me

From *Dave Barry's Greatest Hits* (1988)

I woke up this morning experiencing several important concerns, which I would like to share with you here in the hope that they will add up to a large enough total word count so that I can go back to bed.

CONCERN NUMBER ONE: Mr Lyndon H. LaRouche, Jr.

As you probably know, Mr LaRouche is this person who has started his own political party and wishes to take over the country, which troubles many people because his views are somewhat unorthodox. (What I mean of course, is that he is as crazy as a bedbug. Where you have a brain, Lyndon H. LaRouche, Jr, has a Whack-a-Mole game. But I am not about to state this in print, as I do not wish to have his ardent followers place poison snakes in my sock drawer.)

Those of you who are frequent airline travelers are no doubt already familiar with Mr LaRouche's views, because they are displayed on posters attached to card tables at most major airports. Somehow, a year or so ago, the LaRouche people managed to get the lucrative Airport Lunatic concession away from the Moonies. What I suspect happened is that one day, on a prearranged signal, the LaRouche people sneaked up behind the Moonies and strangled them with their own little book bags, probably in full view of thousands of air travelers, who of course would not have objected. Many of them probably helped out by whapping the Moonies with their carry-on luggage. I know I would have.

But then, two of Mr LaRouche's ardent followers won the Illinois Democratic primary nominations for secretary of state and lieutenant governor. This caused massive nationwide anxiety because of the unorthodoxy of their views, which, as far as we have been able to tell, involve shooting Jane Fonda with a laser beam from space. Not that I personally see anything wrong with these views! No sir! I don't even *have* a sock drawer!

But we do have to ask ourselves if we truly can afford, as a nation, to elect crazy people to a vital state office like lieutenant governor, which involves weighty responsibilities such as wearing a suit and phoning the governor every day to see if he's dead. Because mark my words, if these people win in Illinois, they'll go after higher and higher offices, until someday – I do not wish to alarm you, but we must be aware of the danger – we could have a situation where our top national leaders are going around babbling about laser beams from space. So I have called on you Illinois voters to come to your senses before the general election and take responsible citizen action in the form of moving to a more intelligent state. This is the perfect time to do so, thanks to declining oil prices.

CONCERN NUMBER TWO: Declining oil prices.

Like many of you, I did not realize at first that the decline in oil prices was something to be concerned about. In fact, I viewed it as the first really positive development in this nation since Jimmy Carter was attacked by the giant swimming rabbit. But then I started reading articles by leading nervous economists stating that the oil-price decline is a very bad thing, because it is causing severe hardships for the following groups:

1. The OPEC nations.

2. The US oil industry.

3. The big banks.

4. Texans in general.

When I read this, naturally my reaction as a concerned American, was hahahahaha-hahahaha.

No, seriously, we need to be worried about declining oil prices, and I am going to explain why. The international economy is based on the US dollar, which is trusted and respected throughout the world because it is the only major currency that does not look like it was designed by preschool children. The value of the dollar, in turn, depends on the investment savvy of big US banks, which lend their dollars to the oil-rich Third World, which loses them gambling on rooster fights.

This system worked well until the late 1970s, when the price of oil started to fall. This was caused by a decline in demand, which was caused by the fact that people couldn't get their cars repaired, which was caused by the fact that the oil companies had bought all the independent garages and turned them into 'self-service' stations selling a mutant assortment of retail goods and staffed by surly teenagers, so that God forbid you should have actual *car* trouble at one of these service stations because they would tow you away for blocking the access of customers wishing to purchase nasal spray and Slim Jims.

So now the banks are stuck with a lot of oil, which they are trying to get rid of by converting it into VISA cards, which they offer to my wife. She gets six or seven VISA offers from desperate banks per business day. She got one recently from – I am not making this up – a bank in *South Dakota*. I didn't even know they *had* banks in South Dakota, did you? What would people keep in them? Pelts?

Well I don't know about you, but I am uncomfortable with the idea of having a world economy dependent upon the VISA needs of my wife. She is only one person. That is the law. So I think we need to revamp the whole world economic structure, and the obvious first step is to require banks to repair cars. The supermarkets, which already cash checks, could take over the remaining functions currently performed by banks, such as lending money to the Third World and being closed. You would get your food at service stations, which would be required to get some new sandwiches. You would continue to buy gas at 'convenience' stores. Illinois would be sold to wealthy Japanese investors. All these regulations would be enforced by laser beams from space.

Air Bags for Wind Bags
From *Dave Barry's Greatest Hits* (1988)

Every now and then I like to suggest surefire concepts by which you readers can make millions of dollars without doing any honest work. Before I tell you about the newest concept, I'd like to apologize to those of you who were stupid enough to attempt the previous one, which, as you may recall, involved opening up Electronic Device Destruction Centers.

The idea there was that consumers would bring their broken electronic devices, such as televisions and VCRs, in to the destruction centers, where trained personnel would whack them (the devices) with sledgehammers. With their devices thus permanently destroyed, consumers would then be free to go out and buy new devices, rather than have to fritter away years of their lives trying to have the old ones repaired at so-called factory service centers, which in fact consist of two men named Lester poking at the insides of broken electronic devices with cheap cigars and going, 'Lookit all them *wires* in there!'

I thought the Electronic Device Destruction Center was a surefire concept, but apparently I was wrong, to judge from the unusually large amount of explosives I received in the mail from those of you who lost your life savings and, in some cases, key organs. This made me feel so bad that I have been sitting here for well over five minutes wracking my brains, trying to think of an even *more* surefire money-making concept for you.

One promising concept that I came up with right away was that you could manufacture personal air bags, then get a law passed requiring they be installed on congressmen to keep them from taking trips. Let's say your congressman was trying to travel to Paris to do a fact-finding study on how the French government handles diseases transmitted by sherbet. Just when he got to the plane, his mandatory air bag, strapped around his waist, would inflate – FWWAAAAAAPPPP – thus rendering him too large to fit through the plane door. It could also be rigged to inflate whenever the congressman proposed a law. ('Mr Speaker, people ask me, why should October be designated as Cuticle Inspection Month? And I answer that FWWAAAAAAAPPPP.' This would save millions of dollars, so I have no doubt that the public would violently support a law requiring air bags on congressmen. The problem is that your potential market is very small: There are only around 500 members of Congress, and some of them are already too large to fit on normal aircraft.

But fortunately for you, I have come up with an even *better* money-making concept: The 'Mister Mediocre' fast-food restaurant franchise. I have studied American eating preferences for years, and believe me, this is what people want. They don't want to go into an unfamiliar restaurant, because they don't know whether the food will be very bad, or very good, or what. They want to go into a restaurant that advertises on national television, where they *know* the food will be mediocre. This is the heart of the Mister Mediocre concept.

The basic menu item, in fact the *only* menu item, would be a food unit called the 'patty,' consisting of – this would be guaranteed in writing – 'a hundred percent animal matter of some kind.' All patties would be heated up and then cooled back down in electronic devices immediately before serving. The Breakfast Patty would be a patty on a bun with lettuce, tomato, onion, egg, pretend-bacon bits, Cheez Whiz, a Special Sauce made by pouring ketchup out of a bottle, and a little slip of paper stating: 'Inspected by Number 12.' The Lunch or Dinner Patty would be any Breakfast Patties that didn't get sold in the morning. The Seafood Lover's Patty would be any patties that were starting to emit a serious aroma. Patties that were too rank even to be Seafood Lover's Patties would be compressed into wads and sold as 'Nuggets.'

Mister Mediocre restaurants would have a 'salad bar' offering lettuce, tomato, onion, egg, pretend-bacon bits, Cheez Whiz and a Special House Dressing made by pouring ketchup out of a bottle, tended by an employee chosen on the basis of listlessness, whose job would be to make sure that all of these ingredients had been slopped over into each other's compartments.

Mister Mediocre restaurants would offer a special 'Children's Fun Pak' consisting of a patty containing an indelible felt-tipped marker that youngsters could use to write on their skin.

Also, there would be a big sign on the door that said:

DEPARTMENT OF HEALTH REGULATIONS!
ALL EMPLOYEES MUST WASH HANDS
BEFORE LEAVING THIS RESTAURANT!

If you're a Smart Investor who would like to get a hold of a Mister Mediocre restaurant franchise before the federal authorities get wind of this, all you need to do is send me a fairly large amount of money. In return, I'll send you a complete Startup Package consisting of an unsigned letter giving you permission to use the Mister Mediocre concept. You will also of course be entitled to free legal advice at any time. Like, for example, if you have a situation where your drive-thru customers are taking one bite from their patties and then having seizures that cause them to drive over pedestrians in a fatal manner, you just call me up. 'Hey,' I'll advise you, for free. 'Sounds like you need a lawyer!'

•

SHAUN JOHNSON

Shaun Johnson was born in South Africa in 1959 and educated at Hyde Park High School, Johannesburg; at Rhodes University, Grahamstown; and, as a Rhodes Scholar, at Oxford University. He wrote reportage and political commentary columns for the *Weekly Mail*, the *Star* and the *Saturday Star*. He is now deputy editor and political editor of the *Star*.

The Sound of Shredders Shredding
Saturday Star, 23 May 1992

If you stand on a street corner in Pretoria late at night, I am sure you can hear the sound of shredders shredding. Of assets being stripped. Of pockets being stuffed.

I have become convinced, without the benefit or burden of proof, that a gigantic fraud is being perpetrated on us, the taxpayers. It is happening right now, on an ordinary Saturday morning in the twilight days of the old South Africa. In recent weeks the journalistic rumour mills have been grinding away at bales of conjecture, bags of whispers, and it's got to me. I believe there are two types of South Africans today: those who are In On The Deal, and those who aren't.

Consider our situation objectively. We have still in power – untrammelled power –

a milch cow government and its millions of suckling babes. All are aware that the supply of cream will be cut off in the not-too-distant future. Their choice is to stock up for all the winters of the rest of their lives, or do without. In the past week alone I have been told, *inter alia*, the following stories (names and places omitted to protect the innocent, should there be any).

1. Pension funds administered by a government not a million miles from here are being topped up with vast quantities – truckloads – of crisp, fresh rands. Beneficiaries are being allowed to buy backdated policies, ensuring handsome payouts on (early) retirement – certainly more handsome than the individuals' stations in life would suggest. The taxpayer will foot this bill.

2. Long-term employment contracts are suddenly being signed in government-funded institutions (broadcasting corporations included?). These will ensure that individuals, whose services might – in a future age of unsheltered employment – be found not to be entirely essential, will receive bloated retrenchment payouts, courtesy of the taxpayer.

3. Megabucks parastatals ('strategic' industries?) are suddenly going 'private' and entering the market with new logos, big assets and big plans. It is not clear to whom these assets – paid for, it goes without saying, by the taxpayer – now belong. We are talking billions here.

Many, many similar tales are being whispered. Small wonder that the In On The Deals seem unperturbed by the prospect of the new South Africa. It is probably too late to stop the bulk of the larder-raiding. On a recent visit to Germany, I was chilled to discover how effectively the former East German nomenklatura had laundered their records and their people's money in the brief interlude between the time they saw the writing on the Wall, and when it came crashing down. It was a matter of months. Our transition has been going for two years already, and shows every sign of still having plenty of time to run. German Democratic Republic party grandees managed, under intense pressures of politics and time, to contrive for themselves managing directorships of companies created out of erstwhile corrupt co-operatives. Here, nest eggs can be arranged expertly and at leisure.

Just think about it. If officials of the Department of Development Aid were up to thieving, shamelessly thieving, millions while the going was still good, then what do you imagine they would do when it was clear that the game was up? The snouts-in-troughs analogy has never been more apposite.

If there is an unanswerable, apolitical argument in favour of the immediate installation of a multiparty caretaker government in this country, it is surely that we must do all we can to try to ensure that when the larder door is finally opened, there is more inside than a row of beans. There is a real danger that it will be bare. This is a nauseating prospect for ordinary whites who don't have access to the national autobank, but it must be all but unbearable for blacks who have never had their fair share from the state's coffers.

It is a lot to ask, but what the nation needs now, desperately, is an honest man or woman. Someone who knows what is happening, and is prepared to say so. History would treat them kindly.

Our Noble Compromise
Saturday Star, 11 July 1992

People are talking about leaving again. This time around there are many middle-class blacks among them. The hope that blossomed in 1990 has wilted. The developing trust in each other's intentions is gone. Those who came back from London, Sydney, Houston, Toronto now ask themselves quietly and disbelievingly whether they have made a terrible mistake.

Not even an international soccer tour – involving the one sport which could truly capture the hearts of all South Africans – has made any impact on our free-fall into depression and acrimony. Instead, it has itself become a symbol of our mean-minded crisis of confidence. Vicious exchanges about black plastic armbands serve the same purpose.

In the townships, people are sick of the system and sick of the struggle. They will stick with the struggle if they have to. In the suburbs, the builders are at it again; adding metres of concrete to walls which were first raised in the 1980s. Even when the walls are painted over, you can see where the lines of fear join. It is like reading the inside of a tree trunk: it tells our history. People are hoarding what little money they have, at a loss to know what a 'safe investment' is in the new South Africa. Estate agents plumb the depths in trying to reinvigorate a teetering property market: 'Look Ma, No Squatters!' They might as well say 'no dogs'.

How did we get here? It all seems so very, very stupid. A negotiated settlement is still the most likely political outcome in South Africa. We are not yet on the brink of the Yugoslavia option. What has happened is that we have retreated headlong, in a wake created by the politicians, to the attitudes and circumstances of South Africa pre-1990. On the surface, the exchange of accusatory memoranda between President de Klerk and Mr Mandela differs from what went before only insofar as Mr Mandela is out of prison and Mr P. W. Botha is out of action.

It is below the surface that we must look in order to reach a reasoned assessment of our situation, rather than surrendering to blind panic. From where I sit, I proceed on the assumption that the everyday truth lies at a point somewhere between what the ANC is saying and what the government is saying. That point shifts from day to day, and the challenge is to keep up with it. There are two fundamental, interrelated causes of the current crisis. They are the violence, and the erosion of belief, on both sides, in the sincerity of the other. To deal with the second first: the ANC emerged from Codesa 2 [talks about constitutional change] in shock, suddenly convinced that the government was not after all committed to a truly democratic outcome in negotiations, but rather to a gerrymandered constitution which allowed it to retain power beyond any electoral support it could hope for. The ANC believed it had come close to being suckered, and the suspension of talks coupled with mass action is the result. It now believes it will have to force, rather than talk, Pretoria into an acceptable deal. From the government's side, it believes that the ANC is reverting to fighting for a classical all-or-nothing transfer of power *à la* the decolonizing Africa, with no reference to South Africa's peculiarities.

The magnetic force that will bring both back to the table is the certainty that neither has the power to secure its ideal solution, however much it would like to. But this force can be unleashed only when a degree of trust has been re-established. This is not trust in the sense of fondness for one another, or friendship. It is trust based on the knowledge that both sides' options are limited, and directly reliant upon one another. This brings us to the violence.

It, unlike arguments over special majorities, senates and regional legislatures, is non-negotiable. While the killing continues, there will be no negotiations. Here, at this particular point on the truth continuum, the primary onus falls on the government. President de Klerk does not have the power to put a stop to all the violence, just like that. No one does, either jointly or severally: South Africa is too far gone right now. What he does have the power to do, however, is to take the unambiguous practical steps which many of us in the media, and more recently the Goldstone Commission, have been begging for since mid-1990. These steps, including the banning of the carrying of weapons in public, resolving the hostel tragedy and punishing state miscreants, will certainly save some lives immediately, and have a very good chance of beginning to rebuild shattered trust. They are a key to reconvening Codesa.

The uniqueness of our situation is that an agreement is possible – even probable – whereby one leader, Mr de Klerk, gives more than he is forced to give, while another, Mr Mandela, takes less than he is able to take. That is a shining, noble and deeply hopeful prospect. We the people cannot allow it to be thrown away.

Another Last White Parliament
Saturday Star, 6 February 1993

For the third year running, I find myself attending the opening week of what we annually describe as the 'last white parliament'. It really is going to be embarrassing if we're all back again next year, doing the same thing. But, with the uncertainty of experience, it looks as if finally this is going to be a decisive negotiating year.

There are rough patches ahead (in fact we should be hitting one just as you read this), but nevertheless when parliament reconvenes it will no longer be the expression of white control over our country. It will be something different. Already, this opening of parliament has been different to what went before. One got the distinct impression, listening to the large troupe of performing ministers and deputy ministers, that they were choosing their words carefully. Also, something very familiar was missing from most of the briefings: the ritual savagings of the ANC. Like de Klerk's opening speech itself, the outpourings of the ministers were oddly consensual – as if the speakers were aware that they were talking on behalf of a group wider than just the government. Indeed, it seemed obvious that ministers such as Louis Pienaar were painfully conscious of the fact that they could not make unilateral pronouncements, no matter how much they might want to.

Major speeches, including those of de Klerk, Roelf Meyer and Derek Keys, sounded more like report-backs of what had occurred outside parliament than serious attempts to convince the assembled MPs to support a particular line of action. The old system has not been buried, but it has been partially paralysed. All eyes are now focusing beyond this parliament and on the logical outcome of the reform process, elections. The ANC was too busy to protest at the opening of parliament this year, because it was preparing for elections. Pienaar's Home Affairs ministry is working round the clock . . . registering people so they can vote in elections.

We need these elections, of course, and desperately so. They will be final confirmation to ourselves and the world that we have come up with a rational alternative to racial armageddon. But I wonder if we have any idea of the scale of the exercise we are letting ourselves in for, when we speak blithely of erecting 7,500 polling booths around the country for a ballot towards the end of this year, or early next. Minister Pienaar's labours notwithstanding, I don't believe we are doing nearly enough to prepare the country for its great democratic catharsis.

Time is desperately short, and we need to start now. Not just with the logistics, as daunting as they are, but with drumming into each other's heads democracy's maxims. I sometimes wonder, even, whether it wouldn't be a good idea for the multiparty negotiating forum to commit itself soon to a firm date for elections, but to make that date considerably later than those already proposed – say mid-1995. In this way everybody would have certainty about the ultimate outcome of the process, but we would have much more time to prepare.

Whatever the date settled upon, the Savimbi syndrome remains a frightening prospect. In fact we cannot countenance it. We have to get in place a series of mechanisms which will rule it out. An independent electoral commission, a rule book for elections, an effective monitoring package, agreed and credible security measures, and so much more. It will take time to do this properly.

The politicians have, in many ways, already started their election campaigns. That's OK, but first we need to start a campaign to make elections possible at all.

•

HARRY SHEARER

Harry Shearer was born in Los Angeles. He started out as part of a satirical group called 'The Credibility Gap' and was one of the creators and members of the spoof rock band that starred in the film *This Is Spinal Tap*. For a little over two years, between late 1989 and March 1992, Shearer wrote a weekly column called 'Man Bites Town' for the *Los Angeles Times Magazine*.

'Man Bites Town'
A Funny Thing Happened on the Way to the Poppies
From *Man Bites Town* (1994)

New Yorkers are like nineteenth-century Englishmen. Wherever they go, whatever benighted part of the world they choose to favor with their presence, they seek to re-create as much as possible of the island they left behind.

So, during the past decade, while Southern California has enjoyed its most intense period of colonization from the East, we have reaped the cultural benefits of being Gothamites' home away from home: delis that have been painstakingly modeled on their Manhattan namesakes; out-of-the-way cafés that have suddenly learned how to brew – and pronounce – espresso; and grizzled, angry street people who are just a couple of years away from giving our doorways the distinctive urban perfume of stale human piss.

But while New Yorkers know how to bring, these most sophisticated of our recent visitors don't know how to take. They tend to come out here, congregate in West Holly-wood (because it has what they recognize as street life) or near Ventura Boulevard (because it doesn't) and issue their verdicts on this very small sample of a very large elephant.

Not that Southern California's charms are all that evident to a newcomer. To be fair, I've always been baffled by the desire of people even to make this a vacation destination. Aside from Disneyland, the studios and the beaches during those few weeks when they're not being soiled, this area's most attractive qualities have always seemed to reward only the patient attention of a longtime admirer. This is a Siamese cat of a city.

On weekends, certain sections of the newspaper squirrel away little tips on interesting places to go. A recent arrival not yet trained to root out such truffles of travel might never venture out to the desert – not the Palm Springs desert of white belts and golf and Sonny Bono but the real desert, the place that can frighten you with its seeming emptiness. Some of us go out there to ride dirt bikes over it. I go to see Southern California's answer to fall foliage, the sunlit fireworks of wildflower season.

These days, there are wildflower hot lines to guarantee that a ninety-minute haul out to the Antelope Valley will reward you with more than a view of the newest Builder's Emporium. But my second trip to wildflower country occurred some years ago, and it was the kind of adventure New Yorkers can get only by jogging in Central Park after nightfall.

My TW (Then Wife) and I drove to the Antelope Valley, procured a Lancaster Chamber of Commerce map and headed into the hills. (The wildflowers don't all bloom at once, so you have to seek out the hillsides where your eyes can be overwhelmed.) On the way, we each 'dropped' what we thought was mescaline. I had taken it only a couple of times, officer, on those rare occasions when I ventured out to a Wonder of Nature. I found it to be, as advertised, an extremely mild, almost unnoticeably psychedelic substance. Its chief effect was to point me toward the beauty and keep me from thinking: *Hope we get back in time for the Laker game.*

If you're not way ahead of me, you should be. These days, people don't tell stories about mescaline that end with 'and we both had a groovy time.' Pills can be unknowable little guys, and we had arrived overprepared too late in the season for flowers. Or too early. A restroom break revealed either that the walls of the little structure in the wilderness were crawling with thousands of identical insects or that I was staring at the immobile stucco through the window of something dramatically psychedelic.

Now the TW and I were out in the middle of nowhere, with nothing beautiful to look at and with our minds set on bake. We consulted the map for the quickest route out of wherever it was we were. Like any reasonable chamber of commerce, the Lancaster folks had depicted their beloved city as the largest settlement in the neighborhood and had surrounded it with a big, red heart. This was mighty persuasive to people in our lack of frame of mind, which is why it took us about twenty minutes to realize that, sadly, the route home lay through Palmdale instead.

Then as now, I had a Sunday radio program, which I had taped in advance to free this day for adventure. So, as our car ascended the last hill out of Desert Hell, I was treated to a cliché of the age coming true. I heard my voice on the radio, and it sounded exactly the way voices in bad versions of acid trips always sound – as if it were coming from the bottom of the bathtub drain. Thawawawawawanks for lisssssssening.

We got safely home, and, as I lay on the living-room floor gazing at the light-green walls of my rented house, I had an intense realization: *This is like being in the bottom of an aquarium, and I should repaint this joint pronto.*

It was, and I did. I have been to wildflower country many times since that harrowing Sunday. No mystery pills, no insects, no voice from the drain. For adventure, I now do what the ex-New Yorkers among us do. I go sit in a deli and order the corned beef.

'Man Bites Town'
See You at the Phi Delta Reunion
From *Man Bites Town* (1994)

It's natural for young people to dread the turn of calendar pages that dictates a return to school. It is, perhaps, less natural for teachers to dread it, although nobody likes to kiss a three-month vacation good-bye.

But recent conversations with child-rearing friends have convinced me that our public schools now operate the way they would during the aftermath of an earthquake: nobody's there except the people who have no choice.

Public schools were the children's melting pot, constitutionally proclaimed so by *Brown v. Board of Education*. Now, it seems as though half of the truly unpleasant well-paying jobs around here are held by parents grimly determined to save their kids from the pot, which has long since melted down.

As a public school student, I encountered the standard number of good teachers – two per school – but I was able to convince at least one local university that I had received a semblance of an education. It was during my brief stint as a teacher, though, that I became truly educated about the ways of the public schools.

When I began to teach, I was young enough to talk to students as near-peers, which prompted this advice from the woman who hired me: 'You'll never have a chance if you don't act twenty years old than you are.'

A fellow teacher, old enough not to need that trick, had come up with an even cleverer distancing device: every day, he wore a black three-piece suit to school, with a Phi Beta Kappa key clearly dangling from the watch pocket. Everybody I knew who had made Phi Beta had stashed the key in a desk drawer and forgotten it. Once I asked a teacher who knew Black Suit why he insisted on flaunting his achievement.

'Oh, that's not a Phi Beta Kappa key,' she said. 'It's a Phi *Delta* Kappa key.'

'Uh huh. What's Phi Delta Kappa?'

'It's a national education honorary society.' Ah. In other words, an organization devoted to giving out keys that look like Phi Beta keys. And school principals think Bart Simpson is a bad role model.

Admittedly, these were more innocent days. Kids gathered in the bathroom to do downers, not crack. A young man expelled by another teacher ran into my classroom and punched me in the jaw; he didn't spray the room with automatic-rifle fire.

But some things, I suspect, remain sadly the same. A high school senior sat in one of my classes, asking cogent questions. But he failed every test he took – tanked them pathetically. Other teachers, consulted in the grove of canned tuna and cottage cheese that was the teachers' lounge, confided that the kid was just a dummy, not even worthy of the vaguely optimistic label of Educable Mentally Retarded (known to all the kids as the kiss of brain death – as in, 'Hey, you're an EMR!')

Away from the bracing fragrance of solid-pack albacore, the truth turned out to be even grimmer. The kid had simply made it to the twelfth grade without ever having been taught to read.

What keeps the few good teachers – true heroes who don't even get VA mortgages – in the business is the irreducible satisfaction of working with 'the kids.' After all, at its worst, the way you're taught to do it, teaching is the distribution of a package of educational material to a procession of consumers: year after year, the same lesson plans, just new names on the seating chart. Either through wisdom or through ignorance (my way), some teachers insist on encountering and engaging those students where they are, working toward the curriculum together, as if for the first time – the way a good parent teaches.

Teaching – once the province of women too squeamish for nursing – has been 'professionalized': teachers with twenty years' service can now, in favored districts, earn almost as much as first-year paralegals.

But the process also has cast an aura of pseudoscience around a function that every human is built to perform – teaching something he knows to someone who doesn't. Learning, which we come similarly equipped to do, has been pigeonholed as something you achieve only under the supervision of trained professionals, who in turn are supervised by more trained professionals. Teachers and learners have become practitioners and clients, and very little teaching or learning goes on anymore.

Compulsory public schooling hasn't been around all that long. It's been an experiment, and lately the rats are dying. Maybe it's time to try something – anything – else. When I left the profession, the public schools were a worse argument for a monopoly than cable TV. They still are.

After all, if you watched the addresses at the end of informercials while the announcer yelled them at you, you might eventually learn to read.

●

GEORGE MACKAY BROWN

George Mackay Brown (1921–96), poet, novelist, playwright and short-story writer, was born in Stromness, in the Orkney Islands. The fifth child of a postman and a woman who had come to work in a hotel as a young girl, he was a late developer. In his early years he was dogged by illness, depression and an inability to make something of his life. At around the age of thirty, he started taking evening classes and was accepted at Newbattle Abbey College, an adult education establishment in Dalkeith, and then at Edinburgh University, where he completed a graduate study of the poetry of Gerard Manley Hopkins. All his writings have celebrated the richness of Orcadian life and the spiritual strength of a humble community close to nature. Since 1971 he has written a short weekly essay for the *Orcadian*. He used to pen it on the kitchen table on a Thursday morning, after the breakfast things were cleared away, and it would appear in the following Thursday's edition. At first, from 1971 to 1975, the column was called 'Letter from Hamnavoe' ('Hamnavoe' being the Viking name for Stromness), but when it resumed in 1976, after a break, the heading was changed to 'Under Brinkie's Brae'. His columns have been collected in three volumes: *Letters from Hamnavoe* (1975), *Under Brinkie's Brae* (1979) and *Rockpools and Daffodils: An Orcadian Diary 1979–1991* (1992).

'Under Brinkie's Brae'
Summer is Winding Down
Orcadian, 25 September 1980

Summer winds down. I have never known a summer pass so quickly. But as one gets older the wheel turns faster. A single day is timeless to a child in summer, with sun, insects, birds, sea and stones and sky. To the ageing, years merge together in a grey blur.

Every summer has its different pattern. May was a good month this year; so was June till that black thunderstorm shattered the idyll. After that, the weather was no longer a bale of blue silk unrolling – it was an indifferent patchwork of good days and stormy days and intermediate grey days.

September has brought us far more sunshine than that drab August. The September sun always has a different quality – a sweetness and mellowness. The yard above the sea lay open to the sun, whenever it shone, from May to August. One could sit and drink wine and write letters among congregations of gulls, while three black cats came and lingered and went, softly.

But now, of a bright afternoon, the houses to the west cut shadows into the yard. By four o'clock there is only one bright segment next the sea. The sun goes behind a high chimney-head; the yard is a well of shadows. So the sweet mellow sun of September is touched with melancholy. Summer is over. Ahead lie the darkness and the snow. We have few trees to make autumn vivid and gorgeous. But there's no mistaking the feel of rain that no other season knows. One night I lay awake in the early hours. Outside, the rain surged darkly down, shower after shower with hardly a pause between. The world was being well-scoured of the dust and sweat of summer.

Some creatures at this time of year rouse themselves to last hectic life. Whether the bluebottles are in an agony or an ecstasy, it's difficult to know. But there they are, day after day, bouncing on the windows. ('The blue fly sung in the pane,' wrote Tennyson; and notice how happily he broke the rules of grammar with 'sung' rather than 'sang'.) A fine fortnight or so they have of it, the bluebottles, a hectic feast and a revel before the cold kills them off. Even at night they won't let you read in peace under the lamp: they crash into the bulb, again and again, frenzied with light.

All Nature knows when summer is winding down.

'Under Brinkie's Brae'
A Truncated Meal
Orcadian, 1 October 1981

A new turnip, new potatoes. What better meal than that, with melted butter running through it?

Yet the palate insists on some kind of meat to go with the neep and tatties – why, I don't know.

The only kind of meat in my house that early evening was a tin of Spam. Spam, neep and new tatties – already the digestive juices were burbling in anticipation . . . In a peedie pot the vegetables ramped away.

Then it was only a question of opening the tin of Spam – the simplest thing in the world. There is a key stuck to the bottom of the tin. You insert this key into a minute tin flap, and keep turning the key till the top of the tin comes away – and there is the meat, all ready to be sliced with a sharp knife.

Something went wrong. Three-quarters of the way round the tin, the key (no doubt through carelessness on my part) came off the 'thread'. I wrenched and nagged; nothing happened.

It was very tantalizing. The tin was *almost* open. The Spam was clearly in sight – the delicious smell of the Spam rose into my nostrils. Surely it would be possible to wrench the tin open, somehow.

It was not possible. It was, in fact, clearly dangerous. The exposed edges of the tin were as sharp as lances, and after wrenching at the thing for five sweating, cursing minutes, I realized that one slip would lay the palm of my hand open to the bone, with wellings of blood! Were a few slices of meat worth all that effort and danger?

It must have been as difficult to prise a medieval knight out of his armour.

But the human mind is obstinate. I found a hammer in the cupboard, and struck the tin several resounding blows. Other than acquiring a few dents, the tin remained invulnerable.

I gave up – I was beaten.

Meantime the merry dance of tatties and neep in the pot went on. A prod with a fork showed they were ready.

By inserting a knife I was able to gouge out a few ragged slivers of Spam.

It is very bad for the digestion to eat a meal in a rage. I managed, by a great effort of will, to see that the whole business had been funny; at least, it must have been to an onlooker, if such a one had been present.

With a sauce of wry humour, the truncated meal proved to be most enjoyable.

'Under Brinkie's Brae'
Labyrinth of Books
Orcadian, 6 October 1988

Why are there some days when everything seems to go wrong, like this morning?

I was going to have written so many letters this morning. There was that brief holiday from letter-writing while the postal strike was on. I kept perversely, with one part of me, hoping that the strike would go on for a month or so; so that the work I had to do could flow on unimpeded. But the postman's visits twice a day are so pleasant – the rattle at the letter-box about 9.45 a.m. and again about 3.45 p.m. Sometimes it's only a letter saying I should open it *at once* because if I do I might soon become a millionaire: and such communications go to light the fire. But where would we be without the tidings from dear friends near and far? I got into such a tangle this morning with the letters that had to be written! The birthday present for a friend in Edinburgh wouldn't fit into the padded envelope I had already addressed. Another letter disappeared – what had happened? Maybe I had shoved it into the big birthday envelope by mistake; in which case the so-carefully-sealed envelope would have to be opened again. (Eventually the lost letter was discovered loitering on the couch.)

Then, details had to be copied from a book into an article I had written some time ago – a few factual things; nothing simpler than to fill in the blanks, once the book was located on the shelves. The book refused to be located on the shelf of Orkney books. Blood-pressure rising by the minute, I tore those shelves apart with frantic eyes, looking for *The Ice-Bound Whalers*. Nothing doing. It is there, somewhere, hiding. I could imagine it perversely sniggering from its hidden niche. I could imagine it saying, 'Let this be a lesson to him, once and for all. Let him arrange us books in decent order, not rammed in here and there in utter disregard. Then there's a chance we books might have civilized dealings with him . . .' I admit the justice of these biting remarks. The times I have wasted searching for books in the huge labyrinth of books that I call my library!

Well, I did get one letter written, but that was merely to sign my name on the Electoral Registrar's form. And there may yet be time, before going out to lunch in the Ferry Inn with three friends, to write to Gypsy the cat (who's always first on the list).

Normally the phone keeps a pious silence while I toil at the writing desk. This morning it rang *thrice*, just as a flow of words was building up.

What with looking for lost and missing books and articles, the living-room table is a wild chaos, mixed up with heels-of-loaf and flower petals.

And still, in the next half-hour there's the fire to clean and set.

Hundreds of books mock silently from the wall. The phone looks ready to leap into another wild outburst of ringing at any moment.

I ought, first thing, to have consulted my horoscope.

'Under Brinkie's Brae'
The Lady Nicotine
Orcadian, 16 March 1989

'No-smoking Day' yesterday, all over Britain – and I didn't need to do anything about that because (except for an occasional festive cigar) I threw my collection of pipes into the dustbin eight years ago, and never really missed it, except for a faint pang of desire when I was enjoying a pint of beer.

But cigarettes – that was a different and much more difficult yoke to break out of. Some of us began to smoke 'Wild Woodbines' at the age of twelve, at the beginning purely as a dare and a kind of showing-off, hating every puff and every shred of tobacco that stuck poisonously to the tonsils.

But we persisted, and before we were aware of it the heavy yoke was on us. We were the abject and miserable and furtive slaves of the Lady Nicotine. At the school playtime, we resorted to the boys' toilets with our scraps of 'fags', for each 'Woodbine' was too precious to smoke all at one go – and the lighted match was passed round – and we dragged the blue-grey reek down into our lungs, lingeringly, deep down. And the bell summoned us back to Latin and maths, and the teachers knew well enough what we had been up to by the smell from our hair and jerseys and fingers.

Twopence for a flimsy packet of five 'Woodbines'. Twopences weren't so easily come by in those pre-war days, and so we resorted to many questionable practices to lure or cajole the odd penny, from parents chiefly. 'Oh yes, I'll go for those messages, no trouble . . .' And I would bring the bread or sausages back, with a silent twopence added on for porterage.

The twopence of course was laid on the tobacconist's counter.

But even here, sometimes, there were difficulties; because the tobacconist might say, 'You're not sixteen . . .' Then a lie had to be added to the purloining, and I would hasten to assure the tobacconist that the cigarettes weren't for me – of course not – how could he ever think such a thing? – they were for some neighbour.

A pristine packet of five 'Woodbines'! What a rare jewel to have won, by superlative forethought and deceit! One more day's happiness . . .

The greatest joy in those early days was football, in any field or open space. We couldn't wait to get our hideous homework done (geography or Latin irregular verbs) to be out playing football, South-End *versus* North-End . . . I began to notice, after a year or two, that I couldn't run along the touchline so swiftly or blithely as formerly. Fifteen minutes of play, and I was completely exhausted; the lungs laboured and the legs were like lead.

Curiously, I never connected this sudden disability with the joys of smoking (that had an extra thrill in that it was forbidden, and had to be done subtly and secretly). It just so happened, it seemed to me, that my footballing days were prematurely over.

And then, suddenly, 'My Lady Nicotine' turned and hung heavy chains about me, and threatened me with imminent 'early dark'.

But that's another story.

•

ANNA QUINDLEN

Anna Quindlen was born in 1950 in a New Jersey suburb of Philadelphia, where she wrote for her high school paper and contributed to the *New Brunswick News*. She attended Barnard College and developed an early admiration for the columnist Dorothy Thompson. She also did a summer job on the *New York Post*, and after graduating in 1974 became a reporter there. In 1977 she joined the *New York Times* as a general reporter, as part of an affirmative action employment policy following a lawsuit brought by female employees who claimed they had been discriminated against. Having reported on city hall for a while, she became in 1981 the first woman to write the paper's 'About New York' column on a regular basis, and she was made deputy metropolitan editor that same year. In 1986 she took a long period of maternity leave after the birth of her second child and started to write a column about personal matters called 'Life in the 30s', which ran for three years. This was 'written in a determinedly female voice, and it was considerably off the usual news', but she eventually 'found the relentless self-exposure . . . wearing' – her husband once asked her, 'Could you get up and get me a beer without writing about it?' In 1990 she became the third woman to have an op-ed page column, 'Public & Private', in the *New York Times* (following in the footsteps of Anne O'Hare McCormick and Flora Lewis). In 1992 she won the Pulitzer Prize for commentary and in 1994 she left to pursue a new career as a novelist.

'Life in the 30s'
'I Don't Like that Nightgown'
From *Living Out Loud* (1988)

I have been married for almost ten years to the same person. Sometimes it's hard for me to believe. Neither of us were sure that any human being could be expected to live over the long haul with anyone as stubborn, opinionated and difficult as the other. Somehow it has worked, and it is not a gross exaggeration to say that this is partly due to the fact that I am a much better cook than he is, and he tells much better jokes than I do.

A lot of people don't understand how important these little things are to a marriage. I realized this when I was reading a magazine article about bachelors, many of whom were participating in organized sports instead of having relationships with women, just like their football coaches told them they should do when they were seventeen. Many of these bachelors seemed to think that it would take a lot of compromise and change on the part of both partners to stay married. Nothing could be farther from the truth. One touchstone of marriage is security, and nothing makes you feel more secure than knowing exactly what another person is going to say or do at any given time. If my husband just cut into a slightly pink pork chop and scoffed it down, instead of holding a piece up at eye level, looking at it as though it was a murder suspect, and saying, 'Is this cooked enough?' – well, I'd become pretty suspicious, I can tell you that.

I felt this sense of continuity just the other night. It was a cold night, a wintry night, and I was getting ready to go to sleep when my husband said, 'I don't like that nightgown.' And once again I felt that magic little thrill you always get when you realize that some things in your life are immutable. It was a flannel nightgown I was wearing, one of those little numbers that looks like a fallout shelter and is designed to reveal only that the body beneath possesses ankles. It's warm and comfortable, but I've always known, deep in my heart, that the only person who would consider it seductive would be Buddy Ebsen. Once a year my husband looks at one of these things and says, 'I don't like that nightgown.' I guess if I was what my grandmother used to call a dutiful wife, I wouldn't wear them. But just think how out-of-kilter that would throw my husband's whole existence.

Luckily neither of us ever has to go for long without these little touchstones that keep our relationship solid. More than that, I think they bring home to me constantly the differences between men and women. These are important to keep in mind, because the clearest explanation for the failure of any marriage is that the two people are incompatible – that is, that one is male and the other female. There are all those times when I've purchased a new dress for a special occasion and my husband has glimpsed those telltale price tags in the trash. 'Did you need a new dress?' he will always say, once again illustrating the gender-based distinction between necessity and desire. Or there's the ever-popular 'You look fine without makeup,' usually uttered when I am applying eyeliner five minutes after he has determined we should be in the car. To which the obvious answer is, 'The only place I've ever gone without makeup is to the recovery room.' I think it's worth noting that I was once at a party at which a man said quite loudly, 'You look fine without makeup' and eight women turned around, each thinking it was their husband.

(Of course, these things can backfire on you, too. If I ever am divorced by my husband, for example, it will probably be because I have made it a practise throughout my life never to put the caps back on things. With those grounds and the right judge, he could probably get the kids, the house, the dogs and all the toothpaste tubes, as well as the jar of mayonnaise that has tinfoil molded over the opening.)

However, I am beginning to think that the flannel nightgown is larger than this, figuratively as well as literally. Perhaps it is an extended metaphor for the difference between what men want from a marriage, and what women want. There's a real temptation to say that women want a relationship that is secure, comfortable and enduring, while men are really looking for excitement, sex and black lace. Obviously those are stereotypes. Lots of the bachelors in this magazine piece seemed to be interested in a secure relationship, although some of them had settled for touch football instead. I even have one friend, who previously had the kind of lingerie collection usually confined to a Victoria's Secret catalogue, who fell in love with a man who thinks flannel nightgowns are sexy, in the way the librarian with the bun and the glasses turns out to be something else entirely once she takes her hairpins out. (I know your next question. Forget it. This man is not available. He is taken.) And I know lots of women are interested in having some excitement in their lives, although a great many of the single women I know wish that excitement didn't so often include cheating, lying and uncomfortable undergarments.

It's a little late for me to fall in love with a man who likes cotton flannel and the allure of the dowdy. I'm already taken, too. And I know all his little winning ways, and he knows mine. I believe this is the secret to a successful marriage. It beats me why someone like Madonna, for example, would think she had irreconcilable differences from Sean Penn. Now there's a man you can count on: point a camera and he throws a punch, as predictable and consistent as can be, still spitting and swearing and indulging in fisticuffs, the same guy today as he was the day she married him. I like a certain reliability in a man, and I've got it. I put a plate of radicchio salad on the table, step back, and count to five. 'What is this stuff?' my husband says suspiciously, poking it with his fork. It warms my heart.

'Public & Private'
The Perfect Victim
New York Times, October 16, 1991

She seemed the perfect victim. Or perhaps it is more accurate to say that she was the perfect person to teach us that there are no perfect victims, that no matter how impressive your person, how detailed your story, how unblemished your past, if you stand up and say, 'He did this to me,' someone will find a way to discredit you.

And so it was with Anita Hill. Intelligent, composed, unflappable, religious and attractive, she testified to her sexual harassment by Clarence Thomas and even to her own inadequacies, agreeing that it had taken her too long to come forward, that it was hard to understand why she had kept in touch. And as soon as she left the room, she was portrayed as nut case, romantic loser, woman scorned, perjurer.

Clarence Thomas thundered about the sexual stereotypes of black men, and the Senate gasped obligingly. Little attention was paid to the stereotypes leveled at Professor Hill. Aloof. Hard. Tough. Arrogant. This is familiar shorthand to any successful woman. She wanted to date him. She wasn't promoted. She's being used by his enemies. This is familiar shorthand to anyone who has ever tried to take on the men in power.

African-American women are sometimes asked to choose sides, to choose whether to align themselves with their sisters or with their brothers. To choose whether to stand against the indignities done them as women, sometimes by men of their own race, or to remember that black men take enough of a beating from the white world and to hold their peace. The race card versus the gender card. Clarence Thomas milked the schism.

With his cynical invocation of lynching, he played in a masterly way on the fact that the liberal guilt about racism remains greater than guilt about the routine mistreatment of women. We saw more of Judge Thomas's character last weekend than we ever did during his confirmation hearings. What we learned is that he is rigid, anxious to portray himself as perfect, a man who will not even allow that two men watching a football game might talk differently than they would if there were women in the room.

The members of the Senate took to the floor yesterday and congratulated themselves on educating the American people about sexual harassment. Well, here is what they taught me:

That Senator Orrin Hatch needs to spend more time in the taverns of America if he thinks that only psychopaths talk dirty.

That the party of the Willie Horton commercials is alive and well and continuing to indulge in the deft smear for the simple reason that it works.

That the Democrats behaved in these hearings the way they have in presidential elections, hamstrung by their own dirty linen, ineffectual in their pallid punches, weak advocates for the disfranchised.

I learned that if I ever claim sexual harassment, I will be confronted with every bozo I once dated, every woman I once impressed as snotty and superior, and together they will provide a convenient excuse to disbelieve me. The lesson we learned, watching the perfect victim, is that all of us imperfect types, with lies in our past or spotty job histories, without education or the gift of oratory, should just grin and bear it, and try to stay out of the supply closet. 'This sexual harassment crap,' Senator Alan Simpson called it, evidencing his interest in women's issues.

What I learned from Professor Hill was different. When she returned to Oklahoma, where she may well teach all the rest of her days, unmolested by offers of high appointment because of her status as a historical novelty act, she had a kind of radiance. It seemed to me the tranquility of a person who has done the right thing and who believes that is more important than public perception.

There is only one explanation for her story that seems sensible and logical to me, that does not require conspiracy theories or tortured amateur psychoanalyzing or a member of the United States Senate making himself look foolish by reading aloud from *The Exorcist*. There is only one explanation that seems based not in the plot of some improbable thriller but in the experiences of real life, which the members of the Senate seem to know powerfully little about. That explanation is that she was telling the truth and he was not. Simple as that. She got trashed and he got confirmed. Simple as that.

•

CHRISTOPHER HITCHENS

Christopher Hitchens was born in Portsmouth in 1949. The son of a naval officer, he was educated at the Leys School, Cambridge, and Balliol College, Oxford, where he knew Bill Clinton. He joined the *New Statesman* in the early 1970s and did a number of foreign assignments which led to his appointment as chief foreign correspondent of the *Daily Express*. He went to live in the United States in 1981 and has written for various British and American publications. He has been writing his weekly 'Minority Report' column for the *Nation* since 1981 and also provides a monthly column called 'The Cultural Elite' for *Vanity Fair*. He has written several books and has recently been a visiting professor of English at the University of Pittsburgh.

'Minority Report'
Politically Correct
Nation, October 1991

Of what exhausting phenomenon are the following everyday terms an illustration? 'Bipartisan'; 'partisan'; 'divisive'; 'healing'; 'we look forward to working more closely'; 'I would need to see the full text of those remarks'; 'the business community'; 'the intelligence community'; 'put this behind us'; 'move the country forward'; 'define our agenda'; 'address our concerns'; 'appropriate conduct'; 'inappropriate conduct'; 'I cannot recall at this moment in time'; 'thank you for not smoking'; 'the American people'. These and many other routine fatuities represent the language of political correctness in our day, the prefabricated and conditioned phraseology by which 'we' (it's always 'we' in regular PC talk) express and imbibe the politics of the permissible. I had hoped to avoid writing about this room-temperature, pseudo-intellectual fad, but I realize that it's a fate not to be evaded. Just as those who call for 'English Only' believe themselves to be speaking English when they are mouthing a mediocre patois, and just as those who yell for 'Western civilization' cannot tell Athens, Georgia, from Erasmus Darwin, so those who snicker at the latest 'PC' gag are generally willing slaves to the most half-baked jargon.

Obviously it's tiresome when some loud child who missed the sixties presumes to instruct us all about 'people of colour' or 'persons of gender'. Still, at least there's an element of self-satire in the business; even in the hopeless phrase 'politically correct'. But when every newscaster in the country uses the knee-jerk term 'peace process', or discourses about 'credibility', or describes some bloodsoaked imposter as 'a moderate', the deadening of language has gone so far that it's almost impossible to ironize. Yet this occurs every day, and it's accounted a wonder if the President himself can marshal the clichés in the correct order on his wooden tongue. A person intoxicated by political correctitude might say of capital punishment that it is racist, repressive, fascistic and reminiscent of the worst excesses of the Portuguese Inquisition (or whatever). He or she might even say it was sexist and homophobic – even though it doesn't seem to fall that much upon women and even though the contrived word 'homophobia', as we classicists know, means 'fear of the same', if indeed it means anything at all, which I take leave to doubt. However, all these positions would be preferable in their way to that of Clarence Thomas, who was asked, in a hearing of the world's greatest deliberative body, what he thought of the death penalty and replied that 'philosophically' he foresaw no problem in applying it in 'appropriate' situations. What could be more bipartisan than the use of the word 'philosophical' to mean 'no problem'? The beauty of consensus PC is that it makes differences on matters of principle almost unsayable. A bit of a blow, however, had perhaps been dealt to the Platonic foundations of our great Western civilization.

In the nondebate over nonissues that goes on here, the hands-down winner is the culture of euphemism. Witnesses before Congress are actually awarded points for their expensively coached lying and emollience. Meanwhile, self-defined radicals sell the pass by announcing that anything is better than being 'offensive'. The two rivulets of drool merge softly and imperceptibly, and we end up with a public language by which almost nobody employs plain speech. One is almost rejoiced to hear a stupid, meaningless, barbarous emphasis – 'Fuck this shit' springs to mind – merely for the sake of its unadorned clarity. The disquieting thing about newscaster-babble or editorial-speak is its ready availability as a serf idiom, a vernacular of deference. 'Mr Secretary, are *we* any nearer to bringing about a *dialogue* in this *process*?' Here is the politically correct language of the consensus, which can be spoken while asleep or under hypnosis by any freshly trained microphone-holder. At least the PC felons are not trying – or not all the time – to 'bring us together' and make-believe we are all one family. However, the trend of their emaciated terminology leads in the direction of a mini-consensus that does not welcome dissent. The fact that this consensus is mostly a laugh doesn't make it, as an effort, any less potentially sinister. Morally, it may pose as a compliment to pluralism and 'diversity', which makes it feel superior to its white-bread senior partner. But politically and socially, it translates as 'watch what you say and don't give offence to anybody', which isn't a serious definition of diversity.

Senator Tom Harkin's kickoff campaign rally, I was interested to see, began with a mass open-air recitation of the Pledge of Allegiance, 'under God' and all, and a grand display of American flags. By these means Harkin hoped to show that Bush couldn't scare him! Yet what was this but a humiliating enactment of the mantras and gestures of official political correctness? A man who is still twitching from lashes inflicted more than three years ago is not a proud man, or an emancipated one. He is hoping, hypocritically, to stay within the admissible bounds of the politically safe (hypocrisy is not the least of the psychic wounds that result from enforced consensus) and to pass for white rather than as a possible friend of Willie Horton. What a country, and what a culture, when the liberals cry before they are hurt, and the reactionaries pose as the brave nonconformists, while the radicals make a fetish of their own jokey irrelevance.

It is not enough to 'have' free speech. People must learn to speak freely. Noam Chomsky remarked in the sixties about short-life ultra-radicals on campus who thought that Marx should have been burning down the British Museum rather than writing and thinking in it. The less political descendants of that faction have now tried to reduce life to a system of empowerment etiquette, and have wasted a lot of their own time and everyone else's in the process. But the real bridle on our tongues is imposed by everyday lying and jargon, sanctioned and promulgated at the highest levels of media and politics, and not by the awkward handful who imagine themselves revolutionaries.

•

LIBBY GELMAN-WAXNER (PAUL RUDNICK)

Paul Rudnick was born in Picastaway, New Jersey, in 1957. His father was a physicist and his mother an arts publicist. Educated at Yale University, where he majored in drama, he settled in New York City. He wrote jacket copy for book publishers and painted sets for the Juilliard School, but his heart was intent on writing for the stage. His first play, *Poor Little Lambs*, was produced in 1982, and *Jeffrey*, a comedy about AIDS and his most successful play, was produced on Broadway in 1993. He wrote the original screenplay for *Sister Act*, but felt that the final version had been bled of its satirical content; he was happier with the films made from his subsequent screenplays, *The Addams Family* (1991) and *Addams Family Values* (1993). As Libby Gelman-Waxner, Rudnick has been writing a film review column for the monthly magazine *Premiere* since 1989. Yet Libby is no ordinary film critic. She is a camp, satirical interpreter of social mores. Her essays are replete with references to her family and friends – her Jewish mother, her Lexington Avenue orthodontist husband, her gay designer cousin who lives in the Village, her own mainstay career as an assistant buyer in Juniors Activewear. Occasionally, Libby is replaced by a stand-in persona, such as her realtor mother, Sondra Krell-Gelman, her seven-year-old daughter Jennifer Waxner, or her psychotherapist, Arlene Cole-Natbaum, MD.

'If You Ask Me'
A New Scourge
From *If You Ask Me* (1994)

World literature – I love it, but with a career, two kids, and my roots staring me in the face, who has the time? I haven't even finished the last Jackie Collins, and my husband, Josh, hasn't open the Tom Clancy I got him for Christmas. Maybe it's for the best. As I told Josh, At least our kinds won't see us reading trash. Thank God for movie adaptations. I felt so proud when I told the sitter I was going to see *The Accidental Tourist*. She knew I wasn't going out just to have fun.

The Accidental Tourist is based on the novel by Anne Tyler. Anne, I'm sure it's a swell book, but seeing the film put me into a coma – I'm not kidding you. All I remember is watching William Hurt sitting in an armchair, blinking his little pink eyes, and the next thing I knew the usher was shaking me awake because the film was over. The usher said that many people have had similar reactions to *The Accidental Tourist*, he said that even crying babies nod right off. That night I had a dream about the movie. In my dream, William Hurt came to my apartment, and he said that if I didn't give him my baby son, Mitchell, he would make me watch *The Accidental Tourist* two more times. Even in my dream, William Hurt was the most Caucasian person I have ever seen; he was like this enormous slice of Tip-Top bread in chinos and wire-rimmed eyeglasses. His hair reminded me of mayonnaise, and he spoke very slowly, like a Mormon on Quaaludes. He was like a huge rubber eraser, an albino Gumby, and he terrified me. William Hurt underplaying is much scarier than Shelley Winters at full blast, let me tell you. Just as I was about to head for the baby's room, I woke up screaming. I told my husband about the dream, and he agreed with me: We can always have more children.

After this experience, I went to see the film version of Tama Janowitz's collection of stories, *Slaves of New York*. This movie is about New Wave artists living in New York's trendy East Village, so I thought it would be lively. But the strangest thing happened. All I remember is someone on the screen saying 'Come up to my loft,' and then the usher was yanking my shoulder. That night I had another dream. Tama Janowitz, this woman with a wild, teased hairdo, came to my apartment wearing a rubber miniskirt and a $2,000 silver lamé motorcycle jacket. She was very sweet, but she started to tell me about her troubles with her sadistic artist boyfriend, and how she has low self-esteem, and how hard it is to finance a halfway decent co-op. And I started to think, Maybe some people *should* have low self-esteem. And then Tama said that if I didn't hand over my husband, she would tell me all about her girlfriend's problems in finding a gallery in which to show her voodoo sculpture and trying to get a man who isn't on cocaine to say 'I love you.' And just as I was tying Josh's wrists with an old pair of panty hose, I woke up in a cold sweat. I decided not to tell him about my dream, even though I knew he would have understood, especially if he had seen Tama's eyeliner.

The next day, I went to see my therapist, Dr Arlene Cole-Natbaum, and I told her about my conking out at the movies and my nightmares, and about Tama's earrings. Dr Cole-Natbaum said that I was suffering from a common condition known as movie-lepsy. Movie-lepsy, it seems, is somewhere between epilepsy and narcolepsy, and it is referred to in certain medical textbooks as Merchant Ivory syndrome. The movie-leptic's chronic napping, Dr Cole-Natbaum explained, can be triggered by any number of cinematic images. William Hurt repressing his emotions, Robert Duvall in a cowboy hat, anything involving a child who has been mute since a parent or pet died, and any pair of zanily mismatched detectives or bank robbers. Dr Cole-Natbaum said the origins of movie-lepsy had been traced to several TV movies in which illiterate adults learn to read.

Dr Cole-Natbaum gave me a remedy for my movie-lepsy. She said that when I start to feel drowsy, that whenever Sissy Spacek opens a screen door, I should practice two visualizations. First, I should think about Barbara Hershey's lips. Barbara had collagen injections in her lips to make them fuller and more pouty, which I first noticed in the film *Beaches*. I've also read about a woman who used a chunk of fat from her own thigh to plump out her upper lip. This struck me as very dangerous: what if the fat decided it had merely headed upstream to spawn? My dear friend Stacy Schiff is considering liposuction in order to combat a saddlebag problem. Stacy says that the procedure sounds very satisfying, that it's what she's always dreamed of – removing her cellulite with a penknife.

If Barbara Hershey's lips don't do the trick, Dr Cole-Natbaum said I might also think about director Peter Bogdanovich's marriage to Dorothy Stratten's younger sister. Peter loved Dorothy, but she was murdered; Peter also paid for the younger sister's plastic surgery. Dr Cole-Natbaum is such a fine therapist; last week she cured a manic-depressive by prescribing Mallomars eaten in bed and a subscription to *US* magazine. Thanks to Dr Cole-Natbaum, my movie-lepsy is under control; as a test, I watched an episode of *The Wonder Years*, a sitcom set in the sixties that has sensitive voice-over narration. I am pleased to report that I didn't drop off even once, and Dr Cole-Natbaum says that any dry cracker will control the retching.

Movie-lepsy can be very serious, and it is not caused only by films adapted from acclaimed novels or plays. Still, it is a good idea to watch out for that kind of thing; remember, if you snooze off while reading a book, at least no one steals your purse or sees you with your mouth open. I would like there to be a Prevent Movie-lepsy Telethon, maybe hosted by Bill Hurt, in which funds could be raised to fight movies set in the Midwest, the outback, or London during the Blitz. I, Libby, am a movie-leptic. I only hope that my frank confession will stop the shame and encourage others to seek counseling, especially those who haven't regained consciousness since watching *Maurice* or any film in which people take tea with their maiden aunts. Helping people is what I'm here for, if you ask me.

'If You Ask Me'
Sex, Drugs, and Extra-strength Excedrin
From *If You Ask Me* (1994)

Personally, I think it's interesting that while there haven't been any wide-screen cinematic biographies of Socrates or Proust or Mother Teresa, we now have a multimillion-dollar film on the life of Jim Morrison, the lead singer of the Doors. Jim lived to be twenty-seven, and he made a few albums that you can still buy if you're really at loose ends. Director Oliver Stone's movie *The Doors* is basically *Jim: The Life of an Alcoholic Moron*. Jim starts out in film school with a befuddled expression and corduroy pants and sideburns; after a few more scenes, he begins wearing leather pants and becomes a drunken, abusive star. For the rest of the movie, every scene is identical: Jim looks dazed, swigs from a bottle of whiskey, and mumbles or lip-synchs. If you ask me, Jim's underlying appeal is very simple: he was pretty, he lived in the sixties, and he died. With this as a guideline, I predict that some day, once nature takes its course, we can look forward to movie biographies of Priscilla Presley and Keith Partridge.

Oliver Stone, who also cowrote *The Doors*, may very well be America's favourite kind of person: the talent-impaired genius. This means each of his films, such as *Platoon* and *Born on the Fourth of July*, is an Important Statement From a Major Artist; this also means that most of his films are loud and endless and that everyone in the audience gets a migraine after the first twenty minutes. In *The Doors*, Oliver wants to create an ecstatic Dionysian frenzy, which means the camera spins around a lot and the actors look like frightened deer, because no one's told them exactly how to act Dionysian and frenzied. Meg Ryan plays Jim's heroin-addicted girlfriend, and she keeps grinning and saying things like Jim Morrison, you get back in here, or Jim Morrison, you can't fool me. I don't blame Meg, but after a while she starts to sound like Harriet Nelson calling the boys for dinner – Ricky Nelson, you get in the house this minute! Put down that syringe!

Meg is also forced to discover Jim's dead body in a Paris hotel room while she's wearing a terrible sixties wig with bangs. *The Doors* is a tribute to bad wigs; Kyle MacLachlan, as another band member, gets to wear at least three different strawberry-blond bath mats on his head. At one point, Jim takes the band into the desert for some sort of mystical drug experience, during which he sees many meaningfully wrinkled Indians in buckskins and war paint. Later, while Jim is being Dionysian onstage at a concert, these Indians reappear as fantasy figures, dancing beside him and the many bare-breasted women who run up from the crowd. The Indians serve the same function they did in *Dances With Wolves*: they make the far more highly paid white movie stars seem soulful and important and in touch with ancient truths. Do Indians enjoy being used this way, as spiritual elves or cosmic merit badges? Has Oliver ever met any Indians outside of Frontierland in Disney World?

To Oliver, the sixties were a period of wild sexuality and orgiastic freedom; he's the Hugh Hefner of directors. If you ask me, the sixties were about two things: Paul

McCartney, the cute Beatle, and Goldie Hawn doing the frug in a bikini with peace symbols painted on her tummy on *Laugh-In*. I was very little during the sixties, but I remember my older sister Shelley, now twice divorced and an executive vice-president in creative concepts at Worldwide Foods, having a terrible fight with my mother over whether John Lennon had shamed his family and all of Liverpool with that haircut. Shelley's first husband was Ira Hirsh, whom she met while they were both seniors at Columbia; Shelley and Ira then moved to a commune in New Hampshire for two years and had a child, Serenity Raga Hirsh. At the time, Ira was a member of the Weather Underground, and he brought Bobby Seale to my cousin Andrew's bar mitzvah and demanded that all of Andrew's Cross Pen and Pencil gift sets be returned to the people. Ira also disrupted the hora during the reception and remolded the chopped-liver swan on the buffet into a clenched fist – it was still quite tasty.

Shelley and Ira divorced after Ira wanted to swap Shelley for Cindy Klausner, the woman who ran the commune's continental-breakfast outreach program, which distributed cappuccino, a choice of brioche or elderberry muffin, and a fabric napkin to the only welfare family in town. Shelley did not want to have sex with Milton Klausner, Cindy's husband, who was also the commune's landscape architect (the commune, one of the very few to be housed in a Georgian-style garden apartment complex, was called the Moonrise Unity Whole Planet Countercollective: An Alternative Lifestyle With Underground Parking and Storage). The commune fell apart after a group acid trip, during which Shelley saw God in the form of a white wicker hamper with a matching Kleenex dispenser; Shelley says that these coordinated bathroom accessories told her that the sixties were over and that business school was Zen Buddhism plus security.

Shelley got custody of Serenity, who demanded to be renamed Allison once she started first grade at Dalton. Shelley's second husband was Carp Carlisle III, by whom she had a son, Carp IV. Carp is an old family nickname – it's short for Carpenter; you can imagine how much all of this pleased my mother, who still refers to Carp III as Satan in Deck Shoes. Carp III was an investment banker who secretly wanted to write show tunes; his dream was to compose music and lyrics for a musical comedy about the history of golf, entitled *Teed Off!* The score, when it was completed, included such numbers as 'Nine Holes in My Heart', 'A Country Club for Two (and Their Descendants),' and 'Over You, Under Par.' Shelley played that last song for the judge at the divorce hearing, which led to a settlement that my mother says almost justifies the anguish she continues to suffer over having a grandchild who sings 'The Little Drummer Boy' and calls her Grandmum. Shelley's new career at Worldwide Foods is booming; she's currently test-marketing International Gums, a group of chewing gums inspired by the palates of many lands, including Hot Curry flavor from India, Sugarless Toffee from England, and Bubble Rice Bran from Japan.

Clearly, Shelley has learned from the sixties in a way that Oliver Stone has not. The point is to keep moving, as Shelley always says. I understand that Oliver's next film is about the Kennedy assassination; what's after that, Ollie – the Judy Carne story? A searching look at both Herman and the Hermits? A savage inquiry into the death of Mama Cass? Though I worship at the shrine of auteur filmmaking, sometimes enough is enough, if you ask me.

•

ALAN WATKINS

Alan Watkins was born in Wales in 1933, the son of a schoolteacher. He was educated at Amman Valley Grammar School and Queen's College, Cambridge. He did his national service in the RAF as an education officer and was called to the Bar of Lincoln's Inn in 1957. However, he experienced an epiphany while reading one of Henry Fairlie's *Spectator* political columns on a train journey: that he would rather be Henry Fairlie than Mr Justice Devlin (then a famous judge) and so he resolved to become a political commentator. After a brief spell as a research assistant at the London School of Economics, he joined the *Sunday Express* in 1959 and during the next few years served variously as its New York correspondent, its acting political correspondent, and its 'Crossbencher' political columnist. In 1964 he joined the *Spectator* as its political correspondent and from 1967 to 1976 he did the same job for the *New Statesman*. He has subsequently been a political columnist for the *Observer* (1976 to 1993) and the *Independent on Sunday* (from 1993 to the present). He has also written a more general column, for the *Sunday Mirror* (1968–9) and the *Evening Standard* (1974–5), as well as a rugby column, at first for the monthly magazine the *Field*, and subsequently a weekly column for the *Independent* since its launch in 1986.

'Spotlight on Politics'
The War of Jenkins's Ego
New Statesman, 2 August 1974

> Let the Special only be so unfortunate as to have a style of its own – let him have a capacity for minute observation, or a gift for picturesque and vivid description; let him be endowed with the power of thinking, and of expressing his thoughts in vivid language – and the whole of Hampstead Heath will be upon him at once . . . to accuse him, if he has dined with a duke or conversed with a general, of being a flunkey, a toady, a Jenkins and a lickspittle.

Thus George Augustus Sala, writing about journalists – special correspondents – and not about politicians. The quotation is interesting chiefly because it illustrates a nineteenth-century usage of 'Jenkins' previously unknown to me. Is it, I wonder, still apposite? Certainly Mr Roy Jenkins has not toadied to Mr Harold Wilson, Mr Ian Mikardo or Mr Tony Benn. And both Mr Denis Healey and Mr Anthony Crosland, whose social-democratic credentials, they believe, are every bit as impressive as his, are extremely annoyed with him. They are annoyed because of the timing of the speech, because it suggested – indeed more than suggested – that Mr Benn's rhetoric represented reality and, not least, because of the extensive publicity it received. And this brings us to the first of many interesting questions about Mr Jenkins. Why is it that, not perhaps his lightest observations, but remarks which come very near to them, are treated with such high seriousness, analysed, commented upon, searched for hidden meanings?

There are, I think, several interconnected answers. One is that ever since the days when Mr John Harris (now Lord Harris of Lewisham) was his press officer he has always taken great pains over the release of his speeches to the newspapers. Like Mr Enoch Powell, he prefers on occasion to by-pass party headquarters, thereby adding to the feeling of expectancy. The word goes out to selected editors and correspondents: Roy is about to pronounce. And lo! there is Mr Ivan Yates with a column of respectful exegesis on the leader page of the *Observer*. Mr Jenkins has always held a fascination for a few editors such as Mr David Astor and Mr William Rees-Mogg, even if Monday's *Times* leader did contain one unexpectedly sharp reference to the absence of any commitment to equality in the Haverfordwest speech.

Nor is this all. For many of Mr Jenkins's set-piece speeches prove on examination to be remarkably short on content. Certainly this was true of last weekend's. This means that they are undemanding, an easy read. Mr Crosland will take a specific problem and deal with it gravely under numbered headings, for which he has a regrettable proclivity. Not so with Mr Jenkins's speeches. Despite the appearance of lucidity and rationality, they appeal to passion rather than understanding, prejudice rather than thought. Perhaps this is the essence of a good speech. It is neither here nor there that the passions aroused, the prejudices appealed to, are shared by right-thinking members of society generally – or those sections of society with whom Mr Jenkins customarily consorts.

Take for example the Common Market, which Mr Jenkins skilfully if somewhat unscrupulously muddled with the Anglo-American alliance. It really will not do to say that anyone who wants Britain out of the Market is lacking in moderation. Nor is it by any means established that the centre group on whom Mr Jenkins is so keen wants Britain to stay in Europe. In any case it is not at all self-evident that centre people want centre policies. Very often they want extreme ones. They would have reintroduced hanging, made the IRA an illegal organization and allowed the Price sisters to die. Thank goodness that in practice Mr Jenkins disregards the centre.

Now Mr Jenkins's command of publicity may account for some of the hostility shown to him. But it cannot be the whole explanation because only a very small number is competing in the same business. Why is it, then – this brings us to the second question – that he arouses the antagonism he does? Because he likes wine? But so do the majority of the Cabinet. In addition the Prime Minister himself is a noted connoisseur of fine old brandies, not to mention Havana cigars; and these civilized tastes appear to do him no harm at all in the eyes of the faithful. Well then: is it because Mr Jenkins is not a Socialist? But Mr Michael Foot is not a Socialist either. That strange nineteenth-century continental creed is as remote from Mr Foot as it is from Mr Jenkins. Or again, is it because Mr Jenkins talks in a fancy way? But then, so also does Mrs Judith Hart, the daughter of a linotype operator, and the best of luck to her. Yet Mrs Hart's character is never assailed on purely linguistic grounds. There seems to be a double standard somewhere.

The third, more immediate question is why Mr Jenkins did it. For some time, ever since his resignation from the shadow Cabinet over the referendum, his friends and supporters have been divisible into aggressors and pacifiers. 'Roy, be a king,' some of them would say; while others would advise him in his own interests to take a seat at the back of the kirk. On this occasion all the weight of advice appears to have been against making the speech. Mr Jenkins nevertheless went ahead and made it, presumably because he was tired not only of Mr Benn's policies but of Mr Benn's publicity. Having been consigned to the Home Office ('the dustbin of politics,' as Iain Macleod once described it) he had to demonstrate not merely to others but to himself that he was still a political force.

And of course Mr Mikardo, Mr Eric Heffer and the rest of them rose to the bait, as the Left always will. Afterwards they calmed themselves remarkably quickly. Well before Mr Wilson's speech on Tuesday, by Monday afternoon in fact, good order and party discipline had been restored. Mr Jenkins has obviously not gained any credit among his colleagues excepting Mr Reg Prentice and Mrs Shirley Williams, and even they seemed to be making the noises expected of them. But it does not follow from this that Mr Jenkins has irreparably harmed Labour's chances at the election. He occupies a position, or creates an impression, comparable in some ways to Mr Powell's before the 1970 contest. He is believed to 'speak his mind', than which nothing in politics is easier. It is in this sense that Mr Jenkins is a toady. He toadies to a simple and popular, indeed populist, view of the nature of political honesty.

However, there is another side. There always is. It may seem unfair to blame Mr Wilson for a speech delivered by Mr Jenkins, but the Home Secretary was surely following a precedent set by other ministers. This is not only one of the ablest but one of the most ill-disciplined governments of modern times. The dissent is healthy enough in its way, and gratifying to libertarians such as myself. Still, there are limits. Mr Heffer attacks Mr James Callaghan on Chile. In the PLP two Foreign Office ministers support the government on nuclear tests, while the other two oppose it. Inside the National Executive anything may happen. Mr Robert Mellish, Mr Healey, Mr Foot and Mr Crosland seem to have entered a public competition in who can push Mr Wilson to the polls first. In fact Mr Crosland said this week, in a phrase more appropriate to a Trollopian villain than to a senior minister, that there would be 'a devil of a row' if the election did not take place in the autumn. The timing of the election may not be a matter for the Prime Minister alone. Indeed it was discussed at Cabinet shortly after the government took office. But neither is it something on which individual ministers should pronounce. As Mr Wilson might have said to the parliamentary party this week – he disappointed me by neglecting to do so – this tomfoolery must stop.

Panic is Not the Way to Manage
Independent, September 1987

Never underestimate an Englishman, my father used to advise me. He might look slow, but he was persistent, had application; he got there in the end. The Welsh, by contrast, embarked on enterprises of one kind or another with tremendous enthusiasm. Then they met with a few reverses and, easily discouraged, would retire from the field. They would return to their firesides to sulk, maintaining that they could easily have beaten the opposition – for they were, after all, clearly the better side – but that they did not think it was worth it. They would then ask mam to pour another cup of tea, saying that they fancied egg and chips for dinner.

Though a patriotic Welshman, my father was a creator of national stereotypes who would have been instantly banned by the Lewisham Council. At the time he was dispensing his advice to me, however, forty-odd years ago, there was a good deal of truth in his generalizations, whether applied to rugby or to other, even more important fields of endeavour.

But in their response to the World Cup, the English have certainly not conformed to the model. The appointment of Mike Weston as a sort of manager strikes me as an act of panic, not an application of that cool, calm deliberation which, as Harold Macmillan used to like to remind his colleagues, unravels every knot. I write that Weston is a 'sort of' manager because he is not going to be given the powers which Sir Alf Ramsey, for example, used to possess. It is all very odd. England's performances last season and in the World Cup were (leaving the players out of account for the moment) primarily the responsibility of Weston and of the coach Martin Green. Time and again they were told where they were going wrong, both in this column and by more exalted authorities.

It was wrong to appoint Richard Hill virtually captain-for-life, rather as the Duke of Marlborough was made commander-for-life, and then to be stuck with someone who was manifestly not up to the job, whether as captain or as scrum-half.

It was a mistake to hail the thuggery of the French match as a sterling English performance, and not to anticipate the troubles of the Welsh match. It was a further error to attempt a half-hearted justification of the English team's behaviour on that muddied occasion.

And it was a humiliation to have the temporary dismissal of several English players forced on you by higher authority. I am usually chary of saying that people should resign. But I should have thought that a public reprimand by the Rugby Football Union to the coach and the chairman of selectors would have entailed the automatic resignation of both of them.

Then came the Scottish match, a false dawn and the World Cup. After last season and its sequel, there were three rational choices: to persist with the old system under the old names; to persist with the old system under new or juggled names, Weston, Green or both dropping out; or to embark on a new, managerial system under a new name. If the last choice had been adopted, the obvious candidate would have been Alan Davies of Nottingham, though Charlie White, formerly of Leicester, and Jack Rowell of Bath would have had their supporters.

But there is nothing whatever to be said for starting a new era under an old and (to be frank) discredited name. Weston even tried to bring Green back into the magic circle, but was, it appears, frustrated in this attempt. I have no animus against Weston. As a centre and utility back he was a pundits' favourite. I thought him a rather boring player whose chief accomplishment was his ability to kick the ball higher than anyone else. When I now observe him at matches his handsome countenance usually bears a puzzled expression – as well it may.

The English are at least doing something, even if it is the wrong thing. The Welsh, on the other hand, are somewhat easily pleased. This is just as much a national characteristic as the disposition to be easily discouraged. But more of this in another column.

'Political Commentary'
Tony the Terrible Takes a Tip from the Tudors,
Independent on Sunday, 8 October 1995

In my desultory reading of history, I have often wondered how the tyrants of the past managed to get away with the most dreadful deeds. Why, for example, in the age of the later Tudors, did people generally tolerate the wholesale plunder and regimented religion, the rigged trials and cruel executions? And why – a more puzzling question – was there a need for a justification of these terrible events by later historians: the sycophantic J. A. Froude, the drivelling John Neale, the quite appalling Geoffrey Elton?

The curious could find answers at Brighton last week. It came down to the worship of prospective power. The equivalents of the Protestant historians were the commentators of our great liberal newspapers. Ms Liz Davies had clearly to be disposed of because Mr Tony Blair, the equivalent of King Henry VIII, did not want her. I am not suggesting – heaven forbid! – that Ms Davies found herself in the position of one of the old monster's unfortunate wives. Rather she was accused of treasonable adherence to the Old Religion.

As Elton wrote of Thomas Cromwell's regime, it was not a question of interfering with anyone's freedom of conscience. It was a simple matter of obeying the law. This was the kind of fraudulent case which Ms Clare Short deployed last week. Having seen to it that her sister was securely tied up, she solemnly told us, before setting light to the faggots, that the lady had been found guilty of being a member of the editorial board of a newspaper, *Labour Briefing*.

It is not, I confess, on my reading list. I make do with the *Spectator* and *Private Eye*. But it is, it appears, always being rude about Labour leaders. If this is true, it demonstrates an admirable consistency of purpose and impartiality of approach. In any case, there is nothing in party rules against editing magazines. Altogether Ms Short's indictment reminded me not only of one of Henry VIII's lackeys but also of the customs officer in Evelyn Waugh's *Vile Bodies*:

> This book on Economics comes under Subversive Propaganda. That you leaves behind
> . . . as for this autobiography, that's just downright dirt, and we burns that straight away,
> see.

We have already been told that this is not the conference some of us have come to love, in much the same way as we guiltily enjoy the boxing on television of a Saturday night. Indeed, there was only one contest. In former times, it would have been a warm-up for the big fight of the evening. Happily for the substantial anti-boxing element in the party, this year there was no big fight. We had to make do with the bout between Mr Roy Hattersley and Mr David Blunkett.

Mr Hattersley is not an embittered man. He feels that life has treated him pretty well on the whole, and so it has. But he is moved by a sense of genuine outrage at what he sees as the abandonment of non-selective education. Mr Blunkett says there is no such desertion. But he is being disingenuous. For how can you have 'foundation schools', or separate schools for the specially gifted in music, mathematics, dancing or whatever, unless you have selection? Labour's education policy has been given a nudge forward – or, according to your point of view, forced to take a step backwards – by Mr and Mrs Blair's decision to send their son not merely to an opted-out school but to one of a highly traditional character.

This brings us to Mr Blair's speech. It has received a warmer reception than any comparable performance since Harold Wilson's oration on science and Socialism in 1963. Indeed, there were conscious echoes of that speech in Mr Blair's own.

Every household in the land is, it appears, to be issued with a compulsory computer. It will be connected to the Internet. In exchange BT will run cables into people's houses giving them an additional choice on their television sets of pornographic films, old black-and-white films, ice-hockey and motor racing. Pornography will also, of course, be available on the Internet.

This column is not censorious. *De gustibus non est disputandum*, or, there is no arguing with tastes: that is the motto here. Mr Blair's fallacy is to imagine that children are going to learn anything by fiddling around with electronic machines, occasionally coming across pieces of misleading information supplied by, well, I suppose, much the same kind of young people who are now bustling about advising Mr Blair.

The speech contained other pieces of nonsense. For instance, it is untrue that you cure unemployment by educating people or making them more skilled. This country is full of skilled engineers. Most of them are out of work. Or again, you cannot spend money on some desirable object by transferring to it cash which the present government is not spending at all and has not even decided to spend. This is what Mr Blair said he was going to do with the money saved by not introducing identity cards. With only slightly more plausibility, he adopted the same approach to the assisted places scheme, on which the government really is spending something, and which Mr Blair promises to abolish.

He does not go as far as the Liberal Democrats in wanting to allocate taxes to specific ends. Instead he assumes large commitments by promising to abolish schemes which are either less expensive or do not exist. If Mr Blair behaved in this way while running a public company he would soon find himself in the Southwark Crown Court, where, after a trial lasting several years and costing millions of pounds, he would doubtless be acquitted, or compelled to do a few hours' community service. As for the minimum wage, Mr Blair told us that this had not been brought about by Wilson, by Attlee or even by Keir Hardie.

'But Keir Hardie was never Prime Minister,' I remarked to Mr John Humphrys, who was standing by my side.

'You cynical journalist, you,' Mr Humphrys replied.

In fact Hardie not only failed to become Prime Minister, as most Labour leaders, after all, have failed to do. He was hopelessly incompetent even as leader, and had to be replaced after a couple of years by Arthur Henderson. Wilson really was a Prime Minister, one of only four Labour occupants of Number 10. This year, following his death, and a lengthy period of conference ostracism, an attempt was made to honour him by having Lady Wilson very publicly take the platform before Mr Blair's speech.

She was approached through Lady Falkender and said she would be delighted to appear. But she did not look very happy about it. To me it was a tasteless, even rather horrible event – a bit like D. G. Rossetti opening up his wife's coffin. The party got away with it. Mr Blair more than got away with his speech later on. But then, I am made of sterner stuff than the susceptible Tory commentators. Having been brought up among the nightingales and psalms of South-west Wales, I early acquired an aversion to Uplift in all its forms.

•

ELLEN GOODMAN

Ellen Goodman was born Ellen Holtz in Newton, Massachusetts, in 1941. She was educated at Radcliffe, where she read modern European history, graduating cum laude in 1963. That year she married and moved to Detroit with her husband, and there she wrote features for the *Free Press*. When they returned to Boston in 1967, she joined the *Boston Globe* as a feature writer and was soon given a column in the features section, called 'At Large'. In 1971 her column was moved to the paper's op-ed page and in 1974 Goodman gave up her other work to concentrate on the column. By 1976, before she joined the Washington Post Writers Group, the column was being modestly syndicated to twenty-five papers. Later, it was to run twice a week and appear in 400 papers. Writing from an essentially feminist perspective, Goodman has succeeded in blending personal reflection with political and social commentary, and in 1980 she received the Pulitzer Prize for commentary.

'At Large'
The Family Legacy
Boston Globe, November 23, 1989

It is my turn now: My aunt, the keeper of Thanksgiving, has passed the baton, or should I say the drumstick? She has declared this a permanent legacy.

Soon, according to plan, my grandmother's dishes will be delivered by cousin-courier to my dining room. So will the extra chairs and the communal chafing dishes. The tradition will also be transplanted.

But this morning, she has come over to personally deliver a piece of this inheritance. She is making stuffing with me.

In one hand, she carries the family Thanksgiving 'bible,' a small blue book that bears witness to the recipes and shopping lists and seating plans of decades past. In the other hand, she carries three loaves of bread, a bag of onions and the appropriate spices.

It must be said that my aunt does not quite trust me to do this stuffing the right way, which is, of course, her way, and her mother's way. She doesn't quite trust my spices or my Cuisinart or my tendency to cut corners. So, like a tribal elder, she has come to instruct me, hands on, to oversee my pilgrim's progress every step of the way.

Together we peel the onions and chop them. Not quite fine enough for her. I chop some more. Together we pull the bread apart and soak it and squeeze it. Not quite dry enough for her. I squeeze again.

Gradually I, the middle-aged mother of an adult child standing in the kitchen of the home I make mortgage payments on, feel myself again a child. Only this time I find amusement in taking such exacting instructions from my elder. More than amusement. I find comfort in still being somebody's young.

But sautéing the onions until they are perfectly brown (my aunt doesn't like white onions in the stuffing), I start divining a subtext to this recipe sharing. It says: Time is passing. Generations pass. One day I will be the elder.

'I don't think I like this whole thing,' I say aloud, sounding like the child I am now. My aunt, who is about to be threescore years and ten, stops stirring the pan for a moment and looks at me. She understands. And for a while it isn't just the fumes of onions that come into our eyes.

The moment passes; I go back to mixing, and my aunt goes back to her favorite activity: bustling. But I no longer feel quite so much the child.

Adulthood arrives in these small sudden exchanges more than in well-heralded major crises. And the final moment of assuming adulthood may be when we inherit the legacy, become the keeper of traditions, the curator of our family's past and future memories. When the holidays are at our houses. The reunions at our instigation. When the traditions are carried on, or cast aside, because of choices that we make.

When we were small, my sister and I used to giggle at assorted holiday tables ruled over by our elders. We would at times squirm under the rule of imposed traditions and best behaviors. A certain prayer, an unfamiliar dish, an eccentric relative could send us to the bathroom laughing.

In time, when we were teenagers and then young parents, we were occasionally rebellious conformists, critical participants at family celebrations. We maintained a slight distance of humorous affection for the habits that the older generation carried on.

We were the ones who would point out that no one really liked mincemeat, that the string beans were hopelessly mushy, the onion-ring topping simply *passé*, that there was altogether too much chicken fat in the stuffing. It was easy to rebel against the things we could count on others maintaining.

Now I see this from another vantage point, that of almost-elder. I see that tradition is not just handed down but taken up. It's a conscious decision, a legacy that can be accepted or refused. Only once it's refused, it disappears.

How fragile is this sinew of generations. How tenuous the ceremonial ties that hold families together over time and generations, while they change as imperceptibly and inevitably as cells change in a single human body.

So it is my turn to accept the bequest, the dishes, the bridge chairs, the recipe book. This year there will be no string beans. Nor will there be ginger snaps in the gravy, forgive me. But the turkey will come with my grandmother's stuffing, my aunt's blessing, and my own novice's promise.

'At Large'
Date and Rape
Boston Globe, May 3, 1991

I am told by those who can find the silver lining in a cloud of squid ink that there is some good news in the media storm centered over Palm Beach. It has focused attention on date rape.

Maybe so, but not every spotlight is truly enlightening. Date rape is the should-be oxymoron that we use to distinguish rapes committed by acquaintances from those committed by strangers. But it is also a phrase that glues together the two sides of the story. His date and her rape.

Which story is the truth this time? What really happened in the Kennedy compound on Easter weekend? If this case gets to trial, I will bet big money on the courtroom scenario. The man will portray steamy sexual intercourse in the grass with just a spicy soupçon of rough stuff. The woman will describe sexual assault and a piercing violation of her will.

Moreover, if both of these parties go to the polygraph machine, it is entirely possible that they will separately and equally pass their lie detector tests with flying colors. Male and female alike may make equally convincing witnesses. Because in fact both may believe what they say.

This is what is so unsettling about this so-called gray area of sexual assault. Two people leave the scene of a sexual encounter, one remembering pleasure, the other pain.

In the most often cited 1985 study of 6,000 college students, University of Arizona professor Mary Koss found that over twenty-five percent of college women had experienced a completed or attempted rape since their fourteenth birthday. Four out of five of these encounters were with men they knew. But among college men, only eight percent admitted to behavior that fit these definitions.

It isn't that the same eight percent of the men are assaulting twenty-five percent of the women. Nor are they necessarily lying. The kernel of the research suggests, rather, that many men simply don't believe they have used force. Not really. Nor do they believe that the women have resisted. Not really.

In alleging date rape, Koss says, 'the women reported that they had said "no" forcefully and repeatedly. The men held out the possibility that "no" meant "yes."

'The women considered the amount of force as moderately severe. The men, though they noticed a degree of resistance, believed it could be consistent with seduction. They believed women enjoyed being roughed up to a certain extent.'

How is it possible that there is such a perceptual gap about 'consent' for sex? It is, in part, the *Gone with the Wind* fantasy: Scarlett O'Hara carried to bed kicking and screaming, only to wake up humming and singing. It is the bodice-ripping gothic novel, rock-and-rape cultural messages. It is the ancient script of the mating game – he persists, she resists – that passes for 'normal' sexual relationships.

All of this leaves the burden of proof on a woman that she didn't really want it or didn't at least accede to it. But Koss asks mischievously and seriously what would happen if the burden of proof were turned around.

'How could a man convince us that he went into the sexual encounter with the intention of a satisfying sexual experience?' she asks. 'Did he try to determine whether she liked sex outdoors, liked it on the ground? What did he find out about disease and pregnancy prevention? Do you see the difference I am trying to suggest?'

What if a woman's pleasure were the standard of consent? And why is that the sort of question only asked by female stand-up comics?

There are women who like 'being roughed up.' There are women who make false accusations. Probably in similar numbers. The FBI estimates that two to four percent of all reported rapes are false and only a small percentage of rapes are reported.

When date rape reaches the courtroom, as it rarely does, says Koss, picking her words carefully, 'the only way to convince a jury that his force went beyond the "normal" male assertiveness in pursuing his sexual agenda, and that her resistance went beyond the "normal" female reticence in the interest of protecting her purity or inexperience, is if she sustained a lot of injury.'

Without such an injury, without a witness, we have only the two and opposing views of a man and a woman. Without a legal recourse, the hope lies on 'crime prevention' and that means closing the gap in sexual perceptions.

So, I am told, the Palm Beach story has focused attention on date rape. But I'm afraid that all we are likely to learn from this celebrated story is that we still live in a culture in which he says date and she says rape. And each fervently calls the other a liar.

•

FRANCIS WHEEN

Francis Wheen was born in Chislehurst, Kent, in 1957. The son of an army officer, he was educated at Harrow and the University of London. He was an office boy at the *Guardian* when he was seventeen and a few years later joined the staff of the *New Statesman*. A regular broadcaster and the author of a biography of the columnist and politician Tom Driberg, Wheen has written columns for several British publications including the *Independent*, the *Independent on Sunday*, the *New Statesman*, the *Guardian*, the *Observer* and *Esquire* magazine. He was named Columnist of the Year in the 1997 *What the Papers Say* awards.

Observer, 8 May 1994

It is a little-known fact that, when not writing this column, I attend to my duties as chairman of a large multinational conglomerate. Statements of the Obvious plc – also known by the acronym 'SO?', since that is what cynics usually say when they see our products – was set up a few years ago to meet the ever-growing demand by many consumers to be told what they already know.

You have probably seen the work of SO? without realizing it. One of our most profitable subsidiaries produces all those market-research 'surveys' which are such a boon to news editors with space to fill. 'Unemployment is damaging families ... according to a survey published yesterday.' (*Guardian*, 13 April 1994) That was one of ours. Then there was the research we conducted for the Women's Royal Voluntary Service a couple of weeks ago, which found that many old people 'said that there had been opportunities they wish they could have taken'. Yet another of our recent triumphs was the disclosure that many children are 'more familiar with computer game heroes Sonic the Hedgehog and Super Mario than with childhood literature characters such as Alice in Wonderland and Little Red Riding Hood'. In February, great publicity was given to our startling discovery that many undergraduates find it difficult to live on their student grants. A couple of months earlier, after interviewing 1,500 people, we revealed that few men share household chores equally with their female partners.

But we don't spend all our time brandishing clipboards on windswept street corners, asking passers-by if they would agree that rich people tend to have more money than poor people, or that nice things are better than nasty things. We are just as likely to be found in the oak-panelled lairs of senior politicians, providing them with ringing phrases for their manifestos ('We must face the challenge of the future' – that always seems to go down well) or tweaking up their rhetorical flourishes. Perhaps you recall John Smith's speech to the Labour Party local government conference last year? Promising 'a new political approach for a new political era ... a new politics that puts people first, that rejects dogma and embraces practical commonsense solutions', he argued that Labour should 'embody the hopes and aspirations of the ordinary people of this country for a better life for themselves and their families. When you get right down to it, that is what they want from politics.' This bold oration was hailed by the press as 'radical' and 'astonishing'; the trade union leader John Edmonds praised it as 'a new vision' which 'burst through some of the tired historical dogma of the Labour Party'. We were happy to let Smith take the credit; but we got the fee.

Our vast database of sonorous but uncontroversial phrases is suitable for use by all political parties on every conceivable occasion. 'We must build, but build surely ... We must grasp the opportunities ... Let us go forward together.' I shouldn't be telling you this, but many of these are pinched from an old Peter Sellers sketch parodying the vacuousness of political rhetoric. Another of our secret sources is Sellers's character Chauncey Gardener, whose simple maxims so impressed the Washington political élite in the film *Being There*. When Bill Clinton was writing his inauguration speech last year, he asked us if we could lend a hand. In a spirit of slight mischief, we dug out one of Chauncey Gardener's best lines: 'After the winter comes the spring.' Imagine our delight when Clinton put the words straight into his address – and nobody sniggered.

Why should they? The market for platitudes is the one sector of the American economy which has continued to thrive throughout the recession. Look at those 'how to be a millionaire' manuals which are such a perennial feature of the *New York Times* best-seller list – *The Seven Habits of Highly Effective People*, *The Art of the Deal*, *Things They Don't Teach You at Harvard Business School* and so forth. Almost all of them are assembled by keen young trainees at our American head office and then sold on to the 'author'. Our biggest success so far is *The Leadership Secrets of Attila the Hun*, which is to be found on the bookshelves of every middle manager in the United States, and has been described as a 'fantastic' guide which 'will help you make the most of your leadership potential'. It includes some of our most thought-provoking suggestions: 'You must have resilience to overcome personal misfortunes, discouragement, rejection and disappointment;' 'When the consequences of your actions are too grim to bear, look for another option.' Who could disagree?

Like any world-beating corporation, we are sometimes the victims of industrial espionage. I was irritated recently to read *Keep Going for It*, in which Victor Kiam – he who liked Remington's razors so much he bought the company – passed on the ideas which had propelled him to success. 'Turn those negatives into positives!' 'A little bit of courtesy and caring. It goes such a long way.' 'Business is a game. Play it to win.' 'When you're an entrepreneur, you don't look a gift horse in the mouth.' 'When opportunity knocks, the entrepreneur is always home.' 'Any job worth doing is worth doing well.' All these *aperçus* were stolen from us. Still, as the senior vice-president of our Cliché Department often observes, imitation is the sincerest form of flattery.

Besides, we remain ahead of the game. Recognizing that not everyone wants to be Victor Kiam or Donald Trump, we have lately diversified into the even more lucrative market for New Age books about 'self-help' and 'personal growth'. Our top title at the moment is Jonathan Lazear's *Meditations for Men Who Do Too Much*, aimed at workaholics who have burned themselves out by reading *Keep Going for It* and *The Leadership Secrets of Attila the Hun*. Here are some of Lazear's wise words, which he bought off-the-peg from Statements of the Obvious. 'Our families, our partners, our extended families, our children will always be there for us if we can make the decision to be there for them.' 'We need to learn to pace ourselves.' 'Wealth doesn't really translate to happiness.' 'Trusting no one can be as dangerous as trusting everyone.' 'We can learn from our failures.' 'No one is happy all of the time.'

Finally, a word about ethics. Some consumer groups have suggested that it is 'immoral' for our company to make a fortune by selling truisms which had hitherto been treated as common property, like the air we breathe. What nonsense. More than 200 years ago, the authors of the American Declaration of Independence prefaced their statement of human rights by announcing 'We hold these truths to be self-evident.' If Thomas Jefferson and his colleagues didn't flinch from stating the obvious, why should we?

SELECTED BIBLIOGRAPHY

Adams, Phillip, *Uncensored Adams*, Melbourne, 1981

—, *The Inflammable Adams*, Melbourne, 1983

—, *Classic Columns*, Sydney, 1994

Ade, George, *The Permanent Ade: The Living Writings of George Ade*, edited by Fred C. Kelly, Indianapolis, 1947

—, *The Best of George Ade*, edited by John T. McCutcheon, Bloomington, Ind., 1985

Allen, Joseph Chase, *The Wheelhouse Loafer: Selections from Joseph Chase Allen's Weekly Log 'With the Fishermen' from the Vineyard Gazette 1940–1965*, edited by Colbert Smith, Boston, 1966

Alsop, Joseph, and Alsop, Stewart, *The Reporter's Trade*, New York, 1958

Anderson, Dave, *The Red Smith Reader*, New York, 1982

Anthony, Edward, *O Rare Don Marquis: A Biography*, New York, 1962

Ashby, Lynn, *As Your Acknowledged Leader*, Austin, Tex., 1983

—, *As I Was Saying*, Austin, Tex., 1984

Baer, Arthur 'Bugs', *The Family Album*, New York, 1925

Baker, Russell, *An American in Washington*, New York, 1961

—, *All Things Considered*, Philadelphia, 1965

—, *So This Is Depravity*, New York, 1980

—, *There's a Country in My Cellar*, New York, 1990

Barkley, William, *William Barkley's Notebook*, London, 1948

Barry, Dave, *Dave Barry's Greatest Hits*, New York, 1988

Beebe, Lucius, *The Lucius Beebe Reader*, edited by Charles Clegg and Duncan Emrich, Garden City, NY, 1967

Belford, Barbara, *Brilliant Bylines*, New York, 1986

Berger, Meyer, *Meyer Berger's New York*, New York, 1960

Berkow, Ira, *Red: The Life and Times of a Great American Writer*, New York, 1986

Bernard, Jeffrey, *Low Life*, London, 1986

—, *More Low Life*, London, 1989

Bernard, Jeffrey, and Taki Theodoracopolous, *High Life – Low Life*, London, 1982

Bierce, Ambrose, *Selections from Prattle by Ambrose Bierce*, edited by Carroll D. Hall, San Francisco, 1936

—, *Skepticism and Dissent: 1898–1901*, edited by Lawrence I. Berkove, Ann Arbor, Mich., 1986

Bishop, Jim, *The Mark Hellinger Story*, New York, 1949

Bode, Carl, *The Young Mencken*, New York, 1973

Bombeck, Erma, *Forever, Erma*, Kansas City, Mo., 1996

Breslin, Jimmy, *The World According to Breslin*, New York, 1984

—, *Damon Runyon*, New York, 1991

Broun, Heywood, *Sitting on the World*, New York and London, 1924

—, *It Seems to Me: 1925–1935*, New York, 1935

—, *Collected Edition of Heywood Broun*, edited by Heywood Hale Broun, New York, 1941

Brown, George Mackay, *Letters from Hamnavoe*, Edinburgh, 1975

—, *Under Brinkie's Brae*, Edinburgh, 1979

—, *Rockpools and Daffodils: An Orcadian Diary, 1979–1991*, Edinburgh, 1992

Bruccoli, Matthew J., and Layman, Richard, *Ring W. Lardner: A Descriptive Bibliography*, Pittsburgh, 1976

Buchwald, Ann, and Buchwald, Art, *Seems Like Yesterday*, New York, 1980

Buchwald, Art, *Getting High in Government Circles*, New York, 1968

—, *I Never Danced at the White House*, New York, 1971

Bywater, Michael, *The Best of Bargepole*, London, 1992

Caen, Herb, *Baghdad-by-the-Bay*, New York, 1949

—, *Don't Call It Frisco*, New York, 1953

—, *Only in San Francisco*, New York, 1960

—, *The Best of Herb Caen, 1960–75*, San Francisco, 1995

Cain, James M., *50 Years of Journalism*, edited by Roy Hoops, Bowling Green, Ohio, 1985

Caldwell, William, *In the Record: The Simeon Stylites Columns of William A. Caldwell*, New Brunswick, NJ, 1971

Cameron, James, *Cameron in the Guardian 1974–1984*, London, 1985

Campbell, Patrick, *An Irishman's Diary*, London, 1950

—, *Waving All Excuses*, London, 1971

—, *35 Years on the Job*, London, 1973

—, *The Campbell Companion: The Best of Patrick Campbell*, edited by Ulick O'Connor, London, 1994

Campbell, Ross, *Daddy, Are You Married?*, Sydney, 1963

—, *Mummy, Who is Your Husband?*, London and Sydney, 1964

Cannon, Jimmy, *Nobody Asked Me, But*, New York, 1951

—, *Who Struck John?*, New York, 1956

—, *Nobody Asked Me, But*, edited by Jack Cannon and Tom Cannon, New York, 1978

Clapper, Raymond, *Watching the World*, edited by Olive Ewing Clapper, London and New York, 1944

Clift, Charmian, *The World of Charmian Clift*, edited by George Johnston, Sydney, 1970

—, *Trouble in Lotus Land, Essays, 1964–1967*, edited by Nadia Wheatley, North Ryde, 1990

—, *Being Alone With Oneself, Essays, 1968–1969*, North Ryde, NSW, 1991

—, *Images in Aspic*, Pymble, NSW, 1992

Comstock, Jim, *Best of Hillbilly: A Prize Collection of 100-Proof Writing from Jim Comstock's West Virginia Hillbilly*, edited by Otto Whittaker, Anderson, SC, 1968

Connor, Robert, *Cassandra: Reflections in a Mirror* [biography of William Connor], London, 1969

Connor, William, *Cassandra at His Finest and Funniest*, edited by Paul Boyle, London, 1967

Conrow, Robert, *Field Days: The Life, Times and Reputation of Eugene Field*, New York, 1974

Davis, Bob, *Over My Left Shoulder*, New York, 1926

—, *Bob Davis Recalls: Sixty True Stories of Love and Laughter and Tears*, New York, 1927

—, *Bob Davis Again! In Many Moods*, New York, 1928

—, *Bob Davis Abroad!*, New York, 1929

—, *Bob Davis at Large*, New York, 1934

—, *People, People Everywhere! Footprints of a Wanderer*, New York, 1936

DeMuth, James, *Small Town Chicago: The Comic Perspective of Finley Peter Dunne, George Ade, and Ring Lardner*, Port Washington, NY, 1980

Driberg, Tom, *Colonnade*, London, 1949

—, *Ruling Passions*, London, 1977

Driscoll, Charles, *Life of O. O. McIntyre*, New York, 1938

Dunne, Finley Peter, *Mr Dooley in Peace and War*, Boston, 1898

—, *Mr Dooley at His Best*, edited by Elmer Ellis, New York, 1949

—, *Mr Dooley: Now and Forever*, edited by Louis Filler, Stamford, Calif., 1954

—, *The World of Mr Dooley*, edited by Louis Filler, New York, 1962

Edson, C. L., *The Gentle Art of Columning: A Treatise on Comic Journalism*, New York, 1920

Elder, Donald, *Ring Lardner: A Biography*, New York, 1956

Ellege, Scott, *E. B. White*, New York, 1984

Ellis, Elmer, *Mr Dooley's America: A Life of Finley Peter Dunne*, New York, 1938

Evans, Trevor (ed.), *The Great Bohunkus: Tributes to Ian Mackay*, London, 1953

Fanning, Charles, *Finley Peter Dunne and Mr Dooley: The Chicago Years*, Louisville, Kentucky, 1978

Farr, Finnis, *Fair Enough: The Life of Westbrook Pegler*, New Rochelle, NY, 1975

Ferril, Thomas Hornsby, *I Hate Thursday*, New York and London, 1944

Field, Eugene, *Sharps and Flats*, edited by Slason Thompson, New York, 1990

Fisher, Charles, *The Columnists*, New York, 1944

Fleming, Peter, *My Aunt's Rhinoceros and Other Reflections*, London, 1956

—, *The Gower Street Poltergeist*, London, 1958

—, *Goodbye to the Bombay Bowler*, London, 1961

Fountain, Charles, *Another Man's Poison: The Life and Writings of Columnist George Frazier*, Chester, Conn., 1984

Frayn, Michael, *The Day of the Dog*, London, 1962

—, *The Book of Fub*, London, 1963

—, *On the Outskirts*, London, 1964

—, *At Bay in Gear Street*, London, 1967

—, *The Original Michael Frayn: Satirical Essays*, edited by James Fenton, London, 1990

Gabler, Neal, *Winchell: Gossip, Power and the Culture of Celebrity*, New York, 1994

Gardiner, A. G., *The War Lords*, London, 1915

—, *Pebbles on the Shore*, London, 1916

—, *Leaves in the Wind*, London, 1919

—, *Windfalls*, London, 1920

—, *Many Furrows*, London, 1924

Gary, Kays, *Kays Gary, Columnist*, Charlotte, NC, 1981

Gellert, Leon, *Week After Week*, Sydney, NSW, 1953

—, *Year After Year*, Sydney, NSW, 1956

Gelman-Waxner, Libby, [Paul Rudnick], *If You Ask Me*, New York, 1994

Gilbreth, Jr, Frank, *Ashley Cooper's Doing the Charleston*, Charleston, SC, 1993

Golden, Harry, *Only in America*, New York, 1958

—, *Carl Sandburg*, Cleveland, 1961

—, *You're Entitle'*, Cleveland, 1962

—, *The Best of Harry Golden*, Cleveland, 1967

—, *The Right Time*, New York, 1969

Goodman, Ellen, *At Large*, New York, 1981

—, *Keeping in Touch*, New York, 1985

Gore, Arthur, [8th Earl of Arran], *Lord Arran Writes*, London, 1964

Gould, John, *The Shag Bag*, Boston, 1972

Grauer, Neil A., *Wits and Sages*, Baltimore, 1984

Hamill, Pete, *Irrational Ravings*, New York, 1971

Hearst, W. R., *Selections from the Writings of W. R. Hearst*, edited by E. F. Tompkins, San Francisco, 1948

Hecht, Ben, *One Thousand and One Afternoons*, New York, 1922

—, *Broken Necks*, Chicago, 1926

—, *1001 Afternoons in New York*, New York, 1941

—, *A Child of the Century* [autobiography], New York, 1954

Hellinger, Mark, *Moon Over Broadway*, New York, 1931
—, *The Ten Million*, New York, 1934
Hitchens, Christopher, *Prepared for the Worst: Selected Essays and Minority Reports*, New York, 1988
—, *For the Sake of Argument: Essays and Minority Reports*, London and New York, 1993
Holtzman, Jerome (ed.), *No Cheering in the Press Box: Recollections – Personal and Professional by Eighteen Veteran American Sportswriters*, New York, 1973
House, Jay, *On Second Thought*, Philadelphia, 1936
Howe, Gene, *Them Texans* [by Kernel E. Rasmus Tack, the Tactless Texan], 4 vols., Amarillo, 1927–1930
Hoyt, Edwin P., *A Gentleman of Broadway* [biography of Damon Runyon], New York, 1964
Hughes, Langston, *Simple Speaks His Mind*, New York, 1950
—, *Simple Stakes a Claim*, New York, 1957
Ingrams, Richard (ed.), *The Bumper Beachcomber*, London, 1991
Jenkins, Peter, *An Anatomy of Decline: The Political Journalism of Peter Jenkins*, edited by Brian Brivati and Richard Cockett, London, 1995
Jennings, Paul, *The Paul Jennings Reader: Collected Pieces 1943–89*, London, 1990
Johnson, Shaun, *Strange Days Indeed*, Johannesburg, 1993
Jones, James A., *Courts Day by Day*, London, 1946
Kelly, Fred C., *But, on the Other Hand – !*, New York, 1928
—, *George Ade: Warmhearted Satirist*, Indianapolis, 1947
Kempton, Murray, *America Comes of Middle Age: Columns, 1950–1962*, New York, 1962
—, *Rebellions, Perversities, and Main Events*, New York, 1994
Ketchum, Robert M., *Will Rogers: His Life and Times*, New York, 1973
Knox, Collie [Collumb Thomas], *Collie Knox Calling*, London, 1937
—, *Collie Knox Again*, London, 1938
—, *It Might Have Been You* [autobiography], London, 1938
—, *Draw Up Your Chair*, London, 1939
—, *Collie Knox Re-calls*, London, 1940
Kramer, Dale, *Heywood Broun: A Biographical Portrait*, New York, 1949
Krock, Arthur, *In the Nation, 1932–1966*, New York, 1966
—, *Memoirs: Sixty Years on the Firing Line*, New York, 1968
Kurth, Peter, *American Cassandra: The Life of Dorothy Thompson*, Boston, 1990
Lardner, Ring W., *What of It?*, New York, 1925
—, *First and Last*, edited by Gilbert Seldes, New York, 1934
Lash, Joseph, *Eleanor: The Years Alone*, New York, 1972
Lawrence, David, *Diary of a Washington Correspondent*, New York, 1942
Leonard, John, *Private Lives in the Imperial City*, New York, 1979
Lerner, Leo A., *The Itch of Opinion*, Chicago, 1956
Lerner, Max, *Public Journal: Marginal Notes on Wartime America*, New York, 1945
—, *Actions and Passions: Notes on the Multiple Revolution of Our Time*, New York, 1949
—, *The Unfinished Country: A Book of American Symbols*, New York, 1959
Levin, Bernard, *Taking Sides*, London, 1979
—, *All Things Considered*, London, 1988
Lewis, D. B. Wyndham, *At the Sign of the Blue Moon*, London, 1924
—, *At the Blue Moon Again*, London, 1925
—, *Take It to Bed*, London, 1944
Liebling, A. J., *The Honest Rainmaker: The Life and Times of Colonel John R. Stingo*, San Francisco, 1989

Lippmann, Walter, *The Essential Lippmann: A Political Philosophy for Liberal Democracy*, edited by Clinton Rossiter and James Lave, New York, 1963

Low Cloud, Charles, *Charles Round Low Cloud: Voice of the Winnebago*, edited by William Leslie Clarke and Walker D. Wyman, Black River Falls, Wis., 1973

Lower, Lennie, *The Best of Lennie Lower*, Melbourne, 1963

—, *Here's Lower*, Sydney, 1983

—, *The Legends of Lennie Lower*, Sydney, 1988

Lynd, Robert, *'Y.Y.': An Anthology of Essays*, London, 1933

—, *In Defence of Pink*, London, 1937

MacAdams, William, *Ben Hecht: The Man Behind the Legend*, New York, 1990

McCabe, Charles, *The Fearless Spectator*, San Francisco, 1970

—, *The Charles McCabe Reader*, San Francisco, 1984

McCarthy, Eugene J., *Complexities and Contraries: Essays of Mild Discontent*, New York, 1982

Macdonald, Alexander, *Don't Frighten the Horses*, Melbourne, 1961

McGill, Ralph, *The Fleas Come with the Dog*, Nashville, Tenn., 1954

—, *The Best of Ralph McGill*, edited by Michael Strickland, Atlanta, 1980

McIntyre, O. O., *Twenty-Five Selected Stories of O. O. McIntyre*, New York, 1929

—, *Another 'Odd' Book: 25 Selected Stories of O. O. McIntyre*, New York, 1932

—, *The Big Town: New York Day-by-Day*, New York, 1935

Mackay, Ian, *The Real Mackay*, edited by Stanley Baron, London, 1953

McKelway, St Clair, *Gossip: The Life and Times of Walter Winchell*, New York, 1940

Marquis, Don, *Hermione and Her Little Group of Serious Thinkers*, New York and London, 1916

—, *The Old Soak and Hail and Farewell*, Garden City, NY, and Toronto, 1921

—, *Archy and Mehitabel*, New York, 1927

—, *Archy Does His Part*, Garden City, NY, 1935

—, *The Best of Don Marquis*, edited by Christopher Morley, New York, 1946

—, *The Lives and Times of Archy and Mehitabel*, New York, 1950

Marshall, Arthur, *Girls Will Be Girls*, London, 1974

—, *I Say!*, London, 1977

—, *I'll Let You Know: Musings from Myrtlebank*, London, 1981

—, *Smiles Please: Further Musings from Myrtlebank*, London, 1982

—, *Follow The Sun: A Further Selection of the Writings of Arthur Marshall*, edited by Peter Kelland, London, 1990

Martin, Harold H., *Ralph McGill, Reporter*, Boston, 1973

Mathias, Fred S., *The Amazing Bob Davis: His Last Vagabond Journey*, New York and Toronto, 1944

Meltzer, Milton, *Langston Hughes: A Biography*, New York, 1968

Mencken, H. L., *A Mencken Chrestomathy*, edited by Alistair Cooke, New York, 1949

—, *The Bathtub Hoax* [H. L. Mencken's *Chicago Tribune* columns], edited by Robert McHugh, New York, 1958

Meyer, Ernest L., *Making Light of the Times*, Madison, Wis., 1928

—, *Hey, Yellowbacks!*, New York, 1934

—, *Bucket Boy: A Milwaukee Legend*, New York, 1947

Meyer, Karl E., *Pundits, Poets & Wits: An Omnibus of American Newspaper Columns*, New York, 1990

Miller, Lee G., *The Story of Ernie Pyle*, New York, 1950

Moos, Malcolm, *Carnival of Buncombe*, Baltimore, 1956

Morton, J. B., *The Adventures of Mr Thake*, London, 1934

—, *Cram Me With Eels!: The Best of Beachcomber's Unpublished Humour*, edited by Mike Barfield, London, 1994

Motsisi, Casey, *Casey & Co.: Selected Writings of Casey 'Kid' Motsisi*, edited by Mothobi Mutloatse, Johannesburg, 1978

Mott, Frank Luther, *American Journalism, A History of Newspapers in the United States through 250 Years, 1690 to 1940*, New York, 1941

Murdoch, Walter, *Moreover*, Sydney, 1932

—, *Collected Essays*, Sydney and London, 1938

—, *My 100 Answers*, Sydney, 1960

Murray, Jim, *Best of Jim Murray*, New York, 1978

Nevins, Allan, *Interpretations, 1933–1935* [Walter Lippmann columns], Boston, 1936

Nicolson, Harold, *Marginal Comment*, London, 1939

—, *People and Things*, London, 1939

Nye, Bill, *Bill Nye and Boomerang*, Chicago, 1881

—, *Forty Liars, and Other Lies*, Chicago, 1882

—, *Baled Hay*, New York, 1884

—, *Remarks by Bill Nye*, New York, 1886

—, *Bill Nye's Thinks*, New York, 1888

—, *Bill Nye's Western Humor*, edited by T. A. Larson, Lincoln, Neb., 1968

Nye, Frank Wilson, *Bill Nye: His Own Life Story*, New York and London, 1926

Oakley, Helen, *Three Hours for Lunch, The Life and Times of Christopher Morley*, New York, 1976

O'Brien, Flann, *Myles na Gopaleen (Flann O'Brien): The Best of Myles, A Selection from 'Cruiskeen Lawn'*, edited by Kevin O. Nolan, London, 1968

O'Brien, Howard Vincent, *So Long, Son*, New York, 1944

—, *All Things Considered: Memories, Expressions and Observations of a Chicagoan*, Indianapolis, 1948

O'Connor, Richard, *Ambrose Bierce: A Biography*, Boston, 1967

—, *Heywood Broun: A Biography*, New York, 1975

O'Daniel, Therman, *Langston Hughes: Black Genius*, New York, 1971

Orwell, George, *The Collected Essays, Journalism, and Letters of George Orwell*, edited by Sonia Orwell and Ian Angus, vol. 3: *As I Please, 1943–1945*, London and New York, 1968

Patner, Andrew, *I.F. Stone: A Portrait*, New York, 1988

Patrick, Walton R., *Ring Lardner*, New York, 1963

Pegler, Westbrook, *'T Aint Right*, New York, 1936

—, *The Dissenting Opinions of Mister Westbrook Pegler*, New York, 1941

—, *George Spelvin, American*, New York, 1942

Pilat, Oliver, *Pegler, Angry Man of the Press*, Boston, 1963

Pyle, Ernie, *Ernie Pyle in England*, New York, 1941

—, *Here Is Your War*, New York, 1943

—, *Brave Men*, New York, 1944

—, *Last Chapter*, New York, 1946

—, *Home Country*, New York, 1947

—, *Ernie's War: The Best of Ernie Pyle's World War II Dispatches*, edited by David Nichols, New York, 1986

—, *Ernie's America: The Best of Ernie Pyle's 1930s Travel Dispatches*, edited by David Nichols, New York, 1989

Quindlen, Anna, *Living Out Loud*, New York, 1988

—, *Thinking Out Loud: On the Personal, the Political, the Public and the Private*, New York, 1993

Rampersad, Arnold, *I Dream a World* [biography of Langston Hughes], New York, 1988

Reston, James, *Sketches in the Sand*, New York, 1967

—, *Washington*, New York, 1986

Riley, Sam G. (ed.), *The Best of the Rest: Non-Syndicated Newspaper Columnists Select Their Best Work*, Westport, Conn., 1993

—, *A Biographical Dictionary of American Newspaper Columnists*, Westport, Conn., 1996

Rogers, Will, *Will Rogers' Daily Telegrams 1926–29*, edited by Steven K. Gragert, Stillwater, Oka., 4 vols., 1978–9

—, *Will Rogers' Weekly Articles 1921–31*, edited by James M. Smallwood and Steven K. Gragert, Stillwater, Oka., 6 vols., 1980–82

Rooney, Andy, *Pieces of My Mind*, New York, 1984

—, *Word for Word*, New York, 1986

—, *Sweet and Sour*, New York, 1992

Roosevelt, Eleanor, *This I Remember*, New York, 1949

—, *Eleanor Roosevelt's My Day*, edited by David Emblidge, New York, 1944

—, *Eleanor Roosevelt's My Day 1936–1945*, edited by Rochelle Chadakoff, New York, 1989

Ross, Ishbel, *Ladies of the Press*, New York, 1936

Royko, Mike, *Up Against It*, Chicago, 1967

—, *I May Be Wrong, But I Doubt It*, Chicago, 1968

—, *Slats Grobnik and Some Other Friends*, New York, 1973

—, *Sez Who? Sez Me*, New York, 1982

—, *Like I Was Sayin'*, New York, 1984

—, *Dr Kookie?, You're Right*, New York, 1989

Royster, Vermont, *A Pride of Prejudices*, New York, 1967

—, *The Essential Royster: A Vermont Royster Reader*, Chapel Hill, NC, 1985

Runyon, Damon, *Short Takes: Readers' Choice of the Best Columns of America's Favorite Newspaperman*, New York and London, 1946

Safire, William, *Safire's Washington*, New York, 1980

—, *On Language*, New York, 1980

—, *I Stand Corrected: More on Language*, New York, 1984

—, *Language Maven Strikes Again*, New York, 1990

—, *Quoth the Maven*, New York, 1993

Salmon, Lucy Maynard, *The Newspaper and the Historian*, New York, 1923

Sandburg, Carl, *Home Front Memo*, New York, 1943

Sanders, Marion K., *Dorothy Thompson: A Legend in Her Time*, Boston, 1973

Schaaf, Barbara C., *Mr Dooley Remembers*, Boston, 1963

—, *Mr Dooley's Chicago*, Garden City, NY, 1977

Seldes, Gilbert, *The Seven Lively Arts*, New York, 1924

Shearer, Harry, *Man Bites Town: Notes of a Man Who Doesn't Take Notes*, New York, 1993

Shepherd, Jean (ed.), *The America of George Ade, 1866–1944*, New York, 1960

Sidebotham, Herbert ['Candidus'], *The Sense of Things*, London, 1938

Singh, Khushwant, *Not a Nice Man to Know: The Best of Khushwant Singh*, New Delhi, 1993

Smith, Red [Walter Wellesley Smith], *Out of the Red*, New York, 1950

—, *Views of Sport*, New York, 1954

—, *The Red Smith Reader*, edited by Dave Anderson, New York, 1982

Starrett, Vincent, *The Column Book*, Chicago, 1957

Steel, Ronald, *Walter Lippmann and the American Century*, Boston, 1980

Stokes, Harold Phelps (ed.), *Simeon Strunsky's America* [Simeon Strunsky's 'Topics of the Times' columns], New York, 1956

Stone, I. F., *The Truman Era*, New York, 1953

—, *The Haunted Fifties*, New York, 1963

—, *In a Time of Torment, 1961–1967*, New York, 1967
—, *The Best of I.F. Stone's Weekly: Pages from a Radical Newspaper*, New York, 1973
—, *The I.F. Stone's Weekly Reader*, edited by Neil Middleton, New York, 1973
Strout, Richard L., *TRB: Views and Perspectives on the Presidency*, New York, 1979
Stuart, Lyle, *Secret Life of Walter Winchell*, New York, 1953
Thompson, Dorothy, *Let the Record Speak*, Boston, 1939
Thompson, Slason, *Life of Eugene Field, The Poet of Childhood*, New York, 1928
Trillin, Calvin, *Uncivil Liberties*, New York, 1982
—, *With All Disrespect*, New York, 1985
—, *If You Can't Say Something Nice*, New York, 1987
Tweedie, Jill, *Letters from a Fainthearted Feminist*, London, 1982
Van Doren, Carl, *Many Minds*, New York, 1924
Vaughan, Bill, *Bird Thou Never Wert*, New York, 1962
—, *Half the Battle*, New York, 1963
—, *Sorry I Stirred It*, New York, 1964
—, *The Best of Bill Vaughan*, edited by Kirk W. Vaughan and Robert W. Butler, Independence, Mo., 1979
Waterhouse, Keith, *Mondays, Thursdays* [columns from the *Daily Mirror*], London, 1976
—, *Sharon & Tracey & the Rest: The Best of Keith Waterhouse in the Daily Mail*, London, 1992
Watkins, Alan, *Sportwriter's Eye: An Anthology*, London, 1989
Watson, Morris, and Meyer, Ernest L., *Heywood Broun: As He Seemed to Us*, New York, 1940
Waugh, Auberon, *Four Crowded Years: The Diaries of Auberon Waugh 1972–1976*, edited by N. R. Galli, London, 1976
—, *A Turbulent Decade: The Diaries of Auberon Waugh 1976–1985*, edited by Anne Galli-Pahlavi, London, 1985
—, *Another Voice, An Alternative Anatomy of Britain*, London, 1986
Weiner, Ed, *The Damon Runyon Story*, New York, 1948
—, *Let's Go to Press: A Biography of Walter Winchell*, New York, 1955
Wharton, Michael [Peter Simple], *The Thoughts of Peter Simple* [extracts from 'Way of the World' column in the *Daily Telegraph*, 1969–71], London, 1971
—, *The Stretchford Chronicles: 25 Years of Peter Simple*, London, 1980
Wheen, Francis, *Tom Driberg: His Life and Indiscretions*, London, 1990
White, E. B., *One Man's Meat*, New York, 1944
Winchell, Walter, *Winchell Exclusive – Things That Happened to Me – and Me to Them*, Englewood Cliffs, NJ, 1975
Worsthorne, Peregrine, *Peregrinations*, London, 1980
—, *Tricks of Memory*, London, 1993
Yardley, Jonathan, *Ring* [biography of Ring Lardner], New York, 1977
Zion, Sidney, *Read All About It! The Collected Adventures of a Maverick Reporter*, New York, 1982
—, *Trust Your Mother But Cut the Cards*, New York, 1993